**PETER A. FRIED**
Carleton University

# readings in perception
## principle and practice

D. C. HEATH AND COMPANY
Lexington, Massachusetts   Toronto   London

Copyright © 1974 by D.C. Heath and Company.

All rights reserved. No part of this publication may be reproduced or transmitted in any form or by any means, electronic or mechanical, including photocopy, recording, or any information storage or retrieval system, without permission in writing from the publisher.

Published simultaneously in Canada.

Printed in the United States of America.

International Standard Book Number: 0-669-89367-6

Library of Congress Catalog Card Number: 73-22501

Consulting Editor
**Mark R. Rosenzweig**
University of California, Berkeley

# readings in perception

# CONTENTS

PREFACE   xi

## Part I Input-Output

**WHAT GOES IN — MUST IT COME OUT?**   2

1. THE CONCEPT OF THE STIMULUS IN PSYCHOLOGY   5
    James J. Gibson

2. OPERATIONISM AND THE CONCEPT OF PERCEPTION   21
    Wendell R. Garner   Harold W. Hake
    Charles W. Eriksen

3. SENSORY ORGANIZATION   29
    Wolfgang Köhler

4. THE FIRST STAGE OF PERCEPTION: GROWTH OF THE CELL ASSEMBLY   36
    D. O. Hebb

5. EFFECTS OF DIFFERENTIAL EXPERIENCE ON DENDRITIC SPINE COUNTS IN RAT CEREBRAL CORTEX   41
    Albert Globus   Mark R. Rosenzweig
    Edward L. Bennett   Marian C. Diamond

6. CURRENT TRENDS AND ISSUES IN ADAPTATION-LEVEL THEORY   52
    Harry Helson

7. EFFECT OF INITIAL SELLING PRICE ON SUBSEQUENT SALES   61
    Anthony N. Doob   J. Merrill-Carlsmith
    Jonathan L. Freedman   Thomas K. Landauer
    Soleng Tom, Jr.

8. SOME INFORMATIONAL ASPECTS OF VISUAL PERCEPTION    70
    Fred Attneave

9. PERCEPTUAL RESTORATION OF MISSING SPEECH SOUNDS    77
    R. M. Warren

10. DECISION PROCESSES IN PERCEPTION    80
    John A. Swets    Wilson P. Tanner, Jr.
    Theodore G. Birdsall

11. SUBLIMINAL STIMULATION: AN OVERVIEW    97
    James V. McConnell    Richard L. Cutler
    Elton B. McNeil

12. THE EFFECT OF SUBLIMINAL SHOCK UPON THE JUDGED INTENSITY OF WEAK SHOCK    121
    Roger W. Black    William Bevan

13. TO KNOW A FLY    127
    V. G. Dethier

# Part II  Perceptual Development

**WAS SHE PUSHED OR DID SHE FALL?    134**

14. SUMMATION AND LEARNING IN PERCEPTION    140
    D. O. Hebb

15. VISUAL SCANNING OF TRIANGLES BY THE HUMAN NEWBORN    154
    Philip Salapatek    William Kessen

16. STUDIES IN PERCEPTUAL DEVELOPMENT: II. PART-WHOLE PERCEPTION    165
    D. Elkind    R. R. Koegler    E. Go

17. PERCEPTUAL LEARNING: DIFFERENTIATION OR ENRICHMENT?    175
    J. J. Gibson    E. J. Gibson

18. ASSOCIATION THEORY AND PERCEPTUAL LEARNING    187
    Leo Postman

CONTENTS

19. MATURATION OF PATTERN VISION IN INFANTS DURING THE FIRST SIX MONTHS    198
    R. L. Fantz    J. M. Ordy    M. S. Udelf

20. PATTERN VISION IN NEWBORN INFANTS    218
    R. L. Fantz

21. ATTENTION AND PSYCHOLOGICAL CHANGE IN THE YOUNG CHILD    221
    Jerome Kagan

22. A COMPARATIVE AND ANALYTICAL STUDY OF VISUAL DEPTH PERCEPTION    236
    Richard D. Walk    Eleanor J. Gibson

23. VISUAL PERCEPTION APPROACHED BY THE METHOD OF STABILIZED IMAGES    246
    R. M. Pritchard    W. Heron    D. O. Hebb

24. SPATIAL AND TEXTURAL CHARACTERISTICS OF THE GANZFELD    257
    Walter Cohen

25. PERCEPTUAL CHANGES AFTER PROLONGED SENSORY ISOLATION (DARKNESS AND SILENCE)    266
    J. P. Zubek    D. Pushkar    W. Sansom    J. Gowing

26. STUDYING PERCEPTUAL DEVELOPMENT USING THE TECHNIQUE OF SENSORY DEPRIVATION    284
    Austin H. Riesen

27. LEARNING TO LOVE    290
    Harry F. Harlow    Margaret Harlow

28. ADULT STATUS OF CHILDREN WITH CONTRASTING EARLY LIFE EXPERIENCES: A FOLLOW-UP STUDY    300
    H. M. Skeels

29. RECEPTIVE FIELDS OF CELLS IN STRIATE CORTEX OF VERY YOUNG, VISUALLY INEXPERIENCED KITTENS    303
    David H. Hubel    Torsten N. Wiesel

30. CONSEQUENCES OF MONOCULAR DEPRIVATION ON VISUAL BEHAVIOR IN KITTENS    313
    P. B. Dews    T. N. Wiesel

31. VISUAL EXPERIENCE MODIFIES DISTRIBUTION OF HORIZONTALLY AND VERTICALLY ORIENTED RECEPTIVE FIELDS IN CATS   332
    H. V. B. Hirsch   D. N. Spinelli

32. ADVANTAGE OF EARLY OVER LATE PERCEPTUAL EXPERIENCE IN IMPROVING FORM DISCRIMINATION   338
    Ronald H. Forgus

33. MOVEMENT-PRODUCED STIMULATION IN THE DEVELOPMENT OF VISUALLY GUIDED BEHAVIOR   348
    Richard Held   Alan Hein

34. INDEPENDENCE OF THE CAT'S SCOTOPIC AND PHOTOPIC SYSTEMS IN ACQUIRING CONTROL OF VISUALLY GUIDED BEHAVIOR   356
    Alan Hein   Rhea M. Diamond

35. ABSENCE OF SIZE CONSTANCY IN VISUALLY DEPRIVED RATS   369
    Donald P. Heller

# Part III   Higher Perceptual Processes

## THE BRAIN — DOES IT HAVE A MIND OF ITS OWN?   376

36. STORAGE AND RETRIEVAL PROCESSES IN LONG-TERM MEMORY   380
    R. M. Shiffrin   R. C. Atkinson

37. THE MIND OF A MNEMONIST: HIS MEMORY   390
    A. R. Luria

38. SELECTIVE ATTENTION IN MAN   398
    Anne M. Treisman

39. EMOTIONALITY AND PERCEPTUAL DEFENSE   408
    Elliott McGinnies

40. RESPONSE SUPPRESSION IN PERCEPTUAL DEFENSE   418
    Robert B. Zajonc

41. PAIRED COMPARISON SCALING OF BRIGHTNESS JUDGMENTS: A METHOD FOR THE MEASUREMENT OF PERCEPTUAL DEFENSE   430
    A. G. Worthington
42. EIDETIC IMAGERY: I. FREQUENCY   438
    Ralph Norman Haber   Ruth B. Haber
43. SEEING MOVEMENT   447
    R. L. Gregory
44. VISUAL MOTION PERCEPTION: EXPERIMENTAL MODIFICATION   454
    R. H. Masland
45. HEMISPHERE DECONNECTION AND UNITY IN CONSCIOUS AWARENESS   459
    R. W. Sperry
46. NEURAL PROCESSING OF BACKWARDS-SPEECH SOUNDS   477
    D. Kimura   S. Folb
47. AUDITORY BACKWARD INHIBITION IN CONCERT HALLS   480
    Georg von Békésy
48. DIFFERENCES IN PERCEIVED COLOR AS A FUNCTION OF CHARACTERISTIC COLOR   498
    John L. Delk   Samuel Fillenbaum
49. REINFORCEMENT AND EXTINCTION AS FACTORS IN SIZE ESTIMATION   504
    William W. Lambert   Richard L. Solomon   Peter D. Watson
50. OBESITY AND EATING   510
    Stanley Schachter
51. A CROSS-CULTURAL STUDY OF PERCEPTUAL PREDOMINANCE IN BINOCULAR RIVALRY   525
    James W. Bagby
52. DERMO-OPTICAL PERCEPTION: A PEEK DOWN THE NOSE   532
    Martin Gardner

INDEX   542

# Preface

The purpose in preparing this book is to make available to undergraduate students taking their first course in perception some of the source material upon which textbooks and lectures on this subject are based. The selection of articles in this volume was guided by several, often somewhat conflicting, criteria.

First, an effort was made to present influential theories and issues as described by the authors who did the original work. For the selected articles to be comprehensible to students with few psychology courses, it was occasionally necessary to present either an abridged version of the topic or a nontechnical overview by a researcher involved in the subject. In these cases, however, care was taken to provide enough detailed information so that students can see the development of an idea, how it is investigated, and how the results are interpreted. Hopefully, this will not only provide something generally missing from textbook summaries and often difficult to give in a lecture format but also will result in the opportunity for students to evaluate critically conclusions drawn from the research. In those instances where portions of an article were deleted, the bibliographic references allow for further investigation if desired.

The readings were chosen also to touch on a wide variety of topics rather than to delve exhaustively into a few. It was felt that exposing new students to the diverse aspects of behavior to which perception is relevant would help convey the excitement and importance of the topic. Students to whom this feeling is communicated can then pursue a particular interest in considerable depth, using as a starting point references obtained from the collected articles. In addition, an occasional review article is included to present various sides of a controversial issue.

This book is divided into three parts, more for ease of organization than to suggest a clear delineation of three areas within perception. The first part presents work dealing with the problem of defining the stimuli and intervening variables in perception and sets forth different theoretical approaches to the question of relating input to output. Part II deals with the topic of perceptual learning and the physiological mechanisms underlying perception, and Part III considers such topics as memory, attentional mechanisms, and individual differences. Each of the three parts is preceded by a brief description of the articles, summarizing the work and suggesting the continuity between the readings. In some cases, additional articles are suggested for interested students.

Compiled so as to maximize its flexibility, this book could be assigned either in its entirety or selectively and could be used by the instructor either to supplement the conventional textbook in perception or to replace it.

If this book does contribute to the readers' knowledge of perception, its success must be attributed to the contributing authors. The permission of these individuals and the original publishers to reprint the articles is gratefully acknowledged. It is with pleasure that I express my gratitude to my colleagues, particularly John Barefoot, Brian Laver, Bill Petrusic, and Bruce Ferguson, for their numerous suggestions. I also wish to thank my research assistants, Carol Husband, Stephanie Gillespie, and Bob Young, for helping in innumerable ways; and my wife, whose editorial comments and patience are affectionately appreciated. The advice and encouragement of Mark R. Rosenzweig of the University of California, Berkeley, and the support of the Carleton University Faculty of Arts Publication Fund is acknowledged.

# iNPUT-OUTPUT

Part I

# WHAT GOES IN — MUST IT COME OUT?

Perception can be defined in many ways. One of the most general definitions, and one which indicates how other aspects of psychology could be considered to be subsets of perception, terms it the study of the relation between stimulus input and behavioral output. The first article, by Gibson, clearly demonstrates the difficulty of deciding what is input. The close association of perception with other disciplines such as philosophy and physiology becomes evident as the author deals with such questions as, Is a stimulus that which *does* activate a sense organ or that which *can* activate a sense organ? Is a visual pattern a single stimulus or a number of separate stimuli? After considerable discussion, Gibson concludes that one should speak in terms of *effective* stimuli that arouse some sort of response at either a micro (for instance, cellular) level or at a molar (for example, overt behavioral) level, with the response criterion determined by the experimenter. Thus, whether a potential stimulus is effective depends upon the nature of the receiver—his receptor system, its state of readiness, and other individual characteristics. Many of the theoretical arguments put forth by Gibson are presented in greater detail in later readings.

Whereas Gibson's article emphasizes the stimulus and response, the second paper describes a way in which the intervening variables between input and output may be examined. The authors, Garner, Hake, and Eriksen, suggest that most perceptual experimental results may be interpreted in a variety of ways, so that a number of operations rather than a single one is needed to determine which of several alternative hypotheses is the most satisfactory. Such a procedure, termed converging operations, may be used to consider concepts or intervening processes that are not directly observable.

The third reading is by one of the foremost proponents of Gestalt psychology, Wolfgang Köhler. The Gestalt school of psychology places emphasis on sensory organization that, it is argued, causes stimuli to be grouped and perceived in particular ways determined by innate laws of organization. The consequence of this organization is that things are not perceived as being composed of individual stimuli but are perceived as a whole. Thus the "whole is greater than the sum of its parts." The excerpt chosen is not a description of the specific Gestalt laws of perception (which are described in almost every introductory textbook in psychology and perception) but rather a development of the argument for considering the perception of an integrated whole as being relatively independent of prior learning and experience.

In contrast to this view, the article by Hebb approaches the problems of perception by emphasizing the importance of learning. His theorizing is based upon the following postulate: If several neurons make functional contact with and excite another cell, a physical change will occur, which increases the probability of the single neuron being excited when the impinging neurons are. The cellular associations and changes are determined by the experiences of the organism rather than by innate factors. Hebb argues that two steps are needed for an event to become permanent and thereby affect future perception: (1) There must be a temporary neurological record of the stimulus, achieved by a "reverberatory trace"; that is, neurons can persist, in the absence of the original stimulus, in exciting one another by means of a self-maintaining circuit. (2) This reverberatory loop is required while structural changes are being accomplished at the neuronal level that result in permanent storage. The excerpt chosen for this book describes a possible mechanism for these neurological alterations. Although this theory was proposed over 20 years ago and has been subsequently modified (see, for example, Milner [1]), research inspired and influenced by Hebb's theorizing has been, to a considerable degree, in accord with it.

The selection following the excerpt by Hebb is an example of recent work supporting his hypothesis. Thus study, by Globus and others, demonstrates that cortical neurons of a rat undergo physical change as a consequence of exposure to a stimulating environment early in life. Discussions of some of the questions of innate and learned factors in perception raised by Köhler and Hebb can be found in Part II.

The sixth reading is an overview of adaptation-level theory by its originator, Helson. This theory emphasizes the importance of considering a stimulus as a member of a particular class of stimuli. The perception of the particular stimulus is based upon several factors, including prior experience with other stimuli in that class. Adaptation-level theory was not proposed to replace other theories but rather to supplement them. An example of its wide range of applicability is given in the seventh article: Although originally conducted to examine a theoretical position in social psychology, the study by Doob and others can be interpreted as providing striking support for Helson's adaptation-level theory.

Attneave's article raises the interesting point that much of the information that impinges upon an organism is redundant. In his review, Attneave manages to tie together much of Köhler's, Hebb's, and Helson's theorizing by discussing how an organism copes with redundancy.

Following this theoretical piece, there is a short, recent study by Warren that investigates redundancy in speech.

Whereas Attneave emphasizes redundancy in information processing, Swets, Tanner, and Birdsall extend the question of information processing into a theory of signal detection, that is, how the observer determines whether what is perceived is *signal* or *noise* (interference). The variables influencing this decision, such as payoff and strength of the signal, are discussed in detail. Readers are urged not to be discouraged by the few formulas presented. They are quite straightforward and are explained in a very lucid, step-by-step fashion. One question that clearly emerges from this signal-detection approach is whether a sensory threshold exists and, if it does, whether it is a meaningful and useful concept. For further detail, readers may wish to read an article by Swets, "Is There a Sensory Threshold?" [2].

Both the McConnell and the Black readings deal with research examining the influence of stimuli that are below the level of "awareness." Again the concept of sensory threshold has to be questioned; both articles demonstrate that in certain circumstances subliminal (below threshold) stimuli affect perception of supraliminal stimuli.

The final article of Part I is an excerpt from Vincent Dethier's marvelous book *To Know a Fly*. Although delivered in a very light vein, the writer's insight cannot help but impress the reader.

REFERENCES

1. P. M. Milner. The cell assembly: Mark II. *Psychol. Rev.*, 1957, 64, 242–252.
2. J. A. Swets. Is there a sensory threshold? *Science*, 1961, 134, 168–177.

# 1
# THE CONCEPT OF THE STIMULUS IN PSYCHOLOGY

James J. Gibson

It seems to me that there is a weak link in the chain of reasoning by which we explain experience and behavior, namely, our concept of the stimulus. The aim of this paper is to find out what psychologists mean by the term stimulus, with the hope of deciding what they *ought* to mean by it. After a short look at the history of the term, I will try to uncover the sources of confusion in modern usage. In the end, perhaps, the concept will be clarified. If not, certain contradictions will have been brought to light.

The experimental study of the stimulus began in the eighteenth century, so far as I can tell, with an investigation of the curious things that could be done to make a frog's leg twitch. The experimenters discovered what is now called the nerve-muscle preparation. Galvani and later Volta gave their names to electricity as well as to physiology by their experiments. In the early nineteenth century Johannes Müller applied these discoveries to the philosophers' problem of the human senses, the gates of knowledge. The nerves of sense, he pointed out, can be excited by a variety of unnatural agencies such as electrical current. Since the mind is acquainted only with the qualities specific to the sensory nerves, not with the stimuli, how it gets knowledge of the material world became more puzzling than ever. Later in the century, Sherrington was to emphasize the extent to which receptors are naturally protected against such irrelevant stimuli by the structural specialization of sense organs. But meanwhile it had been discovered that the skin would yield sensations only at certain discrete points. Here was a fresh puzzle. The separate receptor cells of all the sense organs came to be seen under the microscope, and the punctate character of the sensory process seemed to be established.

During all this time, the physical scientists were discovering the laws of energy and triumphantly measuring it in its various forms, electricity, momentum, light, heat, sound, and the results of chemical reaction. It became possible to measure certain variables of energy at sense organs, at least the simple ones like frequency and amount. Thresholds of re-

Source: *American Psychologist,* 1960, *15,* 694–703. Copyright 1960 by the American Psychological Association. Reprinted by permission.

portable sensation were established. Fechner, following Weber, conceived the grand scheme of a measurement formula for consciousness, relating its judged intensity to a simple variable of the stimulus. Psychophysics was born.

Whatever could be controlled by an experimenter and applied to an observer could be thought of as a stimulus. In the growing science of human psychology, it became evident that this was the independent variable of an experiment, to be isolated and systematically varied. Much more complex things than physical energies could be presented to the sense organs—words for instance. These were also called stimuli, although the stimulus conditions manipulated, recency, frequency, meaningfulness, were vastly different from the variables of the psychophysical experiment.

In the latter part of the nineteenth century the concept of the reflex arc was applied to the adaptive behavior of animals. It had been thought to explain the strictly mechanical actions of the body ever since Descartes. Reflexes had stimuli. The situations of animals could be systematically altered and the reactions observed. Organisms obviously responded to such stimuli, and the experimenter could apply them more freely than he could venture to do with human beings. To shorten a long story, such experiments came to be merged with human experiments and the outcome was a general stimulus-response psychology. This was a great success, especially in America. But stimuli for animal psychologists were not the same as stimuli for sensory physiologists, and stimuli were still different for the students of perception and learning.

Enough has been said to show that in the twentieth century we have inherited a mixed batch of ideas about the stimulus. We constantly use the word but seldom define it. We take it for granted. We have behavior theory in full bloom, and perception theory in ripened complexity, but who ever heard of stimulus theory? As a preliminary effort in this direction, I have made a survey of what modern writers seem to mean by the term. Some writers define it, but not many. My method was to collect quotations from books. I then put them in opposition to one another. The ways of conceiving the stimulus are often in flat contradiction. Occasionally one book can be quoted against itself. The issues interlock, of course, but I have separated them into eight areas of disagreement and will treat them separately. In what follows, I will quote without comment, for the most part, keeping my own opinions to the end.

*I.* For Freud, the only use of the term stimulus that is discoverable in the *Collected Papers* [3] is to refer to a motivating force. This, after all, is the dictionary meaning of the word—something that arouses or impels to action. In ordinary speech we refer to the stimulus of hunger or fear, which may compel extreme forms of behavior. Freud does not often use the term, but when he does, a stimulus is something to be satisfied or warded off.

Psychologists and physiologists, however, have generally used the term for the arousing of a sense organ instead of a whole individual. But they do not wholly agree about this. Some accept both meanings. Neal Miller asserts that "any stimulus has some drive value" [15, p. 59]. However, Skinner believes that "a drive is not a stimulus," and that although "the term has the unfortunate connotation of a goal or spur to action," we must not be misled by this popular meaning of the word [19, p. 375]. Here, then, is a first area of disagreement in our way of conceiving the stimulus: *Does a stimulus motivate the individual or does it merely trigger a response?*

*II.* Pavlov said that "a stimulus appears to be connected with a given response as cause with effect" [18, p. 10]. This is a forthright assertion. Similarly Watson took as the whole aim of psychology the predicting of the response, given the stimulus, and the specifying of the stimulus, given the response [26, p. 10]. But contrast this with the caution of Hilgard and Marquis. "We refer to a stimulus as an instigator [and] no more is intended than that the stimulus is in some sense the occasion for the response [8, p. 73]. Evidently what Pavlov and Watson meant by a stimulus is not what Hilgard and Marquis meant. Nearly all psychologists now follow the second line. It is allowed that a stimulus may cause a reflex, but not an act. Woodworth was one of the first to emphasize that the stimulus does not in itself determine the response; factors in the organism intervene to help determine it. The discussion of intervening variables or mediating processes has by now filled volumes.

The same rule is taken to hold for experience. It is allowed that a stimulus may cause a sensation, but not a perception. M. D. Vernon, for example, states that "the nature of the percept is not ... determined by the physical qualities of the stimulus, but is largely a function of constructive tendencies in the individual [25, p. 47]. But I have been arguing the opposite for some time, that the percept is in very good correspondence with the physical variables of the stimulus. *Can a stimulus be taken as the sufficient cause of a response, or can it not?* This is a second area of confusion in our concept of the stimulus.

*III.* Skinner has recently noted that "we frequently define the stimulus by the very doubtful property of its ability to elicit the response in question, rather than by any independent property of the stimulus itself" [20, p. 355]. He suggests no remedy, however, for this doubtful scientific behavior, and he seems to be confessing a sin without pointing the way to salvation. In truth, many psychologists do give a circular definition of the stimulus. Skinner himself believed in his first book that "neither term [stimulus or response] can be defined as to its essential properties without the other" [19, p. 9]. Neal Miller has said "a response is any activity by or within the individual which can become functionally connected with an antecedent event through learning; a stimulus is any event to which a response can become so connected" [15, p. 59]. Miller, in fact, has argued that this circular definition of the stimulus is not only necessary but is theoretically desirable [12, p. 239]. He seems to have abandoned completely the specifying of a stimulus by variables of physical energy. But listen to Estes. "By *stimulus,* I refer to environmental conditions, describable in physical terms without reference to the behavior of an organism" [12, p. 455], and Hayek says, "the distinction between different stimuli must be independent of the different effects they have on the organism" [7, p. 9].

Here is a disagreement. The student of psychophysics will argue that we must define our stimulus by certain operations of physical science, not by the judgments of our subject. Otherwise how are we ever to discover what stimuli can be discriminated and what cannot? When the stimulus is difficult to specify in objective physical terms, however, investigators tend to avoid the difficulty and describe it as that which is responded to, or that which is perceived. A few go further and, by arguing that an experimenter cannot define the stimulus anyway except in terms of *his* perception, reach a philosophical position of subjectivism. There is an ancient puzzle to which students of philosophy are treated—whether there exists any sound when a tree crashes in the forest with no living being there to hear it. It is a question of how to conceive the auditory stimulus. It seems to remain a puzzle for a good many psychologists.

I think the central question is the following. Is a stimulus that which *does* activate a sense organ or that which *can* activate a sense organ? Some writers imply that a stimulus not currently exciting receptors is not a stimulus at all. Others imply that a stimulus need not excite receptors to be called such. They allow of *potential stimuli.* Witness Guthrie's assertion that stimuli are "potential occasions" for the initiation of sensory activity, and that "the physical stimuli, though present, may not be effective [12, p. 178]. The former conception allows physical energy to be called a stimulus only when some response can be observed; the latter allows of the possibility that stimulus energy may be present without necessarily being responded to. The latter seems the better concept. With the former meaning, one could never speak of a subthreshold stimulus, and this is a useful term. An effective stimulus on one occasion may be ineffective on another. And there are various response criteria by which a threshold can be measured.

The distinction between effective and potential stimuli is made by a few theorists, but its implications have not been traced, and the idea remains undeveloped. The concept of a permanent environment of *objects* is widely accepted, but not the concept of a permanent environment of *potential stimuli.*

The third area of disagreement is this: *Must a stimulus be defined independently of the response it produces—in physical terms rather than terms of behavior or sensory process?*

*IV.* For Pavlov a stimulus could be anything in the terrestrial world. Any event he could think of to use in an experiment he would call a stimulus, and he employed tones, bells, the sound of bubbling water, lights, rotating objects, pictures on a screen, acid in the mouth, food, a scratch on the back, or electric shock. This commonsense usage of the term persists among a good many behaviorists. Spence has said that the term stimulus means to him, "the physical or world situation, with its different aspects or features" [21, p. 39]. For Neal Miller anything that is discriminable is a stimulus or, as he calls it, a cue, these terms having the same meaning. For Skinner, a stimulus is simply "a part, or modification of a part, of the environment" [19, p. 235]. To be sure, he says, it must "refer to a class of events the members of which possess some property in common" (p. 34). Because stimuli have this "generic nature," the practice of calling a bell an auditory stimulus and a book a visual stimulus is, as he puts it, "frequently successful" (p. 235). All these writers persist in believing that somehow the things of the environment can *stimulate* us, and they refuse to be worried by the paradox that only receptors at the skin of an individual can actually be stimulated.

This definition of the stimulus is considered naive by perception psychologists. Stimuli are energies, not objects. In Troland's words, "the stimulus may be defined as the specific physical force, energy, or agency which brings about the stimulation of the given receptor system" [23, p. 9]. This conception has the authority of a century's research on the senses. In 1834 Johannes Müller argued that a stimulus was whatever excited one of the "nerves of sense." To the modern neurophysiologist, a stimulus is energy that depolarizes a living cell—especially, but not exclusively, a nerve cell. For Jennings in 1906, studying the amoeba, a stimulus was a type of change in the immediate environment that produced a change in behavior [11, p. 19], and there existed precisely five types: chemical, mechanical, thermal, photic, or electrical. Woodworth says that "a stimulus is any form of energy acting upon a sense organ and arousing some activity of the organism" [27, p. 223]. Koffka wishes to call stimuli "the causes of the excitations of our sense organs" [13, p. 79], but he, more than any other theorist, faced up to the contradictory meanings of the term and proposed a formal distinction between the "proximal" stimulus and the "distal" or "distant" stimulus. He made us consider the paradox that although perception and behavior seem to be determined by the distal object, they can in fact only be aroused by the proximal stimulus.

Not all psychologists are willing to grapple with this paradox and, in truth, it is baffling. If the proximal stimulus for a given object is altered with every change of the observer's position in space, if it is different on different occasions, we are faced with an absurdity. We must suppose that a countless family of different stimuli can all arouse the same percept. Most behaviorists speak of the stimulus-object as if, by hyphenating two words with different meanings, the absurdity were removed. As men of common sense they see the need of reducing to one the countless number of stimuli that can arouse a single percept, and in this surely they have a point. But perceptionists, being unable to take this easy way out, struggle to construct theories of how different stimuli might arouse the same percept, the theories of perceptual constancy. So far, no theory has been agreed on. Is it possible that common sense is right without knowing it, and that every family of proximal stimuli arising from one object *is*, in a sense, one stimulus?

Here is a fourth disagreement: *Do stimuli exist in the environment or only at receptors?* There is a suggestion that both usages of the term are somehow correct, but it has not been explained.

V. Osgood says that "a stimulus may be defined as that form of physical energy that activates a receptor" [17, p. 12]. But he does not tell us whether he means by a receptor a single cell or a mosaic of receptor cells, that is, a sense organ. Others besides Osgood are undecided about this question, or have not thought about it. Hull knew what he thought. For him, the retinal image was a pattern of stimuli [10, p. 37] and a single light ray was a stimulus (p. 33). "A stimulus element is a stimulus energy which activates a single receptor-organ" (p. 349). This is straightforward. Woodworth says that "of course the light entering the eye and striking many rods and cones is a collection of stimuli rather than a single stimulus," but in the next paragraph he suggests that "the sudden cessation of a light" is a stimulus [27, p. 28]. Köhler was fairly explicit on the question, saying that an organism responds to "an objective constellation of millions of stimuli" [14, p. 179], and Koffka also assumed that stimuli on the retina or the skin were local events [13]. But Nissen, on the other hand, asserts that "a stimulus involves a pattern of stimulation, spatial or temporal" [22, p. 374]. Many other writers define stimuli as the occasions for activation of a sense organ, not of a receptor cell, and speak as if a pattern were a stimulus. There is a vast difference between a pattern of stimuli and a stimulus pattern, but we have not sufficiently thought about it. Is a pattern a single stimulus or is it a number of separate stimuli?

The notion that a stimulus is what excites a cell, and is therefore *punctate*, seems to many theorists the only rigorous definition. On this account Hull had to introduce the postulate of afferent neural interaction to explain molar behavior as distinguished from molecular responses. The Gestalt psychologists had to develop the theory of sensory organization in order to explain perception. But Lashley once said that

> the stimulus to any reaction above the level of a spinal reflex involves not the excitation of certain definite sensory cells but the excitation of *any* cells of a system in certain ratios, and the response may be given to the ratio even though the particular cells involved have not previously been excited in the same way [16, p. 476].

This passage suggests the idea that higher levels of reaction require us to define higher orders of stimulation. Lashley seems to be saying that a ratio may be itself a stimulus, not just a relation between two stimuli. But note that the Gestalt theorists, by conceiving all stimuli as local events, did not come to think in this way.

A controversy has long been going on over the question of how an individual could respond to a relation. It began with Köhler's evidence that a chick will select the brighter of two gray papers instead of the absolute brightness of a particular paper. Köhler thought it demonstrated a relational process in the brain; Spence has gone to great lengths to show that it could be explained in terms of absolute responses to each piece of paper, subject to the so-called principle of stimulus generalization. But the simplest explanation would be that the effective stimulus in the experiment was the direction of the difference in brightness in the field of view. In line with this solution to the problem, students of vision conceive that a margin is a visual stimulus, perhaps *the* visual stimulus, and a margin in the array of light to an eye is strictly a ratio, that is, a relation between measured intensities.

Here is a fifth source of confusion: *When is a pattern or relation to be considered a single stimulus and when a number of separate stimuli?*

VI. The notion that a stimulus can only be something punctate is related to the notion that a stimulus can only be something momentary. The gestalt psychologists pointed out that a melody is perceived, but they never suggested that a melody was a stimulus. The notes of the melody were taken to be the stimuli. But what about the transitions between notes, or the "transients" of acoustical engineering? Are they stimuli? The investigators of speech sounds seem to think so, but the auditory literature of sensation is vague on this question. And if a short transition is a stimulus, why not a long transition or temporal pattern?

In vision, experimenters have not been able to make up their minds as to whether an optical motion was a stimulus or a series of stimuli. The retina and also the skin are very sensitive to motion. It ought to be simple, but the facts of the stroboscope and the phi-phenomenon have been interpreted to imply that it is complex. Motion is taken to be change of location, as it is in classical physics, and it is then reasoned that the impression of location must be fundamental to any perception of a change of location.

On the other hand, the generalization is frequently met with that a stimulus is always a change. This is very confusing, in fact it is one confusion piled on another. I think that writers who make this assertion have in mind the experiments showing that an unchanging stimulus soon ceases to be effective for perception. They are thinking of sensory adaptation. What changes in that case is not the stimulus but the process of excitation. For the retina, the skin, and the olfactory organ, sensory adaptation does occur. For example, the steady application of an image to a human retina, by the method of artificially stabilizing the image, eventuates in a wholly ineffective stimulus. But note that the steady application of focusable light to a human eye does not. This stimulus never becomes wholly ineffective, even with the best voluntary fixation, because of slight movements of the eye itself. This means that retinal stimulation is by no means the same thing as optical stimulation. They are different stages in the chain of events that leads to vision. A "change in stimulation" means something quite different when it is produced by some adjustment of the sense organ itself than when it is produced by an external event.

Is optical motion, then, meaning a change in the pattern of focusable light to the eye, to be considered a stimulus? Experiments based on this assumption are beginning to appear. In the recent Cornell research with optical transformation [4] we not only think of this as a stimulus, we have come to think of nonchange of pattern as simply a special case. Stability, after all, is only definable as absence of motion. Similarly, a form is definable as a nontransformation. In this conception, sequence is a dimension of stimulation whether or not change occurs.

The great virtue of this conception of sequence is that it suggests a simple solution to the puzzle of perceptual constancy. Two types of nonchange are distinguishable, first, nonmotion of a pattern and, second, invariance of a pattern during motion. The invariant contained in a family of the perspectives arising from a single object is a single stimulus. Hence there is only one stimulus for a single object, and the common sense opinion is right after all.

The sixth conceptual issue is this: *When does a sequence constitute a single and when a number of separate stimuli; also, can a single enduring stimulus exist throughout a changing sequence?*

VII. Users of the Rorschach test assume that a stimulus field can be either structured or, as they put it, *unstructured*. I could find no explicit definition of unstructured stimulation in the literature but only examples of the material to which the term is applied—inkblots and other items used in the so-called projective tests. The idea of structured stimulation comes from Gestalt theory but only from a vague, tentative, and undeveloped hypothesis of Gestalt theory—the external forces of organization as distinguished from the internal forces of organization. Koffka, for example, was so preoccupied with the ways in which the individual structured his stimulus field that he scarcely considered the ways in which it might already have structure [13]. In fact, he wrote sometimes as if it had none, as if all structure had to be imposed on it, because the stimuli themselves were meaningless points.

This uncertainty about the existence of structure in the stimulus for perceived form still persists. But since Koffka's time, and partly inspired by him, some experimenters are beginning simply to assume it, and to apply mathematics to the structure of a stimulus. They would not agree that an inkblot is in any sense an unstructured stimulus. A picture has one structure, an inkblot has another, but it does not lack structure. That can be said only of a film color or the cloudless blue sky. The structure of an array may have ambiguous or equivocal components, as Koffka showed, but that is not the same thing. The capacity of light to carry structure to an eye may be impoverished or reduced experimentally but it remains. The structure of light may not specify anything familiar to the subject, or to any observer, but it is a geometrical fact. The subject may be unable to register the structure because it is nonsense to him, or he overlooks it, or he was not told to look for it, or his eyes are defective, or he is too young, or for a dozen other reasons, but it is still in the light. So, at least, some experimenters would argue.

What can be meant by an unstructured stimulus field is thus a matter of disagreement. The seventh question is: *How do we specify the structure of a stimulus?*

VIII. The conception of stimuli as physical energies seems to imply that, in themselves, they have no significance or meaning. Especially if they are considered to be only spots of energy at brief moments of time it is clear that they specify little or nothing about the environment. Light, heat, mechanical, acoustical, chemical, and electrical energy are far from being objects, places, events, people, words, and symbols, but nevertheless they are the only stimuli that can affect receptors. This theory of the meaningless stimulus has been an accepted doctrine for a long, long time in the study of the senses. It leads to the notion of the sense datum—the bare sensation, or raw sensory impression, and thence to the persistent problem of how animals and men can be supposed to perceive objects, places, events, and one another.

Students of behavior, however, without questioning the doctrine of the empty stimulus, often act as if they did not believe it. Beach speaks for comparative psychologists when he says, in describing how birds feed their offspring, "young birds exhibit a gaping response which *stimulates* the parent to place food in the nestling's mouth" [22, p. 415]. He takes it for granted that light rays can specify the event called gaping and refuses to worry about it further. Students of perception do worry about this question, but they are not consistent. On the one hand, they firmly assert that nothing gets into the eye but light of variable wave length and intensity, not objects, or events, or facts of the environment. On the other hand, they often say that light "carries" information about the environment, or that stimuli "provide" information to the perceiver. If this is so, the stimuli must specify something beyond themselves, and they cannot be empty of meaning.

A sort of compromise between the informative stimulus and the empty stimulus is provided by the use of the term *cue*. According to

Woodworth, "a cue, as used in psychology, is a stimulus which serves as a sign or signal of something else, the connection having previously been learned" [28, 60]. Stimuli are conceived by analogy with messages, or communication in code. Brunswik thought of stimuli as *indicators* of environmental facts, by analogy with pointer readings, emphasizing, however, that they had only a probable connection with the fact in question [1]. Boring has suggested that stimuli may be taken as *clues,* and this term points to Helmholtz's theory of unconscious rational inference from the sense data [6].

Merely to call the stimulus a cue, sign, signal, message, indicator, or clue does not tell us what we need to know. The question is to what extent does the stimulus specify its source, and how does it do so? Is it possible that the use of these verbal metaphors only prevents us from facing the problem? Or consider the use by modern information theorists of a neutral term like *input*. When they compare the organism to a communication system or to a black box, the internal working of which has to be discovered, are they avoiding the obligation to consider the environment of an organism and the relation of stimuli to the environment?

The problem of the connection between stimuli and their natural sources has not been taken seriously by psychologists. Stimuli have not even been classified from this point of view, but only with respect to the sense organs and the types of energy which carry stimuli. It is a problem of ecology, as Brunswik realized when he wrote about the "ecological validity" of cues [1]. I think the problem has been obscured, and our recognition of it delayed, by our failure to separate it into parts. The connection between natural stimuli and their sources is not the same as the connection between social stimuli and their sources, for example, the connection between words and their referents. This latter problem, surely, is distinct. Semantics is one thing, ecology is another; and a science of environmental stimuli may not prove to be as difficult as a science of symbols, once we put our minds to it.

I have maintained that optical stimuli, for example, gradients of texture in the light to an eye, specify environmental objects by the relation of *projection*. To me this is not at all the same as the relation by which words specify objects, which I would call one of *coding*. But however this may be, we face another unanswered question, the eighth: *Do stimuli carry information about their sources in the world, and how do they specify them?*

## SOME POSITIVE HYPOTHESES

Can anything useful be salvaged from these various contradictory usages and definitions? No one could be blamed for being pessimistic about it. S. S. Stevens, who has thought hard and long about stimuli, concluded that it is futile even to attempt a general definition of the stimulus in psychology. Psychology as a whole, he says, can be equated with the problem of defining the stimulus, that is, giving a complete definition of the stimulus for a given response. To be able to do so would require that we specify "all the transformations of the environment, both external and internal, that leave the response invariant." And "for no response have we yet given a complete definition of the stimulus" in this sense [22, pp. 31f.]. If I understand him, what Stevens chiefly had in mind is the puzzle of constancy. He was saying that we do not know how to specify, in the chaos of literal proximal-energy stimulation, the actual cause of a given response. This is a discouraging truth.

But, unlike Stevens, I have hopes, and even some positive hypotheses to suggest. Once the contradictory assumptions about stimulation are made explicit, we can try to resolve them. For one thing, we might search for an invariant component in the bewildering variety of functionally equivalent stimuli. Perhaps there is an invariant stimulus for the invariant response, after all. Many sorts of higher order variables of energy may exist, only awaiting mathematical description. They will have to be described in appropriate terms, of course, not as simple functions of frequency and amount. We must not confuse a stimulus with the elements used for its analysis. We must learn to conceive an array not as a mosaic of stimuli but as a hierarchy of forms within forms, and a flux not as a chain of stimuli but as a hierarchy of sequences within longer sequences.

**Molar Stimuli**

Ever since Tolman, behavior theorists have been agreeing that psychology is concerned with molar responses, not molecular ones. Accordingly we try to observe and measure what an organism is doing, not how all its muscles are contracting. With this kind of observation on the response side there should be a corresponding kind of observation on the stimulus side. We should try to discover what an organism is responding to, not what excites all the little receptors. Of course, the muscles may be contracting and all the receptors may be excited, but observation at that level is the job of the physiologists.

The same recommendation can be made for the study of perception. The Gestalt theorists have demonstrated the fact of molar experience, but they did not look for molar stimuli. These may very well exist outside the laboratory and, with ingenuity, can perhaps be isolated in the laboratory. If so, we shall have a new and powerful kind of psychophysics.

This conception of molar stimuli is not wholly new. Forty-five years ago, E. B. Holt was convinced that cognition, along with behavior, was a constant function of stimulation. In this he agreed with Pavlov and Watson. But Holt emphasized that the stimulus of which cognitive behavior was a function was more abstract and more comprehensive than the stimulus of classical psychophysics. As one passes from reflexes to behavior, the effective stimulus "recedes," as Holt put it [9, passim]. By the *recession* of the stimulus he meant that it seems to be located far out in the environment rather than close by in the receptors. And he also meant that as cognition develops, the stimulus of which it is a function recedes more and more. Following this suggestion, one might conclude that a change in response implies a change in the stimulus to which the response is made. Learning would then involve not only an alteration of behavior but also an alteration in the effective stimulus. Presumably its molar character has gone up a stage in the hierarchy.

**Potential Stimuli**

Evidently the hypothesis of potential stimulation, accepted casually by some theorists, has quite radical but unrecognized implications. We have long acknowledged the almost unlimited possibilities for new responses in learning theory; why not equally vast possibilities of new stimuli? The environment, so considered, would consist of a sort of reservoir of possible stimuli for both perception and action. Light, heat, sound, odor, gravity, and potential contacts with objects surround the individual. But this sea of energy has variables of pattern and sequence which can be registered by sense organs. They can be explored, either at one station-point or by moving around in the environment. The fields of radiating sound and odor, together with the flux of light rays reflected from surfaces, make it possible to respond to things at a distance. The changes of pattern in time serve as controlling stimuli for locomotion and manipulation. The variables and covariables and invariables of this stimulus environment are inexhaustible.

Surprisingly little has been written about potential stimuli. The sensory physiologists, of course, have read their physics and chemistry. But physical science portrays a sterile world. The variables of physics make uninteresting stimuli. Why is this true? I think it is because psychologists take for stimuli only the variables of physics as they stand in the textbooks. We have simply picked the wrong variables. It is our own fault. After all, physicists are not primarily concerned with stimuli. They have enough to do to study physical energies without worrying about stimulus energies. I think that we will have to develop the needed discipline on a do-it-yourself principle. It might be called ecological physics, with branches in optics, acoustics, dynamics, and biochemistry. We cannot wait for the physical scientists to describe and classify potential stimuli. The variables would seem to them inelegant, the mathematics would have to be improvised, and the job is not to their taste. But it is necessary. And if successful, it will provide a basis for a stimulus-response psychology, which otherwise seems to be sinking in a swamp of intervening variables.

Consider, for example, the physics (that is to say the acoustics) of speech sounds. As recently as 1951, in the *Handbook of Experimental Psychology* [22, p. 869], the fact that a word is perceptually the same when whispered as it is when shouted was taken to prove that the physical characteristics of sound waves, frequency, intensity, and so on, cannot tell us about speech. Speech perception would require a psychological theory, not physical measurement. But the invention of the sound spectrograph seems to have shown that certain higher order variables of acoustic energy are the critical constituents of speech and the stimuli for hearing it. These newly discovered invariant patterns of sound are completely physical, even if they had not previously been studied in physics. What was needed to understand the psychophysics of hearing words was not more psychology but more physics.

For another example consider the optics of an array of light. The physical variables applying to the point source and the image point do not explain the seeing of a surface. But my own work shows that the variables of an optical *texture* do account for the seeing of a surface, and that by manipulating textures an experimenter can produce synthetic perceptions of objects [5]. Gradients, patterns, and other invariants are not part of existing geometrical optics, but they are physical facts. What was needed for a psychophysics of visual perception was not more theorizing about cues but more attention to geometrical optics.

**Effective Stimuli**

An effective stimulus can now be defined. It is one which arouses receptor activity, or recorded neural impulses, or sense organ adjustments, or overt responses, or verbal judgments—whichever criterion one chooses. Note that the idea of fixed innate thresholds of sensation is rejected. It always was a myth, for every psychophysical experimenter knows that the threshold obtained depends on the method used and the response criterion chosen.

In short, whether or not a potential stimulus becomes effective depends on the individual. It depends on the species to which he belongs, on the anatomy of the sense organs, the stage of maturation, the capacities for sense organ adjustment, the habits of attention, the activity in progress, and the possibilities of educating the attention of the individual. Such facts make up the field of perceptual development and perceptual learning. At the lower levels they are called facts of sensory physiology; at the higher levels, facts of attention or exploration, but they are all one problem. Animals seem to be driven to make potential stimuli effective. They use their receptor equipment, probably, in as great a variety of ways as they use their motor equipment. From this point of view, it seems to me, the senses begin to make sense.

**Stages of Specificity**

Johannes Müller began the study of the way in which the modes of experience are specific to the excitations of nerve fibers. Sherrington and others showed how the excitations of fibers were generally specific to the patterns of the stimulus. Ecological physics will tell us the extent to which the proximal stimuli are specific to their sources in the world. If experience is specific to excitation, and excitation to stimulation, and stimulation to the external environment, then experience will be specific to the environment, within the limits of this chain of specificities. The first two stages have long been under investigation. The last is ripe for study. There has been a controversy over whether or not visual stimuli can specify their objects (for example, Cantril) [2], but it can be settled, for the facts are discoverable, and arguments should await evidence.

### The Informative Capacity of Molar Stimuli

If the structure and sequence of stimulus energy can be analyzed, potential stimuli can be described and arranged in a hierarchy. There will be subordinate stimuli and superordinate stimuli, of lower order and higher order. So conceived it is reasonable to assume that stimuli *carry information* about the terrestrial environment. That is, they specify things about objects, places, events, animals, people, and the actions of people. The rules by which they do so are to be determined, but there is at least enough evidence to warrant discarding the opposite assumption under which we have been operating for centuries—that stimuli are necessarily and intrinsically meaningless.

### Natural Stimuli, Pictorial Stimuli, and Coded Stimuli

I have suggested that, instead of continuing to employ the careless analogies of our present loose terminology for stimuli—cues, clues, signals, signs, indicators, messages, inputs, and the like—we make a systematic study of the laws by which stimuli specify their sources. We need to know the laws of stimulus information. Almost certainly these will not be the laws which govern the transmission of information in human systems of communication. The natural world does not literally communicate with the sense organs. The potential physical stimuli arising from an event are not to be compared to the physical stimulus arising from the word for that event. We cannot hope to understand natural stimuli by analogy with socially coded stimuli, for that would be like putting the cart before the horse. Just this, however, is what we tend to do when we speak of the "signs" for depth perception and the "messages" of the senses. We cannot afford to speak of coded information for the sense organs when we mean stimuli, for some of these are coded and some are not.

A systematic study of the specifying power of stimuli will put the problem of meaning in perception on a new footing. It will take several forms, depending on the kinds of relations discovered. My guess is that there will be at least three, corresponding to the stimuli from things, from pictures, and from words. It is true that men, besides learning to perceive objects, also learn to apprehend things by way of perceiving pictures and words. These mediated perceptions get mixed with direct perceptions in the adult. But we shall have to disentangle them before we can have a complete theory of human perception.

## CONCLUSION

The foregoing distinctions and assumptions seem promising to me. But I would agree that a stimulus theory cannot be established by merely asserting it. The scientific question is whether all these new kinds of stimuli exist. I suggest that we look for them in the environment and then try to bring them into the laboratory.

It is still true that the stimulus is the prime independent variable of a psychological experiment. I quote from Underwood:

> One may vary more than one stimulus condition in a given experiment... but to draw a conclusion about the influence of any given variable, that variable must have been systematically manipulated alone somewhere in the design. Nothing in analysis of variance, covariance, Latin squares, Greco-Latin squares, or Greco-Arabic-Latin squares has abrogated this basic principle [24, p. 35].

If Underwood is right, the secret of a good experiment is to discover the relevant stimulus before doing the experiment. The moral of my argument is that a systematic search for relevant stimuli, molar stimuli, potential stimuli, invariant stimuli, specifying stimuli, and informative stimuli will yield experiments with positive results. Perhaps the reservoir of stimuli that I have pictured is full of elegant independent variables, their simplicity obscured by physical complexity, only waiting to be discovered.

## REFERENCES

1. E. Brunswik. *Perception and the representative design of experiments.* Berkeley: University of California Press, 1956.
2. H. Cantril. *The "why" of man's experience.* New York: Macmillan, 1950.
3. S. Freud. *Collected papers.* London: Hogarth Press, 1949.
4. J. J. Gibson and E. J. Gibson. Continuous perspective transformations and the perception of rigid motion. *J. exp. Psychol.,* 1957, 54, 129–138.
5. J. J. Gibson, J. Purdy, and L. Lawrence. A method of controlling stimulation for the study of space perception: The optical tunnel. *J. exp. Psychol.,* 1955, 50, 1–14.
6. R. S. Harper and E. G. Boring. Cues. *Amer. J. Psychol.,* 1948, 61, 343–351.
7. F. A. Hayek. *The sensory order.* Chicago: University of Chicago Press, 1952.
8. E. R. Hilgard and D. G. Marquis. *Conditioning and learning.* New York: Appleton-Century-Crofts, 1940.

9. E. B. Holt. *The Freudian wish.* New York: Holt, 1915.
10. C. L. Hull. *Principles of behavior.* New York: Appleton-Century-Crofts, 1943.
11. H. S. Jennings. *Behavior of the lower organisms.* New York: Columbia University Press, 1906.
12. S. Koch (ed.). *Psychology: A study of a science.* Vol. 2. New York: McGraw-Hill, 1959.
13. K. Koffka. *Principles of Gestalt psychology.* New York: Harcourt, Brace, 1935.
14. W. Köhler. *Gestalt psychology.* New York: Liveright, 1929.
15. N. E. Miller and J. Dollard. *Social learning and imitation.* New Haven: Yale University Press, 1941.
16. C. Murchison. *Handbook of general experimental psychology.* Worcester: Clark University Press, 1934.
17. C. E. Osgood. *Method and theory in experimental psychology.* New York: Oxford University Press, 1953.
18. I. P. Pavlov. *Conditioned reflexes.* Trans. G. V. Anrep. London: Oxford University Press, 1927.
19. B. F. Skinner. *The behavior of organisms.* New York: Appleton-Century-Crofts, 1938.
20. B. F. Skinner. *Cumulative record.* New York: Appleton-Century-Crofts, 1959.
21. K. W. Spence. *Behavior theory and conditioning.* New Haven: Yale University Press, 1956.
22. S. S. Stevens (ed.). *Handbook of experimental psychology.* New York: Wiley, 1951.
23. L. T. Troland. *Psychophysiology.* Vol. 2. New York: Van Nostrand, 1930.
24. B. Underwood. *Psychological research.* New York: Appleton-Century-Crofts, 1957.
25. M. D. Vernon. *A further study of visual perception.* Cambridge: Cambridge University Press, 1952.
26. J. B. Watson. *Psychology from the standpoint of a behaviorist.* Philadelphia: Lippincott, 1924.
27. R. S. Woodworth. *Psychology.* New York: Holt, 1929.
28. R. S. Woodworth. *Dynamics of behavior.* New York: Holt, 1958.

# 2
# OPERATIONISM AND THE CONCEPT OF PERCEPTION

Wendell R. Garner
Harold W. Hake
Charles W. Eriksen

The attitude of contemporary operationists toward perceptual research has been well characterized recently by Allport. He has described their attitude by stating "that a perception can be regarded as nothing more nor less than a discriminatory response" [1, p. 53]. In even simpler terms, the "reaction is the perception," and thus the role of the researcher is simply to determine the conditions under which a discriminatory response is obtained. These conditions then define perception. Unfortunately, we have to agree that many psychologists who consider themselves operationists do in fact accept this position toward perception. However, this position is not necessary from the tenets of operationism. In fact, we believe that this viewpoint is a perversion of the fundamentals of operationism as stated by its originators.

The essence of the above position is that a concept of perception is not distinguishable from the operations on which it is based, and thus that perception is indistinguishable from the responses which indicate its existence and character. This idea springs from a restricted interpretation of Bridgman's writings. For example, Bridgman states, "The concept is synonymous with the corresponding set of operations" [4, p. 5]. This widely quoted statement has been used by psychologists to justify their unwillingness to distinguish between perceptions and responses, and to support their position that any set of responses leads to a concept about the properties of the perceptual system. However, to state that a concept is synonymous with a set of operations is not to state that any operation can produce a concept.

Furthermore, psychologists have ignored the fact that Bridgman is talking about a *set* of operations, not a single experimental operation. He later emphasizes this distinction, stating,

---

Source: *Psychological Review*, 1956, 63, 149–159. Copyright 1956 by the American Psychological Association. Reprinted by permission.

Note: The preparation of this report was supported in part under Contract N5ori–166, Task Order 1, between the Office of Naval Research and The Johns Hopkins University. This is Report No. 166-I-201 under that contract.

Operational definitions, in spite of their precision, are in application without significance unless the situations to which they are applied are sufficiently developed so that at least two methods are known of getting to the terminus. Definition of a phenomenon by the operations which produced it, taken naked and without further qualification, has an entirely specious precision, because it is a description of a single isolated event [3, p. 248].

Many operationists accept the sterile point of view described by Allport, and consider perception not to have any operationally determinable properties other than discrimination. It seems to us that the above quotations from Bridgman do not require such a narrow point of view. It is true that if the only operation allowed were the discriminating reaction, then it would be impossible to determine whether the perceptual process had any properties other than discrimination. But it is equally unjustifiable to state that perception is nothing more than the discriminating reaction, since other possibilities have not been excluded. Surely the perceptual process has more richness than simple discrimination.

It seems clear that many operationists who nominally subscribe to the narrow operational position also feel that perception is more than discrimination, since they do in fact ascribe other properties to the perceptual process. It is equally unjustifiable to ascribe such additional properties, when they are ascribed on the basis of single experiments whose designs are inadequate to determine the nature of these additional properties. It is our contention that additional properties of the perceptual system can and must be considered, but that operational experiments of a particular type are necessary to determine the nature of these properties.

## PERCEPTION AS A CONCEPT

We conceive of perception as an intervening process between stimuli and responses, as schematically iillustrated in Figure 2-1. We can directly observe only stimuli and responses, and therefore perception can

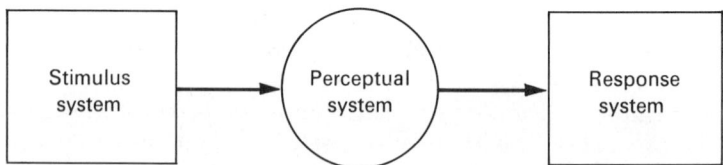

FIGURE 2-1 A schematic of the perceptual problem. The three systems operate in a causal relationship as indicated, although there may be interdependencies. Each system, however, may have independent properties. The properties of the stimulus and response systems can be directly observed; those of the perceptual system must be inferred.

be known only as a concept whose properties are induced from objectively determined relations between stimuli and responses. This statement does not in any sense imply that perception is identical to responses (or to stimuli). Indeed it is the purpose of this paper to indicate the kinds of operations which make it possible to distinguish perception from responses, and to show that these operations are necessary if the concept of perception is to have any use or meaning.

## The Discriminating Reaction

We agree with contemporary operationists that the fundamental and prerequisite operation in any experiment on perception is to demonstrate a discrimination between stimuli on the basis of responses. In other words, it must be demonstrated that there is a contingency relationship between stimuli and responses. If such a relation is demonstrated, we know that a subject can use the same label for the same stimulus within a certain error tolerance.

This operation alone, however, assures us only that we have a system which is operating and which is reliably assigning responses to the various stimuli. This operation provides us with so little information about perception that indeed we cannot distinguish between perceptual and response processes. However, if perception is considered a concept separate from the response system, there are rules for inductively determining the properties of that concept, and they are the same as those for determining the properties of any concept.

## Converging Operations

The necessary condition which makes possible the determination of particular characteristics of any concept (including the concept of perception) is the use of what have been called converging operations [6]. Converging operations may be thought of as any set of two or more experimental operations which allow the selection or elimination of alternative hypotheses or concepts which could explain an experimental result. They are called converging operations because they are not perfectly correlated and thus can converge on a single concept.

To illustrate, let us assume an experiment similar to one reported by McGinnies [11] in which visual thresholds are determined for words with different emotional content. In our hypothetical experiment, we present four alternative stimulus words, tachistoscopically—*fire, save, shit, fuck*. The responses to these words are the verbal pronunciation of them. We find that the two vulgar words have higher thresholds than the two non-vulgar words. Such a result has usually been interpreted as indicating that the perceptual system differentially discriminates on the basis of the emotional content of the perceived stimuli. There is, however, at least one other alternative explanation of these results—namely, that the difference in threshold is a result of a characteristic of the response system, which inhibits the verbalizing of some of these words. A converging operation which would discriminate between the two alternative hypotheses would be to present the same stimuli as before, but to pair these stimuli with responses such that vulgar responses are used for nonvulgar stimuli, and vice versa. This experiment in conjunction with that of the first would allow us to decide which of the two hypotheses is correct, or if some combination of them is. It should be noted that the two operations taken together provide the convergence. One experiment does not converge on the other, but rather the two converge on a mutually acceptable result.

Ideally, converging operations would be orthogonal (completely independent), since such operations are the most efficient. In practice, however, it is difficult to obtain truly orthogonal operations, because the world is so organized that all variables cannot be controlled completely independently. This fact does not seriously change the nature of the problem, because a sufficient number of partially converging operations can still provide precise delimitation of alternative concepts.

Nevertheless, sets of operations can be considered more or less efficient in allowing the formation of definitive concepts. One class of operations can be excluded entirely from consideration. This class can be called *parallel operations*. These operations select among alternative hypotheses along the same dimension, and thus cannot converge to a single concept. In our example above, we could do the entire experiment again using different words, but in which two are still vulgar and two nonvulgar. If this experiment produces the same result as the first, we still do not know whether the difference in threshold is due to a characteristic of the perceptual system or of the response system.

There are two special types of parallel operation which deserve mention. One of these is the *repeat operation,* in which the same experiment is repeated at another time. Such an experiment does not allow convergence to a single concept unless the concept involves time as a variable. Another special type of parallel operation is the *transform operation,* in which one variable is simply a transformation of another. Again, in the illustration we have been using, suppose we retain the original set of words as the stimuli, but use four synonyms as responses—*burn, keep, crap, screw*. These synonyms used as responses can be considered transforms of the original words used as responses, and this experiment will not allow us to determine whether the differential effect exists in the perceptual system or in the response system.

It should be obvious from the above discussion that the value of a set of converging operations depends more on the nature of the operations themselves than on the alternative hypotheses or properties which are being considered. For example, we mentioned above the use of synonyms as an example of a transform operation. If, however, the synonyms were used as the stimuli, this experiment in conjunction with the first would converge to determine whether the differential thresholds were due to the letter configurations of the original words, rather than to their meanings. Thus these two experiments would be converging for that purpose, but would not be converging for purposes of determining whether the effect was in the perceptual system or in the response system.

Although a minimum of two converging operations may define a concept, in practice it is rare that two are sufficient. In the first place, there are usually more alternative hypotheses than can be delimited with two converging operations. In the second place, converging operations are rarely orthogonal, but are usually only partially converging. If there are enough partially converging operations, we can still arrive at a single, well-defined concept, but more than two such operations will be necessary.

It is quite legitimate to use assumed converging operations in place of operations actually carried out. We know from previous research that many of the possible converging operations would work in a particular way if we actually tried them, and thus there is little point in trying them again. The fact that we use assumptions, however, should not allow us to lose sight of the fact that the validity of our concepts rests entirely on the validity of the operations, whether carried out or assumed. A concept has no meaning other than that derived from the operations on which it is based, and unless these operations are known, the concept cannot be known either.

## OPERATIONAL DISTINCTION BETWEEN RESPONSE AND PERCEPTION

An important use of converging operations is to distinguish effects which exist in the response system from those which exist in the perceptual system. Since the primary function of perceptual research is to determine something about the properties of the perceptual system, a major requirement in such research is to use converging operations which will eliminate the possibility that the outcome of an experiment is due to properties of the response system rather than of the perceptual system.

One of the more important properties of the response system which can affect the outcome of a perceptual experiment (and possible interpretations about properties of the perceptual system) is that of *response differentiation*. For example, if only one response is available to a subject, it is clearly impossible to demonstrate anything about perceptual discrimination. This principle is quite obvious when stated in such an extreme form, but it can also operate in other less obvious ways. For example, if the number of response categories is too small to demonstrate the perceptual discrimination capacity of a subject, then the outcome of the experiment will be limited by a property of the response system rather than by a property of the perceptual system. Thus, a converging operation which is required in many experiments is one which demonstrates that discrimination is invariant with respect to the number of response categories and with respect to the discriminability or differentiation of these categories. Such converging operations must either be carried out or be assumed before we can state anything about the limits of perceptual discrimination; if they are assumed, then the validity of the conclusion is limited by the validity of the assumption.

A second major property of the response system which can affect interpretation of experimental results is that of *response availability*. To some extent this property can be considered as a special case of response differentiation. If a subject fails to use a particular response which is defined as appropriate to a particular stimulus, we cannot state that there was a failure of the perceptual system. The failure of response can be due to sheer motor inability. It can also be due to such things as response inhibition (as in the case of vulgar words). That is to say, the response system can be affected by emotional factors just as well as the perceptual system can.

There are other ways in which response availability can operate. For example, it is known that human subjects (and rats too) have a preference for some responses over others. These preferences can affect the apparent nature of the relation between stimuli and responses, and unless they are taken into account, can lead to misinterpretations about properties of the perceptual system. Subjects also exhibit sequential effects in their responses and, if preferred sequences of responses conflict with the sequences of stimuli presented, misinterpretations can again occur. This factor is commonly taken into consideration in psychophysical experiments, where truly random sequences of stimuli are rarely used. Rather, modified random sequences are used which prevent long runs, since most subjects do not believe that long runs can occur by chance and thus are unwilling to use them.

In summary, then, there are many ways in which properties of the response system can affect the outcome of a perceptual experiment and, unless converging operations are used to delimit an effect specifically to the perceptual system, properties can be incorrectly ascribed to that system.

## CONVERGING OPERATIONS AND SOME CURRENT PROBLEMS IN PERCEPTION

To illustrate more specifically the implications of this discussion for research on perception, we shall discuss [an] experiment in these terms, pointing out the kinds of converging operations which are necessary before the results of experiments can reasonably be ascribed to particular properties of the perceptual system. . . .

**Perceptual Set**

Many experiments have demonstrated that the nature of the relation between stimuli and responses changes when the response system changes. A common interpretation of such experiments is that the set of responses provided the subject serves to produce a perceptually selective set. In many of these experiments, however, the necessary converging operations have not been undertaken to justify delimitation of the effect to the perceptual system.

Suppose an experiment similar to one by Hyman and Hake [9], in which subjects are required to identify the form of stimuli presented tachistoscopically. In one condition subjects are told prior to the stimulus exposure that the form will be one of two particular alternatives. In another condition they are told that the form will be one of four. When the duration of exposure required for identification of the form is shorter with just two stimuli, a possible conclusion is that subjects adopt a more accurate perceptual set with the smaller number of stimuli.

There is, however, an alternative explanation which requires no assumptions about the accuracy of the perceptual process, namely, that the amount of error in the response system decreases with a decrease in number of response categories. One necessary converging operation, then, is to run another experiment in which four stimuli are presented, but only two response categories are allowed. If the accuracy of identification in this case is identical to the two stimulus-two response case, then we must assume that the effect is due entirely to a characteristic of the response system. To complete the set of converging operations, it would be necessary also to present two stimuli but to allow four response categories. If the responses, however, are direct descriptions of the stimuli, this last operation would be meaningless to carry out.

Actually, there is still another set of converging operations necessary if two responses are used with four stimuli. If the nature of the responses and stimuli are such that the subject can observe one of two aspects of the stimulus, then this operation is parallel to that of using two stimuli and two responses. For example, suppose that the four stimuli were red square, blue square, red circle, blue circle; and the two responses were red, blue. For all practical purposes, there are just two stimuli, not four, and this operation would not allow us to determine where the effect exists. If the responses were abstract, such as letters of the alphabet, and were not assigned to the stimuli by just color or form, the operation would be converging. One system for handling this problem is to use the two responses with all possible pairs of the four stimuli to determine the extent to which meaningful grouping of the stimuli affects discrimination. . . .

## SUMMARY

Perception is conceived as a process intervening between stimuli and responses. As such it can be viewed as a concept whose properties may be delimited by converging operations. Converging operations are any set of experimental operations which eliminate alternative hypotheses and which can lead to a concept which is not uniquely identified with any one of the original operations, but is defined by the results of all operations performed. Thus converging operations can lead to concepts of processes which are not directly observable. For example, converging operations can be used to describe properties of the perceptual process which are distinct from those of the response system directly observed.

Illustrations from current experimental problems in perception indicate how some response characteristics may be isolated from perceptual properties, and vice versa. Some of these properties have been ascribed to perception without supporting converging operations by researchers dissatisfied by the sterility of operationism as it is commonly, but mistakenly, conceived.

## REFERENCES

1. F. H. Allport. *Theories of perception and the concept of structure.* New York: Wiley, 1955.
2. P. D. Bricker and A. Chapanis. Do incorrectly perceived tachistoscopic stimuli convey some information? *Psychol. Rev.,* 1953, *60,* 181–188.
3. P. W. Bridgman. Some general principles of operational analysis. *Psychol. Rev.,* 1945, *52,* 246–249.
4. P. W. Bridgman. *The logic of modern physics.* New York: Macmillan, 1927.
5. C. W. Eriksen. Subception: fact or artifact? *Psychol. Rev.,* 1956, *63,* 74–80.
6. W. R. Garner. Context effects and the validity of loudness scales. *J. exp. Psychol.,* 1954, *48,* 218–224.
7. W. R. Garner. A technique and a scale for loudness measurement. *J. acoust. Soc. Amer.,* 1954, *26,* 73–88.
8. E. J. Gibson and R. Bergman. The effect of training on absolute estimation of distance over the ground. *J. exp. Psychol.,* 1954, *48,* 473–482.
9. R. Hyman and H. W. Hake. *Form recognition as a function of the number of forms which can be presented for recognition.* USAF, WADC Tech. Rep. 54-164.
10. R. S. Lazarus and R. A. McCleary. Autonomic discrimination without awareness: A study of subception. *Psychol. Rev.,* 1951, *58,* 113–122.

11. E. McGinnies. Emotionality and perceptual defense. *Psychol. Rev.*, 1949, 56, 244–251.
12. E. P. Reese, T. W. Reese, J. Volkmann and H. H. Corbin. *Psychophysical research: Summary report 1946.* USN, Spec. Dev. Cent. Tech. Rep. SDC–131–1–5. 1953.
13. S. S. Stevens. The direct estimation of sensory magnitudes-loudness. *Amer. J. Psychol.*

# 3

# SENSORY ORGANIZATION

## Wolfgang Köhler

... The visual field exhibits two kinds of order. One is the order with which the machine theory is occupied when it tries to explain how a given process keeps its right place between its neighbors, and does not go astray. There is, however, another order in the field which tends to escape our attention, although it is no less important than the first. In most visual fields the contents of particular areas "belong together" as circumscribed units from which their surroundings are excluded....

On the desk before me I find quite a number of circumscribed units or things: a piece of paper, a pencil, an eraser, a cigarette, and so forth. The existence of these visual things involves two factors. What is included in a thing becomes a unit, and this unit is segregated from its surroundings. In order to satisfy myself that this is more than a verbal affair, I may try to form other units in which parts of a visual thing and parts of its environment are put together. In some cases such an attempt will end in complete failure. In others, in which I am more successful, the result is so strange that, as a result, the original organization appears only the more convincing as a visual fact.

The reader will say: "Of course, you are talking about psychological facts; but something may be a psychological fact without for this reason belonging to sensory experience. Surely, you will admit that a piece of paper, a pencil, a cigarette are objects which are known by use. For many

Source: *Gestalt Psychology* by Wolfgang Köhler. Copyright (R) 1956 by Liveright Publishing Corp. Reprinted by permission of the publisher.

years you have handled such objects. Thus you have had more opportunity than you needed for learning that they are units in a practical sense. This previously acquired knowledge you now project into your field of vision. Why, then, do you lay so much stress upon your observation? It is widely known and, as just shown, quite satisfactorily explained. Probably it was known, and so explained, when Aristotle wrote his textbook of psychology."

My answer will take more time than this argument does. So long as arguments of this kind are still accepted, even the most elementary theses of Gestalt psychology will not be adequately understood. To be sure, the piece of paper, the pencil, and so forth, are well-known objects. I will also grant without hesitation that their uses and their names are known to me from numerous contacts in previous life. Much of the meaning which the objects now have unquestionably comes from this source. But from these facts there is a large step to the statement that papers, pencils, and so forth, would not be segregated units without that previously acquired knowledge. How is it proved that before I acquired this knowledge the visual field contained no such units? When I see a green object, I can immediately tell the name of the color. I also know that green is used as a signal on streets and as a symbol of hope. But from this I do not conclude that the color green as such can be derived from such knowledge. Rather, I know that, as an independently existent sensory fact, it has acquired secondary meanings, and I am quite willing to recognize the advantages which these acquired meanings have in practical life. In exactly the same fashion, Gestalt psychology holds, sensory units have acquired names, have become richly symbolic, and are now known to have certain practical uses, while nevertheless they have existed as units before any of these further facts were added. Gestalt psychology claims that it is precisely the original segregation of circumscribed wholes which makes it possible for the sensory world to appear so utterly imbued with meaning to the adult; for, in its gradual entrance into the sensory field, meaning follows the lines drawn by natural organization; it usually enters into segregated wholes.

If the empiristic explanation were correct, specific entities would be segregated in the field only to the extent to which they represent known objects. This is by no means the case. When I look into a dark corner, or when I walk through mist in the evening, I frequently find before me an unknown something which is detached from its environment as a particular object, while at the same time I am entirely unable to say what kind of thing it is. Only afterwards may I discover its nature in this sense. Actually, such visual things will sometimes remain unrecognized for minutes. It follows that my knowledge about the practical significance of things cannot be responsible for their existence as detached visual units. The same argument may be restated in a more general form. Whenever we say to ourselves or others: "What may that something be, at the foot of that hill, just to the right of that tree, between those two houses, and so on?" we ask about the empirical meaning or use of a seen object and demonstrate by our very question that as a matter of principle, segregation of visual things is independent of knowledge and meaning.

Yet many are so fond of their empiristic convictions that in this predicament their explanation will immediately assume another form. "The unknown entity which you see in the mist," they will say, "appears as something separate because it is darker than the gray mist around. In other words, no special knowledge about particular groups of sensations as meaning specific objects need be assumed in our explanation. You seem to underrate the extraordinary achievements of learning, if you restrict its effects to specific instances. Since early childhood we have often observed that sets of sensations which have approximately the same color, and differ in this respect from their environment, tend to behave as units, that is, to move and to be moved, to appear and disappear, at the same time. Such is the case with stones, with papers, with plates, with shoes, with many animals, with the leaves of plants. Approximately homogeneous sets of sensations tend to correspond to physical objects which behave as units for physical reasons. It is only an example of the well-known generalizing power of memory if, as a result of such experiences, we treat all homogeneously colored areas as units until we actually seem to see them as such units. It is therefore not astonishing that, in the mist, for instance, an area of darker nuance is seen as an individual something, although we may not recognize it as a particular kind of thing."

I do not believe that this modification of the theory is satisfactory. In a great many cases units are formed and segregated under circumstances to which the explanation does not apply. Take all visual units which consist of separate parts. If on a clear night we look up at the sky, some stars are immediately seen as belonging together, and as detached from their environment. The constellation Cassiopeia is an example, the Dipper is another. For ages people have seen the same groups as units, and at the present time children need no instruction in order to perceive the same units. Similarly, in Figure 3-1 the reader has before him two groups of patches. Why not merely six patches? Or two other groups? Or three groups of two members each? When looking casually at this pattern everyone beholds the two groups of three patches each. What about generalized effects of learning in these instances? No previous learning can have separated Cassiopeia from the other fixed stars around it. As far as

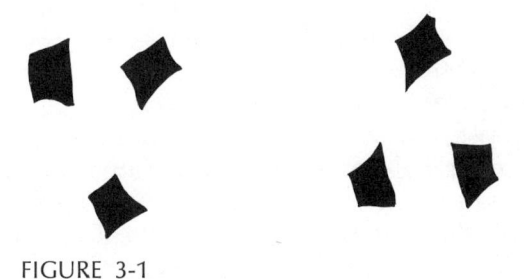

FIGURE 3-1

everyday experience goes, all fixed stars move together. Quite generally, one cannot possibly assert that we have learned to regard a number of separate similar patches as one group because they regularly move together. They are very far from doing so. On a table I now see five flies which, from my distance, appear as black dots. Presently these dots begin to move separately, and to move in different directions. So do three yellow leaves which a breeze lifts from the ground; so again three similar stones which my hand moves one after the other. My general experience is that, as often as not, similar members of a group are movable, and move, independently. If nevertheless in such cases groups are again formed and segregated, this happens in spite of our previous knowledge about the actual behavior of their members.

When discrete entities unite in a group, the part which equality (or similarity) plays in the unification cannot be explained in terms of learning. But the same factor has a unifying influence in the case of continuous areas, whether or not they represent known objects. Consequently it is futile to apply the empiristic explanation to this formation of continuous homogeneous things; for the formation of groups proves that equality favors grouping quite irrespective of acquired knowledge. . . .

The nature of grouping as an elementary sensory fact was most convincingly demonstrated in experiments which Hertz made with a certain species of birds *(Garrulus glandarius)*. A number of small flower pots were put on the ground upside down. The tame bird, perched on the branch of a tree, was allowed to see how food was placed under one of the pots by the experimenter. Soon he would come down, lift the pot, and take the food. This is, of course, a simple form of "delayed reaction" as investigated by Hunter years ago. In the present experiments, however, the main point was not so much the delay of the reaction as its dependence upon particular patterns in the field. The bird reacted without difficulty when there was one pot only. But when there were more than one, everything depended upon the question whether or not the right pot was an outstanding and specifically characterized member of the totality. If it was put in a straight line with the others so that, for human vision, it became absorbed as an indifferent member of the whole series, the bird lifted one pot after another in a haphazard fashion. This happened even when the distance between the pots was as large as 25 cm. As soon, however, as in human vision the right pot became something strikingly segregated from the rest, the bird selected the right object at once. So, for instance, in the case of Figure 3-2, in which the right pot was 10 cm removed from the straight line of the other pots. Apparently in his vision, too, this line was a compact whole from which the right pot could readily be distinguished as a thing by itself. Even in the situation of Figure 3-3, where the right object stood 6 cm from the next, and this 2 cm from the last, grouping was clear enough to permit correct reaction. But in the case of Figure 3-4, where the right object was only 3 cm distant from the next, and this 2 cm from the last, responses became a matter of

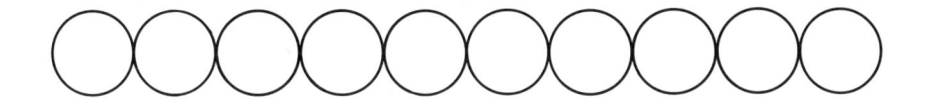

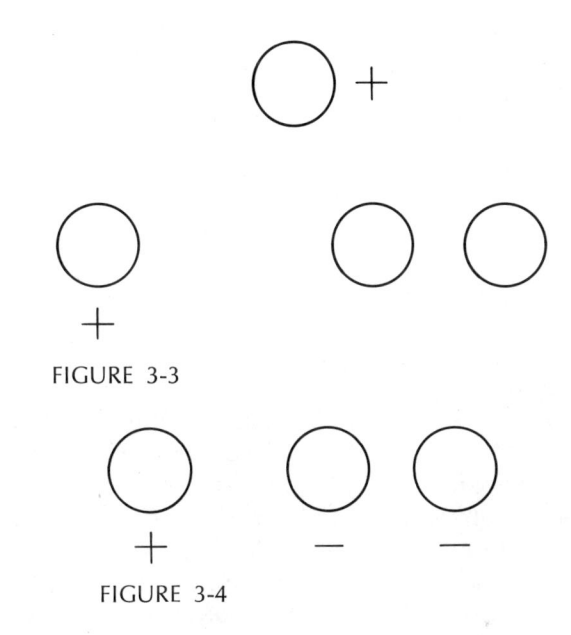

FIGURE 3-2

FIGURE 3-3

FIGURE 3-4

chance. Quite generally, the bird was unable to single out the right pot unless quite specific grouping helped him to do so. On the other hand, so long as grouping was entirely clear in human vision, the bird reacted promptly and correctly even when the right object was in immediate contact with its next neighbor. In the situation of Figure 3-5, for instance,

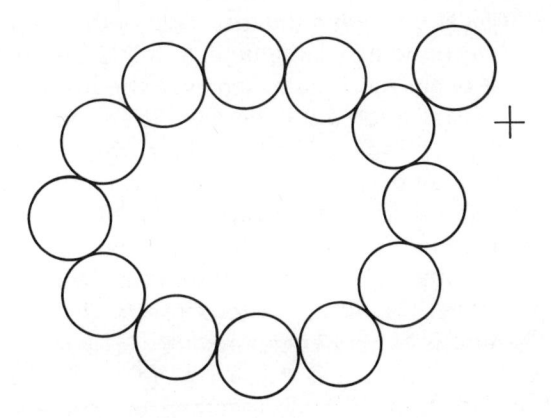

FIGURE 3-5

twelve pots were arranged in the form of an ellipse, and the right pot was put close to one of the other twelve. In the visual field of the experimenter the situation appeared as one compact group to which a single object was added outside. In this situation the bird chose the right object at once. The example is particularly instructive in showing that individual distances as such are not the decisive factors. The grouping which results in the pattern as a whole determines the bird's responses....

One can easily show that the factors on which grouping depends in time are about the same as those on which it depends in space. Suppose that I knock three times at short intervals on my table, and that after waiting for a second I repeat the performance, and so forth. People who hear this sequence of sounds experience groups in time. Physically, all these sounds are, of course, independent events. They are about as unrelated as the stars of Cassiopeia. In other words, there is no grouping in the physical sequence. Also, from a purely logical point of view, other forms of grouping are quite as possible as the one which is actually heard. But these do not occur in the experience of an observer who listens in a passive attitude. The groups as actually heard are therefore instances of psychological and, according to the thesis of isomorphism, also of physiological organization. In the present example, the operating principle is that of proximity in time, which is, of course, strictly analogous to the principle of proximity in spatial grouping. If the intervals between sounds are made equal, groups will again be formed as soon as differences of intensity or quality are introduced in the series, especially if they occur in regular repetition. Thus, equality plays the same role in the organization of temporal sequences as it does in a stationary visual field....

Now it will also be clearly understood why the stimulus-response formula, which sounds at first so attractive, is actually quite misleading. In fact, it has so far appeared acceptable solely because behaviorists use the term stimulus in such a loose fashion. We have seen that when the term is taken in its strict sense, it is not generally "a stimulus" which elicits a response. In vision, for instance, the organism tends to respond to millions of stimuli at once; and the first stage of this response is organization within a correspondingly large field. In many cases reactions of the effector organs will begin soon; but often even the first of these reactions depend upon the organization of the field as it develops at the time. Take eye movements as an example. The laws of visually determined eye movements refer to the boundaries of segregated entities, to the location of these entities in the field, and so forth. Apart from eye movements, a man's actions are commonly related to a well-structured field, most often to particular thing-units. The right psychological formula is therefore: *pattern of stimulation—organization—response to the products of organization*. The operations of the nervous system are by no means restricted to primitive local processes; it is not a box in which conductors with separate functions are somehow put together. It responds to a situation, first, by dynamic sensory events which are peculiar to it as a system, that is, by organization, and then by behavior which depends upon the results of the organization. Suppose that somewhere in a factory $HNO_3$ were produced out of its elements, and that in another part of the factory the acid were used to dissolve silver—would it be right to say that the silver reacts to nitrogen, hydrogen, and oxygen? Surely, such a statement would be utterly wrong, because what happens to the silver depends upon the chemical organization of the acid and cannot be understood as a reaction to those elements or to their sum. Similarly, we ought not to speak of behavior as though it were a reaction to "a stimulus" or to "some stimuli." The last expression, too, is at least ambiguous, because it might mean that the behavior in question results from several stimuli which operate independently at the same time.

Once I tried to convince a behaviorist that when, in speaking of a male bird, he referred to a female as "a stimulus" he ignored the problems and facts of organization. All my efforts were useless. Although (or because) he treated sensory experience as something without any interest for psychology, he committed the experience error so persistently that he could not see why the female should *not* be called a stimulus. How often have a mouse, a door, the experimenter, and so on, been called stimuli. The expression may be harmless when those who are fully aware of the problem of organization use it as an abbreviation. But when authors who have not yet learned to avoid the experience error use the same term, the consequences will be most unfortunate. Such people may never understand what we mean by organization.

REFERENCES

1.  Z. Hertz. *Vergl. Physiol.,* 1928, 7.

# 4

# THE FIRST STAGE OF PERCEPTION: GROWTH OF THE CELL ASSEMBLY

### D. O. Hebb

**THE POSSIBILITY OF A DUAL TRACE MECHANISM**

Hilgard and Marquis [3] have shown how a reverberatory, transient trace mechanism might be proposed on the basis of Lorente de Nó's conclusions, that a cell is fired only by the simultaneous activity of two or more afferent fibers, and that internuncial fibers are arranged in closed (potentially self-exciting) circuits. Their diagram is arranged to show how a reverberatory circuit might establish a sensorimotor connection between receptor cells and the effectors which carry out a conditioned response. There is, of course, a good deal of psychological evidence which is opposed to such an oversimplified hypothesis, and Hilgard and Marquis do not put weight on it. At the same time, it is important to see that something of the kind is not merely a possible but a necessary inference from certain neurological ideas. To the extent that anatomical and physiological observations establish the possibility of reverberatory aftereffects of a sensory event, it is established that such a process would be the physiological basis of a transient "memory" of the stimulus. There may, then, be a memory trace that is wholly a function of a pattern of neural activity, independent of any structural change.

Hilgard and Marquis go on to point out that such a trace would be quite unstable. A reverberatory activity would be subject to the development of refractory states in the cells of the circuit in which it occurs, and external events could readily interrupt it. We have already seen ... that an "activity" trace can hardly account for the permanence of early learning, but at the same time one may regard reverberatory activity as the explanation of other phenomena.

There are memories which are instantaneously established, and as evanescent as they are immediate. In the repetition of digits, for example, an interval of a few seconds is enough to prevent any interference from one series on the next. Also, some memories are both instantaneously established and permanent. To account for the permanence, some struc-

Source: *Organization of Behavior* by D. O. Hebb. Copyright 1949 by John Wiley & Sons. Reprinted by permission of John Wiley & Sons, Inc.

tural change seems necessary, but a structural growth presumably would require an appreciable time. If some way can be found of supposing that a reverberatory trace might cooperate with the structural change, and *carry the memory until the growth change is made,* we should be able to recognize the theoretical value of the trace which is an activity only, without having to ascribe all memory to it. The conception of a transient, unstable reverberatory trace is therefore useful, if it is possible to suppose also that some more permanent structural change reinforces it. There is no reason to think that a choice must be made between the two conceptions; there may be traces of both kinds, and memories which are dependent on both.

## A NEUROPHYSIOLOGICAL POSTULATE

Let us assume, then, that the persistence or repetition of a reverberatory activity (or *trace*) tends to induce lasting cellular changes that add to its stability. The assumption can be precisely stated as follows: *When an axon of cell A is near enough to excite a cell B and repeatedly or persistently takes part in firing it, some growth process or metabolic change takes place in one or both cells such that A's efficiency, as one of the cells firing B, is increased.*

The most obvious and I believe much the most probable suggestion concerning the way in which one cell could become more capable of firing another is that synaptic knobs develop and increase the area of contact between the afferent axon and efferent soma. (*Soma* refers to dendrites and body, or all of the cell except its axon.) There is certainly no direct evidence that this is so, and the postulated change if it exists may be metabolic, affecting cellular rhythmicity and limen; or there might be both metabolic and structural changes, including a limited neurobiotaxis. There are several considerations, however, that make the growth of synaptic knobs a plausible conception. The assumption stated above can be put more definitely, as follows:

When one cell repeatedly assists in firing another, the axon of the first cell develops synaptic knobs (or enlarges them if they already exist) in contact with the soma of the second cell. This seems to me the most likely mechanism of a lasting effect of reverberatory action, but I wish to make it clear that the subsequent discussion depends only on the more generally stated proposition italicized above.

It is wise to be explicit on another point also. The proposition does not require action at any great distance, and certainly is not the same as Kappers' [4] conception of the way in which neurobiotaxis controls axonal and dendritic outgrowth. But my assumption is evidently related to Kappers' ideas, and not inconsistent with them. The theory of neurobiotaxis has been severely criticized, and clearly it does not do all it was once thought to do. On the other hand, neurobiotaxis may still be one factor determining the connections made by neural cells. If so, it would cooperate very neatly with the knob formation postulated above. Criticism has been directed at the idea that neurobiotaxis directs axonal growth throughout its whole course, and that the process sufficiently accounts for all neural connections. The idea is not tenable, particularly in view of such work as that of Weiss [7] and Sperry [6].

But none of this has shown that neurobiotaxis has *no* influence in neural growth; its operation, within ranges of a centimeter or so, is still plausible. Thus, in Figure 4-1, the multiple synaptic knobs of fiber 2 on cell C might be outgrowths from a fiber passing the cell at a distance, and determined by the fact of repeated simultaneous excitations in the two. Again, the course followed by fiber 7 in the neighborhood of cell D may include deflections from the original course of the fiber, determined in the same way.

The details of these histological speculations are not important except to show what some of the possibilities of change at the synapse might be and to show that the mechanism of learning discussed here is not wholly out of touch with what is known about the neural cell. The changed facilitation that constitutes learning might occur in other ways without affecting the rest of the theory. To make it more specific, I have chosen to assume that the growth of synaptic knobs, with or without neurobiotaxis, is the basis of the change of facilitation from one cell on another, and this is not altogether implausible. It has been demonstrated by Arvanitaki [1] that a contiguity alone will permit the excitation aroused in one cell to be transmitted to another. There are also earlier experiments, reviewed by Arvanitaki, with the same implication. Even more important, perhaps, is Erlanger's [2] demonstration of impulse transmission across an artificial "synapse," a blocked segment of nerve more than a millimeter in extent. Consequently, in the intact nervous system, an axon that passes close to the dendrites or body of a second cell would be capable of helping to fire it, when the second cell is also exposed to other stimulation at the same point. The probability that such closely timed coincidental excitations would occur is not considered for the moment but will be returned to. When the coincidence does occur, and the active fiber, which is merely close to the soma of another cell, adds to a local excitation in it, I assume that the joint action tends to produce a thickening of the fiber—forming a synaptic knob—or adds to a thickening already present.

Lorente de Nó [5] has shown that the synaptic knob is usually not a terminal structure (thus the term end foot or end button is misleading), nor always separated by a stalk from the axon or axon collateral. If it were, of course, some action at a distance would be inevitably suggested, if such connections are formed in learning. The knob instead is often a rather irregular thickening in the unmyelinated part of an axon near its

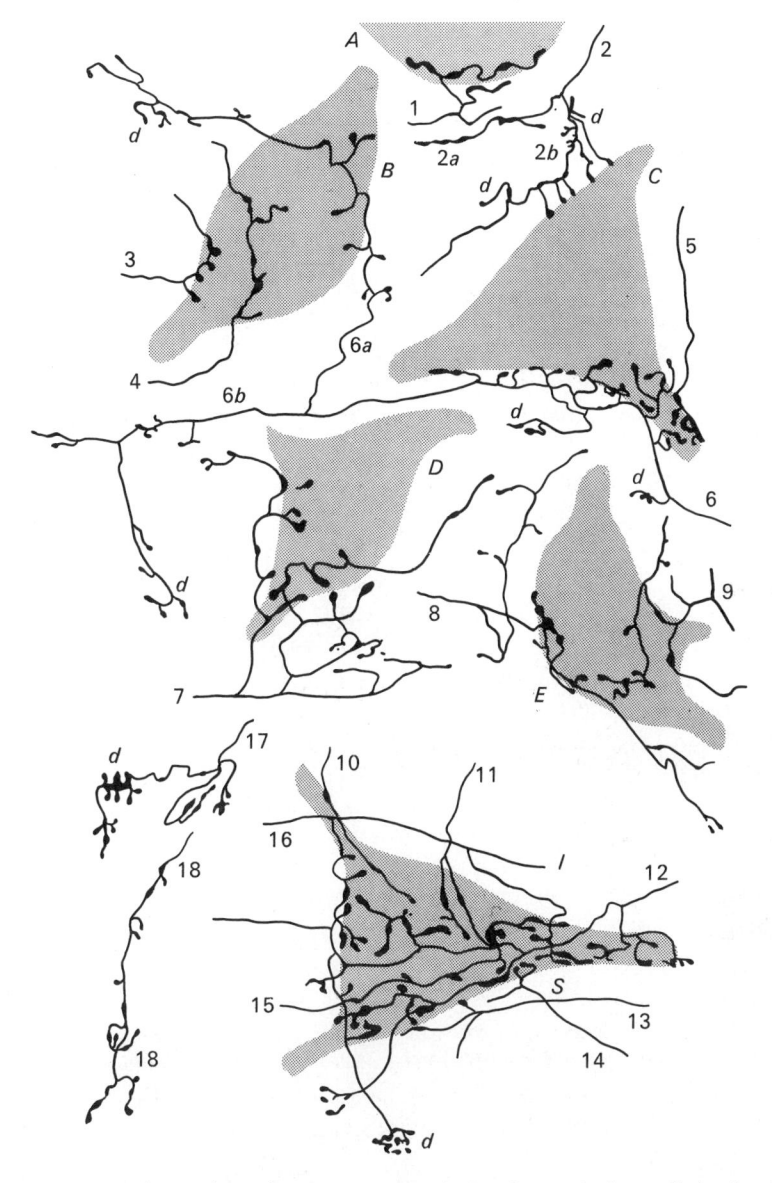

FIGURE 4-1 Relationships between synaptic knobs and the cell body. From Lorente de Nó [5]. Courtesy of Charles C Thomas and R. Lorente de Nó.

ending, where it is threading its way through a thicket of dendrites and cell bodies. The point in the axon where the thickening occurs does not appear to be determined by the structure of the cell of which it is a part but by something external to the cell and related to the presence of a second cell. The number and size of the knobs formed by one cell in contact with a second cell vary also. In the light of these facts it is not implausible to suppose that the extent of the contact established is a function of joint cellular activity, given propinquity of the two cells.

Also, if a synapse is crossed only by the action of two or more afferent cells, the implication is that the greater the area of contact the greater the likelihood that action in one cell will be decisive in firing another.[1] Thus three afferent fibers with extensive knob contact could fire a cell that otherwise might be fired only by four or more fibers; or fired sooner with knobs than without.

In short, it is feasible to assume that synaptic knobs develop with neural activity and represent a lowered synaptic resistance. It is implied that the knobs appear in the course of learning, but this does not give us a means of testing the assumption. There is apparently no good evidence concerning the relative frequency of knobs in infant and adult brains, and the assumption does *not* imply that there should be none in the newborn infant. The learning referred to is learning in a very general sense, which must certainly have begun long before birth.

### REFERENCES

1. A. Arvanitaki. Effects evoked in an axon by the activity of a contiguous one. *J. Neurophysiol.*, 1942, 5, 89–108.
2. J. Erlanger. The initiation of impulses in axons. *J. Neurophysiol.*, 1939, 2, 370–379.
3. E. R. Hilgard and D. G. Marquis. *Conditioning and learning.* New York: Appleton-Century-Crofts, 1940.
4. C. U. P. Kappers, G. C. Huber and E. C. Crosby. *The comparative anatomy of the nervous system of vertebrates, including man.* Vol. 1. New York: Macmillan, 1936.
5. R. Lorente de Nó. Synaptic stimulation of motoneurons as a local process. *J. Neurophysiol.*, 1938, 1, 195–206.
6. R. W. Sperry. Visuomotor coordination in the newt (*Triturua viridescens*) after regeneration of the optic nerve. *J. comp. Neurol.*, 1943, 79, 33–55.
7. P. Weiss. Nerve patterns: The mechanics of nerve growth. *Growth* (Third Growth Symposium), 1941, 5, 163–203.

---

[1] One point should perhaps be made explicit. Following Lorente de Nó, two afferent cells are considered to be effective at the synapse, when one is not, only because their contacts with the efferent cell are close together so their action summates. When both are active, they create a larger region of *local* disturbance in the efferent soma. The larger the knobs in a given cluster, therefore, the smaller the number that might activate the cell on which they are located. On occasion, a single afferent cell must be effective in transmission. It is worth pointing this out, also, because it might appear to the reader otherwise that there is something mysterious about emphasis on the necessity of activity in two or more cells to activate the synapse. All that has really been shown is that in some circumstances two or more afferent cells are necessary. However, this inevitably implies that an increase in the number of afferent cells simultaneously active must increase the reliability with which the synapse is traversed.

# 5

# EFFECTS OF DIFFERENTIAL EXPERIENCE ON DENDRITIC SPINE COUNTS IN RAT CEREBRAL CORTEX

Albert Globus
Mark R. Rosenzweig
Edward L. Bennett
Marian C. Diamond

*Effects of 30 days of differential experience in enriched conditions (EC) or impoverished conditions (IC) were measured on pyramids in the rat occipital cortex in forty littermate pairs in four replication experiments. Using the rapid Golgi method, counts were made of dendritic spines, and the lateral width of basal dendrites was measured. The density of spines was greater in EC than in IC rats on basal dendrites (9.7% p < .01); oblique and terminal dendrites showed barely significant effects in favor of EC (3.6% and 3.1%, respectively; p < .05). No significant effects were measured in spine densities in the apical dendrites or in the lateral width. Weights of cortical sections yield significant EC–IC difference. The results are compared to those of other investigators.*

This study is one of a series in which we have sought to determine how the brain changes as a consequence of experience. In previous studies we have found that exposing rats to enriched or impoverished environmental conditions for periods ranging from a few weeks to a few months brings about differences in brain enzymes and in cortical weight [2, 14], in cortical depth [4], in the ratio of glial cells to neurons [5], and most recently, in the size and number of synaptic junctions [12]. The present experiments on dendritic spines represent another way of measuring cortical connectivity as a function of differential experi-

Source: *Journal of Comparative and Physiological Psychology*, 1973, 82, 175–181. Copyright 1973 by the American Psychological Association. Reprinted by permission.
Note: This research was supported by National Science Foundation Grant GB-5537. The authors thank Pamela Kaups for her diligent assistance in making the counts of dendritic spines.

ence. We will attempt to relate our findings to those of other experiments, although the discussion will make clear that there are few strictly comparable reports in the literature.

## METHOD

### Behavioral Procedure

All subjects were male rats of the Berkeley $S_1$ strain, bred and born in the psychology department colony. The environmental conditions were the enriched condition (EC) and the impoverished condition (IC). To enrich experience above the level of the standard colony environment, EC animals were housed in a group of ten in a large cage (70 × 70 × 46 cm). The cage was provided with stimulus objects ("toys") from a standard pool. Each day there were six or more toys in the EC cage; some were in new positions from the previous day and some were newly taken from the pool. (Rats in an EC cage are shown in Figure 1 of Bennett et al. [2]; the pool of objects is shown in Figure 1 of Rosenzweig and Bennett [13]). Each day the EC animals were placed for 30 min in the field of a Hebb–Williams apparatus (75 × 75 cm) where the pattern of barriers was changed daily. During this time the selection and arrangement of objects in the EC cage were changed.

To reduce experience from the colony base line, IC animals were housed in individual cages (32 × 20 × 20 cm) with solid sidewalls so that the animals could not see each other. The IC cages were placed in a separate, quiet, and dimly illuminated room. In these special IC cages, the floors were made of wire bars; pans of shavings below the cages were changed without touching the animals.

Both EC and IC animals had laboratory pellets and water available ad lib. All animals were weighed regularly, usually at weekly intervals.

In each experiment littermate pairs were assigned at weaning (about 25 days of age), semirandomly to two groups. Assignment was semirandom to insure that the distributions of body weights among groups would be similar. Runts and animals whose weight departed more than 15% from the littermate were excluded. The groups were assigned at random to the experimental conditions. Animals remained in the experimental conditions for 30 days.

Animals of experiment 1 were sacrificed on April 26, 1967, and of experiment 2 on October 19, 1967. Experiments 3A and 3B were run simultaneously, and their sacrifice date was December 12, 1968.

### Dissection of Brain Samples

Animals were brought to sacrifice under code numbers that did not reveal to the analysts the behavioral condition of any subject; littermates were sacrificed in immediate succession, the EC rat being first in some pairs and the IC first in others. The brain was divided rapidly by dissection into these six samples: (a) sample of occipital cortex, (b) sample of somesthetic cortex, (c) remaining dorsal cortex, (d) ventral cortex and adjacent tissues, including corpus callosum, hippocampus, and amygdala, (e) cerebellum and medulla, and (f) the rest of the subcortex, including the olfactory bulbs. For standard removal of the sample of occipital and somesthetic cortex, these were defined with our standard small calibrated plastic T-square, as described and diagrammed in Bennett et al. [2]. The samples were weighed to 0.1 mg. Following weighing, only the occipital cortical blocks were immediately immersed in the fixative for dendritic spine counts.

## Fixing and Staining Techniques

After fixation in an aqueous solution of 0.5% osmium tetraoxide and 2.5% $K_2CR_2O_7$ for 10 to 12 days, the blocks were removed and immersed in 0.5% silver nitrate for 24 to 48 hr. After washing in absolute ethanol they were "shelled" in paraffin and cut on a sliding microtome at 70 to 100 $\mu$. The coronal sections were aligned perpendicular to the pia. From each occipital block a central core of approximately 1.5-mm square was studied. The counts were taken from several sections from each block, usually numbering ten to fifteen. In experiment 1 counts were taken from the left hemisphere; all other counts were taken from the right hemisphere. The sections were washed twice in absolute ethanol, twice in methylsalicylate, and twice in xylene. They were mounted under nitrocellulose only in experiments 1 and 2 and under nitrocellulose and cover slips in experiments 3A and 3B.

## Measurements of Pyramidal Cells

Counts of dendritic spines were performed at 450× with a 50-$\mu$ reticule in experiment 1 and at 500× with a 60-$\mu$ reticule in experiment 2. In experiments 3A and 3B we used a magnification of 600× with a 91.2-$\mu$ reticule. The reticule was centered on the dendrites except for the terminal dendrite in the following fashion. To avoid bias, dendrites for use in counting the spines were selected at a low power. A segment free of artifacts and blood vessels was selected which was nearest the midpoint of the dendrite. The higher objective was used to perform the counts. No attempt was made to distinguish normal from abnormally shaped spines [7, 8, 9, 10], but all the visible spines were counted. For counting terminal dendrites, the procedure was similar, except that the reticule was aligned to the dendrite nearest the pia and with the end of the reticule at the end of the dendrite. The numerical value of spines/$\mu$ refers to the number of spines per micron only on the side of the dendrite in opposition to the reticule. These values must be multiplied by 2 to be comparable to those values for spines/$\mu$ reported by Schapiro and Vukovich [18] or by Globus and Scheibel [7, 8, 9, 10]. For the most part the pyramidal neurons had their somas in layer 4 or 5, but no generalization in relationship to their exact position of the soma is possible due to the nature of the rapid Golgi preparations. Accurate estimation of cortical depth was difficult due to the lack of generalized staining of somas and fibers. At least one or the other of these structures must be stained uniformly in order to determine the relevant layer of the cortex. All the counts of dendritic spines are reported in terms of the number of spines per linear micron.

The lateral width of a pyramidal cell is a measure of the diameter of the cylinder whose surface is defined by the ends of the terminal, oblique and basal dendrites [8]. The measure is taken along a line perpendicular to the axon and apical dendrite and in the plane of the section; it extends from the point where the axon leaves the axon hillock to the lateral-most tip of any uncut dendrite. This is illustrated in Figure 5-1. The measure of lateral width will be given in microns.

The code for the slides was broken only after the counts were completed.

## RESULTS

### Weights of Brain Samples

On weights of brain samples, these experiments yielded results consistent with those of ten other experiments from our laboratories in which rats of the same strain were given the same behavioral treatment. Table 5-1 presents the EC–IC brain weight differences. The combined results of the four present experiments agree well with those of the other ten similar experiments, as Table 5-1 shows. In all but experiment 1, the EC–IC percentage difference in occipital cortex is larger than in any other brain area, as we have found consistently [15]; this difference was statistically significant in each of the present individual experiments. It should be noted that the brain weights were greater in the EC groups; body weights were greater in their IC littermates in each experiment.

### Counts of Dendritic Spines

Table 5-2 presents several measures of dendrites. Clearly significant effects of differential environment on spine counts were found in the basal dendrites. In experiments 1 and 3A, the EC–IC differences were 19.7% ($p < 0.05$) and 10.1% ($p < 0.05$), respectively; experiments 2 and 3B showed differences in the same direction, but they were nonsignificant. The combined values show EC to exceed IC by 9.7% ($p < 0.01$). In twenty-seven of the forty littermate pairs the EC value exceeded that of the IC

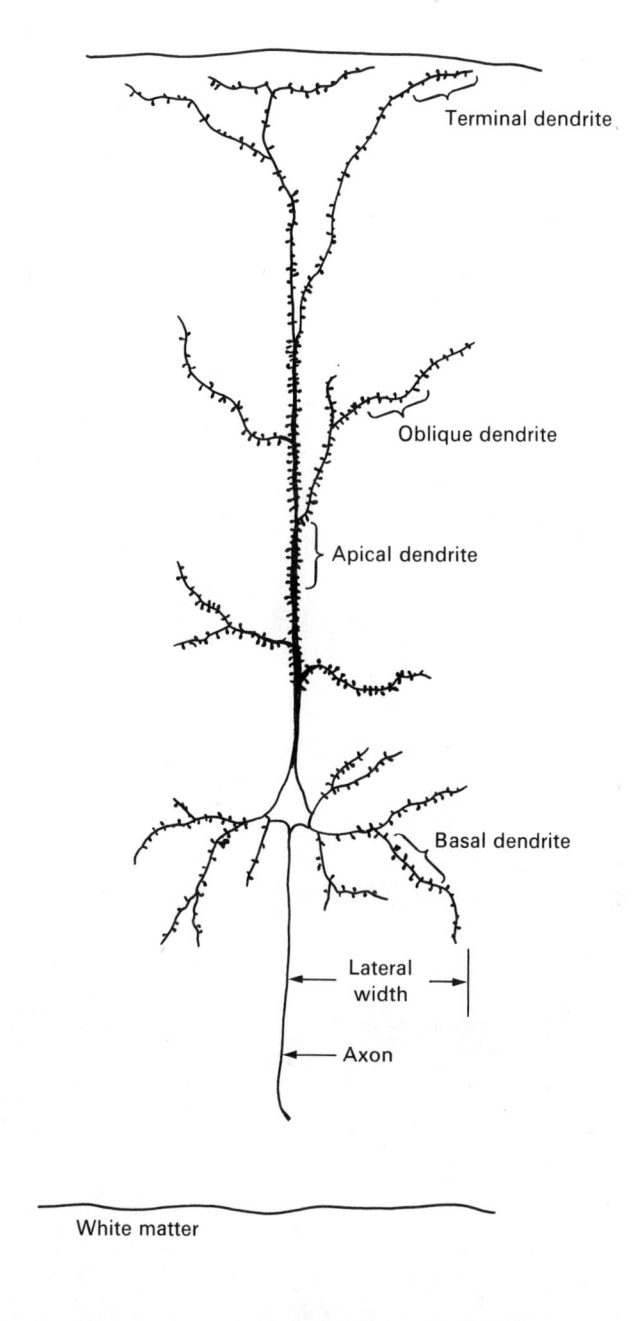

FIGURE 5-1  Counting stations on the pyramidal neuron. Brackets indicate where the reticule was aligned in order to count the dendrite spines. Counting stations were situated on the end of the terminal dendrite, but in the middle of the apical, oblique, and basal dendrites. Lateral width refers to the distance between the axon and the extent of the basal dendrites.

TABLE 5-1  Brain Weights and EC–IC Percentage Differences in Weights

|  | Cortex | | | | | Rest of Brain | Total Brain | Cortex/Rest Body Weight | |
|---|---|---|---|---|---|---|---|---|---|
| Experiment | Occipital | Somesthetic | Remaining Dorsal | Ventral | Total | | | | |
| 1 (n = 10) | | | | | | | | | |
| EC M | 63.1 | 54.4 | 296.8 | 272.1 | 686.4 | 862.4 | 1,548.8 | 0.7968 | 198.2 |
| % EC–IC difference | 7.4** | 3.4 | 10.3*** | 9.9* | 9.3** | 4.0* | 6.3** | 5.3** | −4.9 |
| 2 (n = 10) | | | | | | | | | |
| EC M | 64.6 | 56.8 | 294.6 | 280.5 | 696.4 | 847.8 | 1,544.2 | 0.8220 | 167.6 |
| % EC–IC difference | 15.9** | 8.4** | 5.8* | 6.0* | 7.0*** | 1.3 | 3.8** | 5.7*** | −7.8* |
| 3A (n = 10) | | | | | | | | | |
| EC M | 64.3 | 52.1 | 290.4 | 224.5 | 631.3 | 777.5 | 1,408.8 | 0.8117 | 142.2 |
| % EC–IC difference | 12.8** | 9.4** | 4.2 | −0.8 | 3.6 | −1.6 | 0.7 | 5.0** | −10.1 |
| 3B (n = 10) | | | | | | | | | |
| EC M | 65.1 | 50.9 | 296.9 | 231.5 | 644.3 | 794.5 | 1,438.8 | 0.8112 | 142.0 |
| % EC–IC difference | 11.3*** | 3.9 | 7.7*** | 1.2 | 5.3** | 1.7 | 3.3* | 3.6** | −5.2 |
| Combination (N = 40) | | | | | | | | | |
| EC M | 64.3 | 53.5 | 294.6 | 252.1 | 664.6 | 820.6 | 1,485.2 | 0.8104 | 162.5 |
| % EC–IC difference | 11.8*** | 6.2*** | 7.0*** | 4.3** | 6.3*** | 1.4 | 3.5*** | 4.9*** | −6.9* |
| Ten similar EC–IC experiments (N = 115) | | | | | | | | | |
| EC M | 66.4 | 53.4 | 297.4 | 266.8 | 684.1 | 841.9 | 1,525.9 | 0.8219 | 178.6 |
| % EC–IC difference | 10.3*** | 4.5*** | 5.4*** | 4.7*** | 5.5*** | 0.2 | 2.5*** | 5.3*** | −12.1*** |

Note: Means are in mg for brain weights and in g for body weights.
 * $p < 0.05$.
 ** $p < 0.01$.
 *** $p < 0.001$.

TABLE 5-2 Measures of Dendrites

| Treatment | Dendritic Spines/$\mu$ |  |  |  | Lateral Width (in $\mu$) |
|---|---|---|---|---|---|
|  | Apical | Oblique | Basal | Terminal Dendrites |  |

*Experiment 1*

| EC | 0.38 | 0.28 | 0.33 | 0.24 | 126.2 |
|---|---|---|---|---|---|
| IC | 0.39 | 0.28 | 0.28 | 0.23 | 128.2 |
| % difference | −2.7 | 0.4 | 19.7* | 5.0 | −1.7 |
| EC > IC | 4/10 | 5/10 | 6/10 | 5/10 | 4/10 |

*Experiment 2*

| EC | 0.39 | 0.30 | 0.30 | 0.24 | 126.2 |
|---|---|---|---|---|---|
| IC | 0.38 | 0.29 | 0.28 | 0.22 | 125.0 |
| % difference | 2.9 | 4.4 | 7.7 | 5.3 | 1.0 |
| EC > IC | 6.5/10 | 6.5/10 | 7/10 | 6/10 | 5/10 |

*Experiment 3A*

| EC | 0.41 | 0.36 | 0.36 | 0.40 | 134.2 |
|---|---|---|---|---|---|
| IC | 0.40 | 0.32 | 0.33 | 0.39 | 129.8 |
| % difference | 2.6 | 9.5† | 10.1* | 3.1 | 3.4 |
| EC > IC | 6/10 | 8/10 | 8/10 | 7/10 | 6/10 |

*Experiment 3B*

| EC | 0.35 | 0.29 | 0.30 | 0.36 | 133.6 |
|---|---|---|---|---|---|
| IC | 0.36 | 0.29 | 0.30 | 0.36 | 129.7 |
| % difference | −2.1 | −0.6 | 1.7 | 0.6 | 3.0* |
| EC > IC | 2/10 | 4/10 | 6.5/10 | 6.5/10 | 7/10 |

*Combination*

| EC | 0.38 | 0.31 | 0.32 | 0.31 | 130.0 |
|---|---|---|---|---|---|
| IC | 0.38 | 0.30 | 0.30 | 0.30 | 128.2 |
| % difference | 0.2 | 3.6* | 9.7** | 3.1* | 1.4 |
| EC > IC | 18/10 | 23.5/10 | 27.5/40 | 24.5/40 | 22/40 |

Note: % difference = 100 (EC $M$ − IC $M$)/IC $M$; EC > IC is number of pairs in which EC value is greater than IC value, a fractional value representing a tie.
† $p < 0.10$.
* $p < 0.05$.
** $p < 0.01$.

value, and in one pair they were identical; therefore Table 5-2 shows EC exceeding IC in 27.5 cases. In all four experiments, the EC values exceeded that of the IC for the basal dendrites.

In the case of the oblique dendrites, EC–IC percentage differences ranged −0.6 to 9.5. The difference of 9.5% in experiment 3A was significant only at the 0.10 level. The combined result for oblique dendrites just reached statistical significance (3.6%; $p < 0.05$); the EC values were greater than the IC values in only 23.5 of the forty littermate pairs. In the case of terminal dendrites, EC–IC percentage differences ranged 0.6 to 5.3; although none of the individual experiments yielded significant results, the combined value of 3.1% reached the 0.05 confidence limits. In the case of the apical dendrites, EC–IC percentage differences ranged −2.7 to 2.9. For all experiments combined the effect was only 0.2%.

**Lateral Width**

Lateral width measurements were greater in experiments 2, 3A, and 3B in EC than in IC rats. Combined values show the EC mean width to be greater than the IC mean width by 1.4%, but the difference is nonsignificant.

**DISCUSSION**

It has been reported by Schapiro [17, 18] that early environmental stimulation significantly increases the number of dendritic spines on pyramidal cells in the visual cortex of rat pups. Their techniques for counting dendritic spines were similar to ours, and their conclusion concerning an increase in spine density is consistent with our own, but differences as well as similarities between Schapiro's studies and ours should be considered.

One striking difference is in the types of stimulation employed. We have used rather gentle treatment of rats, calling on abilities within their normal repertoire, and we have demonstrated that stress does not account for our results [16]. On the contrary, in Schapiro's studies a variety of stimulation was used, several aspects of which are likely to have been stressors. Three to five times a day, beginning at birth, his rat pups were stimulated for periods of 20 to 30 min: "they were handled and stroked, shaken on a mechanical shaker; placed in warm and cold water and on cold and then warm metal; and subjected to noise and flashing lights and to short periods of electric shock" [18, p. 293].

A second difference between Schapiro's experiments and ours is in the age of the subjects. While both he and we were interested in effects of experience on behavior, he chose to use newly born rat pups, whereas we used weanlings, 25 days of age. The rat pup is born in a fragile state, hairless and unable to regulate body temperature. Normally it remains sheltered in the nest almost constantly until about 2 weeks of age, and if it tumbles out of the nest, it is usually retrieved promptly by the mother. The rat's eyes and ear canals open at about 14 days of age, and it achieves temperature regulation at about this time. It is questionable, therefore, whether the rat pup has been capable of integrating much sensory experience if it is sacrificed at 8 days of age [18] or even at 13 days [17].

The magnitude and the pattern of the effects also differ between Schapiro's results and ours. Schapiro and Vukovich [18] found rather large and significant effects on almost all types of dendrites: The density of spines in the five stimulated pups exceeded that in the five nonstimulated pups by 10% (ns) in apical dendrites, by 33% ($p < 0.01$) in oblique dendrites, by 28% ($p < 0.05$) in terminal dendrites, and by 33% ($p < .001$) in basal dendrites. On the contrary, we found a moderately large effect only for basal dendrites and this amounted to only 9.7% ($p < 0.01$). Furthermore, only two of the four experiments yielded statistically significant effects even for basal dendrites, although ten pairs were used in each experiment. Overall, as we have reported, the effect in basal dendrites was significant at beyond the 0.01 level of confidence. Perhaps the large magnitude of Schapiro's effects occurred because they represent both effects of stress on very young animals as well as effects of experience.

We are inclined to offer the following interpretations for the fact that in our experiments the only moderately large change in density of spines occurred on the basal dendrites, with oblique dendrites and terminal dendrites showing only 3% differences. The basal dendrites receive principally intracortical connections, and one of several postulated ways [16] in which the nervous system may change to meet an increased multisensory demand is by an increase in numbers of connections among cortical neurons. That the basal dendrites receive most of their afferents from other cortical cells was demonstrated by degeneration of spines after intracortical stab wounds [6]. In contrast, spines on apical dendrites receive their afferents from the specific afferent radiation, the lateral geniculate body in the case of the visual cortex [10, 19]; on the oblique dendrites, the spines receive mainly callosal afferents [9]. The enriched condition involves variation of stimulation in several sensory modalities—visual, tactual, kinesthetic, auditory, and olfactory. The fact that the occipital area of the rat is multisensory is indicated by the following finding: Although the brain weight effects are largest in the occipital area, we have found that EC–IC effects of similar size occur in the occipital area even if the experiment is run in total darkness or if the rats are blinded [13]. Thus the demand of integration of complex multisensory information could result in an increase of intracortical connections—ramification of axon terminals, growth of dendritic spines, formation of new synapses and enlargement of others. The fact that cortical volume is greater in EC than in IC is probably not so much dependent upon these alterations in connections as upon presumably related secondary changes such as those in glial number and in size of perikarya.

Measures of dendritic length and branching in EC and IC rats were made by Holloway [11] using Golgi–Cox preparations. He followed the Sholl method of counting interactions of dendrites with circles concentric around the perikaryon. Preliminary results based on fifteen EC and fifteen IC littermates indicated a greater number of intersections in EC than in IC but no difference in dendritic lengths. This was interpreted to mean that EC dendrites showed greater numbers of branches. The lack of a difference in dendritic length in his study is consistent with our finding of no EC–IC difference in lateral width of dendrites.

Our finding of greater number of spines, and presumably of synapses, in EC versus IC rats may seem to run counter to reported stability of synaptic number in rat cortex after 30 days of age [1]. Upon close examination it is not clear that a discrepancy exists. The measures of Aghajanian and Bloom were made in layer 1 of the parietal area; we have found no EC–IC differences in thickness of layer 1 in the occipital area. Furthermore, it should be noted that Aghajanian and Bloom measured number of junctions per mm$^3$ in layer 1. The volume of cortex continues to increase after 30 days of age. If layer 1 is similar to the other layers in this respect, then the total number of synapses probably increases even though the number per unit volume remains stable.

Although we would like to be able to relate the present findings of changes in spine counts with our recently reported changes in synaptic number and length measured in electron microscopic preparations [12], differences in the measures make this impossible. The Møllgaard study reported differences in synaptic frequency and size between rats exposed to EC and IC environments as in the present study. Asymmetrical axodendritic synapses were measured in the occipital cortex, mainly in layer 3. EC rats, when compared to IC littermates, showed only two-thirds as many synapses, but their mean cross-sectional length was one and one-half times as great. The EM measures were made without regard to whether the synapses occurred on terminal, apical, oblique, or basal dendrites; only serial reconstruction could have established this. The spine counts, however, sampled only apical dendrites at layer 3. Thus the dendritic spine counts were sparse and perhaps unrepresentative in layer 3 where the EM synaptic measures were made; therefore a lack of correspondence between the spine and synaptic measures may not be meaningful. It would be worthwhile in further work to measure spines on basal dendrites in the upper half of the cortex. Cragg [3] has, in fact, reported that changes in synaptic number and dimensions with sensory stimulation may go in opposite directions in the upper and lower halves of the cortex.

## REFERENCES

1. G. K. Aghajanian and F. E. Bloom. The formation of synaptic junctions in developing rat brain: A quantitative electron microscopic study. *Brain Res.,* 1967, *6,* 716–727.
2. E. L. Bennett, M. C. Diamond, D. Krech, and M. R. Rosenzweig. Chemical and anatomical plasticity of brain. *Science,* 1964, *146,* 610–619.
3. B. G. Cragg. Are there structural alterations in synapses related to functioning? *Proc. Royal Soc. (ser. B),* 1968, *171,* 319–323.
4. M. C. Diamond, D. Krech, and M. R. Rosenzweig. The effects of an enriched environment on the histology of the rat cerebral cortex. *J. comp. Neurol.,* 1964, *123,* 111–119.
5. M. C. Diamond, F. Law, H. Rhodes, B. Lindner, M. R. Rosenzweig, D. Krech, and E. L. Bennett. Increases in cortical depth and glia numbers in rats subjected to enriched environment. *J. comp. Neurol.,* 1966, *128,* 117–125.
6. A. Globus. Neuronal ontogeny: Its use in tracing connectivity. In M. B. Sterman, D. J. McGinty, and A. M. Adinolfi (eds.). *Brain development and behavior.* New York: Academic Press, 1971.
7. A. Globus and A. B. Scheibel. Effect of visual deprivation on cortical neurons: A Golgi study. *Exp. Neurol.,* 1967, *19,* 331–345.
8. A. Globus and A. B. Scheibel. Pattern and field in cortical structure: The rabbit. *J. comp. Neurol.,* 1967, *131,* 155–172.
9. A. Globus and A. B. Scheibel. Synaptic loci on parietal cortical neurons: Terminations of corpus callosum fibers. *Science,* 1967, *156,* 1127–1129.
10. A. Globus and A. B. Scheibel. Synaptic loci on visual cortical neurons of the rabbit: The specific afferent radiation. *Exp. Neurol.,* 1967, *18,* 116–131.
11. R. L. Holloway, Jr. Dendritic branching in rat visual cortex: Effects of extra environmental complexity and training. *Brain Res.,* 1966, *2,* 393.
12. K. Møllgaard, M. C. Diamond, E. L. Bennett, M. R. Rosenzweig, and B. Lindner. Quantitative synaptic changes with differential experience in rat brain. *Int. J. Neuroscience,* 1971, *2,* 113–128.
13. M. R. Rosenzweig and E. L. Bennett. Effects of differential environments on brain weights and enzyme activities in gerbils, rats, and mice. *Devel. Psychol.,* 1969, *2,* 87–95.
14. M. R. Rosenzweig, E. L. Bennett, and M. C. Diamond. Chemical and anatomical plasticity of brain: Replications and extensions, 1970. In J. Gaito (ed.). *Macromolecules and behavior.* 2d ed. New York: Appleton-Century-Crofts, 1972.
15. M. R. Rosenzweig, E. L. Bennett, M. C. Diamond, S.-Y. Wu, R. W. Slagle, and E. Saffran. Influences of environmental complexity and visual stimulation on development of occipital cortex in rat. *Brain Res.,* 1969, *14,* 427–445.
16. M. R. Rosenzweig, K. Møllgaard, E. L. Bennett, and M. C. Diamond. Negative as well as positive synaptic changes may store memory. *Psychol. Rev.,* 1972, *79,* 93–96.
17. S. Schapiro. Hormonal and environmental influences on rat brain development and behavior. In M. B. Sterman, D. J. McGinty, and A. M. Adinolfi (eds.). *Brain development and behavior.* New York: Academic Press, 1971.

18. S. Schapiro and K. R. Vukovich. Early experience effects upon cortical dendrites: A proposed model for development. *Science,* 1970, *167,* 292–294.
19. F. Valverde. Structural changes in the area striata of the mouse after enucleation. *Exp. Brain Res.,* 1968, *5,* 274–292.

# 6

# CURRENT TRENDS AND ISSUES IN ADAPTATION-LEVEL THEORY

## Harry Helson

... Workers in the tradition of classical psychophysics have tried to establish pure scales relating physical and psychological magnitudes by ruling out series, anchor, and order effects. In this approach each sense modality is presumed to have its own fixed sensitivity predetermined by the nature of the receptor mechanism. Each scale is supposed to have unique constants giving rise to negatively or positively accelerated functions. According to this view, the organism acts only as a meter or transducer of energy; any variations due to series, contextual, background, or residual stimuli are considered errors that must be gotten rid of at all costs.

In contrast to the classical approach, adaptation-level theorists believe that complex factors determining psychophysical judgments must be taken into account, and a broader base must be incorporated in psychophysical laws. Contrasted with classical psychophysics, or the psychophysics of stimuli, is the psychophysics of classes, or frame of reference psychophysics. In this approach stimuli are regarded not as isolated events but as members of classes, and interest centers in the way stimuli are ordered in the classes to which they belong. Each class of stimuli is judged with respect to internal norms which can be objectively and quantitatively specified. Judgments are relative to prevailing norms or

Source: *American Psychologist,* 1964, *19,* 26–38. Copyright 1964 by the American Psychological Association. Reprinted by permission.
Note: Preparation of this paper was supported in part by the Office of Naval Research under Contract Nonr–3634(01) with Kansas State University. The studies of reaction time, contrast and assimilation, and anchor effects in recall were supported by grants from the Bureau of General Research of Kansas State University.

adaptation levels. Thus a 4-oz fountain pen is heavy, but a baseball bat to be heavy must weigh over 40 oz. What is called heavy or light cannot be attributed merely to a change in scale modulus or to semantic set or to judgmental relativity, because different bodily members, different sets of muscles, and a different stance are used to swing a baseball bat and to write with a fountain pen. Even within the same sense modality different scales have to be used for different classes of objects if they are referred to different internal norms. Thus a single scale will not suffice for judging the sizes of rectangles or cubes under laboratory conditions and judging the sizes of houses. A large house is judged according to a different internal norm from that used in judging large rectangles. Functional considerations also influence internal norms: A house that is large for a family of three is small for a family of eight. Psychophysics cannot ignore the role of internal norms except at its own peril. By internal norms we refer to the operationally defined concept of adaptation level.

The concept of adaptation level may be defined by at least three different sets of operations:

1. Adaptation levels appear as neutral or indifferent zones in bipolar responses. The bipolar nature of behavior has been recognized in almost all systems of psychology, for example, by Lewin [33] in his positive and negative valences; by Pavlov [40] in his concept of facilitation and inhibition; by Koffka [32] in his concept of the "demand" character of objects which Boring [10] put into behavioral terms as "that which attracts or repels us"; by N. E. Miller [36] in his concept of approach-avoidance gradients; and in the concepts of positive and negative reinforcers used by learning theorists. Descriptively, we find positive and negative afterimages in sensory processes, and pleasant and unpleasant feelings in the domain of affects. If we measure bipolar properties of behavior on continua, then it is immediately evident that there are neutral zones between opposite qualities and opposed modes of behavior. Operationally, the stimuli or conditions eliciting neutral responses furnish a measure of prevailing levels. In 1924 Hess [28] pointed out that the earthworm, *Lumbricus terrestris,* avoids certain intensities of light above a certain level, approaches weaker intensities, and remains quiescent at some intermediate intensity. In the most primitive responses objects are grossly dichotomized into approach-ignore-avoid, good-indifferent-bad, pleasant-neutral-unpleasant. This is the simplest form of categorizing or scaling, and all scaling methods, whether they require the use of language or some other type of response, are fundamentally bipolar rating scales in which the neutral or zero is fixed by the organism. Adaptation levels are revealed in all forms of behavior whether they are sensory, motor, or cognitive verbal in nature.

2. We may deduce the concept of adaptation level (AL) from a set of assumptions regarding the nature of psychophysical judgments, as was

done by Michels and Helson [35] in reformulating the Fechner law. Less strict than the derivation of AL by logicomathematical reasoning is the incorporation of a parameter in empirical equations to make the organism's functional zero the zero of psychological continua. In such cases the best values of AL can be determined from all judgments of a set of stimuli by curve fitting, linear interpolation, and so on. This has been done both by means of the reformulated Fechner law and also in using other types of equations, for instance, in the determination of the loci of achromatic points in strongly chromatic illuminances [25].

3. We may arrive at the concept of AL in the time-honored way found so fruitful in mathematics, physics, and chemistry, that is, by definition. There are many advantages in defining a concept besides the important one that we then know what we are talking about. AL as a weighted log mean derives much of its value, like many concepts in physics, in being defined so that constants appropriate to specific cases can be determined. Like the general differential equation relating resistance, capacitance, and inductance in electrical circuits, which can be used to solve any number of specific problems, so the definition of AL as a weighted mean can be used to obtain quantitative answers to many different questions.

This definition has provided a number of deductions such as the pooling or integrative nature of most types of responses, the decentered position of stimuli eliciting neutral psychophysical judgments, the nonlinearity of stimulus-response functions, and AL as the moving zero of psychophysical and other functions. In addition, it has accounted for such experimentally determined facts as the tendency of organisms to match level of output with level of input, variability of response with constant stimulation, and effects of anchors, context, and residual factors in perception and judgment.

We have found that the weighted log mean definition of AL is the best approximation to the neutral or indifferent region for sensory magnitudes. In estimates of the averages of series of numbers, Parducci, et al. [39] have stressed the role of mid, median, and end points of the series in determining AL. I prefer the weighted log mean because it brings in all the stimuli, not just the mid and end stimuli, because of its greater theoretical power and greater generality, and because this definition requires fewer arbitrary constants than any other definition so far proposed. As an example, let us consider a recent application by Bevan, Barker, and Pritchard [4] of this definition to handle an effect Stevens has called hysteresis, which means "lagging behind." These writers point out:

> When one asks what it is that lags, the concept of adaptation level presents itself for consideration. According to this point of view, the apparent dif-

ference in magnitude between two successively presented stimuli depends not simply upon a difference between the intensitive processes representing the first (standard) and the second (variable), but upon the difference between an internal norm evolved from a combination, on the one hand, of all of the relevant prior inputs including the standard and, on the other, the process representing the variable. If a sequence of inputs is nonrandom (that is, ascending or descending), then we may expect that there will be a lag in the shift of the internal norm in contrast to the shift in standard stimuli. If the norm evolves from successive presentations of an ascending series, it may be expected that the bowing will be upward; if a descending series is used, the expected bowing is downward [pp. 103–104].

Using lifted weights, Bevan, Barker, and Pritchard obtained concave upward curves in light-to-heavy order and concave downward curves in heavy-to-light order. Stevens' assumption [47] that bowing is due to poorer discrimination at the higher end of the scale, resulting in greater use of upper categories, cannot, they show, explain positively accelerated curves, because in these cases discrimination is better at the high than at the low end of the continuum. Hence this argument can apply only to negatively accelerated curves. Excellent fits were obtained to experimental data by taking as the effective stimulus not the physical value of the stimulus being judged, but the difference between the stimulus judged and the adaptation level, calculated as a weighted log mean of preceding stimuli, with the immediately preceding stimulus as standard. On this basis upward bowed curves were obtained for ascending series and downward bowed curves for descending series. No new assumptions had to be made in this application of the weighted mean definition to explain upward and downward bowing with ascending and descending orders of stimulus presentation.

Let us now turn to some other studies that reveal current trends and bear on fundamental issues in adaptation-level theory.

## ANCHORING EFFECTS OF SUBLIMINAL STIMULI

In this connection it was found by Black and Bevan[1] [7] that experimental subjects judged a set of five electric shocks ranging from 1,500 to 2,700 $\mu$a as more intensive following a subliminal anchor shock than did a control group which received the five supraliminal shocks without the subliminal anchor. Since the subliminal shocks were not detected by GSR measures, it appears that a behavioral measure, judgment, may be more sensitive to the influence of stimulation than a widely used physiological indicator.

---

[1] See selection 12 in this book.

Reinforcing effects of 2,300 μa shocks were found by Bevan and Adamson [3] to be most effective when the preadaptation electric shock was below 2,300 μa, least effective when the preadaptation shock was above, and intermediate in effectiveness when the preadaptation shock was the same as in the learning series. These findings were replicated with rat subjects in a subsequent study by Black, Adamson, and Bevan [6] using running speed to escape shock at the criterion. It is difficult to believe that rats are subject to semantic sets, judgmental relativity, or change in scale modulus, as proposed by Stevens [48] as alternatives to adaptation-level theory. It seems simpler to assume that shocks following preadapting weak shocks are effectively more intense, and shocks following preadapting strong shocks are effectively less intense because of their effects on prevailing adaptation levels.

## RESIDUAL EFFECTS OF ANCHORS IN MEMORY AND RECALL

Using a null method that did not require judgment in terms of language responses, Steger and I (unpublished study) have found that effects of anchors persist over a period of time and influence recall as as well as conditions during immediate impression of stimuli. In the first study four groups of subjects judged a series of black squares on white background during the impression or learning series. The squares ranged from 1.0 to 3.82 in. on a side and were judged in terms of a rating scale from very, very small to very, very large. The initial conditions for the four groups were as follows: (a) without anchor stimulus; (b) with an anchor at the geometric center of the series (1.96 in.); (c) with a 9.0-in. anchor; and (d) with a 0.30-in. anchor. The average size judgments are shown in Figure 6-1 and are in line with expectations from known anchor effects: The squares were judged smallest with the largest anchor, largest with the smallest anchor, and intermediate with the anchor at the center of the series and with the no anchor condition. One week later subjects were called back to the laboratory and asked to identify the smallest, middle, and largest stimuli in the series from a much more extended series that ranged from 0.10 in. to 14.56 in. on a side presented in ascending and descending orders. As shown in Figure 6-2 (p. 58), the residual effects of the anchors in the impression trials are evident after 1 week: The 9.0-in. anchor group picked the smallest set of three; the 0.30-in. group picked the largest set of three; while the two control groups picked sets intermediate in size between those of the other two groups.

The first experiment was replicated and extended in a second experiment with four new groups of subjects to determine the relative potency of anchors as residuals, that is, anchors given during the impression phase, versus anchors present during the recall phase. Two control groups were not given anchors during the impression phase but were

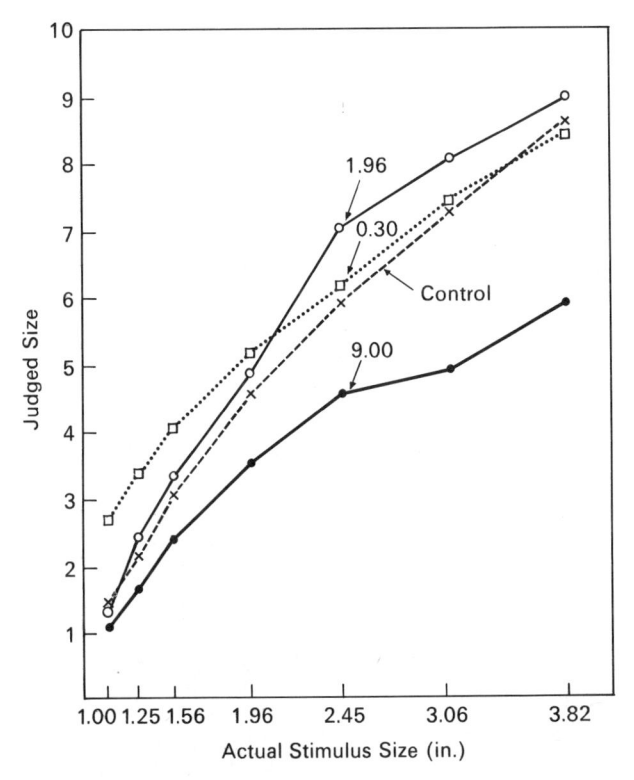

FIGURE 6-1  Judged size of stimuli in the impression phase showing expected anchor effects with small (0.30 in.), intermediate (1.96 in.), and large (9.0 in.) anchors and under the control condition in which no anchor was employed.

exposed to the 0.30- and 9.0-in. anchors during the recall phase. One experimental group was given the 9.0-in. anchor during the impression phase and the 0.30-in. anchor during the recall phase; conversely, the other experimental group was given the 0.30-in. anchor in the impression session and the 9.0-in. anchor in the recall session. The results again show expected effects of anchors, as seen in Figure 6-3, where the stimuli recalled with the 9.0-in. anchor present were smaller (curves coded V and VIII) than stimuli recalled with the 0.30-in. anchor (curves coded VI and VII). Comparison of the curves for groups VI and VII show that the 0.30-in. anchor during recall was more effective if it followed 9.0-in. anchor during the impression phase 1 week earlier than if no anchor was present during the impression phase. However the 9.0-in. anchor in the recall phase following 0.30-in. anchor in the impression phase did not yield significantly lower recall choices than under the control condition (groups V and VIII).

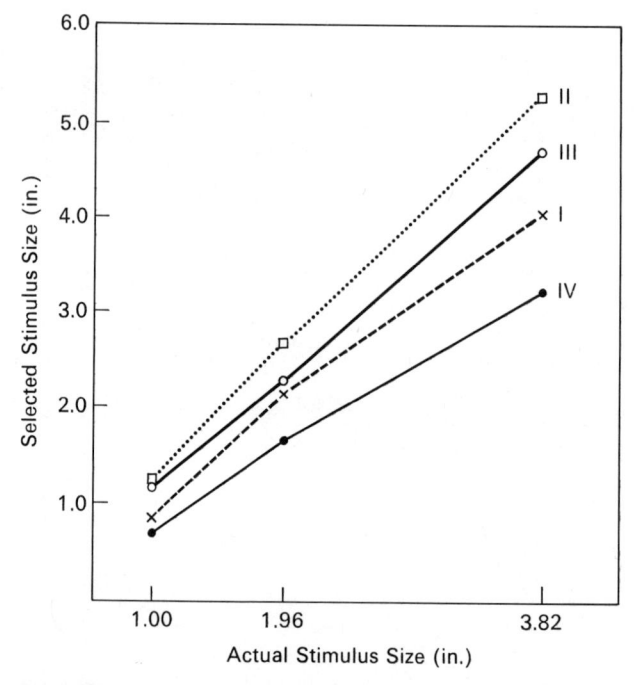

FIGURE 6-2 Smallest, middle, and largest stimuli of the series recalled 1 week after initial presentation.

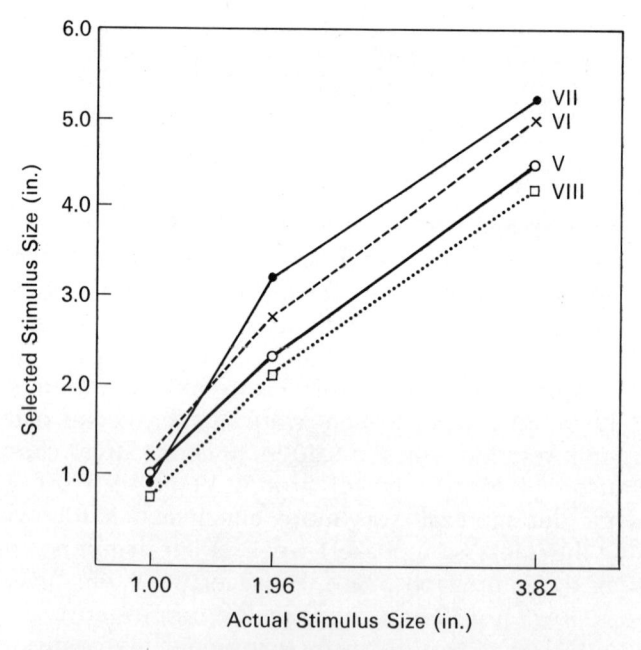

FIGURE 6-3 Smallest, middle, and largest stimuli recalled 1 week after initial impression with large (small) anchor if small (large) anchor was employed during the impression phase.

## REFERENCES

1. J. Behar and W. Bevan. The perceived duration of auditory and visual intervals: Cross-modal comparison and interaction. *Amer. J. Psychol.*, 1961, 74, 17–26.
2. W. Bevan. The pooling mechanism and the phenomena of reinforcement. In O. J. Harvey (ed.). *Motivation and social interaction*. New York: Ronald Press, 1963.
3. W. Bevan and R. Adamson. Reinforcers and reinforcement: Their relation to maze performance. *J. exp. Psychol.*, 1960, 59, 226–232.
4. W. Bevan, H. Barker, and J. F. Pritchard. The Newhall scaling method, psychophysical bowing, and adaption level. *J. gen. Psychol.*, 1963, 69, 95–111.
5. W. Bevan and J. F. Pritchard. Effect of "subliminal" tones upon the judgment of loudness. *J. exp. Psychol.*, 1963, 66, 23–29.
6. R. W. Black, R. Adamson, and W. Bevan. Runway behavior as a function of apparent intensity of shock. *J. comp. physiol. Psychol.*, 1961, 54, 270–274.
7. R. W. Black and W. Bevan. The effect of subliminal shock upon the judged intensity of weak shock. *Amer. J. Psychol.*, 1960, 73, 262–267.
8. W. Block. A conceptual framework for the clinical test situation. *Psychol. Bull.*, 1964, 61.
9. W. K. Boardman and S. Goldstone. Effects of subliminal anchors upon judgments of size. *Percept. mot. Skills*, 1962, 14, 475–482.
10. E. G. Boring. Koffka's *Principles of Gestalt psychology*. *Psychol. Bull.*, 1936, 33, 59–69.
11. D. T. Campbell, W. Hunt, and N. A. Lewis. The effects of assimilation and contrast in judgments of clinical materials. *Amer. J. Psychol.*, 1957, 70, 347–360.
12. D. T. Campbell, N. A. Lewis, and W. A. Hunt. Context effects with judgmental language that is absolute, extensive, and extra-experimentally anchored. *J. exp. Psychol.*, 1958, 55, 220–228.
13. A. Dollin and J. M. Sakoda. The effect of order of presentation on perception of TAT pictures. *J. consult. Psychol.*, 1962, 26, 340–344.
14. S. Goldstone, J. L. Goldfarb, J. Strong, and J. Russell. Replication: The effect of subliminal shock upon the judged intensity of weak shock. *Percept. mot. Skills*, 1962, 14, 222.
15. S. Goldstone and J. L. Goldfarb. Adaptation level, personality theory, and psychopathology. *Psychol. Bull.*, 1964, 61.
16. D. A. Grant and L. M. Schipper. The acquisition and extinction of conditioned eyelid responses as a function of the percentage of fixed-ratio random reinforcement. *J. exp. Psychol.*, 1952, 43, 313–320.
17. J. F. Hall. *Psychology of motivation*. Philadelphia: Lippincott, 1961.
18. H. Helson. Fundamental problems in color vision. I. The principle governing changes in hue, saturation, and lightness of nonselective samples in chromatic illumination. *J. exp. Psychol.*, 1938, 23, 439–476.
19. H. Helson. Studies of anomalous contrast and assimilation. *J. opt. Soc. Amer.*, 1963, 53, 179–184.

20. H. Helson, R. R. Blake, and J. S. Mouton. Petition-signing as adjustment to situational and personal factors. *J. soc. Psychol.*, 1958, *48*, 3–10.
21. H. Helson, R. R. Blake, J. S. Mouton, and J. A. Olmstead. Attitudes as adjustments to stimulus, background, and residual factors. *J. abnorm. soc. Psychol.*, 1956, *52*, 314–322.
22. H. Helson and V. Joy. Domains of lightness assimilation and contrast effects in vision. *Psychol. Beit.*, 1962, *6*, 405–415.
23. H. Helson, D. B. Judd, and M. H. Warren. Object-color changes from daylight to incandescent-filament illumination. *Illum. Engr.*, 1952, *47*, 221–233.
24. H. Helson, D. B. Judd, and M. Wilson. Color rendition with fluorescent sources of illumination. *Illum. Engr.*, 1956, *51*, 329–346.
25. H. Helson and W. C. Michels. The effect of adaptation on achromaticity. *J. opt. Soc. Amer.*, 1948, *38*, 1025–1032.
26. H. Helson and F. H. Rohles, Jr. A quantitative study of reversal of classical lightness-contrast. *Amer. J. Psychol.*, 1959, *72*, 530–538.
27. H. Helson and J. A. Steger. On the inhibitory effects of a second stimulus following the primary stimulus to react. *J. exp. Psychol.*, 1962, *63*, 201–205.
28. W. Hess. Reactions to light in the earthworm, *Lumbricus terrestris*. *J. morphol. Physiol.*, 1924, *39*, 515–542.
29. C. I. Hovland and M. Sherif. Judgmental phenomena and scales of attitude measurement: Item displacement in Thurstone scales. *J. abnorm. soc. Psychol.*, 1952, *47*, 822–832.
30. D. B. Judd. Basic correlates of the visual stimulus. In S. S. Stevens (ed.). *Handbook of experimental psychology*. New York: Wiley, 1951.
31. D. B. Judd. Appraisal of Land's work on two primary color projections. *J. opt. Soc. Amer.*, 1960, *50*, 254–268.
32. K. Koffka. *Principles of Gestalt psychology*. New York: Harcourt, Brace, 1935.
33. K. Lewin. *Field theory in social science*. New York: Harper, 1951.
34. F. H. Logan. *Incentive*. New Haven: Yale University Press, 1960.
35. W. C. Michels and H. Helson. A reformulation of the Fechner law in terms of adaptation-level applied to rating-scale data. *Amer. J. Psychol.*, 1949, *62*, 355–368.
36. N. E. Miller. Liberalization of basic S-R concepts: Extensions to conflict behavior, motivation, and social learning. In S. Koch (ed.). *Psychology: A study of a science*. New York: McGraw-Hill, 1959. Vol. 2.
37. K. F. Muenzinger. Reward and punishment. *U. Colo. Stud., gen. Sec.*, 1946, *27* (no. 4), 1–16.
38. A. Parducci. Sequential effects in judgment. *Psychol. Bull.*, 1964, *61*, 163–167.
39. A. Parducci, R. C. Calfee, L. M. Marshall, and L. P. Davidson. Context effects in judgment: Adaptation level as a function of the mean, midpoint, and median of the stimuli. *J. exp. Psychol.*, 1960, *60*, 65–77.
40. I. P. Pavlov. *Conditioned reflexes*. Trans. G. V. Anrep. London: Oxford University Press, 1927.
41. J. E. Podell. A comparison of generalization and adaptation level as theories of connotation. *J. abnorm. soc. Psychol.*, 1961, *62*, 593–597.

42. W. W. Rambo and E. L. Johnson. Practice effects and the estimation of adaption level. *Amer. J. Psychol.,* 1964, *77,* 106–110.
43. M. Rosenbaum. The effect of stimulus and background factors in the volunteering response. *J. abnorm. soc. Psychol.,* 1956, *53,* 118–121.
44. B. Russell. *Human knowledge.* New York: Simon and Schuster, 1948.
45. M. Sherif and C. I. Hovland. *Social judgment.* New Haven: Yale University Press, 1961.
46. M. Sherif, D. Taub, and C. I. Hovland. Assimilation and contrast effects of anchoring stimuli on judgments. *J. exp. Psychol.,* 1958, *55,* 150–155.
47. S. S. Stevens. On the psychophysical law. *Psychol. Rev.,* 1957, *64,* 153–181.
48. S. S. Stevens. Adaptation level vs. the relativity of judgment. *Amer. J. Psychol.,* 1958, *71,* 633–646.
49. H. H. Young, W. H. Holtzman, and W. D. Bryant. Effects of item context and order on personality ratings. *Educ. psychol. Measmt.,* 1954, *14,* 499–517.

# 7

# EFFECT OF INITIAL SELLING PRICE ON SUBSEQUENT SALES

Anthony N. Doob
J. Merrill Carlsmith
Jonathan L. Freedman
Thomas K. Landauer
Soleng Tom, Jr.

*Five field experiments investigated the effect of initial selling price on subsequent sales of common household products. Matched pairs of discount houses sold the same product at either a discounted price or the regular price for a short period of time. The prices were then made the same for all stores. The results were consistent with the prediction*

Source: *Journal of Personality and Social Psychology,* 1969, *11,* 345–350. Copyright 1969 by the American Psychological Association. Reprinted by permission.
Note: This study was supported in part by National Science Foundation grants to Carlsmith and to Freedman. The authors thank management and personnel of the discount chain for their cooperation in this research.

*from dissonance theory that subsequent sales would be higher where the initial price was high.*

The "introductory low price offer" is a common technique used by marketers. A new product is offered at a low price for a short period of time, and the price is subsequently raised to its normal level. Since the goal naturally is to maximize final sales of the product, the assumption behind this technique is that it will accomplish this goal. An economic model based entirely on supply and demand would of course predict that the eventual sales would not be affected by the initial price. The lower price would be expected to attract many marginal buyers and produce greater sales; but as soon as the price is raised, these buyers should drop out of the market. The hope of the marketer, however, is that some of these marginal buyers will learn to like the product enough so that they will continue to purchase it even at the higher price.

Unfortunately for the marketer, this may be a vain hope. There are various psychological reasons why we might expect the introductory low price to have an opposite effect from that which the marketers intend, such that the introductory low price would reduce rather than increase eventual sales. Since this technique is so widespread, it provides an unusual opportunity to investigate the applicability of social psychology in a natural setting and to compare the marketer's predictions with that of social psychology.

The most interesting analysis of this situation is based on the theory of cognitive dissonance [2]. One of the clearest deductions from the theory is that the more effort in any form a person exerts to attain a goal, the more dissonance is aroused if the goal is less valuable than expected. The individual reduces this dissonance by increasing his liking for the goal, and therefore the greater the effort, the more he should like the goal. This prediction has received some substantiation in laboratory experimentation (for example, Aronson and Mills [1]; Gerard and Mathewson [3]). Its applicability to the marketing situation is straightforward: the theory predicts that the higher the price a person initially pays for a product, the more he will come to like it. Presumably this greater liking will produce "brand loyalty" in the form of repeat purchases. Thus, when the initial price is high, a higher *proportion* of buyers should continue to purchase the product than when the initial price is low. Accordingly, although the introductory price will initially attract more customers, we may expect the sales curves for the two conditions to cross at some later point, and the higher brand loyalty induced by the dissonance involved in paying a high price to manifest itself in higher final sales in that condition.

Five experiments were performed to demonstrate that introducing a new brand of a product at a low price for a short time and then raising it to the normal selling price leads to lower sales in the long run than introducing the product at its normal selling price. The general design of all the experiments was to introduce the new brand at a low price in one set of stores and, after the price is raised to the normal selling price, compare sales with matched stores where the product was introduced at the normal selling price and held there throughout the course of the experiment.

All of the experiments that are to be reported here were done in a chain of discount houses. All sales figures have been multiplied by a constant in order to maintain confidentiality.

This chain of discount houses differs from most others in a number of important ways. They do not advertise much, and what advertising they do does not include prices on specific items. Price changes occur very seldom in these stores and are usually not advertised. In most cases, prices are lowered because an item is overstocked, and unless the customer remembers the regular selling price, he has no way of knowing that the price is lower than usual. Management in most of these stores is under direct control of the central office. When the manager receives orders from the central office, he has little or no power to change them.

The chain sells a large number of "house brands" at prices lower than the equivalent name brands. These house brands have the same registered trademark and constitute a brand which customers can easily identify with the store. Generally, the quality of the house brand item is as high as the equivalent name brand, the differences usually being in characteristics which do not directly affect the usefulness of the item (for instance, mouthwash bottles are not as attractive as those of the name brand; the average grain size of powdered detergent is larger than that of the name brand, which is chemically equivalent).

The products used in the studies reported here were house brands. All were being introduced into the stores at the time when the study was being run. The particular products used and the price differential were both determined by management.

## EXPERIMENT I

### Method

Twelve pairs of discount houses, matched on gross sales, were randomly assigned to one of two experimental conditions. In one store of each pair, the house brand of mouthwash was introduced at $0.25 per quart bottle. The price was held at this level for 9 days (two weekends and the intervening days), and then the price was brought up to $0.39 for all stores. In the other store, it was introduced at its normal selling price of $0.39.

None of the managers had any reason to believe that the price of mouthwash at his store was not the same as in all other stores in the chain. No one was given any special instructions beyond the place in the store where the item was to be sold and its selling price. The location was essentially identical for all stores. In stores where mouthwash was introduced at the low price, the manager received a memo at the end of the first week instructing him to change the price to $0.39 after that weekend.

**Results**

Sales were recorded by the sundries buyer as he replenished stock. At the end of each week these figures were sent to the central office and then relayed to the experimenters. Average sales for the twelve matched stores in each condition are shown in Figure 7-1. It is estimated that at

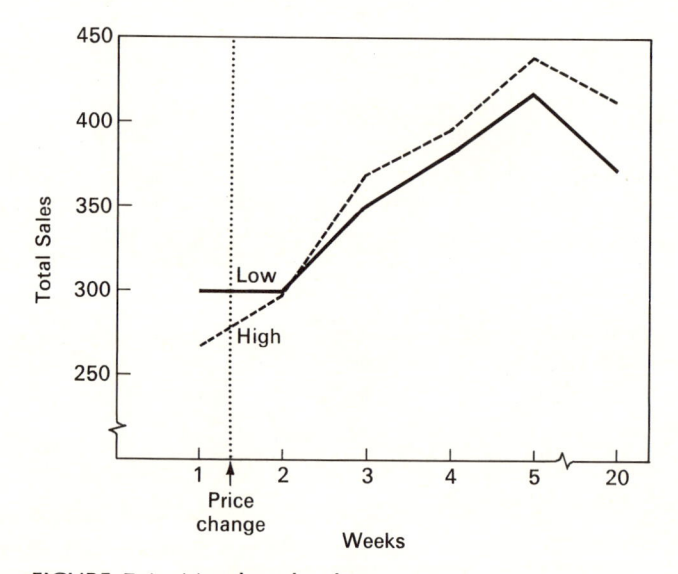

FIGURE 7-1 Mouthwash sales.

least 2 weeks had to pass before customers would return to buy more mouthwash, and therefore one would not expect there to be any difference between the height of the curves until the third week. In fact, the curves cross at this point, and after this point, it is clear that the stores where the initial selling price was high were selling more mouthwash than stores where the initial price was low. This is true in spite of the fact that more mouthwash was sold the first week in stores where the price was low. Unfortunately, for a variety of reasons, the authors were not able to collect continuous data. They were able, however, to check sales 19 weeks after the price change, and clearly the difference still existed. When sales for weeks 3, 4, 5, and 20 are combined, sales of mouthwash were higher in the store where the initial selling price was high in ten of the twelve pairs of stores ($p = 0.02$).

Sales in the two sets of stores during weeks 3, 4, 5, and 20 (pooled) were also compared by use of a $t$ test, resulting in a $t$ of 2.11 ($df = 11$, $p < 0.10$). Thus stores where the initial selling price was low sold less mouthwash than did stores where the initial selling price was the same as the final selling price.

## REPLICATIONS

The same experiment was repeated four times, using different products. The procedures were very similar in all cases. In each experiment, the stores were rematched and randomly assigned independent of all other replications.

### Experiment II: Toothpaste

Six pairs of stores were matched on the basis of sundries sales and randomly assigned to conditions in which the selling price for the first 3 weeks was either $0.41 or $0.49 for a "family size" tube of toothpaste. After 3 weeks, the price in all stores was set at $0.49. The results are presented in Figure 7-2. When the sales of the last 4 weeks are combined as

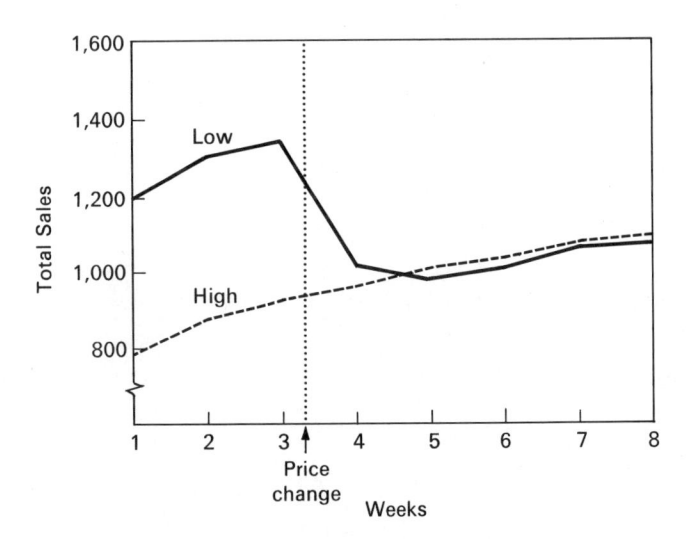

FIGURE 7-2 Toothpaste sales.

in the previous experiment, four of the six pairs show differences in the predicted direction ($p = 0.34$). When the more sensitive $t$ test is done on the data from these 4 weeks, the $t$ is 2.26 ($df = 5, p < 0.10$).

## Experiment III: Aluminum Foil

Seven pairs of stores were matched on the basis of grocery sales and randomly assigned to conditions in which the selling price for the first 3 weeks was either $0.59 or $0.64 for a 75-ft roll of foil. After 3 weeks, the price in all stores was set at $0.64. The results are presented in Figure 7-3.

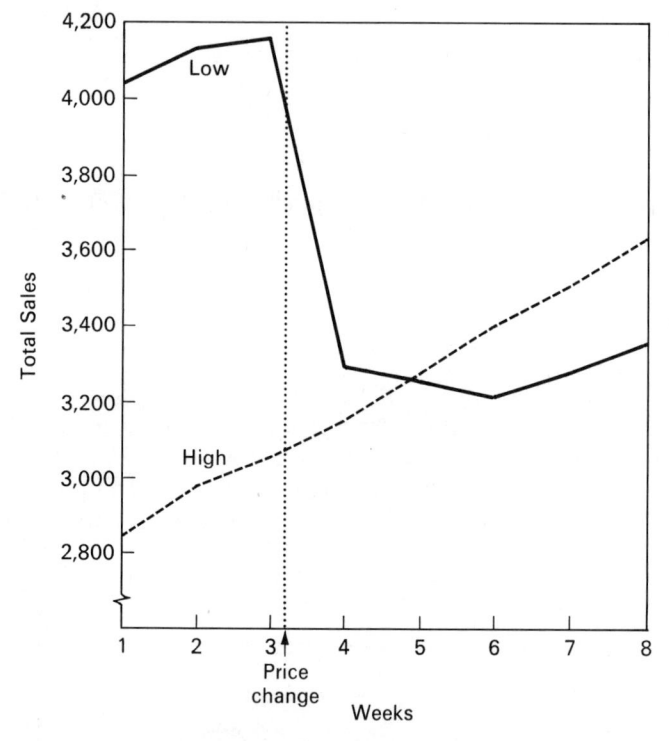

FIGURE 7-3  Aluminum foil sales.

For weeks 5 to 8 combined, all seven pairs ($p = 0.01$) show differences in the predicted direction ($t = 5.09$, $df = 6$, $p < 0.005$).

## Experiment IV: Light Bulbs

Eight pairs of stores were matched on the basis of hardware sales and randomly assigned to conditions in which selling price for the first week was either $0.26 or $0.32 for a package of light bulbs. After 1 week, the price was brought up to $0.32 in all stores. The results are presented in Figure 7-4. For weeks 3 and 4 combined, six of the eight pairs ($p = 0.15$) show differences in the predicted direction ($t = 0.837$, $df = 7$). Although this difference is not significant, it might be noted in Figure 7-4 that there was the predicted reversal, even though initial sales were almost 50% higher at the low price.

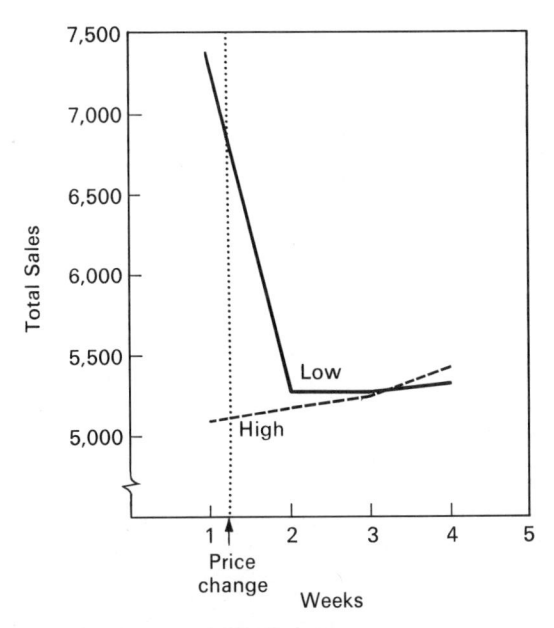

[Figure: graph showing Total Sales vs Weeks with Low and High conditions, price change marker between weeks 1 and 2]

FIGURE 7-4  Light bulb sales.

## Experiment V: Cookies

Eight pairs of stores were matched on the basis of grocery sales and randomly assigned to conditions in which the selling price for the first 2 weeks was $0.24 or $0.29 for a large bag of cookies. After 2 weeks, the price was at $0.29 for all stores. The results are presented in Figure 7-5. For weeks 4 to 6 combined, six of the eight pairs show differences in the predicted direction ($t = 0.625$, $df = 7$).

## RESULTS

When the results of all five experiments are combined into one test of the hypothesis, a $z$ of 3.63 ($p < 0.0002$) is obtained. Clearly, so far as this has been tested, the practice of introducing a product at a low price is not a good strategy for this chain of stores to use.

## Discussion

These studies indicate that introducing products at a lower than usual price is harmful to final sales. It was earlier argued that one possible reason for this is the lower proportion of buyers who return to a product

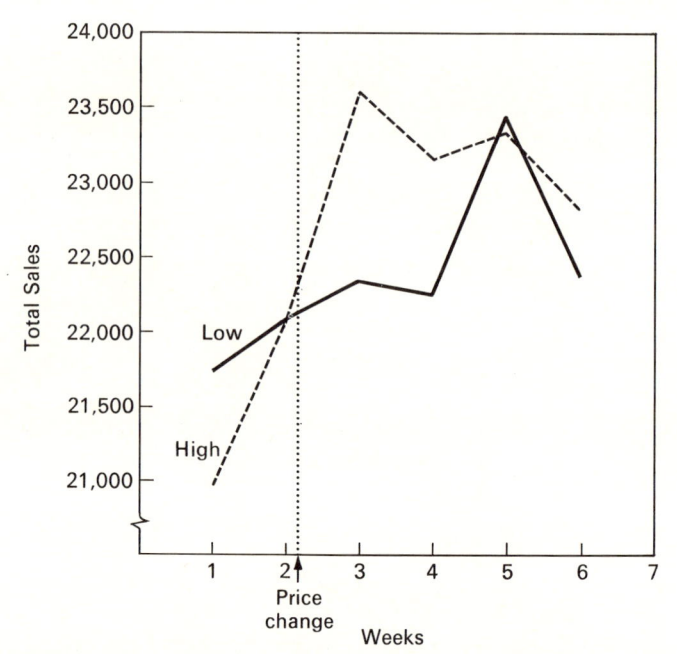

FIGURE 7-5  Cookie sales.

when the initial price is lower than the normal price. Whether or not this causes eventual sales actually to be lower when the initial price is low is not critical to the argument. If, for example, there is an extremely large difference in initial sales, even a lower proportion of returning buyers may produce an advantage for the initial low price. Similarly, if the product has some special feature which would be expected to produce loyalty merely from exposure, it would be beneficial to maximize initial sales by the use of low introductory offers. In the experiments reported here, neither of these possibilities seems to have been present. For the range of prices studied, even a 50% increase in sales due to the lower price was not enough to overcome the increased consumer loyalty engendered by the higher price. Because of the presence of other identical brands, differing only in price, exposure alone was not enough to produce loyalty.

Whether or not eventual sales are actually lower when the initial price is low is not critical to the argument. From a theoretical point of view, the only essential comparison is the relative proportion of repurchases in the two conditions. A stringent method of showing that this proportion is higher when the initial price is high is to demonstrate that the absolute volume of eventual sales is greater for the high-price condition, even though initial sales are lower. For the products and prices studied here, this was true.

There are at least two alternative explanations of this result. The first is that in the low-initial-price stores the market is glutted after the first few weeks, and it takes a long time for there to be any need to repurchase the product. This might be a partial explanation of the difference between the conditions, but seems implausible as a total explanation. For all the products except light bulbs the length of time that the sales curves were followed exceeded by a goodly margin the marketer's estimate of the normal time until repurchase. Indeed, with mouthwash, for which the repurchase period is about 2 weeks, the difference between conditions is still present 19 weeks after the price switch. Customers might have stocked up by buying more than their usual supply of a product, but pricing practices of this chain of stores makes this unlikely. These stores have rarely used low introductory price offers, and they were not advertised as such for the products studied. Buyers therefore had no reason to believe that the "low price" was a special price and accordingly had little reason to stock up on the product. Thus, although one cannot entirely rule out this "glutting the market" explanation, it is not convincing.

A second and more interesting alternative is in terms of what might be called the customers' adaptation level regarding the particular product. When mouthwash is put on sale at $0.25, customers who buy it at that price or notice what the price is may tend to think of the product in terms of $0.25. They say to themselves that this is a $0.25 bottle of mouthwash. When, in subsequent weeks, the price increases to $0.39, these customers will tend to see it as overpriced and are not inclined to buy it at this much higher price. Therefore, sales drop off considerably. In the $0.39 steady condition, initial sales are lower, but there is no reason for them to drop off due to this effect. Therefore, introducing it at the ultimate price results in greater sales in the long run than does introducing it at the low price. This explanation fits the data as nicely as does the one in terms of cognitive dissonance. In many ways, they are quite similar and are difficult to distinguish experimentally.

It should be noted that the adaptation level and dissonance explanations are by no means mutually exclusive. It is entirely possible that both mechanisms are operating to some extent. In any case, the basic result stands—the introduction of a product at a low price tended to decrease subsequent sales, and this effect lasted for at least 20 weeks.

## REFERENCES

1. E. Aronson and J. Mills. The effect of severity of initiation on liking for a group. *J. abnorm. soc. Psychol.*, 1959, 59, 177–181.
2. L. Festinger. *A theory of cognitive dissonance.* Stanford, Calif.: Stanford University Press, 1957.
3. H. B. Gerard and G. C. Mathewson. The effects of severity of initiation on liking for a group: A replication. *J. of exp. soc. Psychol.*, 1966, 2, 278–287.

# 8

# SOME INFORMATIONAL ASPECTS OF VISUAL PERCEPTION

### Fred Attneave

The ideas of information theory are at present stimulating many different areas of psychological inquiry. In providing techniques for quantifying situations which have hitherto been difficult or impossible to quantify, they suggest new and more precise ways of conceptualizing these situations (see Miller [12] for a general discussion and bibliography). Events ordered in time are particularly amenable to informational analysis; thus language sequences are being extensively studied, and other sequences, such as those of music, plainly invite research.

In this paper I shall indicate some of the ways in which the concepts and techniques of information theory may clarify our understanding of visual perception. When we begin to consider perception as an information-handling process, it quickly becomes clear that much of the information received by any higher organism is *redundant*. Sensory events are highly interdependent in both space and time: if we know at a given moment the states of a limited number of receptors (that is, whether they are firing or not firing), we can make better-than-chance inferences with respect to the prior and subsequent states of these receptors, and also with respect to the present, prior, and subsequent states of other receptors. The preceding statement, taken in its broadest implications, is precisely equivalent to an assertion that the world as we know it is lawful. In the present discussion, however, we shall restrict our attention to special types of lawfulness which may exist in space at a fixed time and which seem particularly relevant to processes of visual perception.

**THE NATURE OF REDUNDANCY IN VISUAL STIMULATION: A DEMONSTRATION**

Consider the very simple situation presented in Figure 8-1. With a modicum of effort, the reader may be able to see this as an ink bottle on

Source: *Psychological Review*, 1954, 61, 183–193. Copyright 1954 by the American Psychological Association. Reprinted by permission.
Note: The experimental work for this study was performed as part of the United States Air Force Human Resources Research and Development Program. The opinions and conclusions contained in this report are those of the author. They are not to be construed as reflecting the views or endorsement of the Department of the Air Force.

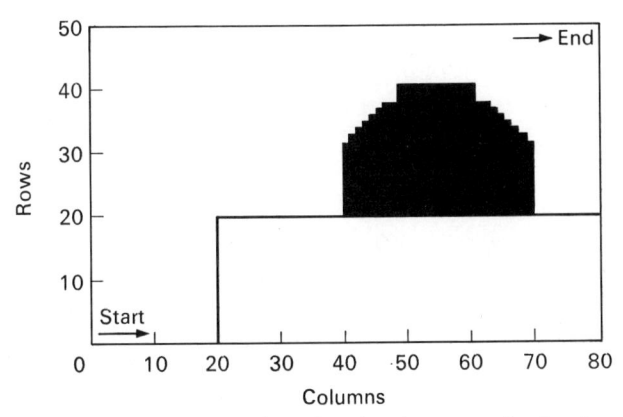

FIGURE 8-1  Illustration of redundant visual stimulation.

the corner of a desk. Let us suppose that the background is a uniformly white wall, that the desk is a uniform brown, and that the bottle is completely black. The visual stimulation from these objects is highly redundant in the sense that portions of the field are highly predictable from other portions. In order to demonstrate this fact and its perceptual significance, we may employ a variant of the "guessing game" technique with which Shannon [17] has studied the redundancy of printed English. We may divide the picture into arbitrarily small elements which we "transmit" to a subject in a cumulative sequence, having him guess at the color of each successive element until he is correct. This method of analysis resembles the scanning process used in television and facsimile systems, and accomplishes the like purpose of transforming two spatial dimensions into a single sequence in time. We are in no way supposing or assuming, however, that perception normally involves any such scanning process. If the picture is divided into fifty rows and eighty columns, as indicated, our subject will guess at each of 4,000 cells as many times as necessary to determine which of the three colors it has. If his error score is significantly less than chance [$2/3 \times 4,000 + 1/2 \;(2/3 \times 4,000) = 4,000$], it is evident that the picture is to some degree redundant. Actually, he may be expected to guess his way through Figure 8-1 with only fifteen or twenty errors. It is fairly apparent that the technique described, in its present form, is limited in applicability to simple and somewhat contrived situations. With suitable modification it may have general usefulness as a research tool, but it is introduced into the present paper for demonstrational purposes only.

Let us follow a hypothetical subject through this procedure in some detail, noting carefully the places where he is most likely to make errors, since these are the places in which information is concentrated. To begin, we give him an 80 × 50 sheet of graph paper, telling him that he is to guess whether each cell is white, black, or brown, starting in the lower left corner and proceeding across the first row, then across the second, and so on to the last cell in the upper right corner. Whenever he makes an error, he is is allowed to guess a second and, if necessary, a third time until he is correct. He keeps a record of the cells he has been over by filling in black and brown ones with pencil marks of appropriate color, leaving white ones blank.

After a few errors at the beginning of the first row, he will discover that the next cell is "always" white, and predict accordingly. This prediction will be correct as far as column 20, but on 21 it will be wrong. After a few more errors he will learn that "brown" is his best prediction, as in fact it is to the end of the row. Chances are good that the subject will assume the second row to be exactly like the first, in which case he will guess it with no errrors; otherwise he may make an error or two at the beginning, or at the edge of the "table," as before. He is almost certain to be entirely correct on row 3, and on subsequent rows through 20. On row 21, however, it is equally certain that he will erroneously predict a transition from white to brown on column 21, where the *corner* of the table is passed.

Our subject's behavior to this point demonstrates two principles which may be discussed before we follow him through the remainder of his predictions. It is evident that redundant visual stimulation results from either (a) an area of homogeneous color ("color" is used in the broad sense here, and includes brightness), or (b) a contour of homogeneous direction or slope. In other words, information is concentrated along contours (that is, regions where color changes abruptly),[1] and is further concentrated at those points on a contour at which its direction changes most rapidly (that is, at angles or peaks of curvature).

Evidence from other and entirely different situations supports both of these inferences. The concentration of information in contours is illustrated by the remarkably similar appearance of objects alike in contour and different otherwise. The "same" triangle, for example, may be either white on black or green on white. Even more impressive is the familiar fact that an artist's sketch, in which lines are substituted for sharp color gradients, may constitute a readily identifiable representation of a person or thing.

An experiment relevant to the second principle—that information is further concentrated at points where a contour changes direction most rapidly—may be summarized briefly.[2] Eighty subjects were instructed to

---

[1] Our "scanning" procedure introduces a certain artifact here, in that a particular subject will make errors at a linear contour only the first few times he crosses it. It is fairly obvious that if the starting point of the sequence and the direction of scan were varied randomly over a large number of subjects, summated errors would be distributed evenly along such a straight contour.

[2] This study has been previously published only in the form of a mimeographed note: "The Relative Importance of Parts of a Contour," Research Note P&MS 51–8, Human Resources Research Center, November 1951.

draw, for each of sixteen outline shapes, a pattern of ten dots which would resemble the shape as closely as possible, and then to indicate on the original outline the exact places which the dots represented. A good sample of the results is shown in Figure 8-2. Radial bars indicate the relative frequency with which dots were placed on each of the segments into which the contour was divided for scoring purposes. It is clear that subjects show a great deal of agreement in their abstractions of points best representing the shape, and most of these points are taken from regions where the contour is most different from a straight line. This conclusion is verified by detailed comparisons of dot frequencies with measured curvatures on both the figure shown and others.

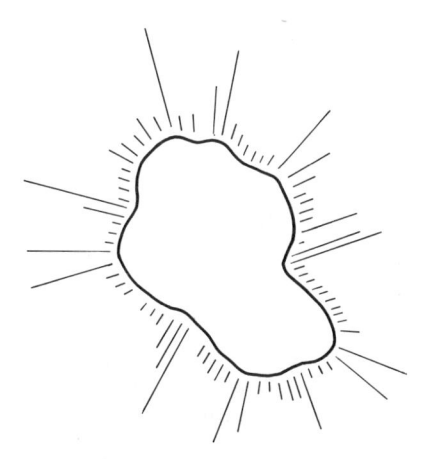

FIGURE 8-2 Subjects attempted to approximate the closed figure shown above with a pattern of ten dots. Radiating bars indicate the relative frequency with which various portions of the outline were represented by dots chosen.

Common objects may be represented with great economy, and fairly striking fidelity, by copying the points at which their contours change direction maximally and then connecting these points appropriately with a straightedge. Figure 8-3 was drawn by applying this technique, as mechanically as possible, to a real sleeping cat. The informational content of a drawing like this may be considered to consist of two components: one describing the positions of the points, the other indicating which points are connected with which others. The first of these components will almost always contain more information than the second, but its exact share will depend upon the precision with which positions are designated, and will further vary from object to object.

Let us now return to the hypothetical subject whom we left between the corner of the table and the ink bottle in Figure 8-1. His

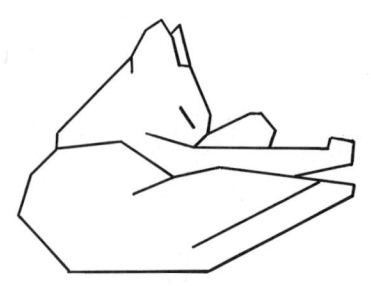

FIGURE 8-3 Drawing made by abstracting thirty-eight points of maximum curvature from the contours of a sleeping cat, and connecting these points appropriately with a straightedge.

errors will follow the principles we have just been discussing until he reaches the serrated shoulders of the bottle. (A straight 45° line would be represented in this way because of the grain of the coordinate system but we shall consider that the bottle is actually serrated, as it is from the subject's point of view.) On the left shoulder there are thirteen right angles, but these angles contain considerably less than thirteen times the information of an angle in isolation like the corner of the table. This is true because they fall into a pattern which is repetitive, or redundant in the everyday sense of the term. They will cease to evoke errors as soon as the subject perceives their regularity and extrapolates it. This extrapolation, precisely like the subject's previous extrapolations of color and slope, will have validity only over a limited range and will itself lead to error on row 38, column 48.

At about the same time that he discovers the regularity of the stair-step pattern (or perhaps a little before), our subject will also perceive that the ink bottle is symmetrical, that the right contour is predictable from the left one by means of a simple reversal. As a result he is very unlikely to make any further errors on the right side above row 32 or 33. Symmetry, then, constitutes another form of redundancy.[3]

It should be fairly evident by now that many of the gestalt principles of perceptual organization pertain essentially to information distribution. The *good gestalt* is a figure with some high degree of internal redun-

---

[3] The reader may be comforted to know that six subjects have actually been run on the task described. Their errors, which ranged in number from thirteen to twenty-six, were distributed as suggested above, with a single interesting exception: four of the six subjects assumed on row 1 that the brown area would be located symmetrically within the field, and guessed "white" on column 61. By the use of Shannon's formulas [17] it was estimated that the field contains between 34 (lower limit) and 156 (upper limit) bits of information, in contrast to a possible maximum of 6,340 bits. The redundancy is thus calculated to be between 97.5 and 99.5%.

dancy. That the grouping laws of *similarity, good continuation,* and *common fate* all refer to conditions which reduce uncertainty is clear enough after the preceding discussion, and we shall presently see that *proximity* may be conceptualized in a like manner. It is not surprising that the perceptual machinery should "group" those portions of its input which share the same information. Any system handling redundant information in an efficient manner would necessarily do something of the sort. Musatti [20] came very close to the present point when he suggested that a single principle of *homogeneity* might subsume Wertheimer's laws as special cases. All of our hypothetical subject's extrapolations have involved some variety of homogeneity (or invariance), either of color, of slope, or of pattern.

The kinds of extrapolation that have been discussed certainly do not exhaust the repertory of the human observer. For example, if the brightness of a surface were changed at a constant rate along some spatial extent, an observer could probably extrapolate this change with a fair degree of accuracy (given an appropriate response medium, such as choosing from a set of Munsell color patches). Likewise, we may reasonably suppose that a contour, the direction of which changes at a constant rate (for instance, the arc of a circle), could be extrapolated. Any sort of physical invariance whatsoever constitutes a source of redundancy for an organism capable of abstracting the invariance and utilizing it appropriately, but we actually know very little about the limits of the human perceptual machinery with respect to such abilities. A group of psychophysical studies determining the accuracy with which observers are able to extrapolate certain discrete and continuous functions of varying complexity must be carried out before we can usefully discuss any but the simplest cases.[4]

A troublesome question arises in this connection: Where does perception leave off and inductive reasoning begin? The abstraction of simple homogeneities from a visual field does not appear to be different, in its formal aspects, from the induction of a highly general scientific law from a mass of experimental data. Certain subjective differences are obvious enough: thus reasoning seems to involve conscious effort, whereas perception seems to involve a set of processes whereby information is

---

[4] There is, however, a great deal more that can be said about the simplest cases. Vernier acuity demonstrates that, under optimal conditions, error of extrapolation may be less than the "minimum separable." It has been found by Salomon [16] that the error made in "aiming" a line at a point some constant distance from its end is a decreasing, negatively accelerated function of the line's length. This may be taken to mean that increasing the length of a line adds information about its extension, but at a decreasing rate, somewhat as increasing the length of a passage of English text adds decreasing increments of information about the next letter [13, 17]. Dr. Karl Zener, under whose direction the Salomon study was done, is at present (1954) conducting a program of related psychophysical experiments which may answer some of the questions raised above.

predigested before it ever reaches awareness. When extrapolations are required of a subject in an experimental situation, however, it is difficult or impossible for the experimenter to be certain whether the subject is responding on an "intuitive" or a "deliberative" basis. I do not know any general solution to this problem, and can only suggest that a limited control may be exercised by way of the establishment of a desired set in the subject.

# REFERENCES

1. F. Attneave and P. W. McReynolds. A visual beat phenomenon. *Amer. J. Psychol.,* 1950, *63,* 107–110.
2. E. Brunswik. *Systematic and representative design of psychological experiments: with results in physical and social perception.* Berkeley: University of California Press, 1947.
3. E. Brunswik. *The conceptual framework of psychology.* Chicago: University of Chicago Press, 1952.
4. E. Brunswik and J. Kamiya. Ecological cue-validity of "proximity" and of other gestalt factors. *Amer. J. Psychol.,* 1953, *66,* 20–32.
5. J. T. Culbertson. *Consciousness and behavior.* Dubuque: Wm. C. Brown, 1950.
6. J. J. Gibson. *The perception of the visual world.* Boston: Houghton Mifflin, 1950.
7. D. O. Hebb. *Organization of behavior.* New York: Wiley, 1949.
8. H. Helson. Adaptation level as frame of reference for prediction of psychophysical data. *Amer. J. Psychol.,* 1947, *60,* 1–29.
9. W. H. Ittelson. *The Ames demonstrations in perception.* Princeton: Princeton University Press, 1952.
10. K. Koffka. *Principles of Gestalt psychology.* New York: Harcourt, Brace, 1935.
11. J. C. R. Licklider and G. A. Miller. The perception of speech. In S. S. Stevens (ed.). *Handbook of experimental psychology.* New York: Wiley, 1951. Pp. 1040–1074.
12. G. A. Miller. What is information measurement? *Amer. Psychologist,* 1953, *8,* 3–11.
13. E. B. Newman and L. S. Gerstman. A new method for analyzing printed English. *J. exp. Psychol.,* 1952, *44,* 114–125.
14. S. L. Polyak. *The retina.* Chicago: University of Chicago Press, 1941.
15. N. Rashevsky. *Mathematical biophysics.* Chicago: University of Chicago Press, 1948.
16. A. D. Salomon. Visual field factors in the perception of direction. *Amer. J. Psychol.,* 1947, *60,* 68–88.
17. C. E. Shannon. Prediction and entropy of printed English. *Bell Syst. tech. J,* 1951, *30,* 50–64.

18. G. W. Snedecor. *Statistical methods*. Ames: Iowa State College Press, 1946.
19. D. W. Thompson. *Growth and form*. New York: Macmillan, 1942.
20. R. S. Woodworth. *Experimental psychology*. New York: Holt, 1938.

# 9

# PERCEPTUAL RESTORATION OF MISSING SPEECH SOUNDS

## R. M. Warren

*When an extraneous sound (such as a cough or tone) completely replaces a speech sound in a recorded sentence, listeners believe they hear the missing sound. The extraneous sound seems to occur during another portion of the sentence without interfering with the intelligibility of any phoneme. If silence replaces a speech sound, the gap is correctly localized and the absence of the speech sound detected.*

We frequently listen to speech against a background of extraneous sounds. Individual phonemes may be masked, yet comprehension is possible. In a study of the effect of transient masking sounds, it was found that replacement of a phoneme in a recorded sentence by a cough resulted in illusory perception of the missing speech sound. Further, the cough did not seem to coincide with the restored sound.

In the first experiment exploring this phonemic restoration effect, twenty undergraduate psychology students were tested. The stimulus was a tape recording of the sentence, "The state governors met with their respective legislatures convening in the capital city," with a 120-msec section deleted and replaced with a recorded cough of the same duration.

Source: *Science*, 1970, *167*, 392–393. Copyright 1970 by the American Association for the Advancement of Science.
Note: Supported by PHS Grant NB05998–03 and by the University of Wisconsin-Milwaukee Graduate School. The author thanks C. J. Obusek for assistance.

The speech sound removed (as determined by slow movement past the playback head and confirmed by a sound spectrograph) was the first *s* in the word *legislatures* together with portions of the adjacent phonemes which might provide transitional cues to the missing sound. The subjects were told that, after listening to a cough occurring somewhere in a sentence, they would be given a typewritten statement of the sentence so that they could circle the exact position at which the cough occurred. They were told also that they would be asked whether or not the cough replaced completely the circled sounds. The stimulus was heard binaurally through headphones in an audiometric room at 80 db (peak), and the cough was heard at 86 db (peak) above 0.0002 microbars.

Nineteen subjects reported that all speech sounds were present (the single subject reporting a missing phoneme selected the wrong one). The illusory perception of the absent phoneme was in keeping with the observations of others (graduate students and staff), who, despite knowledge of the actual stimulus, still perceived the missing phoneme as distinctly as the clearly pronounced sounds actually present.

No subject identified correctly the position of the cough, and half the subjects circled positions beyond the boundaries of the word *legislatures*. The median distance separating responses from the true position was five phonemes. These errors were rather symmetrically distributed in time, with eleven subjects placing the cough early, and nine late.

In order to determine whether phonemic restorations could be obtained with another extraneous sound, a second group of twenty subjects was tested under the same procedure except that the cough was replaced by a 1,000-H tone (intensity equal to the peak intensity of the cough). Results similar to those of the first experiment were obtained.

Every subject reported that all speech sounds were present, and no subject identified the position of the tone correctly. Eight subjects circled positions beyond the boundaries of the word *legislatures,* the median distance separating responses from the true position was three phonemes, and most subjects (thirteen) placed the tone earlier than its actual position, although this tendency to early placement was not statistically significant.

The inability to identify the position of extraneous sounds in sentences has been reported [1, 2]. In these studies very brief intrusive sounds (clicks and hisses) were used, and as considerable care was taken to ensure that no phoneme was obliterated or masked, phonemic restorations were not observed. Inability to identify temporal order is more general than had been thought; it occurs with sequences consisting solely of nonspeech sounds such as hisses, tones, and buzzes. It was suggested that accurate perception of order may be restricted to items which may be linked temporarily to form speech or music [4].

Phonemic restorations are linked to language skills, which enable the listener to replace the correct sound. The experiments involving the deletion of the first *s* in *legislatures* did not permit the listener familiar with English any choice (that is, no other sound could produce an English word). But, Sherman [3] found that when a short cough was followed immediately by the sounds corresponding to *ite,* so that the word fragment could have been derived from several words, such as *kite* or *bite,* the listener used other words in the sentence to determine the phonemic restoration; when the preceding and following context indicated that the incomplete word was a verb referring to the activity of snarling dogs, the ambiguous fragment was perceived quite clearly as either *bite* or *fight*.

Phonemic restorations are not restricted to single phonemes but may involve deleted clusters of two or three sounds. Also, extraneous sounds other than coughs and tones (for example, buzzes) may be used to produce the illusion. But, when a speech sound was deleted and not replaced with an extraneous sound, the gap was recognized in its proper location, and illusory perception of the missing sound did not occur. Of course, unlike extraneous sounds, a silence would not occur normally unless produced by the speaker. Also, silent intervals have functions akin to phonemes, requiring their accurate identification and localization for speech comprehension.

The ability to understand speech with masked phonemes is not surprising; the redundancy of language can account readily for this. However, our lack of awareness of restorative processes—our illusory perception of the speaker's utterance rather than the stimulus actually reaching our ears—reflects characteristics of speech perception which may help us understand the perceptual mechanisms underlying verbal organization.

## REFERENCES

1. T. G. Bever, J. R. Lackner, and R. Kirk. *Percept. Psychophys.,* 1969, *5,* 225 ff.
2. P. Ladefoged and D. E. Broadbent. *Quart. J. exp. Psychol.,* 1960, *12,* 162 ff.
3. G. Sherman. Unpublished study.
4. R. M. Warren, C. J. Obusek, R. M. Farmer, and R. P. Warren. *Science,* 1969, *164,* 586 ff.

# 10

# DECISION PROCESSES IN PERCEPTION

John A. Swets
Wilson P. Tanner, Jr.
Theodore G. Birdsall

                 About 5 years ago, the theory of statistical decision was translated into a theory of signal detection.[1] Although the translation was motivated by problems in radar, the detection theory that resulted is a general theory, for, like the decision theory, it specifies an ideal process. The generality of the theory suggested to us that it might also be relevant to the detection of signals by human observers. Beyond this, we were struck by several analogies between this description of ideal behavior and various aspects of the perceptual process. The detection theory seemed to provide a framework for a realistic description of the behavior of the human observer in a variety of perceptual tasks.

    The particular feature of the theory that was of greatest interest to us was the promise that it held of solving an old problem in the field of psychophysics. This is the problem of controlling or specifying the criterion that the observer uses in making a perceptual judgment. The classical methods of psychophysics make effective provision for only a single free parameter, one that is associated with the sensitivity of the observer. They contain no analytical procedure for specifying independently the observer's criterion. These two aspects of performance are confounded, for example, in an experiment in which the dependent variable is the intensity of the stimulus that is required for a threshold re-

---

Source: *Psychological Review*, 1961, 68, 301–340. Copyright 1961 by the American Psychological Association. Reprinted by permission.

Note: This paper is based upon Technical Report No. 40, issued by the Electronic Defense Group of the University of Michigan in 1955. The research was conducted in the Vision Research Laboratory of the University of Michigan with support from the United States Army Signal Corps and the Naval Bureau of Ships. The authors thank H. R. Blackwell and W. M. Kincaid for their assistance in the research, and D. H. Howes for suggestions concerning the presentation of this material. This paper was prepared in the Research Laboratory of Electronics, Massachusetts Institute of Technology, with support from the Signal Corps, Air Force (Operational Applications Laboratory and Office of Scientific Research), and Office of Naval Research. This is Technical Report No. ESD-TR-61-20.

[1] For a formal treatment of statistical decision theory, see Wald [33]; for a brief and highly readable survey of the essentials, see Bross [5]. Parallel accounts of the detection theory may be found in Peterson, Birdsall, and Fox [18] and in Van Meter and Middleton [32].

sponse. The present theory provides a quantitative measure of the criterion. There is left, as a result, a relatively pure measure of sensitivity. The theory, therefore, promised to be of value to the student of personal and social processes in perception as well as to the student of sensory functions. A second feature of the theory that attracted us is that it is a normative theory. We believed that having a standard with which to compare the behavior of the human observer would aid in the description and in the interpretation of experimental results and would be fruitful in suggesting new experiments.

This paper begins with a brief review of the theory of statistical decision and then presents a description of the elements of the theory of signal detection appropriate to human observers.

## THE THEORY

### Statistical Decision Theory

Consider the following game of chance. Three dice are thrown. Two of the dice are ordinary dice. The third die is unusual in that on each of three of its sides it has three spots, whereas on its remaining three sides it has no spots at all. You, as the player of the game, do not observe the throws of the dice. You are simply informed, after each throw, of the total number of spots showing on the three dice. You are then asked to state whether the third die, the unusual one, showed a 3 or a 0. If you are correct—that is, if you assert a 3 showed when it did in fact, or if you assert a 0 showed when it did in fact—you win $1. If you are incorrect—that is, if you make either of the two possible types of errors—you lose $1.

How do you play the game? Certainly you will want a few minutes to make some computations before you begin. You will want to know the probability of occurrence of each of the possible totals 2 through 12 in the event that the third die shows a 0, and you will want to know the probability of occurrence of each of the possible totals 5 through 15 in the event that the third die shows a 3. Let us ignore the exact values of these probabilities, and grant that the two probability distributions in question will look much like those sketched in Figure 10-1.

Realizing that you will play the game many times, you will want to establish a policy which defines the circumstances under which you will make each of the two decisions. We can think of this as a *criterion* or a cutoff point along the axis representing the total number of spots showing on the three dice. That is, you will want to choose a number on this axis such that whenever it is equaled or exceeded you will state that a 3 showed on the third die and such that whenever the total number of spots showing is less than this number, you will state that a 0 showed on the third die. For the game as described, with the a priori probabilities of

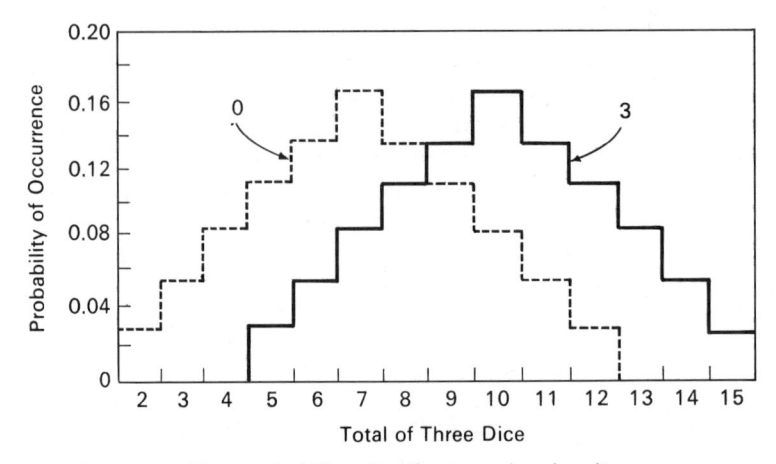

FIGURE 10-1  The probability distributions for the dice game.

a 3 and a 0 equal, and with equal values and costs associated with the four possible decision outcomes, it is intuitively clear that the optimal cutoff point is that point where the two curves cross. You will maximize your winnings if you choose this point as the cutoff point and adhere to it.

Now, what if the game is changed? What, for example, if the third die has three spots on five of its sides and a 0 on only one? Certainly you will now be more willing to state, following each throw, that the third die showed a 3. You will not, however, simply state more often that a 3 occurred without regard to the total showing on the three dice. Rather, you will lower your cutoff point: You will accept a smaller total than before as representing a throw in which the third die showed a 3. Conversely, if the third die has three spots on only one of its sides and 0's on five sides, you will do well to raise your cutoff point—to require a higher total than before for stating that a 3 occurred.

Similarly, your behavior will change if the values and costs associated with the various decision outcomes are changed. If it costs you $5 every time you state that a 3 showed when in fact it did not, and if you win $5 every time you state that a 0 showed when in fact it did (the other value and the other cost in the game remaining at $1), you will raise your cutoff to a point somewhere above the point where the two distributions cross. Or if, instead, the premium is placed on being correct when a 3 occurred, rather than when a 0 occurred as in the immediately preceding example, you will assume a cutoff somewhere below the point where the two distributions cross.

Again, your behavior will change if the amount of overlap of the two distributions is changed. You will assume a different cutoff than you did in the game as first described if the three sides of the third die showing spots now show four spots rather than three.

This game is simply an example of the type of situation for which the theory of statistical decision was developed. It is intended only to recall the frame of reference of this theory. Statistical decision theory—or the special case of it which is relevant here, the theory of testing statistical hypotheses—specifies the optimal behavior in a situation where one must choose between two alternative statistical hypotheses on the basis of an observed event. In particular, it specifies the optimal cutoff, along the continuum on which the observed events are arranged, as a function of (a) the a priori probabilities of the two hypotheses, (b) the values and costs associated with the various decision outcomes, and (c) the amount of overlap of the distributions that constitute the hypotheses.

According to the mathematical theory of signal detectability, the problem of detecting signals that are weak relative to the background of interference is like the one faced by the player of our dice game. In short, the detection problem is a problem in statistical decision; it requires testing statistical hypotheses. In the theory of signal detectability, this analogy is developed in terms of an idealized observer. It is our thesis that this conception of the detection process may apply to the human observer as well. The next several pages present an analysis of the detection process that will make the bases for this reasoning apparent.[2]

## Fundamental Detection Problem

In the fundamental detection problem, an observation is made of events occurring in a fixed interval of time, and a decision is made, based on this observation, whether the interval contained only the background interference or a signal as well. The interference, which is random, we shall refer to as *noise* and denote as $N$; the other alternative we shall call *signal plus noise*, $SN$. In the fundamental problem, only these two alternatives exist—noise is always present, whereas the signal may or may not be present during a specified observation interval. Actually, the observer, who has advance knowledge of the ensemble of signals to be presented, says either "yes, a signal was present" or "no, no signal was present" following each observation. In the experiments reported below, the signal consisted of a small spot of light flashed briefly in a known location on a uniformly illuminated background. It is important to note that the signal is always observed in a background of noise; some, as in the present case,

---

[2] It is to be expected that a theory recognized as having a potential application in psychophysics, although developed in another context, will be similar in many respects to previous conceptions in psychophysics. Although we shall not, in general, discuss explicitly these similarities, the strong relationship between many of the ideas presented in the following and Thurstone's earlier work on the scaling of judgments should be noted [30, 31]. The present theory also has much in common with the recent work of Smith and Wilson [21] and of Munson and Karlin [16]. Of course, for a new theory to arouse interest, it must also differ in some significant aspects from previous theories—these differences will become apparent as we proceed.

may be introduced by the experimenter or by the external situation, but some is inherent in the sensory processes.

## Representation of Sensory Information

We shall, in the following, use the term *observation* to refer to the sensory datum on which the decision is based. We assume that this observation may be represented as varying continuously along a single dimension. Although there is no need to be concrete, it may be helpful to think of the observation as some measure of neural activity, perhaps as the number of impulses arriving at a given point in the cortex within a given time. We assume further that any observation may arise, with specific probabilities, either from noise alone or from signal plus noise. We may portray these assumptions graphically, for a signal of a given amplitude, as in Figure 10-2. The observation is labeled $x$ and plotted on the

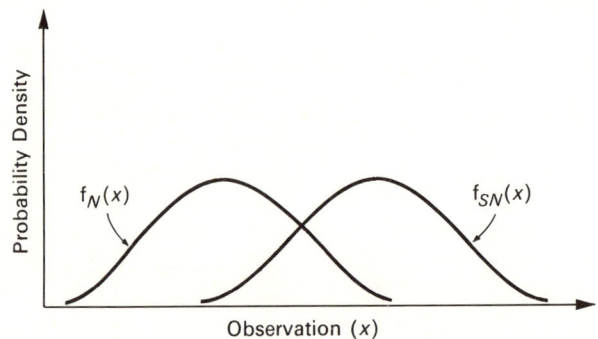

FIGURE 10-2 The probability density functions of noise and signal plus noise.

abscissa. The left-hand distribution, labeled $f_N(x)$, represents the probability density that $x$ will result given the occurrence of noise alone. The right-hand distribution, $f_{SN}(x)$, is the probability density function of $x$ given the occurrence of signal plus noise. (Probability density functions are used, rather than probability functions, since $x$ is assumed to be continuous.) Since the observations will tend to be of greater magnitude when a signal is presented, the mean of the *SN* distribution will be greater than the mean of the *N* distribution. In general, the greater the amplitude of the signal, the greater will be the separation of these means.

## Observation as a Value of Likelihood Ratio

It will be well to question at this point our assumption that the observation may be represented along a single axis. Can we, without serious violation, regard the observation as unidimensional, in spite of the fact that the response of the visual system probably has many dimensions?

The answer to this question will involve some concepts that are basic to the theory.

One reasonable answer is that when the signal and interference are alike in character, only the magnitude of the total response of the receiving system is available as an indicator of signal existence. Consequently, no matter how complex the sensory information is in fact, the observations may be represented in theory as having a single dimension. Although this answer is quite acceptable when concerned only with the visual case, we prefer to advance a different answer, one that is applicable also to audition experiments, where, for example, the signal may be a segment of a sinusoid presented in a background of white noise.

So let us assume that the response of the sensory system does have several dimensions, and proceed to represent it as a point in an $m$-dimensional space. Call this point $y$. For every such point in this space there is some probability density that it resulted from noise alone, $f_N(y)$, and similarly, some probability density that it was due to signal plus noise, $f_{SN}(y)$. Therefore, there exists a likelihood ratio for each point in the space, $\lambda(y) = f_{SN}(y)/f_N(y)$, expressing the likelihood that the point $y$ arose from $SN$ relative to the likelihood that it arose from $N$. Since any point in the space, that is, any sensory datum, may be thus represented as a real, non-zero number, these points may be considered to lie along a single axis. We may then, if we choose, identify the observation $x$ with $\lambda(y)$; the decision axis becomes likelihood ratio.[3]

Having established that we may identify the observation $x$ with $\lambda(y)$, let us note that we may equally well identify $x$ with any monotonic transformation of $\lambda(y)$. It can be shown that we lose nothing by distorting the linear continuum as long as order is maintained. As a matter of fact we may gain if, in particular, we identify $x$ with some transformation of $\lambda(y)$ that results in Gaussian density functions on $x$. We have assumed the existence of such a transformation in the representation of the density functions, $f_{SN}(x)$ and $f_N(x)$, in Figure 10-2. We shall see shortly that the assumption of normality simplifies the problem greatly. We shall also see that this assumption is subject to experimental test. A further assumption incorporated into the picture of Figure 10-2, one made quite tentatively, is that the two density functions are of equal variance. This is equivalent to the assumption that the $SN$ function is a simple translation of the $N$ function or that adding a signal to the noise merely adds a constant to the $N$ function. The results of a test of this assumption are also described below.

To summarize the last few paragraphs, we have assumed that an ob-

---

[3] Thus the assumption of a unidimensional decision axis is independent of the character of the signal and noise. Rather, it depends upon the fact that just two decision alternatives are considered. More generally, it can be shown that the number of dimensions required to represent the observation is $M - 1$, where $M$ is the number of decision alternatives considered by the observer.

servation may be characterized by a value of likelihood ratio, $\lambda(y)$, that is, the likelihood that the response of the sensory system $y$ arose from $SN$ relative to the likelihood that it arose from $N$. This permits us to view the observations as lying along a single axis. We then assumed the existence of a particular transformation of $\lambda(y)$ such that on the resulting variable, $x$, the density functions are normal. We regard the observer as basing his decisions on the variable $x$.

## Definition of the Criterion

If the representation depicted in Figure 10-2 is realistic, then the problem posed for an observer attempting to detect signals in noise is indeed similar to the one faced by the player of our dice game. On the basis of an observation, one that varies only in magnitude, he must decide between two alternative hypotheses. He must decide from which hypothesis the observation resulted; he must state that the observation is a member of the one distribution or the other. As did the player of the dice game, the observer must establish a policy which defines the circumstances under which the observation will be regarded as resulting from each of the two possible events. He establishes a criterion, a cutoff $x_c$ on the continuum of observation, to which he can relate any given observation $x_i$. If he finds for the $i$th observation, $x_i$, that $x_i > x_c$, he says yes; if $x_i < x_c$, he says no. Since the observer is assumed to be capable of locating a criterion at any point along the continuum of observations, it is of interest to examine the various factors that, according to the theory, will influence his choice of a particular criterion. To do so requires some additional notation.

In the language of statistical decision theory the observer chooses a subset of all of the observations, namely the critical region $A$, such that an observation in this subset leads him to accept the hypothesis $SN$, to say that a signal was present. All other observations are in the complementary subset $B$; these lead to rejection of the hypothesis $SN$, or, equivalently, since the two hypotheses are mutually exclusive and exhaustive, to the acceptance of the hypothesis $N$. The critical region $A$, with reference to Figure 10-2, consists of the values of $x$ to the right of some criterion value $x_c$.

As in the case of the dice game, a decision will have one of four outcomes: the observer may say yes or no and may in either case be correct or incorrect. The decision outcome, in other words, may be a hit ($SN \cdot A$, the joint occurrence of the hypothesis $SN$ and an observation in the region $A$), a miss ($SN \cdot B$), a correct rejection ($N \cdot B$), or a false alarm ($N \cdot A$). If the a priori probability of signal occurrence and the parameters of the distributions of Figure 10-2 are fixed, the choice of a criterion value $x_c$ completely determines the probability of each of these outcomes.

Clearly, the four probabilities are interdependent. For example, an increase in the probability of a hit, $p(SN \cdot A)$, can be achieved only by accepting an increase in the probability of a false alarm, $p(N \cdot A)$, and decreases in the other probabilities, $p(SN \cdot B)$ and $p(N \cdot B)$. Thus a given criterion yields a particular balance among the probabilities of the four possible outcomes; conversely, the balance desired by an observer in any instance will determine the optimal location of his criterion. Now the observer may desire the balance that maximizes the expected value of a decision in a situation where the four possible outcomes of a decision have individual values, as did the player of the dice game. In this case, the location of the best criterion is determined by the same parameters that determined it in the dice game. The observer, however, may desire a balance that maximizes some other quantity—a balance that is optimum according to some other definition of optimum—in which case a different criterion will be appropriate. He may, for example, want to maximize $p(SN \cdot A)$ while satisfying a restriction on $p(N \cdot A)$, as we typically do when as experimenters we assume an 0.05 or 0.01 level of confidence. Alternatively, he may want to maximize the number of correct decisions. Again, he may prefer a criterion that will maximize the reduction in uncertainty in the Shannon [20] sense.

In statistical decision theory, and in the theory of signal detectability, the optimal criterion under each of these definitions of optimum is specified in terms of the likelihood ratio. That is to say, it can be shown that if we define the observation in terms of the likelihood ratio, $\lambda(x) = f_{SN}(x)/f_N(x)$, then the optimal criterion can always be specified by some value $\beta$ of $\lambda(x)$. In other words, the critical region $A$ that corresponds to the criterion contains all observations with likelihood ratio greater than or equal to $\beta$, and none of those with likelihood ratio less than $\beta$.

We shall illustrate this manner of specifying the optimal criterion for just one of the definitions of optimum proposed above, namely, the maximization of the total expected value of a decision in a situation where the four possible outcomes of a decision have individual values associated with them. This is the definition of optimum that we assumed in the dice game. For this purpose we shall need the concept of *conditional probability* as opposed to the *probability of joint occurrence* introduced above. It should be stated that conditional probabilities will have a place in our discussion beyond their use in this illustration; the ones we shall introduce are, as a matter of fact, the fundamental quantities in evaluating the observer's performance.

There are two conditional probabilities of principal interest. These are the conditional probabilities of the observer saying *yes*: $p_{SN}(A)$, the probability of a yes decision conditional upon, or given, the occurrence of a signal; and $p_N(A)$, the probability of a yes decision given the occurrence of noise alone. These two are sufficient, for the other two are simply their complements: $p_{SN}(B) = 1 - p_{SN}(A)$ and $p_N(B) = 1 - p_N(A)$. The conditional and joint probabilities are related as follows:

$$p_{SN}(A) = \frac{p(SN \cdot A)}{p(SN)}$$

$$p_N(A) = \frac{p(N \cdot A)}{p(N)} \qquad (10\text{-}1)$$

where $p(SN)$ is the a priori probability of signal occurrence and $p(N) = 1 - p(SN)$ is the a priori probability of occurrence of noise alone.

Equation 10-1 makes apparent the convenience of using conditional rather than joint probabilities—conditional probabilities are independent of the a priori probability of occurrence of the signal and of noise alone. With reference to Figure 10-2, we may define $p_{SN}(A)$, or the conditional probability of a hit, as the integral of $f_{SN}(x)$ over the critical region $A$; and $p_N(A)$, the conditional probability of a false alarm, as the integral of $f_N(x)$ over $A$. That is, $p_N(A)$ and $p_{SN}(A)$ represent, respectively, the areas under the two curves of Figure 10-2 to the right of some criterion value of $x$.

To pursue our illustration of how an optimal criterion may be specified by a critical value of likelihood ratio $\beta$, let us note that the expected value of a decision (denoted $EV$) is defined in statistical decision theory as the sum, over the potential outcomes of a decision, of the products of probability of outcome and the desirability of outcome. Thus, using the notation $V$ for positive individual values and $K$ for costs or negative individual values, we have the following equation:

$$EV = V_{SN \cdot A} p(SN \cdot A) + V_{N \cdot B} p(N \cdot B) - K_{SN \cdot B} p(SN \cdot B) - K_{N \cdot A} p(N \cdot A) \qquad (10\text{-}2)$$

Now if a priori and conditional probabilities are substituted for the joint probabilities in equation 10-2 following equation 10-1, for example, $p(SN)p_{SN}(A)$ for $p(SN \cdot A)$, then collecting terms yields the result that maximizing $EV$ is equivalent to maximizing:

$$p_{SN}(A) - \beta p_N(A) \qquad (10\text{-}3)$$

where

$$\beta = \frac{p(N)}{p(SN)} \cdot \frac{(V_{N \cdot B} + K_{N \cdot A})}{(V_{SN \cdot A} + K_{SN \cdot B})} \qquad (10\text{-}4)$$

It can be shown that this value of $\beta$ is equal to the value of likelihood ratio, $\lambda(x)$, that corresponds to the optimal criterion. From equation 10-3 it may be seen that the value $\beta$ simply weights the hits and false alarms, and from equation 10-4 we see that $\beta$ is determined by the a priori probabilities of occurrence of signal and of noise alone and by the values associated with the individual decision outcomes. It should be noted that equation 10-3 applies to all definitions of optimum. Equation 10-4 shows the determinants of $\beta$ in only the special case of the expected-value definition of optimum.

Return for a moment to Figure 10-2, keeping in mind the result that $\beta$ is a critical value of $\lambda(x) = f_{SN}(x)/f_N(x)$. It should be clear that the optimal cutoff $x_c$ along the $x$ axis is at the point on this axis where the ratio of the ordinate value of $f_{SN}(x)$ to the ordinate value of $f_N(x)$ is a certain number, namely $\beta$. In the symmetrical case, where the two a priori probabilities are equal and the four individual values are equal, $\beta = 1$ and the optimal value of $x_c$ is the point where $f_{SN}(x) = f_N(x)$, where the two curves cross. If the four values are equal but $p(SN) = 5/6$ and $p(N) = 1/6$, another case described in connection with the dice game, then $\beta = 1/5$ and the optimal value of $x_c$ is shifted a certain distance to the left. This shift may be seen intuitively to be in the proper direction—a higher value of $p(SN)$ should lead to greater willingness to accept the hypothesis $SN$, that is, a more lenient cutoff. To consider one more example from the dice game, if $p(SN) = p(N) = 0.5$, if $V_{N \cdot B}$ and $K_{N \cdot A}$ are set at \$5 and $V_{SN \cdot A}$ and $K_{SN \cdot B}$ are equal to \$1, then $\beta = 5$ and the optimal value of $x_c$ shifts a certain distance to the right. Again intuitively, if it is more important to be correct when the hypothesis $N$ is true, a high, or strict, criterion should be adopted.

In any case, $\beta$ specifies the optimal weighting of hits relative to false alarms: $x_c$ should always be located at the point on the $x$ axis corresponding to $\beta$. As we pointed out in discussing the dice game, just where this value of $x_c$ will be with reference to the $x$ axis depends not only upon the a priori probabilities and the values but also upon the overlap of the two density functions, in short, upon the signal strength. We shall define a measure of signal strength within the next few pages. For now, it is important to note that for any detection goal to which the observer may subscribe, and for any set of parameters that may characterize a detection situation (such as a priori probabilities and values associated with decision outcomes), the optimal criterion may be specified in terms of a single number, $\beta$, a critical value of likelihood ratio.[4]

## Receiver-Operating-Characteristic

Whatever criterion the observer actually uses, even if it is not one of the optimal criteria, can also be described by a single number, by some value of likelihood ratio. Let us proceed to a consideration of how the observer's performance may be evaluated with respect to the location of his criterion, and at the same time we shall see how his performance may be evaluated with respect to his sensory capabilities.

---

[4] We have reached a point in the discussion where we can justify the statement made earlier that the decision axis may be equally well regarded as likelihood ratio or as any monotonic transformation of likelihood ratio. Any distortion of the linear continuum of likelihood ratio, which maintains order, is equivalent to likelihood ratio in terms of determining a criterion. The decisions made are the same whether the criterion is set at likelihood ratio equal to $\beta$ or at the value that corresponds to $\beta$ of some new variable. To illustrate, if a criterion leads to a yes response whenever $\lambda(y) > 2$, if $x = [\lambda(y)]^2$ the decisions will be the same if the observer says yes whenever $x > 4$.

As we have noted, the fundamental quantities in the evaluation of performance are $p_N(A)$ and $p_{SN}(A)$, these quantities representing, respectively, the areas under the two curves of Figure 10-2 to the right of some criterion value of $x$. If we set up a graph of $p_{SN}(A)$ versus $p_N(A)$ and trace on it the curve resulting as we move the decision criterion along the decision axis of Figure 10-2, we sketch one of the arcs shown in Figure 10-3.

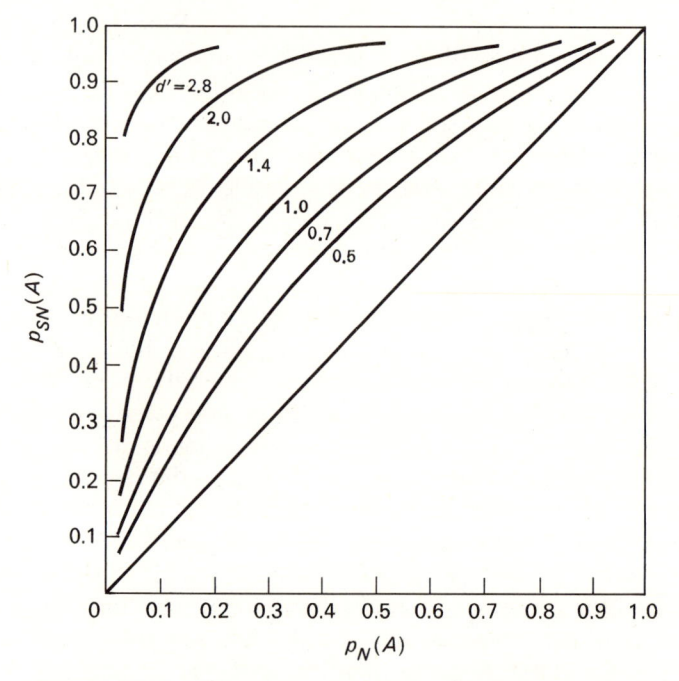

FIGURE 10-3 The receiver-operating-characteristic curves. These curves show $p_{SN}(A)$ versus $p_N(A)$ with $d'$ as the parameter. They are based on the assumptions that the probability density functions, $f_N(x)$ and $f_{SN}(x)$, are normal and of equal variance.

Ignore, for a moment, all but one of these arcs. If the decision criterion is set way at the left in Figure 10-2, we obtain a point in the upper right-hand corner of Figure 10-3: both $p_{SN}(A)$ and $p_N(A)$ are unity. If the criterion is set at the right end of the decision axis in Figure 10-2, the point at the other extreme of Figure 10-3, $p_{SN}(A) = p_N(A) = 0$, is obtained. In between these extremes lie the criterion values of more practical interest. It should be noted that the exact form of the curve shown in Figure 10-3 is not the only form which might result, but it is the form which will result if the observer chooses a criterion in terms of likelihood ratio and the probability density functions are normal and of equal variance.

This curve is a form of the *operating characteristic* as it is known in statistics; in the context of the detection problem it is usually referred to as the *receiver-operating-characteristic,* or ROC, curve. The optimal "operating level" may be seen from equation 10-3 to be at the point of the ROC curve where its slope is $\beta$. That is, the expression $p_{SN}(A) - \beta p_N(A)$ defines a utility line of slope $\beta$, and the point of tangency of this line to the ROC curve is the optimal operating level. Thus the theory specifies the appropriate hit probability and false alarm probability for any definition of optimum and any set of parameters characterizing the detection situation.

It is now apparent how the observer's choice of a criterion in a given experiment may be indexed. The proportions obtained in an experiment are used as estimates of the probabilities, $p_N(A)$ and $p_{SN}(A)$; thus, the observer's behavior yields a point on an ROC curve. The slope of the curve at this point corresponds to the value of likelihood ratio at which he has located his criterion. Thus we work backward from the ROC curve to infer the criterion that is employed by the observer.

There is, of course, a family of ROC curves, as shown in Figure 10-3, a given curve corresponding to a given separation between the means of the density functions $f_N(x)$ and $f_{SN}(x)$. The parameter of these curves has been called $d'$, where $d'$ is defined as the difference between the means of the two density functions expressed in terms of their standard deviation,

$$d' = \frac{M_{f_{SN}(x)} - M_{f_N(x)}}{\sigma_{f_N(x)}} \qquad (10\text{-}5)$$

Since the separation between the means of the two density functions is a function of signal amplitude, $d'$ is an index of the detectability of a given signal for a given observer.

Recalling our assumptions that the density functions $f_N(x)$ and $f_{SN}(x)$ are normal and of equal variance, we may see from equation 10-5 that the quantity denoted $d'$ is simply the familiar normal deviate, or $x/\sigma$ measure. From the pair of values $p_N(A)$ and $p_{SN}(A)$ that are obtained experimentally, one may proceed to a published table of areas under the normal curve to determine a value of $d'$. A simpler computational procedure is achieved by plotting the points $[p_N(A), p_{SN}(A)]$ on graph paper having a probability scale and a normal deviate scale on both axes.

We see now that the fourfold table of the responses that are made to a particular stimulus may be treated as having two independent parameters—the experiment yields measures of two independent aspects of the observer's performance. The variable $d'$ is a measure of the observer's sensory capabilities, or of the effective signal strength. This may be thought of as the object of interest in classical psychophysics. The criterion $\beta$ that is employed by the observer, which determines the $p_N(A)$ and $p_{SN}(A)$ for some fixed $d'$, reflects the effect of variables which have been variously called the set, attitude, or motives of the observer. It is the ability to distinguish between these two aspects of detection performance that comprises one of the main advantages of the theory proposed here. We have noted that these two aspects of behavior are confounded in an experiment in which the dependent variable is the intensity of the signal that is required for a threshold response.

### Relationship of d' to Signal Energy

We have seen that the optimal value of the criterion, $\beta$, can be computed. In certain instances, an optimal value of $d'$, that is, the sensitivity of the mathematically ideal device, can also be computed. If, for example, the exact wave form and starting time of the signal are determinable, as in the case of an auditory signal, then the optimal value of $d'$ is equal to $\sqrt{2E/N_o}$, where $E$ is the signal energy and $N_o$ is the noise power in a one-cycle band [18]. A specification of the optimal value of $d'$ for visual signals has been developed very recently.[5] Although we shall not elaborate the point in this paper, it is worth noting that an empirical index of detectability may be compared with ideal detectability, just as observed and optimal indices of decision criteria may be compared. The ratio of the squares of the two detectability indices has been taken as a measure of the observer's sensory efficiency. This measure has demonstrated its usefulness in the study of several problems in audition [27].

### Use of Ideal Descriptions as Models

It might be worthwhile to describe at this point some of the reasons for the emphasis placed here on optimal measures, and, indeed, the reasons for the general enterprise of considering a theory of ideal behavior as a model for studies of real behavior.[6] In view of the deviations from any ideal which are bound to characterize real organisms, it might appear at first glance that any deductions based on ideal premises could have no more than academic interest. We do not think this is the case. In any study, it is desirable to specify rigorously the factors pertinent to the study. Ideal conditions generally involve few variables and permit these to be described in simple terms. Having identified the performance to be expected under ideal conditions, it is possible to extend the model to include the additional variables associated with real organisms. The ideal performance, in other words, constitutes a convenient base from which to explore the complex operation of a real organism.

In certain cases, as in the problem at hand, values characteristic of ideal conditions may actually approximate very closely those characteris-

---

[5] W. P. Tanner, Jr., and R. C. Jones, personal communication, November 1959.

[6] The discussion immediately following is, in part, a paraphrase of one in Horton [13].

tics of the organism under study. The problem then becomes one of changing the ideal model in some particular so that it is slightly less than ideal. This is usually accomplished by depriving the ideal device of some particular function. This method of attack has been found to generate useful hypotheses for further studies. Thus, whereas it is not expected that the human observer and the ideal detection device will behave identically, the emphasis in early studies is on similarities. If the differences are small, one may rule out entire classes of alternative models and regard the model in question as a useful tool in further studies. Proceeding on this assumption, one may then in later studies emphasize the differences, the form and extent of the differences suggesting how the ideal model may be modified in the direction of reality.

## Alternative Conceptions of the Detection Process

The earliest studies that were undertaken to test the applicability of the decision model to human observers were quite naturally oriented toward determining its value relative to existing psychophysical theory. As a result, some of the data presented below are meaningful only with respect to differences in the predictions based upon different theories. We shall, therefore, briefly consider alternative theories of the detection process.

Although it is difficult to specify with precision the alternative theories of detection, it is clear that they generally involve the concept of the *threshold* in an important way. The development of the threshold concept is fairly obscure. It is differently conceived by different people, and few popular usages of the concept benefit from explicit statement. One respect, however, in which the meaning of the threshold concept is entirely clear is its assertion of a lower limit on sensitivity. As we have just seen, the decision model does not include such a boundary. The decision model specifies no lower bound on the location of the criterion along the continuous axis of sensory inputs. Further, it implies that any displacement of the mean of $f_{SN}(x)$ from the mean of $f_N(x)$, no matter how small, will result in a greater value of $p_{SN}(A)$ than $p_N(A)$, irrespective of the location of the criterion.

To permit experimental comparison of decision theory and threshold theory, we shall consider a special version of threshold theory [1]. Although it is a special version, we believe it retains the essence of the threshold concept. In this version, the threshold is described in the same terms that are used in the description of decision theory. It is regarded as a cutoff on the continuum of observations (see Figure 10-2) with a fixed location, with values of x above the cutoff always evoking a positive response, and with discrimination impossible among values of x below the cutoff. This description of a threshold in terms of a fixed cutoff and a stimulus effect that varies randomly, it will be noted, is entirely equivalent to the more common description in terms of a randomly varying cutoff and a fixed stimulus effect. There are several reasons for assuming that the hypothetical threshold cutoff is located quite high relative to the density function $f_N(x)$, say at approximately $+3\sigma$ from the mean of $f_N(x)$. We shall compare our data with the predictions of such a "high threshold" theory and shall indicate their relationship to predictions from a theory assuming a lower threshold. We shall, in particular, ask how low a threshold cutoff would have to be to be consistent with the reported data. It may be noted that if a high threshold exists, the observer will be incapable of ordering values of $x$ likely to result from noise alone and hence will be incapable of varying his criterion over a significant range.

If a threshold exists that is rarely exceeded by noise alone, this fact will be immediately apparent from the ROC curves (see Figure 10-3) that are obtained experimentally. It can be shown that the ROC curves in this case are straight lines from points on the left-hand vertical axis—$p_{SN}(A)$—to the upper right-hand corner of the plot. These straight-line curves represent the implication of a high threshold theory that an increase in $p_N(A)$ must be effected by responding *yes* to a random selection of observations that fail to reach the threshold rather than by a judicious selection of observations, that is, a lower criterion level. If we follow the usual procedure of regarding the stimulus threshold as the signal intensity yielding a value of $p_{SN}(A) = 0.5$ for $p_N(A) = 0$, then an appreciation of the relationship between $d'$ and $p_N(A)$ at threshold may be gained by visualizing a straight line in Figure 10–3 from this point to the upper right-hand corner. If we note which of the ROC curves drawn in Figure 10-3 are intersected by the visualized line, we see that the threshold decreases with increasing $p_N(A)$. For example, a response procedure resulting in a $p_N(A) = 0.02$ requires a signal of $d' = 2.0$ to reach the threshold, whereas a response procedure yielding a $p_N(A) = 0.98$ requires a signal of $d' < 0.5$ to reach the threshold. A graph showing what threshold would be calculated as a function of $p_N(A)$ is plotted in Figure 10-4. The calculated threshold is a strictly monotonic function of $p_N(A)$ ranging from infinity to zero.

The fundamental difference between the threshold theory we are considering and decision theory lies in their treatment of false alarm responses. According to the threshold theory, these responses represent guesses determined by nonsensory factors; that is, $p_N(A)$ is independent of the cutoff which is assumed to have a fixed location. Decision theory assumes, on the other hand, that $p_N(A)$ varies with the temporary position of a cutoff under the observer's control; that false alarm responses arise for valid sensory reasons and that therefore a simple correction will not eliminate their effect on $p_{SN}(A)$. A similar implication of Figure 10-4 that should be noted is that reliable estimates of $p_{SN}(A)$ or of the stimulus threshold are not guaranteed by simply training the observer to maintain a low, constant value of $p_N(A)$. Since extreme probabilities cannot be estimated with reliability, the criterion may vary from session to session

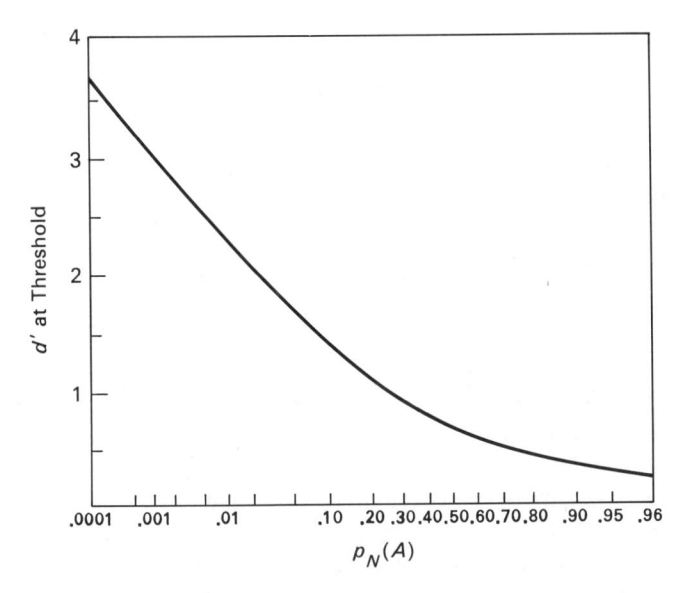

FIGURE 10-4  The relationship between $d'$ and $p_N(A)$ at threshold.

with the variation having no direct reflection in the data. Certainly, false alarm rates of 0.01, 0.001, and 0.0001 are not discriminable in an experimentally feasible number of observations; the differences in the calculated values of the threshold associated with these different values of $p_N(A)$ may be seen from Figure 10-4 to be sizable.

# REFERENCES

1. H. R. Blackwell. *Psychophysical thresholds: Experimental studies of methods of measurement.* Bull. Eng. Res. Inst. U. Mich. No. 36. 1953.
2. H. R. Blackwell, B. S. Pritchard, and T. G. Ohmart. Automatic apparatus for stimulus presentation and recording in visual threshold experiments. *J. opt. Soc. Amer.,* 1954, 44, 322–326.
3. E. G. Boring. *A history of experimental psychology.* 2d ed. New York: Appleton-Century-Crofts, 1950.
4. P. D. Bricker and A. Chapanis. Do incorrectly perceived tachistoscopic stimuli convey some information? *Psychol. Rev.,* 1953, 60, 181–188.
5. I. D. J. Bross. *Design for decision.* New York: Macmillan, 1953.
6. F. R. Clarke, T. G. Birdsall, and W. P. Tanner, Jr. Two types of ROC curves and definitions of parameters. *J. acoust. Soc. Amer.,* 1959, 31, 629–630.
7. L. R. Decker and I. Pollack. Confidence ratings and message reception for filtered speech. *J. acoust. Soc. Amer.,* 1958, 30, 432–434.

8. J. P. Egan. Monitoring task in speech communication. *J. acoust. Soc. Amer.*, 1957, *29*, 482–489.
9. J. P. Egan and F. R. Clarke. Source and receiver behavior in the use of a criterion. *J. acoust. Soc. Amer.*, 1956, *28*, 1267–1269.
10. J. P. Egan, F. R. Clarke, and E. C. Carterette. On the transmission and confirmation of messages in noise. *J. acoust. Soc. Amer.*, 1956, *28*, 536–550.
11. J. P. Egan, A. I. Schulman, and G. Z. Greenberg. Operating characteristics determined by binary decisions and by ratings. *J. acoust. Soc. Amer.*, 1959, *31*, 768–773.
12. I. Goldiamond. Indicators of perception: I. Subliminal perception, subception, unconscious perception: An analysis in terms of psychophysical indicator methodology. *Psychol. Bull.*, 1958, *55*, 373–411.
13. J. W. Horton. *Fundamentals of sonar.* Annapolis: United States Naval Institute, 1957.
14. D. H. Howes. A statistical theory of the phenomenon of subception. *Psychol. Rev.*, 1954, *61*, 98–110.
15. J. G. Miller. *Unconsciousness.* New York: Wiley, 1942.
16. W. A. Munson and J. E. Karlin. The measurement of the human channel transmission characteristics. *J. acoust. Soc. Amer.*, 1956, *26*, 542–553.
17. C. E. Osgood. *Method and theory in experimental psychology.* New York: Oxford University Press, 1953.
18. W. W. Peterson, T. G. Birdsall, and W. C. Fox. The theory of signal detectability. *IRE Trans.*, 1954, PGIT-4, 171–212.
19. I. Pollack and L. R. Decker. Confidence ratings, message reception, and the receiver operating characteristic. *J. acoust. Soc. Amer.*, 1958, *30*, 286–292.
20. C. E. Shannon. The mathematical theory of communication. *Bell Syst. tech. J.*, 1948, *27*, 379–423.
21. M. Smith and E. A. Wilson. A model of the auditory threshold and its application to the problem of the multiple observer. *Psychol. Monogr.*, 1953, *67* (9, whole no. 359).
22. J. A. Swets. Indices of signal detectability obtained with various psychophysical procedures. *J. acoust. Soc. Amer.*, 1959, *31*, 511–513.
23. J. A. Swets and T. G. Birdsall. The human use of information: III. Decision making in signal detection and recognition situations involving multiple alternatives. *IRE Trans.*, 1956, IT-2, 138–165.
24. J. A. Swets and D. M. Green. Sequential observations by human observers of signals in noise. In C. Cherry (ed.). *Fourth symposium on information theory.* London: Butterworth, 1961. Pp. 177–195.
25. J. A. Swets, E. F. Shipley, M. J. McKey, and D. M. Green. Multiple observations of signals in noise. *J. acoust. Soc. Amer.*, 1959, *31*, 514–521.
26. W. P. Tanner, Jr. A theory of recognition. *J. acoust. Soc. Amer.*, 1956, *28*, 882–888.
27. W. P. Tanner, Jr., and T. G. Birdsall. Definitions of $d'$ and $\eta$ as psychophysical measures. *J. acoust. Soc. Amer.*, 1958, *30*, 922–928.

28. W. P. Tanner, Jr., and J. A. Swets. A decision-making theory of visual detection. *Psychol. Rev.*, 1954, *61*, 401–409.
29. W. P. Tanner, Jr., J. A. Swets, and D. M. Green. *Some general properties of the hearing mechanism.* U. Mich. Electronic Defense Group Tech. Rep. No. 30. 1956.
30. L. L. Thurstone. A law of comparative judgment. *Psychol. Rev.*, 1927, *34*, 273–286.
31. L. L. Thurstone. Psychophysical analysis. *Amer. J. Psychol.*, 1927, *38*, 368–389.
32. D. Van Meter and D. Middleton. Modern statistical approaches to reception in communication theory. *IRE Trans.*, 1954, PGIT-4, 119–145.
33. A. Wald. *Statistical decision functions.* New York: Wiley, 1950.

# 11

# SUBLIMINAL STIMULATION: AN OVERVIEW

James V. McConnell
Richard L. Cutler
Elton B. McNeil

Seldom has anything in psychology caused such an immediate and widespread stir as the recent claim that the presentation of certain stimuli below the level of conscious awareness can influence people's behavior in a significant way. The controversy was precipitated primarily by a commercial firm which claimed that the subliminal presentation of the words "Eat Popcorn" and "Drink Coca-Cola" fantastically stimulated the respective sales of these products among the motion picture audiences who received the stimulation. Despite the fact that detailed reports of the experiment have not been made directly available in any published form, this technique was seized upon as the newest of the "new look" promises of the application of psychology to advertising. While such claims and demonstrations will be considered in greater detail below, it is important to note here that they have given rise to a

Source: *American Psychologist*, 1958, *13*, 229–242. Copyright 1958 by the American Psychological Association. Reprinted by permission.

series of charges and countercharges, the effects of which have reached the United States Congress and the Federal Communications Commission [7, 117].

Rarely does a day pass without a statement in the public press relating to the Utopian promise or the 1984 threat of the technique [8, 17, 29, 37, 42, 45, 118, 132]. Since the process of choosing up sides promises to continue unabated, it appears wise to provide the potential combatants with a more factual basis for arriving at their positions than presently seems available. Meanwhile, the present writers have cautiously sought to avoid aligning themselves behind either of the barricades.

Obviously, the notion that one may influence the behavior of another individual without the individual's knowing about it is a fascinating one. It is of extreme interest, not only to psychologists and advertisers, but also to politicians, psychiatrists, passionate young men, and others, whose motives would be considered more or less sacred by the larger society. Equally obvious is the need for a clarification of the issues surrounding the application of subliminal perception. This clarification must involve the assessment of available scientific evidence, the answering of a series of technical questions, and the examination of what, if any, levels of behavior may indeed be influenced. Finally, a series of extremely complex ethical issues needs to be explored. It is the purpose of the present paper to undertake this task, in the hope of providing information upon which possible decisions involving its application may be based.

## RECENT HISTORY OF THE TECHNIQUE

The custom of providing a chronological review of the literature will be violated in this paper, inasmuch as three separate threads of investigation seem worth tracing: (a) the recent demonstrations by advertisers which first aroused large-scale public interest in subliminal perception, (b) systematic research by psychologists relating directly to the influencing of behavior without the individual's awareness that he is being influenced, and (c) psychological research concerned primarily with the influence of inner states of the organism upon the threshold for conscious recognition of certain stimuli.

### Recent Advertising Demonstrations

While the advertising possibilities of subliminal stimulation were recognized by Hollingworth [59] as early as 1913, the intensive work in its application to this area has been carried out within the past two years. In 1956, BBC-TV, in conjunction with one of its regular broadcasts, transmitted the message "Pirie Breaks World Record" at a speed assumed to be subliminal [85]. At the conclusion of the regular program, viewers were asked to report whether they had noticed "anything unusual" about the program. While no reliable statistical data are available, it seems possible that those few viewers responding to the message possessed sufficiently low thresholds so that for them the message was supraliminal.

A demonstration by the commercial enterprise which has been most vocal in its claims for the advertising promise of the technique consisted of projecting, during alternate periods, the words "Eat Popcorn" and "Drink Coca-Cola" during the regular presentation of a motion picture program. As a result of this stimulation, reports contend,[1] popcorn sales rose more than 50% and Coca-Cola sales 18%, as compared to a "previous period." Despite the likelihood of serious methodological and technical defects (exposure time was reported as 1/3,000 sec, far faster than any previously reported stimulation), this demonstration has been the one which has caused the most stir in both the fields of advertising and psychology. There were no reports, however, of even the most rudimentary scientific precautions, such as adequate controls, provision for replication, and so on, which leaves the skeptical scientist in a poor position to make any judgment about the validity of the study.

In a later demonstration for the press, technical difficulties permitted the viewers to become consciously aware of the fact that they were being stimulated. Although described as a purposeful and prearranged part of the demonstration, it left many of the reporters present unconvinced that the technical difficulties inherent in the technique have been surmounted.

The FCC, turning its attention to the problem, has reported that one TV station (WTWO, Bangor, Maine) has experimented with the transmission of public service announcements at subliminal levels, with "negative results" [117].

The uncontrolled and unsystematic nature of the demonstrations reported above makes very difficult the task of reaching a trustworthy conclusion about the effectiveness of subliminal stimulation in advertising. Whether the technique represents a promising means of communicating with the individual at a level of his unconsciousness or whether it reflects only the hyperenthusiasm of an entrepreneurial group remain unanswered questions.

### Research on Behavior Without Awareness

In the hope of providing a more substantial foundation upon which to base judgments of the validity of advertising claims for subliminal stimulation, a systematic review of relevant scientific work was undertaken. While we believe that our review was comprehensive, we have decided not to provide an extensive critical discussion of the various

---

[1]The essential facts of this study have not been reported in any journal. The discussion of this experiment and the findings reported by the commercial enterprise responsible for the study is based on reports in several general news accounts appearing in the popular press [7, 8, 16, 17, etc.].

studies, choosing instead to present summative statements and conclusions based upon what seems to be sufficient evidence and consensus in the literature.²

The work of experimental psychologists in subliminal stimulation dates from Suslowa [119] in 1863, as reported by Baker [5]. Suslowa's experiments concerned the effect of electrical stimulation upon subjects' ability to make two-point threshold discriminations. He found that, even when the intensity of the electrical stimulation was so low that the subjects were not aware of its presence, their ability to discriminate one- from two-point stimulation was somewhat reduced.

In 1884, Peirce and Jastrow [94] were able to show that subjects could discriminate differences between weights significantly better than chance would allow, even though the differences were so small they had no confidence whatsoever in their judgments.

Numerous experimenters have relied upon this criterion of "zero confidence" to establish that discrimination of stimuli presented below the level of conscious awareness is possible. For example, Sidis [107] showed that subjects could reliably distinguish letters from numbers, even when the stimuli were presented at such a distance from them that the subjects thought they were relying on pure guesswork for their judgments.

In what was essentially a replication of Sidis' research, Stroh, Shaw, and Washburn [116] found evidence to support his conclusions. They found similar results when auditory stimuli (whispers) were presented at a distance such that the subjects were not consciously aware that they were hearing anything.

Several experiments have provided further support for Peirce and Jastrow's initial conclusions [44, 127]. Baker [5] found subjects able to discriminate diagonal from vertical crossed lines, and a dot-dash from a dash-dot auditory pattern. Miller [88] presented five geometric figures at four different levels of intensity below the threshold and found that while subjects could discriminate which was being presented a significant proportion of the time, their ability to discriminate was reduced as the intensity of stimulation was further reduced. More recently, a series of studies by Blackwell [11] has shown that subjects can reliably identify during which of four time periods a subliminal spot of light is presented upon a homogeneous field. Blackwell, however, stresses that reliability of discrimination decreases as the intensity of the stimulus is further lowered. Several other supporting studies are available [28, 97, 130] which show essentially the same results, namely, that even when subjects have zero confidence in their judgments, they can discriminate reliably (though not perfectly) between stimuli.

---

² The reader who wishes a more complete technical critique of studies in the field is referred to reviews by Adams [1], Collier [27], Coover [28], Lazarus and McCleary [76], and Miller [90].

In his review, Adams [1] points out certain general weaknesses inherent in studies of this type, but agrees with the present authors that discrimination can occur under certain circumstances. However, it is interesting to note that in nearly all studies reporting relevant data, the reliability of the subjects' judgments increases directly with the intensity of the stimuli. If a valid extrapolation can be drawn from this finding, it would be that accuracy of perception increases as the stimulation approaches a supraliminal level.

A second series of studies has involved presenting subjects with variations of the Mueller-Lyer illusion, in which the angular lines have differed, subliminally, in hue or brightness from the background. The first of these studies, reported by Dunlap in 1909 [36], gave clear evidence that the subjects were influenced in their judgments of line length, even though they could not "see" the angular lines. Several replications of this study have been carried out, and while at least three have found partial support for Dunlap's conclusions [14, 59, 86], others have failed to find the phenomenon [123]. In another experiment conducted by Sidis in 1898 [107], subjects asked to fixate on a number series in the center of a card, and then asked to pick a number from this series, systematically chose that number which was written in the periphery of the card, even though they were not consciously aware of its presence. Coover [28] in 1917 showed essentially the same results by asking subjects to pick a number at random while they were fixating on a letter in the upper right portion of a card. He found that subjects tended to pick the number printed in the lower left of the card, even though they did not *usually* know it was there. In similar experiments, Collier [27] and Perky [95] showed that subjects could be made to produce drawings, even though they were not aware that they were being influenced in their actions. While these studies are not unequivocal in their findings, nor generally rigorous in their methodology, they too seem to support the contention that behavior of a sort can be influenced by subliminal means. However, they require cautious interpretation, since the degree of the subject's attention to the stimuli seems clearly to be a factor. Further, as contrasted to those studies where the subject is actually aware in advance of at least the general nature of the stimulation, these studies reveal a somewhat less pronounced effect of subliminal stimulation upon the subject's behavior.

While the studies reported above seem to indicate that discrimination without awareness may occur, it may reasonably be asked whether stimulation below the level of conscious awareness can produce any but the most simple modifications in behavior. A series of studies [24, 26, 73, 109], beginning with Newhall and Sears in 1933 [92], has attempted to show that it is possible to condition subjects to subliminal stimuli. Newhall and Sears found it possible to establish a weak and unstable conditioned response to light presented subliminally, when the light had been previously paired with shock. Baker [6] in 1938 reported the successful conditioning of the pupillary reflex to a subliminal auditory stimulus, but later experimenters have failed to replicate his results [57, 128]. In a now classic experiment, McCleary and Lazarus [79] found that nonsense syllables which had previously been associated with shock produced a greater psychogalvanic reflex when presented tachistoscopically at subliminal speeds than did nonshock syllables. Deiter [34] confirmed the McCleary and Lazarus findings and showed further that when verbal instructions were substituted for the shock, no such differences were produced. Bach and Klein [4] have recently reported that they were able to influence subjects' judgments of whether the line drawing of a face (essentially neutral in its emotional expression) was angry or happy by projecting the appropriate words at subliminal speeds upon the drawing.

A series of related studies [58, 65, 89, 99, 105, 121, 122] has shown that even when the subject is not aware that any cue is being given, certain responses can be learned or strengthened during the experimental process. For example, Cohen and others [25] showed that when the experimenter said *right* to any sentence which the subject started with *I* or *We*, the number of such sentences increased significantly. Klein [69] was able to produce both conditioning and extinction without awareness, using the Cohen technique.

Several experimenters have used subliminal or "unnoticed" reward-punishment techniques to modify subjects' responses in a variety of situations, including free or chained association tasks, performance on personality tests, and interview elicited conversation [35, 41, 50, 56, 72, 78, 93, 120, 125, 126]. Typical is the work of Greenspoon [48], who reinforced the use of plural nouns by saying *mm-humm* after each plural mentioned by the subject. He found that even though none of his subjects could verbalize the relationship between their response and his reinforcement, their use of plural nouns doubled. Sidowski [108] demonstrated essentially the same thing using a light, of which the subject was only peripherally aware, as a reinforcer for the use of plural words. Weiss [129], however, failed to find any increase in the frequency of "living things" responses, using a right-wrong reinforcement to free associations by the subjects.

This evidence suggests that subjects may either (a) "learn" certain subliminally presented stimuli or (b) make use of subliminal reinforcers either to learn or strengthen a previously learned response. Again, the critical observations of Adams [1] and the introduction of other possible explanations by Bricker and Chapanis [15] make necessary a cautious interpretation of these results.

### Effects of Inner States upon Thresholds

Whatever the possibility that subliminal stimulation may significantly alter behavior, there is excellent evidence that certain inner states of the organism, as well as externally induced conditions, may significantly alter the recognition threshold of the individual. This, of course, has important implications for the susceptibility of the individual to the effects of subliminal stimulation. It is well known that physiological factors, such as fatigue, visual acuity, or satiation, may change the threshold of an individual for various kinds of stimuli.

Recent evidence has accumulated to show that in addition to these physiological factors, certain "psychological states," such as psychological need, value, conflict, and defense, may also significantly influence thresholds, as well as other aspects of the perceptual process. Early work in this area is reported by Sanford [102, 103], who showed that subjects who had been deprived of food were more prone to produce "food-relevant" responses to a series of ambiguous stimuli. McClelland and Atkinson [80] showed that levels of the hunger drive were systematically related to the ease with which food responses were made when no words were presented on the screen.

While a complete review of the experimental work on "perceptual defense" and "selective vigilance" would take us too far afield, it seems wise to indicate, by example, some of the inner state factors which allegedly produce variations in recognition threshold. Bruner and Postman [19, 20, 21] and Bruner and Goodman [18] were able to show that such factors as symbolic value, need, tension and tension release, and emotional selectivity were important in the perceptual process. Ansbacher [3] had earlier demonstrated that the perception of numerosity was significantly affected by the monetary value of the stimuli. Rees and Israel [101] called attention to the fact that the mental set of the organism was an important factor in the perceptual process. Beams and Thompson [9] showed that emotional factors were important determiners of the perception of the magnitude of need-relevant objects. Other studies bearing upon the issue of inner state determiners of perception are reported by Carter and Schooler [23], Cowen and Beier [31, 32], and Levine, Chein, and Murphy [77].

More specifically related to the issue of altered recognition thresholds is a study by McGinnies [82] in which he demonstrated that emotionally toned words had generally higher thresholds than neutral words. Blum [13] has shown that subjects tend to be less likely to choose conflict-relevant stimuli from a group presented at subliminal speeds than to choose neutral stimuli. Lazarus, Ericksen, and Fonda [75] have shown that personality factors are at least in part determiners of the recognition threshold for classes of auditory stimuli. Reece [100] showed that the association of shock with certain stimuli had the effect of raising the recognition threshold for those stimuli.

While many writers have contended that the variations in threshold can be accounted for more parsimoniously than by introducing "motivational" factors such as need and value [60, 61, 111], and while the issue of the degree to which need states influence perception is still unresolved [22, 39, 40, 62, 74, 83], it is apparent that the recognition threshold is not a simple matter of intensity nor speed of presentation. Recent work by Postman and others [47, 96, 98], which has sought to illuminate the prerecognition processes operating to produce the apparent changes in threshold, does not alter the fact that individual differences in the perceptual process must be taken into account in any further work on the effects of subliminal stimulation.

## UNANSWERED METHODOLOGICAL QUESTIONS

Having now concluded that under certain conditions, the phenomenon of subliminal perception does occur, we turn our attention next to the many unanswered questions which this conclusion raises. For example, what kinds of behavior can be influenced by subliminal stimulation? What types of stimuli operate best at subthreshold intensities? Do all subliminal stimuli operate at the same "level of unconsciousness," or do different stimuli (or modes of stimulation) affect different levels of unconsciousness? What characteristics of the perceiver help determine the effectiveness of subliminal stimulation? All of these questions, as well as many others of a technological nature, will be discussed in the ensuing paragraphs.

A few words of caution concerning the word *subliminal* seem in order, however. It must be remembered that the psychological limen is a statistical concept, a fact overlooked by far too many current textbook writers. The common definition of the limen is "that stimulus value which gives a response exactly half the time" [44, p. 111]. One of the difficulties involved in analyzing the many studies on subliminal perception is the fact that many experimenters have assumed that because the stimuli which they employed were below the statistical limen for a given subject, the stimuli were therefore never consciously perceivable by the subject. This is, of course, not true. Stimuli slightly below the statistical limen might well be consciously perceivable as much as 49% of the time. Not only this, but thresholds vary from moment to moment, as well as from day to day. All this is not to deny that stimuli which are so weak that they are never consciously reportable under any circumstances may not indeed influence behavior. We simply wish to make the point that the range of stimulus intensities which are in fact subliminal may be smaller than many experimenters in the past have assumed. It has been commonly assumed that the several methods of producing subliminal stimuli —reducing intensity, duration, size, or clarity—are logically and methodologically equivalent. While this may be true, it remains to be demonstrated conclusively.

### Types of Behavior Influenced by Subliminal Stimulation

One of the first questions that springs to mind concerns the types of response which can be elicited with subliminal stimulation. Let us assume for the moment that the below-threshold advertisements used in commercial demonstrations were the sole cause of increased popcorn buying among the movie audiences subjected to the ads. How did this come about? Did the stimulus "Eat Popcorn" elicit an already established response in some members of the audience? Or did the frequent repetitions of the stimulus message cause a shift in attitude towards popcorn eating which eventually resulted in the purchase of popcorn at the first opportunity the audience had? Did the ads merely raise an already existing, presumably learned, but weak need for popcorn to an above the action-threshold level, or did the ads actually create a need for popcorn where no need had existed beforehand? Did members of the audience rise like automatons during the course of the movie and thus miss part of the feature in order to satisfy a sudden craving for popcorn or in order to respond to a suddenly evoked stimulus-response connection? Or did they wait until a "rest period" to do their purchasing? How many patrons bought popcorn only after they had seen the film and were heading home? How many people purchased popcorn on their way *in* to see the next movie they attended? How many of those who purchased popcorn did so for the first time in their lives, or for the first time in recent memory? What if the message presented had been "Buy Christmas Seals," which are available only in one season? How many people failed to buy popcorn at the theater, but purchased it subsequently at the local supermarket?

Unfortunately, these pertinent questions have yet to be answered. Let us tentatively accept this demonstration that impulse buying of inexpensive items such as popcorn and Coca-Cola can be influenced by subliminal advertising, without yet knowing what the mechanism involved is. It remains to be demonstrated, however, that such ads could make a person of limited means wreck himself financially by purchasing a Cadillac merely because the ads told him to do so. Nor do we know if deep-seated, strongly emotional attitudes or long established behavior patterns can be shifted one way or another as a result of subliminal stimulation. The answers to these questions must come from further experimentation.

As we have already seen, people can make use of subthreshold stimuli in making difficult perceptual judgments in situations where they are required to call up images of various objects [95] and in situations where they are asked to "read the experimenter's mind" [88]. Kennedy [68] believes that some extrasensory-perception (ESP) experimenters may have obtained positive results because the senders unconsciously transmitted slight auditory and visual cues to their receivers, and offers many experimental findings to back up his belief. Kennedy's studies also point up the difficult dilemma faced by people who object to subliminal stimulation as being an immoral or illegal attempt to influence other people. All of us, apparently, are constantly attempting to influence the people around us by means of sounds and movements we are unconscious of making. Correspondingly, all of us make some unconscious use of the cues presented to us by the people around us.

It also seems fairly clear that learning can take place when the stimuli to which the organism must respond are presented subliminally. Hankin [51] learned to predict changes in the flight of birds by utilizing wing-tip adjustments which were too slight to be consciously (reportably) noticeable. As we stated previously, Baker [6] obtained a conditioned pupillary response to subliminal auditory stimuli, although other investigators failed to replicate his findings. Miller [89] had subjects look at a mirror while trying to guess geometrical forms in an ESP type of experiment. Stimuli far below the statistical limen were projected on a mirror from behind. When the subjects were rewarded by praise for correct guesses and punished by electric shock for wrong guesses, learning took place. It is interesting to note that neither punishment alone nor reward alone was sufficient to produce learning.

Whether different types of learning than those reported above can take place using subliminal stimulation, and indeed how broad a range of human behavior can be influenced in any way whatsoever by subliminal stimulation, are questions which remain unanswered.

## Levels of Unconsciousness Affected by Subliminal Stimulation[3]

We must now differentiate between stimuli which a subject cannot bring to awareness under any conditions (completely subliminal stimuli) and those stimuli of which he is merely not aware at the moment but could be made aware of should his set be changed. At any given moment, a vast conflux of stimuli impinges upon a subject's receptors. Few of the sensations arising from this stimulation ever enter the focus of attention. As Dallenbach was fond of reminding his freshman classes: "Until I mentioned it, you were quite unaware that your shoes are full of feet." A great many experimenters have demonstrated that subjects could make use of stimuli well above the threshold of awareness but which could not be consciously reported on. Thus in one phase of her experiment, Perky [95] raised the intensity of the visual stimuli she was using to such a level that other psychologists who had not participated in the study apparently refused to believe that the subjects had not been aware of the stimuli. Perky's subjects, however, operating under a set to call up "images" of the stimuli presented, did not notice even relatively intense stimuli. Correspondingly, Newhall and Dodge [91] presented visual stimuli first at below-threshold intensities, then increased the intensities so slowly that the subjects were not aware of them even when the stimuli were well above the threshold. When the stimuli were turned off suddenly, however, the subjects experienced after-images. Thus certain stimuli may be well above threshold and yet be subliminal in the

---

[3] For an excellent review of the many meanings of the word *unconsciousness*, readers are referred to Miller's book of the same name [90].

sense that they cannot be reported on under certain experimental conditions.

There are other levels of "unconsciousness" which are deserving of our attention, however. Much work has been done at the animal level in which conditioning has been attempted upon animals with various parts of the brain removed [33, 43]. The same is true of animals under various types of anesthesia [106, 115]. Miller, in summarizing the experimental data dealing with conditioning and consciousness, concludes:

1. That conditioning can take place in other parts of the nervous system than the cortex—even in the spinal cord.

2. That, if conditioned responses are evidences of consciousness, then consciousness is not mediated solely by the cortex.

3. That it may be possible to develop conditioning ... at more than one level of the nervous system at the same time.

4. And that ... animals are conditionable even when anesthetized [90, p. 100].

The nervous system has many levels of anatomical integration. Should we be surprised to discover that incoming stimuli may have an effect on a lower level and not on a higher and that under certain conditions this effect can later be demonstrated in terms of behavioral changes? We shall not be able to speak clearly of the effects of subliminal stimulation upon the various "levels of unconsciousness" until we have some better method of specifying exactly what these levels are and by what parts of the nervous system they are mediated. Experimentation is badly needed in this area.

## Technological Problems Involved in Stimulating Subjects Subliminally

The paucity of data presented by those dealing with subliminal perception on a commercial basis, as well as the equivocal nature of their results, suggests that there are many technological problems yet to be solved by these and other investigators. For example, during a two-hour movie (or a one-hour television show), how many times should the stimulus be repeated to make sure that the message gets across to the largest possible percentage of the audience? Should the stimulus be repeated every second, every five seconds, only once a minute? Is the effect cumulative, or is one presentation really enough? Is there a satiation effect, such that the audience becomes "unconsciously tired" of the stimulation, and "unconsciously blocks" the incoming subliminal sensations? Should the stimuli be presented between frames of the movie (that is, when the shutter of the film projector is closed and the screen momentarily blank as it is twenty-four times each second), or should the message be presented only when the screen already has a picture on it? How close to the threshold (statistical or otherwise) should the stimuli be? How many words long can the message be? If the message must be short, could successive stimulations present sequential parts of a longer advertisement? How much of the screen should the stimuli fill? Should the stimuli be presented only during "happier" moments in the film, in order to gain positive affect? Does any affect transfer at all from the film to the ad? Should one use pictures, or are words best? Must the words be familiar ones? And what about subliminal auditory, cutaneous, and olfactory stimulation?

As we have stated before, there has been so much talk and so little experimentation, and much of what experimentation has been done is so inadequately reported, that we can merely hazard guesses based on related but perhaps not always applicable studies.

To begin with, we can state with some assurance that the closer to the threshold of awareness the stimuli are, the more effect they are likely to have. Study after study has reported increased effectiveness with increased intensity of stimulation [5, 14, 88, 97, 104]. The main difficulty seems to be that thresholds vary so much from subject to subject [112], and from day to day [114], that what is subliminal but effective for one person is likely to be subliminal but ineffective for a second, and supraliminal for a third. As is generally the case, anyone who wishes to use the technique of subliminal stimulation must first experiment upon the specific group of people whom he wishes to influence before he can decide what intensity levels will be most efficacious.

Somewhat the same conclusion holds for the question of how many times the stimuli should be presented. While under some conditions subliminal stimuli which did not influence behavior when presented only once seemed to "summate" when presented many times [10, 66], Bricker and Chapanis [15] found that one presentation of a stimulus slightly below the (statistical) limen was enough to increase the likelihood of its being recognized on subsequent trials. We interpret this to mean that too many presentations may well raise the subliminal stimuli above the limen of awareness if the stimuli themselves are not carefully chosen.

As for the physical properties of the message itself, we can but guess what the relevant issues are. Both verbal and pictorial presentations apparently are effective in the visual modality, but no one has tested the relative effectiveness of these two types of stimulation. Quite possibly subsequent experimentation will show that words are best for some situations (such as direct commands), while pictures are best for others.[4] It can be stated unequivocally, however, that advertisers should look to their basic English when writing their subliminal commercials. Several studies have shown that the more familiar a subject is with the stimulus

---

[4] Perhaps much of the work on sensory preconditioning is applicable here. When Ellson [38] presented his subjects with both a light and a buzzer for many trials, then presented the light alone, subjects "heard" the buzzer too.

he is to perceive, the more readily he perceives it [22, 54, 63, 110]. We interpret these studies to mean that unfamiliar stimuli may be ineffective when presented subliminally, even though familiar messages may "get through."

The exact length the message should be, its composition, and the background in which it should be presented are variables upon which no work has been done and about which no conclusions can presently be drawn. Suffice it to say, however, that a message which would be short enough to be perceived by one person might be too long for another person to perceive under any conditions.

Which modalities are most useful for subliminal stimulation? While most of the work has been done on the visual modality, Vanderplas and Blake [124] and Kurland [71] have found subthreshold auditory stimuli to be effective, and earlier in this paper we have reported similar studies with cutaneous stimulation. Advertisers who wish to "sneak up on" their patrons by presenting subliminal stimuli in one modality while the patrons are attending to supraliminal stimuli from another modality are probably doomed to failure, however. Collier [27] presented subliminal geometric forms simultaneously with the visual and the cutaneous modalities and found little, if any, lowering of thresholds. Correspondingly, it should be remembered that Hernandez-Peon et al. [55] found that some part of the nervous system acts as a kind of gating mechanism, and when an organism is attending strongly to one modality, the other modalities are probably "shut off" to most incoming stimuli.

Even if experimenters succeed in finding answers to many of the questions raised above concerning the physical characteristics of the stimuli to be employed, it is quite probable that they will have succeeded in discovering the source of only a small part of the variance operant in subliminal perception. For, as always, the major source of variance will come from the perceiver himself.

## Characteristics of the Perceiver Which Affect Subliminal Perception

The following section of this paper might well be considered a plea for the recognition that individual differences exist and that they must be taken into account by anyone who wishes to deal with individuals. We know next to nothing about the relationships between such factors as age, sex, social class, and so forth, and subliminal perception. Perhaps only one study is relevant: Perky [95] found that children were as much influenced by subthreshold visual stimulation as were naive adults. It is quite likely that many differences in the perception of subliminal stimuli do exist between individuals of differing classes, ages, and sexes. As always, only experimentation can determine what these differences are.

We do have some idea, however, of how what might be called personality factors influence subliminal perception. First and foremost, there seems little doubt but that a high need state affects perception. Gilchrist and Nesberg [46] found that the greater the need state, the more their subjects tended to overestimate the brightness of objects relevant to that need. It should be noted that they were dealing with difference limens, not absolute limens, but other studies to be quoted later show the same effect for absolute limens. It should be noted also that Gilchrist and Nesberg apparently overlooked evidence in their own data that a strong need affects judgments of non-need-related objects in the same direction (but not as much) as it does need-related objects. Wispe and Drambarean, dealing with visual duration thresholds, concluded that "need-related words were recognized more rapidly as need increased" [131, p. 31]. McClelland and Lieberman [81] found that subjects with high need achievement scores had lower visual thresholds for "success" words than did subjects not scoring as high on need achievement. Do all of these findings mean that subliminal ads will work only when some fairly strong need (of any kind) is present in the viewers? Only experimentation can answer this question.

What about abnormalities of personality? What effect do they have? Kurland [71] tested auditory recognition thresholds using emotional and neutral words. He found that hospitalized neurotics perceived the emotional words at significantly lower thresholds than did a group of normal subjects. Does this mean that neurotics are more likely to respond to low-intensity subliminal commands than normals? Should advertisers take a "neurotic inventory" of their audiences?

A more pertinent problem is posed by the findings of Krech and Calvin [70]. Using a Wechsler Vocabulary Score of 30.5 as their cutting point, they found that almost all college students above this score showed better visual discriminations of patterns presented at close to liminal values than did almost all students scoring below the cutting point. Does this mean that the higher the IQ, the better the subliminal perception? What is the relationship between the value of the absolute limen and intelligence? Will advertisers have to present their messages at such high intensities (in order that the "average man" might perceive the message) that the more intelligent members of the audience will be consciously aware of the advertising?

One further fascinating problem is posed by Huntley's work [64]. He surreptitiously obtained photographs of the hands and profiles of his subjects, as well as handwriting samples and recordings of their voices. Six months later each subject was presented with the whole series of samples, among which were his own. Each subject was asked to make preference ratings of the samples. Huntley reports evidence of a significant tendency for subjects to prefer their own forms of expression above all others, even though in most cases they were totally unaware that the samples were their own and even though many subjects were unable to identify their own samples when told they were included in the series. If an advertiser is making a direct appeal to one specific individual, it would seem then that he should make use of the photographs and recordings of that individual's behavior as the subliminal stimuli. If an advertiser is making an appeal to a more general audience, however, it might be that he would find the use of pictures and recordings of Hollywood stars, and so on, more efficacious than mere line drawings, printed messages, and unknown voices.

Nor can the advertiser afford to overlook the effects of set and attention. Miller [88], Perky [95], and Blake and Vanderplas [12], among others, discovered that giving the subject the proper set lowered the recognition threshold greatly. In fact, in many cases the stimulus intensity which was subliminal but effective for sophisticated subjects was far too subliminal to have much, if any, effect upon naive subjects. Thus advertisers might do well to tell their audiences that subliminal messages were being presented to them, in order to bring all members of that audience closer to a uniform threshold. Does this not, however, vitiate some of the effect of subliminal advertising?

As for attentional effects, we have presented evidence earlier [46] that strong needs seem to have an "alerting" effect upon the organism, lowering recognition thresholds for *all* stimuli, not just need-related stimuli. In addition to this, two studies by Hartmann [52, 53], as well as two by Spencer [113, 114], lead us to the belief that subliminal stimuli might best be presented when either the television or movie screen was blank of other pictures. Perhaps, then, subliminal commercials in movie houses should be shown between features; while on television the commercials should consist of an appropriate period of apparent visual silence, during which the audience would not be aware of the subliminal stimulation presented but might react to it later.

One fact emerges from all of the above. Anyone who wishes to utilize subliminal stimulation for commercial or other purposes can be likened to a stranger entering into a misty, confused countryside where there are but few landmarks. Before this technique is used in the marketplace, if it is to be used at all, a tremendous amount of research should be done, and by competent experimenters.

## THE ETHICS OF SUBLIMINAL INFLUENCE

From its beginnings as a purely academic offshoot of philosophy, psychology has, with ever increasing momentum, grown in the public perception as a practical and applied discipline. As psychologists were called upon to communicate and interpret their insights and research findings to lay persons, it was necessary to make decisions about what constituted proper professional behavior, since it was evident that the misuse of such information would reflect directly on the community of psychologists. As a growing number of our research efforts are viewed as useful to society, the problem of effective and honest communication becomes magnified, although its essential nature does not change. Recently, to our dismay, the announcement of a commercial application of long established psychological principles has assumed nightmarish qualities, and we find ourselves unwillingly cast in the role of invaders of personal privacy and enemies of society. A kind of guilt by association seems to be occurring, and as future incidents of this kind will, it threatens to undermine the public relations we have built with years of caution and concern for the public welfare. The highly emotional public reaction to the "discovery" of subliminal perception should serve as an object lesson to our profession, for in the bright glare of publicity we can see urgent ethical issues as well as an omen of things to come. When the theoretical notion $E = MC^2$ became the applied reality of an atom bomb, the community of physicists became deeply concerned with social as well as scientific responsibility. Judging from the intensity of the public alarm when confronted with a bare minimum of fact about this subliminal social atom, there exists a clear need for psychologists to examine the ethical problems that are a part of this era of the application of their findings.

The vehemence of the reaction to the proposed use of a device to project subliminal, or from the public's point of view "hidden," messages to viewers indicates that the proposal touches a sensitive area. One of the basic contributors to this reaction seems to be the feeling that a technique which avowedly tampers with the psychological status of the individual ought to be under the regulation or control of a trusted scientific group. As a professional group, psychologists would fit this description, for in the *Ethical Standards of Psychologists* [2] there is a clear statement of their motives and relationship to society:

> Principle 1.12-1 The psychologist's ultimate allegiance is to society, and his professional behavior should demonstrate an awareness of his social responsibilities. The welfare of the profession and of the individual psychologist are clearly subordinate to the welfare of the public....

Both this statement and the long record of responsible behavior of the members of the profession would certainly seem to be sufficient to reduce any anxiety the public might have over the possible unscrupulous use of this or any other device. It is precisely the fact that the public *is* aware that decisions about the use of subliminal perception devices rest not with psychologists but with commercial agencies that may be distressing to the public. The aura of open-for-business flamboyance and the sketchily presented percentages in the first public announcement tended to reinforce existing apprehensions rather than allay them.

Although subliminal perception happens now to be the focus of a great deal of reaction, it is merely the most recent in a succession of perturbing events to which the public has been exposed. It has become the focus of, and is likely to become the whipping boy for, a host of techniques which now occupy the twilight zone of infringement of personal psychological freedom. It must be remembered that to the lay person the notion of an unconscious part of the mind is eerie, vague, and more than a little mysterious. Unable fully to comprehend the systematic and theoretical aspects of such a concept, he must be content with overly popularized and dramatic versions of it. In every form of mass media the American public has been exposed to convincing images of the bearded hypnotist (with piercing eye) who achieves his nefarious ends by controlling the unconscious of his victim. It has been treated to the spectacle of the seeming reincarnation of Bridey Murphy out of the unconscious of an American housewife and, in *Three Faces of Eve,* to complex multiple personalities hidden in the psychic recesses of a single individual. With such uncanny and disturbing images as an emotional backdrop, the appearance of *The Hidden Persuaders* on the best seller lists formed the indelible impression of the exploitation of the unconscious for purposes of profit and personal gain. In combination, this growth of emotionally charged attitudes toward the unconscious and the suspicions about commercial morality came to be a potentially explosive set of tensions which was triggered off by the first commercial use of subliminal techniques.

What is to be the psychologist's position in regard to future developments with subliminal perception? The apparent discrepancy between the claims being made for the technique and the available research evidence suggests a need for considerable scientific caution as well as extensive investigation. The responsibility of psychologists in this instance is clearly indicated in the code of ethics:

> Principle 2.12-1 The psychologist should refuse to suggest, support, or condone unwarranted assumptions, invalid applications, or unjustified conclusions in the use of psychological instruments or techniques.

The flurry of claim and opinion about the effectiveness of subliminal methods seems to be based more on enthusiasm than controlled scientific experimentation, and it is here that psychology can be of service. Until acceptable scientific answers are forthcoming, we believe psychologists should guard against a premature commitment which might jeopardize public respect for them. The course of scientific history is strewn with the desiccated remains of projects pursued with more vigor than wisdom.

Scientific caution is essential, but it falls short of meeting the ethical issue raised by the nature of subliminal perception itself. The most strident public objections have been directed toward the possibility that suggestions or attempts to influence or persuade may be administered without the knowledge or consent of the audience. Assurances that widespread adoption of this technique would provide increased enjoyment through the elimination of commercial intrusions, or that the users will establish an ethical control over the content of the messages presented, can only fail to be convincing in light of past experience. The suggestion that the public can be taught means of detecting when it is being exposed to a planned subliminal stimulation is far from reassuring, since such a suggestion implies that the ability to defend oneself warrants being attacked. A captive audience is not a happy audience, and even the plan to inform the viewers in advance concerning the details of what is to be presented subliminally may not prevent the public from reacting to this technique as a demand that it surrender an additional degree of personal freedom. Fresh from similar encounters, the public may not allow this freedom to be wrested from it.

Finally, the argument that a great deal of our normal perception occurs on the fringe of conscious awareness and that subliminal events are no more effective than weak conscious stimuli rests on opinion and not fact. This seems particularly dangerous clinical ground on which to tread, since the effect on behavior of stimuli which may possibly be inserted directly into the unconscious has yet to be explored. Assurances that this technique can only "remind" a person of something he already knows or "support" a set of urges already in existence but cannot establish a completely new set of urges or needs are reckless assertions having no evidence to support them. So it seems that the aspect of subliminal projection which is marked by the greatest potential risk to the individual's emotional equilibrium is the aspect about which the least is scientifically known.

The psychologist's ethical quandary, then, stems directly from the inescapable implication of deviousness in the use of such a technique. The appropriate guidelines for conduct are provided in this ethical statement:

> Principle 2.62-2 It is unethical to employ psychological techniques for devious purposes, for entertainment, or for other reasons not consonant with the best interests of a client or with the development of psychology as a science.

It is obvious that "devious purposes" and "the best interests . . . of psychology as a science" are not self-defining terms and must be interpreted by the individual psychologist in light of the circumstances of each situation. It is a trying and complex decision to make. If in his mature judgment the intended uses of the principles of subliminal perception do not meet acceptable ethical standards, the psychologist is obligated to disassociate himself from the endeavor and to labor in behalf of the public welfare to which he owes his first allegiance. In this respect, the responsibility of the social scientist must always be that of watchdog over his own actions as well as the actions of those to whom he lends his professional support.

The furore which promises to accompany the further application of a variety of devices involving subliminal perception is certain to embroil psychology in a dispute not of its own choosing. The indiscriminate and uncontrolled application of psychological principles is increasing at a fearsome rate in the form of motivation research, propaganda, public relations, and a host of other "useful" practices based on the work of psychologists. In a very real sense this era of applied psychology will be a test of the workability of the psychologist's code of ethics and promises to stimulate the profession to give further consideration to its responsibility for assisting society to use its findings wisely.

## REFERENCES

1. J. K. Adams. Laboratory studies of behavior without awareness. *Psychol. Bull.*, 1957, *54*, 383–405.
2. American Psychological Association, Committee on Ethical Standards for Psychology. *Ethical standards of psychologists*. Washington: APA, 1953.
3. H. Ansbacher. Perception of number as affected by the monetary value of the objects. *Arch. Psychol.*, 1937, *30* (no. 215).
4. S. Bach and G. S. Klein. Conscious effects of prolonged subliminal exposures of words. *Amer. Psychologist,* 1957, *12,* 397. (Abstract)
5. L. E. Baker. The influence of subliminal stimuli upon verbal behavior. *J. exp. Psychol.*, 1937, *20,* 84–100.
6. L. E. Baker. The pupillary response conditioned to subliminal auditory stimuli. *Psychol. Monogr.*, 1938, *50* (3, whole no. 223).
7. Ban on subliminal ads, pending FCC probe, is urged. *Adv. Age*, 1957, *28* (no. 45).
8. P. Battelle. The lady objects to id tampering. *Publishers Auxiliary,* 1957, *92* (no. 40).
9. H. L. Beams and G. G. Thompson. Affectivity as a factor in the perception of the magnitude of food objects. *Amer. Psychologist,* 1952, *7,* 323. (Abstract)
10. R. J. Beitel, Jr. Spatial summation of subliminal stimuli in the retina of the human eye. *J. gen. Psychol.*, 1934, *10*, 311–327.
11. H. R. Blackwell. Personal communication, 1958.
12. R. R. Blake and J. M. Vanderplas. The effects of prerecognition hypotheses on veridical recognition thresholds in auditory perception. *J. Pers.*, 1950–1951, *19*, 95–115.
13. G. S. Blum. Perceptual defense revisited. *J. abnorm. soc. Psychol.*, 1955, *56,* 24–29.
14. J. Bressler. Illusion in the case of subliminal visual stimulation. *J. gen. Psychol.*, 1931, *5*, 244–250.
15. P. D. Bricker and A. Chapanis. Do incorrectly perceived tachistoscopic stimuli convey some information? *Psychol. Rev.*, 1953, *60,* 181–188.
16. S. H. Britt. Subliminal advertising—fact or fantasy? *Adv. Age,* 1957, *28,* 103.
17. J. Brooks. The little ad that isn't there. *Consumer Rep.*, 1957, *23* (no. 1).
18. J. S. Bruner and C. C. Goodman. Value and need as organizing factors in perception. *J. abnorm. soc. Psychol.*, 1947, *42,* 33–44.
19. J. S. Bruner and L. Postman. Emotional selectivity in perception and action. *J. Pers.*, 1947, *16,* 69–77.
20. J. S. Bruner and L. Postman. Tension and tension release as organizing factors in perception. *J. Pers.,* 1947, *16,* 300–308.

21. J. S. Bruner and L. Postman. Symbolic value as an organizing factor in perception. *J. soc. Psychol.,* 1948, *27,* 203–208.
22. J. S. Bruner and L. Postman. Perception, cognition, and behavior. *J. Pers.,* 1949, *18,* 14–31.
23. L. F. Carter and K. Schooler. Value, need, and other factors in perception. *Psychol. Rev.,* 1949, *56,* 200–207.
24. H. Cason and N. Katcher. An attempt to condition breathing and eyelid responses to a subliminal electric stimulus. *J. exp. Psychol.,* 1934, *16,* 831–842.
25. B. D. Cohen, H. I. Kalish, J. R. Thurston, and E. Cohen. Experimental manipulation of verbal behavior. *J. exp. Psychol.,* 1954, *47,* 106–110.
26. L. H. Cohen, E. R. Hilgard, and G. R. Wendt. Sensitivity to light in a case of hysterical blindness studied by reinforcement-inhibition and conditioning methods. *Yale J. Biol. Med.,* 1933, *6,* 61–67.
27. R. M. Collier. An experimental study of the effects of subliminal stimuli. *Psychol. Monogr.,* 1940, *52* (5, whole no. 236).
28. J. E. Coover. Experiments in psychical research. *Psychical Res. Monogr.,* 1917 (no. 1).
29. N. Cousins. Smudging the subconscious. *Saturday Rev.,* 1957, *40* (no. 40), 20.
30. E. L. Cowen and E. G. Beier. The influence of "threat-expectancy" on perception. *J. Pers.,* 1950–1951, *19,* 85–94.
31. E. L. Cowen and E. G. Beier. A further study of the "threat-expectancy" variable in perception. *Amer. Psychologist,* 1952, *7,* 320–321. (Abstract)
32. E. L. Cowen and E. G. Beier. Threat-expectancy, word frequencies, and perceptual prerecognition hypotheses. *J. abnorm. soc. Psychol.,* 1954, *49,* 178–182.
33. E. Culler and F. A. Mettler. Conditioned behavior in a decorticate dog. *J. comp. Psychol.,* 1934, *18,* 291–303.
34. J. Deiter. The nature of subception. Unpublished doctoral dissertation, University of Kansas, 1953.
35. K. Diven. Certain determinants in the conditioning of anxiety reactions. *J. Psychol.,* 1937, *3,* 291–308.
36. K. Dunlap. Effect of imperceptible shadows on the judgments of distance. *Psychol. Rev.,* 1900, *7,* 435–453.
37. G. DuShane. The invisible word, or no thresholds barred. *Science,* 1957, *126,* 681.
38. D. G. Ellson. Hallucinations produced by sensory conditioning. *J. exp. Psychol.,* 1941, *28,* 1–20.
39. C. W. Eriksen. The case for perceptual defense. *Psychol. Rev.,* 1954, *61,* 175–182.
40. C. W. Eriksen. Subception: Fact or artifact? *Psychol. Rev.,* 1956, *63,* 74–80.
41. C. W. Eriksen and J. L. Kuethe. Avoidance conditioning of verbal behavior without awareness: A paradigm of repression. *J. abnorm. soc. Psychol.,* 1956, *53,* 203–209.
42. A. A. Fink. Questions about subliminal advertising. New York: Author, 1957.
43. J. P. Foley, Jr. The cortical interpretation of conditioning. *J. gen. Psychol.,* 1933, *9,* 228–234.

44. G. S. Fullerton and J. M. Catteli. *On the perception of small differences.* U. Penn. Publ., Philos. Ser., No. 2. 1892.
45. "Ghost" ads overrated. *Sci. Newsltr.,* 1957, *72* (no. 17).
46. J. C. Gilchrist and L. S. Nesberg. Need and perceptual change in need-related objects. *J. exp. Psychol.,* 1952, *44,* 369–376.
47. J. Goodnow and L. Postman. Probability learning in a problem-solving situation. *J. exp. Psychol.,* 1955, *49,* 16–22.
48. J. Greenspoon. The reinforcing effect of two spoken sounds on the frequency of two responses. *Amer. J. Psychol.,* 1955, *68,* 409–416.
49. J. P. Guilford. *Psychometric methods.* New York: McGraw-Hill, 1936.
50. E. A. Haggard. Experimental studies in affective processes: I. Some effects of cognitive structure and active participation on certain autonomic reactions during and following experimentally induced stress. *J. exp. Psychol.,* 1943, *33,* 257–284.
51. H. Hankin. *Common sense.* New York: Dutton, 1926.
52. G. W. Hartmann. The increase of visual acuity in one eye through the illumination of the other. *J. exp. Psychol.,* 1933, *16,* 383–392.
53. G. W. Hartmann. Changes in visual acuity through simultaneous stimulation of other sense organs. *J. exp. Psychol.,* 1933, *16,* 393–407.
54. M. Henle. An experimental investigation of past experience as a determinant of visual form perception. *J. exp. Psychol.,* 1942, *30,* 1–21.
55. R. Hernandez-Peon, H. Scherrer, and J. Michel. Modification of electrical activity of cochlear nucleus during "attention" in unanesthetized cats. *Science,* 1955, *123,* 331–332.
56. D. C. Hildum and R. W. Brown. Verbal reinforcement and interviewer bias. *J. abnorm. soc. Psychol.,* 1956, *53,* 108–111.
57. E. R. Hilgard, J. Miller, and J. A. Ohlson. Three attempts to secure pupillary conditioning to auditory stimuli near the absolute threshold. *J. exp. Psychol.,* 1941, *29,* 89–103.
58. E. R. Hilgard and G. R. Wendt. The problem of reflex sensitivity to light studied in a case of hemianopsia. *Yale J. Biol. Med.,* 1933, *5,* 373–385.
59. H. L. Hollingworth. *Advertising and selling.* New York: Appleton, 1913.
60. D. Howes. A statistical theory of the phenomenon of subception. *Psychol. Rev.,* 1954, *61,* 98–110.
61. D. Howes. On the interpretation of word frequency as a variable affecting speed of recognition. *J. exp. Psychol.,* 1954, *48,* 106–112.
62. D. Howes and R. L. Solomon. A note on McGinnies' "Emotionality and perceptual defense." *Psychol. Rev.,* 1950, *57,* 235–240.
63. D. Howes and R. L. Solomon. Visual duration threshold as a function of word probability. *J. exp. Psychol.,* 1951, *41,* 401–410.
64. C. W. Huntley. Judgments of self based upon records of expressive behavior. *J. abnorm. soc. Psychol.,* 1953, *48,* 398–427.
65. F. W. Irwin, K. Kaufman, G. Prior, and H. B. Weaver. On "Learning without awareness of what is being learned." *J. exp. Psychol.,* 1934, *17,* 823–827.
66. H. W. Karn. The function of intensity in the spatial summation of subliminal stimuli in the retina. *J. gen. Psychol.,* 1935, *12,* 95–107.

67. J. L. Kennedy. Experiments on "unconscious whispering." *Psychol. Bull.,* 1938, *35,* 526. (Abstract)
68. J. L. Kennedy. A methodological review of extrasensory perception. *Psychol. Bull.,* 1939, *36,* 59–103.
69. G. S. Klein, D. Meister, and H. J. Schlesinger. The effect of personal values on perception: An experimental critique. *Amer. Psychologist,* 1949, *4,* 252–253. (Abstract)
70. D. Krech and A. Calvin. Levels of perceptual organization and cognition. *J. abnorm. soc. Psychol.,* 1953, *48,* 394–400.
71. S. H. Kurland. The lack of generality in defense mechanisms as indicated in auditory perception. *J. abnorm. soc. Psychol.,* 1954, *49,* 173–177.
72. J. I. Lacey and R. L. Smith. Conditioning and generalization of unconscious anxiety. *Science,* 1954, *120,* 1045–1052.
73. J. I. Lacey, R. L. Smith, and A. Green. Use of conditioned autonomic responses in the study of anxiety. *Psychosom. Med.,* 1955, *17,* 208–217.
74. R. S. Lazarus. Subception: Fact or artifact? A reply to Eriksen. *Psychol. Rev.,* 1956, *63,* 343–347.
75. R. S. Lazarus, C. W. Eriksen, and C. P. Fonda. Personality dynamics and auditory perceptual recognition. *J. Pers.,* 1950–1951, *19,* 471–482.
76. R. S. Lazarus and R. A. McCleary. Autonomic discrimination without awareness: A study of subception. *Psychol. Rev.,* 1951, *58,* 113–122.
77. R. Levine, I. Chein, and G. Murphy. The relation of the intensity of a need to the amount of perceptual distortion. *J. Psychol.,* 1942, *13,* 283–293.
78. W. Lysak. The effects of punishment upon syllable recognition thresholds. *J. exp. Psychol.,* 1954, *47,* 343–350.
79. R. A. McCleary and R. S. Lazarus. Autonomic discrimination without awareness: An interim report. *J. Pers.,* 1949, *18,* 171–179.
80. D. C. McClelland and J. W. Atkinson. The projective expression of needs: I. The effect of different intensities of the hunger drive on perception. *J. Psychol.,* 1948, *25,* 205–222.
81. D. C. McClelland and A. M. Lieberman. The effect of need for achievement on recognition of need-related words. *J. Pers.,* 1949, *18,* 236–251.
82. E. McGinnies. Emotionality and perceptual defense. *Psychol. Rev.,* 1949, *56,* 244–251.
83. E. McGinnies. Discussion of Howes' and Solomon's note on "Emotionality and perceptual defense." *Psychol. Rev.,* 1950, *57,* 229–234.
84. G. Mandler and W. K. Kaplan. Subjective evaluation and reinforcing effect of a verbal stimulus. *Science,* 1956, *124,* 582–583.
85. M. Mannes. Ain't nobody here but us commercials. *Reporter,* 1957, *17* (no. 6).
86. H. M. Manro and M. F. Washburn. Effect on imperceptible lines on judgment of distance. *Amer. J. Psychol.,* 1908, *19,* 242–243.
87. Michigan State prof. tells weaknesses of invisible commercials. *Publishers Auxiliary,* 1957, *92* (no. 40).
88. J. G. Miller. Discrimination without awareness. *Amer. J. Psychol.,* 1939, *52,* 562–578.

89. J. G. Miller. The role of motivation in learning without awareness. *Amer. J. Psychol.*, 1940, *53*, 229–239.
90. J. G. Miller. *Unconsciousness.* New York: Wiley, 1942.
91. S. M. Newhall and R. Dodge. Colored afterimages from unperceived weak chromatic stimulation. *J. exp. Psychol.*, 1927, *10*, 1–17.
92. S. M. Newhall and R. R. Sears. Conditioning finger retraction to visual stimuli near the absolute threshold. *Comp. psychol. Monogr.*, 1933, *9* (no. 43).
93. A. M. Nuthmann. Conditioning of a response class on a personality test. *J. abnorm. soc. Psychol.*, 1957, *54*, 19–23.
94. C. S. Peirce and J. Jastrow. On small differences of sensation. *Mem. Nat. Acad. Sci.*, 1884, *3*, 73–83.
95. C. W. Perky. An experimental study of imagination. *Amer. J. Psychol.*, 1910, *21*, 422–452.
96. E. B. Philbrick and L. Postman. A further analysis of "learning without awareness." *Amer. J. Psychol.*, 1955, *68*, 417–424.
97. R. P. Pillai. A study of the threshold in relation to the investigations on subliminal impressions and allied phenomena. *Brit. J. educ. Psychol.*, 1939, *9*, 97–98.
98. L. Postman and R. F. Jarrett. An experimental analysis of "learning without awareness." *Amer. J. Psychol.*, 1952, *65*, 244–255.
99. G. Razran. Stimulus generalization of conditioned responses. *Psychol. Bull.*, 1949, *46*, 337–365.
100. M. M. Reece. The effect of shock on recognition thresholds. *J. abnorm. soc. Psychol.*, 1954, *49*, 165–172.
101. H. J. Rees and H. E. Israel. An investigation of the establishment and operation of mental sets. *Psychol. Monogr.*, 1935, *46* (6, whole no. 210).
102. R. N. Sanford. The effects of abstinence from food upon imaginal processes: A preliminary experiment. *J. Psychol.*, 1936, *2*, 129–136.
103. R. N. Sanford. The effects of abstinence from food upon imaginal processes: A further experiment. *J. Psychol.*, 1937, *3*, 145–159.
104. T. H. Schafer. Influence of the preceding item on units of the noise masked threshold by a modified constant method. *J. exp. Psychol.*, 1950, *40*, 365–371.
105. R. R. Sears and L. H. Cohen. Hysterical anesthesia, analgesia, and astereognosis. *Arch. Neurol. Psychiat.*, 1933, *29*, 260–271.
106. T. Settlage. The effect of sodium amytal on the formation and elicitation of conditioned reflexes. *J. comp. Psychol.*, 1936, *22*, 339–343.
107. B. Sidis. *The psychology of suggestion.* New York: Appleton, 1898.
108. J. B. Sidowski. Influence of awareness of reinforcement on verbal conditioning. *J. exp. Psychol.*, 1954, *48*, 355–360.
109. A. Silverman and L. E. Baker. An attempt to condition various responses to subliminal electrical stimulation. *J. exp. Psychol.*, 1935, *18*, 246–254.
110. K. L. Smoke. An objective study of concept formation. *Psychol. Monogr.*, 1932, *42* (4, whole no. 191).
111. R. L. Solomon and D. H. Howes. Word frequency, personal values, and visual duration thresholds. *Psychol. Rev.*, 1951, *58*, 256–270.

112. R. L. Solomon and L. Postman. Frequency of usage as a determinant of recognition thresholds for words. *J. exp. Psychol.*, 1952, *43*, 195–201.
113. L. T. Spencer. The concept of the threshold and Heymans' law of inhibition: I. Correlation between the visual threshold and Heymans' coefficient of inhibition of binocular vision. *J. exp. Psychol.*, 1928, *11*, 88–97.
114. L. T. Spencer and L. H. Cohen. The concept of the threshold and Heymans' law of inhibition. II. *J. exp. Psychol.*, 1928, *11*, 194–201.
115. K. Sterling and J. G. Miller. Conditioning under anesthesia. *Amer. J. Psychol.*, 1941, *54*, 92–101.
116. M. Stroh, A. M. Shaw, and M. F. Washburn. A study in guessing. *Amer. J. Psychol.*, 1908, *19*, 243–245.
117. Subliminal ad okay if it sells: Lessler; FCC peers into subliminal picture on TV. *Adv. Age*, 1957, *28* (no. 48).
118. Subliminal ads wash no brains, declare Moore, Becker, developers of precon device. *Adv. Age*, 1957, *28* (no. 48).
119. M. Suslowa. Veränderungen der Hautgefuhl unter dem Einflusse electrischer Reizung. *Z. Rationelle Med.*, 1863, *18*, 155–160.
120. C. Taffel. Anxiety and the conditioning of verbal behavior. *J. abnorm. soc. Psychol.*, 1955, *51*, 496–501.
121. E. L. Thorndike. *The fundamentals of learning*. New York: Teachers College, Columbia University, 1932.
122. E. L. Thorndike and R. T. Rock. Learning without awareness of what is being learned or intent to learn it. *J. exp. Psychol.*, 1934, *17*, 1–19.
123. E. B. Titchner and W. H. Pyle. Effect of imperceptible shadows on the judgment of distance. *Proc. Amer. phil. Soc.*, 1907, *46*, 94–109.
124. J. M. Vanderplas and R. R. Blake. Selective sensitization in auditory perception. *J. Pers.*, 1949, *18*, 252–266.
125. W. S. Verplanck. The control of the content of conversation: Reinforcement of statements of opinion. *J. abnorm. soc. Psychol.*, 1955, *51*, 668–676.
126. W. S. Verplanck. The operant conditioning of human motor behavior. *Psychol. Bull.*, 1956, *53*, 70–83.
127. W. E. Vinacke. The discrimination of color and form at levels of illumination below conscious awareness. *Arch. Psychol.*, 1942, *38* (no. 267).
128. C. H. Wedell, F. V. Taylor, and A. Skolnick. An attempt to condition the pupillary response. *J. exp. Psychol.*, 1940, *27*, 517–531.
129. R. L. Weiss. The influence of "set for speed" on "learning without awareness." *Amer. J. Psychol.*, 1955, *68*, 425–431.
130. A. C. Williams. Perception of subliminal visual stimuli. *J. Psychol.*, 1938, *6*, 187–199.
131. L. G. Wispe and N. C. Drambarean. Physiological need, word frequency, and visual duration thresholds. *J. exp. Psychol.*, 1953, *46*, 25–31.
132. J. D. Woolf. Subliminal perception is nothing new. *Adv. Age*, 1957, *28* (no. 43).

# 12

# THE EFFECT OF SUBLIMINAL SHOCK UPON THE JUDGED INTENSITY OF WEAK SHOCK

Roger W. Black
William Bevan

From the inception of psychophysics, it has been held that the absolute threshold provides the limiting criterion in the identification of the stimulus correlates of the several magnitudes of sensory experience. The validity of Fechner's law, in its general form, depends, for example, on two assumptions: that the stimulus may be integrated and that it equals zero at threshold. Similarly, it relates to the limits of the reciprocity principle—a stimulus below a critical intensity will not produce a response, regardless of its duration. Fechner's law has, from time to time, come in for its full share of criticism on a variety of grounds, the most serious, perhaps, being that it ignores two important classes of variables—background and past experience—which influence the magnitude of the psychophysical judgment. This charge is supported by data from studies of the central-tendency effect, series effects, interpolated stimuli, anchoring, category limens, and adaptation level [5; 6; 8, pp. 362–367; 12; 14; 15]. Here still, however, one notes the persistence, at least tacitly, of the assumption that the population of inputs which give rise to a judgment is supraliminal.

Meanwhile, an experimental interest in the relation of subliminal stimuli to behavior goes back a number of years. There have been, for example, the studies of the nonrandomness of response to subliminal inputs, of conditioning with subliminal stimuli, and, more recently, of perceptual defense and subception [1, 2, 4, 9, 10, 11, 13]. These studies have in common a preoccupation with the thesis that the organism responds to inputs of which it is not aware. If this proposition is accepted, one is forced to a re-examination of the status of the threshold assumption. By placing the problem in the psychophysical setting, one is prompted to ask not only if the organism responds to subliminal stimuli but also if subliminal stimuli influence responses to supraliminal stimuli. Accordingly, the present experiment was intended to answer two questions. Do subliminal stimuli interpolated between supraliminal stimuli influence judgments of the latter; and if so, is their effect similar to that associated with anchors above threshold?

Source: *American Journal of Psychology*, 1960, 73, 262–267.

The dimension chosen for study was response to shock, since an electrical stimulus can be easily controlled and because it constitutes input for which a range of readily available subliminal intensities exists. A preliminary experiment was done with seven observers making judgments under both control (supraliminal series alone) and experimental (supraliminal series with interpolated subliminal shocks) conditions and orders counterbalanced. While no significant-conditions main effect was observed, two reliable interactions—shocks × conditions and observers × conditions—suggested the possible fruitfulness of further experimentation. Thus the present simple two-group design was carried out.

## OBSERVERS

Forty-six students in introductory psychology (twenty men and twenty-six women) were randomly divided into two groups, the ratio of men to women in each being approximately equal. All were informed that they would be required to judge intensities of shock, but no mention of subliminal input was made. None gave any evidence of being cognizant of its use.

## APPARATUS

All shocks presented were square-wave pulses delivered by an Applegate Model 226 B Electronic Stimulator. Shock duration, as well as the interval between shocks, was controlled by two Hunter Model 111-C timers wired to recycle themselves. Shocks were given through two silver disks, 2 cm in diameter, covered by saline-saturated sponge. One electrode was attached to the right wrist on the proximal side, the other on the distal side, by means of an elastic wrist-band. In addition, a 1 × 4 in. saline-moistened, sponge-covered, copper-screen electrode was attached to each ankle for the recording of changes in skin resistance. The GSRs were recorded on a Brown Electronik continuous recorder with advances controlled by a third Hunter timer. Each advance was initiated 2 sec before the onset of shock and terminated with the presentation of shock.

## PROCEDURE

An observer was seated on a classroom chair with his back to the apparatus, the electrodes attached, and an estimate of his absolute threshold obtained by means of the method of limits with four ascending and four descending series. Shocks were 200 msec in duration presented in increments of 100$\mu$a with a pulse rate of 50 per sec. Next, a seven-category rating scale, varying from very strong through medium to very weak, was placed on the arm of the observer's chair and instructions were provided for its use. Each observer was reassured that the shocks would be mild, varying from a "prick" to a "twitch" or "sting." He was cautioned to make his judgments only with reference to the shocks received during the experiment and was informed that if additional categories were needed they could be added to either end of the scale. Finally, he was asked to report a judgment each time a shock was felt.

Each observer received a series of 100 supraliminal 200-msec shocks spaced at 20-sec intervals. The series consisted of five intensities, 1,500; 1,800; 2,100; 2,400; and 2,700 $\mu$a, each presented twenty times in random order. In addition, observers in the experimental group received a 200-msec subliminal stimulus, with an intensity of 50% of the individual observer's threshold, at the midpoint of the 20-sec interval between suprathreshold stimuli. In addition to the observer's judgments, GSR deflections were recorded for all stimuli in the series, as well as for the intervals between these stimuli. Basal resistances were noted after every fourth shock. The GSR apparatus was set at maximal sensitivity (change of 1,000$\Omega$ for full-scale deflection, 100$\Omega$ for single-unit deflection). At the end of the session, the absolute threshold again was determined. Because of apparatus failures, GSR data were obtained only for eighteen observers in one group and twenty in the other.

## RESULTS

The results, which were analyzed by Alexander's method [1], are summarized graphically in Figure 12-1. The fact that all points on the curve for the experimental group lie above their counterparts on the control curve suggests an affirmative answer to the first question asked in this experiment, and the reliability of this difference is demonstrated by the highly significant mean variance between groups ($p < 0.001$). Interpolation of imperceptible stimuli appears to enhance the judged intensity of the perceptible series stimuli. It may be objected that since the absolute threshold represents a range of stimulus values from the rarely perceptible to the always perceptible, the observer may, on certain occasions, have been aware of the interpolated shocks and this awareness altered the judged magnitude of the series shocks. We are inclined to reject this possibility for several reasons. Each observer had been instructed to make judgments of *all* shocks which he felt, but no judgments were ever given for the interpolated shocks. Interrogation of the observers after testing failed to reveal any knowledge of the interpolated stimulus. Finally, no GSRs could be linked with any confidence to the occurrence of these shocks. The enhancement seen in the experimental group appears to have occurred in the face of sensory adaptation. While both groups displayed an increase in threshold as a result of testing, the post-test threshold of the experimental group, which received twice the number of shocks given the control group, was slightly higher than that of the control. The present data are inconsistent with the traditional psychophysical assumption that the absolute threshold is a limiting value in the generation of psychophysical functions.

Inspection of Figure 12-1 also suggests that the interpolated stimulus behaved like a supraliminal anchor introduced below the series. It

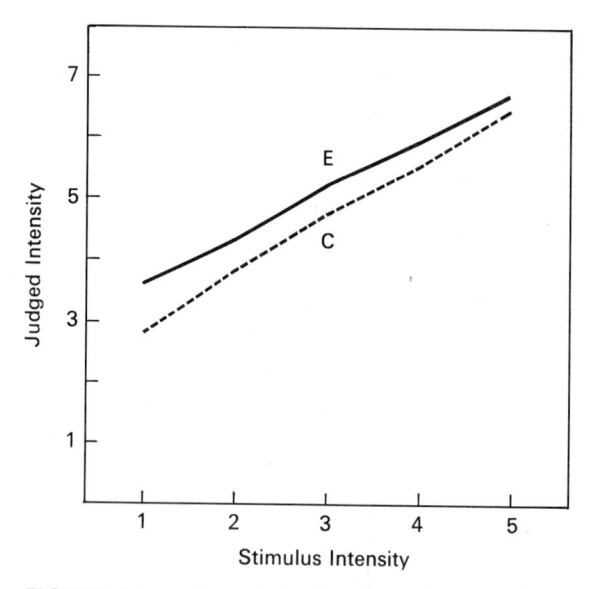

FIGURE 12-1 Average judgments of intensity of five supraliminal stimuli with and without the interpolation of a subliminal anchor. The physical intensities varied from 1,500 to 2,700 µa in 300 µa steps.

drew the Indifference Point toward itself, but its effect was asymmetrical, being greatest upon the weaker of the series inputs situated closer to it on the stimulus continuum. (The variance for slopes between groups was significant at the 5% level.) Thus it would appear that the organism may incorporate subliminal along with supraliminal stimuli in the derivation of subjective norms for judgment, and the criterion of perceptibility cannot be applied in defining the properties of input relevant for pooling.[1]

---

[1] The obtained Indifference Point for the control group was 1,841 µa, for the experimental group, 1,671 µa. Three estimates of the subjective norm were computed to test the adequacy of the quantitative aspect of the theory of adaptation level: the arithmetic mean; the logarithmetic mean with Helson's correction (+0.75d) applied for interval size; and the exponential or power mean. The corrected log mean and the power mean predicted with approximately the same efficiency, but only moderately well (error = 15%). Corrected log mean: C = 2,281, E = 1,486; power mean: C = 2,181, E = 1,458. Since, at this point, we are not preoccupied with precise quantitative prediction, no attempt has been made to determine constants for purpose of correction. Meanwhile, it would appear that the subliminal anchor is less potent than a supraliminal counterpart might be.

Lastly, with the GSR apparatus set at maximal sensitivity, deflections were observed in 92.2% of the 10-sec intervals following series stimuli, in only 9.5% of the 10-sec intervals following interpolated shock in the experimental group, and in 9% of the corresponding "empty" intervals for the control group. The difference between frequency of GSRs observed in the supraliminal and subliminal or empty intervals is highly reliable. Chi-squares computed for individual observers all were highly significant, the smallest being 37.2. Meanwhile, the average frequency of response by the experimental group during the subliminal period was not reliably in excess of that seen in the controls during the "empty" period ($U = 176$, $m/n = 20/18$, $p > 0.10$).

It would thus appear that GSRs during the subliminal interval were "spontaneous" and not systematically related to the subthreshold shock. This failure for the subliminal shock to produce a GSR, although it produced a significant change in judgment, points up two things. First, this is another instance in which a behavioral measure appears to be more sensitive than a widely used physiological measure as an index of the influence of a physical variable. Secondly, the notion of arousal, so closely linked, at least since the time of Cannon, to the autonomic nervous system, warrants more definitive formulation. It may not be inappropriate to suggest relating the present findings to the function of the thalamic portion of the reticular activating system, while those from the studies of perceptual defense may be thought to reflect the activity of the basal diencephalic and midbrain parts of this same complex.

## SUMMARY

The present experiment investigated the effect of subliminal electrical shocks upon the judged intensity of supraliminal shocks. Two groups of observers received 100 shocks above threshold, 20 at each of five intensities, to be rated on a seven-point scale. One group, in addition, received shocks of 50% threshold intensity interpolated between the series stimuli. GSR deflections were recorded for both supra- and subliminal presentations.

The mean intensity of the series judgments for the group receiving the interpolated shock was significantly greater than for the control group. Further, the interpolated shock behaved like an anchor below the series, effecting the greatest enhancement for the series stimuli closest to it on the stimulus continuum. While GSR deflections occurred consistently with the presentation of the series stimuli, none could be confidently related to the presentation of the subliminal stimuli. The implications of these data for pooling theory and for the concept of arousal were noted.

## REFERENCES

1. H. W. Alexander. A general test for trend. *Psychol. Bull.,* 1946, *43,* 533–557.
2. L. E. Baker. The influence of subliminal stimuli upon verbal behavior. *J. exp. Psychol.,* 1937, *20,* 84–100.
3. L. E. Baker. The pupillary response conditioned to subliminal auditory stimuli. *Psychol. Monogr.* 1938, *50* (no. 223).
4. R. C. Davis. Motor responses to auditory stimuli above and below threshold. *J. exp. Psychol.,* 1950, *40,* 107–120.
5. J. P. Guilford and D. G. Park. The effect of interpolated weight upon comparative judgments. *Amer. J. Psychol.,* 1931, *43,* 588–599.
6. H. Helson. Adaptation level as a basis for a quantitative theory of frame of reference. *Psychol. Rev.,* 1948, *55,* 297–313.
7. H. Jasper. Reticular-cortical systems and theories of the integrative action of the brain. In H. F. Harlow and C. N. Woolsey (eds.). *Biological and biochemical bases of behavior.* Madison: University of Wisconsin, 1958. Pp. 37–63.
8. D. M. Johnson. *The Psychology of thought and judgment.* New York: Harper, 1955.
9. R. S. Lazarus and R. A. McCleary. Autonomic discrimination without awareness: A study of subception. *Psychol. Rev.,* 1951, *58,* 113–122.
10. E. McGinnies. Emotionality and perceptual defense. *Psychol. Rev.,* 1949, *56,* 244–251.
11. J. G. Miller. Discrimination without awareness. *Amer. J. Psychol.,* 1939, *52,* 562–578.
12. S. Rogers. The anchoring of absolute judgments. *Arch. Psychol.,* 1941, *36* (no. 261), 1–42.
13. F. W. R. Taylor. The discrimination of subliminal visual stimuli. *Canad. J. Psychol.,* 1953, *7,* 12–20.
14. M. E. Tresselt. The influence of amount of practice upon the formation of a scale of judgment. *J. exp. Psychol.,* 1947, *37,* 251–260.
15. H. Woodrow. Weight discrimination with a varying standard. *Amer. J. Psychol.,* 1933, *45,* 391–416.

# 13

# TO KNOW A FLY

### V. G. Dethier

*i scurry around
gutters and sewers
and garbage cans
said the fly and
gather up the germs of
typhoid influenza
and pneumonia on my
feet and wings . . .*

*then i carry the germs
into the households of
men*

*. . . . . . .
. . . it is my mission
to help rid the world
of these wicked persons
i am a vessel of righteousness
scattering seeds of justice
and serving the noblest
uses*

Don Marquis, The Lives and Times of Archy and Mehitabel

A properly conducted experiment is a beautiful thing. It is an adventure, an expedition, a conquest. It commences with an act of faith, faith that the world is real, that our senses generally can be trusted, that effects have causes, and that we can discover meaning by reason. It continues with an observation and a question. An experiment is a scientist's way of asking nature a question. He alters a condition, observes a result, and draws a conclusion. It is no game for a disorderly mind (although the ranks of science are replete with confused thinkers). There are many ways of going astray. The mention of two will suffice.

The most commonly committed scientific sin is the lack of proper experimental control. The scientist must be certain that the result he obtains is a consequence of the specific alteration he introduced and not of some other coincidental one. There is the case of the gentleman who had trained a flea to leap at the command "Jump!"

"Now," said the clever gentleman, "I shall do an experiment to discover where the flea's ears are located. First I shall amputate his feelers." Whereupon, the operation having been completed and the flea having

Source: Chapter 3 of *To Know a Fly* by V. G. Dethier (San Francisco: Holden-Day, 1962).

recovered, the command "Jump!" was given. The flea jumped. "Ah," said the gentleman, obviously pleased, "he does not hear with his antennae. I shall now amputate his forelegs." With each succeeding operation the flea leaped on command until only the hindmost legs remained. When they were removed, the flea failed to jump. "You see," concluded the gentleman triumphantly, "he hears with his hind legs."

Or there is the well-known case of the chap who wondered which component of his mixed drink caused his inevitable intoxication. He tried bourbon and water, rum and water, scotch and water, rye and water, gin and water and concluded, since every drink had water as a constant, that water caused his drunkenness. He then gritted his teeth and tried water alone—with negative results. When I last saw him he had concluded that the glass was the intoxicating agent, and he was about to begin another series of experiments employing paper cups.

FIGURE 13-1  Insecticides?

Of course even controls can be carried to absurd extremes, as in the case of the atheistic scientist who seized upon the opportunity afforded by the birth of twins to test the efficacy of religion. He had one baby baptized and kept the other as a control.

Another common fallacy is that of confusing correlation with cause and effect. This is exemplified by the case of the gentleman who was extricated from the rubble of an apartment house immediately after an earthquake. "Do you know what happened?" his rescuers inquired.

"I am not certain," replied the survivor. "I remember pulling down the window shade and it caused the whole building to collapse."

The kind of question asked of nature is a measure of a scientist's intellectual stature. Too many research workers have no questions at all to ask, but this does not deter them from doing experiments. They become enamored of a new instrument, acquire it, then ask only "What can I do with this beauty?" Others ask such questions as "How many leaves are there this year on the ivy on the zoology building?" And having counted them do not know what to do with the information. But some questions can be useful and challenging. And meaningful questions can be asked of a fly.

Between the fly and the biologist, however, there is a language barrier that makes getting direct answers to questions difficult. With a human subject it is only necessary to ask: What color is this? Does that hurt? Are you hungry? The human subject may, of course, lie; the fly cannot. However, to elicit information from him it is necessary to resort to all kinds of trickery and legerdemain. This means pitting one's brain against that of the fly—a risk some people are unwilling to assume. But then, experimentation is only for the adventuresome, for the dreamers, for the brave.

It is risky even at higher levels. I am reminded of the eminent professor who had designed experiments to test an ape's capacity to use tools. A banana was hung from a string just out of reach. An assortment of tools, that is, boxes to pile up, bamboo poles to fit together, and so on, were provided, and the ape's ability was to be judged by his choice of method. To the chagrin of the professor, the ape chose a method that had never even occurred to that learned gentleman.

Extracting information from a fly can be equally challenging. Take the question of taste, for example. Does a fly possess a sense of taste? Is it similar to ours? How sensitive is it? What does he prefer?

The first fruitful experimental approach to this problem began less than fifty years ago with a very shrewd observation, namely, that flies (and bees and butterflies) walked about in their food and constantly stuck out their tongues. The next time you dine with a fly (and modern sanitary practice has not greatly diminished the opportunities), observe his behavior when he gavots across the top of the custard pie. His proboscis, which is normally carried retracted into his head like the landing gear of an airplane, will be lowered, and like a miniature vacuum cleaner he will suck in food. For a striking demonstration of this, mix some sugared water and food coloring and paint a sheet of paper. The first fly to find it will leave a beautiful trail of lip prints, hardly the kind suitable for lipstick ads but nonetheless instructive.

Proboscis extension has been seen thousands of times by thousands of people but few have been either struck by the sanitary aspects of the act or ingenious enough to figure out how they might put the observation to use to learn about fly behavior.

The brilliant idea conceived by the biologist who first speculated on why some insects paraded around in their food was that they tasted with their feet. In retrospect it is the simplest thing in the world to test this idea. It also makes a fine parlor trick for even the most blasé gathering.

The first step is to provide a fly with a handle, since nature failed to do so. Procure a stick about the size of a lead pencil. (A lead pencil will do nicely. So will an applicator stick, the kind that a physician employs when swabbing a throat.) Dip one end repeatedly into candle wax or paraffin until a fly-sized gob accumulates. Next anesthetize a fly. The least messy method is to deposit him in the freezing compartment of a refrigerator for several minutes. Then, working very rapidly, place him backside down on the wax and seal his wings onto it with a hot needle.

Now for the experimental proof. Lower the fly gently over a saucer of water until his feet just touch. Chances are he is thirsty. If so, he will lower his proboscis as soon as his feet touch and will suck avidly. When thirst has been allayed, the proboscis will be retracted compactly into the head. This is a neat arrangement because a permanently extended proboscis might flop about uncomfortably during flight or be trod upon while walking.

Next, lower the fly into a saucer of sugared water. In a fraction of a second the proboscis is flicked out again. Put him back into water (this is the control), and the proboscis is retracted. Water, in, sugar, out. The performance continues almost indefinitely. Who can doubt that the fly can taste with his feet? The beauty of this proboscis response, as it is called, is that it is a reflex action, almost as automatic as a knee jerk. By taking advantage of its automatism, one can learn very subtle things about a fly's sense of taste.

For example, who has the more acute sense of taste, you or the fly? As the cookbooks say, take ten saucers. Fill the first with water and stir in one teaspoon of sugar. Now pour half the contents of the saucer into another, which should then be filled with water. After stirring, pour half of the contents of the second saucer into a third and fill it with water. Repeat this process until you have a row of ten saucers. Now take a fly (having made certain that he is not thirsty) and lower him gently into the most dilute mixture. Then try him in the next and so on up the series until his proboscis is lowered. This is the weakest sugar solution that he can taste.

Now test yourself. If you are the sort of person who does not mind kissing his dog, you can use the same saucers as the fly. Otherwise make up a fresh series. You will be surprised, perhaps chagrined, to discover that the fly is unbelievably more sensitive than you. In fact, a starving fly is ten million times more sensitive.

FIGURE 13-2 "I've lost my appetite for pistachio mousse."

You console yourself with the thought that he may be less versatile, less of a gourmet, than you. Well, this too can be tested. Try him on other sugars; there are any number of sugars; cane sugar, beet sugar, malt sugar, milk sugar, grape sugar. Each is chemically different; each has for you a different sweetness. It is only necessary to determine for each the most dilute solution that will cause the fly to lower his proboscis. Then when the sugars are listed in order of decreasing effectiveness, it turns out that the order is the same for you and the fly: grape sugar, cane sugar, malt sugar, milk sugar, beet sugar. In one respect the fly is less gullible; he is not fooled by saccharine or any other artificial sweeteners.

But, you may argue, I can distinguish many other kinds of tastes. This is only partly correct. You can distinguish many kinds of flavors, but to assist you in this you recruit your nose. Flavor is a mixture of tastes, odors, and textures. With taste alone you are pretty much restricted to sweet, salt, sour, and bitter.

The old adage that one can catch more flies with honey than with vinegar has a sound basis in physiology. Leaving aside for the moment the fact that flies react differently to different odors, the truth remains that flies accept materials that taste sweet to us and reject those that taste salt, sour, or bitter to us. This fact, too, can be demonstrated with the proboscis response, but the only way for a fly to say *no* is to retract his proboscis, and it can be retracted only if it is first extended. Accordingly, one prepares several saucers of sugared water. A pinch of salt is added to one, two pinches to another, three pinches to a third, and so on. As before, the fly is lowered gently into the saucer with the least salt. He responds, as expected, by extending his proboscis. He is then allowed to taste the next dish, and the next, and the next. At one of these dishes he will stubbornly refuse to extend his proboscis. Since this dish contains the same amount of sugar as the rest, one must conclude that it is the salt that is being rejected. The test can be repeated with vinegar, lemon juice, or quinine water. It can even be tried with aspirin, whiskey, bicarbonate of soda, tobacco juice—anything that will dissolve in water. If you wish to be really sophisticated, you can test the relative sensitivity of his legs and mouth by standing him in one solution and allowing his proboscis to come down into a different one. A friend of mine who once wished to study the stomach of the fly and to color it so it could be seen more easily under the microscope hit upon the idea of standing a fly in sugar but arranging for its mouth to come down in dye. As a result the fly's insides were stained beautifully. This is one example of a physiological way to coat a pill.

# PART II

# PERCEPTUAL DEVELOPMENT

# WAS SHE PUSHED
# OR DID SHE FALL?

Part II considers some aspects of the role of experience in the ontogeny of perception. This is a facet of the old "nature-nurture" issue: To what extent is perception genetically determined and to what degree is it modified by individual experience? The wide range of studies included in Part II should not be interpreted by the reader as representing a comprehensive overview of the topic. Rather, it is an attempt to give the student of perception a feeling for the breadth of the issues, the various experimental procedures, and the sorts of variables that experimenters have considered relevant in the area of perceptual learning.

The first article, by Hebb, proposes a distinction between innate and acquired aspects of perception. This theoretical paper is based on data derived from reports of congenitally blind adults who have had their sight restored, and from animal studies in which subjects were raised in restricted sensory environments prior to testing. Hebb distinguishes between figural unity and figural identity. The former, he states, is the ability to segregate a figure from the background and is an innate property of the nervous system. The latter requires that the figure be separated from the background and also be identified as similar to some stimuli and dissimilar to others. Figural identity is thought to depend to a large extent on experience. Hebb emphasizes, however, that perception cannot be considered an exclusive product of either innate or learned factors.

Salapatek and Kessen describe a recent study in which they examined the response of human newborns to a triangle, with particular emphasis on those aspects of the stimulus upon which the infant spent time scanning. This investigation bears directly upon Hebb's theory of how an individual learns to perceive a triangle. However, in relating the data of adults with newly restored vision to the development of vision in infants much caution must be exercised: The adult has already made extensive use of his other senses, and this is totally different from the infant who starts with very little experience in all sense modalities.

The proposal of Piaget [1] that perception in a young child is determined by gestalt principles is explored in the interesting study of

Elkind, Koegler, and Go. They investigated whether stimulus figures made up of identifiable parts would be perceived by children of various ages as wholes or as parts. The results suggest that the question of part-whole perception in children cannot be answered without taking into account the nature of the particular stimulus.

The next two papers present divergent opinions on what is learned during perceptual learning. In Gibson and Gibson's view, perceptual learning involves a differentiation phenomenon, with subjects becoming able to perceive more of the stimulus as they gain experience. That is, perception "consists of responding to variables of physical stimulation not previously responded to." In contrast to this, Postman proposes an association or enrichment theory. He argues that perceptual learning occurs if there is "a change in the nature of responses evoked by a particular configuration or sequence of stimuli." This arises, according to Postman, because discernible memories become associated with various stimuli. These two papers are somewhat difficult for new students of perception, but because of the importance of the issues raised, readers experiencing difficulty are encouraged to focus on the main line of the arguments and skim through the details.

In order to examine the genesis of perceptual phenomena it is necessary to know the perceptual capabilities of young organisms. Several methodological procedures have been used to pursue this goal, and examples of them can be found in the remaining selections of Part II. In general, the experimental techniques can be divided into two broad categories: (1) studies that have involved testing organisms at a very early age, and (2) studies in which organisms have been tested after varying degrees of stimulus deprivation or enrichment. The first category is represented by the two studies of children by Fantz and his colleagues and the one by Kagan. The work of Fantz is an investigation of visual acuity and pattern perception in very young infants and is a clear demonstration that the newborn's visual world is far from a "blooming, buzzing confusion," as was suggested by William James at the beginning of the century. The study by Kagan examines how the perception of infants, as measured by attentional behavior, alters during the first few years. An important aspect of Kagan's research is the finding that stimuli that are somewhat discrepant from established, expected schema have the greatest power to maintain a child's attention. This fact can be related to the adaptation-level theory discussed in Part I, since investigators [2] have found that stimuli that differ slightly from the norm or adaptation level are perceived as being more pleasant than stimuli that are exactly equal to the adaptation level.

The next study is an excerpt from a classic study by Walk and Gibson in which depth perception was examined in a number of species at a very early age. The test situation was the "visual cliff." In the excerpt selected for this book, both young rats and children were observed to be capable of discriminating depth at an early age using only visual cues.

In portions of the monograph not included here, Walk and Gibson found that motion parallax (the fact that if you are moving past various stimuli, near objects apparently move faster than far objects) is a more important cue for depth perception in young animals than the apparent change in texture density that occurs when stimuli are perceived at varying distances.

Besides testing the organism soon after birth, workers have attempted to investigate influences on perception in older subjects by manipulating the experiences of the subjects. One of the many ways in which this can be done is to place subjects in a special set of experimental circumstances—one that restricts the opportunity for stimulus change in one or several sensory modalities. Pritchard, Heron, and Hebb describe an ingenious method of projecting a visual image on the retina, such that the stimulus always impinges upon the same receptor cells. This constant stimulation results in very interesting "disappearances" of images, which are far from being random but are rather determined by an apparent interaction of gestalt principles and previous learning. Another method used in this type of research is the production of a *Ganzfeld,* a perfectly homogeneous stimulation over the entire visual field. The consequences of such stimulation and of introducing a heterogeneous stimulus are described in the study by Cohen.

Zubek and others also investigated stimulus homogeneity, but in this case in the form of sensory isolation. Subjects were kept a week or longer under visual and auditory isolation and then tested in a variety of perceptual-motor tasks. The primary deficit observed was in a visual vigilance task. Little impairment was observed in depth perception, size constancy, auditory discrimination, or reversible figures. In another study, Zubek and others examined intellectual abilities following sensory isolation [8]. Only recent memory was found to be significantly impaired.

While the previous three readings dealt with one form of sensory deprivation, that of restricting stimulus variability, the next five papers are concerned with more direct forms of stimulus deprivation. Perhaps the best known of this type of work are the studies by the Harlows; an overview of their work with monkeys deprived of mother and peer contacts from birth for various periods of time is given in the selection included here. The most striking effect of this sort of deprivation is long-term social maladjustment. There are striking similarities between the work of the Harlows with the rhesus macque monkeys and a study reported by Skeels, who observed human infants raised in environments in which there was a dearth of close social relationships. A summary of Skeels' findings is included in paper 28 so that the comparison can be made by the reader. Although this work may not be considered to deal directly with perception, it has obvious tangential importance, as the type of deprivation described by these authors has a profound influence —both immediate and long-term—on an organism's reaction to stimuli.

For ethical reasons there is a limit to the degree of sensory isolation one can impose on human subjects, so that much of this kind of work must be restricted to animals. An example of this procedure and the results obtained in kittens and primates is given in the paper by Riesen. The development of visually guided behavior is examined in animals deprived of vision during growth. The results indicate that visual-motor coordination involves the learning of complex perceptual relations between stimuli and motor responses. A description of the physiological deterioration that follows such deprivation has been presented by Riesen [5], and the physiological changes following an enriched environment have also been investigated (for example, by Rosenzweig [6]). Both of these articles are somewhat beyond the scope of this book, but interested readers with some background in physiology or physiological psychology will have little difficulty in reading them.

One aspect of perceptual learning and deprivation that has received much attention is the question of the physiological mechanisms underlying visual pattern perception. This line of research obtained its major impetus from the fascinating paper by Hubel and Wiesel [3] in which they demonstrated that in adult cats there is a form of coding in the visual cortex involving the abstraction of certain features of objects. The authors demonstrated that there are cells that respond to specific types of stimuli, such as edges and contours moving in certain directions, and that these cells have quite well-defined receptive fields (the area of the retina to which a neuron is receptive). The study included here is a continuation of that work and investigates whether such coding cells exist in young kittens prior to any visual stimulation. The principal finding is that these complex cells do not seem dependent upon any learning experience. Other work by Hubel and Wiesel [4] has shown that monocular closing in kittens between 4 and 8 weeks of age results in a significant decrease in the number of cells responsive to that eye when it was reopened. If the monocular deprivation lasted for as long as 3 months, very little recovery was observed, even after 5 years. Similar deprivation in adult cats did not result in such effects. However, if both eyes are closed [7] for several months in kittens, responsive cells are found in the cortex, although many of the cells respond abnormally. The authors conclude that deterioration following monocular closing results not only from disuse but depends also on the interaction of the pathways of the two eyes.

An investigation of visual behavior following monocular deprivation in kittens, undertaken by Dews and Wiesel, is included as the next reading in this part. An interesting comparison can be made between the physiological findings of the Hubel-Wiesel selection and the behavioral consequences described in the Dews-Wiesel study. The next selection by Hirsch and Spinelli is a short study demonstrating the effect of selective deprivation on the shape of the receptive field of visual cortical cells. Taken together, the Riesen, Hubel, and Dews, and Hirsch and Spinelli readings provide a good example of the progress in a particular area of research in perceptual learning. A logical sequel to the preceding articles is the selection by Forgus. The author asks whether there is a differential effect of perceptual experience in subsequent learning tasks as a function of the age of a rat. The results suggest that experience early in life is more beneficial than a similar experience occurring when the animals are older. The theoretical implications of this finding are discussed by Forgus.

One form of deprivation used in a number of studies involves the prevention of movement-produced feedback. This is usually done by restricting the subject in a particular situation to passive movements, for instance, being wheeled around in a wheelchair. Held and Hein have shown that a number of perceptual deficits occur in kittens raised in a situation that permitted only passive movement when the environment was well lit. The Hein-Diamond article pursues this topic further by limiting the interaction of visual feedback and self-induced movement to dim-light conditions (scotopic vision) and not allowing such interaction during bright-light conditions (photopic vision). The animals were then tested under photopic conditions for visually guided behavior and were observed to be impaired. This finding, as well as the results of several earlier readings, indicate how varied experience (or deprivation) can affect specific aspects of subsequent perceptual learning.

The final work in Part II examines the effect of visual deprivation on a specific perceptual phenomenon—size constancy. This term refers to the fact that as the distance between a stimulus and an observer changes, the size of the retinal image changes, yet the perceived size of the stimulus does not alter. In the study by Heller, normally raised and dark-raised rats were compared in size discrimination, depth perception, and size constancy. The results suggest that visual deprivation resulted in a loss of size constancy, although it reappeared after 10 days of normal visual exposure.

## REFERENCES

1. J. H. Flavell. *The developmental psychology of Jean Piaget.* Princeton, N.J.: D. Van Nostrand, 1963.
2. R. N. Haber. Discrepancy from adaptation level as a source of affect. *J. exp. Psychol.,* 1958, *56,* 370–375.
3. D. H. Hubel and T. N. Wiesel. Receptive fields, binocular interaction, and functional architecture in the cat's visual cortex. *J. Physiol.,* 1962, *160,* 106–154.
4. D. H. Hubel and T. N. Wiesel. The period of susceptibility to the physiological effects of unilateral eye closure in kittens. *J. Physiol.,* 1970, *206,* 419–436.
5. A. H. Riesen. Sensory deprivation. In E. Stellar and J. M. Sprague (eds.). *Progress in physiological psychology.* New York: Academic Press, 1966. Vol. 1, pp. 117–147.
6. M. R. Rosenzweig. Environmental complexity, cerebral change, and behavior. *Amer. Psychologist,* 1966, *21,* 321–332.

7. T. N. Wiesel and D. H. Hubel. Extent of recovery from the effects of visual deprivation in kittens. *J. Neurophysiol.*, 1965, *28*, 1060–1072.
8. J. P. Zubek, W. Sansom, and A. Prysiazniuk. Intellectual changes during prolonged perceptual isolation (darkness and silence). *Canad. J. Psychol.*, 1960, *14*, 233–243.

# 14

# SUMMATION AND LEARNING IN PERCEPTION

### D. O. Hebb

### DISTINCTION OF PRIMITIVE UNITY FROM OTHER PROPERTIES OF THE PERCEIVED FIGURE

As a preliminary, certain terms must be defined. I want to show that simple figures do not always act as wholes, innately. But it is undoubtedly true that they sometimes do so in one respect—in the figure-ground relationship: So this property of a perceived figure is to be distinguished from others, in which summation and learning are important. Accordingly, the following are distinguished: the conceptions of (1) a primitive, sensorily determined unity, (2) a nonsensory unity, affected by experience, and (3) the identity (also affected by experience), of a perceived figure.

The *primitive unity* of a figure is defined here as referring to that unity and segregation from the background which seems to be a direct product of the pattern of sensory excitation and the inherited characteristics of the nervous system on which it acts.

Rubin [18] elaborated the conception of the figure-ground relationship, in a study of visual perception of patterns with clearly marked boundaries. In order to elucidate the relation of figure to ground (the relation of the perceived object or surface to other objects and surfaces which make up the background) he put particular stress on "ambiguous" figures (Figure 14-1). This is the special case in which either of two parts of a diagram may be seen as figure, each alternating as part of the ground when the other is figure. The principles he established, however, are most fully operative in the unambiguous figure, made up of a homogeneous zone of color surrounded by another color and having a sharply defined boundary—an abrupt transition in brightness from one zone to the other at all points. Such a figure may or may not be regular. It is as well illustrated by a splash of ink or by a silhouette of an animal as by a white circle on a black stimulus card.

An area thus sensorily delimited is seen as *one*, unified and distinct from its surroundings, by any normal person, by the congenitally blind on the first occurrence of vision following operation for cataract [19], by the normal rat [12], and apparently also at first vision by the rat that has been

Source: *Organization of Behavior* by D. O. Hebb. Copyright 1949 by John Wiley & Sons. Reprinted by permission of John Wiley & Sons, Inc.

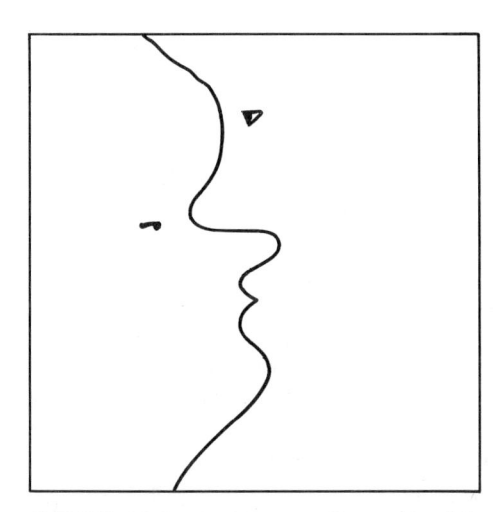

FIGURE 14-1 Ambiguous figure. In this diagram it is possible to see either of two profiles, but only rarely can the two be seen simultaneously; they alternate instead. When a figure appears on the left, the profile of a rather chubby man, the white area on the left appears as a more solid surface and one that is nearer to the observer. This relationship is reversed when a figure appears on the right—the profile of one suffering from gigantic tumors of the neck and of the frontal bone. The theoretical importance of such reversals of figure-ground relationships has been stressed by Gestalt psychologists, though there is considerable difficulty in subsuming the instability under perceptual theory.

reared in darkness [6]. The unity and distinctiveness of such figures from their background, then, is independent of experience, or "primitive."

It is not possible to specify exactly the stimulating conditions which determine the primitive figure-ground organization. I do not exclude as nonprimitive the perception of groupings; nor the segregation of a patch of color which has ill-defined boundaries. There are suggestions in Senden's [19] monograph and in rat behavior that the perception of such units in the visual field may also be independent of experience. Senden's monograph is of the first importance for understanding the perceptual process, but in several respects the evidence is far from clear. The earlier writers whose reports are summarized did not recognize some of the psychological problems to which their observations are relevant. What Senden does show, in the fact that patients always responded to certain objects as wholes and could on occasion detect differences between objects even in spite of nystagmus, is that there is a primitive or innate figure-ground mechanism. He does not make it possible to state its limiting conditions.

## THE NONSENSORY FIGURE

The *nonsensory figure ground organization* is defined as one in which the boundaries of the figure are not fixed by gradients of luminosity in the visual field. It is affected by experience and other nonsensory factors, and is not inevitable in any perception. In contrasting the primitive and the nonsensory figure, however, one need not imply that a perceived figure must be either of one or the other kind. They are rather two extremes, and in most perceptions both sensory and nonsensory factors affect figure-ground organization.

Even commoner in everyday perception is the perceived entity in which both sensory and nonsensory factors cooperate. Here the figural boundary may follow one of a number of possible luminosity gradients in the field, the particular one that is effective being usually determined by experience in one form or another. This is illustrated by Leeper's experiment [14], which demonstrated a lasting control, *by earlier experience,* of the particular perception that is made with Boring's ambiguous figure, "My wife and my mother-in-law" [1]. Another illustration is the process of slow learning to see a configuration in a particular way, as in the gradual decrease of the difficulty a novice has in following the boundaries of a thalamic nucleus that are obvious to the expert.

There is reason to believe that the rat, as well as man, finds some figure-ground relations obvious and inescapable, and detects others only after prolonged experience. That is, the distinction of primitive and nonsensory figures applies also to the rodent's perception. Lashley [12, pp. 156, 185] points out that success in discrimination and generalization evidently depends on the rat's finding a differentiating characteristic between two figures, or one that is common to a pattern already known and the new one which is presented in the testing situation. It is equally clear that the distinctive part of the test pattern is not obvious to the rat at once. This part, whatever it is, is what determines the response and becomes the true figure (as contrasted with what the experimenter meant to be the figure), the rest merging into ground.

In general, Gestalt writers on the organization of the figure have been concerned to show that it cannot be reduced to experience and learning, and have thus selected cases for discussion in which sensory dynamics alone is enough to produce an effective figure-ground organization. They have, that is, concentrated attention on the primitive figure, and they give the impression that the spontaneity of its organization is a property of any figure. True, one can find many passages in the literature on gestalten that refer to figures not sensorily delimited, but no stress on the fact that this implies some role of learning in the delimitation.

Köhler [9], for example, has written: "Since 'real form' presupposes a segregated whole, the existence of 'form' depends upon factors *of stimulation* similar to those upon which the segregation and organization of wholes depend. Again, definite relations in the total constellation *of retinal stimuli* are found to be decisive for the existence of real form" (p. 202; my italics draw attention to the stress put on sensory factors). Again, after referring to Gottschaldt's experiments, Köhler says: "After these results, whoever defends the automatic influence of past experience upon our seeing definite forms, will have incumbent upon him the task of supporting his theory by other experiments. *If such an influence exists, it must be restricted to rather special cases*" (p. 208; italics mine).

Attention is drawn to this aspect of Gestalt theory because it helps one to define the point at which one can diverge from the theory without failing to recognize the great contribution it has made to modern psychology, which has been shaped to a great extent by the impact of Gestalt ideas on behaviorism. There are few psychologists who would not own a debt of this kind to *Gestalttheorie,* and few who do not also feel the need of qualifying the theory in some way, though it is not easy to see just how this is to be done without losing the values that have been obtained with its help.

In the pages from which the passage above is taken, Professor Köhler, I believe, provides the necessary clue. His argument appears to depend on a complete antithesis of experience and innate sensory dynamics, and it is this antithesis that we may avoid. The question that is asked by Köhler is whether sensory organization is wholly innate, or wholly experiential.[1] If these are the only two alternatives, the argument is unanswerable. Köhler and Koffka and Lashley have unquestionably slain the dragon of pure learning theory, in the field of perception, and no one today would argue that perceptual organization is wholly acquired; there is some innate organization. But this of course does not show that the organization is entirely innate. There is always a possibility that perception has a partly innate, partly learned organization; and that besides the figure that has a primitive unity there are nonsensory figures in which experience has an important role.

I propose, then, that Gestalt theory made an essential contribution when it showed that there are innate factors in perception, but that it has tended to carry the argument too far in denying that learning and experience have any important role in the perception of simple configurations (apart, of course, from learning the *meaning* of the configurations). This, as we have seen, has led to emphasis on a dominant role of sensory dy-

---

[1] In the monograph of Köhler and Wallach [10, pp. 316, 323] there are also passages that seem not intelligible unless one is thinking in terms of such an extreme dichotomy between completely organized sensory processes (innately) and completely unorganized ones. This does not do justice, either to current learning theory, or to the effectiveness of the earlier Gestalt arguments in favor of an innate sensory organization.

namics; important as sensory processes are, however, they do not completely dominate either behavior or perception.

Furthermore, Gestalt emphasis on the primitive figure, which has a marked stability, obscures the fact that in ordinary perception any figure-ground relationship is a highly unstable one, with a practically constant fluctuation from one organization to another. Even when one perceives the compact, clearly delimited figure which is such that any observer at once sees it, one finds that the stability of the figure-ground relation is not great; or, better, that its stability consists of a continual *recurrence*, instead of a constancy, of the figure. It is notorious that attention wanders, and this is another way of saying that in perception any figure is unstable; one looks at this part of the configuration and that, and notices its corners or smooth contour, in the intervals between seeing the figure as a whole. In ordinary perception, moreover, the instability is far greater [2, 16].

An adequate account of perception cannot be given in terms of a figure-ground organization that has any great duration in time, even when gaze is fixated at a single point in a configuration. The fluctuations of attention which occur point directly to a fundamental importance, in any perception, of nonsensory factors. This of course has already been demonstrated for complex indeterminate figures by Carmichael, Hogan, and Walter [3] and by Zangwill [23]; I propose that the same factors must be taken into account in the perception of square or circle as well.

## IDENTITY IN PERCEPTION

*Identity* is defined here as referring to the properties of association inherent in a perception. The reference has two aspects: first, a figure is perceived as having identity when it is seen immediately as similar to some figures and dissimilar to others—that is, when it falls at once into certain categories and not into others. This similarity can be summed up as spontaneous association, since it may occur on the first exposure to the stimulus object. Secondly, the object that is perceived as having identity is capable of being associated readily with other objects or with some action, whereas the one that does not have identity is recalled with great difficulty or not at all, and is not recognized or named easily. Identity of course is a matter of degree and, as I shall try to show, depends on a considerable degree of experience; it is not innately given.

Thorndike [21, p. 87] has presented an approach to this conception, using the term identifiability, and has proposed that identifiability promotes the formation of associations. If one carries the analysis a little further, it appears that the proposition is circular. Identifiability is not merely a perceptible difference of one figure from another when the two are side by side, but implies a rememberable difference—identifiability is clearly, in the instances Thorndike gives, recognizability; and recognition is one form of association. Thus Thorndike's proposition is that associability affects the occurrence of associations.

The real point at which he is driving seems to be that there are genuine differences of associability in different patterns. Also, more is involved in these differences than the number of trials necessary to establish recognition; there are also the spontaneous associations referred to in speaking of similarity. Recognizability goes with selective similarity, or generalization: the figure that is readily remembered is also perceived as belonging to a particular class of figures, and remembered so.

An irregular mass of color or a pattern of intersecting lines drawn at random has some coherence and unity, but one such figure is not readily recognized and distinguished from others when it is seen a second time, and generalization (or similarity) is not selective among a number of such stimuli. There is not a total lack of distinctiveness and of generalization, however. Two of Thorndike's figures which lack identity are not indistinguishable when seen together; and mistaking one figure for another can be called generalization. Lashley and Wade [13] distinguish between the "so-called generalization" which means only a failure to observe differences and the generalization which involves perception of both similarities and differences. The amorphous figure, lacking in identity, is generalized in the first sense only.

A further illustration of these points is found in the development of identity in the perception of chimpanzee faces by one who has seen no chimpanzees before. Two animals seen side by side are obviously different in details, but the inexperienced observer is not able easily to remember one selectively. Also, all chimpanzees at this stage look alike; the "so-called generalization" occurs. With experience the perception of identity increases. Similarity is still perceived between animals, and confusion between some animals is still possible; but there is a marked change in the perception, as shown in a much more selective similarity of one animal to others, and in the radical increase of the observer's capacity to associate even a new chimpanzee with a specific name. Thus identity is a matter of degree: readiness of recognition, and the extent to which generalization is selective.

This discussion has been meant to establish the conception of identity as an important property of perception which should be kept carefully distinct from the unity of the perceived figure (as well as from its meaning). Unity may be innately determined, an immediate property of sensory dynamics, whereas identity is dependent on a prolonged experience. Because these two things have not been separated in the past, it has appeared that perceptual organization is innate. Some aspects of the organization *are* present, apparently, at the first experience; but others are not.

## INDEPENDENCE OF UNITY AND IDENTITY IN SIMPLE FIGURES

The examples of the preceding section dealt with complex perceptions. I wish next to review the evidence that shows that unity and identity have separate determinants even in quite simple perceptions. Seeing a circle as a single coherent object is not the same as seeing it as a distinctive object, selectively recognizable.

First, the evidence for man. It has already been said that the figure-ground segregation is good at the initial occurrence of human vision, as shown by Senden's reports [19], at the very time when perception of identity appears to be practically nil. Unity then can be perceived without identity. Investigators (of vision following operation for congenital cataract) are unanimous in reporting that the perception of a square, circle, or triangle, or of sphere or cube, is very poor. To see one of these as a whole object, with distinctive characteristics immediately evident, is not possible for a long period. The most intelligent and best-motivated patient has to seek corners painstakingly even to distinguish a triangle from a circle. The newly seeing patient can frequently find a difference between two such figures shown together, just as the normal adult can readily detect differences between two of Thorndike's figures lacking identifiability, but the differences are not remembered. There is for weeks a practically zero capacity to learn names for such figures, even when tactual recognition is prompt and complete.

Another facet of the same lack of capacity is the failure to generalize as normal persons do. When the patient first gets to the point of being able to name a simple object promptly, recognition is completely destroyed if the object is slightly changed or put into a new setting. The patient who had learned to name a ring showed no recognition of a slightly different ring; having learned to name a square, made of white cardboard, could not name it when its color was changed to yellow by turning the cardboard over; and so on. These reports consistently indicate that the perceived whole at first vision is *simultaneously unified and amorphous*. There is not a single instance given in which the congenitally blind after operation had trouble in learning color names; but a great number in which the perception of identity in a simple figure was poor indeed [19, pp. 135–141].

A second evidence comes from species differences in the perception of identity. For coherent patterns and simple groupings the figure-ground relationship appears to be the same from rat to man, so the significant differences of perceptual generalization (one aspect of identity) argue strongly that figural unity and identity have separate bases. (a) The discrimination of simple geometrical figures by man and chimpanzee is unaffected by reversal of brightness relations between figure and ground [5]; a white triangle on a black ground is generalized by these anthropoids to include a black triangle on a white ground. For the rat, such a reversal completely disrupts discrimination, and no amount of training with the white triangle alone will produce recognition of a black one. There is some uncertainty about the phylogenetic level at which the capacity for this generalization appears [12, p. 144; 15; 20], but between the rat, and chimpanzee or man, the difference in this respect seems complete (although for simple figures only; human perception of more complex figures in reversed brightness is definitely defective, as in recognition of photographic negatives). (b) The perception of a triangle or square by the rat is not generalized, without specific training, to include a similar rotated figure (Fields, 1932) but is generalized so by chimpanzee and by 2-year-old children, although a corresponding head rotation also occurs [5]. (c) Perception of a triangle is not generalized either by rat or chimpanzee to include a triangle made up of small circles, but the generalization is made by 2-year-old children [5, 12].

Thus the perception of identity is different in different mammals; the perception of primitive unity is practically the same.

Further evidence of the independence of unity and identity is found in the peculiar "equivalences" or generalizations often observed in rat behavior, and in the anomalies to be found in the relative difficulty with which the rat learns to discriminate between certain patterns. Two discriminations that are equally easy, from the human point of view, present very unequal difficulty for the rat. For normal man a square and a circle are no less obviously distinct than erect and inverted triangles; yet the rat readily learns to discriminate between the triangles and consistently has trouble with circle versus square [12, pp. 155, 156]. Some animals that have learned other patterns (thus showing that their acuity is sufficient for the task) show no sign of discriminating circle and square at all. A five-pointed star and an H are for man clearly, inevitably distinct, while the rat distinguishes them with difficulty and no faster learning occurs than with quite irregular figures [12, p. 157]. Such facts mean a great difference of rat from man in perceiving the identity of simple, regular figures.

The same is evident in the patterns which may be "equivalent" for individual rats, and in some failures of equivalence. One animal may transfer his response from an erect triangle (versus an inverted one) to a single horizontal line low on the stimulus card (versus another higher on the card), while another animal fails to discriminate the complete triangles with which he was trained, when a slight change is made of their positions on the respective stimulus cards. It is very doubtful in such cases that the rat has perceived the pattern as a distinctive whole, and it seems that a response is frequently determined by only a part of a figure as simple as a triangle.

Lashley [12, p. 182] has recognized this, but interpreted it by comparing the rat to a ski-jumper who does not pay attention in his jump to nonessentials such as the shape of a spectator's hat. The general interpretation was made that there is little significant difference in the perception of simple figures by rat and man, but this conclusion is not supported by the evidence.

When identity is distinguished from unity, we find great species differences in the perception of identity and not in what is seen as a primitive unity. The analogy between the rat's perceiving all the detail of a triangle in the jumping apparatus, and the ski-jumper's perception of a hat, is valid—except that it sets the human subject a much more difficult task. It is inconceivable that a ski-jumper would not perceive a large triangle as such, fully structured, if it lay close to and marked the point of safe landing in an otherwise plain field, as it does for the rat in the jumping apparatus. The rat, however, may respond selectively to only the part of the figure which lies nearest the point to which he jumps, although his field of vision is wide and although (as Lashley has demonstrated) he perceives much more than he has to in making a discrimination.

These considerations are the more convincing because the evidence of the rat's frequent failure to see the triangle as a distinctive whole figure coincides with Senden's description of the congenitally blind after acquiring vision—the normally reared rat, and a man seeing for the first time, both have precisely the same kind of difficulty.

It is reasonable to conclude that the perception of identity (as defined) follows the same principles in rat and man but is much more highly developed in normal man. Since there is no evidence of any clear difference of the primitive figure-ground organization perceived by these two species, but strong suggestions that it is the same for both, the evidence is consistent with the idea that identity and figural unity have separate physiological bases. They are, that is, psychologically independent. This makes it possible to suppose that additive processes may occur in the development of identity without denying that the figure has a primitive unity.

## LEARNING TO PERCEIVE SIMPLE FIGURES

The facts already adduced in the last section have indicated a role of learning in the perception of triangle or square as distinctive wholes. The idea that one has to learn to see a triangle must sound extremely improbable, and so I shall now present the evidence to this effect more systematically.

We have seen that the perceptions of the congenitally blind after operation are almost completely lacking in identity. Senden [19, pp. 155–157] reports cases in which there was an immediate perception of differences in two figures seen together, but also one definite instance in which even this was not possible. Thus the patient sometimes saw differences between a sphere and cube, sometimes not (p. 90). Color has been found to dominate form persistently in the first vision of these patients.

Eleven months after operation the color names learned by a patient in hospital were retained, but the little that had been learned of form was forgotten (p. 135). An egg, potato, and cube of sugar were seen by a patient repeatedly, until naming was prompt, but then were not recognized when put into colored light; the cube of sugar was well named when it was seen on the table or in the investigator's hand but not recognized when suspended by a thread with a change of background (p. 138).

Such patients, when learning has proceeded far enough, manifest the characteristic generalizations of the normal person, so the initial difficulties are not to be put down to structural defects of the sensory apparatus [19, pp. 173–175].

Riesen [17] has fully confirmed the conclusion that ordinary visual perception in higher mammals presupposes a long learning period. His observations concerning the almost complete visual incapacity of chimpanzees reared in darkness, and the slowness of learning, are of the greatest importance. They show that Senden's similar results with man are not due to some inadequacy of the clinical tests, not peculiarly human.

The course of perceptual learning in man is gradual, proceeding from a dominance of color, through a period of separate attention to each part of a figure, to a gradually arrived at identification of the whole as a whole: an apparently simultaneous instead of a serial apprehension. A patient was trained to discriminate square from triangle over a period of 13 days and had learned so little in this time "that he could not report their form without counting corners one after another.... And yet it seems that the recognition process was beginning already to be automatic, so that some day the judgment 'square' would be given with simple vision, which would then easily lead to the belief that form was always simultaneously given" [19, p. 160]. The shortest time in which a patient approximated to normal perception, even when learning was confined to a small number of objects, seems to have been about a month.

It is possible then that the normal human infant goes through the same process, and that we are able to see a square as such in a single glance only as the result of complex learning. The notion seems unlikely, because of the utter simplicity of such a perception to the normal adult. But no such argument can be valid, since Lashley [11] has shown that subjective simplicity and immediacy may be very deceptive as an index of physiological simplicity. There are moreover residual traces of learning in normal perception, and hints of its complexity.

Gellerman [5] reports that chimpanzees and 2-year-old children recognized a triangle that had been rotated through 120° from the training position, but (in the one protocol that is given) responded selectively only *after* a head rotation; and persistent head rotation continued in the later discriminations. Older human subjects do not need to make the same receptor adjustment to recognize the figure in two positions, and so this generalization may be a learned capacity, simple as it seems to us.

Consider also the following evidence, which is suggestive though perhaps not conclusive. When a simple figure such as square, circle, or triangle, subtending a retinal angle of from 2° to 10°, is fixated at one point, it tends in a second or so to become almost amorphous except near the point of fixation. The effect is not due to fatigue alone, nor to poor acuity outside the macular zone: since (1) a single straight line does not suffer nearly as much, (2) shifting fixation back and forth between two corners of a triangle does not restore the clarity with which the third is seen, and (3) an 8° circle drawn with a line 2 mm wide, and a 4° circle drawn with a line 1 mm wide, seem to give approximately the same effect.

The factors involved are evidently complicated; it will be found, for example, that with a large figure merely *imagining* eye movements (of following the contours) will restore definition of the figure. Also, these "imaginary" eye movements, or subliminal activations of the motor system, occur more frequently and are less easy to control in looking at a smaller than at a larger figure, and it is hard to be sure that the size of the figure is unimportant. But this at least seems definite, that a stable, clear, and effective perception of circle or square is more possible with eye movement than without. Once the question is asked, anyone can verify for himself the falsity of the implicit assumption (usually made in the study of perception) that the figure acts always as one, without a reinforcing perception of its parts as distinct from the whole.

My point is not that eye movements are essential to perception by a sophisticated observer (nor, in the following paragraph, that they are completely necessary for an image); but that the perception is definitely clearer, more effective, with them than without. This is really an evident fact. It is to be interpreted in the light of all evidence, cited above, showing that the perception of square or circle is slowly learned *and depends originally on multiple visual fixations.*

Directly in line with such phenomenological observations are the following introspections. I find it very difficult to have a clear image of a triangle, square, or circle without imagining or actually making a series of eye movements. Several others, asked to make observation on this point, have reported the same thing. It is hard or impossible, that is, to have a clear image of a triangle as fixated at one point. Eye movements definitely improve the image. They do not take the form, necessarily, of following the figure's contours, but are apt to jump from point to point, perhaps three to four points in all. Thus the distinctiveness of the image is not merely in the eye movement pattern, for approximately the same series of eye movements may contribute to a good image either of circle or square. Activation of the motor system, overt or implicit (even possibly within the cerebrum alone, with no activity of the final common paths), *contributes essentially to the development of visual integration without being sufficient to it.* As I have said, such evidence is hard to evaluate, but it points to the same conclusion as Senden's evidence, already cited, and is supported by it.

Clark and Lashley [4] have confirmed the observations of Kennard and Ectors [8] and Kennard [7] and have provided what appears to be an independent confirmation of the argument above. Kennard found a one-sided loss of vision by monkeys on extirpation of the opposite frontal eyefield, a cortical motor area for head-and-eye movement. Clark and Lashley have demonstrated this phenomenon convincingly, with an adequate method of testing. The most significant and striking observation was startle by the monkey when an object was passed from the blind side into the seeing side, at the moment of passing the midline. One might have argued that the animal could "see" an object in his apparently hemianopic field but was not able to move his eyes toward it. The observation referred to rules that interpretation out, and other observations showed that the hemianopia is a genuine failure to see (though it is transient, disappearing in a week or two).

## CONCLUSIONS

Animal experiments and the human clinical data alike indicate that the perception of simple diagrams as distinctive wholes is not immediately given but slowly acquired through learning. Introspective observations which would not carry much weight in themselves appear to agree fully with other evidence, showing vestiges of a summative process involved in perceiving the identity of circle or triangle; although such a figure is seen by the adult clearly and is effectively discriminated at a single glance, there are still traces left of complexities such as the learning process described by Senden would produce, which for normal persons must have occurred in early infancy and which makes the unified perception possible.

The subjective experience of an irreducible simplicity in the perception of square or circle may then be fully analogous to the illusion of the image of the letter-square [22, p. 42], where the subject thinks he has an actual image of the square but can be shown not to have.[2] Although the

---

[2] The experiment is as follows. The subject is shown a diagram such as

```
x e a q
r l i s
o f z g
d y u p
```

and studies it until he has, apparently, an image of the whole square and can "look at" it and read the letters off, one by one. If he really has such an image, it will not matter in what direction he is asked to "read." Actually, it is found that the subject cannot reproduce the letters as fast from right to left as from left to right, or promptly give the four letters, p, z, l, x, that make up the diagonal from lower right to upper left. So what seems a simple, immediately given image of the whole is actually a serial reconstruction of parts of the figure. An image of triangle or square is simpler, longer practiced, but may be fundamentally the same. The perception of such figures, also, may involve a temporal sequence.

perception of identity is good at a glance, it is improved by several glances at different parts of the figure. This process of successive part reinforcement, as an *aid* to perception, exists at the same time as an essential unity of the whole; and theory must provide for the additive process, with its motor elements, as well as for the primitive unity.

This argument is not in any way a return to the old idea that sensory integration occurs solely through motor activity, or that the distinctiveness of a perception is solely or mainly due to distinctive eye movement. We know that this is not true. But there are three theoretical possibilities, not two: (1) perceptual integration is wholly the result of motor activity; (2) it is wholly independent of motor activity; and (3) the motor activity is important but not all-important—the position that is taken here.

Grant fully that visual integration cannot be reduced to a synthesis of unrelated elements through effector activity, and the question remains, how much significance the motor factor may still have. Receptor adjustment (head-and-eye movement) is the most prominent feature of visual perception whether in rat, chimpanzee, or man—*except* in long-practiced habits. The assumption has been tacitly made that the adjustments are unimportant for theory (once it was shown that they were not the whole answer). The fact of eye movement has been treated only as a further (negative) evidence that the locus of excitation in the retina is unimportant, since the changing retinal projection does not disturb perception. But obviously another point of view is possible. The thesis of this chapter is that eye movements in perception are not adventitious. They contribute, constantly and essentially, to perceptual integration, even though they are not the whole origin of it.

## REFERENCES

1. E. G. Boring. A new ambiguous figure. *Amer. J. Psychol.*, 1930, *42*, 444–445.
2. E. G. Boring. *The physical dimensions of consciousness.* New York: Century, 1933.
3. L. Carmichael, H. P. Hogan, and A. A. Walter. An experimental study of the effect of language on the reproduction of visually perceived form. *J. exp. Psychol.*, 1932, *15*, 73–86.
4. G. Clark and K. S. Lashley. Visual disturbances following frontal ablations in the monkey. *Anat. Rec.*, 1947, *97*, 326.
5. L. W. Gellerman. Form discrimination in chimpanzees and two-year-old children: I. Form (triangularity) per se. *J. genet. Psychol.*, 1933, *42*, 3–27.
6. D. O. Hebb. The innate organization of visual activity: I. Perception of figures by rats reared in total darkness. *J. genet. Psychol.*, 1937, *51*, 101–126.
7. M. A. Kennard. Alterations in response to visual stimuli following lesions of frontal lobe in monkeys. *Arch. Neurol. Psychiat.*, 1939, *41*, 1153–1165.
8. M. A. Kennard and L. Ectors. Forced circling in monkeys following lesions of the frontal lobes. *J. Neurophysiol.*, 1938, *1*, 45–54.

9. W. Köhler. *Gestalt Psychology*. New York: Liveright, 1929.
10. W. Köhler and H. Wallach. Figural after-effects: An investigation of visual processes. *Proc. Amer. phil. Soc.*, 1944, *88*, 269–357.
11. K. S. Lashley. Functional determinants of cerebral localization. *Arch. Neurol. Psychiat.*, 1937, *38*, 371–387.
12. K. S. Lashley. The mechanism of vision: XV. Preliminary studies of the rat's capacity for detail vision. *J. gen. Psychol.*, 1938, *18*, 123–193.
13. K. S. Lashley and M. Wade. The Pavlovian theory of generalization. *Psychol. Rev.*, 1946, *53*, 72–87.
14. R. W. Leeper. A study of a neglected portion of the field of learning—the development of sensory organization. *J. genet. Psychol.*, 1935, *46*, 41–75.
15. C. C. Neet. Visual pattern discrimination in the *Macacus rhesus* monkey. *J. genet. Psychol.*, 1933, *43*, 163–196.
16. W. B. Pillsbury. "Fluctuations of attention" and the refractory period. *J. Phil. Psychol. Sci. Meth.*, 1913, *10*, 181–185.
17. A. H. Riesen. The development of visual perception in man and chimpanzee. *Science*, 1947, *106*, 107–108.
18. E. Rubin. *Visuall wahrgenommene Figuren: Studien in psychologischer Analyse*. Teil 1. Berlin: Gyldendalske Boghandel, 1921.
19. M. V. Senden. *Raum- und Gestaltauffassung bei operierten Blindgeborenen vor und nach der Operation*. Leipzig: Barth, 1932.
20. K. U. Smith. Visual discrimination in the cat: III. The relative effect of paired and unpaired stimuli in the discriminative behavior of the cat. *J. genet. Psychol.*, 1936, *48*, 29–57.
21. E. L. Thorndike. *Human learning*. New York: Century, 1931.
22. R. S. Woodworth. *Experimental psychology*. New York: Holt, 1938.
23. O. L. Zangwill. A study of the significance of attitude in recognition. *Brit. J. Psychol.*, 1937, *28*, 12–17.

# 15

# VISUAL SCANNING OF TRIANGLES BY THE HUMAN NEWBORN

Philip Salapatek
William Kessen

*Ten human newborns were shown a homogeneous black visual field and ten newborns were shown a large black triangle on a white field. Ocular orientation to within approximately ±5° of visual angle was measured by scoring infrared photographs of corneal reflections. The infants showed much less dispersion of scanning in the presence of the triangle than in the presence of the homogeneous field. Moreover, ocular orientations were directed toward a vertex of the presented triangle. The results were related to Hebb's theory of perceptual development, to analyzer theories of discrimination, and to studies of complexity and preference in the human newborn.*

It is only through a detailed study of ocular responses in the newborn child that critical questions about the nature of perceptual development can be resolved. Recent studies (for example [5, 6, 9, 10]) have indicated that the human infant will usually look longer at certain visual patterns than at others during the first few days of life. These findings have generally been explained as representing a preference for differing levels of stimulus complexity; unfortunately, different experimenters have found that preference is greatest for low complexity, for moderate complexity, and for high complexity. Variation in empirical outcome may be accounted for in part by variation from study to study in the stimulus dimensions that were under investigation. Of more consequence, however, is the difficulty in determining with the procedures

Source: *Journal of Experimental Child Psychology*, 1966, 3, 155–167. Copyright 1966 by Academic Press.

Note: The research reported in this paper was supported in part by USPHS research grant HD-0890 (formerly MH-1787). The writers are deeply indebted to Marshall M. Haith and Adrienne Salapatek and to the nursing staff of the Maternity Service of Grace-New Haven Community Hospital.

used in these studies whether or not the infant was responding to the dimension defined by the experimenter. For example, in studies of preference for visual forms, the child may have been responding to the preferred figure as a whole or only to certain parts of it; that is, the preferred figure may have more of what the infant wants to look at or the preferred figure may have something uniquely attractive which the less well preferred figure does not have. In addition, although the finding of differential orientation in a paired-comparison design indicates a discrimination of the preferred figure from its surround, lack of preference does not necessarily indicate a lack of discrimination [13]. This paper describes a procedure which permits more detailed specification of the ocular orientation of human infants than has been available heretofore with dichotomous left-right or yes-no judgments of orientation. A measure of looking accurate to within a few degrees of visual angle will illuminate the processes that underlie preference and discrimination of form in the human newborn.

A large solid black triangle in the center of a white field was shown to human newborns in the present study. It was expected that a central stimulus would capture the infant's regard and that a solid figure on a contrasting field would not demand fine acuity. Further, if the contours of a figure influence ocular orientation, orientations toward the contours would be more readily discernible if the figure was large, that is, if the contours were at some distance from the center of the field. Of the many figures that might have been selected for initial study, the triangle was chosen because it has received detailed consideration in theoretical treatments of perception in the newborn [8].

## METHOD

### Subjects

Subjects for the experiment were twenty awake, alert newborn infants under 8 days of age from the nursery of the Grace-New Haven Community Hospital. The subjects were randomly selected from the babies available and awake in the nursery at the time of observation. Records obtained from forty-nine other babies could not be used either because the infants fell asleep during the observation or because the film was badly processed and unscorable. Observations on the ten babies in the experimental group were completed before observations on the ten babies in the control group were begun. The experimental group was made up of five males and five females ranging in age from 23 to 177 hr with a mean age of 68.1 hr. The control group was made up of six males and four females ranging in age from 23 to 137 hr with a mean age of 77.6 hr.

## Apparatus and Procedure

All subjects were observed approximately 20 min before their regular feeding at 9:30 a.m. or their regular feeding at 5:30 p.m. in a quiet room under moderate illumination. Each subject was brought into the observation room by a nurse, placed in a head-restraining cradle [9], and given a pacifier. The experimental group was shown a solid black equilateral triangle 8 in. on each side. The triangle was painted on wire window screen and was centered in a circular white background of aluminum 23 in. in diameter. The stimulus was approximately 9 in. above the infant's eyes. From the baby's side, the wire-screen triangle appeared solid in color. However, enough light passed through the screen to permit photography of the eyes by a camera directly behind the wire screen. Figure 15-1 shows a schematic drawing of the apparatus. Infrared marker

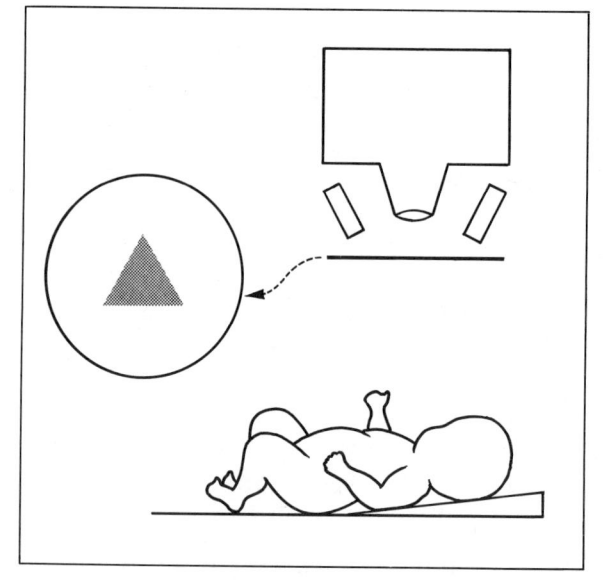

FIGURE 15-1 Schematic representation of the apparatus used in determining ocular orientation.

lights, invisible to adult observers from the position of the baby's eyes, were placed behind the stimulus panel at each vertex of the triangle. The marker lights were Bausch and Lomb Nicholas illuminators fitted with Kodak Wratten 87C filters. An Automax Model G-2 35-mm variable-speed camera, also invisible to adult observers from the position of the baby's eyes, was mounted behind the stimulus panel in the exact center of the wire screening that formed the triangle. The camera was loaded with Kodak high-speed infrared-sensitive film (HIR 417). Another Bausch and Lomb illuminator, fitted with a Wratten 87C filter in which a pinhole was drilled, was mounted approximately 2 in. to the temporal side and out of line with subject's eyes. The diffuse red and infrared illumination from this illuminator heightened the contrast shown on the film between subject's iris and pupil. One of the baby's eyes was centered under the camera and was photographed through a Pentax 105-mm Takumar lens fitted with three extension rings. Usually the lens was opened to an f-stop of 2.8. The field photographed in this way was approximately 1½ × 1½ in., and the depth of field was less than 1 in. Therefore, subject's eye had to be exactly centered, and at a fixed distance from the stimulus or the record of ocular orientation was lost. Once each second during each observation a picture of the infant's centered eye was taken through the wire screen stimulus; in nineteen cases, the right eye was photographed. The noise of the solenoid in the camera which advanced the shutter permitted the experimenter to count the number of pictures taken. At least 100 pictures of the infant's open eye were taken with the triangle in an upright position. The camera was then stopped, the triangle was rotated 180°, and at least 100 pictures were taken of the infant's open eye with the triangle inverted. Order of rotation of triangle was balanced across subjects. If the subject fell asleep during an observation, the experimenter stopped the camera and tried to wake the subject up. If he was successful, a note was made of the interruption in the record and the observation continued until 100 pictures had been taken of the baby's open eye. The procedure did not produce an equal number of pictures for all subjects or a constant duration of observation; the observation continued until at least 100 frames of film had been taken of each rotation of the triangle with the baby's eye open.

The control group was treated just like the experimental group with these exceptions. Instead of being shown a black triangle on a white field, the control group was shown a homogeneous circular black field 21 in. in diameter. The infrared marker lights remained mounted behind the stimulus panel at the vertices of a hypothetical equilateral triangle, 8 in. to a side. After at least 100 pictures had been taken of the baby's open eye (at the standard rate of one frame per second) with the marker lights in one rotation, the camera was stopped, the baby's eye was covered for a second or two, and the marker lights were rotated 180°. Then, at least 100 pictures were taken of its open eye with the marker lights in the second rotation.

## RESULTS

### Scoring

Ocular orientation was determined by calculating the deviation of the corneal reflections of the infrared marker lights from the center of the subject's pupil. The distance from a given marker light to the center of the pupil changes as the baby looks at different parts of the field. Moreover, this measure of ocular orientation is not affected by head movement of up to ½ in. from central visual axis [1]. Each 35-mm film frame was scored either on a Vanguard Motion Analyzer or on a semiautomatic scoring device invented by Haith [7]. Both of these instruments provide rectilinear coordinates for the center of the pupil and for a single preselected marker light. The relative position of the center of the pupil was obtained for each film frame by subtracting the marker light coordinates for a particular frame from the pupil-center coordinates for the same frame. The first 100 successive positions of pupil orientation obtained in this way were fed to an EAI Dataplotter which plotted the points with a reference marker light as origin and joined them to provide a record of visual scanning. Therefore, all records of visual scanning were based on exactly 100 positions of pupil orientation.

Scoring with both instruments yielded inter- and intrascorer reliability coefficients ($r$) of over +0.90. Both instruments were also calibrated to detect a change in ocular orientation of less than 1 in. on the stimulus panel (approximately 5° of visual angle). Ocular orientation could be measured as far as 45° from the center of the stimulus panel.

## Patterns of Ocular Orientation

Twenty records of ocular orientation for the ten babies in the control group—those who were shown a homogeneous black field—are presented in Figure 15-2. The triangle shown in each record is a hypothetical one, 8 in. on each side, formed by joining the positions of the infrared marker lights behind the field; the triangle is drawn in to permit easy comparison with records of ocular orientation in experimental subjects. Ocular orientations among control subjects were generally widely distributed through the field; there was no evidence that the infrared marker lights systematically influenced the orientation of control subjects. Twenty records of ocular orientation for the ten babies in the experimental group —those who were shown a black equilateral triangle in a white field—are presented in Figure 15-3. The inner triangle in each record is again a hypothetical one drawn to indicate the positions of the invisible infrared marker lights; the outer triangle, 8 in. on each side, represents the stimulus actually shown to the infants. As can be seen, when subjects were presented with a solid black triangle on a white field, their ocular orientation tended to cluster, and more, tended to cluster near the vertices of the triangle. Relatively few orientations were directed toward the center of the triangle. It seems clear, from a comparison of Figures 15-2 and 15-3 that the ocular orientation of the human newborn is to some degree controlled by visual form.

Some experimental records show a clustering of orientations at a slight distance from a vertex. This pattern of orientation may be accounted for by the fact that the babies had both eyes open, but only one eye was photographed. It is plausible to suspect that occasionally the unphotographed eye was "on target" and the photographed eye slightly misaligned [2, 9, 14, 16].

### Analysis of Preference for Sides and Vertices

In order to assess more precisely the overall influence of contour on ocular orientation and the differential influence on orientation of angles (vertices) and linear contours (sides), the real triangles on the experimental records and the hypothetical but metrically equivalent triangles on the control records were partitioned into linear and angular components. An orientation was scored as on contour if it fell within 1 in. of a side of the triangle or within 1½ in. of a vertex. Neither order nor rotation of the stimulus field (triangle base down or base up) significantly influenced on-contour score; therefore, all results are presented with records combined from the two presentations of the stimulus field for each subject.

Each baby was given an overall on-contour score. Significantly more experimental subjects scored above the median on this measure than did control subjects ($p < 0.025$, Fisher's exact test). As inspection of Figures 15-2 and 15-3 indicates, this overall effect is largely an expression of the experimental group's orientation toward the vertices of the triangle. Each baby was scored on the ratio of the number of orientations within 1½ in. of a vertex to the total number of orientations remaining on his record after the number of orientations on contour other than the vertices had been subtracted out. This measure is a ratio of orientations on vertex to orientations altogether off contour. A significantly greater number of experimental subjects fell above the median on this measure than did control subjects ($p < 0.025$, Fisher's exact test). A similar test of the ratio of orientations within 1 in. of linear contours of the triangle to orientations altogether off contour provided no significant difference between experimental and control groups. The division of contour for scoring purposes into angular components (vertices) and linear components (sides) gave considerably greater total area for linear components. Of course, the linear components (sides) were also nearer the center of the visual field than were the vertices and, presumably, more easily accessible to ocular orientation. In spite of these possible biases in favor of linear components of the figures, it was the vertices and not the sides that significantly attracted ocular orientation in the experimental group. Figure 15-3 also shows that experimental subjects typically looked toward a *single* vertex although the particular vertex chosen varied both between and within subjects.

### Dispersion of Ocular Orientation

The tendency of babies to orient their eyes toward the vertices of the presented triangle is part of a more general characteristic of ocular

**160** PERCEPTUAL DEVELOPMENT

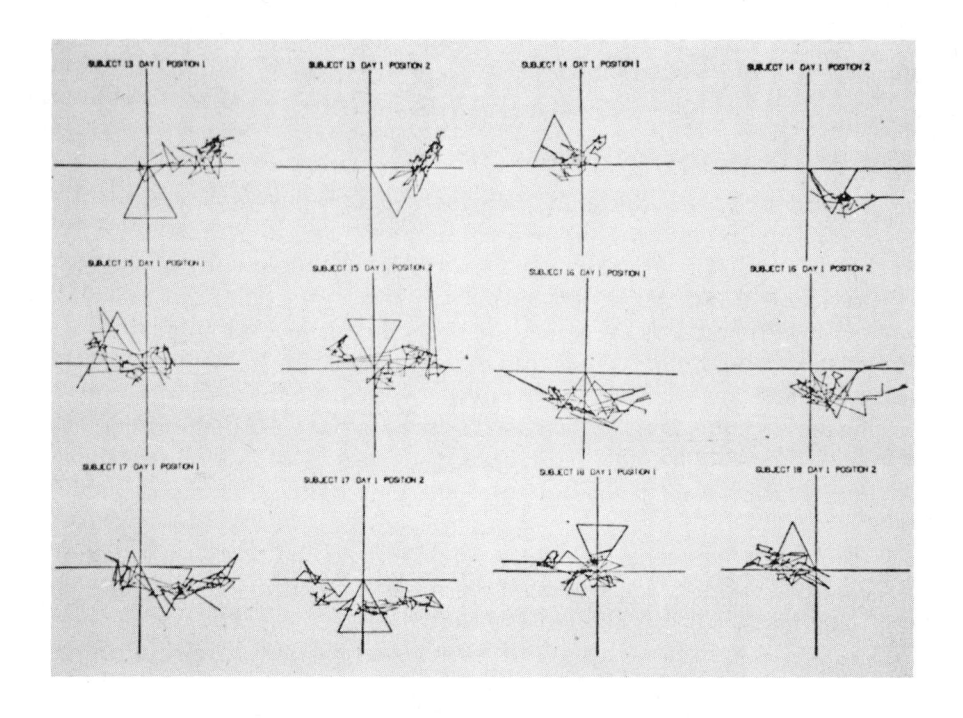

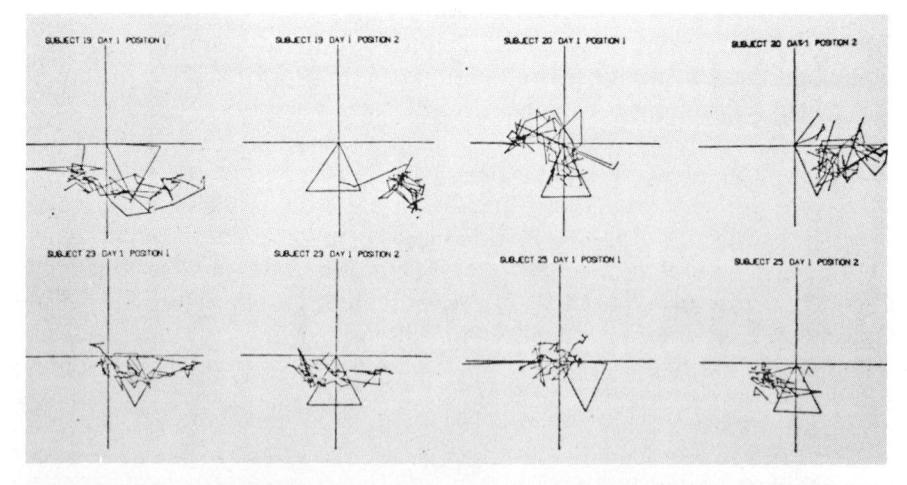

FIGURE 15-2 Records of ocular orientation for subjects in the control group. The triangle on each record is a *hypothetical* one metrically equivalent (8 in. on each side) to the triangle presented to the experimental subjects.

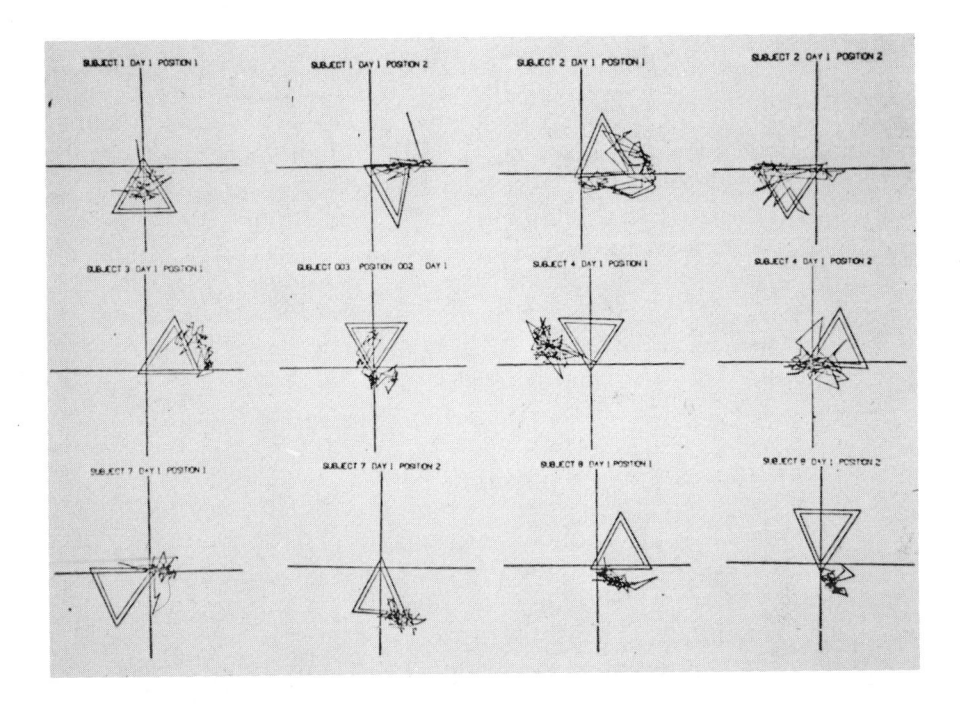

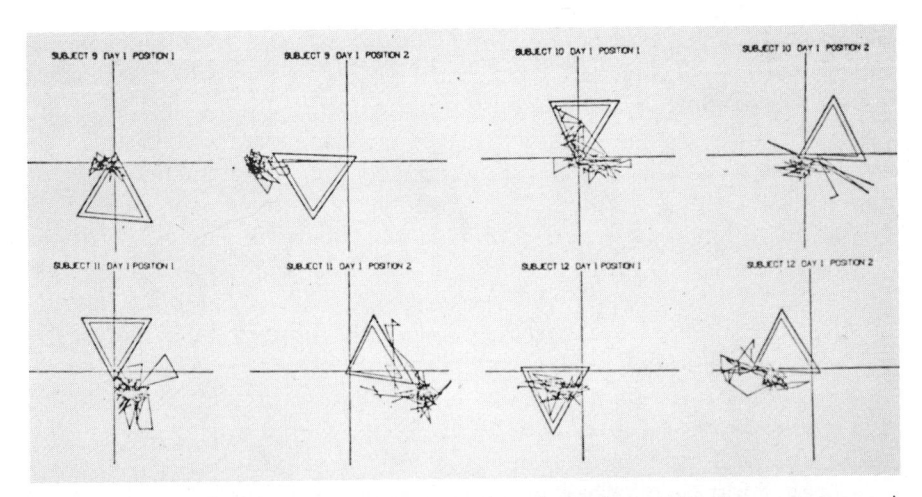

FIGURE 15-3 Records of ocular orientation for subjects in the experimental group. The outer triangle on each record represents the outline of the solid black equilateral triangle, 8 in. to a side, presented to the experimental subjects.

orientation in the experimental group. As an examination of Figures 15-2 and 15-3 will indicate, babies in the experimental group showed much less dispersion of orientations through the stimulus field. To put the finding another way, the presence of a triangular form reduced the tendency of the baby's eye to wander. An analysis of variance was performed on log standard deviation of positions of ocular orientation in both the $x$ and the $y$ dimensions for experimental and control subjects. Control subjects showed much more dispersion of ocular orientation ($F = 29.80$; $df = 1$, 18; $p < 0.001$). There was also a significant overall tendency for dispersion in the horizontal dimension to be greater than dispersion in the vertical dimension of orientation measurements ($F = 52.66$; $df = 1, 18$; $p < 0.001$). Finally, there was a stable interaction between group differences on the one hand (experimental versus control) and the direction of spread (horizontal versus vertical) on the other ($F = 9.51$; $df = 1, 18$; $p < 0.01$). The significant interaction represents a tendency for the triangle to reduce the superiority of horizontal dispersion over vertical dispersion in the experimental group. In brief, then, both groups of babies showed a wider range of variation through the horizontal dimension of the field than through the vertical; the experimental subjects showed both less overall dispersion in orientation and relatively less dispersion in the horizontal dimension.

## SUMMARY AND DISCUSSION

When infants under 8 days of age were shown a homogeneous black field, their visual scanning tended to be widely dispersed with a greater dispersion in the horizontal than in the vertical dimension. This selective dispersion suggests that horizontal scanning is easier for the newborn than is vertical, although it should also be noted that the infants were able to scan widely in both dimensions. The introduction of a large, solid, central triangle into the infant's field of view markedly reduced the overall dispersion of scanning and also reduced the predominance of horizontal over vertical scanning. Of greatest consequence for perceptual theory, the infants responded to only part of the figure. The ocular orientations of the infants were not distributed haphazardly over the triangle but tended to cluster at the vertices. Not only did their orientations cluster at vertices; there were extremely few orientations in the center of the triangle, the region in which it would be expected that a substantial number of orientations would lie if the infants were responding to the figure as a whole. Moreover, they typically looked toward a single vertex of the figure, the preferred vertex varying from subject to subject. There was little indication that for any particular subject, orientation was toward more than one element of the figure, for instance, orientations divided between two vertices or between a vertex and a side.

If one tries to explain the obtained results in the light of Hebb's theory [8] about the acquisition of the concept of "triangle" by linkage through visual scanning of the elements comprising the figure, one is led toward one or another of the following conclusions:

1.  The newborn babies, either because of a lack of maturation or of experience, were at a "pre-linkage" stage, capable of responding to elements but incapable of linking the elements through scanning.
2.  A *solid* triangular figure is defined by contour and may not be analyzed by the visual system into the elements—sides and angles—that are fundamental to Hebb's theory.
3.  The figure used in the present study was too large to permit the integration of elements. Obviously, the influence on ocular orientation of age, visual experience, and the size and nature of the figure must be studied before the role of scanning in the construction of form can be fully assessed.

What mechanism may underlie the response of the newborn to vertices of a triangle? The obtained results are compatible with at least three interpretations. It is possible that newborns respond to transitions in brightness and that the orientation toward a vertex is directed by the presence of two brightness transitions. Secondly, the infants may respond to vertices through a mechanism specifically tuned to angles. This interpretation is congruent with analyzer theories of discrimination (for example, [3, 4, 15]), and may suggest the presence in young infants of neurophysiological coding mechanisms analogous to the contour operators described for the visual system of cats [11, 12]. Thirdly, it is possible that the infants were responding to an optimal level of brightness [9] that is only to be found near a vertex.

The results of the present study are relevant to an interpretation of the ambiguous relation found between complexity and preference in the human newborn [6, 9, 10]. The results presented here suggest that the human newborn orients toward preferred elements in his visual field and does not respond to a figure as a whole. Therefore, a preferred figure may well be one in which there is a predominant number of attractive elements.

# REFERENCES

1.  A. Cowey. The basis of a method of perimetry with monkeys. *Quart. J. exp. Psychol.*, 1963, *15* (part 2), 81–90.
2.  G. O. Dayton, Jr., and Margaret H. Jones. Analysis of characteristics of fixation reflex in infants by use of direct current electrooculography. *Neurology*, 1964, *14*, 1152–1156.
3.  J. A. Deutsch. *The structural basis of behavior.* Chicago: University of Chicago Press, 1960.

4. P. C. Dodwell. A coupling system for coding and learning in shape discrimination. *Psychol. Rev.,* 1964, *71,* 148–159.
5. R. L. Fantz. The origin of form perception. *Sci. Amer.,* 1961, *204,* 459–463.
6. R. L. Fantz. Studying visual perception and the effects of visual exposure in early infancy. Paper read at meetings of American Psychological Association, Philadelphia, August 1963.
7. M. M. Haith. A semiautomatic procedure for measuring changes in position, *J. exp. child Psychol.,* 1966, *3,* 289–295.
8. D. O. Hebb. *The organization of behavior.* New York: Wiley, 1949.
9. M. Hershenson. Visual discrimination in the human newborn. *J. comp. physiol. Psychol.,* 1964, *58,* 270–276.
10. M. Hershenson, H. Munsinger, and W. Kessen. Preference for shapes of intermediate variability in the newborn human. *Science,* 1965, *147,* 630–631.
11. D. H. Hubel and T. N. Wiesel. Receptive fields, binocular interaction, and functional architecture in the cat's visual cortex. *J. Physiol.,* 1962, *160,* 106–154.
12. D. H. Hubel and T. N. Wiesel. Receptive fields of cells in striate cortex of very young, visually inexperienced kittens. *J. Neurophysiol.,* 1963, *26,* 994–1002.
13. W. Kessen and M. Hershenson. Ocular orientation in the human newborn infant. Paper read at meetings of American Psychological Association, Philadelphia, August 1963.
14. B. Ling. A genetic study of sustained visual fixation and associated behavior in the human infant from birth to six months. *J. genet. Psychol.,* 1942, *61,* 227–277.
15. N. S. Sutherland. Stimulus analyzing mechanisms. In *Mechanisation of thought processes.* London: HMSO, 1959. Vol. 2, pp. 575–609.
16. B. L. White. Plasticity in perceptual development during the first six months of life. Paper read at meetings of American Association for the Advancement of Science, Cleveland, December 1963.

# 16
# STUDIES IN PERCEPTUAL DEVELOPMENT: II. PART-WHOLE PERCEPTION

D. Elkind
R. R. Koegler
E. Go

*One hundred and ninety-five children from 4 to 9 years of age were tested for their ability to perceive both parts and wholes in drawings wherein both parts and wholes had independent meanings. Results showed (a) regular increase with age in ability to perceive part and whole, (b) parts perceived at an earlier age than wholes, and (c) part and whole integration present in a majority (75%) of children by age 9. The results were interpreted from the standpoint of Piaget's genetic theory of perception.*

This is the second in a series of studies devoted to the systematic exploration of Piaget's [11] theory of perception as it applies to meaningful materials. According to Piaget, the perception of the young child is "centered" in the sense that its organization is dominated by the gestalt-like principles of proximity, closure, and good form, and so on, which Piaget calls field effects. With age, however, and the development of new mental structures, the child's perception is progressively freed from its domination by field effects and becomes increasingly logical in form. (That is, the older child is able to differentiate the elements of a configuration and can organize and reorganize them as if he employed operations analogous to those of logic and mathematics.) Piaget's decentering theory was originally formulated in relation to illusions and constancy phenomena, but it has also been found to apply to figure ground reversal involving the identification of meaningful figures [6, 7]. The present study seeks to determine whether the decentering of perception can also be demonstrated in the development of part-whole perception when both parts and wholes have different and independent meanings.

Source: *Child Development*, 1964, *35*, 81–90. Copyright 1964 by the Society for Research in Child Development, Inc.

Although a number of studies [8, 9, 12, 13] have investigated part-whole perception, only one, a study by Meili-Dworetzki [10], used figures in which both parts and wholes had different meanings. For example, in one of her drawings Meili-Dworetzki had a number of fruits drawn so that in their entirety they resembled a man. Meili-Dworetzki presented her figures to both children and adults and found a regular increase with age in the percentage of subjects who saw both parts and wholes. She also found that, for her figures, wholes were perceived at an earlier age than were the parts and that a majority of her subjects (75%) did not perceive both part and whole until adulthood.

Despite the fact that Meili-Dworetzki's study was not carried out in relation to Piaget's theory (she was concerned with the genetic analysis of Rorschach responses), her results do bear on Piaget's position. The increased ability with age of Meili-Dworetzki's subjects to perceive both part and whole is in keeping with Piaget's decentering hypothesis, which would also predict that the ability to attribute different meanings to the same perceptual form should develop gradually with age. On the other hand, Meili-Dworetzki's finding that it was not until adulthood that a majority (75%) of subjects perceived both parts and wholes conflicts with Piaget's hypothesis that perceptual regulations, permitting the perception of both part and whole, are well developed by middle childhood. Likewise, her finding that wholes were perceived earlier than parts does not necessarily support the Piaget position. According to Piaget's theory, whether wholes or parts are perceived is determined by the field effects produced by the stimulus configuration and not by whole or part tendencies in young children.

One possible explanation of Meili-Dworetzki's findings (that part and whole were not perceived until adulthood and that wholes were perceived at an earlier age than parts) is that her stimulus materials were such as to favor a continued centering on wholes rather than on parts. Examination of Meili-Dworetzki's figures makes this interpretation a reasonable possibility. Several features of her drawings may have favored continued centering by children. For one thing, the parts were often superimposed so that they were not always clearly represented. Secondly, the parts and wholes were drawn schematically with some common identifying characteristics left out of the figures. Finally the parts were sometimes objects, such as sewing-basket items, which are not always familiar to children. If this stimulus explanation of Meili-Dworetzki's results is correct and if Piaget's theory of perceptual decentering does apply to the development of part-whole perception, then changing some of the features of the stimulus materials should lead to results consistent with the decentering hypothesis. Such an alteration of the stimulus figures was attempted in the present study. The figures used (Figure 16-1) contained parts which were taken from nursery-school books, were clearly drawn with all identifying characteristics, were not superimposed, and were generally (as determined by pilot studies with nursery-school children)

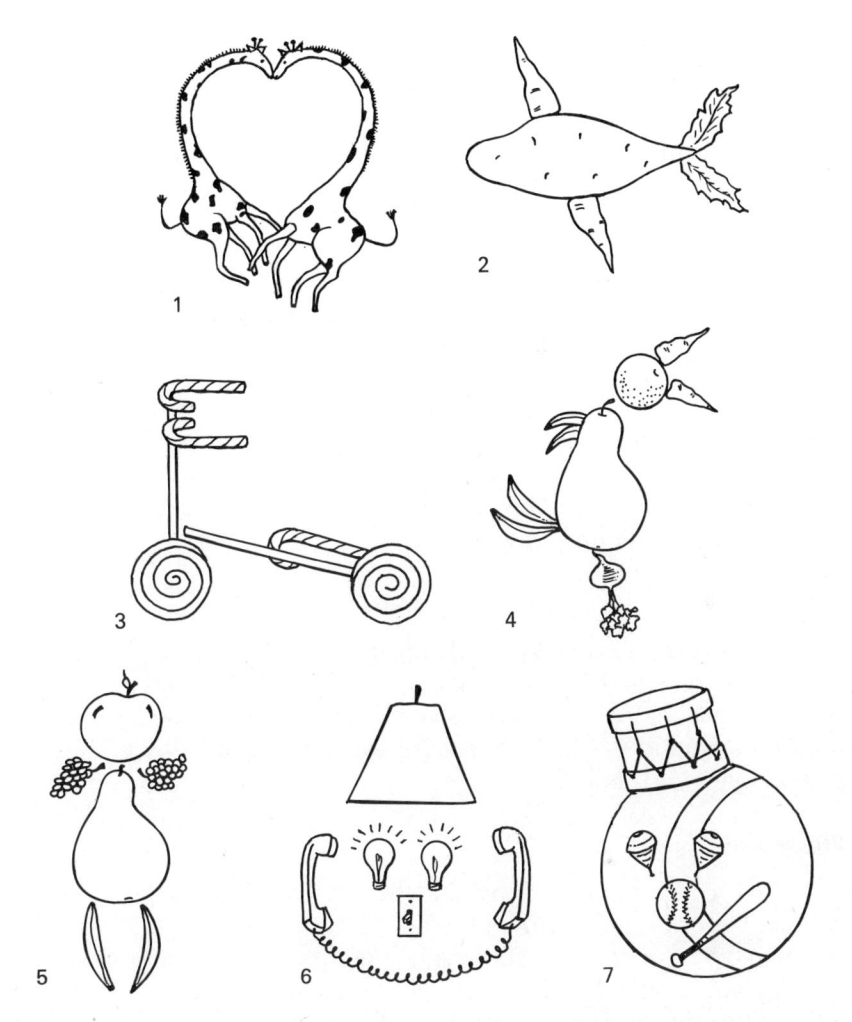

FIGURE 16-1  Drawings used in the study of part-whole perception.

easier to recognize than the wholes. Using these figures with children at different age levels, three questions were asked: (a) Is there a regular increase with age in the ability of children to perceive both parts and wholes? (b) With figures in which the field effects favor part perception, will parts be perceived earlier than wholes? (c) With figures containing parts and wholes which are familiar and easily identified, will both parts and wholes be perceived by a majority of children (75%) during middle childhood? Control tests for sex and IQ differences were also carried out.

## METHOD

### Subjects

Two groups of subjects were used. One group consisted of a nursery-school class and the first three grades of the university elementary school at UCLA, a total of 95 children. The nursery-school youngsters were of the same socioeconomic (and presumably the same intellectual) level of the elementary-school children. For the elementary-school group as a whole, the mean IQ (Stanford-Binet) was 122. Mean ages for the four age groups were 63 months, 79 months, 91 months, and 103 months, respectively.

The second group of subjects were the first four grades, a total of 100 children, of an elementary school in a lower-middle-class neighborhood of Los Angeles. The mean IQ of this group was 100. Mean ages for the four age groups in this sample were 78 months, 91 months, 104 months, and 115 months, respectively.

### Tests

The figures used in the study are shown in Figure 16-1. We call the set as a whole the Picture Integration Test (PIT). The figures were pretested on groups of nursery-school children (not those used in the study), and it was found that the parts were easily recognized by a majority of 4- and 5-year-old children.

### Procedure

Each child was tested individually. The cards were shown one at a time in the order indicated by the numbers in Figure 16-1. The child was instructed, "I am going to show you some pictures one at a time. I want you to look at them and tell me what you see, what they look like to you." After the child's response to the first card, he was asked (if he had not seen either the parts or the whole), "Do you see anything else?" Thereafter no further questions, other than to clarify a response, were asked, and only spontaneous responses were recorded.

### Scoring

The child was given a W for every whole response, a D for every part response (regardless of the number of parts mentioned), and a W + D for every whole and part response.

## RESULTS

### Age and Perception

*Age Increase in Part-Whole Perception.* As shown in Table 16-1,

TABLE 16-1 Percentage of Part, Whole, and Part-Whole Responses for Five Age Levels and for Groups of Average (A) and Above-Average (AA) Intelligence

| IQ Group | N | D | W | W + D |
|---|---|---|---|---|
| Age 4.5 | | | | |
| AA | 23 | 71.4 | 17.4 | 11.2 |
| A | — | — | — | — |
| Age 6 | | | | |
| AA | 24 | 49.4 | 27.4 | 23.2 |
| A | 20 | 50.0 | 8.6 | 41.4 |
| Age 7 | | | | |
| AA | 24 | 48.2 | 14.9 | 36.9 |
| A | 26 | 42.9 | 7.1 | 50.0 |
| Age 8 | | | | |
| AA | 24 | 32.3 | 7.5 | 60.2 |
| A | 26 | 35.2 | 2.2 | 62.6 |
| Age 9 | | | | |
| AA | — | — | — | — |
| A | 28 | 21.4 | 0.0 | 78.6 |
| Total | | | | |
| AA | 95 | | $\chi^2 = 109.6$** | |
| A | 100 | | $\chi^2 = 264.9$** | |

** Significant beyond the 0.01 level.

there was a regular increase with age in the percentage of children who perceived both parts and wholes.

*Age Sequence of Whole-Part Perception.* Contrary to Meili-Dworetzki's results, Table 16-1 also indicates that children of average and above-average intelligence perceived parts more readily than they perceived wholes.

*Age of Part-Whole Integration.* Although Meili-Dworetzki did not find part-whole integration in a majority of her subjects until adulthood, a majority (78.6%) of the 9-year-old children in this study were able to make such an integration, and close to a majority (60.2 and 62.6%) of 8-year-olds were also able to make such an integration.

## Control Measures

*Gross Socioeconomic and Intellectual Factors.* Table 16-1 indicates that despite the socioeconomic and intellectual differences between the two groups used in the present study, there were no significant differences between them (by chi-square tests) with respect to the age at which part and whole were perceived nor with respect to the order of part and whole responses.

*IQ and Part-Whole Perception.* To test the relation between part-whole perception and intelligence more directly, the scores of the university elementary-school subjects, for whom Stanford-Binets (Form LM) were available, were translated into numerical scores. Each part response was given a score of 1, each whole response was given a score of 2 (since nursery-school children saw parts and not wholes, we assumed wholes were more difficult to see and so gave them a higher numerical score), and each part and whole response was given a score of 3. The rank difference correlations at the three age levels were age 6, $+ 0.41$; age 7, $- 0.01$; age 8, $- 0.05$. The average was 0.11.

*Sex Differences.* Sex differences for order and age of part-whole perception were checked at each age level by means of chi-square. No significant differences between boys and girls with respect to part-whole perception were found at any of the age levels studied.

## DISCUSSION

The results of our study have shown that (a) there is a regular increase with age in the ability of children to perceive parts and wholes involving the identification of meaningful figures; (b) when the figures are such that the laws of closure, good form, and so on, favor the perception of parts, the parts will be perceived at an earlier age than the wholes; (c) when the parts and wholes are easily identified and familiar even to nursery-school children, the perception of both parts and wholes can be accomplished by a majority (75%) of 9-year-old children. Each of these findings will be commented on in the present section, but we will take them up in reverse order.

### Age of Part-Whole Perception

According to Piaget, the decentering of perception comes about in middle childhood as a consequence of the development of perceptual regulations which free the child's perception from its earlier domination by field effects. In our study, we found that 78.6% of the 9-year-old children were able to perceive both part and whole in agreement with Piaget's position and with the results of our other studies [6, 7], which have also shown that the 7- to 8-year level is the point of most abrupt perceptual improvement.

In view of this finding, that part and whole can both be perceived by a majority of youngsters in middle childhood, it seems plausible to attribute Meili-Dworetzki's results (part and whole perceived only at the adult level) to factors other than an incapacity of children to integrate meaningful parts and wholes. The finding that children of average and above-average intelligence perform in a similar fashion and that there is little correlation between IQ and part-whole perception also seems to rule out intelligence as the condition making for the difference between Meili-Dworetzki's findings and our own. Cultural differences are also probably not the answer, because a number of studies [1, 2, 3, 4] have shown that there is considerable similarity between European and American children in the age stages of conceptual development and presumably in stages of perceptual development as well. In sum, it seems reasonable to conclude that the differences between Meili-Dworetzki's findings and our own with regard to the age of part-whole integration are attributable to differences in the stimulus materials and not to differences in the subjects.

### Sequence of Part-Whole Perception

The theory of perceptual decentering holds that the perception of the young child is determined by gestalt-like laws of closure, good form, and so on. According to this theory, whether a child perceives parts or wholes depends upon the configural character of the stimulus materials. In our study the parts, which were more closed and had better (more recognizable) form than did the wholes, were perceived at an earlier age. In view of these results, Meili-Dworetzki's finding [10] that wholes were perceived earlier than parts cannot be attributed to inborn tendencies to perceive wholes. On the contrary, her findings seem most reasonably ascribed to the fact that her figures favored whole over part perception. It may be that in perception, as in embryology and development generally, growth is sometimes from whole to part and sometimes from part to whole and that generalizations regarding the sequence of part-whole perception cannot be made without adding some specific information as to the characteristics of the stimuli employed. At any rate, this is the implication of Piaget's theory, and it is supported by Meili-Dworetzki's results as well as our own.

### Age Increase in Part-Whole Perception

Centering, as it is used by Piaget, implies not only a domination by field effects but also a kind of fixation on the dominant figure and an inability spontaneously to shift perspective so as to perceive the configuration in a new way. Decentering is in fact the spontaneous shift of focus from one perceptual organization to another which is made possible by the development of perceptual regulations. In part-whole perception, decentering involves a shift of focus from whole to part or vice versa. Our finding that there is a general increase with age in the ability of children to perceive both part and whole is therefore in accord with the decentering position. It remains, however, to describe the regulational mechanisms of this decentering in part-whole perception, and that is the task of the present section. Unfortunately, Piaget has not dealt with the problem of part-whole perception involving the identification of meaningful figures, and the interpretation given below is our application of his theory to this new situation. To paraphrase a popular slogan, what follows is not necessarily the view of Piaget.

From the regulational standpoint, the problem of perceiving both whole and part would seem to be analogous to the problem of forming disjunctive classes on the plane of conception. Disjunctive classes are formed by means of the operation of logical multiplication. Logical multiplication requires, from the standpoint of intension, the formation of a new property by the joining of the properties of two independent classes. For example the logical multiplication of the property "Protestant" and the property "American" results in the new property "Protestant American." Looked at from the standpoint of extension, logical multiplication requires the subject to attribute two properties to the same object at the same time. For example, the subject must be able to attribute to one and the same person the properties of being Protestant and American.

Now, it seems to us, that with respect to part and whole perception somewhat the same requirements hold true. The child must be able, from the standpoint of intension, to combine, say, the percept of a head with the percept of an apple, the percept of a banana with that of an arm, and so on. He must also, from the standpoint of extension, be able to attribute both percepts to one and the same perceived form. Put differently, the perception of both part and whole would seem to involve the formation of a new percept just as the recognition of an American Protestant requires the formation of a new concept. If this analysis of part-whole perception is correct, we would expect to find stages in the development of logical multiplication in perception analogous to those found in the realm of conception. Such stages were indeed found and are described below.

*Stage 1a.* At the first stage (usually age 5 to 6) there was *complete centration* in the sense that children saw the parts (with the exception of a few who saw the wholes but not the parts) and did not respond at all to the wholes.

Jan (5–9) (card 1) "Two giraffes." "Anything else?" "No."
Rose (5–8) (card 3) "Some candy suckers and candy canes."

*Stage 1b.* This stage appeared in only a few children (usually age 6) and seemed to be a transitional stage. These children mentioned the whole and then the parts, but then denied seeing the whole. Operationally they had succeeded in decentering, but apparently the operational mechanism was still so undeveloped that when challenged it could not be sustained and the youngsters fell back to the centered position.

Bob (5–6) (card 5) "A man, I mean fruit." Can you show me the man?" "No."
Sal (6–5) (card 3) "A scooter, I mean candy." "Can you show me the scooter?" "No."

*Stage 2.* Children at the second stage (usually age 7 to 8) made an *intuitive decentration* in the sense that they mentioned both wholes and parts but without trying to integrate them in any way.

Tom (7–2) (card 3) "A scooter, candy canes, suckers."
Art (8–10) (card 5) "Some fruit. Oh! a clown."

These children responded as if they saw the parts and then the whole in alternation and not simultaneously. At this stage the logical multiplication is performed but in slow motion, so that the child is not aware of the contradiction of attributing two different meanings to the same perceived form.

*Stage 3.* At this stage (usually age 8 or 9) there was *complete regulational decentration* in the sense that not only were the part and whole both perceived but they were also simultaneously attributed to the same perceived form.

Ben (8–3) (card 5) "A man made of fruit."
Ed (9–5) (card 3) "A scooter made of candy."

Third-stage children recognized that the same form had two different meanings and integrated these meanings at the verbal level. As far as we could tell, there were no transitional stages between the second and third stages, which may mean that verbal resolution of the contradiction (for instance, scooter made of candy) of perceiving two meanings in the same form is attained simultaneously with the instantaneous action of logical multiplication. It is important to emphasize, however, that the verbal resolution follows and does not precede the perceptual integration. Even nursery children know that a scooter can be made of candy, but they do not perceive it as such until the appropriate operations are attained.

In the preceding discussion nothing was said about individual differences in part-whole perception other than that such differences seem not to be related to intelligence. It is likely that there is some relation between Piaget's notion of perceptual decentering and the Field Independence-Dependence dimension of personality described by Witkin [13], but this relation is a problem for future research. In our study we have only argued that the age changes in whole-part perception involving the identification of meaningful figures are in accord with Piaget's developmental theory of perception.

# REFERENCES

1. D. Elkind. Children's discovery of the conservation of mass, weight and volume. Piaget replication study II. *J. genet. Psychol.*, 1961, *98*, 219–227.
2. D. Elkind. The development of the additive composition of classes in the child. Piaget replication study III. *J. genet. Psychol.*, 1961, *99*, 51–57.

3. D. Elkind. The child's conception of brother and sister. Piaget replication study IV. *J. genet. Psychol.*, 1961, *99*, 269–276.
4. D. Elkind. The child's conception of right and left. Piaget replication study V. *J. genet. Psychol.*, 1961, *99*, 269–276.
5. D. Elkind. Discrimination, seriation and numeration of size differences in young children. Piaget replication study VI. *J. genet. Psychol.*, 1964, *104*, 275–296.
6. D. Elkind, R. R. Koegler, and E. Go. Effects of perceptual training at three age levels. *Science*, 1962, *137*, 755-756.
7. D. Elkind and L. Scott. Studies in perceptual development: I. The decentering of perception. *Child Develop.*, 1962, *33*, 619–630.
8. L. Ghent. Perception of overlapping and imbedded figures by children of different ages. *Amer. J. Psychol.*, 1956, *69*, 575–587.
9. E. S. Gollin. Developmental differences in visual recognition under conditions of reduced cues. *Percept. mot. Skills*, 1960, *II*, 289–298.
10. G. Meili-Dworetzki. The development of perception in the Rorschach. In B. Klopfer (ed.). *Developments in the Rorschach technique*. World Book, 1956. Pp. 108–176.
11. J. Piaget and A. Morf. Les isomorphismes partiels entre les structures logiques et les structures perceptives. In J. Piaget (ed.). *Études d'épistémologie génétique*. Paris: Presses Universitaires de France, 1958. Vol. 6, pp. 51–116.
12. C. D. Smock. The influence of psychological stress on the perception of incongruity. *J. abnorm. soc. Psychol.*, 1955, *50*, 354–356.
13. A. A. Witkin. Individual differences in ease of perception of embedded figures. *J. Pers.*, 1950, *19*, 1–15.

# 17

# PERCEPTUAL LEARNING: DIFFERENTIATION OR ENRICHMENT?

J. J. Gibson
E. J. Gibson

The term perceptual learning means different things to different psychologists. To some it implies that human perception is, in large part, learned—that we learn to see depth, for instance, or form, or meaningful objects. In that case the theoretical issue involved is *how much* of perception is learned, and the corresponding controversy is that of nativism or empiricism. To others the term implies that human learning is in whole or part a matter of perception—that learning depends on comprehension, expectation, or insight, and that the learning process is to be found in a central process of cognition rather than in a motor process of performance. In this second case, the theoretical issue involved is whether or not one has to study a man's perceptions before one can understand his behavior, and the controversy is one of long standing which began with old-fashioned behaviorism.

These two sets of implications are by no means the same, and the two problems should be separated. The problem of the role of learning in perception has to do with perception and the effect of past experience or practice on it. The problem of the role of perception in learning has to do with behavior and the question of whether we can learn to do something by perceiving, or whether we can only learn by doing it. The questions, then, are these: (a) In what sense do we learn to perceive? (b) In what sense can we learn by perceiving? Both questions are important for the practical problems of education and training, but this paper will be concerned with the former.

## IN WHAT SENSE DO WE LEARN TO PERCEIVE?

This question has roots in philosophy and was debated long before experimental psychology came of age. Does all knowledge (information is the contemporary term) come through the sense organs or is some knowledge contributed by the mind itself? Inasmuch as sensory psychol-

Source: *Psychological Review*, 1955, 62, 32–43. Copyright 1955 by the American Psychological Association. Reprinted by permission.

ogy has been unable to explain how as much information about the world as we manifestly do obtain is transmitted by the receptors, some theory is required for this unexplained surplus. There has been a variety of such theories ever since the days of John Locke. An early notion was that the surplus is contributed by the rational faculty (rationalism). Another was that it comes from innate ideas (nativism). In modern times there have been few adherents to these positions. The most popular theory over the years has been that this supplement to the sensations is the result of learning, and that it comes from past experience. A contemporary formula for this explanation is that the brain stores information—possibly in the form of traces or memory images, but conceivably as attitudes, or mental sets, or general ideas, or concepts. This approach has been called empiricism. It preserves the dictum that all knowledge comes from experience by assuming that past experience somehow gets *mixed with* present experience. It assumes, in other words, that experience *accumulates,* that traces of the past somehow exist in our perception of the present. One of its high-water marks was Helmholtz's theory of unconscious inference, which supposes that we learn to see depth by interpreting the clues furnished by the depthless sensations of color. Another was Titchener's context theory of meaning, which asserts that we learn to perceive objects when a core of sensations acquires by association a context of memory images.

Over a generation ago this whole line of thought was challenged by what seemed to be a different explanation for the discrepancy between the sensory input and the finished percept—the theory of sensory organization. The Gestalt theorists made destructive criticisms of the notion of *acquired* linkages among sensory elements and their traces. Instead they asserted that the linkages were *intrinsic,* or that they arose *spontaneously,* taking visual forms as their best example. Perception and knowledge, they said, were or came to be *structured*.

The theory of sensory organization or cognitive structure, although it generated a quantity of experimentation along new lines, has not after 30 years overthrown the theory of association. In this country the old line of empiricist thinking has begun to recover from the critical attack, and there are signs of a revival. Brunswik [2, pp. 23 ff.] has followed from the start the line laid down by Helmholtz. Ames and Cantril and their followers have announced what might be called a neoempiricist revelation [3, 11, 14]. Other psychologists are striving for a theoretical synthesis which will include the lessons of Gestalt theory but retain the notion that perception is learned. Tolman, Bartlett, and Woodworth began the trend. Leeper took a hand in it at an early date [15]. The effort to reconcile the principle of sensory organization with the principle of determination by past experience has recently been strenuously pursued by Bruner [1] and by Postman [16]. Hilgard seems to accept both a process of organization governed by relational structure and a process of association governed by the classical laws [10]. Hebb has recently made a systematic full-scale attempt to combine the best of Gestalt theory and of learning theory at the physiological level [9]. What all these theorists seem to us to be saying is that the organization process and the learning process are not inconsistent after all, that both explanations are valid in their way, and that there is no value in continuing the old argument over whether learning is really organization or organization is really learning. The experiments on this issue (beginning with the Gottschaldt experiment) were inconclusive, and the controversy itself was inconclusive. Hence, they argue, the best solution is to agree with both sides.

It seems to us that all extant theories of the perceptual process, including those based on association, those based on organization, and those based on a mixture of the two (including attitudes, habits, assumptions, hypotheses, expectation, images, contexts, or inferences) have at least this feature in common: They take for granted a discrepancy between the sensory input and the finished percept and they aim to explain the difference. They assume that somehow we get more information about the environment than can be transmitted through the receptor system. In other words, they accept the distinction between sensation and perception. The development of perception must then necessarily be one of supplementing or interpreting or organizing.

Let us consider the possibility of rejecting this assumption altogether. Let us assume tentatively that the stimulus input contains within it everything that the percept has. What if the flux of stimulation at receptors *does* yield all the information anyone needs about the environment? Perhaps all knowledge comes through the senses in an even simpler way than John Locke was able to conceive—by way of variations, shadings, and subtleties of energy which are properly to be called stimuli.

## THE ENRICHMENT THEORY VERSUS THE SPECIFICITY THEORY

The entertaining of this hypothesis faces us with two theories of perceptual learning which are clear rather than vague alternatives. It cuts across the schools and theories, and presents us with an issue. Is perception a creative process or is it a discriminative process? Is learning a matter of enriching previously meager sensations or is it a matter of differentiating previously vague impressions? On the first alternative we might learn to perceive in this sense: that percepts change over time by acquiring progressively more memory images, and that a context of memories accrues by association to a sensory core. The theorist can substitute attitudes or inferences or assumptions for images in the above Titchenerian proposition, but perhaps all this does is to make the theory less neat while making the terminology more fashionable. In any case, perception is progressively in *decreasing correspondence with stimulation*. The latter point is notable. Perceptual learning, thus conceived, necessarily consists of experience becoming more imaginary, more assumptive, or more inferential. The dependence of perception on learning seems to be contradictory to the principle of the dependence of perception on stimulation.

On the second alternative we learn to perceive in this sense: that percepts change over time by progressive elaboration of qualities, features, and dimensions of variation; that perceptual experience even at the outset consists of a world, not of sensation, and that the world gets more and more properties as the objects in it get more distinctive; finally, that the phenomenal properties and the phenomenal objects correspond to physical properties and physical objects in the environment *whenever learning is successful.* In this theory perception gets richer in differential responses, not in images. It is progressively in *greater* correspondence with stimulation, not in less. Instead of becoming more imaginary it becomes more discriminating. Perceptual learning, then, consists of responding to variables of physical stimulation not previously responded to. The notable point about this theory is that learning is always supposed to be a matter of improvement—of getting in closer touch with the environment. It consequently does not account for hallucination or delusions or, in fact, for any kind of maladjustment.

The latter kind of theory is certainly worth exploring. It is not novel, of course, to suggest that perceptual development is a matter of differentiation. As phenomenal description this was asserted by some of the Gestalt psychologists, notably Koffka and Lewin. (Just how differentiation was related to organization, however, was not clear.) What *is* novel is to suggest that perceptual development is always a matter of the correspondence between stimulation and perception—that it is strictly governed by the relationships of the perceiver to his environment. The rule would be that as the number of distinct percepts a man can have increases, so also the number of different physical objects to which they are specific increases. An example may clarify this rule. One man, let us say, can identify sherry, champagne, white wine, and red wine. He has four percepts in response to the total possible range of stimulation. Another man can identify a dozen types of sherry, each with many varieties, and numerous blends, and so on for the others. He has 4,000 percepts in response to the range of stimulation. The crucial question to ask about this example of differentiated perception is its relation to stimulation.

Stimulus is a slippery term in psychology. Properly speaking, stimulation is always energy at receptors, that is, proximal stimulation. An individual is surrounded by an array of energy and immersed in a flow of it. This sea of stimulation consists of variation and invariants, patterns and transformations, some of which we know how to isolate and control and others of which we do not. An experimenter chooses or constructs a sample of this energy when he performs a psychological experiment. But it is easy for him to forget this fact and to assume that a glass of wine is a stimulus when actually it is a complex or radiant and chemical energies which is the stimulus. When the psychologist refers to stimuli as cues, or clues, or carriers of information he is skipping lightly over the problem of how stimuli come to function as cues. Energies do not have cue properties unless and until the differences in energy have correspondingly different effects in perception. The total range of physical stimulation is very rich in complex variables, and these are theoretically capable of becoming cues and constituting information. This is just where learning comes in.

All responses to stimulation, including perceptual responses, manifest some degree of specificity and, inversely, some degree of nonspecificity. The gentleman who is discriminating about his wine shows a high specificity of perception, whereas the crude fellow who is not shows a low specificity. A whole class of chemically different fluids is equivalent for the latter individual; he can't tell the difference between claret, burgundy, and chianti; his perceptions are relatively undifferentiated. What has the first man learned that the second man has not? Associations? Memories? Attitudes? Inferences? Has he learned to have perceptions instead of merely sensations? Perhaps, but a simpler statement might be made. The statement is that he has learned to taste and smell more of the qualities of wine, that is, he discriminates more of the variables of chemical stimulation. If he is a genuine connoisseur and not a fake, one combination of such variables can evoke a specific response of naming or identifying and another combination can evoke a different specific response. He can consistently apply nouns to the different fluids of a class and he can apply adjectives to the differences between the fluids.

The classical theory of perceptual learning, with its emphasis on subjective determination of perception in contrast to stimulus determination, gets its plausibility from experiments on errors in form perception, from the study of illusions and systematic distortions, and from the fact of individual differences in and social influences on perception. The learning process is assumed to have occurred in the past life of the experimental subject; it is seldom controlled by the experimenter. These are *not* learning experiments insofar as they do not control practice or take measures before and after training. True perceptual learning experiments are limited to those concerned with discrimination.

One source of evidence about discriminative learning comes from the study of the cues for verbal learning. The analysis of these cues made by one of the authors in terms of stimulus generalization and differentiation [4] suggests the present line of thought. It has also led to a series of experiments concerned with what we call *identifying responses*. Motor reactions, verbal reactions, or percepts, we assume, are identifying responses if they are in specific correspondence with a set of objects or events. Code learning [13], aircraft recognition [7], and learning to name the faces of one's friends are all examples of an increasingly specific correspondence between the items of stimulation presented and the items of response recorded. As a given response gains univocality, the percept is reported to gain in the feeling of familiarity or recognition and to acquire meaning.

## AN ILLUSTRATIVE EXPERIMENT

In order to provide a clear example of such learning, we studied the development of a single identifying response. The subject was presented with a visual item consisting of a nonsense scribble; his recognition of it was tested when it was interspersed in a series of similar scribbles, and then the single showing and the multiple presentation were repeated until the item could be identified. We devised a set of seventeen scribbles intended to be indistinguishable from the critical item on the first trial, and another set of twelve items intended to be distinguishable from the critical item on the first trial.

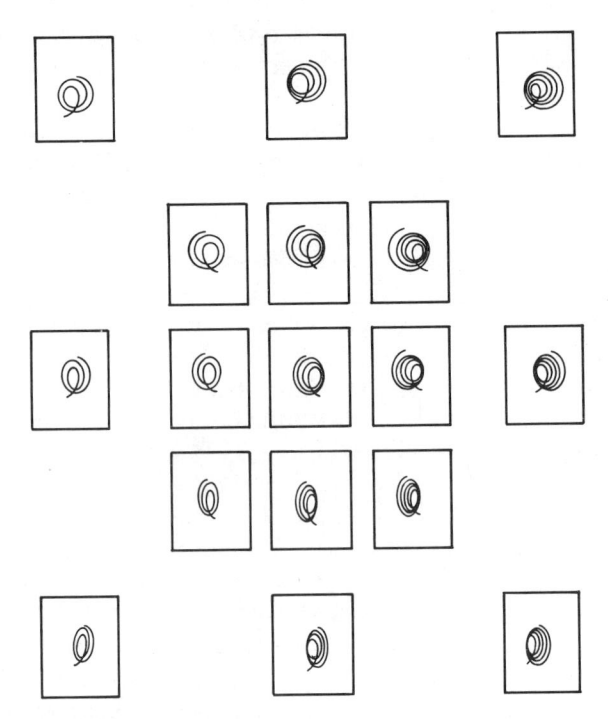

FIGURE 17-1 Nonsense items differing in three dimensions of variation.

The items which had to be differentiated are shown in Figure 17-1. The critical item, a four-coil scribble, is in the center and sixteen other items are arranged outward from it. The eighteenth item (a reversal of the critical item) is not shown. It may be noted that there are three dimensions of variation from the critical item: (a) number of coils—three, four, or five, (b) horizontal compression or stretching, and (c) orientation or right-left reversal. The latter two kinds of variations were produced by photographic transformation. There are three degrees of coil frequency, three degrees of compression, and two types of orientation, which yields eighteen items. Since one of these is the critical item, seventeen remain for use in the experiment. The reader may observe that when these differences are verbally specified and the figures are displayed for immediate comparison, as in Figure 17-1, they are clearly distinguishable. The subjects of the experiment, however, saw the items only in succession.

The twelve additional items presented on each recognition trial are shown in Figure 17-2. Each differs from every other and from all of the set of eighteen. The differences from the scribbles were intended to be sufficient to make them appear different at the outset to subjects with a normal amount of experience with drawn forms. The thirty items (twelve plus eighteen) were printed photographically on stiff 2 × 4 in. cards with black borders, and made into a pack. The material available for any one

FIGURE 17-2 Nonsense items differing in many dimensions of variation.

learning trial consisted of the critical item plus a shuffled pack of cards among which were interspersed four replicas of the critical item.

The subject was shown the critical item for about 5 sec and told that some of the items in the pack would be exactly like the one shown. The series of thirty-four was then presented, each with a 3-sec exposure, and the subject was asked to report which of them were the same figure. The identifying response recorded was any report such as "that's it" or "this is the one I saw before." The subject was never told whether an identification was correct or incorrect. A record was kept not only of the identifying responses but also of any spontaneous descriptions offered by the subject, which were later classified as *naming* responses and *qualifying* responses.

At the end of the first trial the critical figure was presented a second time and another shuffled pack was run through. The procedure of examining a figure and then trying to identify it when mixed with a series including figures of both great and little similarity was continued until the subject made only the four correct identifications in one trial. Three groups took part in the experiment: twelve adults, ten older children (8½ to 11 years), and ten younger children (6 to 8 years).

## Results

In this experiment, learning is taken to be an increase in the specificity of an identifying response or, in other words, a decrease in the size of the class of items that will elicit the response. The data therefore consist of the number of items (out of a probable maximum of seventeen) reacted to as if they were the critical figure. As will be evident, this class of undifferentiated items was reduced as a result of repetition. The three groups of subjects, however, began to learn at very different levels and learned at very different rates. The results are given in Table 17-1. For

TABLE 17-1 Increase in Specificity of an Identifying Response for Three Age Groups

| Variable | Adults (N = 12) | Older Children (N = 10) | Younger Children (N = 10) |
|---|---|---|---|
| Mean number of undifferentiated items on first trial | 3.0 | 7.9 | 13.4 |
| Mean number of trials required for completely specific response | 3.1 | 4.7 | 6.7 † |
| Percentage of erroneous recognitions for items differing in *one* quality | 17 | 27 | 53 |
| Percentage of erroneous recognitions for items differing in *two* qualities | 2 | 7 | 35 |
| Percentage of erroneous recognitions for items differing in *three* qualities | 0.7 | 2 | 28 |

† Only two of the younger children achieved a completely specific identification. The mean number of undifferentiated items on the last trial was still 3.9.

adults, the class of undifferentiated items at the outset was small (mean = 3.0), and only a few trials were needed before this class was reduced to the critical item alone (mean = 3.1). Two of these adults were able to make no other than correct identifying responses on the first trial. Both were psychologists who could have had previous acquaintance with nonsense figures. The learning task was so easy for this group that not much information about the learning process could be obtained. At the other extreme, however, the younger children "recognized" nearly all of the scribbles on the first trial (mean = 13.4), which is to say that the class of undifferentiated items was large. The number of trials needed to reduce this class to the correct item was so great that most of the subjects could not be required to complete the experiment. Two out of ten reached the criterion, but for the remainder the trials had to be stopped for reasons of fatigue. After an average of 6.7 trials the mean number of undifferentiated items was still 3.9. One child had so much difficulty with the task that the experimenter finally gave differential reinforcement by saying *right* or *wrong* after each presentation of a card. Although this procedure helped, wholly specific identifications were never achieved. The failures of the younger children to discriminate did not seem to be due merely to "inattention"; they understood that they were to select only the figures which were *exactly* the same as the critical figure.

For the older children (between 8½ and 11 years of age) the results were intermediate between these extremes. For them the particular task and the particular items were neither too hard nor too easy. The average number of undifferentiated items on the first trial was 7.9, and all children succeeded in reducing this to a single item after a mean of 4.7 trials.

Table 17-1 also indicates for each group an important fact about the unspecific responses: They tend to occur more often as the differences between the test item and the critical item become fewer. As Figure 17-1 shows, a given scribble may differ in *one* quality or dimension (thickness, coil frequency, or orientation), or in *two* of these qualities, or in all *three* of them. Five of the scribbles differ in one feature, eight differ in two features, and four differ in three features. It will be recalled that the twelve additional forms shown in Figure 17-2 differed from the critical item with respect to *more* than three features. Amount of difference can be usefully stated as number of differing qualities or, conversely, amount of sameness as the fewness of differing qualities.[1] The lower half of Table 17-1 gives the percentage of occurrence of false recognitions in the case of scribbles with one quality different, with two qualities different, and with three qualities different. These percentages are based on the number of times the items in question were presented during the whole series of trials. The dissimilar figures, which had many qualities different, yielded a zero percentage of false recognitions except for a few scattered instances among the younger children.

## Discussion

The results show clearly that the kind of perceptual learning hypothesized has occurred in this experiment. A stimulus item starts out by being indistinguishable from a whole class of items in the stimulus universe tested, and ends by being distinguishable from all of them. The

---

[1] Experiments on primary stimulus generalization have usually varied the magnitude of a *single* difference, not the number of differences, between the critical stimulus and the undifferentiated stimulus. However, our method of quantifying amount of difference has much to recommend it.

evidence for this assertion is that the specificity of the subject's identifying response has increased. What has happened to produce this result?

The subjects were encouraged to describe all the items of each series as they were presented, and a special effort was made to obtain and record these spontaneous verbal responses for seven of the older children. In general they tended to fall into two types, either naming responses or qualifying responses. Considering only the responses to the seventeen scribbles, the record showed that the frequency of the latter type increased during the progress of learning. Examples of the former are nouns like *figure 6, curl, spiral, scroll*. Examples of the latter are adjectival phrases like *too thin, rounder, reversed*. It is notable that the latter are responses not to the item as such but to the relation between it and the critical item. They are analogous to differential judgments in a psychophysical experiment. An adjective, in general, is a response which is specific not to an object but to a property of two or more objects. It is likely, then, that the development of a specific response to an item is correlated with the development of specific responses to the qualities, dimensions, or variables that relate it to other items. The implication is that for a child to identify an object, he must be able to identify the differences between it and other objects, or at least that *when* he can identify an object he *also* can identify its properties.

The verbal reactions of the children to the seventeen scribbles, both naming and qualifying, could be categorized by the experimenter as specific or nonspecific to the item in question. These judgments were necessarily subjective, but they were carried out with the usual precautions. Although a single adjective cannot be specific to a single item, a combination of adjectives can be. An example of a nonspecific reaction is "another curlicue," and of a specific reaction is "this one is thinner and rounder." The latter sort may be considered a spontaneously developing identifying reaction, not of the "that's it" type, it is true, but nevertheless fulfilling our definition. The mean number of such verbal reactions on the first trial was 7.7 out of 17, or 45%. The mean number of such reactions on the last trial was 16.5, or 97%. This suggests that as a single identifying response becomes increasingly specific to one member of a group of similar items, verbal identifying responses also tend to become specific to the other members of the group. As the class of indistinguishable items which will elicit one response is diminished, the number of responses which can be made to the class increases.

## OTHER EVIDENCE

Another source of experimental evidence about perceptual learning comes from psychophysics. Contrary to what might be expected, psychophysical experimenters over the years have shown a lively interest in perceptual learning, or at least in the bettering of perceptual judgments with practice. One of the authors has recently surveyed this neglected literature insofar as it concerns improvement of perception or increase in perceptual skills [5]. There is a great quantity of evidence about progressive change in acuity, variability, and accuracy of perception, including both relative judgments and absolute judgments. It proves beyond a shadow of doubt that the notion of fixed thresholds for a certain set of innate sensory dimensions is oversimplified. Discrimination gets better with practice, both with and without knowledge of results. An example may be taken from the two-point threshold on the skin.

As long ago as 1858 it was discovered that there is a certain distance at which two points are felt double by a blindfolded subject that is characteristic of the area of the skin tested. At the same time, it was found that only a few hours of practice in this discrimination had the effect of reducing the distance to half of what it had been [17]. Later experiments showed that the lowering of the threshold continued slowly for thousands of trials; for instance, it might go from 30 mm to 5 mm during 4 weeks of training. Moreover, the improved discrimination transferred to other untrained areas of the skin, transfer being nearly complete for the bilaterally symmetrical area. It was found that blind subjects had very much lower thresholds than seeing subjects even at the beginning of testing [12, 18]. The experimental improvement was largely lost after a period of disuse. It seemed to depend on confirmation or correction of the judgment or, in the absence of that, on the development of a sort of scale from "close together" to "far apart" [5]. It is clear that any theory of supposedly distinct sensations of oneness and twoness never had any support from these data. As one writer put it, the observer adopts different and finer *criteria of doubleness*. What might these criteria be? We suggest that the stimulation is complex, not simple, and that the observer continues to discover higher-order variables of stimulation in it. The percept becomes differentiated.

## CONCLUSION

There is no evidence in all of this literature on perceptual learning, nor is there evidence in the experiment reported in the last section, to *require* the theory that an accurate percept is one which is enriched by past experience, whereas a less accurate percept is one *not* enriched by past experience. Repetition or practice is necessary for the development of the improved percept, but there is no proof that it incorporates memories. The notion that learned perception is less and less determined by external stimulation as learning progresses finds no support in these experiments. The observer sees and hears more, but this may be not because he imagines more, or infers more, or assumes more, but because he discriminates more. He is more sensitive to the variables of the stimulus array. Perhaps the ability to summon up memories is merely incidental to perceptual learning and the ability to differentiate stimuli is basic. Perhaps the dependence of perception on learning and the dependence of perception on stimulation are not contradictory principles after all.

This theoretical approach to perceptual learning, it must be admitted, has points of weakness as well as points of strength. It accounts for veridical perception, but it does not account for misperception. It says nothing about imagination or fantasy or wishful thinking. It is not an obviously useful approach for the study of abnormal behavior or personality, if one is convinced that a man's perceptions are the clues to his motives. But if one is concerned instead with the practical question of whether training can affect favorably a man's perception of the world around him, a very productive field for theory and experiment is opened up.

## REFERENCES

1. J. S. Bruner. Personality dynamics and the process of perceiving. In R. R. Blake and G. V. Ramsey (eds.). *Perception: an approach to personality*. New York: Ronald, 1951. Pp. 121–147.
2. E. Brunswik. The conceptual framework of psychology. *Int. Encycl. unif. Sci.* 1952. Vol. 1, No. 10.
3. H. Cantril, A. Ames, Jr., A. H. Hastorf, and W. H. Ittelson. Psychology and scientific research. *Science*, 1949, *110*, 461–464, 491–497, 517–522.
4. E. J. Gibson. A systematic application of the concepts of generalization and differentiation to verbal learning. *Psychol. Rev.*, 1940, *47*, 196–229.
5. E. J. Gibson. Improvement in perceptual judgments as a function of controlled practice or training. *Psychol. Bull.*, 1953, *50*, 401–431.
6. E. J. Gibson and J. J. Gibson. The identifying response: a study of a neglected form of learning. *Amer. Psychologist*, 1950, *7*, 276. (Abstract)
7. J. J. Gibson (ed.). *Motion picture testing and research*. AAF Aviat. Psychol. Pgm. Res. Rep. No. 7. 1947.
8. J. J. Gibson and E. J. Gibson. Perceptual learning in relation to training. In *Symposium on psychology of learning basic to military training problems*. Dept. of Defense Rep. HR-HTD-201–1. 1953. Pp. 151–159.
9. D. O. Hebb. *The organization of behavior*. New York: Wiley, 1949.
10. E. R. Hilgard. The role of learning in perception. In R. R. Blake and G. V. Ramsey (eds.). *Perception: an approach to personality*. New York: Ronald, 1951. Pp. 95–120.
11. W. H. Ittelson. The constancies in perceptual theory. *Psychol. Rev.*, 1951, *58*, 285–294.
12. J. Jastrow. Psychological notes on Helen Keller. *Psychol. Rev.*, 1894, *1*, 356–362.
13. F. S. Keller. Studies in International Morse Code. I. A new method of teaching code reception. *J. appl. Psychol.*, 1943, *27*, 407–415.

14. F. P. Kilpatrick. *Human behavior from the transactional point of view.* Hanover, N. H.: Institute for Associated Research, 1952.
15. R. Leeper. A study of a neglected portion of the field of learning—the development of sensory organization. *J. genet. Psychol.,* 1935, *46,* 41–75.
16. L. Postman. Toward a general theory of cognition. In J. H. Rohrer and M. Sherif (eds.). *Social psychology at the crossroads.* New York: Harper, 1951. Pp. 242–272.
17. A. Volkmann. Über den Einfluss der Übung auf das Erkennen raumlicher Distanzen. *Ber. d. Sachs. Ges. d. Wiss., math. phys. Abth.,* 1858, *10,* 38–69.
18. G. M. Whipple. *Manual of mental and physical tests.* I. *Simpler processes.* Baltimore: Warwick and York, 1924.


# 18

# ASSOCIATION THEORY AND PERCEPTUAL LEARNING

## Leo Postman

The theoretical discussion of perceptual learning has received a welcome impetus from a recent critical analysis by Gibson and Gibson [6]. These writers focus on two opposing interpretations of perceptual learning which they designate as the *enrichment theory* and the *specificity theory.* Enrichment theory is presented as the embodiment of associationistic thinking about perceptual learning, whereas specificity theory represents the hypothesis of psychophysical correspondence. The Gibsons' argument is directed at a refutation of the associationistic position in general and the enrichment theory in particular. At the same time, a strong plea is made for the hypothesis of psychophysical correspondence, as represented by the specificity theory. This paper will attempt to state the case for the associationistic position.

"Is perception a creative process or is it a discriminative process? Is learning a matter of enriching previously meager sensations or is it a matter of differentiating previously vague impressions?" [6, p. 34]. These are the questions to which the enrichment theory and the specificity theory are said to provide diametrically opposed answers. According to enrichment theory, perceptual learning results from the association of

Source: *Psychological Review,* 1955, *62,* 438–446. Copyright 1955 by the American Psychological Association. Reprinted by permission.

sensory elements with memories of past experiences. These memories may be conceived as images, or as physiological traces. The essential point is that sensory elements produced by stimulation are assumed to be enriched by the arousal of such memories. As the fringe of associated memories grows, a constant sensory input gives rise to progressively more complex and more diversified experiences. This is Titchener's context theory or its modern equivalent. Such a view faces two major difficulties: (a) It perpetuates the distinction between sensation and perception, and hence inherits the thankless task of specifying the bare sensations to which memorial associations accrue. (b) It implies that perception comes to be in *"decreasing correspondence with stimulation"* [6, p. 34]. The richer the context which accrues to the sensory core, the further removed the percept is from the sensory data transmitted through the receptor system.

By contrast, the specificity theory holds that perceptual learning consists of the "progressive elaboration of qualities, features, and dimensions of variation" [6, p. 34]. Such elaboration becomes possible because the organism responds to more and more variables of physical stimulation. Perceptual discrimination becomes more subtle and more refined because the stimulus variables with which it stands in psychophysical correspondence become more subtle and more refined. This view is said to avoid both of the difficulties upon which associationistic theory has foundered. It is (a) no longer necessary to distinguish between sensation and perception, for perception is from the beginning and is always a matter of psychophysical discrimination; and (b) whenever perceptual learning occurs, it means increasing rather than decreasing correspondence with the variables of stimulation. Note, however, that no mechanism is proposed to account for the progressive changes in psychophysical relationships which constitute perceptual learning. At this point, the specificity theory is essentially the statement of an assumption or expectation, namely, that all perception follows a strict law of psychophysical correspondence. If perceptions change, there *must* be changes in the effective stimulus variables.

In developing our own discussion of the theory of perceptual learning, we shall find it useful to reaffirm the historical distinction between two facets of the associationistic position: the psychological and the physiological. Psychological associationism refers to the language in which the facts of learning are stated and the experimental problems are formulated. The conception of learning as consisting of linkages between ideas, or between stimuli and responses, exemplifies psychological associationism. Experimentally, the study of learning becomes the investigation of the conditions under which such linkages are established. Physiological associationism, on the other hand, refers to a class of hypotheses concerning the mechanisms which mediate the observed changes in experience or behavior. Thus, the hypotheses that learning depends on lowered synaptic resistances or on the formation of cell assemblies are examples of physiological associationism. We would expect to find the two kinds of associationism to be highly correlated in the thinking of psychological theorists. Physiological hypotheses which are associationistic in nature will necessarily be reflected in coordinate descriptions of behavior. It is possible, however, to argue for a psychological associationism without committing oneself to a specific physiological hypothesis. Such is precisely the position in which we shall find ourselves with respect to the problem of perceptual learning.

In their critique of the associationistic point of view, Gibson and Gibson have bracketed both its psychological and physiological implications. While stressing this distinction, we shall state our disagreement with the Gibsons' thesis on three counts: (a) The enrichment hypothesis discussed by them represents merely one historical stage in the associationistic approach to perceptual learning, and in some of its major aspects has long since been superseded by the formulations of behavior theory. Associationistic theory need not stand or fall with the historical version of the enrichment hypothesis. (b) Experimental methodology favors a formulation of the facts and problems of perceptual learning in the language of psychological associationism. (c) The specificity theory fails to generate testable hypotheses concerning the conditions and mechanisms of perceptual learning. We shall conclude that the specificity hypothesis has failed to challenge the associationistic position on either logical or empirical grounds.

## ASSOCIATIONISM AND THE ENRICHMENT HYPOTHESIS

The enrichment hypothesis, as exemplified by Titchener's context theory, represents the associationism of the structuralists and the introspectionists. The hypothesis had both a psychological and physiological component, and Titchener was careful to distinguish between them. Psychologically, a perception was regarded as a complex mental event which resolves into a number of sensations supplemented by images. Perceptual learning has occurred when an imaginal fringe has accrued to the sensory core, so that the complement of images, "puts more in the perception than the sensory stimuli can account for" [12, p. 115]. Both the nucleus and the fringe can be discovered by introspection. But, adds Titchener, "we perceive more than is furnished us by sensations and images.... Every perception is shaped and moulded by the action of nerve-forces which show themselves neither in sensation nor in image" [12, p. 115]. The sensations and the images are the descriptive psychological data; the causative physiological factors behind them are dispositions in the central nervous system. In fact, in the case of well-practiced perceptions, the imaginal fringe may all but disappear and the meaning of a percept be carried by the neural dispositions alone. Thus, Titchener draws a sharp distinction between the givens of consciousness and the neural processes underlying them, between the "law of nervous action" and the "law of mental connection." He quotes with approval James's dictum: "Association, so far as the word stands for an *effect,* is between things *thought of.* ... And so far as association stands for a *cause,* it is between *processes in the brain*—it is these which, by being associated in certain ways, determine what successive objects shall be thought" [9, p. 554]. And Titchener sums up succinctly, *"The brain associates and meanings are associated"* [12, p. 149].

Thus, the structuralist position encompassed both a psychological and a physiological associationism. The arguments of Gibson and Gibson are directed against both these historical views. However, contemporary associationists have lost interest in Titchener's "law of mental connection" and have substituted for it a new psychological associationism. At the same time, many of them have continued the search for a "law of nervous action." We must evaluate the validity of the Gibsons' arguments not against the historical position of structuralism but against the psychological and physiological associationism of present behavior theory.

## PSYCHOLOGICAL ASSOCIATIONISM AND THE CRITERIA OF PERCEPTUAL LEARNING

Associationists have long since left behind the introspective pursuit of bare sensations and accruing imaginal contexts. The timeworn arguments of the behaviorists and operationists which led to rejection of the introspective method need not be repeated here. The contemporary associationist deals neither with sensory cores nor with images. On the contrary, he would naturally begin by formulating the problem of perceptual learning in terms of stimuli and responses. The behavioral criterion of perceptual learning is a change in the nature of the responses evoked by a particular configuration or sequence of stimuli, where stimuli are defined in terms of physical operations. The two major classes of such responses with which we are concerned in experiments on perceptual learning with human subjects are (a) identifying responses, such as naming or labeling; and (b) discriminative responses such as *same* or *different, larger* or *smaller, higher* or *lower*—in short, the types of responses which we obtain in conventional psychophysical experiments.[1] We assert that perceptual learning has taken place when the relative frequencies of such responses undergo significant changes under controlled conditions of practice.

Experimentally, then, perceptual learning is defined by changes in stimulus-response relationships under controlled conditions of practice.

---

[1] As I have suggested elsewhere [10], our conclusions concerning the parameters of perceptual discrimination gain in generality if they are based on observations using more than one class of discriminatory responses.

We see no alternative formulation, short of recourse to introspection or the vague language of phenomenology. Once the problem has been so formulated, the relevance of the variables governing stimulus-response association to perceptual learning becomes clear. Examination of the literature shows that such principles as frequency, recency, effect, and associative interference are relevant to perceptual learning just as they are to verbal and motor learning [5, 10]. The psychological associationism of a stimulus-response formulation serves to emphasize the continuity between perceptual learning and other types of learning, with respect to both experimental operations and functional relationships. Descriptively, perceptual learning *is* the attachment of new responses, or a change in the frequency of responses, to particular configurations or sequences of stimuli.

There are undoubtedly those who will say that insistence on a stimulus-response formulation robs the study of perception of its very core and, indeed, its fascination, for it looks away from the richness and subtlety of perceptual experience. We do not share this anxiety. There is no reason why all the valid facts of perception cannot eventually be translated into the language of stimulus-response relationships. In the meantime, the unpopular pedantry of insisting on stimulus-response formulations may serve a healthy purpose. In arguing for a stimulus-response formulation of perceptual experiments, Graham writes: "... it may be argued that it does not provide a description of perception. Certainly it does not describe perception if by that term is meant any area of knowledge that exists between the limits of sensory nerve impulses on the one hand and the language responses ('private experience') of the patient on the other. Such a usage, of course, deprives the term of any significance or specificity" [7, p. 69]. We agree with Graham that a stimulus-response formulation helps to make perception an integral part of the study of behavior. By the same token, the problem of perceptual learning, formulated in terms of changing stimulus-response relationships, becomes part of the broader problem of associative learning.

The psychological associationism of stimulus and response avoids the two major difficulties which were raised in criticism of the psychological associationism of Titchener. (a) As Graham has pointed out, in terms of a stimulus-response formulation, "any presumed differences between 'sensory' and 'perceptual' research evaporate. Both types of research give rise to the same sort of stimulus-behavior function." [7, p. 69]. (b) As for the question of whether learning results in increasing or decreasing psychophysical correspondence, the present formulation does not require us to give an a priori answer. We may adopt one of two positions. We can, as a matter of definition, restrict the term learning to those cases in which controlled practice results in improved discrimination. Preferably, however, we can leave the question open, and let the facts decide whether and under what conditions changes produced by training do or do not result in improved discrimination. The question of psychophysical correspondence cannot be decided by fiat except at the peril of begging the question.

## THE PROBLEM OF ASSOCIATIVE MECHANISMS

One may well object at this point that we have defended the associationistic position by means of a restatement in operational terms which avoids the problem on which the analysis of Gibson and Gibson has focused, namely, the problem of enrichment versus differentiation. However, our insistence on a reformulation of the problem of perceptual learning in stimulus-response terms is an essential step in the development of the argument for two major reasons: (a) It was necessary to divorce once and for all the associationistic position from the concepts and methods of introspectionism, modern or old-fashioned. (b) It was equally essential to emphasize the fact that a theory of perceptual learning, of whatever persuasion, cannot sidestep the fact that discriminative *responses*—words, movements, autonomic responses, and so on—change as a result of training. Gibson and Gibson appear to take it for granted that appropriate responses will be somehow attached to the differentiated perceptions developed in the course of learning. We wish to stress the fact that the changes in response are part and parcel of the problem of perceptual learning. The need to account for changes in response inevitably endows the problem of perceptual learning with an associative component.

The problem of mediating mechanisms, however, remains. One may, to be sure, rest content with the psychological associationism of stimulus and response, and pursue the specifications of the conditions of perceptual learning within this framework. I take it that this is essentially the position advocated by Graham. For those who have, like the present writer, failed to be convinced by the explanatory powers of current theories of mediation, the position has much to recommend for itself. It is true, nevertheless, that there is an old and continuing tradition of physiological associationism, and we must examine its logical status in the light of the criticisms advanced by Gibson and Gibson. Historically, the enrichment hypothesis does, indeed, represent a major strand in the tradition of physiological associationism. In evaluating the physiological facet of the enrichment hypothesis, we must stress again that a "law of nervous action" can stand as an independent hypothesis, divorced from assumed correlations with introspective content. There are modern formulations of the enrichment hypothesis which confirm its independence of introspective data. A good example is provided by Spence's schematic analysis of perception into a series of events, beginning with sense reception and followed by the redintegration of past sensory events, which in turn leads to anticipatory responses, manipulations, or verbal responses [11]. In Spence's analysis, however, the associations aroused by the sensory events have the status of hypothetical constructs anchored to stimulus variables and observable responses, and do not depend for their validity on introspective or phenomenological evidence. It is possible to hold to a physiological enrichment hypothesis without implying an introspective distinction between sensation and perception. Nor does such a physiological associationism prejudge the question of increasing or decreasing psychophysical correspondence.

Physiological associationism does not necessarily take the form of an enrichment hypothesis. Consider Hebb's neurophysiological theory of perceptual learning. The fundamental assumptions of the theory are associationistic, but the process of perceptual learning is not described as the enrichment of invariant sensory events but rather in terms of progressive modifications of the central activities produced by stimulation. "According to the schema, the perception is constituted by a temporal sequence of activity in suprasensory (or association-area) structures which owe their organization to change at the synapse" [8, p. 102]. The changes at the synapse which constitute the physiological mechanism of learning govern the central transformations of sensory input.

The main point to be stressed concerning such physiological hypotheses is that one may assume an associative mechanism of perceptual learning without insisting that the events which are associated retain their identity or remain recoverable in perceptual analysis. This point is by no means new in the history of associationism. In contrasting the mental chemistry of John Stuart Mill with the mental compounding of James Mill, Boring writes: "... we never know about any element that *all* which we think ideally would enable us to predict the laws of the compound. We have always to study the compound directly, independently of its known or supposed elemental composition ... even when we know the generative process, we cannot deduce the law of the resultant: those laws must be found in every case from direct experiment" [1, pp. 230 ff.]. While Boring's remarks are directed specifically at the difference between two versions of psychological associationism, they apply to hypotheses about mediating mechanisms as well. Associationistic hypotheses about the mechanism of perceptual learning may be formulated without affirming that the associated elements must retain their identity in the resultant. What they must do is entail testable predictions about the resultant. Hebb and his associates have, indeed, been able to make specific predictions concerning the development of perceptual acuity which lend support to their assumptions concerning the generative process [8, pp. 49 ff.].

It must be recognized, however, that the body of facts supporting associationistic theories of the *mechanism* of perceptual learning remains small. For example, the perceptual constancies which are a mainstay of Helmholtzian empiricism continue to present a puzzle to physiological associationism or, for that matter, to any physiological theory of perception. It is true that the organism acts as though it had learned to make inferences about sizes, colors, and forms, but what the associative processes might be which underline such inferential learning is far from clear. We can specify the cues which the organism appears to use in the attainment of the distal properties of objects [3], but we know little about how the organism comes to use certain stimuli as cues or about the mechanisms which make the utilization of these cues possible. It is easy to agree with Brunswik [4] that hypotheses about specific mediating mechanisms of perception may be premature at the present stage of development.

Much of the experimental work on perceptual learning has been done under conditions of impoverished stimulation. In such cases it is particularly plausible to conceive of a neural redintegrative process initiated by a fragmentary sensory input. However, the components of the redintegrative chain have never been sufficiently specified to constitute a testable theory of mediating mechanisms. This essential vagueness and invulnerability is shared by other physiological and neurological theories of perceptual learning, such as, for example, the Gestalt theory of traces. The experimental facts have been all too ineffective in checking the elaboration of physiological fancies. However, to recognize that physiological associationism is as yet in a highly undeveloped state is very different from denying its possibility on a priori or logical grounds. We see no compelling reasons for such rejection.

## DIFFERENTIATION VERSUS ASSOCIATION

From the defense of associationism—psychological associationism now and physiological associationism as a possibility for the future—we turn to a reexamination of the specificity hypothesis. The critical difference between associationism and the specificity point of view appears to concern the degree of psychophysical correspondence assumed by the two positions. According to the specificity hypothesis, perceptual learning consists of "responding to variables of stimulation not previously responded to," and hence, "perceptual development is always a matter of correspondence between stimulation and perception" [6, p. 34]. By contrast, association theory is said to stress the enrichment of constant stimulus effects by the organism. It is our contention that the specificity position can be maintained only at the expense of avoiding or begging the question of learning.

What are the exact implications of the statement that perceptual learning consists of *responding* to variables of stimulation not previously responded to? If we take this statement at its face value, it would seem to assert that as a result of practice with certain stimuli new responses are associated with these stimuli. These responses, whatever their specific nature, have the function of mediating the differentiation of new qualities. We might, for example, conceive of such responses as receptor adjustments ensuring optimal exposure to the stimuli, such as focusing, scanning, and so on. It is clear, however, that such an interpretation is not intended by the specificity theory, for perceptual learning is said to consist not of the attachment of responses to stimuli but of the elaboration of new qualities. Thus, contrasting the connoisseur of wines with a man whose untutored palate cannot tell the difference between Chianti and claret, Gibson and Gibson write: "What has the first man learned that the second man has not? . . . he has learned to taste and smell more of the qualities of wine, that is, he discriminates more of the variables of chemical stimulation" [6, p. 35]. But if his learning is mediated neither by new receptor adjustments nor by centrally aroused associations, how are we to account for the acquisition of new differential responses? Surely we cannot assume that the stimuli have changed, for the stimuli are whatever they are. The fact that the organism has learned to discriminate more qualities is *the very fact that we need to explain*. The end result—the improvement in discrimination—cannot be accepted as a description of the learning process. It appears that the specificity hypothesis achieves its overriding emphasis on psychophysical correspondence by avoiding the critical problem of perceptual learning, namely, the nature of the processes which mediate the increased differentiation of the stimuli. Improvement in discrimination cannot be invoked to explain improvement in discrimination.

## INHERENT LIMITATIONS OF THE SPECIFICITY HYPOTHESIS

Even though the specificity hypothesis may not qualify as a theory of perceptual *learning,* one may wish to uphold it as a descriptive generalization to the effect that after practice as well as before practice "the stimulus input contains within it everything that the percept has" [6, p. 34]. Quite apart from the problem of mediating mechanisms, this generalization would assert that all the *results* of perceptual learning can be described adequately—and, indeed, exhaustively—as changes in psychophysical correspondence. Although such a generalization is logically tenable, its empirical adequacy is doubtful. The inherent limitations of the doctrine of psychophysical correspondence are brought out most clearly with reference to the perception of signs and symbols.

### The Perception of Sign Properties

Environmental events do not occur in complete independence of each other; the occurrence of one event implies, with some degree of probability, the occurrence of others. The existence of these sequential linkages makes it possible for the organism to learn means-end relationships, to respond to objects as signs of absent significates [13, pp. 135 ff.]. Tolman and Brunswik speak of the causal texture of the environment in which the organism is immersed and which is reflected in his perceptions and cognitions [14]. A general theory of perceptual learning must account for the development of sign perception. But the discrimination of sign properties necessarily depends on commerce with environmental sequences. Hence, sign perception would appear to be, almost by definition, an associative phenomenon: an object can be perceived as a sign only by virtue of the fact that the organism has associated the sign object with the object signified. The fact of sign perception makes it difficult to accept the impassable barrier between perception and memory erected by the specificity theorists. It is, indeed, the analysis of sign perception which led Tolman to conclude that "the differences between perceptions and mnemonizations are probably, in actuality, always differences in degree only . . . there are probably no actual cases of pure perceptions—i.e., perceptions unaided by any memory—save in newborn organisms" [13, p. 139]. The only alternative open to the specificity theorist is to assert that the facts of environmental linkage somehow become part of the *physical* stimulus pattern which constitutes the sign object! This would be tantamount to saying that the organism's past experiences somehow become translated into physical properties of stimuli, or at least that the organism comes to discover stimulus variables which carry the sign properties of the stimulus object in all their specific details. Every possible stimulus would have to have physical properties adequate for signifying every possible significate.

### The Perception of Symbols

Consideration of the perception of symbols similarly points to a breakdown of the specificity hypothesis. An important segment of the man-made perceptual world consists of symbols, of which words and numbers are the most familiar and frequent. Here are marks and sounds which the individual learns to perceive so that they carry meaning and significance. This is a case of perceptual learning par excellence, the environmental determination of which cannot be questioned. Little as we may know about the development of symbol perception, the very facts seem to demand an associationistic interpretation. Marks and sounds which are initially meaningless and undifferentiated come to be discriminated and identified by virtue of their appearance and usage in specific sequences and contexts. Again the specificity theory would have to maintain that all that is encompassed in the recognition or identification of a letter, a word, or a series of numbers or mathematical symbols is somehow carried by high-order stimulus variables. And, indeed, since any arbitrary mark or sound can be made into a symbol, all possible marks and sounds would have to have physical properties that can carry all possible connotations!

Thus, the historical problem of meaning in perception raises serious difficulties for the specificity position. It is precisely here that stimulus-response analysis comes into its own. As Boring pointed out in discussing the behavioristic analysis of meaning, "Response is the context which gives the stimulus its meaning for the responding organism. One sees, therefore, that a theory of perception lies implicit in modern psychological positivism" [2, pp. 18 ff.]. A theory of perceptual learning is equally implied. The organism has learned to perceive the meaning of a stimulus when it has learned to make the appropriate response.

## SUMMARY

We have examined two contrasting approaches to the problem of perceptual learning—traditional associationism and the specificity hypothesis of Gibson and Gibson, which ascribes all perceptual learning to the increasing effectiveness of stimulus variables. The case for the associationistic position has been reaffirmed, and the adequacy of the specificity formulation has been questioned. The argument stresses three major points: (a) Perceptual learning is a problem of behavior change, and experimentally reduces to the study of stimulus-response associations. (b) Associationistic hypotheses about the mechanism of perceptual learning can be entertained without reference to introspective evidence, without commitment to a particular epistemological position and without prejudice to the problem of psychophysical correspondence. (c) The specificity hypothesis assumes, but does not account for, improvement in discrimination, and does not entail a testable theory of perceptual learning.

## REFERENCES

1. E. G. Boring. *A history of experimental psychology*. 2d ed. New York: Appleton-Century-Crofts, 1950.
2. E. G. Boring. *Sensation and perception in the history of experimental psychology*. New York: Appleton-Century, 1942.
3. E. Brunswik. *Systematic and representative design of psychological experiments*. U. Calif. Syllabus Ser. No. 304. 1947.
4. E. Brunswik. *The conceptual framework of psychology*. Chicago: University of Chicago Press, 1952.
5. E. J. Gibson. Improvement in perceptual judgments as a function of controlled practice or training. *Psychol. Bull.*, 1953, *50*, 401–431.
6. J. J. Gibson and E. J. Gibson. Perceptual learning—differentiation or enrichment? *Psychol. Rev.*, 1955, *62*, 32–41.
7. C. H. Graham. Behavior and the psychophysical methods: An analysis of some recent experiments. *Psychol. Rev.*, 1952, *59*, 62–70.
8. D. O. Hebb. *Organization of behavior*. New York: Wiley, 1949.
9. W. James. *Principles of psychology*. Vol. 1. New York: Dover, 1950.
10. L. Postman. Experimental analysis of motivational factors in perception. In *Current theory and research in motivation*. Lincoln: University of Nebraska Press, 1953. Pp. 58–108.

11. K. W. Spence. Cognitive versus stimulus-response theories of learning. *Psychol. Rev.*, 1950, *57*, 159–172.
12. E. B. Titchener. *A beginner's psychology*. New York: Macmillan, 1915.
13. E. C. Tolman. *Purposive behavior in animals and men*. New York: Appleton-Century, 1932.
14. E. C. Tolman and E. Brunswik. The organism and the causal texture of the environment. *Psychol. Rev.*, 1935, *42*, 43–77.

# 19

# MATURATION OF PATTERN VISION IN INFANTS DURING THE FIRST SIX MONTHS

R. L. Fantz
J. M. Ordy
M. S. Udelf

Studies of the vision of young infants have been confined largely to the stimulus variables of intensity, wave length, and movement. This is apparently due to two assumptions: first, that tests of pattern vision are not feasible during the early months; and second, that negative results would be obtained in any case due to the immaturity of the eye and brain, which is presumed to prevent the focusing of an image on the retina, to interfere with precise retinal reception and neural transmission, and to exclude "cortical vision" [11, 15, 19].

Both assumptions have been challenged by studies comparing the visual attention given to stimuli differing only in form or pattern. Consistent differential response to patterns was shown by infants throughout the first 6 months [6] and as early as 1 day of age [17]. These studies, using large patterns, indicated that although pattern vision may be very poor in the early months, it is not absent. Data on visual acuity at various ages were needed to clarify the issue. The resolution of visual detail in-

Source: *Journal of Comparative and Physiological Psychology*, 1962, *55*, 907–917. Copyright 1962 by the American Psychological Association. Reprinted by permission.
Note: This research was supported by Grants M-2497 and M-5284 from the National Institute of Mental Health, United States Public Health Service. It was carried out with the cooperation of DePaul Infant Home.

volves most of the structures and functions underlying pattern and spatial vision. Thus visual acuity can provide a behavioral measure of the maturation of the basic visual mechanism as a foundation for studying the development of adaptive responses to specific visual patterns.

A so-called acuity test described by Gesell, Ilg, and Bullis [8] consists of placing a small sugar pellet at a certain distance in front of the infant and noting any reaction to it. A technique developed by Schwarting [16] requires the visual pursuit of a fine wire moving across a lighted area. A more sensitive technique involving visual pursuit, often used to test the acuity of animals, consists of observing the reflex eye and head movements to a large field of moving stripes and decreasing the width of stripes until this optokinetic nystagmus response is no longer present [13]. Recently Gorman, Cogan, and Gellis [9], using this technique with infants under 5 days of age found that 93 of 100 infants responded to stripes subtending a visual angle of 33.5 min, while few responded to stripes one-third as wide.

Although this result indicates a much better developed visual system in the newborn infant than had been assumed, its meaning for the maturation of pattern vision is uncertain. Structures which are important in the mediation of pattern vision—the central retina and the cerebral cortex— are not essential for the nystagmic response to patterned stimulation, at least in the adult animal [13, 18]. Furthermore, the reflex response to a moving pattern covering most of the visual field is a very different type of visual performance from the "voluntary" attention to the pattern of localized stationary objects. The latter response, representing a closer approach to the way pattern vision functions in most adaptive behavior of the adult, formed the basis for the acuity test in the present experiments. The optokinetic technique was used for comparison with the differential fixation test in the second study.

Young infants tend to look at patterned surfaces in preference to homogeneous ones [1, 6, 17]. If we present a graded series of patterns and find the smallest which elicits a differential ocular response, we know that visual detail at least that fine can be resolved. This method was shown to be feasible in a preliminary study [7]. Infants from 2 to 5 months responded to stripes subtending a visual angle as small as 18 min, while younger infants did not respond consistently to the sizes of pattern used.

## EXPERIMENT 1

The main aim was to obtain more complete data on the early development of acuity by using a larger sample of infants and a wider range of pattern size. A second aim was to find the effect of testing distance on the level of acuity to provide information on the maturation of accommodation for nearby distances. A third aim was to try to separate two parts of the total visual response to pattern: reflex responses to a peripheral pattern, and maintenance of a central fixation of the pattern.

## Method

*Procedure.* The procedure was to place an infant in a crib inside a test chamber and to expose above him a striped pattern and a plain gray comparison object for 20 sec. Ocular responses were observed through a peephole and recorded on timers and counters. A second exposure was made with reversed object positions. The initial positions were determined randomly. Stripes of varying widths were presented in this way in random order during a single test session. Within 2 weeks or less, each infant was given three such tests but with the distance of the stimulus objects changed. The order of testing at the three distances was varied systematically for all age levels.

*Apparatus.* The test chamber was basically a wooden box 2 ft sq and 30 in. high, resting on a low table. The lower half of the front side of the chamber was open so that a small hammock-type crib could be rolled underneath until the infant's head was directly under an observation hole in the center of the ceiling. The stimulus objects were attached to the ceiling to the right and left of this ¼-in. peephole. For the 5- and 10-in. distances, the objects extended down from the ceiling on dowel rods which were slanted so as to not be visible to the infant. Fine adjustments of the distance were made for each subject by raising or lowering the crib.

The objects were placed in position in the chamber through rectangular openings 14 × 5 in. high along the top of the right and left sides of the chamber. These openings also gave additional space needed for the 20-in. separation of the 8-in. stimulus objects. The ceiling of the chamber extended over the side openings to prevent the infant's seeing into the room (see Figure 19-1). The inside of the chamber was a nonglossy, dark saturated blue color which tended to quiet the infants and gave a contrasting background for the lighter achromatic objects.

The illumination of objects at each distance came through a horizontal slit in the back of the chamber from two 25-w projection bulbs not visible to the infant. They were directed obliquely to the object surfaces to eliminate glare, resulting in only about 4 ft-c of light reflected from the objects according to an illumination meter. The lights were equidistant from the test and comparison objects and also from the objects at the three test distances, to equate illuminance. Background illuminance was also held constant.

The objects were hidden from view between exposures by drawing two window shades horizontally across the middle of the chamber. A 2-in. hole in the center of the closed shades served to attract the infant's

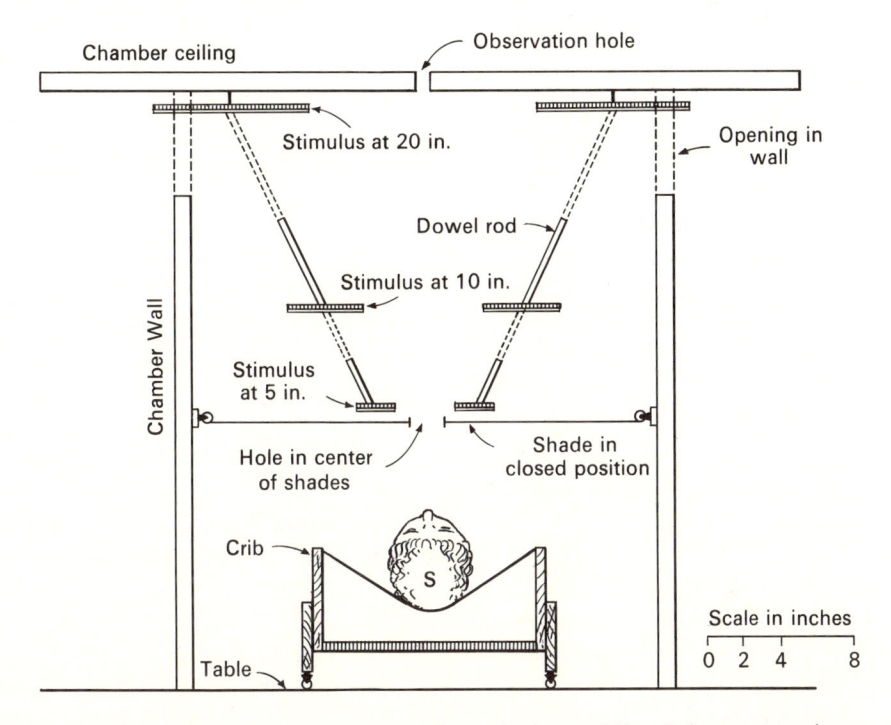

FIGURE 19-1  Schematic cross-section through the middle of the testing chamber, with the stimulus objects used at the three test distances superimposed on the same drawing. The drawing is to scale except for the ¼-in. observation hole.

gaze to the center and, at the same time, allowed the experimenter to wait until the gaze was midway between the objects before opening the shades, in order to minimize position preferences.

*Stimulus Objects.* The test patterns were squares with vertical black and white stripes of equal width. A series of five pattern sizes was used, each presented with the same gray square, matched in luminous reflectance. All objects were nonglossy photographic prints glued to posterboard. The original striped patterns were made by a scale-making machine tool accurate to 0.0001 in. Stimulus objects of a different size were used for each test distance (measured from the infant's eyes to the point midway between the test and comparison objects). For the 5-in. distance, the objects were 2-in. squares placed 5 in. apart, center to center; for the 10-in. distance, 4-in. squares 10 in. apart; for the 20-in. distance, 8-in. squares 20 in. apart. This resulted in a constant visual angle of 20° subtended by each test object and a constant visual angle of 53° between the two objects presented together (see Figure 19-1). The width of stripes also increased in proportion to distance, as shown in Table 19-1, to give a constant retinal size.

*Response Measure.* The subject's eyes were observed through the hole in the ceiling of the chamber. Tiny reflections of the stimulus objects

TABLE 19-1  Pattern Sizes for Each Testing Distance

| Visual Angle Subtended by Stripe (min) | Width of Stripe (in.) | | |
|---|---|---|---|
| | 5-in. Distance 2-in. Square | 10-in. Distance 4-in. Square | 20-in. Distance 8-in. Square |
| 5  | 1/128 | 1/64 | 1/32 |
| 10 | 1/64  | 1/32 | 1/16 |
| 20 | 1/32  | 1/16 | 1/8  |
| 40 | 1/16  | 1/8  | 1/4  |
| 80 | 1/8   | 1/4  | 1/2  |

were clearly visible on the cornea, under the given conditions of contrasting figures against a homogeneous ground. The location of one of these reflections over the pupil provided a simple criterion of fixation. If the left reflection was over the pupil, for example, the infant was looking at the object on the left. Since coordination of the two eyes was not always good in the early months, the location of a reflection over either pupil was accepted to indicate fixation as long as the reflection of the other object was not over the pupil of the other eye (which rarely occurred).

A reliability check of this criterion of fixation was made in an earlier study using photographic recordings [5]. Good agreement in the relative attention given to different objects was shown in independent analyses of the photographs. Direct observation of responses was used in the present experiments for greater clarity of observation and simplicity of procedure.

Fixations of the right and left objects were recorded by pressing the right or left of two telegraph-key switches. Each switch activated a Veedor counter when first pressed, to record the number of separate fixations, and also started a Thompson stopclock, to record the accumulated duration of fixations of the object during a 20-sec exposure. Timers and counters stopped automatically at the end of the exposure.

*Subjects.* The subjects were thirty-seven infants 1 to 22 weeks of age and included all infants under 6 months available at a foundling home at the time of the experiment excepting six who persistently cried or otherwise made testing impossible. The infants had been screened for gross abnormalities of any sort upon admittance to the home and, in addition, after the study had an ophthalmological examination which indicated no apparent ocular pathology.

In order to be able to finish a test session before the infant became fussy or fell asleep, the smaller pattern sizes were omitted for the younger infants and the largest pattern was omitted for the older ones. This selection was based on preliminary results suggesting the acuity level at each age.

## Results and Discussion

The scores for the two consecutive test periods with reversed right and left positions of the striped and plain objects were combined to balance out the position preferences shown by a number of the infants. Even a consistent tendency to look more at the right or at the left object did not in most cases prevent the infant from also showing consistent differential object fixation with the position effect controlled.

The main data analysis is based on the relative fixation time for patterned and unpatterned objects. Table 19-2 gives the consistency of pre-

TABLE 19-2 Visual Fixation Responses to Successive Pattern Sizes by Infants of All Ages at Each Distance

| Test Distance (in.) | No. of Infants Responding More to Stripes (in min of visual angle) Versus No. for Gray Comparison Object (G)† | | | | |
|---|---|---|---|---|---|
| | 5/G | 10/G | 20/G | 40/G | 80/G |
| 5 | 10/6 | 14/15 | 29/6*** | 27/7*** | 17/1*** |
| 10 | 6/11 | 16/14 | 28/8*** | 33/3*** | 14/5* |
| 20 | 10/7 | 19/11 | 25/10* | 28/8*** | 17/2*** |
| Total ‡ | 8/9 | 16/14 | 29/8*** | 34/3*** | 18/2*** |

† Since not all pattern sizes were used at each age level, the total N varies with stimulus pair.
‡ Based on combined scores for each infant at the three distances.
* $p < 0.05$ level.
*** $p < 0.001$ level.

dominant responses to stripes for infants of all ages. At each distance the three larger pattern sizes were each significantly differentiated from gray according to one-tailed sign tests. Thus, the tendency shown in previous studies for infants to attend more to patterned objects was verified under the present conditions to provide the necessary basis for estimating how fine a pattern can be resolved.

*Age.* The results for the three tests at different distances were included together for the analysis of age differences. With a criterion of 75% of the tests showing longer response to the patterned than to the plain object, the minimum separable visual angle for both the first and second month of age was 40 min; for each of the next 2 months, 20 min; and over 4 months, this criterion was almost reached (73%) for 10 min. That these data actually measure a sensory threshold was suggested by an abrupt change at the criterion point from a near-chance result (equal tests favoring stripes and gray) to a consistent choice of stripes over gray. Such a change was shown by all but the oldest group, in which case a majority of tests showed a choice of even the finest stripes presented.

The consistency of choice of the two above-threshold patterns by the youngest group is particularly noteworthy in view of the supposed absence of the ability to fixate as well as to see pattern in the neonate. The 80-min stripes were visually selected over gray in fifteen of eighteen tests; the 40-min stripes in thirteen of seventeen tests; while the 20-min stripes were selected in half the tests.

Another basis for estimating the threshold for pattern at each age level is the average strength of the response differential for each size of pattern, shown in Figure 19-2. Again there is a clear separation between

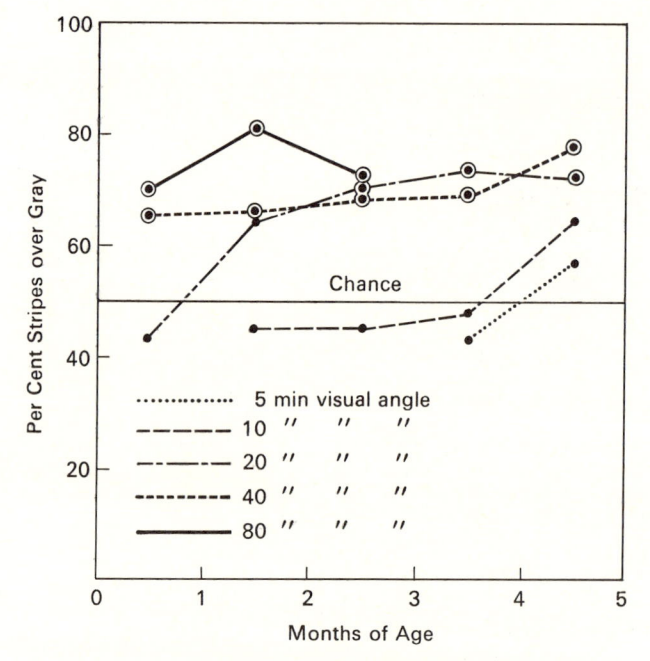

FIGURE 19-2 Differential strength of visual fixation response to squares with varying angular fineness of pattern, averaged for tests at three distances for all infants at a given age. Encircled points indicate that 75% of individual tests showed predominant response to pattern.

the close-to-chance response level (equal duration of fixation of stripes and gray) for most below-threshold results and the uniformly high differential response to above-threshold patterns. A lower threshold was suggested for the second month; otherwise there is agreement with the frequency criterion.

*Distance.* One possible cause of less acute vision during the first month or two than later on is inability of the optical mechanism to focus a clear retinal image of a near object. It is known from ophthalmological measurements that the young infant is hyperopic ("farsighted"), which has been attributed to the short distance between lens and retina [12].

The hyperopic eye requires accommodation of the lens to focus at any distance and especially at a short distance. However, it is often stated that the neonatal infant has little if any power of accommodation [11, 15]. If true, this would mean a blurred retinal image, with consequent loss of acuity at short test distances. This blurring would be expected to be accentuated by the low illumination used in this study due to the resultant large pupillary opening and reduction in depth of focus.

However, test distance had no noticeable effect on the response to pattern of a given retinal size for the range of sizes and distances used. This is shown in Table 19-2 for all ages combined. Likewise, the data for successive age groups did not reveal any relation between distance and visual acuity. In particular, the infants under 1 month of age attended equally to above-threshold patterns when placed at the three distances: stripes subtending 80 min received an average of 70%, 73%, and 69% of the fixation time at 5, 10, and 20 in., respectively, while the corresponding figures for stripes half as wide were 63%, 65%, and 64%. Gorman et al. [9] found a similar level of acuity in newborn infants tested at 6 in. for optokinetic nystagmus.

These results give behavioral evidence that the neonatal infant, in spite of being hyperopic, can focus sharply enough at a very short distance to resolve a near-threshold pattern, thus implying considerable power of accommodation. This is in agreement with anatomical and ophthalmological information [12, 14] suggesting that the optical system of the eye is functional at birth.

Since binocular coordination on a nearby object is not perfected for several months after birth, it is an interesting question why this would not impair visual acuity at close range. The answer may be that the doubling of the retinal image of an object due to lack of convergence need not obscure the pattern of either image provided it is superimposed on a homogeneous background.

*Central Fixation Versus Peripheral Reflex.* Two other developmental factors which have been cited as causes of poor vision in the early months are the late maturation of the central retina compared with the periphery, and the supposed late appearance of nonreflex visual responses. Information on these factors was given by analyzing the fixation-time data into two component responses:

1. The *number* of separate fixations of each object during a test period, showing the number of times a stimulus falling on the peripheral retina elicits eye and head movements to bring the stimulus to the center of the visual field. The relative number of fixations of patterned and plain objects thus measures peripheral vision and reflex response tendencies.

2. The average *length* of fixation, derived by dividing the accumulated fixation time by the number of fixations, showing the length of time central fixation was maintained by interest in the object. The relative length of fixation of patterned and unpatterned objects thus measures vision in

a more central area of the retina and the tendency to inhibit movements to peripheral stimuli.

Both measures indicated greater responsiveness to a visible pattern than to gray, but the differential for length of fixation was more pronounced and more consistent than for number of fixations. The relative consistency of the two measures is shown in Table 19-3, based only on

TABLE 19-3 Comparison of the Differential Response to a Near-Threshold Pattern Based on Three Different Measures of Visual Fixation

| Age (months) | N | Width of Stripes (min) | No. of Fixations‡ | Mean Length of Fixation | Resultant Fixation Time |
|---|---|---|---|---|---|
| 0–1 | 7 | 40 | 4/3 | 5/2 | 6/1 |
| 1–2 | 6 | 40 | 4/1 | 6/0 | 6/0 |
| 2–3 | 7 | 20 | 4/3 | 6/1 | 6/1 |
| 3–4 | 7 | 20 | 5/1 | 7/0 | 7/0 |
| 4–5 | 10 | 10 | 7/2 | 8/2 | 8/2 |
| Total | 37 | | 24/10 | 32/5 | 33/4 |

No. of Infants Favoring Stripes Versus Gray for Each Measure†

† Based on total scores for each infant on three tests at different distances.
‡ Total N is lower due to three tie scores.

data from the finest pattern discriminated by each age group. The frequencies for length of fixation are almost identical to those for total response time, while the differential for number of fixations is less consistent.

Figure 19-3 compares graphically the strength of the selectivity for a patterned object as measured by the average number of eye movements toward a peripheral stimulus and by the average duration of a central fixation. The relative responsiveness to gray and to stripes for each measure is shown by the relative distances along the scale. The areas enclosed by the two coordinates represent the resultant total response time for gray or for stripes during 40 sec of testing. The stripes-gray differential is proportionally greater along the horizontal axis than along the vertical axis, especially for the infants under 3 months, for whom fixations were longer in general than for older infants.

These results do not prove that macular vision was more acute than peripheral vision, since the stimulus objects were so large that nonmacular parts of the retina may have contributed to the acuity shown by the central fixation component of the visual response. What these results do mean is that the overall response to fine patterns must be attributed primarily to sustained visual interest in a patterned stimulus once it falls on

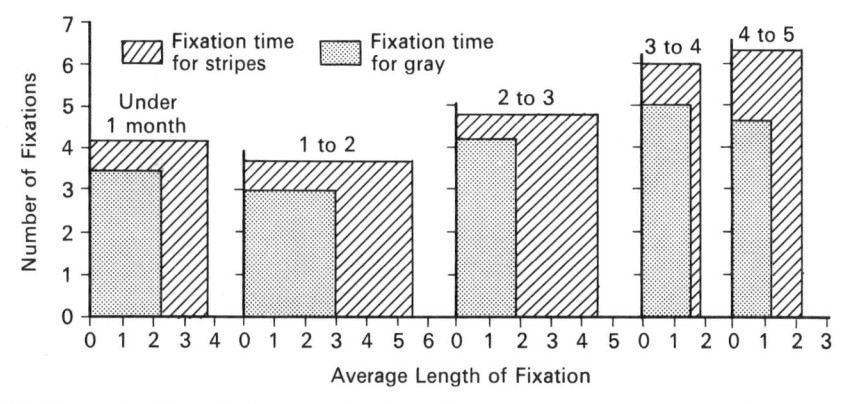

FIGURE 19-3 The relative contribution of two component responses (measured along the two coordinates) to the resultant total fixation time for patterned and for plain stimuli (area of the striped and of the gray portion) averaged for all pattern sizes and test distances.

a broad central region of the retina, rather than to the peripheral response component. Stirnimann's results with newborns also imply sustained fixation of patterns. This central attentiveness to fine details, which might be considered the voluntary part of the fixation response, is thus present in immature form from the first month of life. Further development of this response and further maturation of the macula are undoubtedly important causes of the improvement in visual acuity during the early months.

## EXPERIMENT 2

The pattern-fixation test of acuity was compared with a more conventional acuity test based on the optokinetic nystagmus response to a moving striped field. It was hoped that the two different techniques would provide a check on each other and perhaps also clarify the role of various factors in the development of acute vision. The testing was done by another investigator using mostly new subjects.

### Method

*Optokinetic Test.* The apparatus was similar to that used by Gorman et al. [9]. A roll of 16-in.-wide heavy paper had four 6-ft sections of vertical black and white stripes alternating with 2-ft sections of plain gray. The width of the stripes in the successive sections was 1/8 in., 1/16 in., 1/32 in., and 1/64 in., respectively. This paper was rolled from one drum to another around semicircular, 1-in.-wide strips of metal at either edge of the paper and in the middle, thus forming a half-cylinder chamber under the paper and between the drums. The hammock crib used in the first study was placed in such a position in this chamber that the subject's eyes were in the center and about 10 in. from the paper all around the arc. Gray boards extended part way down from either edge of the paper to restrict the infant's view into the room and thus keep his attention on the moving stripes. The drums were turned by a hand crank so the speed could be easily varied. Fairly uniform illumination of the stripes was provided by a 25-w incandescent bulb placed near the center of the chamber and level with the infant's head.

The procedure was to move the section of ⅛-in. stripes slowly around the arc and observe the response from the front or back of the chamber. If pursuit eye and head movements in the direction of the stimulus movement were clearly present, followed by saccadic eye movements in the opposite direction, the next finer stripes were used, and so on. If the response was negative or uncertain, the same section of stripes was moved back and forth a number of times at varying speeds in the attempt to elicit a nystagmic response. When the response was in doubt, the test was repeated later. Two levels or qualities of nystagmic response were recorded: "Poor" responses were counted as positive in the data analysis when there was agreement between two separate tests given before and after the pattern-fixation test; a "good" response on either test was counted.

*Pattern-Fixation Test.* The apparatus was the same as for experiment 1. Only the 4-in. squares were used, at a distance of 10 in. and 10 in. apart. The largest pattern was omitted so that the same four widths of stripes were used as in the optokinetic test. For each infant the test started with the ⅛-in. pattern paired with the gray comparison object; then the objects were reversed for another 20-sec exposure. Successively smaller patterns were presented in the same manner. Only the accumulated fixation time for each object was recorded. Illumination was given by a single 25-w incandescent bulb level with the infant's head and equidistant from the two stimuli. The amount of light reflected from the stripes was almost as much as in the optokinetic test and about the same as for the fixation test in experiment 1.

*Subjects.* The subjects were forty-six healthy infants 4 days to 6 months of age, of which ten had been used 3 months earlier in the first study.

**Results and Discussion**

The results are presented in Table 19-4 for each month of age and for each size of pattern. The data for the two techniques have a somewhat different meaning. For the fixation test, a close-to-equal frequency of infants responding more to stripes and more to gray indicates lack of discrimination; for the optokinetic test, a "zero" first frequency indicates lack of nystagmic response to that pattern size, while an intermediate value has no certain interpretation and could mean individual differences or fluctuations in sensory threshold or motor coordination, or errors of

TABLE 19-4  Comparison of Visual Acuity Data from Pattern-Fixation (F) and Optokinetic (O) Nystagmus Tests of Same Infants

| Age (months) | Test | \multicolumn{4}{c}{No. of Infants Responding to Stripes of Each Size (in min) Versus No. Not Responding} | | | |
|---|---|---|---|---|---|
| | | 5 | 10 | 20 | 40 |
| 0–1 | F | 2/3 | 2/3 | **6/1** | **6/1** |
|     | O | 0/7 | 0/7 | **7/0** | **7/0** |
| 1–2 | F | 5/4 | 6/4 | 6/4 | **10/0** |
|     | O | 0/10 | 6/4 | **10/0** | **10/0** |
| 2–3 | F | 3/4 | 5/3 | 7/2 | **8/1** |
|     | O | 0/9 | 3/6 | **9/0** | **9/0** |
| 3–4 | F | **6/1** | **7/1** | **8/0** | **8/0** |
|     | O | 1/7 | 6/2 | **8/0** | **8/0** |
| 4–5 | F | 4/3 | **6/1** | **7/0** | **7/0** |
|     | O | 3/4 | **7/0** | **7/0** | **7/0** |
| 5–6 | F | **4/1** | **5/0** | **5/0** | **5/0** |
|     | O | **5/0** | **5/0** | **5/0** | **5/0** |
| All ages | F | 24/16 | 31/12 | **39/7** | **44/2** |
|          | O | 9/37 | 27/19 | **46/0** | **46/0** |

Note: Entries in boldface indicate stripe response frequencies meeting the 75% criterion.

observation due to ambiguity of the response. However, for either technique a high percentage of response to pattern is indicative of visual resolution. A criterion of 75% was chosen to give a rough comparison of the threshold value for the two techniques. According to this criterion, the threshold differs only at two age levels—lower for the optokinetic test from 1 to 2 months and lower for the fixation test from 3 to 4 months.

This close correspondence is surprising in view of the small samples and the difference in mechanism underlying the two responses. It is possible that factors which might be expected to favor better performance on the fixation test (that is, a stationary stimulus pattern falling on the retinal area of most acute vision), were balanced by factors which might tend to result in poorer performance by young infants on the fixation test (that is, a nonreflex and more variable type of response, requiring better oculomotor coordination and a greater degree of cortical involvement than does optokinetic nystagmus). Whether or not this is the correct interpretation, the agreement between the two techniques gives support for the results of the pattern fixation test.

An interesting methodological comparison was brought out in the process of recording the two different responses to pattern. Optokinetic nystagmus was often fleeting and irregular with the younger subjects and the finer stripes. Consequently, qualitative judgments were necessary, and these judgments for near-threshold patterns varied considerably in repeated observations. The expected objectivity of the optokinetic test was not apparent. In contrast, the fixation test of acuity involved a simple, unambiguous criterion of fixation at each moment, and a quantitative criterion of differential response for each test.

Table 19-5 combines the fixation-test results of the first two studies, using 2-month intervals. With this increase in sample size, the results are very consistent. The threshold pattern size for the first 2 months is 40 min; for the next 2, 20 min; and the for the last 2 months, 10 min of visual angle.

TABLE 19-5 Combined Fixation Acuity Data for the First and Second Studies

| Age (months) | N† | \multicolumn{5}{c}{No. of Infants Favoring Stripes Versus No. Favoring Gray (in min)} |
| --- | --- | --- | --- | --- | --- | --- |
| | | 5/G | 10/G | 20/G | 40/G | 80/G |
| 0–2 | 30 | 7/7 | 10/11 | 18/12 | 28/2*** | 12/1** |
| 2–4 | 31 | 11/10 | 18/12 | 28/3*** | 28/3*** | 6/1 |
| 4–6 | 22 | 14/8 | 19/3*** | 22/0*** | 22/0*** | — |
| Total | 83 | 32/25 | 47/26** | 68/15*** | 78/5*** | 18/2*** |

† Number in each cell often is less than total N, since all pattern sizes were not used at each age level in the first study and the 80-min pattern was not used at all in the second study.
** $p < 0.01$ level (sign test).
*** $p < 0.001$ level (sign test).

## EXPERIMENT 3

The last study was undertaken primarily to make certain of the reliability of the differential fixation test of acuity. The visual responses of each infant were observed and recorded independently by two people. Repeatability was determined from two tests of each infant under the same conditions. A further control consisted of using two shades of gray as comparison object—one lighter and one darker than the striped patterns—instead of matching the reflectance as previously. The illumination was increased to see if the threshold would be lowered.

### Method

The apparatus was the same as in experiment 2 with these exceptions. Instead of attaching stimulus objects to the ceiling of the chamber, stripes and gray were visible through two holes in the ¼-in. ceiling, each

7 × 5 in. wide, and 12 in. apart, center to center. New striped and gray stimuli were used, placed 15½ in. from the infant's eyes. They were larger than the holes and were placed directly on top of the chamber so as to cover the holes. This arrangement permitted quick changing of the objects between test periods.

Observations were made through two ¼-in. holes, one adjacent to the lower edge (toward the infant's feet) of each stimulus object. The two observers, one on each side of the chamber, each recorded the fixation times by means of silent finger switches and timers out of sight of the other observer. During the first series of tests, the observer on the left of the chamber placed the stimulus objects in position without the other observer knowing which was the striped pattern or the width of stripes. In the repeat series of tests, the observer on the right handled the objects. The scores of the two observers were not compared until after the series of tests was completed.

Four widths of stripes (1/64, 1/32, 1/16, and 1/8 in.) were used with each infant in random sequence. Two consecutive 20-sec periods were given with each pattern size. For the second period, the right and left positions were reversed and a different gray comparison object was used. The initial positions and the gray used first were determined randomly. One gray had a slightly higher, the other a slightly lower, luminous reflectance than the striped patterns. Both stripes and grays had a mat finish to eliminate glare.

Four 60-w incandescent lamps with reflectors were placed in the bottom four corners of the chamber, below the infant's eyes. To give further diffusion of the light and reduce glare on the chamber walls above the lights, the walls were covered with finely knit, medium blue jersey cloth. The ceiling was a lighter blue than in the previous studies to reduce the figure-ground contrast and thus favor acute vision. The ceiling was just enough darker than the stimulus surfaces to make reflections of the latter clearly visible in the infant's eyes. The lights were connected to a Powerstat set at 90% voltage, which seemed to give about the maximum of light without discomfort to the younger infants. An illumination meter measured about 12 ft-c close to the stimulus surfaces, roughly three times as much as in the first study.

*Subjects.* The subjects were twenty-three healthy infants ranging from 7 to 29 weeks of age. (Younger infants were not available at this time.) Each was given two complete tests within 2 weeks or less, at median ages of 14 and 15 weeks.

## Results and Discussion

*Reliability.* The differential responsiveness to stripes was remarkably consistent between the simultaneous recordings of two observers and also between repeated tests of the same infants. In terms of the frequency of choice of stripes and of gray, the three larger patterns were responded to significantly (0.01 level, sign test) for all four sets of data. There was no appreciable difference in the results from observers with and without knowledge of the stimuli.

Figure 19-4 gives a comparison of the four sets of data in terms of average strength of responsiveness to patterned surfaces over plain. The four curves are very similar, each showing differential response for all but the finest stripes.

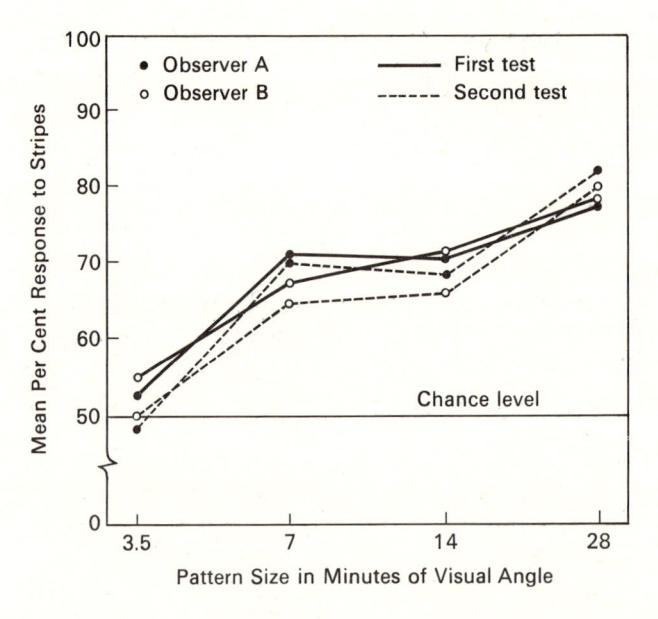

FIGURE 19-4 Reliability of the differential-fixation test of acuity as shown by similarity in results of two tests of the same infants, each recorded independently by two observers.

These results indicate reliability of the testing technique and response measurement. They further show that very similar responses were observed through different peepholes, one close to each stimulus. This is of interest because a change in the observer's position theoretically can displace the corneal reflection of an object relative to the pupil, which indicates whether or not the object is fixated. When the observer is in line with the object and the infant, a fixated object is reflected directly over the pupil. This superposition is not always exact when the observer is to one side of the object, depending on the degree of curvature of the cornea and the distance between cornea and pupil for a particular subject. While any resulting error should be equalized for right and left objects when the observer is in the center, the position of the observers in this study would accentuate any such error by increasing the left observer's error for the right object and vice versa. Since the observers agreed nevertheless, the influence of this factor in the previous studies, using a center observation hole, may be dismissed.

*Reflectance Control.* When the test periods with different comparison objects were analyzed separately, no difference was shown. About an equally low amount of visual attention was directed toward the gray with higher reflectance than the stripes (an average of 33% of the response time for all infants and tests) and toward the gray with lower reflectance than the stripes (31% of response time). In terms of the numbers of infants favoring stripes or gray, a significant response to pattern was shown both for pairings with the light gray and the dark gray. This was true in each test and for each pattern size except the smallest, which was not differentiated in the combined results. Thus, the differential response was clearly due to the presence or absence of pattern, not to a brightness difference. Similarly, Berlyne [1] found no significant difference in the visual attention given by infants to white, gray, and black, while differences in pattern aroused differential responses.

*Age and Illumination.* Table 19-6 gives an age breakdown of the results, averaged for the two observers. The frequencies are the numbers of tests favoring stripes or gray, including the two tests for each infant described above, as well as preliminary tests given to the same and to six additional infants. The larger patterns were differentiated at all age levels while the narrowest stripes, subtending only 3.5 min, elicited increasing visual response with age and passed the 75% criterion during the sixth month. If the several tests for each infant over 5 months are averaged and combined with the same age group in experiment 2, ten of twelve infants show a differential response to either 3.5- or 5-min stripes, the finest used in the respective studies.

The threshold for pattern suggested by the data in Table 19-6 is lower at each age level than in the earlier experiments (Table 19-5). Al-

TABLE 19-6 Visual Fixation Responses to Patterns of Successive Sizes by Infants at Various Age Levels with Increased Illumination (Includes One to Three Tests of Each Infant)

| Age (months) | N† | No. of Tests Favoring Stripes Versus No. Favoring Gray ||||
|---|---|---|---|---|---|
| | | 3.5/G | 7/G | 14/G | 28/G |
| 2–3 | 14 | 11/11 | **16/6** | **17/5** | **18/4** |
| 3–4 | 12 | 11/7 | **14/4** | **15/2** | **16/2** |
| 4–5 | 10 | 7/4 | **9/3** | **11/1** | **12/0** |
| 5–6 | 8 | **9/3** | **11/1** | **10/2** | **12/0** |

Note: Entries in boldface indicate stripe response frequencies meeting the 75% criterion.
† The total N was 28 since some infants were tested at several age levels.

though there were several changes in conditions, this is most likely due to better illumination of the stimuli and background, since illumination is known to affect the acuity of adults markedly.

## GENERAL DISCUSSION

The results of the various acuity tests give a far different picture of the development of pattern vision than the common view that the young infant can see only vague masses of light and dark, or is lacking in pattern vision until several months of age due to immaturity of the visual system or the need for visual experience. Instead, pattern vision becomes progressively more acute, starting with the ability of the neonate to see stripes as narrow as ⅛ in. at a 10-in. distance. By 6 months, 1/64-in. stripes can be resolved at 10 or at 15 in.

These figures cannot be taken as absolute limits of visual resolution at the various age levels without knowing the optimal testing conditions, such as illumination, figure-ground contrast, type of pattern, size of field, and so on, and without data from a large, representative sample of infants using a wide range of pattern sizes. Even so, these studies show much more acute vision than previous studies. For subjects at 4 months, Chavasse [3] found an acuity of 20/2,560 in the Snellen notation, based on the reaction to a small pellet, while the present results would correspond roughly to 20/200 or better at this age. For subjects at 6 months, Chavasse found an acuity of 20/960, and Schwarting [16] gives the figure of 20/400 based on the pursuit of a fine line, compared with 20/100 or 20/70 according to the pattern-fixation test results above.

The only comparable result was obtained by Gorman et al. [9] based on optokinetic nystagmus to moving stripes. They found an acuity of 20/670 in newborn infants, compared with 20/400 in the present optokinetic test and 20/800 in the fixation test of infants under one month with lower illumination. When all ages are considered, the present results for the optokinetic and fixation tests are similar (Table 19-4).

The above comparison of present results with previous ones justifies the unconventional use of a stimulus preference method for determining a sensory threshold. The usual arguments against such a method are that negative results do not necessarily mean inability to discriminate, and that even if positive results are obtained they would be more variable and show lower sensitivity than methods providing better motivation, as by means of reward or instructions or by using a reflex response. However, the differential-fixation test of acuity has revealed much finer visual resolution than other methods based on a "voluntary" response and about equal to those based on a reflex response. Futhermore, one could hardly ask for less variability among subjects than shown by the visual choice of a near-threshold pattern in preference to gray by twenty-eight of thirty infants under 2 months of age (Table 19-5); or less variability in repeated tests or between independent observations than shown by the similar curves in Figure 19-4. The differential-fixation method thus is a sensitive and reliable test of visual acuity in spite of being based on free choice rather than forced or reinforced behavior; in fact *because* it is based on an innate and yet nonreflex response, the method gets meaningful results with subjects too immature for traditional tests of pattern vision.

The infant has the ability to see fairly fine patterns from the first month of life; to see equally well at 5, 10, and 20 in.; and to respond to patterns by continuing to gaze voluntarily at a pattern falling on the central retina as well as by reflexly turning toward a peripheral pattern or following a large moving pattern with eyes and head. These facts imply that all parts of the visual system, from the optical apparatus of the eye to the visual centers of the brain, are functional soon after birth, however structurally immature they are. This conclusion is in essential agreement with the best available anatomical, neurophysiological, ophthalmological, and behavioral information. Contrary to some reports, studies of newborn infants have shown that some degree of fixation and accommodation is present [8, 14], that retinal hemorrhages are rare [2], and that electrophysiological activity of the retina and visual cortex is elicited by visual stimulation [4, 10]. The arguments purporting to prove the lack of cortical vision in the young infant are inconclusive, while the present data are sufficient evidence for cortical vision, since pattern vision is completely absent in mammals from rats to humans without visual cortex [13].

The marked increase in the precision of pattern vision during the first 6 months, from a threshold of 40 to 5 min or less, is easily explained by the extensive maturation of the visual apparatus during this period. Probably of most importance are the increased density of macular receptors, completed myelinization of nerve fibers, maturation of the visual cortex, and improved skill in foveal fixation.

Neither visual learning nor postnatal maturation are necessary for the infant to see and respond to a patterned stimulus when the response is innate and the stimulus intrinsically interesting. Knowing this and knowing the approximate acuity at various ages should make it easier to find out how and when pattern vision comes to be used to perceive objects and space and to direct more complex behaviors.

## SUMMARY

The differential-fixation test of visual acuity was used to determine the ability of the young infant to resolve and attend to fine patterns. It was based on the natural tendency of infants to fixate a striped stimulus more than a gray stimulus. Each of a series of patterns with different widths of stripes was exposed to the infant in a controlled fashion to determine the finest pattern differentiated from gray according to relative duration or number of fixations.

In experiment 1, thirty-seven infants were tested at three distances with patterns subtending the same visual angle. No difference in acuity was shown at 5, 10, and 20 in., suggesting the ability to accommodate for near vision from early infancy. Under 1 month, the minimum separable visual angle was 40 min (1/8-in. stripes at 10 in.); by 5 months, this was reduced to 10 min. The total visual response to pattern was due primarily to maintaining the central fixation of a pattern rather than to reflex fixation of a peripherally seen pattern.

Experiment 2, using forty-six infants, showed about the same level of acuity for differential fixation of patterns as for optokinetic nystagmus to a moving striped field. The fixation test supported experiment 1 and suggested a pattern threshold of 5 min by 6 months of age.

In experiment 3, twenty-three infants over 2 months old were tested twice with responses recorded independently by two observers. The four sets of data were very similar in frequency of choice of each size of pattern and in average strength of differential responsiveness to pattern, indicating the reliability of the testing method. A lower threshold for pattern was shown than in the other studies, probably due to better illumination.

The results refute the common opinion that the young infant is lacking in pattern vision or can see only vague masses of light and dark. The results imply that all parts of the visual mechanism, from cornea to cortex, function to some degree in the neonate, although further development of visual structures and functions during the first 6 months causes progressively more acute vision.

## REFERENCES

1. D. E. Berlyne. The influence of the albedo and complexity of stimuli on visual fixation in the human infant. *Brit. J. Psychol.*, 1958, 49, 315–318.
2. R. R. Chase, K. K. Merritt, and M. Bellows. Ocular findings in the newborn. *Arch. Ophthal., Chicago*, 1950, 44, 236–242.
3. F. B. Chavasse. *Worth's squint or the binocular reflexes and the treatment of strabismus.* 7th ed. Philadelphia: Blakiston, 1939.
4. R. J. Ellingson. Electroencephalograms of normal, full-term newborns immediately after birth with observations on arousal and visual evoked responses. *EEG clin. Neurophysiol.*, 1958, 10, 31–50.
5. R. L. Fantz. A method for studying early visual development. *Percept. mot. Skills*, 1956, 6, 13–15.
6. R. L. Fantz. Pattern vision in young infants. *Psychol. Rec.*, 1958, 8, 43–47.
7. R. L. Fantz and J. M. Ordy. A visual acuity test for infants under six months of age. *Psychol. Rec.*, 1959, 9, 159–164.

8. A. Gesell, F. L. Ilg, and G. E. Bullis. *Vision: Its development in infant and child.* New York: Hoeber, 1949.
9. J. J. Gorman, D. G. Cogan, and S. S. Gellis. An apparatus for grading the visual acuity of infants on the basis of optokinetic nystagmus. *Pediatrics,* 1957, *19,* 1088–1092.
10. G. P. M. Horsten and J. E. Winkelman. Development of the ERG in relation to the histological differentiation of the retina in man and animals. *Arch. Ophthal., Chicago,* 1960, *63,* 232–242.
11. M. B. McGraw. *The neuromuscular maturation of the human infant.* New York: Columbia University Press, 1943.
12. I. Mann. *The development of the human eye.* New York: Grune & Stratton, 1950.
13. C. T. Morgan and E. Stellar. *Physiological psychology.* New York: McGraw-Hill, 1950.
14. A. Peiper. *Die Eigenart der Kindlichen Hirntätigkeit.* Leipzig: Thieme, 1949.
15. K. C. Pratt. The neonate. In L. Carmichael (ed.). *Manual of child psychology.* New York: Wiley, 1946. Pp. 190–254.
16. B. H. Schwarting. Testing infants' vision. *Amer. J. Ophthal.,* 1954, *38,* 714–715.
17. F. Stirnimann. Über das Farbenempfinden Neugeborener. *Ann. Paedia.,* 1944, *163,* 1–25.
18. F. B. Walsh. *Clinical neuro-ophthalmology.* Baltimore: Williams & Wilkins, 1957.
19. J. P. Zubek and P. A. Solberg. *Human development.* New York: McGraw-Hill, 1954.

# 20
# PATTERN VISION IN NEWBORN INFANTS

R. L. Fantz

*Human infants under 5 days of age consistently looked more at black-and-white patterns than at plain colored surfaces, which indicates the innate ability to perceive form.*

It is usually stated or implied that the infant has little or no pattern vision during the early weeks or even months, because of the need for visual learning or because of the immature state of the eye and brain, or for both reasons [1, 5, 6]. This viewpoint has been challenged by the direct evidence of differential attention given to visual stimuli varying in form or pattern [2, 4]. This evidence has shown that during the early months of life, infants: (a) have fairly acute pattern vision (resolving ⅛-in. stripes at a 10-in. distance); (b) show greater visual interest in patterns than in plain colors; (c) differentiate among patterns of similar complexity; and (d) show visual interest in a pattern similar to that of a human face.

The purpose of the present study was to determine whether it was possible to obtain similar data on newborn infants and thus further exclude visual learning or postnatal maturation as requirements for pattern vision. It is a repetition of a study of older infants which compared the visual responsiveness to patterned and to plainly colored surfaces [3]. The results of the earlier study were essentially duplicated, giving further support for the above conclusions.

The subjects were eighteen infants ranging from 10 hr to 5 days old. They were selected from a much larger number on the basis of their eyes remaining open long enough to be exposed to a series of six targets at least twice. The length of gaze at each target was observed through a tiny hole in the ceiling of the chamber and recorded on a timer. The fixation

Source: *Science*, 1963, *140*, 296–297. Copyright 1963 by the American Association for the Advancement of Science.

Note: Supported by National Institute of Mental Health Grant M-5284. The author is indebted to Booth Memorial Hospital for making the subjects available; to Major Purser, Caroline Holcombe, R.N., Dr. R. C. Lohrey, and other staff members for their cooperation; and to Isabel Fredericson for invaluable assistance.

time started as soon as one or both eyes of the infant were directed towards the target, using as criterion the superposition over the pupil of a tiny corneal reflection of the target; it ended when the eyes turned away or closed.[1] The six targets were presented in random order for each infant, with the sequence repeated up to eight times when possible. Only completed sequences were included in calculating the percentage of total fixation time for each target.

The targets were circular, 6 in. in diameter, and had nonglossy surfaces. Three contained black-and-white patterns—a schematic face, concentric circles, and a section of newspaper containing print 1/16 to 1/4 in. high. The other three were unpatterned—white, fluorescent yellow, and dark red. The relative luminous reflectance was, in decreasing order; yellow, white, newsprint, face and circles, red. Squares containing the patterns or colors were placed in a flat holder which slid horizontally into a slightly recessed portion of the chamber ceiling to expose the pattern or color to the infant through a circular hole in the holder. The chamber and underside of the holder were lined with blue felt to provide a contrasting background for the stimuli and to diffuse the illumination (between 10 and 15 ft-c) from lights on either side of the infant's head. The subject was in a small hammock crib with head facing up directly under the targets, 1 ft away.

The results in Table 20-1 show about twice as much visual attention to patterns as to plainly colored surfaces. Differences in response to the

TABLE 20-1  Relative Duration of Initial Gaze of Infants at Six Stimulus Objects in Successive and Repeated Presentations

| Age Group | N | Face | Circles | News | White | Yellow | Red | P[†] |
|---|---|---|---|---|---|---|---|---|
| Under 48 hrs | 8 | 29.5 | 23.5 | 13.1 | 12.3 | 11.5 | 10.1 | 0.005 |
| 2 to 5 days | 10 | 29.5 | 24.3 | 17.5 | 9.9 | 12.1 | 6.7 | 0.001 |
| 2 to 6 months [‡] | 25 | 34.3 | 18.4 | 19.9 | 8.9 | 8.2 | 10.1 | 0.001 |

[†] Significance level based on Friedman analysis of variance by ranks.
[‡] From an earlier study [4].

six stimulus objects are significant for the infants both under and over 2 days of age; results from these groups do not differ reliably from each other and are similar to earlier results from much older infants. The selectivity of the visual responses is brought out still more strikingly by tabu-

---

[1] High reliability of a similar technique, using the same criterion of fixation, was shown with older infants [1, 5, 6]. Since eye movements are less coordinated and fixations less clear-cut in newborn infants, a further check of the response measurement is desirable; I plan to do this by photographic recordings.

lating the longest-fixated target for each newborn infant: 11 for face, 5 for concentric circles, 2 for newsprint, and 0 for white, yellow, and red. For comparison, the first choices of infants 2 to 6 months were distributed as follows: 16, 4, 5, 0, 0, 0.

Three infants under 24 hr could be tested sufficiently to indicate the individual consistency of response. Two of these showed a significant (0.005 and 0.05) difference among the targets in successive sets of exposures, one looking longest at the face pattern in seven of eight exposures, the other looking longest at the "bull's-eye" in three of six exposures. The third infant 10 hr after birth looked longest at the face in three of eight exposures.

It is clear that the selective visual responses were related to pattern rather than hue or reflectance, although the latter two variables are often thought to be primary visual stimuli. Specification of the prepotent configurational variables is unwarranted at this time. The results do not imply "instinctive recognition" of a face or other unique significance of this pattern; it is likely there are other patterns which would elicit equal or greater attention.[2] Longer fixation of the face suggests only that a pattern with certain similarities to social objects also has stimulus characteristics with considerable intrinsic interest or stimulating value; whatever the mechanism underlying this interest, it should facilitate the development of social responsiveness, since what is responded to must first be attended to.

Substantiation for the visual selection of patterned over unpatterned objects is given in an independent study of newborn infants in which more visual attention was given to a colored card with a simple figure, when held close to the infant, than to a plain card of either color [7].

The results of Table 20-1 demonstrate that pattern vision can be tested in newborn infants by recording differential visual attention; these and other results call for a revision of traditional views that the visual world of the infant is initially formless or chaotic and that we must learn to see configurations.

## REFERENCES

1. Evelyn Dewey. *Behavior development in infants*. New York: Columbia University Press, 1935.
2. R. L. Fantz. Pattern vision in young infants. *Psychol. Rec.*, 1958, *8*, 43–47.
3. R. L. Fantz. The origin of form perception. *Sci. Amer.*, 1961, *204*, 66–72.

---

[2] I chose the targets for their expected attention value for the older infants of the earlier study; this may be different for newborn subjects: response to the newsprint may be decreased by less acute vision (although some patterning would be visible without resolution of individual letters); "bull's-eye" elicited strong differential attention only over 2 months of age in another study [3]; and blue is preferred to red and yellow by newborns [4]. The face pattern might for these reasons have a relative advantage for newborns.

4. R. L. Fantz, J. M. Ordy, and M. S. Udelf. Maturation of pattern vision in infants during the first six months. *J. comp. Physiol. Psychol.*, 1962, *55*, 907–917.
5. K. C. Pratt. The Neonate. In L. Carmichael (ed.). *Manual of child psychology.* New York: Wiley, 1954. Pp. 215–294.
6. B. Spock. *Baby and child care.* New York: Pocket Books, 1957.
7. F. Stirnimann. Über das Farbenempfinden Neugeborener. *Ann. Paedia.*, 1944, *163*, 1–25.


# 21

# ATTENTION AND PSYCHOLOGICAL CHANGE IN THE YOUNG CHILD

## Jerome Kagan

One of the great unanswered psychological questions concerns the mechanisms responsible for the transformations in organization of behavior and cognitive structure that define growth and differentiation. Until recently most of these changes were viewed as the product of learning. The child was presumably born unmarked, and the imposing hand of experience taught him the structures that defined him. Hence, many behavioral scientists agreed that learning was the central mystery to unravel, and conditioning was the fundamental mechanism of learning. There is a growing consensus, however, that conditioning may be too limited a process to explain the breadth and variety of change characteristic of behavioral and psychological structures. What was once a unitary problem has become a set of more manageable and theoretically sounder themes.

### CATEGORY OF CHANGE

It is always desirable to categorize phenomena according to the hypothetical processes that produced them. But since psychology has not

Source: *Science*, 1970, *170*, 826–832. Copyright 1970 by the American Association for the Advancement of Science.

Note: This work was supported by grants from the National Institute of Child Health and Human Development (HD 4299) and the Carnegie Corporation of New York. I thank Robert McCall, Marshall Haith, and Philip Zelazo for comments on the manuscript.

discovered these primary mechanisms, it is often limited to descriptive classifications. One category includes alterations in the probability that a stimulus will evoke a given response, which is a brief operational definition of conditioning. Half a century of research on the acquisition of conditioned responses has generated several significant principles, some with developmental implications. It is generally true, for example, that the acquisition of a conditioned response proceeds faster as the child matures [22]. Although the explanation of this fact is still not settled, it is assumed that, with age, the child becomes more selectively attentive and better able to differentiate the relevant signal from background noise. Thus a newborn requires about thirty-two trials before he will turn his head to a conditioned auditory stimulus in order to obtain milk; a 3-month-old requires about nine trials [2].[1]

A second category of change refers to the delayed appearance of species-specific behaviors after exposure to a narrow band of experience. A bird's ability to produce the song of its species [29] or a child's competence with the language of his community [3] requires only the processing of particular auditory events, with no overt response necessary at the time of initial exposure. The environment allows an inherited capacity to become manifest. Close analysis indicates that the development of these and related behaviors does not seem to conform to conditioning principles, especially to the assumption that the new response must occur in temporal contiguity with the conditioned stimulus. This class of phenomena suggests, incidentally, the value of differentiating between the acquisition of a disposition to action and the establishment of and successive changes in cognitive structures not tied directly to behavior. This distinction between behavioral performance and cognitive competence is exemplified by the difference between a child's learning to play marbles and his ability to recognize the faces of the children with whom he plays.

A third category of change, and the one to which this essay is primarily devoted, involves the initial establishment and subsequent alteration of representations of experience, called schemata (singular: schema). A schema is a representation of experience that preserves the temporal and spatial relations of the original event, without being necessarily isomorphic with that event. It is similar in meaning to the older term engram.

---

[1] Infants over 3 months old who had learned the conditioned response continued to turn their head to the auditory stimulus even though they were completely satiated for milk and did not drink. This phenomenon replicates similar observations with pigeons and rats who, after having acquired a conditioned response to obtain food, continued to respond even though ample food was available without any effort [4, 27]. One interpretation of this phenomenon assumes that when an organism is alerted or aroused, for whatever reason, he issues those responses that are prepotent in that context. This view is congruent with the demonstration that intracranial stimulation of the hypothalamus elicits behaviors appropriate to the immediate situation [33]. If food is available, the rat eats; if water, he drinks; if wood chips, he gnaws. Intracranial stimulation, like transfer from the home to the experimental chamber, alerts the animal, and prepotent behavior is activated.

Like the engram, the construct of schema was invented to explain the organism's capacity to recognize an event encountered in the past. Although the process of recognition is not clearly understood, the neurophysiologist's suggestion that a cortical neuronal model is matched to current experience captures the essential flavor of the concept [27]. It is important to differentiate between the notion of schema as a representation of a sensory event and the hypothetical process that represents the organism's potential action toward an object. Piaget [31] does not make this differentiation as sharply as we do, for his concept of *sensory-motor scheme* includes the internal representation of the object as well as the organized action toward it.

There is some evidence that some form of primitive representation of experience can be established prior to or soon after birth. Grier, Counter, and Shearer [12] incubated eggs of White Rock chickens (*Gallus gallus*) from 12 to 18 days under conditions of quiet or patterned sound. Within 6 hr after hatching, each chick was tested for responsiveness to two auditory stimuli, the 200-H tone presented prenatally and a novel 2,000-H sound. The control chicks moved equivalent distances toward both sounds; the experimental chicks moved significantly closer to the 200-H sound than to the novel one. Similarly, infant laughing gulls (*Larus atricilla*) 6 to 13 days old seem able to form representations of their parents' calls, for they orient toward and approach the calls of their own parents but orient away from the calls of other adult gulls [1].

A central assumption surrounding early schema formation states that the first schemata represents invariant stimulus patterns that are part of a larger context characterized by high rate of change (movement, contour contrast, and acoustic shifts). Hence a schema for the human face should develop early, for the face is characterized by an invariant arrangement of eyes, nose, and mouth within a frame that moves and emits intermittent, variable sounds. Experimental observations of young infants suggest that the face is one of the earliest representations to be acquired. Since the establishment of a schema is so dependent upon the selectivity of the infant's attention, understanding of developmental priorities in schema formation should be facilitated by appreciation of the principles governing the distribution of attention. These principles will be considered in the sections that follow.

## CONTRAST, MOVEMENT AND CHANGE

Ontogenetically, the earliest determinant of duration of orientation to a visual event is probably inherent in the structure of the central nervous system. The infant naturally attends to events that possess a high rate of change in their physical characteristics. Stimuli that move, have many discrete elements, or possess contour contrast are most likely to attract and hold a newborn's attention. Hence, a 2-day-old infant is more attentive to a moving or intermittent light than to a continuous light source; to a solid black figure on a white background than to a stimulus that is homogeneously gray [9, 10, 14, 32]. The newborn's visual search behavior seems to be guided by the following rules [15]:

1. If he is alert and if light is not too bright, his eyes open up.
2. If his eyes are open but no light is seen, he searches.
3. If he sees light but no edges, he keeps searching.
4. If he sees contour edges, he holds and crosses them.

The preference for the study of contour is monitored, however, by the area of the stimulus field, and there seems to be an optimum amount of contour that maintains attention at a maximum. Four-month-old infants exposed to meaningless achromatic designs with variable contour length were most attentive to those with moderately long contours [23]. Karmel [17] has reported that among young infants, duration of attention to meaningless achromatic figures is a curvilinear function of the square root of the absolute amount of black-white border in the figure.

The behavioral addiction to contour and movement is in accord with neurophysiological information on ganglion potentials in vertebrate retinas. Some cells respond to movement; others, to onset of illumination, to offset, or to both. Objects with contour edges should function better as onset stimuli than do solid patterns, because the change in stimulation created by a sharp edge elicits specialized firing patterns that may facilitate sustained attention [19].

There is some controversy over the question of whether contour or complexity exerts primary control over attention in the early months, where complexity is defined in terms of either redundancy or variety or number of elements in the figure and where contour is defined in terms of the total amount of border contained in the arrangement of figures on a background. Existing data support the more salient role of contour over complexity. McCall and Kagan [23] found no direct relation, in 4-month-olds, between fixation time and number of angles in a set of achromatic meaningless designs. Rather, there was an approximate inverted-U relation between attention and total length of contour in the figure. Similarly, fixation time in 5-month-old infants was independent of degree of asymmetry and irregularity in the arrangement of nine squares; however, when these indices of complexity were held constant but area and amount of contour were varied, fixation times were a function of contour. Finally, the average evoked cortical potentials of infants to checkerboard and random matrix patterns were independent of redundancy of pattern, but they displayed an inverted-U relation with density of contour edge [18].

Although indices of attention to auditory events are considerably more ambiguous than those used for vision, it appears that stimuli that have a high rate of change, such as intermittent sounds, produce more quieting and, by inference, more focused attention than continuous sounds [2, 7]. Nature has apparently equipped the newborn with an initial bias in the processing of experience. He does not, as the nineteenth-century empiricists believed, have to learn what he should examine. The preferential orientation to change is clearly adaptive, for the locus of change is likely to contain the most information about the presence of his mother or of danger.

## DISCREPANCY FROM SCHEMA

The initial disposition to attend to events with a high rate of change soon competes with a new determinant based largely on experience. The child's attentional encounters with events result, inevitably, in a schema. Somewhere during the second month, duration of attention comes under the influence of the relation between a class of events and the infant's schema for that class. One form of this relation, called the discrepancy principle, states that stimuli moderately discrepant from the schema elicit longer orientations than do either minimally discrepant (that is, familiar) events or novel events that bear no relation to the schema. The relation between attention and magnitude of discrepancy is assumed to be curvilinear (an inverted U). Although an orientation reflex can be produced by any change in quality or intensity of stimulation, duration of sustained attention is constrained by the degree of discrepancy between the event and the relevant schema. Consider some empirical support for the discrepancy principle.

One-week-old infants show equivalent fixations to an achromatic representation of human faces (see Figure 21-1) and a meaningless achromatic design, for contour is assumed to be the major determinant of attention at this early age. Even the 8-week-old shows equivalent fixations to a three-dimensional representation of a face and an abstract three-dimensional form [5]. But a 4-month-old shows markedly longer attention to the regular achromatic face than to the design [23], presumably because he has acquired a schema for a human face, and the laboratory representation is moderately discrepant from that schema. If the representation of the face is too discrepant, as when the facial components are rearranged (see Figure 21-1), fixation times are reduced [13, 16, 21].

Fixation times to photographic representations of faces drop by over 50% after 6 months and are equivalent to both regular and irregular faces during the last half of the first year [13, 16, 21]. This developmental pattern is in accord with the discrepancy principle. During the opening few weeks of life, before the infant has established a schema for a human face, photographs of either regular or irregular faces are so discrepant from the infant's schema that they elicit equivalent epochs of attention. As the schema for a human face becomes well established, between 2 and 4 months, the photograph of a strange face becomes optimally discrepant from that schema. During the latter half of the first year, the face

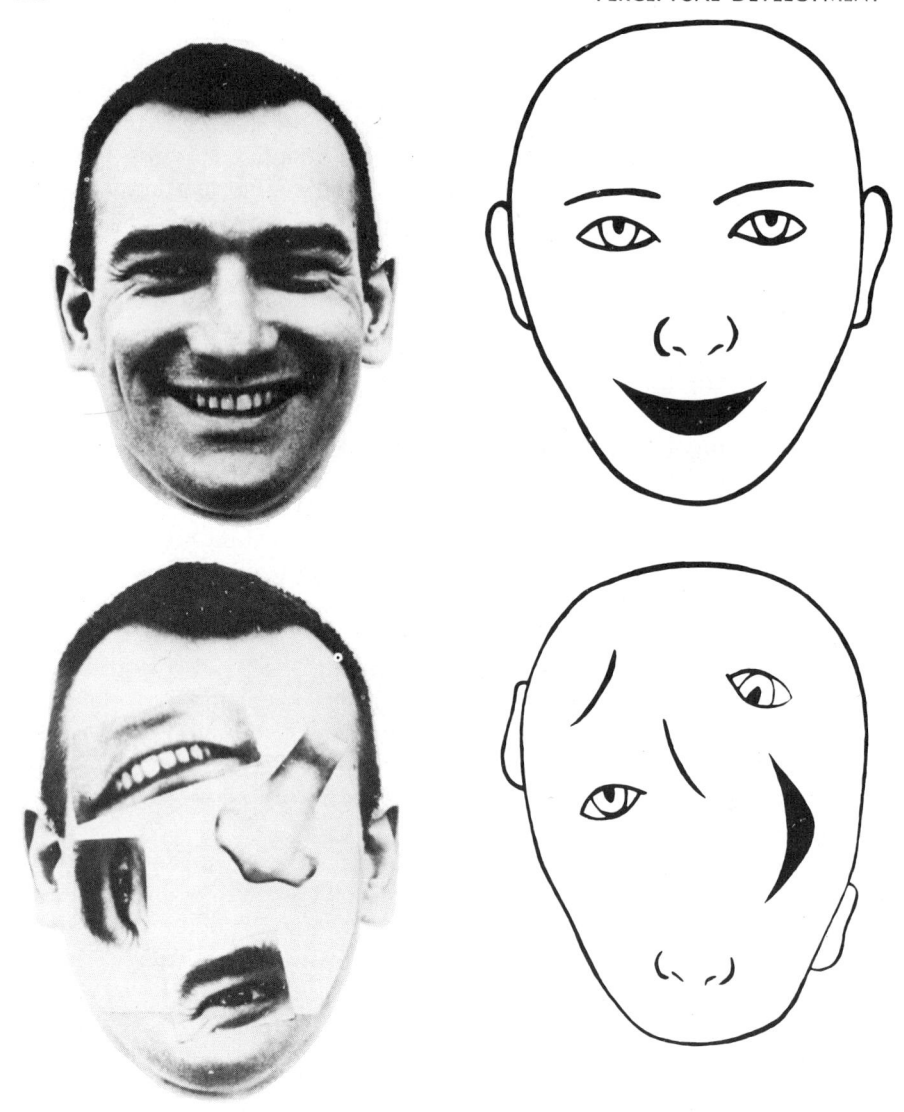

FIGURE 21-1 Achromatic representations of four facelike stimuli shown to infants.

schema becomes so well established that photographs of regular or irregular faces, though discriminable, are easily assimilated and elicit short and equivalent fixations.

A second source of support for the discrepancy principle comes from research designs in which familiarity and discrepancy are manipulated through repeated presentation of an originally meaningless stimulus, followed by a transformation of the standard. Fixation times are typically longer to the transformation than to the last few presentations of the habituated standard [26]. For example, 4-month-old infants were shown three objects in a triangular arrangement for five repeated trials. On the sixth trial, infants saw a transformation of the standard in which one, two, or three of the original objects were replaced with new ones. Most infants displayed longer fixations to the transformation than to the preceding standard. When the analysis was restricted to the forty-two infants who displayed either rapid habituation or short fixations to the last four presentations of the standard trials 2 through 5), an increasing monotonic relation emerged between amount of change in the standard (one, two, or three elements replaced) and increase in fixation from the last standard to the transformation [25].

Although fixation time cannot be used as an index of sustained attention to auditory stimuli, magnitude of cardiac deceleration, which covaries with motor quieting, provides a partial index of focused attention. Melson and McCall repeated the same eight-note ascending scale for eight trials to 5-month-old girls; this repetition was followed by transformations, in which the same eight notes were rearranged. The magnitude of cardiac deceleration was larger to the discrepant scale than to the preceding standard. The curvilinear form of the discrepancy principle finds support in an experiment in which 5½-month-old male infants were shown a simple stimulus consisting of five green, three-dimensional elements arranged vertically on a white background (far left in Figure 21-2). The order of the stimulus presentation was *SSSSSSSSTSSTSSTS*, in which *S* was the standard and *T* was one of three transformations of differing discrepancy from the standard. Each infant was shown only one of the three transformations in Figure 21-2. The magnitude of cardiac deceleration was larger to the moderate transformation of the standard (oblique arrangement of the five elements in Figure 21-2, second from left) than to the two more serious transformations [26]. This finding is partially congruent with an earlier study on younger infants that used the same stimuli but established the schema over a 4-week period. The girls, but not the boys, displayed larger decelerations to the transformations than to the standard [24].

The most persuasive confirmation of the curvilinear relation between attention and discrepancy was revealed in an experiment in which firstborn, 4-month-old infants were shown a three-dimensional stimulus composed of three geometric forms of different shape and hue for twelve half-minute presentations [33]. Each infant was then randomly assigned to one of seven groups. Six of these groups were exposed to a stimulus at home that was of varying discrepancy from the standard viewed in the laboratory. The seventh was not exposed to any experimental stimulus. The mother showed the stimulus to the infant, in the form of a mobile above his crib, 30 min a day for 21 days. The seven experimental groups are summarized in Figure 21-3.

Three weeks later each subject returned to the laboratory and saw exactly the same stimulus he viewed initially at the age of 4 months. The

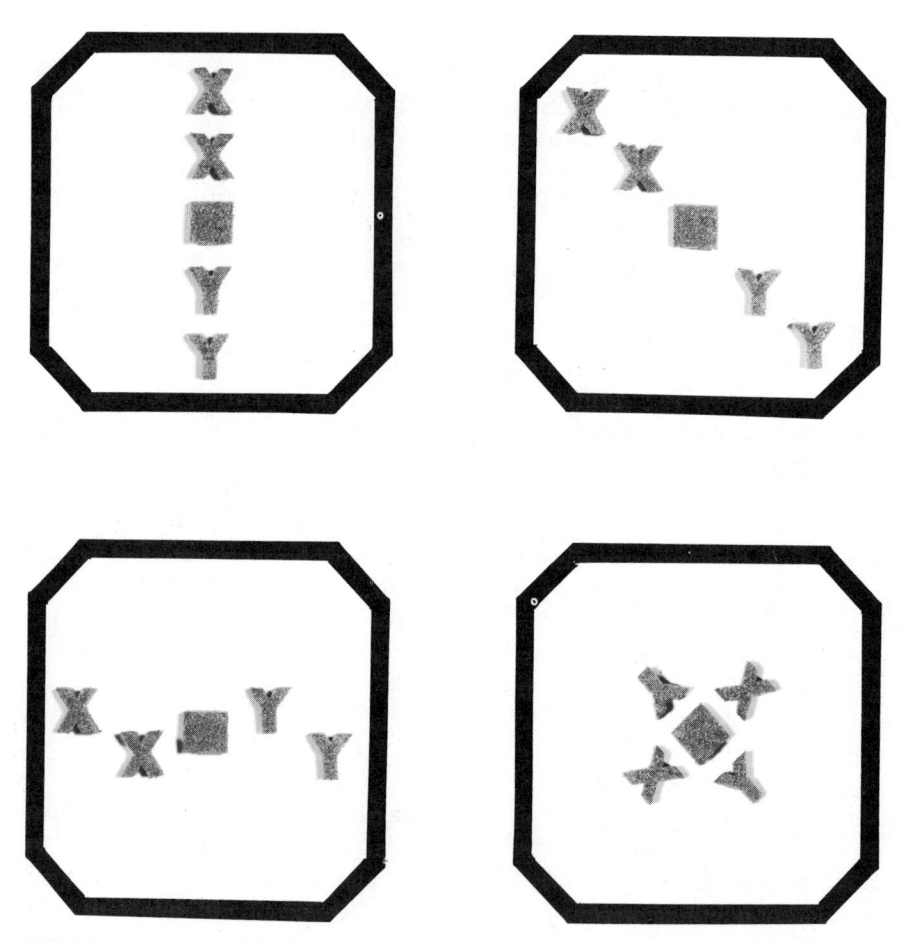

FIGURE 21-2 Standard (far left) and three transformations shown to infants in study of reaction to discrepancy.

major dependent variable was the *change in fixation time* between the first and second test sessions. Figure 21-4 illustrates these change scores for total fixation time across the first six trials of each session.

The infants who saw no mobile at home showed no change in fixation time across the 3 weeks, which indicates that the laboratory stimulus was as attractive on the second visit as it had been on the first. The infants who had an opportunity to develop a schema for the asymmetric and vertical rotation mobiles and therefore could experience a moderate discrepancy on the second visit, showed the smallest drop in attention across the 3 weeks. By contrast, the infants who experienced a minor or major discrepancy showed the greatest drop in interest ($F = 5.29$, $p < 0.05$). There was a curvilinear relation between attention and stimulus-schema discrepancy.

The incidence of smiling to familiar and discrepant stimuli also supports the discrepancy principle. It is assumed that the infant is likely to

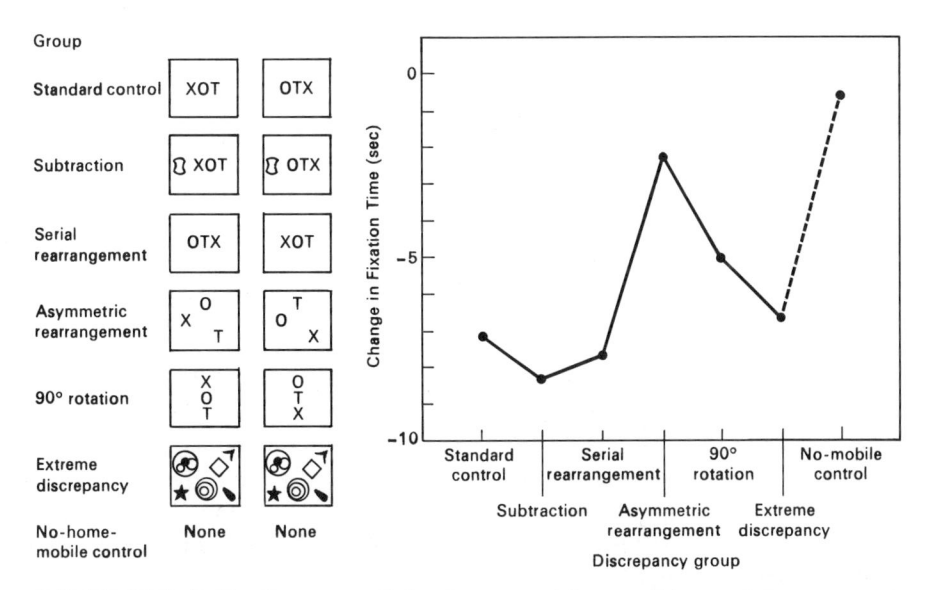

FIGURE 21-3 (left) Summary of the home mobile conditions of the seven experimental groups. The drawings illustrate in schematic form the stimulus to which each child was exposed at home.
FIGURE 21-4 (right) Change in mean total fixation time across the two test sessions for each of the seven experimental groups.

smile as he assimilates an initially discrepant event [31]. Hence, very familiar and totally novel stimuli should elicit minimum smiling, whereas moderately discrepant events should elicit maximum smiling. The smile to a human face or a pictorial representation of a face during the first 7 months is most frequent at 4 months of age among infants from varied cultural settings [11]. It is assumed that, prior to 4 months, the human face is too discrepant to be assimilated, and after this time it is minimally discrepant and easily assimilated. The smile of assimilation is not restricted to human faces. Three different auditory stimuli (bronze bell, toy piano, and nursery rhyme played by a music box) were presented to 13-week-old infants in two trial blocks on each of two successive days [35]. Frequency of smiling was lowest on the first block of trials on day 1, when the sounds were novel, and on the second block on day 2, when they had become very familiar, but highest on the two intermediate blocks, when the infant presumably was able to assimilate them after some effort.

A final illustration of the display of the smile as a sign of assimilation comes from a study in progress in which sixty children, 5½ to 11½ months old, watched a hand slowly move an orange rod clockwise in an arc until it contacted a set of three differently colored light bulbs. As the rod touched one of the lights, all three turned on. This 11-sec sequence was repeated eight or ten times (depending upon the age of the child) during which most children remained very attentive. Each child then saw only one of four transformations for five successive trials; (a) The bulbs did not light when the rod touched them; (b) the hand did not appear; (c) the rod did not move; or (d) no hand appeared and no bulbs lit, but the rod moved. After the fifth presentation, the original sequence was repeated three more times. The proportion of infants who smiled was largest on the sixth repetition of the standard and on the third presentation of the transformation. Figure 21-5 illustrates the pattern of smiling to this episode for one 7½-month-old girl who displayed maximum smiling on trials 4 and 5 of the initial familiarization series and trials 3, 4, and 5 of the transformation series, during which the hand did not appear. Thus both duration of fixation and probability of smiling seem to be curvilinearly related to degree of discrepancy between an event and the child's schema for that event. Moreover, the child seems to become most excited by moderately discrepant events that are perceived as transformations of those that produced the original schema. If the infant does not regard a new event as related to a schema, he is much less excited by it. To illustrate, seventy-two infants, 9½ and 11½ months old, were exposed to one of two different transformations after six repeated presentations of a 2-in. (5-cm) wooden orange cube. The infants exposed to the novel event saw a yellow, rippled, plastic cylinder differing from the standard in color, size, texture, and shape. The infants exposed to the moderate transformation saw a 1-in. (2.54-cm) wooden orange cube, in which only size was altered. Almost half (43%) of the females in the moderate group displayed an obvious increase in vocalization when the smaller cube appeared, suggesting they were excited by this transformation. By contrast, only one female exposed to the novel yellow form showed increased vocalization, and most showed no change at all ($p < 0.05$). There was no comparable difference for boys.

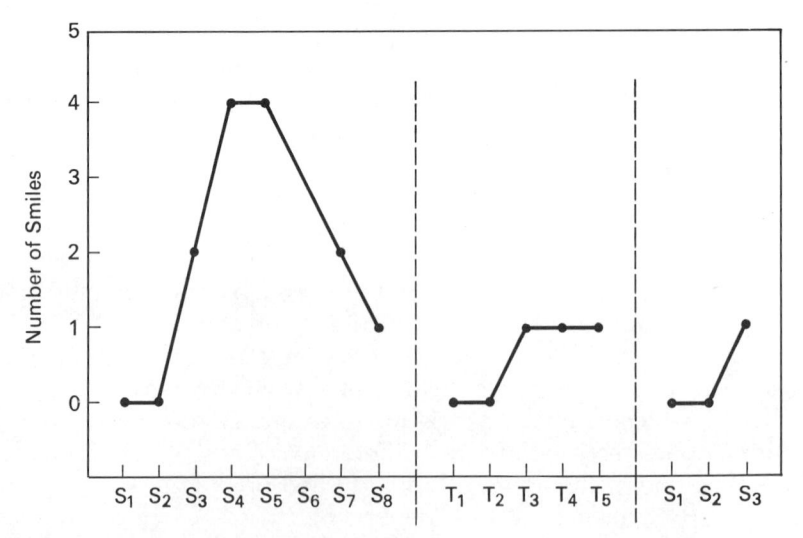

FIGURE 21-5 Frequency of smiling to the light episode for a 7½-month-old girl (S, standard presentation; T, transformation).

The onset of a special reaction to discrepancy at about 2 months may reflect the fact that structures in the central nervous system have matured enough to permit long-term representation or retrieval of such representations. It is probably not a coincidence that a broad band of physiological and behavioral phenomena also occur at this time. The latency of the visual evoked potential begins to approach adult form, growth of occipital neurons levels off, alpha rhythm becomes recognizable [8], the Moro reflex begins to disappear, habituation to repeated presentations of a visual event becomes a reliable phenomenon [6], and three-dimensional representations of objects elicit longer fixations than two-dimensional ones [9].

## ACTIVATION OF HYPOTHESES

Two empirical facts require the invention of a third process that influences attention and, subsequently, produces change in cognitive structures. The relation between age and fixation time to masklike representations of a human face (see Figure 21-6) decreases dramatically across the period from 4 to 12 months, but it increases, just as dramatically, from 12 to 36 months [16]. If discrepancy from schema exerted primary control over attention, increased fixation times after 1 year should not have occurred, for the masks should have become less discrepant with maturity. Furthermore, educational level of the infant's family was independent of fixation time prior to 1 year but was positively correlated with fixation time (correlation coefficient of 0.4) after 1 year [16]. These data suggest the potential usefulness of positing the emergence of a new cognitive structure toward the end of the first year. This structure, called a *hypothesis*, is the child's interpretation of a discrepant event accomplished by mentally transforming it to a form he is familiar with, where the "familiar form" is the schema. The cognitive structure used in the transformation is the hypothesis. To recognize that a particular sequence of sounds is human speech rather than a series of clarinet tones requires a schema for the quality of the human voice. Interpretation of the meaning of the speech, on the other hand, requires the activation of hypotheses which, in this example, are linguistic rules. The critical difference between a schema and a hypothesis is analogous to the difference between the processes of recognition and interpretation and bears some relation to Piaget's complementary notions of assimilation and accommodation [31].

It is assumed that the activation of hypotheses to explain discrepant events is accompanied by sustained attention. The more extensive the repertoire of hypotheses, the longer the child can work at interpretation and the more prolonged is his attention. The interaction between discrepancy and the activation of hypotheses is illustrated in the pattern of fixation times of 2-year-olds to four related stimuli: a doll-like representation

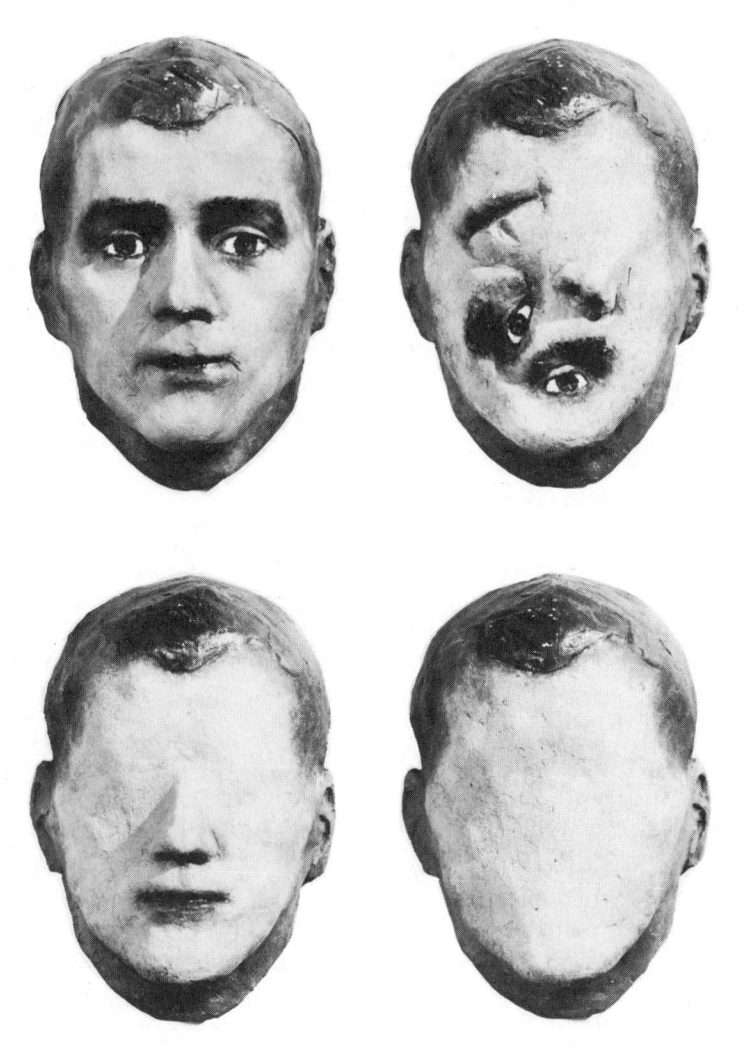

FIGURE 21-6  Facelike masks shown to infants from 4 to 36 months of age.

of a male figure; the same figure with the head placed between the legs; the same figure with the head, arms, and legs rearranged in an asymmetric pattern; and an amorphous free form of the same color, size, and texture as the other three. Duration of fixation was significantly longer to the two moderately discrepant forms (8.5 sec) than to the regular figure (7 sec) or to the free form (5.5 sec) [16].

In sum, events that possess a high rate of change, that are discrepant from established schemata, and that activate hypotheses in the service of interpretation elicit the longest epochs of attention. These events are most likely to produce changes in cognitive structures, for the attempt to assimilate a transformation of a familiar event inevitably leads to alterations in the original schema.

## SUMMARY

This article began by suggesting that different processes are likely to mediate alterations in behavior and cognitive structure and that conditioning principles do not seem sufficient to explain all the classes of change. Although the acquisition of conditioned responses, the potentiation of inborn capacities, and the establishment of schemata probably implicate different processes, all three involve selective attention to sensory events, whether these events function as conditioned stimuli, releasers of innate response dispositions, or the bases for mental representations. Hence, better understanding of the forces that control selectivity and duration of attention should provide insights into the nature of psychological growth, especially the lawful alterations in cognitive structure that seem to occur continually as a function of the child's encounter with discrepant events. The heart of this article was devoted to this theme. It was argued that events that possessed a high rate of change in their physical characteristics, that were moderately discrepant from established schemata, and that activated hypotheses in the service of assimilation had the greatest power to recruit and maintain attention in the young child.

Unfortunately, quantification of the fragile process of attention is still inelegant, for an infant displays a small set of relatively simple reactions to an interesting event. The infant can look at it, vocalize, be quiet, thrash, smile, or display changes in heart rate, respiration, or pattern of electrocortical discharge. Each of these variables reflects a different aspect of the attention process. Fixation time provides the clearest view and seems controlled by movement, contour, discrepancy, and the activation of hypotheses. Smiling seems to reflect the state that follows effortful assimilation. Cardiac deceleration occasionally accompanies attention to discrepant events, but not always, and vocalization can index, among other things, the excitement generated by a stimulus that engages a schema. It is important to realize, however, that a specific magnitude for any of these responses serves many different forces. The future mapping of these magnitudes on a set of determinants will require a delicate orchestration of rigorous method, ingenious theory, and a keen sensitivity to nature's subtle messages.


## REFERENCES

1.  C. G. Beer. Laughing gull chicks: Recognition of their parents' voices. *Science,* 1969, *166,* 1030–1032.
2.  Y. Brackbill, G. Adams, D. H. Crowell, and M. C. Gray. Arousal level in newborns and preschool children under continuous auditory stimulation. *J. exp. Child Psychol.,* 1966, *3,* 176–188.
3.  R. W. Brown and U. Bellugi. Three processes in the child's acquisition of syntax. *Harvard Educ. Rev.,* 1964, *34,* 135–151.

4. B. Carder and K. Berkowitz. Rats' preference for earned in comparison with free food. *Science,* 1970, *167,* 1273–1274.
5. G. C. Carpenter. Paper presented at the Merrill-Palmer Infancy Conference, Detroit, February 1969.
6. C. Dreyfus-Brisac, D. Samson, C. Blanc, and N. Monod. L'électroencéphalogramme de l'enfant normal de moins de 3 ans. *Étud. Néo-natales,* 1958, *7,* 143–175.
7. R. B. Eisenberg, E. J. Griffin, D. B. Coursin, and M. A. Hunter. Auditory behavior in the human neonate: A preliminary report. *J. Speech Hear. Res.,* 1964, *7,* 245–269.
8. R. J. Ellingson. The study of brain electrical activity in infants. In L. P. Lipsitt and C. C. Spiker (eds.). *Advances in child development and behavior.* New York: Academic Press, 1963. Pp. 53–97.
9. R. L. Fantz. Pattern discrimination and selective attention as determinants of perceptual development from birth. In A. H. Kidd and J. L. Rivoire (eds.). *Perceptual development in children.* New York: Int. Universities Press, 1966. Pp. 163–173.
10. R. L. Fantz and S. Nevis. Pattern preferences and perceptual-cognitive development in early infancy. *Merrill-Palmer Quart.,* 1967, *13,* 88–108.
11. J. L. Gewirtz. The course of infant smiling in four child-rearing environments in Israel. In B. M. Foss (ed.). *Determinants of infants behaviour.* London: Methuen, 1965. Pp. 205–260.
12. J. B. Grier, S. A. Counter, and W. M. Shearer. Prenatal auditory imprinting in chickens. *Science,* 1967, *155,* 1692–1693.
13. R. A. Haaf and R. Q. Bell. A facial dimension in visual discrimination by human infants. *Child Develop.,* 1967, *38,* 893–899.
14. M. M. Haith. The response of the human newborn to visual movement. *J. exp. Child Psychol.,* 1966, *3,* 235–243.
15. M. M. Haith. Paper presented at meeting of the Society for Research in Child Development, Clark University, Worcester, Mass., March 1968.
16. J. Kagan. *Change and continuity in infancy.* New York: Wiley, 1971.
17. B. Z. Karmel. Complexity, amounts of contour, and visually dependent behavior in hooded rats, domestic chicks, and human infants. *J. comp. Physiol. Psychol.,* 1969, *69,* 649–657.
18. B. Z. Karmel, C. T. White, W. T. Cleaves, and K. J. Steinsiek. Paper presented at meeting of Eastern Psychological Association, Atlantic City, N. J., April 1970.
19. S. W. Kuffler. Neurons in the retina: organization, inhibition and excitation problems. *Cold Spring Harbor Symp. Quant. Biol.,* 1952, *17,* 281–292.
20. S. W. Kuffler. Discharge patterns and functional organization of mammalian retina. *J. Neurophysiol.,* 1953, *16,* 37–68.
21. M. Lewis. Infant responses to facial stimuli during the first year of life. *Develop. Psychol.,* 1969, *1,* 75–86.
22. L. P. Lipsitt. Learning in the first year of life. In L. P. Lipsitt and C. C. Spiker (eds.). *Advances in child development and behavior.* New York: Academic Press, 1963. Pp. 147–196. Vol. 1.

23. R. B. McCall and J. Kagan. Attention in the infant: Effects of complexity, contour, perimeter and familiarity. *Child Develop.,* 1967, *38,* 939–952.
24. R. B. McCall and J. Kagan. Stimulus-schema discrepancy and attention in the infant. *J. exp. Child Psych.,* 1967, *5,* 381–390.
25. R. B. McCall and J. Kagan. Individual differences in the infant's distribution of attention to stimulus discrepancy. *Develop. Psychol.,* 1970, *2,* 90–98.
26. R. B. McCall and W. H. Melson. Attention in infants as a function of magnitude of discrepancy and habituation rate. *Psychonom. Sci.,* 1969, *17,* 317–318.
27. H. W. Magoun. Advances in brain research with complications for learning. In K. H. Pribram (ed.). *On the biology of learning.* New York: Harcourt, Brace, & World, 1969. Pp. 171–190.
28. A. J. Neuringer. Animals respond to food in the presence of free food. *Science,* 1970, *166,* 399–401.
29. F. Nottebohm. Ontogeny of bird song. *Science,* 1970, *167,* 950–956.
30. H. Papousek. Experimental studies of appetitional behavior in human newborns and infants. In H. W. Stevenson, B. H. Hess, H. L. Rheingold (eds.). *Early behavior.* New York: Wiley, 1967. Pp. 269–278.
31. J. Piaget. *The origins of intelligence in children.* New York: Int. Universities Press, 1952.
32. P. Salapetek and W. Kessen. Visual scanning of triangles by the human newborn. *J. exp. Child Psychol.,* 1966, *3,* 155–167.
33. C. Super, J. Kagan, F. Morrison, M. Haith, and J. Weiffenbach. Unpublished manuscript.
34. E. S. Valenstein, V. C. Cox, and J. W. Kakolewski. Reexamination of the role of the hypothalamus in motivation. *Psychol. Rev.,* 1970, *77,* 16–31.
35. P. R. Zelazo and J. M. Chandler. Unpublished manuscript.

# 22

# A COMPARATIVE AND ANALYTICAL STUDY OF VISUAL DEPTH PERCEPTION

Richard D. Walk
Eleanor J. Gibson

**HISTORICAL BACKGROUND**

Several methods used in the study of animal behavior have taken for granted that an animal will discriminate and avoid a drop-off. The elevated maze is useful because the rat does not jump off. The jumping stand requires that the animal gauge his jump to a platform, and that he avoid falling into a net below. But only a few studies have been made of the avoidance of the drop itself. We shall refer arbitrarily to such a discrimination as perception of *depth,* to differentiate discrimination of depth downward, or a drop-off, from perception of distance ahead. . . .

To conduct a comparative study of the visual discrimination of depth downward, an apparatus fulfilling the following requirements is necessary: It must permit control of all cues other than optical ones, no pretraining should be required, and substantially the same apparatus should be adaptable for testing many different species. . . .

The apparatus designed for the present experiments, which we named the *visual cliff,* uses the principle of a drop-off or graduated heights, but gives the animal a choice between a short drop-off on one side of a center board and a long drop-off on the other side. A terrestrial animal, if it detected the difference, should prefer the short drop-off at a safe depth to the long drop-off at a dangerous depth. To eliminate non-visual cues that might permit detection of the difference, such as auditory, olfactory or temperature differentials[1] from near or distant surfaces, a sheet of glass was inserted under the center board where the organism was placed, so as to extend outward across both the shallow (safe) drop and the deep (dangerous) one. The glass was placed over the shallow side as well as the deep side to equate stimulation produced by the glass itself, if any (for instance, reflections), and to equalize tactual cues for locomotion.

Source: *Psychological Monographs,* 1961, 75 (15 whole no. 519), 2–34. Copyright 1961 by the American Psychological Association. Reprinted by permission.

[1] Of these cues, the only one reliably demonstrated to be a cue for distance is echolocation [17, 29].

Patterned material (wallpaper, linoleum, and so on) could be placed directly under the glass on the shallow side and on the floor below, at any desired distance, on the deep side. Information in the light coming to the animal's eye from the patterns on either side, in combination with stimulation produced by the animal's own motion and ocular equipment constituted the stimulus basis for visually differentiating the two sides. Figure 22-1 shows diagrammatically the situation created by the apparatus.

In summary, the subject was allowed to descend to either an optically shallow or to an optically deep surface from a center board between the two surfaces. If the subject could not or would not locomote, of course no data could be obtained.

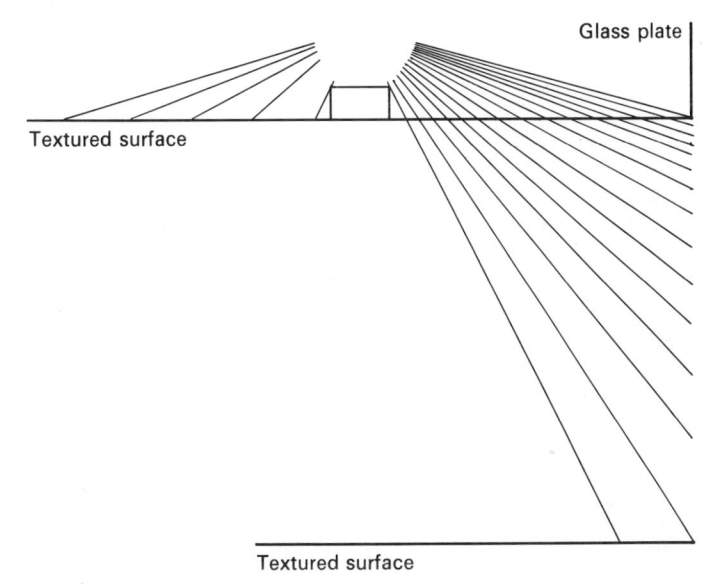

FIGURE 22-1  Diagram of the visual cliff, in cross-section. The animal is placed on a raised board in the center. On the left side is a patterned surface only a short drop below his feet—the shallow side—and on the right is the same patterned surface placed much further below—the deep side. Glass extends across both sides from the base of the center starting board.

The general procedure was as follows: The animal was placed on the center board, normally by hand, although the first experiments with rats placed the animal on the board in a small box to eliminate handling bias. To equate for position preferences half of the animals were started from one end of the board, half from the other. Observation periods varied for each species but were adequate to permit descent from the board. Descent to the glass surface was whenever possible left to the natural exploratory tendency of the subject. At the end of the observation period, the animal was removed and the board and glass surface cleaned with a damp sponge. To equate odor cues the sponge was used on the glass surface over both the shallow and deep sides regardless of the side of descent. . . .

## BASIC EXPERIMENTS AND VALIDATION OF THE CLIFF

This section will be devoted to a report of basic experiments with the visual cliff and a number of control experiments run to provide validation for the technique. The purpose of all the control experiments was to demonstrate that the animals were responding to the visual cues provided by the textured surfaces at different depths below the animal. The possibility of choices depending on other factors, such as brightness, reflections, and position of the experimenters had to be ruled out. The experiments included here also varied textures, heights, and the apparatus design itself. The subjects for these experiments were all hooded rats. (Long-Evans stock) reared in the laboratory colony. Hooded rats were chosen for their availability in large numbers, their small size, which made control of apparatus and environmental factors practical, and the fact that their natural exploratory drive solved the motivation problem. A rat was never run more than once unless it is specifically stated in the experiment.

### Original Experiment

The first experiment [38] was run on the original apparatus (model I). The measures taken were side chosen on first descent, time spent on either side, and number of crossings back and forth (if any). The textured material was directly under the glass on one side (shallow), 3 in. below the surface of the center board. On the other side (deep), the textured material was on the floor, 53 in. below the surface of the center board. The animal was placed on the center board and then observed for 5 min. A second group of animals was run under a control condition in which the textured paper was placed directly under the glass on both sides. The side which was deep for the experimental group is referred to similarly (Table 22-1) for this group as well, for purposes of comparison. If the animals had a preference for one side or the other, due to irrelevant factors such as the position of the experimenters, the control group's behavior should reveal it. The experimenters actually stood closest to the shallow side.

*Results.* It can be seen in Table 22-1 that the experimental group tended strongly to descend on the shallow side, did not cross back and forth at all, and passed a majority of its time on the same side. The preference for the shallow side is especially convincing in view of the closeness of the experimenters to that side.

The control group, on the other hand, showed no preference for either side in first descents, did in a number of cases cross back and forth,

TABLE 22-1 Comparison of Experimental and Control Groups on the Visual Cliff Apparatus

|  | Experimental Group (N = 29) | Control Group (N = 10) |
|---|---|---|
| Percentage descending on shallow side | 88.5 | 50.0 |
| Mean number of crossings in 5 min | 0.0 | 1.70 |
| Percentage of time on: |  |  |
| shallow side | 76.0 | 24.1 |
| deep side | 10.0 | 61.5 |
| board | 14.0 | 14.4 |

and spent more time on the side which was deep for the experimental group.

This experiment led us to the conclusion that hooded rats will avoid a visual cliff—a long visual drop-off as compared with a short one. It should follow, therefore, that animals placed on a center board with the textured surface far below the glass on both sides should be hesitant in descending either way. We next set up such an experiment. The same rats were run under two conditions: first, in the control condition already described, with the checked pattern directly under the glass on both sides; and second, in a new control condition with the checked pattern far below the glass on the floor on both sides. The animals were placed on the center board and observed for 3 min. The number of animals descending in 3 min and the median time to descend are presented in Table 22-2.

TABLE 22-2 Number of Descents and Latency of Descending Under Two Control Conditions, Both Sides Identical (N = 11)

| Control Condition | Number of Animals Descending | Median Latency (sec) |
|---|---|---|
| Pattern directly under glass | 9 (81.8%) | 9 |
| Pattern on floor | 4 (36.4%) | 120 |

As would be expected, the animals were much slower to descend when the patterned surface was on the floor (53 in. below) than when it was directly under the glass. The majority of animals did not descend at all in this condition, although they were being run for the second time. . . .

## COMPARATIVE EXPERIMENTS

The visual cliff was designed to permit comparison of the behavior of different species and ages of animals in depth discrimination. While some alterations had to be made in adapting the apparatus for some species, a common visual stimulus was present, and the same procedure was used for all. . . .

### Human Infants

After the large visual cliff was first constructed, and a 50-lb weight had been placed on the glass to make sure it was safe for infants, an 18-month-old male infant, who had been walking since he was 10 months old, was placed on the center board. He crawled off the center board to the shallow side and stood up. He could not be persuaded to walk across the glass of the deep side, but he was then picked up, placed on the glass of the deep side, and coaxed toward the center board. He firmly clutched the wooden support with one hand, curled his toes and hitched himself cautiously toward the experimenter. When he reached the center board he crawled up on it and ran over the glass on the shallow side (Figure 22-2).

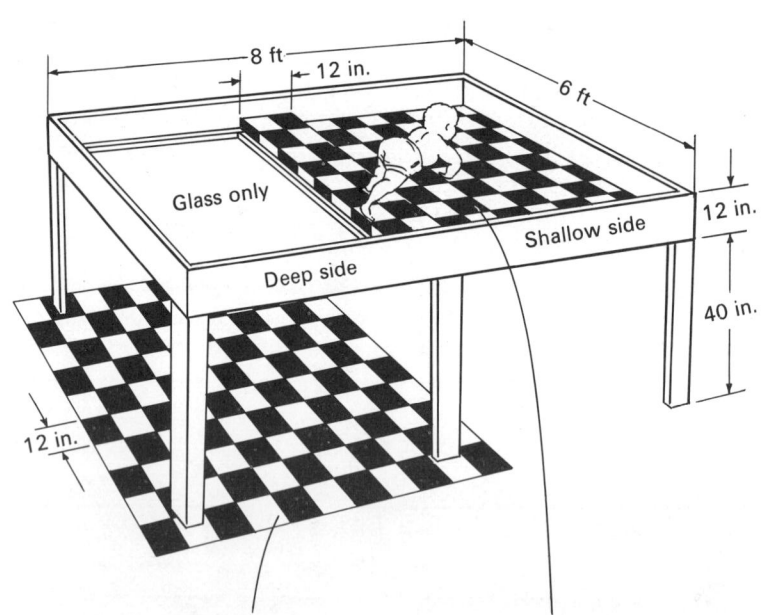

FIGURE 22-2 Drawing of the visual cliff, model III. This cliff differed from model II chiefly in size and strength. Because of its weight, it was supported by legs. An infant is starting from the center board toward the shallow side. The entire floor of the room is covered with the checkered linoleum identical with that on the cliff.

But this child was 18 months old, and had fallen, according to his parents, from cribs, beds, sofas, chairs, and so on, on to the hard floor or the bare ground. Would children who had just learned to crawl behave similarly to this child? Or had this child learned caution from falling? The following report describes the testing of thirty-six infants, 6 to 14 months old, that were crawling, according to their mothers.

The first infants were placed on the center board and observed for several minutes, a procedure that had worked well with animals. The

FIGURE 22-3 This mother has just placed her child on the center board in preparation for testing the infant.

mother was placed behind a screen where the child could not see her. A toy (red, white, and blue pinwheel) was placed at the end of both sides. It rotated slowly and emitted a tinkling sound as it turned. The protocols of the two subjects tested with this procedure follow:

$S_1$: Girl, 9 months old. Looked a number of times to both sides and at both pinwheels, touched shallow side but wouldn't go either way. (Mother behind screen. Total testing time 8 min.)

$S_2$: Girl, 6 months old. Looked mostly at experimenter, a little at pinwheels; crawled halfway across board, slipped on shallow side, back to board, then off on shallow again, near experimenter at west side of room by now, cries and is picked up by experimenter; put face down to glass on deep side during testing, peered under. (Mother behind screen. Testing time 7 min.)

The third subject marked a change in procedure. After the infant would not move, the mother was put at the shallow side. She turned the pinwheel and talked to the child. The protocol follows:

S₃: Male, 10½ months old. (Mother at shallow side, experimenter at deep side.) Child cries a little; at 4 min 50 sec from time of first starting testing gets off board toward mother, goes to lure, touches it. (Mother at deep side, experimenter at shallow side.) Cries when put back on board; knee on shallow side toward experimenter but won't go further, cries.

The standardized procedure evolved was as follows: The mother stood twice at each side, alternating, some mothers starting at the shallow side, some at the deep. The mother stood for 2 min at each side unless the child got off the board and reached a lure. If this happened, the child was put back on the board and the mother switched sides. An experimenter stood at each end of the board so as not to influence the way the infant crawled. If the child crawled away from the mother the experimenter went toward the infant to safeguard him.

The use of this standardized procedure clearly showed that the babies discriminated depth. They crawled toward the mother when she stood at the shallow side and refused to cross the glass to her when she stood at the deep side. Many infants crawled to the shallow side when the mother stood at the deep side twirling the pinwheel and urging him to come to her. Eleven subjects did this; no subject crawled away from the mother across the deep side when she stood at the shallow. Some of the babies cried when the mother stood at the deep side and would not go to her. In such cases, the 2-min observation period from the deep side was usually terminated at 1 min.

Once the procedure was standardized, from subject 10 on, the infants tended to behave very consistently. They crawled to the shallow side twice; in only two cases did the child go but once to the shallow side. The three negative cases, all boy infants, were also consistent; each child crawled twice to the mother across the deep side, twice to her at the shallow side.

When thirty subjects had been run, there were five subjects in the youngest (6 to 7 months) age group. Of these infants, three had not moved from the center board, one had gone to the shallow side only and one to both sides. Even though two cases is not a large sample, one of the two had crawled across the deep side and it seemed possible, a trend that had to be checked, that very young infants could not discriminate depth as adequately as older ones. Consequently, telephone calls were made to mothers in the city with infants 6 to 7½ months old. Very few of these infants were crawling, but five subjects were added to the youngest group. Of these five children, two remained on the center board and three crawled only to the shallow side. The indication was, therefore, that younger infants have as adequate depth perception, if they can be tested, as the older ones.

The results on the first thirty-six subjects run are shown in Table 22-3. The only age trend is the inadequate locomotor ability of the

TABLE 22-3   Behavior of Human Infants on the Visual Cliff

| Response of S | 6-7 | 8-9 | 10-11 | 12-14 | Total | % |
|---|---|---|---|---|---|---|
| Did not move off center board | 5 | 2 | 1 | 1 | 9 | 25 |
| To shallow side only | 4 | 7 | 8 | 5 | 24 | 67 |
| To deep side only | 0 | 0 | 0 | 0 | 0 | 0 |
| To both sides | 1 | 1 | 1 | 0 | 3 | 8 |
| Total | 10 | 10 | 10 | 6 | 36 | 100 |

Age of Infant (months)

younger subjects. They evidently crawled at home but not in a strange place. One must recognize that Table 22-3 is not a random sample of babies at the indicated ages, but a sample of infants whose mothers say they crawl. It is probably slightly skewed toward younger developers in the 6- to 7-months-old group.

There is much interesting behavior to be observed in this situation. The babies were attracted by the lure and when they reached it, played with it eagerly. They peered down through the glass, sometimes patted it or leaned on it with their faces, yet refused to cross. Some used the deep side for support with one knee, others backed partly out across it (in first locomotion in the human infant the child often goes in reverse when he means to go forward), yet they still refused to cross. It was as if the infant could not recognize the consequences of his own actions, since he had already been where he now refused to go. The attitudes of the mothers were interesting as well. The predominant impression among mothers seemed to be that the child had failed the "test" because he did not have enough sense to realize the glass was safe to crawl over. The glass on the deep side was banged with hands and fists; cigarette boxes, lipsticks, purses, crumpled bits of paper, and other releasers of infant approach behavior were proffered, but the babies still refused to go across the glass of the deep side. . . .

## Conclusion

Comparative studies of depth discrimination on the cliff revealed that all the animals studied (hooded and albino rats, chickens, goats, lambs, pigs, dogs, turtles, cats, monkeys, and human infants) have some capacity for discriminating depth by visual cues alone. . . .

The remarkable fact, indeed, is that animals with such widely differing eyes—a panoramic ocular system in the case of goats and sheep, for instance—show similar behavior in this one respect. The human and the monkey infants, though better able to utilize binocular cues, were certainly not superior to the other young animals tested, some of whom (the chick and the goat, for instance) exhibited highly discriminative behavior a few hours after birth. . . .

## REFERENCES

1. F. A. Brown, Jr. (1959), The rhythmic nature of animals and plants. *Amer. Scientist*, 1959, *47*, 147–168.
2. E. Brunswik. *Perception and the representative design of psychological experiments.* Berkeley: University of California Press, 1956.
3. K. L. Chow, A. H. Riesen, and F. W. Newell. Degeneration of retinal ganglion cells in infant chimpanzees reared in darkness. *J. comp. Neurol.*, 1957, *107*, 27–42.
4. R. M. Cruikshank. The development of visual size constancy in early infancy. *J. genet. Psychol.*, 1941, *58*, 327–351.
5. M. Denis-prinzhorn. Perceptions des distances et constance des grandeurs: étude génétique. *Arch. Psychol., Genève*, 1960, 37 (whole no. 147), 181–309.
6. S. Duke-Elder. The eye in evolution. In S. Duke-Elder (ed.). *System of Ophthalmology.* St. Louis, Missouri: Mosby, 1958. Vol. 1.
7. D. G. Forgays and J. W. Forgays. The nature of the effect of free-environmental experience in the rat. *J. comp. physiol. Psychol.*, 1952, *45*, 322–328.
8. E. J. Gibson. The role of shock in reinforcement. *J. comp. physiol. Psychol.*, 1952, *45*, 18–30.
9. E. J. Gibson and R. Bergman. The effect of training on absolute estimates of distance over the ground. *J. exp. Psychol.*, 1954, *48*, 473–482.
10. E. J. Gibson and R. D. Walk. The "visual cliff." *Sci. Amer.*, 1960, *202*, 64–71.
11. E. J. Gibson, R. D. Walk, and T. J. Tighe. Enhancement and deprivation of visual stimulation during rearing as factors in visual discrimination learning. *J. comp. physiol. Psychol.*, 1959, *52*, 74–81.
12. J. J. Gibson. *The perception of the visual world.* Boston: Houghton Mifflin, 1950.
13. J. J. Gibson. Visually controlled locomotion and visual orientation in animals. *Brit. J. Psychol.*, 1958, *49*, 182–194.
14. J. J. Gibson, P. Olum, and F. Rosenblatt. Parallax and perspective during aircraft landings. *Amer. J. Psychol.*, 1955, *68*, 372–385.
15. A. M. Greenhut. Visual distance discrimination in the rat. *J. exp. Psychol.*, 1954, *47*, 148–152.
16. A. M. Greenhut and F. A. Young. Visual depth perception in the rat. *J. genet. Psychol.*, 1953, *82*, 155–182.
17. D. R. Griffin. *Listening in the dark.* New Haven: Yale University Press, 1958.
18. S. B. Hendricks. Control of growth and reproduction by light and darkness. *Amer. Scientist*, 1956, *44*, 229–247.

19. E. H. Hess. Space perception in the chick. *Sci. Amer.*, 1956, *195*, 71–80.
20. J. E. Hochberg. Nativism and empiricism in perception. In L. Postman (ed.). *Psychology in the making.* New York: Knopf, 1962. Pp. 255–330.
21. B. Hymovitch. The effects of experimental variations on problem solving in the rat. *J. comp. physiol. Psychol.*, 1952, *45*, 313–321.
22. B. Johnson and F. L. Beck. The development of space perception: I. Stereoscopic vision in preschool children. *J. genet. Psychol.*, 1941, *58*, 247–254.
23. M. I. Kurke. The role of motor experience in the visual discrimination of depth in the chick. *J. genet. Psychol.*, 1955, *86*, 191–196.
24. K. S. Lashley and J. T. Russell. The mechanism of vision: XI. A preliminary test of innate organization. *J. genet. Psychol.*, 1934, *45*, 136–144.
25. M. Mishkin, R. D. Gunkel, and H. E. Rosvold. Contact occluders: A method for restricting vision in animals. *Science*, 1959, *129*, 1220–1221.
26. S. M. Nealey and B. J. Edwards. "Depth perception" in rats without pattern vision experience. *J. comp. physiol. Psychol.*, 1960, *53*, 468–469.
27. A. H. Riesen. Arrested vision. *Sci. Amer.*, 1950, *183*, 16–19.
28. A. H. Riesen and L. Aarons. Visual movement and intensity discrimination in cats after early deprivation of pattern vision. *J. comp. physiol. Psychol.*, 1959, *52*, 142–149.
29. D. A. Riley and M. R. Rosenzweig. Echolocation in rats. *J. comp. physiol. Psychol.*, 1957, *50*, 323–328.
30. E. W. Robinson and E. G. Weyer. Visual distance perception in the rat. *U. Calif. Publ. Psychol.*, 1930, *4*, 233–239.
31. J. T. Russell. Depth discrimination in the rat. *J. genet. Psychol.*, 1932, *40*, 136–159.
32. C. Sherrington. *The integrative action of the nervous system.* New Haven: Yale University Press, 1906.
33. A. I. Siegel. Deprivation of visual form definition in the ring dove: I. Discrimination learning. *J. comp. physiol. Psychol.*, 1953, *46*, 115–119.
34. D. A. Spalding. Instinct and acquisition. *Nature, London*, 1875, *12*, 507–508.
35. E. Thorndike. The instinctive reactions of young chicks. *Psychol. Rev.*, 1899, *6*, 282–291.
36. R. Updegraff. The visual perception of distance in young children and adults: a comparative study. *U. Iowa Stud. child Welf.*, 1930, *4* (no. 4).
37. M. C. Van Tuyl. Monocular perception of distance. *Amer. J. Psychol.*, 1937, *49*, 512–542.
38. R. D. Walk, E. J. Gibson, and T. J. Tighe. Behavior of light- and dark-reared rats on a visual cliff. *Science*, 1957, *126*, 80–81.
39. G. L. Walls. *The vertebrate eye.* Bloomfield Hills, Michigan: Cranbrook Institute of Science, 1942.
40. J. Warkentin and K. U. Smith. The development of visual acuity in the cat. *J. genet. Psychol.*, 1937, *50*, 371–399.
41. J. B. Watson. *Psychology from the standpoint of a behaviorist.* Philadelphia: Lippincott, 1919.

42. K. T. Waugh. The role of vision in the mental life of a mouse. *J. comp. neurol. Psychol.*, 1910, 20, 549–599.
43. C. D. Windle, J. S. Ward, K. Nedved, and J. Nathan. The effect of mock tower height in airborne training. *HumRRO Tech. Rep.* no. 29, 1956.
44. R. M. Yerkes. Space perception of tortoises. *J. comp. neurol. Psychol.*, 1904, 4, 17–26.


# 23

# VISUAL PERCEPTION APPROACHED BY THE METHOD OF STABILIZED IMAGES

R. M. Pritchard
W. Heron
D. O. Hebb

The present paper reports some preliminary experiments on the Ditchburn-Riggs effect, which is obtained with stabilized images. Our results are such as to show that the original discovery, made independently by Ditchburn and Riggs and their collaborators about 1952, has opened a new and valuable avenue of approach to the analysis of visual perception.

In normal visual fixation, the image that falls on the retina is never really stable; "physiological nystagmus," the continuous tremor of the normal eye at rest, causes a slight but constant variation in the rods and cones that are excited. It is now known that the variation plays a vital role in perception, for it was shown by Ditchburn and Ginsborg [7] and Riggs et al. [31] that stabilizing the image (experimentally eliminating variabilty of retinal excitation) leads rapidly to the disappearance of the visual object, followed by intermittent reappearance.

Source: *Canadian Journal of Psychology*, 1960, 14, 67–77.
Note: The authors acknowledge invaluable assistance from Myron R. Haugen, Klear Vision Contact Lens Specialists of Canada Ltd., and from Fred J. Kader, McGill University. This study was primarily supported by the Defence Research Board (9401–11), with aid also from the National Research Council of Canada (AP 17) and the U.S. Public Health Service (M–2455).

In their experiments, the target was projected on a screen after being reflected from a small mirror attached to a contact lens worn by the observer. Thus each slight involuntary movement of the "fixated" eye would produce a movement of the target. By having the subject observe through a complex optical system, it was possible to make the two movements correspond exactly: The angular extent and direction of the eye movement were matched by the movement of the target, canceling out the normal tremor of the eye and producing a stabilized retinal image. In these conditions the line of demarcation between the two halves of a 1° field, separately lighted so as to give intensity ratios of up to 3:1, disappears intermittently for 2 to 3 sec, at intervals of about 1 min [7]. Similarly, within a few seconds of stabilized viewing, a thin black line crossing a bright 1° field fades out; coarser lines are seen for longer periods, but still intermittently, the length of time the line remains visible being a direct function of its thickness [31].

Later papers using this technique dealt with other aspects of the phenomenon, still with simple targets. Experimentally controlled movement of the image on the retina, as might be expected, restores the object to view, as does intermittent instead of continuous illumination [4, 5, 6, 18]. Krauskopf also showed that narrow bars need a higher intensity (higher contrast ratio) than broad bars to be seen 50% of the time; Fender [9] and Clowes [3], using colored targets, showed that stabilization affects discrimination of hue as well as saturation and brightness.

Achieving stabilization by reflecting the image off the contact lens, however, has some limitations. The field that can be used is small, mainly because torsional movement is not controlled. The next step in the development of method was to attach the complete optical system to the eyeball itself [8, 21, 32]. Since the optical system produces an apparently distant target, which is viewed with a relaxed eye, gross fluctuations of accommodation due to muscular fatigue could be ruled out as an explanation of fading. More important, larger and more complex figures could be used.

Ditchburn and Pritchard [8] used interference fringes produced by a small calcite crystal between two polaroid sheets, and fastened by a stalk to a contact lens, to get a concentric ring pattern which covered a wide field and was in focus for a fully relaxed normal eye. With this method, it was found that the visual object is present for a very small fraction of the viewing time. Moreover, several observations of great interest were made [26, 28]. It was found, in brief, that stimulation of other senses could affect the amount of time that the target was seen, and that when the subjects attention was directed to a particular part of the target, this part would usually remain in view longer. Also, it was shown that parts of interference fringes might appear and disappear independently of each other. It is these results which lead directly to the experiments which we now report.

## METHOD

In the present investigation the method used to compensate for retinal-image motion produced by the involuntary eye movements is that described by Pritchard [27]. It consists, essentially, of a collimator device (one producing parallel rays of light), carried on a contact lens, as illustrated in Figure 23-1. The target to be viewed is maintained in the focal plane of a high-power glass lens and illuminated by a miniature surgical bulb attached to a diffusing screen. It is seen against a circular patch of light subtending 5° while the rest of the diffuser is blackened to shield the eye from stray light. The assembly of lens, target, and light source is mounted by a ball-socket joint to a stalk carried on a contact lens, corrected for the subject's visual defects, if any. The lens is tight-fitting and thus follows small eye movements accurately [29, 30]. The target is easily changed by unscrewing the top of the collimator assembly and replacing one small circular target by another. When the top is screwed down again, the new target is immediately secured in the focal plane of the high-power lens and no additional focusing is necessary.

The targets are produced by photographing India ink drawings on

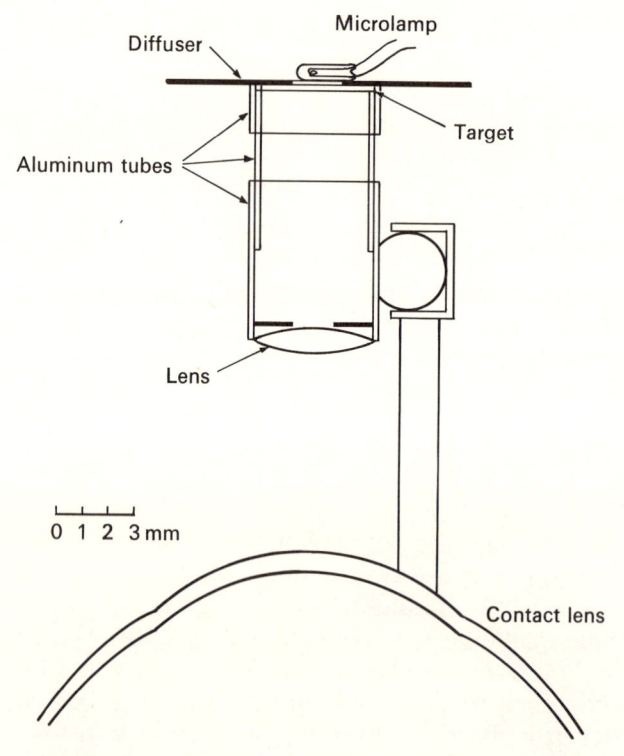

FIGURE 23-1 The apparatus used to produce stabilized images.

white cards, or drawings in white ink on black cards. Then, 5-mm discs of the negative are viewed by the subject through the collimating lens and consequently are seen as if located at infinity. They are in focus, therefore, for the normal relaxed eye.

In the present study all the targets were presented within a central 2° field, in view of the earlier finding [26] of a marked difference between perception within this central region and more peripheral regions. All observations were monocular, the other eye being occluded. The luminance of the brightest parts of the target was maintained at approximately 25 mL, with the experiment room in darkness during the viewing period.

The subject lay on a couch with his head supported, in a partly soundproofed room or in some of the observations, in an ordinary room at times when irregular auditory stimuli were at a minimum (see [28]). The target was then put in position by the experimenter, and a continuous recording was made of the subject's report. Control observations were also made, in which the subject viewed the same targets through the contact lens and collimator system, but without attaching one to the other, so that the image was not stabilized.

It is important to note that the subject must first be habituated to the viewing conditions, and for this reason reports obtained during the first three sessions, of approximately an hour each, were not recorded. For some subjects it is desirable at first to use a local anesthetic to minimize sensations from the contact lens, which tend to produce frequent blinking and jerky movements of the eyeball, causing a slight slipping of the contact lens and loss of stabilization. But further, the visual phenomena themselves are so striking at first that the subject inevitably tries to look at the object that has suddenly vanished or equally suddenly popped into vision after having vanished, again destroying stabilization. Only when he has adapted to the phenomena themselves, enough to be able to observe passively, does he begin to obtain the full range of phenomena. When adaptation was achieved, in the present experiment, the subject observed and reported on some fifty different visual objects.

## THE PHENOMENA

The phenomena of perception with stablized images and complex targets seem at first to have a bewildering variety, mostly without precedent in the subject's previous experience, but signs of order begin to appear with continued observation. The phenomena described here are from the reports of four experienced observers; unless otherwise stated, each phenomenon has been independently confirmed at least once, a second observer simply being asked to look at a new figure without being told what the preceding observer had found of interest in it.

When the figure is first presented, it remains intact for a length of time which depends on its complexity. With a single line as target, the line fades and disappears, leaving the more dimly illuminated field only. Eventually this disappears also, replaced by a "rich" or intense black patch. Subsequently it regenerates. A more complex target may behave similarly or it may instead lose one or more of its parts, in ways that will be described.

The time of the first disappearance varies, perhaps because of different levels of attention in the observer or because of variations in the level of unfamiliar auditory stimulation [28], but disappearance is quicker with simpler figures. Also, it has been possible to determine that a simpler figures such as a line is visible for about 10% of viewing time, while a more complex figure such as an unconnected set of curlicues or a facial profile (Figures 2, 3) retains at least one of its parts for as much as 80% of the time. Such a comparison can be made directly by presenting two figures simultaneously (for example, Figure 3); or the comparison may be quantified with repeated separate presentations, during which the observer presses a key whenever the figure is visible [14].

The greater time during which a more complex figure is present cannot be explained by assuming a random fluctuation of threshold in the different parts of the field. One might conclude, on such an assumption, that one or other part of the more complex figure remains visible only because the figure covers more of the field, and therefore is more likely to involve an area in which the visual threshold is, for the moment, lower than elsewhere. But, chaotic as the activity of the figure may seem at first, it still obeys some rules which relate to the form of the figure itself. It is these that we are now concerned with.

The "rules" may be summarized as follows: A meaningful diagram is visible longer than a meaningless one, an effect possibly related to the fact that attending to a diagram keeps it visible longer [28]. A straight line tends to act as a unit (that is, to appear or disappear as a whole) even though it extends across the whole 2° field; if the line breaks up, the break is likely to occur at the point of intersection with another line. The several lines of a triangle, square, and so on, act independently, with the exception that the activity of parallel lines in a figure is correlated. Jagged diagrams are more active, less stable, than rounded ones: a "good" figure [16] is more likely to act as a complete unit than a "poor" figure, and there are occasional observations of completion or regularization of a figure. Finally, there are clearly marked field effects, in which the presence of a figure in one part of the field modifies the activity of parts of a neighboring figure.

These results are illustrated in Figures 3 to 18. Figure 3 shows two curves which are similar except that one is a recognizable profile of a face. When they are seen with the apparent fixation point midway between them, the left curve, without meaning, fades faster and is absent more frequently than the right. Figure 14 combines three meaningful symbols: a 4, a B, and a 3. Fading of the parts of this complex does not occur at random; almost all the time, when any part of the figure is pres-

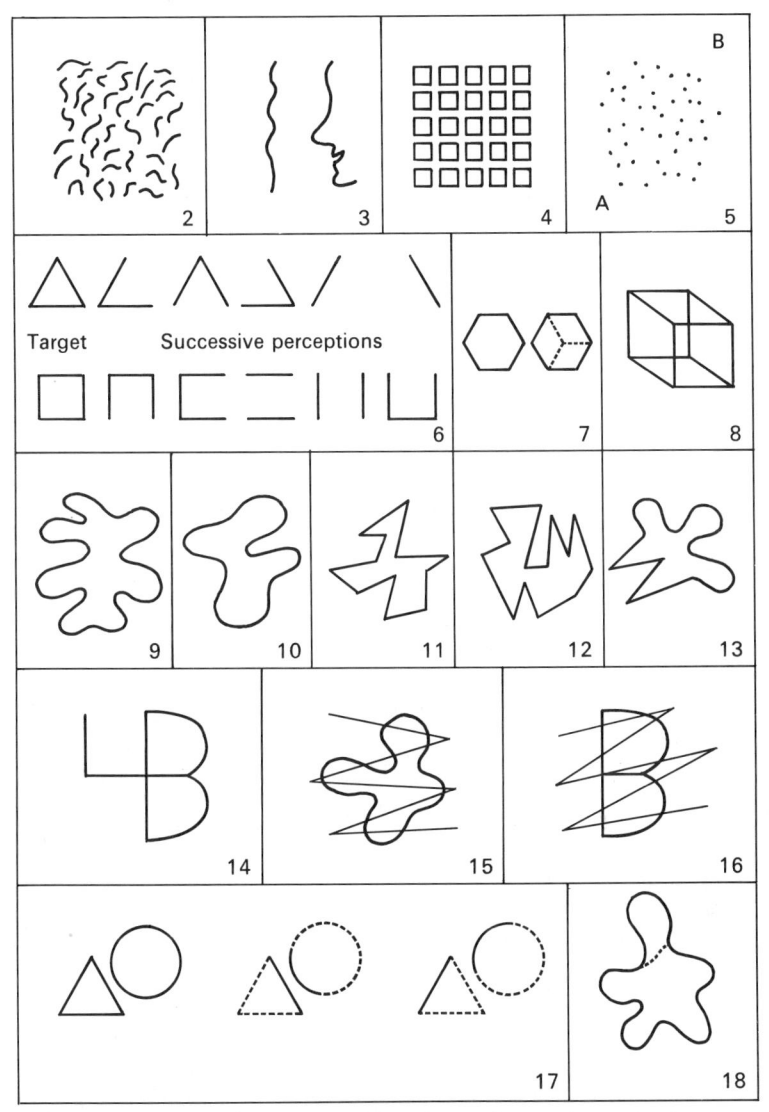

FIGURES 23-2 to 23-18 Examples of visual stimuli used. Figures 6, 7, 17, and 18 also show successive perceptions.

ent, it includes one or more of the symbols, complete. Similarly in Figure 16: The meaningless superimposed lines, over the letter B, act independently of it, and fade more frequently.

Figures 4 and 5 are configurations which behave in such a way as to emphasize the importance of linear organization. This may be horizontal, vertical, or diagonal, but the horizontal is usually predominant. In Figure 4, whole rows of squares may disappear together, leaving one row intact; in Figure 5, a more or less random collection of dots, there is a strong tendency for the dots to organize themselves, so that a line of dots such as that running from A to B may take on unity and repeatedly remain in the field when the others have disappeared. For one observer, one of the rows of Figure 4 at times acquired a further unity which is hard to describe: the squares within the row remained fully distinct visually, but the row became one thing, separate from the other parts of the figure. Possibly this was one of the three-dimensional depth effects discussed below, but the observer could not be certain on the point.

With the diagrams of Figures 6, 7, and 8, the independence of separate straight lines making up a more complex figure is very striking. Figure 6 shows two series of events which might occur with triangle and square respectively. Lines act as units. It is very seldom that an incomplete one is observed, except where a slight trace may occasionally remain at an intersection with another line. None of our data support the assumption made elsewhere [11] that it is the angle or corner that is a perceptual element. In these figures, again, the influence of parallel lines on one another is evident, since opposite sides of square or hexagon (at the left in Figure 7) remain together too frequently for this to be explained as coincidence, whereas with the square it is rare for two adjacent sides only to remain. The parallel-line effect is most striking with the Necker cube; in addition, when the cube is seen in three dimensions (as it always is with the stabilized image), surfaces which are separate but in parallel planes act frequently together. The front and back of the cube may remain in sight, for example, while the other edges (the lines which connect the squares which constitute front and back faces) have disappeared. The parallel-line effect is not invariable, of course, and still less the parallel-surface effect: In addition to complete inversion of the cube (which occurs with the stabilized image as with normal vision) there may be a partial inversion, the same surfaces being seen at right angles to each other.

Our emphasis has been on the independent action of parts of a complex figure, but the figure can also—less frequently—act as a whole, appearing and disappearing as a single unit. The probability that it will do so is principally determined by its shape. A circle, or a diagram such as those of Figures 9 and 10, is relatively stable and quiet, whereas another, as in Figures 11 and 12, is quite unstable and likely to produce an effect of violent motion, as the separate parts appear and disappear in rapid succession. In general, the pattern composed of rounded curves is less active than a jagged one, and more likely to act as whole. The difference between smoothness and jaggedness appears dramatically in a single pattern such as that of Figure 13, in which the angular parts are likely to be active and unpredictable and the rounded parts to form a more stable unit or part figure. This effect is clearly related to the "good" figure of Gestalt psychology, but it must be said that even the circle, the good figure par excellence, frequently acts as though composed of separate perceptual elements (see discussion of Figure 17, below). We have in fact found no other extended figure than an uninterrupted straight line which reliably acts as a unit.

The behavior of wholes is further illustrated by the diagrams of Figures 14, 15, and 16. We have already reported that Figure 14, containing three symbolic patterns, tends to break down in such a way as to leave one or more of the symbols intact. Here an effect of meaning and past experience is evident: similarly in Figure 16, where the B tends to remain for longer periods than the hatching lines, and even when they are present, the B is seen in a separate plane nearer the observer, as a separate entity. The diagram of Figure 15, however, shows that the effect can occur with a figure which lacks both meaning and goodness of form: The closed loop also tends to act as a whole though it is quite irregular.

Figure 17 illustrates a field effect which has been observed repeatedly. There is a marked influence of one of the two figures on the other, seen in two ways. First, the parts of the triangle and the circle which are nearest to each other frequently remain visible while the other parts disappear (Figure 17, first example) and second, less frequently, a side of the triangle which remains is accompanied by an arc of the circle which is "parallel" to it (Figure 17, second and third examples). This, with the tendency of parallel lines to act together which was mentioned earlier, seems clearly to show the existence of an influence of a visual object which extends well beyond the actual area of stimulation.

The final illustration, Figure 18, concerns a completion phenomenon which occurs in several ways, including the special case of closure. When a diagram such as that of Figure 9 or Figure 10 loses one of its limbs, we have obtained several reports of a transient closure which is diagramed in Figure 18. This appears to be a clear case of production of a better figure, and to it we may add the report of one observer that a slightly irregular hexagon became definitely regular. (On the other hand, a circle or other regular figure may be temporarily distorted, with an equally definite change of shape (one observer). The effect is similar to the perceptual distortions reported by subjects who have just come out of isolation [13].) A second example of completion is found in the hallucinatory addition of an eye to the profile of Figure 3 (one observer, but confirmed by a second observer with another profile figure).

Thirdly, a case which is perhaps equivocal as an instance of completion, but is of considerable interest and one which also brings us to our final topic, of depth effects. With the hexagon as presented in Figure 7, left, we have obtained reports of a "strong cube impression," the hexagon being perceived as the outline of a cube in three dimensions. The cube, also, is seen to reverse as the Necker cube does. The diagram at the right of Figure 7 shows how this may occur; the dotted lines do *not* appear in vision, but the figure acts in other respects as if they were present. In this sense, at least, there is completion.

Depth effects are ubiquitous. When the hexagon just referred to is seen as a two-dimensional figure instead of a cube, it is still clearly in a different plane from that of the background, nearly always above the surface, or closer to the observer. The effect is the same whether the figure is brighter than the ground or darker. The squares of Figure 4 have the appearance of a waffle iron, as protrusions from the surface (or, for one observer, occasionally as depressions); a row of circles of about the same dimensions look like a row of craters of small volcanoes. The tridimensionality of the Necker cube is much more definite than with ordinary vision; with prolonged viewing it may deteriorate from the appearance of regular cube, but is still definitely in three dimensions, the interior connecting lines appearing like wires strung over and under each other.

## COMMENT

The phenomena that have been described bear directly on two theoretical approaches to perception: Gestalt theory [16, 17] and the theory of cell assemblies [11, 22] or trace systems [20]. On the one hand, Gestalt ideas concerning the phenomena of perception find further new support; on the other, an independent action of parts even of good figures demonstrates that an exclusively holistic treatment of the percept is not sufficient, so that the explanatory conceptions of Gestalt theory require modification. We believe that the data offer support to both approaches, and qualify them to a greater or less extent; it is too soon to go into detailed analysis, but we may say in general that the holistic ideas become more compatible with analytical ones than was evident previously.

The Gestalt closure that has been described (Figure 18) is most clear-cut and unambiguous, comparable only to what has been observed in cases of hemianopia [10, 19]. There is clear evidence of the functional meaning of the conception of the "good" figure; of the functioning of the whole as a perceptual entity, distinct from part functions; and of groups as entities, and of similarity and contiguity as determinants of grouping. Finally, we have found evidence of marked field effects.

But with this we have found an extraordinary action of parts, independent of the whole. In the conditions of the experiment, this action tends to predominate over the whole in a way that never occurs in normal vision. The phenomena described, we believe, make inevitable the conclusion that perceptual elements (as distinct from sensory elements: [11]) exist in their own right. In conformity with Gestalt ideas, these are organized entities, and the conclusion to be drawn here, perhaps, is not that Gestalt emphasis on organized wholes is erroneous but rather (a) that the wholes in question are often simpler ones than are usually discussed—that is, straight lines or short segments of curves—and (b) that the more complex wholes, such as square or circle, are syntheses of simpler ones though they may also function as genuine single entities. The earlier literature treated perception-by-parts and perception of wholes as antithetical, mutually exclusive ideas. In retrospect, one seems that such a theoretical opposition is quite unnecessary, logically; and our data show that both conceptions are valid and complement one another.

The action of parts that has been described is also a very considerable confirmation of the theory of cell assemblies, in its main lines. As we have said above, the data show a need for revision, no support being provided for the idea that an angle or an intersection of lines is a perceptual element. Revision or development of the theory becomes necessary in other respects; for example, to account for the unexpected influence of contiguity as such, seen with Figure 17. In general terms, however, the phenomena confirm the earlier analysis [11] to a very surprising extent.

Today there are further data to support this approach. Apart from the present experiment, we may cite the auditory "holding" demonstrated by Broadbent [1] and the phenomena of serial order in visual perception [2, 12, 15, 23, 24]. All are intelligible in terms of a semiautonomous activity of closed systems in perception but unintelligible when perception is regarded as a simple input system, and the concept of cell assembly or trace system becomes less remotely speculative than it may have seemed at first, and closer to the realities of behavior. Further experiments of the kind we have reported, with the use of stabilized images, should make it possible to specify in more detail the properties of these closed systems and so provide a new understanding of the perceptual process.

## REFERENCES

1. D. E. Broadbent. Successive responses to simultaneous stimuli. *Quart. J. exp. Psychol.*, 1956, *8*, 145–152.
2. M. P. Bryden. Tachistoscopic recognition of nonalphabetical material. *Canad. J. Psychol.*, 1960, *4*, 74–82.
3. M. B. Clowes. Eye movements and the discrimination of brightness and color. Unpublished doctoral dissertation, University of Reading, 1959.
4. T. N. Cornsweet. Determination of the stimuli for involuntary drifts and saccadic eye movements. *J. opt. Soc. Amer.*, 1956, *46*, 987–993.
5. R. W. Ditchburn and D. H. Fender. The stabilised retinal image. *Opt. Acta*, 1955, *2*, 128–133.
6. R. W. Ditchburn, D. H. Fender, and S. Mayne. Vision with controlled movements of the retinal image. *J. Physiol.*, 1959, *145*, 98–107.
7. R. W. Ditchburn and B. L. Ginsborg. Vision with a stabilised retinal image. *Nature, London*, 1952, *170*, 36–37.
8. R. W. Ditchburn and R. M. Pritchard. Stabilised interference fringes on the retina. *Nature, London*, 1956, *177*, 434.
9. D. H. Fender. The function of eye movements in the visual process. Unpublished doctoral dissertation, University of Reading, 1956.

10. W. Fuchs. Untersuchungen über das Sehen der Hemianopiker und Hemiambliopiker, II. In A. Gelb and K. Goldstein (eds.). *Psychologische Analysen hirnpathologischer Fälle*. Leipzig: Barth, 1920.
11. D. O. Hebb. *The organization of behavior*. New York: Wiley, 1949.
12. W. Heron. Perception as a function of retinal locus and attention. *Amer. J. Psychol.*, 1957, *70*, 38–48.
13. W. Heron, B. K. Doane, and T. H. Scott. Visual disturbances after prolonged perceptual isolation. *Canad. J. Psychol.*, 1956, *10*, 13–18.
14. F. J. Kader. Target complexity and visibility in stabilised images. Unpublished B.A. honors thesis, McGill University, 1960.
15. D. Kimura. The effect of letter position on recognition. *Canad. J. Psychol.*, 1959, *13*, 1–10.
16. K. Koffka. *Principles of Gestalt psychology*. New York: Harcourt, Brace, 1935.
17. W. Köhler. *Gestalt psychology*. New York: Liveright, 1929.
18. J. Krauskopf. Effect of retinal image motion on contrast thresholds for maintained vision. *J. opt. Soc. Amer.*, 1957, *47*, 740–744.
19. K. S. Lashley. Patterns of cerebral integration indicated by the scotomas of migraine. *Arch. Neurol. Psychiat., Chicago*, 1941, *46*, 331–339.
20. K. S. Lashley. Cerebral organization and behavior. *Res. Publ. Ass. nerv. ment. Dis.* 1958, *35*, 1–18.
21. D. M. Mackay. Some further visual phenomena associated with regular patterned stimulation. *Nature, London*, 1957, *180*, 1145–1146.
22. P. M. Milner. The cell assembly: Mark II. *Psychol. Rev.*, 1957, *64*, 242–252.
23. M. Mishkin and D. G. Forgays. Word recognition as a function of retinal locus. *J. exp. Psychol.*, 1952, *43*, 43–48.
24. J. Orbach. Retinal locus as a factor in the recognition of visually perceived words. *Amer. J. Psychol.*, 1952, *65*, 555–562.
25. R. M. Pritchard. Studies of visual perception with a stabilised retinal image. Unpublished doctoral dissertation, University of Reading, 1958.
26. R. M. Pritchard. Visual illusions viewed as stabilised retinal images. *Quart. J. exp. Psychol.*, 1958, *10*, 77–81.
27. R. M. Pritchard. A collimator stabilising system. *Quart. J. exp. Psychol.*, 1961, *13*, 181–183.
28. R. M. Pritchard and D. Vowles. The effects of auditory stimulation on the perception of the stabilised retinal image. 1960.
29. F. Ratliff and L. A. Riggs. Involuntary motions of the eye during monocular fixation. *J. exp. Psychol.*, 1950, *40*, 687–701.
30. L. A. Riggs, J. C. Armington, and F. Ratliff. Motions of the retinal image during fixation. *J. opt. Soc. Amer.*, 1954, *44*, 315–321.
31. L. A. Riggs, F. Ratliff, J. C. Cornsweet, and T. N. Cornsweet. The disappearance of steadily fixated test-objects. *J. opt. Soc. Amer.*, 1953, *43*, 495–501.
32. A. L. Yarbus. On the perception of an image fixed relative to the retina. *Biofizika*, 1957, *2*, 703–712.

# 24
# SPATIAL AND TEXTURAL CHARACTERISTICS OF THE GANZFELD

## Walter Cohen

There have been several partially successful attempts to study the effects of uniform stimulation over the entire visual field. Metzger has reported that under low illumination the entire visual field (*Ganzfeld*) appears as "a mist of light which becomes more condensed at an indefinite distance" [9]. When intensity is increased, the fog becomes a filmy surface separated from the observer by empty space. The distance of the surface is judged to be about the same as its objective distance. With further increase in level of illumination, the distance is judged to be greater, and the filmy curved surface is transformed into a flat plane surface with microstructure. It is difficult to interpret these results, since uniformity of stimulation was not achieved by Metzger. Under high illumination, the physical texture of the surface was perceived.

Gibson and Waddell, using a translucent globe, found that under high illumination their observers described a "sea of light" with something vaguely surfacelike in front of the face [4]. Their naive observers did not consistently report the impression of space-filling fog. Gibson and Waddell attribute the occasional reports of other qualities to central processes rather than to peripheral stimulation.

There have been two basic sources of inhomogeneity in all previous studies dealing with the *Ganzfeld*. First, physical microstructure was present. In addition, parts of the observer's face prevented uniform stimulation of the entire retina—for example, the nose must have produced a shadow on the peripheral nasal area of the visual field. The apparatus developed for the present investigation provided an adequate uniform *Ganzfeld* by eliminating both these sources of inhomogeneity. Although additional information was collected, this paper will be limited to the "mode of appearance" and spatial characteristics of the *Ganzfeld*. The following three questions guided the design of the experiment: (1) In what manner is the appearance of the homogeneous *Ganzfeld* dependent upon intensity and wavelength? (2) How does the appearance of the inhomogeneous *Ganzfeld* differ from that of the homogeneous *Ganzfeld*?

Source: *American Journal of Psychology*, 1957, 70, 403–410.
Note: The author is indebted to Professor Carl R. Brown for his assistance.

(3) How are these differences in appearance related to stimulus distributions?

## METHOD

### Apparatus

A new method was devised which would produce a uniform *Ganzfeld* as well as permit the introduction of a spot into the field. The principle utilized was similar to that of the photometric sphere—as a result of direct illumination of a small part of the inner surface, there is indirect uniform illumination of the entire surface of the sphere.

Two spheres, each having a diameter of 1 m, were joined together (Figure 24-1). The smooth inner walls were sprayed with Benjamin Moore Sphere Paint to produce a diffuse reflecting surface of high albedo and no visible texture at viewing distance. The observer looked into sphere A, and the light entered by way of two openings in sphere B. At the junction of the two spheres was a circular aperture 8 cm in diameter. A special mask was made to fit the contours of the observer's face. The mask formed a removable section of the wall of sphere A and was used as a headrest. Each mask had an opening which permitted unobstructed monocular

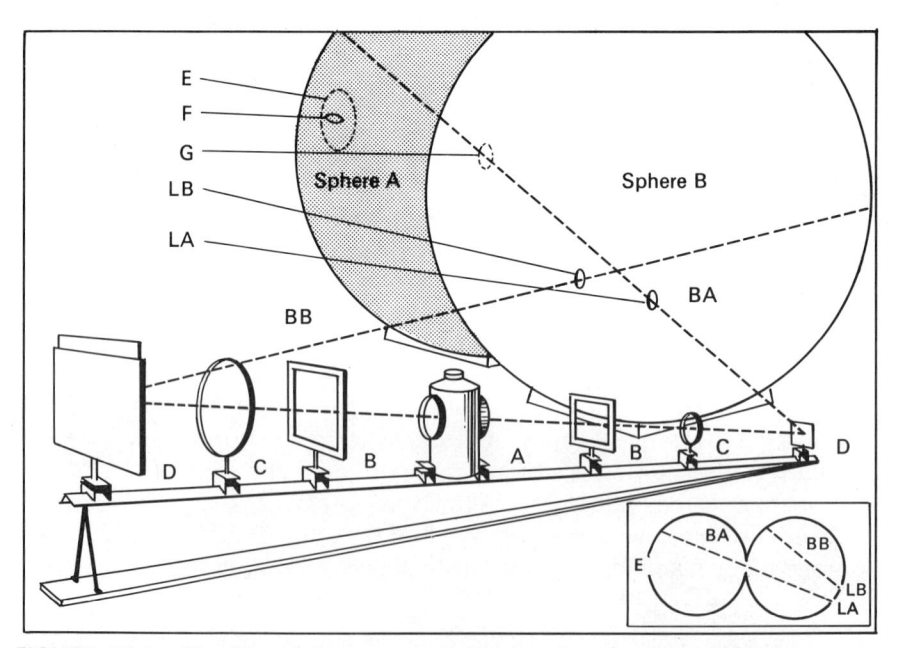

FIGURE 24-1 Diagram of Apparatus: A, light-source; B, filter; C, lens; D, mirror; E, mask; F, eye-piece; G, 8-cm aperture; BA, beam for sphere A; BB, beam for sphere B; LA, opening for BA; LB, opening for BB.

vision. When the observer looked to the right, no part of his mask or face was visible. The left eye was kept in complete darkness. Since the opening of the mask was directly opposite the center of the 8-cm aperture, the observer's line of sight was perpendicular to the plane of the aperture.

A beam of light was projected onto the inner surface of sphere A, 20 cm above the observer's eye. Sphere B was uniformly illuminated by a beam of light that could be independently varied. By use of appropriate filters, the luminosity of both spheres was so controlled as to produce either equality or some desired difference. When the luminous flux density in the two spheres was made equal, the aperture ceased to exist optically, and a uniform *Ganzfeld* was produced. When the luminous flux in the two spheres differed as to dominant wavelength, purity, or intensity, inhomogeneity was produced. Light coming from the aperture area was different from that coming from the rest of the field, and the observer was confronted with a simple inhomogeneity in an otherwise uniform field.

The two beams of light originated from the same source. With appropriate lenses and mirrors, the beams were directed through two 5-cm openings in sphere B. These openings were not visible to observers looking into sphere A. Neutral and colored filters altered the intensity and composition of the light. Chromatic illumination was obtained by the use of the following Wratten filters: (1) red (608 m$\mu$) CC-50R, excitation purity 21%; (2) green (554 m$\mu$) CC-40G, excitation purity 21%; (3) green (554 m$\mu$) CC-30G, excitation purity 16%; (4) blue (461 m$\mu$) CC-30B, excitation purity 20%. The following notation will be used to designate the manner of illumination: The chromatic filters will be designated by the letters *R, G, GX,* and *B* respectively. The letter *A* will signify the absence of a chromatic filter. The luminance will be expressed in millilamberts. Thus, (R2.1-A4.9) signifies a field having a dominant wavelength of 608 m$\mu$ and a brightness of 2.1 mL., with an achromatic spot having a brightness of 4.9 mL.

## Observers

Thirteen men and three women served as observers. The median age of the group, which was made up of three undergraduates, ten graduate students, and three faculty members of the University of Buffalo, was 25 years. Although all specialized in psychology, they were naive as to the purpose of the present study. All had normal color vision, but only six had normal visual acuity.

## Procedure

Each observer was studied in an average of five 1-hr sessions. A complete record of the observer's responses was made with a tape recorder. Tasks of two kinds were performed: (1) The observer was required to compare two situations with respect to fog density, distance, distinctiveness of figure, hue, and saturation. Each of the situations was presented for 20 sec, with an interval of 5 sec between the two members of each pair and an interval of 15 sec between pairs. (2) The observer remained in the experimental situation for 3 min to report on the effects of adaptation. Each situation was followed by a 2-min rest period.

The order of presentation was counterbalanced to control for time error, peactice, and adaptation. Each observer was presented with approximately half of the experimental situations, thus providing an N of 8 for each. There were five basic kinds of visual field with which the observers were presented: (1) homogeneity; (2) inhomogeneity due to a difference in chromaticity between field and spot; (3) inhomogeneity due to a difference in intensity; (4) inhomogeneity due to a difference both in intensity and chromaticity; (5) inhomogeneity due to a difference in purity.

## RESULTS AND DISCUSSION

### Homogeneity

The most characteristic description of the field for all observers was "foglike." Reports as to density and degree of immersion varied. The following phrases are representative: "A diffuse fog." "A hazy insipid yellow." "A gaseous effect." "A milky substance." "Misty, like being in a lemon pie." "Smoky."

The observers of Gibson and Waddell reported other impressions with considerable frequency, a disparity which may be traced to procedure as well as to apparatus [3, pp. 268–269]. Gibson and Waddell used a question and training procedure which may have influenced their observers to seek something other than fog. Failure to control for facial shadows may account for the reports of a boundary. During the present investigation, there were a few descriptions of a "cracked ice effect" or a "weblike structure" which could be eliminated by slight adjustments in the illumination of sphere B. It may be that gradients of intensity which are insufficient for the formation of a spot result in other forms of phenomenal inhomogeneity.

The homogeneous *Ganzfeld* was reported to be "close at hand" by all observers. Only one consistently described the field as being more than 6 in. away, and the modal judgment of distance was 2 in. The fog itself was, however, seen to extend for an indefinite distance. Several observers described an experience of complete immersion in the fog, and, in a few instances, space was internalized, described as being "inside the head." Werner has described a similar internalization of sound [10]. There was a high degree of uncertainty as to distance and most observers were extremely hesitant about making distance judgments.

A nonparametric technique gave no indication, within the range of

1.8-4.9 mL, that either fog density or fog distance was significantly related to intensity of illumination ($p > 0.10$) [2], a result which does not correspond to Metzger's findings [9, p. 14]. This discrepancy may be accounted for by the absence of surface texture in the present experiment. The "blue" field ($B2.4$-$B2.4$) was consistently judged ($p < 0.05$) as less dense than either the "red" field ($R2.1$-$R2.1$) or the achromatic field ($A2.4$-$A2.4$). In addition, the observers reported feeling less immersed in the "blue" field, which suggests that receptors sensitive to long wavelength are more densely concentrated than those sensitive to short.

During the course of adaptation, five of the sixteen observers reported a complete cessation of visual experience. Two reported "blackout" almost every time they were confronted with prolonged, homogeneous stimulation. This was a unique experience which involved a complete disappearance of the sense of vision for short periods of time, and not simply the presence of a dark, undifferentiated visual field. The following description is representative: "Foggy whiteness, everything blacks out, returns, goes. I feel blind. I'm not even seeing blackness. This differs from the black when lights are out." It may be conjectured that the perceptual mechanism has evolved to cope with a differentiated field, and, in the absence of differentiation, there is a temporary breakdown of the mechanism (which might be detected electrophysiologically). Anxiety and fear of blindness under somewhat similar conditions also were reported by Hochberg, Triebel, and Seaman [5].

Although uniform proximal stimulation does not provide a basis for articulation, the separation of the field into a fog in front of a ground occurs. This effect may be related to the process of figure-ground segregation. It should be noted that when hue is experienced in the chromatic *Ganzfeld,* it is seen as a phenomenal characteristic of the fog, whereas the ground behind the fog may appear as neutral.

**Inhomogeneity**

Introduction of inhomogeneity reduced fog density and increased fog distance ($p < 0.05$) in most instances. When figure-ground segregation was poor because of the absence of steep gradients of intensity, the field, as fog, continued to be seen as close, while the figure was seen as far away. Thus, the "normal" relationship between figure and ground was reversed. Distance judgments for the figure under these conditions ranged from 5 in. to 6 ft, with a mode of 2 ft. Increasing the difference in intensity between field and spot resulted in a closer figure and a more distant ground. When the difference in intensity was maximal, judgments of figural distance ranged from "next to the eye" to 3 ft away, with a median of 6 in. The ground usually was judged to be a few inches behind the spot, although a few observers judged it to be several feet behind the spot. Each observer was consistent in his judgments of distance. There were, however, marked differences among observers in the range of values used to describe the distance of the figure. The terms close and far varied considerably in meaning for different observers. For one, an apparent distance of 5 in. was considered far, while for another an apparent distance of 3 ft was considered close.

Inhomogeneity due either to intensitive or to chromatic differences between field and spot reduced fog density and increased fog distance in most cases. There were, however, no consistent differences ($p > 0.10$) between homogeneous and inhomogeneous fields when (1) differences in intensity between field and spot were at about 1 jnd, or (2) inhomogeneity was due to a difference in purity between field and spot. In both cases, the spot was unstable and often disappeared for brief intervals.

The results of comparisons between homogeneous fields are shown in Table 24-1. Increasing the difference in intensity between field and spot tended to decrease the apparent density and to increase the apparent distance of the fog (a, b, c, d). The direction of the difference was not relevant (e). There was no consistent difference between those situations involving both chromatic and intensive inhomogeneity and those involving only intensive inhomogeneity (f, g, h, i). The appearance of the fog of an achromatic field was dependent upon the dominant wavelength of the spot (j, k, l). The fog was reported as denser and closer when the dominant wavelength of the spot was short than when it was long.

An amorphous field, as well as an amorphous figure, appears to characterize those situations in which gradients of intensity are absent. The assertion that gradients of intensity are more effective than chromatic gradients in reducing the amorphous characteristics of the field would not, however, be completely warranted. Such a conclusion would require the comparison of fields in which the two types of gradient were equated as to magnitude. Since such an equation would be arbitrary, and articulation of the field is dependent upon the magnitude of the stimulus gradients, no direct test of this hypothesis is possible [8].

The mode of appearance of the field seems to be related to the definiteness of figure-ground segregation. With increased sharpness of boundary, there is greater definiteness of surface. Gibson and Dibble, in their study of visual surface, found that the steepness of gradients of luminous intensity was a determinant of surface hardness [3]. The same was found to be true in the present study to a limited extent. Even when steep gradients of intensity were present, fog was reported more than 50% of the time. In only a few cases did the observers actually report the ground as appearing hard, but the figure was frequently described as hard when differences in intensity between field and spot were large.

An expansion of the field was experienced when steep gradients were introduced. Koffka suggested that contraction and expansion of space may be a function of "forces" related to articulation of the field [7, p. 119]. In accordance with his formulation, well-articulated fields are perceived as being at a greater distance than those which are poorly articulated.

TABLE 24-1  Relative Fog Density and Fog Distance of the Ground Areas of Inhomogeneous Fields

| | Situations Compared | | Density Judgment | | | | Distance Judgment | | | |
|---|---|---|---|---|---|---|---|---|---|---|
| | 1 | 2 | 1 greater | Equal | 2 greater | p† | 1 nearer | Equal | 2 nearer | p† |
| a | (A2.1–A2.0) | (A2.1–A1.8) | 6 | 2 | 0 | <0.03 | 5 | 3 | 0 | <0.05 |
| b | (A2.1–A1.8) | (A2.1–A0.0) | 8 | 0 | 0 | <0.01 | 6 | 2 | 0 | <0.03 |
| c | (A2.1–A2.2) | (A2.1–A2.4) | 7 | 1 | 0 | <0.03 | 5 | 3 | 0 | <0.05 |
| d | (A2.1–A2.4) | (A2.1–A4.9) | 8 | 0 | 0 | <0.01 | 7 | 1 | 0 | <0.03 |
| e | (A2.1–A2.4) | (A2.1–A1.8) | 2 | 5 | 1 | >0.25 | 1 | 6 | 1 | >0.25 |
| f | (R2.1–A2.2) | (R2.1–R2.2) | 2 | 5 | 1 | >0.25 | 1 | 6 | 1 | >0.25 |
| g | (R2.1–A2.0) | (R2.1–R2.0) | 1 | 6 | 1 | >0.25 | 2 | 6 | 0 | >0.25 |
| h | (R2.1–A1.8) | (R2.1–R1.8) | 3 | 4 | 1 | >0.25 | 4 | 2 | 2 | >0.25 |
| i | (G2.7–A2.4) | (G2.7–G2.4) | 3 | 3 | 2 | >0.25 | 3 | 4 | 1 | >0.25 |
| j | (A2.1–R2.1) | (A2.1–G2.1) | 0 | 3 | 5 | <0.05 | 2 | 3 | 3 | >0.25 |
| k | (A2.1–R2.1) | (A2.1–B2.1) | 0 | 2 | 6 | <0.03 | 0 | 3 | 5 | <0.05 |
| l | (A2.1–G2.1) | (A2.1–B2.1) | 1 | 4 | 3 | >0.25 | 1 | 5 | 2 | >0.25 |

† Sign test.

In most cases, the figure was judged to be about one and one-half times as large as its "real" size. It has been suggested that there is an invariant relationship between phenomenal size and phenomenal distance [1]. If there were such a relationship, the underestimation of the apparent distance of the figure should have been accompanied by an underestimation, rather than an overestimation, of its apparent size. When steepness of the intensive gradients was increased, the figure appeared closer, but there was no systematic change in apparent size. The apparent distance changed without a change either in retinal size or in apparent size. These results are consistent with the conclusion of Kilpatrick and Ittleson that the invariant relationship between size and distance is restricted to special conditions and does not apply to those situations in which the field is poorly articulated [6].

## SUMMARY

The present investigation deals with visual perception when the entire visual field is uniform and when a small differentiated area is introduced into such a field.

The most representative description of the homogeneous *Ganzfeld* is that of close, impenetrable fog. The experience is a unique one, and most observers have difficulty in describing the field in terms usually associated with visual phenomena. In some instances, temporary cessation of visual experience is reported. Variations in wavelength rather than intensity of illumination alter the density and distance of the fog.

A differentiated area in the *Ganzfeld* changes its phenomenal characteristics. When the differentiation results from chromatic gradients alone, a distant, indefinite figure is reported, and modifications in the appearance of the fog are slight. Those situations involving dominant short wavelength seem more indefinite and distant than those involving dominant long wavelength. The addition of an intensive gradient to the chromatic gradient increases definiteness of the figure-ground segregation.

The effect of moderate differences in intensity is to produce a relatively definite separation of figure and ground. The density of fog is considerably reduced. Increased differences in intensity further separate figure and ground. The fog disappears. The figure is seen as closer than the ground. Their modes of appearance differ and a distinct boundary separates them. Those factors which increase the apparent distance of the field consistently decrease the apparent distance of the spot and the density of the fog.

The phenomenal characteristics of the *Ganzfeld* do not appear to be independently determined. Any change in the stimulus distribution that modifies one aspect of experience produces concomitant changes in the other phenomenal characteristics of the *Ganzfeld*. The distribution of stimulation rather than the nature of the local stimulus seems to determine what is experienced.

## REFERENCES

1. E. G. Boring. Visual perception as invariance. *Psychol. Rev.*, 1952, *59*, 141–148.
2. W. J. Dixon and A. M. Mood. The statistical sign test. *J. Amer. statist. Ass.*, 1946, *41*, 557–566.
3. J. J. Gibson and F. N. Dibble. Exploratory experiments on the stimulus conditions for the perception of a visual surface. *J. exp. Psychol.*, 1952, *43*, 414–419.
4. J. J. Gibson and D. Waddell. Homogeneous retinal stimulation and visual perception. *Amer. J. Psychol.*, 1952, *65*, 263–270.
5. J. E. Hochberg, W. Triebel, and G. Seaman. Color adaptation under conditions of homogeneous visual stimulation (*Ganzfeld*). *J. exp. Psychol.*, 1951, *41*, 153–159.
6. F. P. Kilpatrick and W. H. Ittleson. The size-distance invariance hypothesis. *Psychol. Rev.*, 1953, *60*, 223–231.
7. K. Koffka. *Principles of Gestalt psychology.* New York: Harcourt, Brace, 1935.
8. K. Koffka and M. R. Harrower. Colour and organization. *Psychol. Forsch.*, 1931, *15*, 145–275.
9. W. Metzger. Optische Untersuchungen am Ganzfeld. II. Zur Phänomenologie des homogenen Ganzfelds. *Psychol. Forsch.*, 1930, *13*, 6–29.
10. H. Werner. Untersuchungen über Empfindung und Empfinden. *Z. Psychol.*, 1929, *114*, 152–166.

# 25

# PERCEPTUAL CHANGES AFTER PROLONGED SENSORY ISOLATION (DARKNESS AND SILENCE)

J. P. Zubek
D. Pushkar
W. Sansom
J. Gowing

In an earlier report [26] a description was given of the intellectual changes occurring in sixteen subjects during a week of isolation under conditions of constant darkness and silence. In the present paper the concern is largely with the perceptual changes recorded in these same subjects.

## METHOD

The experimental conditions were similar to those previously described [26]. Briefly, they were as follows: The subjects were paid to lie on an air mattress in a dark and soundproofed chamber (70 db attenuation). They constantly wore a pair of earmuffs, which served to reduce any sounds that they might make inside the chamber. They were instructed to lie quietly on the mattress and not to engage in any singing or humming or any other vocal or physical activity. Toilet facilities, a food chamber, a panic button, a two-way intercom system, and an air-conditioning unit are all built into the floor, making it unnecessary for the subject to leave the chamber for any purpose during the isolation period. The subjects were asked to remain in isolation for a week and during this time were prevented as far as possible from determining what time it was. The only intrusion on the experimental condition of darkness and silence was an occasional test session, for purposes of appraising intellectual abilities, of approximately 45 min duration when a 15-w red bulb was put on inside

Source: *Canadian Journal of Psychology,* 1961, 15, 83–100.
Note: This research was supported by the Defence Research Board of Canada, Project 9425-08. The authors express their gratitude to the Children's Hospital, Winnipeg, for making available the facilities of their EEG laboratory, and to Dr. M. G. Saunders of the General Hospital and of the Department of Physiology, University of Manitoba, for his analysis of the EEG records.

the chamber. Since the results of these intellectual tests have already been reported in an earlier publication, they will not be dealt with here.

The experimental group consisted of sixteen subjects (twelve males and four females). Of these, fourteen were in isolation for 7 days, one for 8½ days, and one for 10 days. A control group of subjects was also employed. Further details about these subjects have been given in the earlier publication. The experimental subjects were given a battery of perceptual-motor tests before and immediately after the isolation period. These were all administered outside of the isolation chamber under a constant level of illumination. The control subjects were given the same perceptual tests at the same time intervals as the experimentals.

The battery of perceptual-motor tests consisted of the following:

1. *Visual vigilance* was measured by a modified Mackworth clock test. It consisted of an electric laboratory clock (8 in. in diameter) with a single rotating hand which was briefly stopped (0.10 sec) and then started at eight irregular time intervals during each 30-min period. The "breaks" or signals were presented at intervals of 2, 2, 3, 1, 6, 7, 3, and 5 min. This 30-min cycle was repeated four times. The subject indicated the presence of a signal by pressing a button.

2. *Auditory discrimination.* While the subject was performing the vigilance task he was presented with a continuous tone of 1,100 cycles at 25 db whose frequency and intensity were periodically increased or decreased in magnitude. Six frequency (50 cycles) and six intensity (5 db) changes were made in each of six 20-min periods. The twelve changes or signals were presented at random time intervals in each of the six time periods. The subject again indicated the presence of a signal by pressing a button.

3. *Depth perception* was tested with the Howard-Dohlman apparatus. Each test of depth perception was the mean of four binocular trials where half of the trials started with the movable rod in front of the standard and the other half with it in the back. The subject, whose head was kept immobilized, was at a distance of 12 ft from the apparatus. Scores are recorded in terms of the mean separation, in cm, of the variable rod from the standard (taken as zero).

4. *Size constancy.* A black equilateral triangle, of variable height, was presented at 15 ft. The subject was required to adjust the height of this triangle until it looked the same in size as the near one, the standard triangle. This triangle was 20 cm high and was presented at a distance of 4 ft. Four trials were given.

5. *Reversible figures.* The subject was asked to fixate a point at the center of an ambiguous figure (reversible blocks) for 60 sec, pressing a counter each time the figure changed. Three trials were given. The score was the average number of reversals per minute.

6. *Perception of lines.* The subject was shown a horizontal black line, 10 in. long and ¼ in. wide with a fixation point located 3 in. above and below the center of the line. He was then shown two parallel vertical black lines, each 10 in. long and ¼ in. wide, separated by 2¾ in. with a fixation point located between the two parallel lines. These two sets of lines were presented on a white background at a distance of 3 ft from the subject, who was instructed to "tell me what each figure looks like to you—not what you think it really is, but what it looks like subjectively."

7. *Perception of colors.* The subject was shown six colored, 5-in. squares of paper—red, green, yellow, blue, black and white—and asked to report on any changes in brightness or richness in color.

In addition to these perceptual tests, which were given before and after isolation, or a week apart in the case of the controls, the experimental subjects were required to estimate various intervals of time before and at daily intervals during isolation. Starting at the sound of a buzzer the subjects were asked to signal when 1, 3, 5, 15, 30, 60, and 120 min had elapsed. All time estimates were from zero, that is, the subjects making a 5-min estimate, for example, were told to signal when they felt a total period of 5 min had elapsed rather than the passage of a 2-min period after the 3-min estimate. During all of the time estimates the subjects were told to refrain from any intellectual activity and to keep their minds as blank as possible. In several instances the subjects fell asleep during the test. When this occurred the time estimates were repeated a little later.

The ideal time control subjects for this study would have been the experimentals, retested some months after isolation. However, since many of them had left the city, only eight could be used as controls. They were all tested from 4 to 6 months after isolation. The rest of the controls were made up of subjects as close as possible in age, education, intelligence, and so forth, to the experimentals. Most of the time estimate controls were tested in the isolation chamber. The remainder were tested in a quiet room wearing black goggles and earmuffs. At the completion of the daily time estimates the subjects were kept in the laboratory for a period of time before being allowed to go home. This was done in order to prevent knowledge of results unduly influencing the subsequent daily time estimates.

## RESULTS

### Perceptual Tests

Table 25-1 shows the results of the experimental and control subjects on the tests of depth perception, size constancy, and reversible figures administered before and after a week of isolation or an elapse of a week. The statistical analysis is based on the difference between the mean scores

TABLE 25-1  Mean Scores on Depth Perception, Size Constancy, and Reversible Figures

|  | Experimentals | Controls |
|---|---|---|
| Depth perception |  |  |
| N | 16 | 16 |
| Before | 2.00 cm | 1.97 cm |
| After | 2.83 cm | 1.56 cm |
| Size constancy |  |  |
| N | 15 | 15 |
| Before | 21.9 cm | 20.3 cm |
| After | 23.9 cm | 20.5 cm |
| Reversible figures |  |  |
| N | 15 | 15 |
| Before | 15.8/min | 15.3/min |
| After | 13.4/min | 15.2/min |

of the experimental and control groups after a week, relative to their scores a week earlier. It can be seen that on depth perception the experimental subjects did less well after a week than did the controls. This difference, however, is not reliable ($0.05 < p < 0.10$). On the size constancy test, the experimentals chose larger comparison triangles than did the controls, suggesting a decrease in constancy, but this difference again is not statistically reliable ($0.05 < p < 0.10$). However, since these two sets of results border on significance it is possible that with a larger N they might have reached statistical significance. Finally, on the reversible figures the experimentals showed fewer figural reversals per minute than the controls but this difference again is not reliable ($p > 0.40$).

Figure 25-1 shows the performance of the experimental and control subjects on the auditory discrimination task in terms of percentage detection of signal changes, frequency and intensity combined, occurring in six successive 20-min intervals of time. A statistical analysis based on a comparison of the mean difference scores (between the preisolation and week-later tests) of the two groups shows no reliable difference in performance on the entire 120-min test ($p > 0.10$) nor on any of the six 20-min test periods, although the difference on the sixth 20-min period borders on significance ($0.05 < p < 0.10$). Separate curves for frequency and intensity changes are not shown because no reliable differences were evident between the two measurements.

Figure 25-2 shows the scores of the experimental and control subjects on the visual vigilance task in terms of percentage detection of signal changes occurring in four successive 30-min periods. It can be seen that after a week, the overall vigilance performance of the experimentals is much poorer than that of the controls ($p < 0.001$). Furthermore, their performance on each of the four successive 30-min periods is reliably poorer

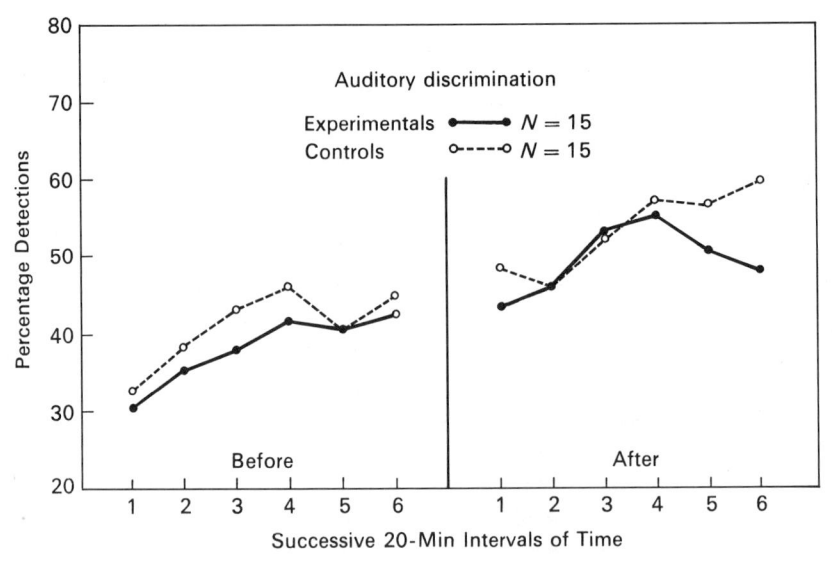

FIGURE 25-1  Performance of experimental and control subjects on an auditory discrimination task in terms of percentage detection of signal changes occurring in six successive 20-min intervals of time.

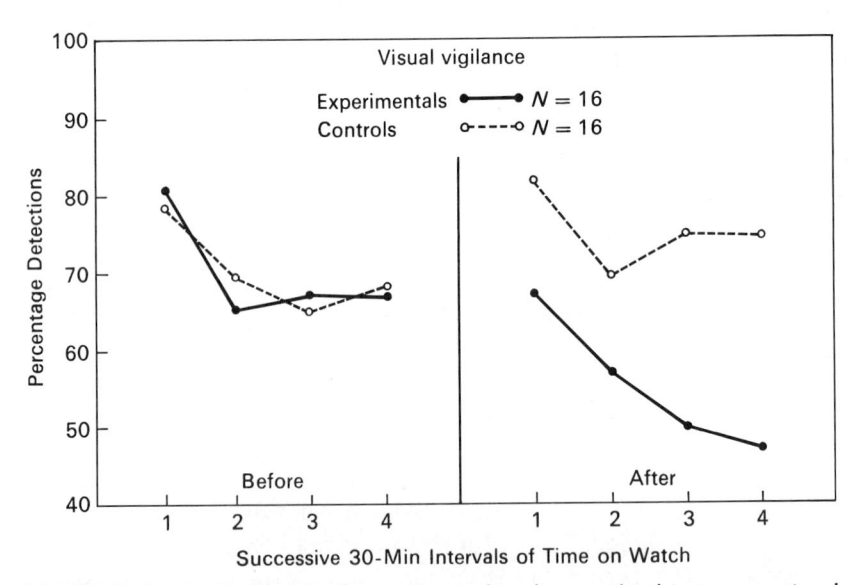

FIGURE 25-2  Performance of experimental and control subjects on a visual vigilance task in terms of percentage detection of signal changes occurring in four successive 30-min intervals of time.

than that of the controls. It is interesting to note that although the vigilance performance of the control subjects has leveled off during the last 60 min, it is still deteriorating in the experimentals.

In the daily time estimation tests it was found that both the experimental and control subjects overestimated [1] the short intervals of time, that is, 1, 3, 5, 15, and 30 min. However, none of the differences between the groups is statistically reliable. On the longer time intervals, that is, 60 and 120 min, both groups of subjects showed an underestimation, with the experimentals showing more underestimation, that is, less accuracy than the controls. However, only on the 120-min estimate is the difference statistically reliable ($0.01 < p < 0.02$).

Some observations of an exploratory nature were also made of the ability of ten of the sixteen subjects to report the time of day. These subjects were asked, at an *average* of once a day, to report the clock time. Their estimates were surprisingly accurate, showing an average error of 105 min ($SD = 76.5$) over the 7 days. No reliable difference was found between the average error of estimate of the first 3 days and that of the last 4 days. However, the error during the first day was significantly greater than that of any of the succeeding days. The general tendency of the errors was in the minus direction, that is, to underestimation. The "accuracy" of these estimates may partly be due to the presence of certain cues, for example from the occasional battery of intellectual tests (given at intervals from 18 to 30 hr) and also to possible vibrations passing into the chamber. Whatever the explanation for this accuracy might be, these results are in agreement with those obtained by MacLeod and Roff [14], who, in perhaps the first experimental study of isolation, confined two subjects in a soundproofed room for 86 and 48 hr and asked them at various intervals to report the clock time. They found that the errors were "surprisingly small." The final error of the 86-hr subject was 40 min, while that of the 48-hr subject was 26 min. Furthermore, they reported an "initial large error of orientation after the first night of sleep, which gradually became reduced and eventually disappeared almost completely." These results are also in line with those of Smith and Lewty [20] on a group of twenty subjects kept in a silent but constantly illuminated room for periods up to 4 days. Their error of estimate ranged from 1/2 to 3 hr. Subjects kept in a tank-type respirator for 36 hr have also revealed an excellent time sense. Their error of estimating the duration of their restriction ranged from 7 min to 2 hr [25]. Goldberger and Holt [9] have also commented on the accuracy of time estimation in their 8-hr isolation experiments.

## Qualitative Observations During Isolation

Changes of an intellectual nature have already been reported in an earlier publication and will, therefore, not be dealt with here. One type of phenomenon, however, about which there has been considerable in-

---

[1] In keeping with the suggestion of Bindra and Waksberg [3], underestimation of time by the production method refers to "subjective temporal units smaller than objective temporal units" whereas overestimation refers to "subjective temporal units larger than objective temporal units."

terest in the literature on sensory deprivation is hallucinatory activity. In order to qualify as a hallucination the experience had to have an "out-thereness"; its appearance and disappearance had to be independent of the subject's volition, and the subject, at least in the beginning, had to be convinced of its reality. These were the criteria employed by Vernon, McGill, and Schiffman [23] in their paper on visual hallucinations occurring during 3 days of darkness and silence. If these criteria are applied to the present study, we can say that eleven out of the sixteen subjects experienced some hallucinatory activity at some time during the period of isolation. When hallucinations were reported, they usually appeared after the third day. The majority of the hallucinations were of the type I variety, a category employed by Vernon, McGill, and Schiffman [23] to describe hallucinations characterized by "flashes of light, flickering lights, dim glowing lights, and so on, which lack shape and usually appear in the peripheral field of vision." A few type II hallucinations consisting of geometric shapes (for example, circles, squares, latticework) were reported, but usually towards the end of the isolation period. Only two instances of type III hallucinations, that is highly structured, integrated scenes of an animated nature, were reported. One of these consisted of a TV screen showing a blurred message which the subject tried to read but was unable to. The other consisted of two moving eyeballs of a "most frightening nature." Both of these were reported during the sixth day.

There was little evidence of increasing hallucinatory complexity with increasing time in isolation. The changes which did take place usually consisted of an increase in the brightness and number of the type I hallucinations present at one time rather than a change in their quality or a transformation to the type II variety. The hallucinations usually were of very short duration, about 5 to 10 sec, although some were reported to last for as long as 15 min. Although most of the subjects showed hallucinatory activity of one degree or another, it is important to note that in general this activity took up only a very small portion of the subject's time in isolation. Many subjects reported only one or two brief hallucinatory periods a day, others only one or two during the entire week and some (five) reported no hallucinatory activity whatsoever.

In addition to visual hallucinations a number of auditory hallucinations were reported. These were usually very realistic in nature, for example, howling dogs, ringing of alarm clocks, sound of typewriter, policeman's whistle, and dripping water. Two hallucinations of a tactual-kinesthetic nature were also reported. One consisted of cold steel pressing on the subject's forehead and cheeks and the other a sensation of someone pulling the mattress from under the subject. These auditory and tactual hallucinations, if present, were usually reported during the last two days of isolation.

There were some *suggestions* that female subjects may be less prone to hallucinations than males. Of twelve male subjects, ten had hallucinations, while out of four female subjects only one reported them. Her hallucinations were of the type I variety and occurred relatively infrequently. Although this sample is too small for any definite conclusions to be drawn, these sex differences are suggestive and should warrant further investigation by workers in the field of sensory deprivation. There are already some suggestions that females can take isolation for longer periods than males [20].

In addition to reporting hallucinatory activity, many subjects reported certain changes in imagery. At various intervals during isolation the subjects were asked to imagine or visualize certain familiar scenes, for example, lakes, countryside, the inside of their homes, and so forth. The majority of the subjects reported that the images which they conjured up were of unusual vividness, were usually characterized by bright colors, and had considerable detail. All these subjects were unanimous in their opinion that their images were more vivid than anything they had previously experienced. Several subjects who normally had great difficulty visualizing scenes could now visualize them almost instantly with great vividness. This enhanced imagery can be illustrated by reference to one subject who could visualize faces of former associates of a few years back with almost picturelike clarity, a thing which he was never able to do previously. This phenomenon usually appeared during the second or third day and, in general, became more pronounced with time. This increased vividness of imagery has been reported by many of the workers on isolation (for example, [2, 7, 9]).

Certain emotional changes were evident in many of the subjects. The most common of these was irritability characterized by annoyance with trivial matters and occasionally with the experimenters. The irritability was usually most noticeable during the second and third days. This emotional change has been reported by many investigators but not by all [20]. In a number of cases, this irritability was followed by feelings of depression, brooding, and dwelling on imaginary injustices. After the fifth day, a quarter of the subjects (four) reported feelings of contentment, well-being, and, in two cases, of euphoria. This state of well-being is not a *typical* isolation effect. Its presence in this experiment may be a result of the very long isolation period or it may be a reaction brought about by the realization that the week is almost up and that a substantial monetary reward is imminent. In all likelihood, both factors are involved.

An attempt was made to record as many dreams as the subjects could remember. These were quite numerous, especially during the first three or four days. They were largely of an anxiety nature whose main theme concerned death—for example, standing on erupting volcano, being surrounded by ferocious Indians, a knife fight with a giant. Another theme, also of an anxiety nature, concerned restricted space—for example, living in a miniature apartment with ceilings 3 ft high. Very few dreams of a pleasant nature were reported or could be remembered. These dreams are similar in nature to those reported by Smith and Lewty [20], who confined their subjects in a soundproofed room for periods up to 4 days.

## Qualitative Observations After Isolation

Upon emerging from isolation all sixteen subjects reported no *gross* perceptual changes of the type reported by Heron, Doane, and Scott [11]. Furthermore, there were no reports of nausea or dizziness, although the subjects did stagger somewhat at first: This was to be expected from the nature of the experimental conditions. When the subjects were asked to fixate on the horizontal and vertical lines presented on the wall, ten out of the sixteen subjects reported some changes. These, however, were barely noticeable and were characterized by a *very slight* wavering, thickening, or change in length of the lines. These changes, when present, lasted for only about a minute. On the color test, half of the subjects reported that the colored papers and the colored objects in the laboratory were much brighter and more vivid. The white and black objects seemed to stand out particularly. However, in view of the unreliability of the color test employed, not too much reliance can be placed on these results.

Approximately half of the subjects reported a loss of motivation to study or to carry out various activities which they would normally do. In almost all of these cases this condition did not persist for more than 1 day. Hyperacuity to sounds was also a very common phenomenon, especially during the first night, when even the slightest sounds could be heard. Furthermore, many sounds which normally might be irritating seemed pleasant and in some cases were even considered delightful. The noise of traffic seemed particularly loud and even somewhat startling.

## Report on Two Special Cases

Two subjects, one male and one female, were permitted to remain in isolation somewhat longer than the other subjects, whose isolation was arbitrarily terminated at the end of a week. In view of certain unusual phenomena which they experienced, they will be singled out for special attention.

*Subject A (10 Days).* This was a male, 34 years of age. During the first 7 days he reported experiences very similar to those of the majority of the subjects. The first indications of hallucinatory activity appeared in the third day and consisted of a few, small cloud formations and several pulsating lights in the peripheral field of vision. With successive days these type I hallucinations (largely pulsating lights) became more numerous, brighter, and of longer duration. During the tenth day the pulsating lights, resembling hundreds of car lights blinking at night, were experienced constantly. They were particularly vivid the first night at home (isolation was terminated at 10 P.M.), so vivid in fact, that the subject was unable to sleep all night because of their almost blinding nature. There was still some evidence of hallucinatory activity the following afternoon (16 hr later) when the subject went into the chamber for further intellectual tests—the dim red light under which he took the tests seemed to pulsate for approximately 10 min, after which the sensation disappeared entirely.

In common with most of the other subjects, irritability was very pronounced, especially from the third to the fifth days. However, the most memorable emotional change was the development of a mildly euphoric state beginning sometime in the eighth day. It was characterized by a state of serenity, peacefulness, "all's well with the world," total absence of any worries, and extremely good humor. This state was occasionally punctuated by feelings of hilarity and playing of pranks on the experimenters. It was also characterized by an absence of any intellectual activity, with the subject spending hours daydreaming and reliving various past experiences. There was little interest in food or in any activity which might interrupt this "idyllic" state. It persisted for about 3 days after termination of isolation. It was an emotional state most unlike anything the subject had ever experienced before.

Upon emerging from isolation the subject experienced no nausea or dizziness nor any gross perceptual changes involving distortion of shapes and objects nor their movement. There was a slight quivering of horizontal and vertical lines but this persisted for only a few seconds. The only noticeable change was in the brightness and vividness of colors, especially blacks and whites, and the two-dimensional nature of the environment. Furthermore, people did not seem like people, but merely lifeless objects moving about a stage with the subject acting as a detached observer. This feeling of detachment or of "not belonging" to the outside world was quite noticeable for the next two days. Furthermore, during this time the subject had a strong craving to go back into the chamber and looked for any pretext to do so again. This feeling or craving was particularly strong the following day, when the subject was required to go back into the chamber to take the last battery of tests. It was only with the greatest effort that he could force himself to leave. It would appear as if some form of addiction had developed. This subject was the only one out of the group who reported this craving or even indicated a desire to go back into isolation. It may be related to his long period of isolation or it may be an individual difference.

Another striking and long-lasting experience was a loss of motivation. Although this was present in a noticeable form during the last half of the isolation period, it was most obvious in the postisolation period, when the subject, who is the head of a university department, had no desire to do even the most urgent academic duties for a period of at least a week. Furthermore, he showed no interest in delegating some of these duties to his colleagues.

EEG records were taken from this subject before and after the 10 days of isolation. The postisolation record consisted mainly of fast activity at 12 to 20 cps (see Figure 25-3). An excess of slow or theta activity also appeared particularly in runs involving the temporal lobes. In some ways the pattern was reminiscent of a person who had taken barbiturates. During the recording, which took place inside the chamber, the subject was hallucinating profusely. An attempt was made, therefore, to relate the hallucinatory activity to variations in the EEG record. The only significant factor was a diminution of some of the alpha activity during some of the hallucinations. A repeat EEG taken two weeks later revealed that the pattern had changed markedly. It was now quite normal, although some temporal lobe slow activity was still evident but not in excess. This suggested abnormality two weeks later may be related to some of the long-lasting postisolation effects reported by this subject.

EEG records were also taken from eight subjects before and within 3 hr after emerging from a week of isolation. Two of them showed normal postisolation records, three showed a slowing of the alpha by one or two cycles, and three showed a slowing of the alpha together with an above-average amount of slow or theta activity. There was a *suggestion* that this theta activity is somewhat more common in the temporal lobe region. The presence of fast activity in the 10-day subject and its absence in the 7-day subjects is most puzzling. It may be an individual difference or it may be a change in electrical activity of the brain which occurs only after a week of isolation. These EEG results, together with others which are being accumulated, will be dealt with in some detail in a subsequent publication.

*Subject B (8½ Days).* This was a female, 24 years of age. The first appearance of hallucinatory activity occurred, as in subject A, during the morning of the third day and was characterized by a single flickering light in the peripheral field of vision. It seemed to last no longer than a minute and appeared and disappeared several times that morning. No further activity was experienced until the next morning, when a number of flashing lights appeared, largely in the left visual field. That evening the subject reported a most disturbing experience. She imagined that one of the experimenters had told her that her husband was severely injured in a car accident. She then imagined him being carried away in an ambulance, removed to the operating theater, and then dying in front of her eyes. This experience was so real that she went through all the emotions one

FIGURE 25-3  EEG tracings from the frontal, central, parietal, and occipital areas of the brain before and after 10 days of isolation (darkness and silence). Runs from the temporal leads are not shown in this tracing. The records were taken with the eyes closed. Note the considerable amount of fast activity in the postisolation record, particularly evident in the right frontal leads. The arrows indicate some of the scattered slow or theta waves. →

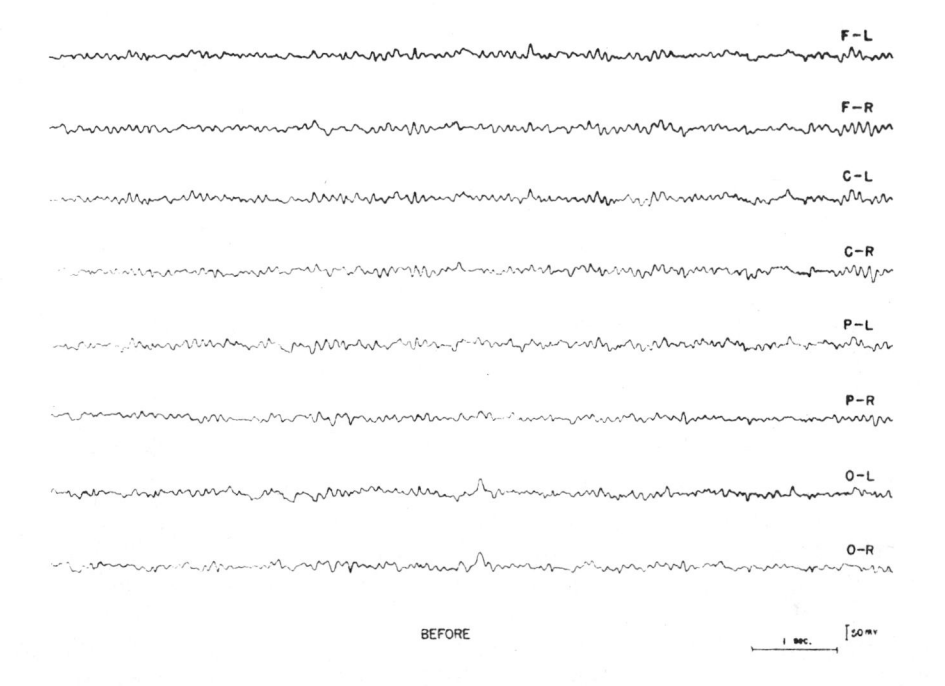

F-L
F-R
C-L
C-R
P-L
P-R
O-L
O-R

BEFORE

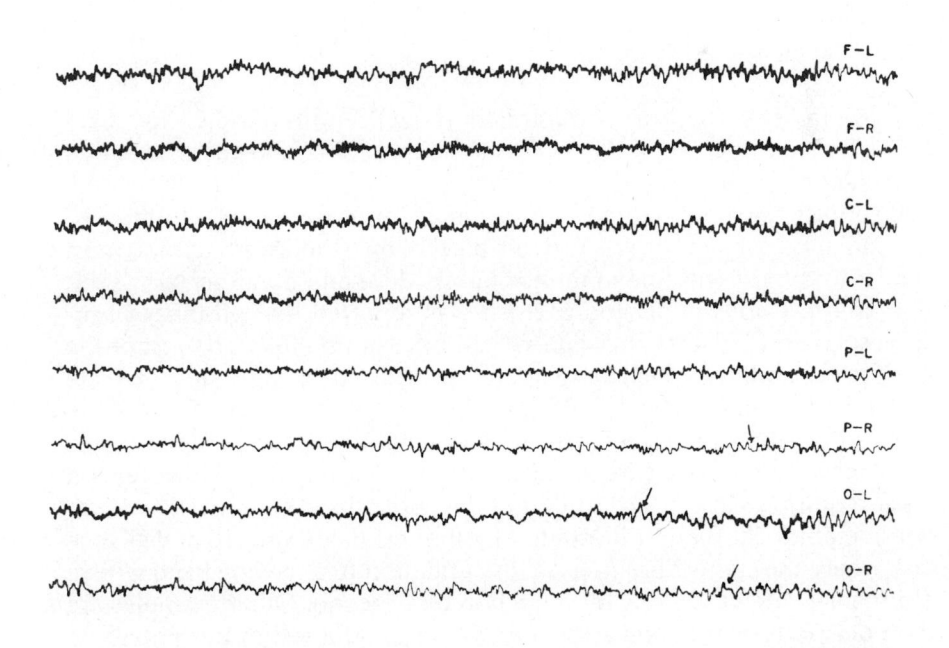

F-L
F-R
C-L
C-R
P-L
P-R
O-L
O-R

AFTER

would go through if the accident had actually happened. It was only with the greatest effort of restraint that she did not terminate her isolation. Following this experience, no further hallucinatory activity was reported except on the seventh day, when several large glowing lights appeared for a few seconds.

In regard to emotional changes, she exhibited some irritability during the third day, followed by feelings of depression and anxiety during the fourth and fifth days brought about, presumably, by the imagined car accident. From the sixth day on and for a day after isolation, she experienced a feeling of "contentment and serenity of a pleasant sort" similar in nature to that of subject A but lacking his periodic feelings of hilarity.

Upon emerging from isolation, the subject reported no perceptual distortions, although colors, especially reds and blacks, seemed brighter than normal. In keeping with subject A, she reported a strong feeling of detachment in which she felt she really was not a part of the world. This feeling of detachment is similar in many respects to the break-off phenomenon reported by pilots at high altitudes [4]. This feeling lasted for about 2 days. The subject also reported a very disturbing memory impairment while at work 2 days after release from isolation. It was characterized by an inability to remember various details of her work. This memory loss was so disturbing that she finished the day in a most distraught state. The impairment was no longer present on the following day. In contrast to subject A, no craving to go back into the chamber nor any long-lasting loss of motivation was reported.

## DISCUSSION

A direct comparison of these findings with those of other investigators is difficult because of differences in method of confinement, duration of isolation, degree of sensory restriction, types of capacities measured, and so forth. However, some valid comparisons can be made. In this discussion the main emphasis will be placed on studies which are most similar to the present one in terms of procedure and duration.

In a previous publication [26] it was reported that prolonged sensory isolation (darkness and silence) had little or no effect on *most* of the intellectual abilities which were appraised. The foregoing results indicate that a similar situation exists with respect to perceptual-motor tasks. There was, for example, no significant impairment of depth perception, size constancy, reversible figures, and auditory discrimination. However, on tasks requiring close visual attention and precision the impairment was considerable. This is best illustrated by the results on the visual vigilance task where the subject has to pay close attention to a moving hand which, at irregular intervals, stops for a fraction of a second. Other examples are the poor performances on a cancellation test and a test of dexterity (fine eye-hand coordination) employed in an earlier study. This differential impairment of perceptual-motor skills is in line with some results obtained at Princeton, where subjects were placed in a dark and soundproof room for periods up to 3 days. In this study depth perception was not impaired, while performance on a mirror drawing and a pursuit rotor task was [24]. Our results also agree to some extent with those obtained at McGill under conditions of diffuse light and noise. The McGill workers reported no impairment in rate of figure reversal, c.f.f., visual acuity, phi-phenomenon, autokinetic effect, and various brightness phenomena. In contrast to our findings they reported an impairment of size constancy [6]. Some differences, however, might be expected, since the sensory conditions in the two experiments were different.

None of our subjects reported any *gross* perceptual changes involving distortion of size and shape of objects immediately upon emerging from isolation. This is in agreement with the Princeton studies [21] and also with those carried out at the Aerospace Medical Laboratory, Ohio, where a group of pilots were kept in a dark, soundproof chamber for periods ranging from 4 hr to a week [17]. These results on darkness and silence are quite different from those reported at McGill, where subjects were exposed to diffuse light and noise for periods ranging from 2 to 6 days. Most of these subjects reported gross distortions of the size and shape of objects present in the laboratory and a fluctuation, drifting, and swirling of objects and surfaces in the visual field [6, 11]. These results provide a further suggestion that prolonged darkness and silence and prolonged diffuse light and noise may produce different behavioral effects.

Although hallucinations were reported by the majority of our subjects, they were almost exclusively of the simple type I variety, were in general of short duration, occurred relatively infrequently, and did not appear until after 2 days in isolation. These hallucinations have been reported by some investigators, but not by others. The presence or absence of hallucinatorylike experiences seems to depend on several variables. One of the more important of these is the amount of movement which the subject is permitted. In experiments where no restriction on movements is applied, hallucinatory phenomena seem to be totally or almost totally absent [17, 20, 23], while in experiments such as ours where the subject is requested to restrict his movements inside the chamber, hallucinatory activity seems to be quite common [2, 7, 9, 19, 25]. Furthermore, when these restrictions on movement are severe, hallucinations may be reported within a few hours [13, 25]. The second factor which is important in determining the presence or absence of hallucinatory phenomena is visual stimulation, especially diffuse unpatterned light. The role of this variable can be clearly seen in one of the McGill experiments. When some of the "good" hallucinators were placed in darkness, their hallucinations either completely disappeared or were greatly diminished. Upon re-exposure to diffuse light the hallucinations returned to their original level of intensity [6]. These results are also in line with those of Ruff and Levy [17], who kept pilots in constant darkness for periods of up to a week. Few hallucinations were reported. The importance of some visual stimulation is also seen in the Princeton studies, in which, during complete blackout conditions, only one out of eleven subjects reported hallucinations. However, in an experiment where the blackout condition was not completely successful, due to light leaks in a faulty blindfold, six out of nine subjects reported the presence of simple hallucinations [23]. These results are in agreement with our findings where simple hallucinations occurred under conditions involving occasional intrusions from a dim red light.

One of the intriguing findings of this study was the presence, in several cases, of some theta activity, particularly in the temporal lobe region. This possible involvement of the temporal lobes is of some interest, since it is in line with some observations of Baldwin, Lewis, and Frost [1]. They found that when chimpanzees were subjected to bilateral removal of the temporal lobes prior to 13 days of isolation (darkness and quiet) they exhibited none of the emotional, perceptual, and motor disturbances which nonoperated control animals showed after the same type of restriction. Furthermore, these operated animals were immune to the effects of lysergic acid, which in controls produced some striking behavioral changes. This experiment suggests that there is some relationship between the possession of normal temporal lobes and the effects of either sensory isolation or lysergic acid in animals. It also suggests that some of the human sensory deprivation effects may have a temporal lobe origin. The impairment of recent memory, which we reported in an earlier paper, may be one of these cases. This suggestion is supported by some research at the Montreal Neurological Institute, where patients with temporal lobe lesions, particularly in the hippocampal region, exhibited severe and long lasting impairments of recent memory [15]. Some of the perceptual changes may also have a temporal lobe origin. This is suggested by reports on the ictal patterns of temporal lobe epilepsy, which are often characterized by illusions of size, shape, color, and depth [12].

Earlier in the discussion it was suggested that prolonged darkness and silence and prolonged diffuse light and noise may produce different perceptual effects. This was indicated by the greater perceptual distortions and more frequent and complex hallucinatorylike experiences which appear under diffuse light and noise. These two conditions also seem to differ in their effects on intellectual processes. Our first experiment on darkness and silence [26] as well as the experiments at Princeton [21, 22] showed little if any impairment of various intellectual abilities, apart from recent memory, whereas experiments on prolonged unpatterned light and noise [18] seem to produce widespread intellectual impairment. Although these differences seem to occur after prolonged isolation, there are indications that they are not present after short isolation intervals. This is indicated in an experiment on recognition thresholds for five-digit numbers where no reliable differences were found between 5 to 30 min periods of blackout and diffuse light conditions [16]. Similarly, Freedman and Greenblatt [7] in an 8-hr isolation experiment reported no differences between blackout and diffuse light conditions in the production of hallucinatorylike imagery or in the kind and amount of cognitive effects. There were, however, more distortions of simple forms under constant diffuse light. In a further study Freedman and Held [8] reported no differences between the two conditions in "perceptual lag." The absence of behavioral differences in these experiments is not surprising in view of the shortness of the isolation periods.

The behavioral differences which occur after prolonged isolation may partly be due to differences in central neural activity brought about by the two types of sensory conditions. This view is supported by some exploratory EEG studies in our laboratory which suggest that although the EEG changes occurring under blackout and diffuse light conditions are not too different with isolation periods up to a week, they may be quite different beyond this period. This can best be illustrated by reference to one subject who at the end of 10 days of darkness and silence showed an EEG pattern characterized mainly by fast activity at 12 to 20 cps together with an abnormal amount of theta activity, particularly in the temporal lobes. However, this same subject when retested a year later showed, after 10 days of diffuse light and white noise, a quite different pattern of EEG activity. It was now characterized by a slowing of the alpha by several cycles together with an excess of theta activity in the temporal lobes. Fast activity of 12 to 20 cps was nowhere in evidence. In view of these differences in the pattern of neural activity, some behavioral differences might be expected. These results, however, are of an exploratory nature and too much reliance cannot be put on them until more EEG data are available.

In summary, we can conclude that exposing subjects to prolonged darkness and silence can result in perceptual changes, appearance of hallucinatorylike experiences, changes in emotionality, impairment of recent memory, and significant changes in EEG activity, all of which point to considerable disorganization of brain function. There is as yet no adequate explanation of these phenomena or of those reported by other investigators. However, one widely held explanation [10] is based on the view that the normal functioning of the brain depends on a continuing arousal reaction produced in the reticular formation, which in turn depends on constantly varying sensory stimulation. When this variability of sensory input is reduced, as it is in constant darkness and silence or diffuse light and noise, these sensory stimuli lose their power of arousal. Under these conditions the activity of the brain may be impaired and disturbances of psychological processes may occur. There is considerable neurophysiological evidence in favor of this view. However, this explanation has to be modified somewhat in the light of an experiment by Davis, McCourt, and Solomon [5], who presented *random* visual stimulation to their subjects confined in a tank type of respirator, and observed emotional disturbances, intellectual impairments, and hallucinatory phenomena similar in nature to those occurring under constant light and noise.

They conclude that "what the brain needs for normal functioning is not quantity or change in sensation per se, but a continuous meaningful contact with the outside world." Freedman and Greenblatt [7], on the basis of their work on blackout and diffuse light conditions, also suggest that it is the "absence of order and/or meaning rather than the specific nature of the stimulus field which tends to degrade perceptual organization." It would appear, therefore, that what is required for normal functioning of the brain is constantly varying *meaningful* stimulation. When meaning is absent or is reduced for long periods of time, for example under darkness, silence, diffuse light, white noise, or random visual stimulation, psychological disturbances, as we already know, will occur. Furthermore, since these sensory conditions are not equal in meaningfulness, they might be expected to produce somewhat different behavioral effects. This has already been shown in some experiments. This explanation, at this stage of our knowledge, can be only an incomplete one. It does not account for many of the sensory deprivation effects. However, when a satisfactory theory eventually emerges, variability and meaningfulness of stimulation will undoubtedly occupy a central role.

## SUMMARY

Sixteen subjects were placed in a dark and soundproofed chamber for a week or longer. A battery of perceptual-motor tests was administered before and immediately after they emerged from isolation. In addition, subjects were asked to estimate the passage of 1, 3, 5, 15, 30, 60, and 120 min at daily intervals during isolation. A carefully matched group of control subjects was given the same tests at the same time intervals. There was no significant impairment of depth perception, size constancy, auditory discrimination, or reversible figures. Furthermore, there were no gross perceptual distortions present when they emerged from isolation. Performance on a visual vigilance task was impaired significantly. There was no impairment on the time estimation tests except on the 120-min interval, in which the experimentals showed more underestimation than did the controls.

Eleven out of the sixteen subjects experienced some hallucinatory phenomena at some time during isolation. They were almost exclusively of the simple type I variety, were in general of short duration, occurred relatively infrequently, and appeared only after at least 2 days of isolation.

## REFERENCES

1. M. Baldwin, S. I. Lewis, and L. L. Frost. Perceptual interference after cerebral ablation. *Percept. Mot. Skills*, 1957, 7, 45–48.

2. W. H. Bexton, W. Heron, and T. H. Scott. Effects of decreased variation in the sensory environment. *Canad. J. Psychol.,* 1954, *8,* 70–76.
3. D. Bindra and H. Waksberg. Methods and terminology in studies of time estimation. *Psychol. Bull.,* 1956, *53,* 155–159.
4. B. Clark and A. Graybiel. The break-off phenomenon. *J. aviat. Med.,* 1957, *28,* 121–126.
5. J. M. Davis, W. F. McCourt, P. Solomon, and S. I. Solomon. The effect of visual stimulation on hallucination and other mental experiences during sensory deprivation. *Amer. J. Psychiat.,* 1960, *116,* 889–892.
6. B. K. Doane, W. Mahatoo, W. Heron, and T. H. Scott. Changes in perceptual function after isolation. *Canad. J. Psychol.,* 1959, *13,* 210–219.
7. S. J. Freedman and M. Greenblatt. *Studies in human isolation.* Tech. Rep. 59-266, Wright-Patterson AFB, Ohio, WADC Aero-Medical Lab., 1959.
8. S. J. Freedman and R. Held. Sensory deprivation and perceptual lag. *Percept. mot. Skills,* 1960, *11,* 277–280.
9. L. Goldberger and R. R. Holt. Experimental interferences with reality contact (perceptual isolation). I. Method and group results. *J. nerv. ment. Dis.,* 1958, *127,* 99–112.
10. W. Heron. The pathology of boredom. *Sci. Amer.,* 1957, *196* (no. 1), 52–56.
11. W. Heron, B. K. Doane, and T. H. Scott. Visual disturbances after prolonged perceptual isolation. *Canad. J. Psychol.,* 1956, *10,* 13–18.
12. F. Kennedy. The symptomatology of temporosphenoidal tumors. *Arch. intern. Med.,* 1911, *8,* 317–350.
13. J. C. Lilly. Mental effects of reduction of ordinary levels of physical stimuli on intact healthy persons. *Psychiat. Res. Rep.,* 1956, *5,* 1–9.
14. R. M. MacLeod and M. F. Roff. An experiment in temporal disorientation. *Acta Psychol.,* 1936, *1,* 381–423.
15. W. Penfield and B. Milner. Memory deficits produced by bilateral lesions in the hippocampal zone. *A.M.A. Arch. Neurol. Psychiat.,* 1958, *79,* 475–497.
16. G. Rosenbaum, S. I. Dobie, and B. D. Cohen. Visual recognitive thresholds following sensory deprivation. *Amer. J. Psychol.,* 1959, *72,* 429–433.
17. G. E. Ruff and E. Z. Levy. Psychiatric research in space medicine. *Amer. J. Psychiat.,* 1959, *115,* 793–797.
18. T. H. Scott, W. H. Bexton, W. Heron, and B. K. Doane. Cognitive effects of perceptual isolation. *Canad. J. Psychol.,* 1959, *13,* 200–209.
19. A. J. Silverman, S. I. Cohen, B. Bressler, and B. M. Shmavonian. Hallucinations in sensory deprivation. Presented at the Symposium on Hallucinations, AAAS meeting, Washington, D.C., December 26–27, 1958.
20. S. Smith and W. Lewty. Perceptual isolation using a silent room. *Lancet,* 1959 (no. 7098), 342–345.
21. J. Vernon and J. Hoffman. Effect of sensory deprivation on learning rate in human beings. *Science,* 1956, *123,* 1074–1075.
22. J. Vernon and T. E. McGill. The effect of sensory deprivation upon rote learning. *Amer. J. Psychol.,* 1957, *70,* 637–639.

23. J. Vernon, T. E. McGill, and H. Schiffman. Visual hallucinations during perceptual isolation. *Canad. J. Psychol.*, 1958, *12*, 31–34.
24. J. Vernon, T. E. McGill, W. L. Gulick, and D. K. Candland. Effect of sensory deprivation on some perceptual and motor skills. *Percept. mot. Skills*, 1959, *9*, 91–97.
25. D. Wexler, J. Mendelson, P. H. Leiderman, and P. Solomon. Sensory deprivation, a technique for studying psychiatric aspects of stress. *Arch. Neurol. Psychiat., Chicago*, 1958, *79*, 225–233.
26. J. P. Zubek, W. Sansom, and A. Prysiazniuk. Intellectual changes during prolonged perceptual isolation (darkness and silence). *Canad. J. Psychol.*, 1960, *14*, 233–242.

# 26

# STUDYING PERCEPTUAL DEVELOPMENT USING THE TECHNIQUE OF SENSORY DEPRIVATION

## Austin H. Riesen

Sensory deprivation of the newborn (or newly hatched) organism has been used as a special condition for the study of perceptual and cognitive arrest which may be correlated with limited opportunities for certain interactions between the developing organism and the environment. Reviews of experimental and case history evidence are available [cf. 2]. Specific results and general conclusions vary with the organism and with the nature of the response indicator employed. The degree, kind, or duration of deprivation can each in turn be shown to have significant effects with some organisms on some indicators. To what extent the results with this procedure represent simple arrest of development or, on the other hand, reflect both initial arrest and a superimposed regressive or atrophic process remains to be more adequately determined. That both types of effect do occur and that they can be separated there is no longer any doubt.

Source: *Journal of Nervous and Mental Disease*, 1961, *132*, 21–25. Copyright 1961 by The Williams & Wilkins Co. Reprinted by permission.
Note: Studies summarized in this paper were supported by Grants B-771 and B-1590 from the National Institute of Neurological Diseases and Blindness of the National Institutes of Health, Public Health Service, by the Yerkes Laboratories of Primate Biology, Inc., Orange Park, Fla., and by the Dr. Wallace C. and Clara M. Abbott Memorial Fund of the University of Chicago.

The developmental approach to visual perception, with or without the use of the technique of visual deprivation, has clearly demonstrated innate neural organizations which govern reflex responses in higher mammalian species. One class of reflexes depends upon changes in the intensity of visual stimulation, and another is related to changes in the distribution of light across the retinal mosaic. Sudden alterations of light intensity produce pupillary and palpebral reflexes, and quick movements of the head and neck which appear and disappear again at certain maturational stages [cf. 10], showing little dependence upon prior conditions of sensory deprivation. Optokinetic responses and associated head rotations depend upon the gradual and continuous shift of sharp light gradients across the retina, and are easily demonstrated after complete visual deprivation.

In our laboratories [1, 7, 8, 9] we have been unable to demonstrate that any of the reflexive behavior that is seen after visual deprivation will directly support locomotion, manipulation, or the finding and eating of food in primates or in cats. There is such evidence, however, for lower mammals such as the rat and for birds. In the present paper further evidence will be presented in support of the hypothesis that with encephalization of the visual sensory system visually guided behavior develops in ontogeny as a function of patterned visual stimulation.

An earlier literature on normally reared cats tends to imply that visual placing is a reflex that matures with the growing nervous system. Warkentin and Smith [11] placed the mean age of first visual placing, the extension of the forelimbs before bodily contact when the animal is brought toward a surface, at 25 days, with a range of 22 to 28 days. These authors also reported tests of visual acuity as measured by the optokinetic response to a moving striated visual field. By day 25 the kittens were responding to stripes so narrow as to subtend only 11 min of visual angle.

Since tactile placing appears quite early, between days 11 and 16, there is no lack of ability to make the limb response involved, and the hypothesis strongly suggested is that visual placing depends, following adequate development of the sensory and effector units, upon the visual-motor learning that is normally supported by an interaction with the visual environment during days 15 to 25.

In our experiments [5] six litters of kittens were used. One or two members of each litter were control animals, the other two or three serving as experimentals. There were fifteen experimental subjects and ten in the control group. Each mother and her kittens remained in normal indoor lighting of the laboratory until the kittens were 18 days of age.[1] They were then put into a darkroom for 23 hr per day. During the other hour they were in light, the control animals without visual restriction, the experimental kittens wearing hoods made of fine percale which diffused the light. Sufficient air for breathing also passed through the cloth, and

---

[1] Each kitten's eyes had opened by 10 days from birth.

the kittens showed no signs of discomfort. All kittens were handled an equal amount each day.

The unhooded kittens were tested for visual placing at the beginning and end of each hour in the light. The hooded kittens were carried through the same movements to further equalize handling. Support of the kitten was given through the body and hind legs, with the head and forelegs free. With a slow even motion the kitten was carried forward and slightly downward toward the edge of the table used as the testing surface. If the forelegs were extended toward the table before any part of the body, limbs, or vibrissae touched it the animal was scored as capable of visual placing. On the day following the first appearance of visual placing in an unhooded kitten its littermates were left unhooded during the hour of light and testing continued as before. For the sixth litter to be carried through this procedure the method was altered so that the mother and kittens remained in the light continuously until the response appeared, testing being done at hourly intervals.

The unhooded (control) kittens first gave placing responses to the visually perceived surface at age 27, 28, or 29 days. No experimental kitten showed the response when the hood was first removed. Remarkable consistency was shown in that each of the fifteen animals of this condition gave its first placing response after 5 hr in the patterned light. This was true whether the 5 hr accrued 1 hr per day or continuously.

During the second unhooded hour the experimental kittens typically spent considerable time sitting straight up and still, staring fixedly at the mother's face. This was one of the first indications of a gradually increasing use of vision that followed.

In other experiments, kittens and primates whose early visual experience was complete with the usual room patterns, but who were not permitted to move freely during such visual exposure, failed to develop either the visual placing or the protective eye blink [1, 7]. These animals did, however, show normal binocular fixation and visual pursuit of other animals or persons moving about in the room.

One may raise the question of whether or not the initial visual-motor reflexes support in some degree the development of the eye-paw or eye-hand coordinations that come about only with motor activity engaged in while the animal is seeing what he approaches. To answer this question is not easy. There is no procedure that will enable us to study the development of the learned coordinations in the absence of the prior reflexes. One alternative approach devised by a graduate student in our laboratories for his doctoral research gives at least a first analytical lever for prying apart the mutual interactions of these two factors.

Harding Bishop [3] has completed experimentation in which kittens were raised while seeing the environment through one eye only, the vision in that eye being either upright or inverted (not with right and left reversed, as in some lens experiments done with human subjects). After these animals, under one or the other condition continuously, achieved plateau levels of performance on a variety of mazes, obstacle courses, and an eye-paw coordination test display, the conditions for each group were interchanged. Readaptation was then followed for a further series of tests lasting several more weeks.

In this experiment the obvious question is, Do the conditions permit equal levels of performance to be achieved in equal periods of time? Innate reflexes would compete with development under the inverted condition. This is particularly clear in the case of pursuit head movements. A downward or upward pursuit movement of the head causes an increased speed of movement of the image projected on the retina when inverting lenses are worn. Without inverting lenses the pursuit reflex tends to slow down or stop movement of the image, that is, it aids fixation. So long as the head does not move up or down, this competition does not occur.

Bishop's results show a surprisingly small difference between performance under the two conditions. Only with pooled data from the test battery does the difference reach significance. The fact of a difference supports the conclusion that the reflexes have something to do with the development of visual-motor coordination. Their rather mild effect emphasizes the important contribution of the learning factor.

Other observations show that the animals we have deprived of vision during initial growth periods must progress thereafter through stages of learning to fixate and pursue moving objects, learning to avoid obstacles, find food, discriminate movement from nonmovement, and so on. Many of these data fit into a stimulus-response conception of the learning process.

When intensity cues are all that need to be discriminated the animals learn as quickly whether or not they have undergone visual deprivation prior to the commencement of discrimination learning [8]. When complex patterns or movements must be discriminated it is obvious that the pattern-deprived animals *begin* the training procedure at a great disadvantage. To me this means that a sensory-sensory (S → S) associative integration has preceded the formal training in the pattern-experienced group. I am quite willing to call this cognitive learning, as many others have done along with Freedman, and with Tolman before him.

We still need more data on the significance *during* the early patterned light experience of active movement (as opposed to passive movement) of the animal or its appendages. Held has effectively demonstrated that this can be crucial to egocentric localization in readaptation following disarrangement of the visual field. Our study of visual movement discrimination [8] showed this kind of activity (locomotion and/or manipulation) to be essential during perceptual development if visual motion is to be discriminated from nonmotion. Body postures and movement and the stimulation consequent to the movement are entering into a kind of response → stimulus learning. The reafferentation principle, as extended to perceptual disarrangement problems by Held, calls for the inversion of our customary S → R formula.

So, by this point I am asserting that we need a theory broad enough to include S → R, S → S, and R → S learning in any complete formulation of perceptual development.

I am not quite sure whether the perceptual changes reported for human subjects following 8 to 48 hr of visual deprivation include a loss of learned integrations. Perhaps something new develops during those hours of "random" input which overlays and competes with previously learned cell assemblies. If so, longer periods should produce greater and more persistent effects.

I can report in this connection two experiments, one done with a monkey which was deprived of visual stimulation from the age of 5 months to the age of 10 months, the other on a chimpanzee deprived of patterned light from 10 to 18 months of age.

Both animals showed loss of recognition for food or food containers. In each case approximately 8 days were required before these animals regained the clear discriminations between pieces of food and inedible objects which they had shown with complete accuracy before the deprivation period.

Both animals showed inaccuracies of distance and direction when making protective eyelid responses and when approaching and reaching for objects. These improved rapidly during the first 3 days postdeprivation.

During initial hours of return to the visually structured environment these animals showed, in addition to the eye-hand inaccuracies, some peculiarities of eye movement and binocular coordinations. A pendular nystagmus of rapid (8 per sec) rate appeared in the chimpanzee youngster and moments of exotropia or divergent squint appeared briefly but repeatedly. The monkey showed occasional eye and head oscillations of a more jerky pattern, that is, faster in one direction than the other. These were transitory and in a matter of a few hours disappeared.

When we saw these incoordinations we were immediately struck by their similarity to what we commonly see in the animals deprived from birth. Infant primates and pattern-deprived kittens take considerably longer, however, than did these two animals to develop steadiness of gaze and the ability to fixate binocularly. Once ocular coordinations are established, they can be regained after disuse with a large savings, as is true of learned behavior generally.

What theoretical implication is inherent in these motor incoordinations? Identical stimulating conditions are not producing the same responses, it is true. However, I do not think that an S → R formulation can, by itself, account for the data. Much of the loss in fixation skill (both monocular and binocular) must be due to a breakdown of coordination within the motor system itself. This can be conceived of as a decomposition of rather fragile response → response associations. Charles Osgood earlier suggested in his *Experimental Psychology* [6, p. 401] that the term motor cell assemblies be applied to integrations between motor units. Eye fixation skills, and I think perhaps also eye-hand coordinations, must involve the development and maintenance of cell assemblies *within* and *between* motor nuclei. In the absence of patterned visual input, autonomous rhythmic activity in these centers appears to gain the upper hand.

In summary, to account for the prolonged refinement of the perceptual control over behavior that higher mammals exhibit in their discriminations in space we need a considerable extension of learning theory. The testing of this theory will involve a much more refined analysis of the neurophysiological and behavioral units which enter into the finished performance. When these units are more adequately isolated experimentally, necessary conditions for their associative integration will be found. I predict that they will be classifiable into S → S, R → R, and R → S groupings in addition to the favorite category of recent learning theories, the S → R bonds.

W. K. Estes [4] has shown us that S → R units may become associated on an all-or-none basis. I suspect that this may some day prove to be true also for the three additional types of unit that I am proposing here to account for effects of sensory deprivation. We need empirical grounding for these views. The chief obstacle standing in our way remains that of studying the behavior of such units in isolation.

# REFERENCES

1. L. Aarons. Visual movement and intensity discrimination in cats after early restriction and deprivation of pattern vision. Unpublished doctoral dissertation, University of Chicago, 1957.
2. F. A. Beach and J. Jaynes. Effects of early experience upon the behavior of animals. *Psychol. Bull.*, 1954, *54*, 239–263.
3. H. E. Bishop. Innateness and learning in the visual perception of direction. Unpublished doctoral dissertation, University of Chicago, 1959.
4. W. K. Estes. Learning theory and the new "mental chemistry." Address given at annual convention, American Psychological Association, Cincinnati, September 3–9, 1959.
5. C. Munro and A. H. Riesen. The development of visual placing in kittens after short term deprivation of pattern vision. Unpublished manuscript, 1960.
6. C. E. Osgood. *Method and theory in experimental psychology*. New York: Oxford University Press, 1953.
7. A. H. Riesen. Plasticity of behavior: Psychological aspects. In H. F. Harlow and C. N. Woolsey (eds.). *Biological and biochemical bases of behavior*. Madison: University of Wisconsin Press, 1958. Pp. 425–450.
8. A. H. Riesen and L. Aarons. Visual movement and intensity discrimination in cats after early deprivation of pattern vision. *J. comp. physiol. Psychol.*, 1959, *52*, 142–149.
9. A. H. Riesen, M. I. Kurke, and J. C. Mellinger. Interocular transfer of habits learned monocularly in visually naive and visually experienced cats. *J. comp. physiol. Psychol.*, 1953, *46*, 166–172.

10. D. Trincker and I. Trincker. Die ontogenetische Entwicklung des Helligkeits- und Farbensehens beim Menschen. I. Die Entwicklung des Helligkeitssehens. *Graefes Arch. Ophthal.,* 1955, *156,* 519–534.
11. J. Warkentin and K. U. Smith. The development of visual acuity in the cat. *J. genet. Psychol.,* 1937, *50,* 371–399.

# 27

# LEARNING TO LOVE

Harry F. Harlow
Margaret Harlow

## EFFECTS OF SOCIAL DEPRIVATION

During the last 5 years we have conducted a series of studies on the effects of social deprivation in early life. From birth onward for predetermined periods of time, monkeys have been denied both mothering and contact with peers. These deprivation studies have taken two forms: In the one form, partial social deprivation, monkeys are housed in individual bare wire cages where they can see and hear other monkeys but make no physical contact with them, as shown in Figure 27-1. We have also subjected monkeys to total social deprivation in the apparatus shown in Figure 27-2. In this situation the subjects see no animal of any kind for the predetermined period even though sensory deprivation is held to a minimum. As would be expected, total social deprivation produces more dramatic and pervasive effects than partial social deprivation, although we now know, somewhat to our surprise, that the differences between these two forms of social deprivation are not nearly as great as we would have predicted, primarily because partial social deprivation is more damaging than we had anticipated.

Two studies show that release of the animals after 3 months of essentially total social deprivation leaves them in a state of emotional shock. Their initial responses are characterized by self-clutching and crouching, as illustrated in Figure 27-3, which resembles a postural expression of human autistic children. If, however, the monkeys can survive the immedi-

Source: *American Scientist,* 1966, *54,* 244–272.
Note: This research was supported by USPHS Grants MH-11894 and FR-0167 from the National Institutes of Health to the University of Wisconsin Primate Laboratory and Regional Primate Research Center, respectively.

FIGURE 27-1 Living situation of infants being raised in semi-isolation in the nursery.

ate emotional trauma of release from total social deprivation and are then allowed to interact with control agemates 30 min. a day in our playroom situation, they very rapidly establish effective social relationships with their peers, as is illustrated in Figure 27-4. Such long-term studies as we have to date point to essentially complete social recovery, normal learning, and normal sexual adjustment in adolescence. We can find no indication in these same animals of any intellectual loss (see Figure 27-5, p. 294), and we doubt that any will be uncovered on laboratory learning problems.

We have limited data showing that 6 months of partial social deprivation greatly impairs the ability of infant monkeys to interact socially with control agemates, and we have data which seem to indicate that these social inadequacies persist over periods of years even when the animals are subsequently given some opportunity to associate continuously with agemates over long periods of time.

We have much more definitive data on the effects of 6 and 12 months of total social isolation. The results clearly indicate that even 6 months of total social isolation leaves the monkeys unable to interact socially with agemates when pairs of them are placed with pairs of controls raised in partial social deprivation and tested in our playroom situation. One com-

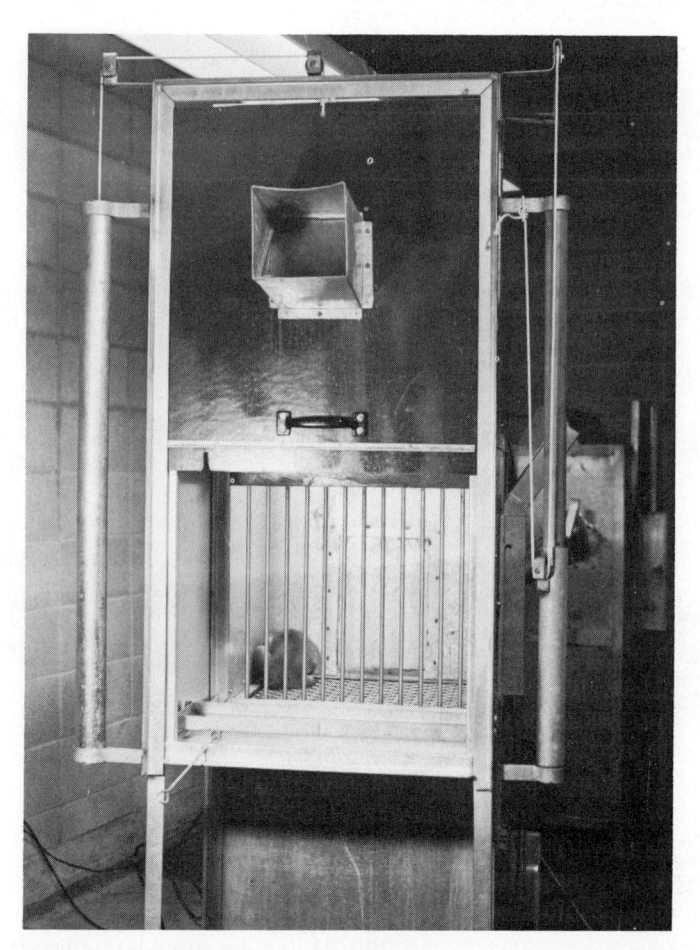

FIGURE 27-2 Total social isolation cabinet with front wall in raised position at the termination of the period of confinement. Light and sound stimulation are provided throughout isolation, but the subject is fed and cared for without ever seeing a monkey or human during the isolation period.

parison of 6-month isolates and their controls in the 2 months following isolation is given in Figure 27-6 (p. 294), and a comparable difference exists for all the social measures. Moreover, the effects persist throughout the period of social coexistence, as illustrated for social threat (Figure 27-7, p. 295). Nonetheless, the isolates do show a small gain in social interactions with each other, but not with the controls, in the course of 6 to 7 months of social testing. Twelve months of total social deprivation, compared with 6 months, produces even more socially devastating results. The 12-month isolates display essentially no social interaction with each other or with controls, as illustrated for the simplest form of play—activity play (Figure 27-8, p. 295). Indeed, in this experiment we had to conclude the social tests after 10 weeks because the control animals were

FIGURE 27-3 Rhesus monkey viewed immediately after raising the wall of the isolation chamber where it was confined from birth to 12 months of age. The monkeys typically retreat to a back corner of the box and display a crouching posture which includes some form of self-clutching and shielding of the eyes. Such postures are also common during confinement and continue after the animals are housed in wire-mesh cages in the nursery.

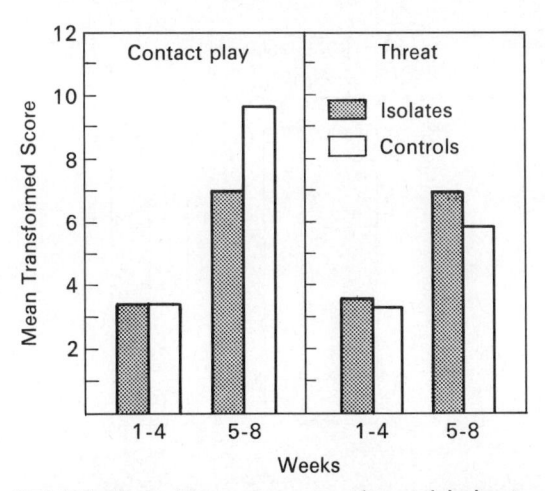

FIGURE 27-4 Two measures of social behavior in the playroom for four monkeys subjected to 3 months of social isolation and four control monkeys. Interactions are for 8 weeks beginning in the subjects' fourth month of life.

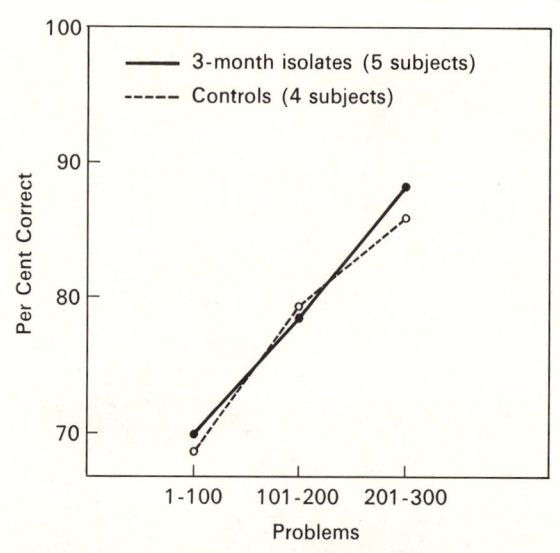

FIGURE 27-5  Performance of 3-month social isolates and control subjects of the same age on 300 discrimination learning set problems administered in the second year of life. Performance is percentage of correct responses on trials 2 to 6 of each problem. Trial 1 is a blind trial that provides the subject information on the correct stimulus. Differences between the groups are not significant ($p > 0.05$).

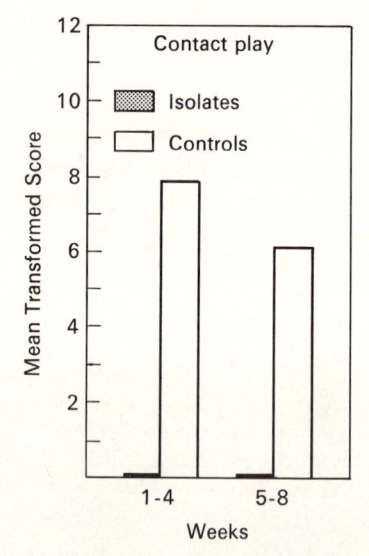

FIGURE 27-6  Contact play in the playroom for 6-month social isolates and controls during the first 8 weeks after experimental subjects were released from isolation. As is apparent, essentially no contact play was exhibited by isolates.

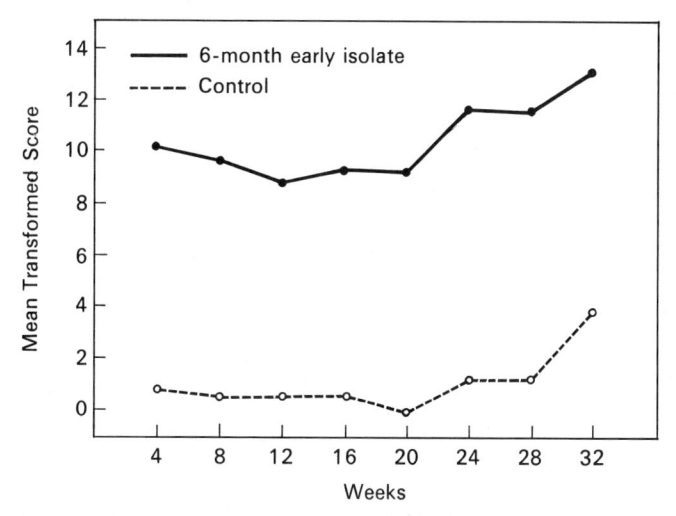

FIGURE 27-7 Social threats in the playroom by 6-month social isolates and control subjects during the course of 32 weeks of interactions in the playroom. Threats exhibited by isolates were entirely directed to other isolates.

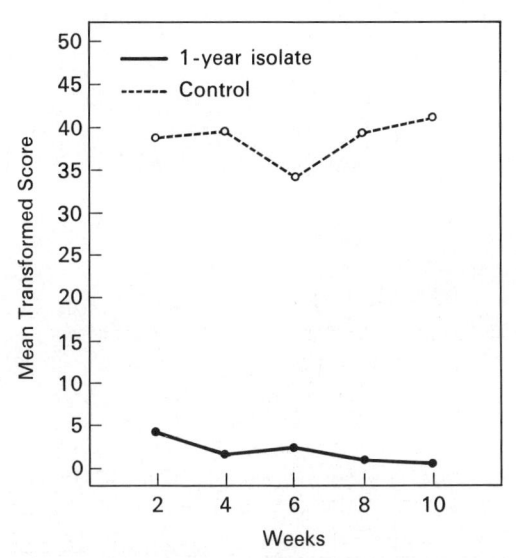

FIGURE 27-8 Activity play, a nonsocial form of play, exhibited by 12-month social isolates and control subjects in 10 weeks of exposure to the playroom. Decreasing frequency of the play in the experimental subjects doubtless reflects their increasing fear of the control subjects.

increasingly abusing the social isolates, and we were convinced that the isolates would have been killed if testing had continued.

Despite the social ineptitude of both the 6- and 12-month social isolates, their intellectual abilities appear to have been spared (Figure 27-9). Like the 3-month isolates (cf. Figure 27-5), the 6- and 12-month isolates were tested on discrimination learning set problems in the second year of life. They performed at a level not statistically different from that of control subjects of the same age. Discrimination learning set performance has been a consistently successful test in differentiating intellectual functioning among rhesus monkeys of different ages, among various genera of primates, and between primates and lower mammals [12].

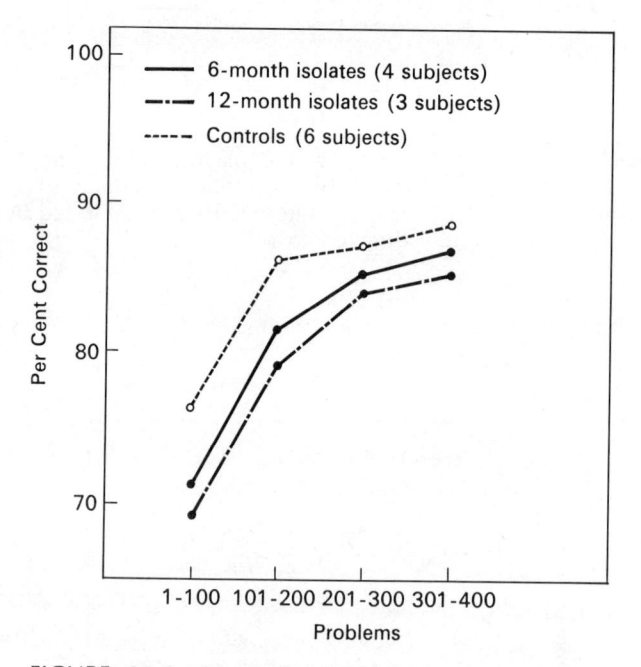

FIGURE 27-9 Discrimination learning set performance of 6-month and 12-month social isolates and control subjects of comparable age during the second year of life. Performance is measured by percentage of correct trial 2 to 6 responses during successive blocks of six-trial problems (cf. Figure 27-5).

We now have a long-term follow-up of animals subjected to 6 and 12 months of total social isolation. As preadolescents and adolescents, they were individually paired in separate tests with a single normal adult, a normal agemate, and a normal young juvenile. The total social isolates showed fear of adults, agemates, and even juveniles, but while showing fear, the 6-month isolates—not the 12-month isolates—also demonstrated, completely to our surprise, violent and abnormal aggressive behaviors. These included aggression against juveniles, a pattern of response seldom or never seen in normal adolescent monkeys, particularly normal adolescent female monkeys, and brief outbursts of suicidal aggression against adults—aggressions which they never displayed more than once, since the bursts of aggression were always unsuccessful; these isolates learned the social facts of life the hard and bloody way. The 12-month isolates, on the other hand, showed no aggression, apparently because fear inhibited its external expression in these animals.

We have a number of studies in which we have raised baby monkeys with cloth surrogate mothers, with brutal abnormal mothers—our so-called "motherless mothers"—or with no mothers whatsoever. In these situations the infants were given opportunities to form agemate or peer affectional relationships, and the data made it appear on first sight that perhaps normal mothering is dispensable as a social variable. We now have some reservations about the earlier conclusion.

Baby monkeys raised with cloth surrogate mothers as compared with real monkey mothers were somewhat slow in forming adequate play patterns with their peers, but by the end of a year they were interacting effectively, and they have made normal heterosexual adjustments with agemates as juveniles and preadolescents. Babies raised with motherless mothers but allowed to interact socially in our playpen situation showed an initial lag in adjusting to their agemates, but this difficulty rapidly ended and there was even precocious heterosexual adjustment.

The babies which we raised with no mothers whatsoever but allowed to interact with agemates form what we have previously called our "together-together" monkeys, and the group which has been studied most intensively is a group of four, one male and three females. These infants showed greatly depressed patterns of play in our playroom situation and showed exaggerated tendencies toward partner clinging even though these clinging responses tended to ameliorate with time. Again, it appeared that heterosexual behavior was normal, even precocious. The first of the females has become a mother and she is a perfectly normal mother, and we hopefully predict that when the other females achieve maternity, they will treat their infants in a kind, tender, and loving manner.

Thus, the three diverse kinds of peer-experienced but mother-deprived groups have made adequate social adjustments though delayed in each case and continuously depressed in the instance of the play of together-together animals. Heterosexual behavior has been adequate or precocious. Maternal behavior will be studied as the females reproduce, with only one of these animals having so far been observed, but the expectation is that mothering will be normal. There is, however, one question that the studies leave unanswered: Could unmothered or inadequately mothered infants with peer experience adjust normally to mothered infants with peer experience? We suspect that during the first year of life, particularly the first 6 months, unmothered or inadequately mothered animals would be disadvantaged in interactions with mothered animals and would likely develop subnormally or abnormally. Their inferiority might well carry over into adolescence and maturity under these conditions. The later the admixture of the mother-deprived and mother-reared infants, however, the less would be the expected differences. There is evidence that, at 18 months of age, surrogate-mothered monkeys raised with each other in the playpen can adjust adequately to monkeys of the same age raised by their natural mothers and with equivalent playpen peer experience. The question of dispensability of mothers, then, hinges on testing the adequacy of mother-deprived infants in interactions in infancy with mothered infants, and the best guess at the present time is that the mother-deprived infants would have marked difficulties. Normal mothering, we believe, confers early social advantages upon the recipients, and these advantages would be expected to facilitate early peer adjustments. Early success might well confer an additional advantage that could be maintained indefinitely, similar to the advantages which seem to accrue to infants whose mothers are favored by dominant males [6].

During the last year an interesting study has been completed by Alexander in which he raised babies with their mothers for periods of 2 weeks (control group), 4 months, and 8 months while depriving them of any opportunity to form agemate or peer affectional relationships. We call these infants our "mother-only" or "mother-captive" infants. After ½, 4 or 8 months of maternal captivity, these infants were permitted daily contacts with their agemates, and the rapidity of their play development was inversely related to their age at the time peer experience began. All three groups developed play and social behavior, but the 4-month group showed greater wariness of close contact and greater aggressiveness than the control group, and the 8-month group showed both characteristics in far greater degree. Cautiousness and hyperaggression in the experimental groups may have resulted from their inability to escape from maternal punishment as the mothers went into the transitional, or ambivalent, maternal stage. These characteristics could have been bolstered by the absence of peer affectional ties when fear matured and the weakness of such ties when social aggression matured. It is possible that these traits might be a social advantage in contention with animals having earlier peer experience, although this has not been tested to date. Be this as it may, it is perfectly obvious that monkey mothers can be infant substitutes or "infant surrogates" for their babies throughout a large part of the first critical year of life, and one would predict that this role would be even more adequately played by the human mother, since she has an interest and a capability in playing with her infant that totally transcend those of the rhesus macaque. The implication, we believe, is that mothering is important not only as a source of social security but also as a very powerful agent in the social training of infants, and we are happy to state that we now believe that real mothering, monkey or human, is a very important social factor and that real mothering is here to stay!

In designing our original studies we tended to contrast the relative importance of mother-infant relationships as opposed to infant-infant affectional relationships in the socialization process. We are now convinced that this is the wrong way to look at these social forces. Both normal mothering and normal infant-infant affectional development are extremely important variables in the socialization of rhesus monkeys and presumably of the higher primates. These variables are interactive, and they interact in a totally orderly sequential manner. Interference with either variable may not of necessity socially destroy an infant monkey if it is subsequently allowed to lead a normal or more or less normal life, but there can be no doubt that the easier and safer way to become a normal monkey is to learn to love and live with both mothers and agemates.

## REFERENCES

1. J. Bowlby. The nature of the child's tie to his mother. *Int. J. Psycho-anal.,* 1958, *39,* 1–24.
2. J. Goodall. My life among wild chimpanzees. *Nat. Geographic,* 1963, *124,* 272–308.
3. H. F. Harlow. Love in infant monkeys. *Sci. Amer.,* 1959, *200,* 68–74.
4. H. F. Harlow and M. K. Harlow. The affectional systems. In A. M. Schrier, H. F. Harlow, and F. Stollnitz (eds.). *Behavior of nonhuman primates.* New York: Academic Press, 1965. Vol. 2, pp. 287–334.
5. H. F. Harlow, M. K. Harlow, and E. W. Hansen. The maternal affectional system of rhesus monkeys. In H. L. Rheingold (ed.). *Maternal behavior in mammals.* New York: Wiley, 1963. Pp. 254–281.
6. K. Imanishi. Social behavior in Japanese monkeys, Macaca fuscata. In C. H. Southwick (ed.). *Primate social behavior.* Princeton, N. J.: Van Nostrand, 1963. Pp. 68–81.
7. P. Jay. Mother-infant relations in langurs. In H. L. Rheingold (ed.). *Maternal behavior in mammals.* New York: Wiley, 1963. Pp. 282–304.
8. C. B. Koford. Population dynamics of rhesus monkeys on Cayo Santiago. In I. DeVore (ed.). *Primate behavior.* New York: Holt, 1965. Pp. 160–174.
9. N. E. Miller and J. Dollard. *Social learning and imitation.* New Haven: Yale University Press, 1941.
10. J. B. Mowbray and T. E. Cadell. Early behavior patterns in rhesus monkeys. *J. comp. physiol. Psychol.,* 1962, *55,* 350–357.
11. G. B. Schaller. *The mountain gorilla: Ecology and behavior.* Chicago: University of Chicago Press, 1963.
12. J. M. Warren. Primate learning in comparative perspective. In A. M. Schrier, H. F. Harlow, and F. Stollnitz (eds.). *Behavior of nonhuman primates.* New York: Academic Press, 1965. Vol. 1, pp. 249–281.

# 28

# ADULT STATUS OF CHILDREN WITH CONTRASTING EARLY LIFE EXPERIENCES: A FOLLOW-UP STUDY

## H. M. Skeels

In the original study, the thirteen children in the experimental group, all mentally retarded at the beginning of the study, experienced the effects of early intervention, which consisted of a radical shift from one institutional environment to another. The major difference between the two institutions, as experienced by the children, was in the amount of developmental stimulation and the intensity of relationships between the children and mother-surrogates. Following a variable period in the second institution, eleven of the thirteen children were placed in adoptive homes.

The contrast group of twelve children, initially higher in intelligence than the experimental group, were exposed to a relatively nonstimulating orphanage environment over a prolonged period of time.

Over a period of 2 years, the children in the experimental group showed a marked increase in rate of mental growth, whereas the children in the contrast group showed progressive mental retardation. The experimental group made an average gain of 28.5 IQ points; the contrast group showed an average loss of 26.2 IQ points.

The first follow-up study was made 2½ years after the termination of the original study. The eleven children in the experimental group that had been placed in adoptive homes had maintained and increased their earlier gains in intelligence, whereas the two not so placed had declined in rate of mental growth. Over the 3-year postexperimental period, the children in the contrast group showed a slight mean gain in IQ but were still mentally retarded to a marked degree. In those children that showed gains in intelligence, the gains appeared to be associated with improved environmental experiences that occurred subsequent to the original study.

In the adult follow-up study, all cases were located and information obtained on them, after a lapse of 21 years.

The two groups had maintained their divergent patterns of competency into adulthood. All thirteen children in the experimental group

Source: *Monographs of The Society for Research in Child Development,* 1966 (ser. 105), *31,* 54–59. Copyright 1966 by The Society for Research in Child Development, Inc.

were self-supporting, and none was a ward of any institution, public or private. In the contrast group of twelve children, one had died in adolescence following continued residence in a state institution for the mentally retarded, and four were still wards of institutions, one in a mental hospital, and the other three in institutions for the mentally retarded.

In education, disparity between the two groups was striking. The contrast group completed a median of less than the third grade. The experimental group completed a median of the twelfth grade. Four of the subjects had one or more years of college work, one received a B.A. degree and took some graduate training.

Marked differences in occupational levels were seen in the two groups. In the experimental group all were self-supporting or married and functioning as housewives. The range was from professional and business occupations to domestic service, the latter the occupations of two girls who had never been placed in adoptive homes. In the contrast group, four (33%) of the subjects were institutionalized and unemployed. Those who were employed, with one exception (case 19), were characterized as "hewers of wood and drawers of water." Using the $t$ test, the difference between the status means of the two groups (based on the Warner Index of Status Characteristics applied to heads of households) was statistically significant ($p < 0.01$).

Educational and occupational achievement and income for the eleven adopted subjects in the experimental group compared favorably with the 1960 U. S. Census figures for Iowa and for the United States in general. Their adult status was equivalent to what might have been expected of children living with natural parents in homes of comparable sociocultural levels. Those subjects that married had marriage partners of comparable sociocultural levels.

Eleven of the thirteen children in the experimental group were married; nine of the eleven had a total of twenty-eight children, an average of three children per family. On intelligence tests, these second-generation children had IQs ranging from 86 to 125, with a mean and median IQ of 104. In no instance was there any indication of mental retardation or demonstrable abnormality. Those of school age were in appropriate grades for age.

In the contrast group, only two of the subjects had married. One had one child and subsequently was divorced. Psychological examination of the child revealed marked mental retardation with indications of probable brain damage. Another male subject (case 19) had a nice home and family of four children, all of average intelligence.

The cost to the state for the contrast group, for whom intervention was essentially limited to custodial care, was approximately five times that of the cost for the experimental group. It seems safe to predict that for at least four of the cases in the contrast group costs to the state will continue at a rate in excess of $200 per month each for another 20 to 40 years.

## REFERENCES

1. H. C. Dawe. A study of the effect of an educational program upon language development and related mental functions in young children. *J. exp. Educ.*, 1942, *11*, 200–209.
2. J. M. Hunt. The psychological basis for using preschool enrichment as an antidote for cultural deprivation. *Merrill-Palmer Quart.*, 1964, *10*, 209–248.
3. S. A. Kirk. *Early education of the mentally retarded.* Chicago: University of Illinois Press, 1958.
4. R. B. Kugel. Familial mental retardation: Some possible neurophysiological and psychosocial interrelationships. In A. J. Solnit and Sally Provence (eds.). *Modern perspectives in child development.* New York: Int. Universities Press, 1963. Pp. 206–216.
5. L. W. Schenke and H. M. Skeels. An adult follow-up of children with inferior social histories placed in adoptive homes in early childhood. 1965.
6. H. M. Skeels. The mental development of children in foster homes. *J. genet. Psychol.*, 1936, *49*, 91–106.
7. H. M. Skeels. Mental development of children in foster homes. *J. con. Psychol.*, 1938, *2*, 33–43.
8. H. M. Skeels. Some Iowa studies of the mental growth of children in relation to differentials of the environment: A summary. In *Intelligence: Its nature and nurture.* 39th Yearbook, Part II. National Society for the Study of Education, 1940. Pp. 281–308.
9. H. M. Skeels. A study of the effects of differential stimulation on mentally retarded children: A follow-up report. *Amer. J. ment. Defic.*, 1942, *46*, 340–350.
10. H. M. Skeels and H. B. Dye. A study of the effects of differential stimulation on mentally retarded children. *Proc. Addr. Amer. Assoc. ment. Defic.*, 1939, *44*, 114–136.
11. H. M. Skeels and E. A. Fillmore. The mental development of children from underprivileged homes. *J. genet. Psychol.*, 1937, *50*, 427–439.
12. H. M. Skeels and M. Skodak. Techniques for a high-yield follow-up study in the field. *Pub. Health Rep.*, 1965, *80*, 249–257.
13. H. M. Skeels, R. Updegraff, B. L. Wellman, and H. M. Williams. A study of environmental stimulation: An orphanage preschool project. *U. Iowa Stud. child Welf.*, 1938, *15* (no. 4).
14. M. Skodak. Children in foster homes: A study of mental development. *U. Iowa Stud. child Welf.*, 1939, *16* (no. 1).
15. M. Skodak and H. M. Skeels. A follow-up study of children in adoptive homes. *J. genet. Psychol.*, 1945, *66*, 21–58.
16. M. Skodak and H. M. Skeels. A final follow-up study of one hundred adopted children. *J. genet. Psychol.*, 1949, *75*, 85–125.
17. U. S. Bureau of the Census (1960). *Methodology and scores of socioeconomic status.* Working Paper No. 15. Washington, D. C.: Govt. Ptg. Off., 1963. P. 13.
18. U. S. Bureau of the Census. U. S. Census Population (1960). Vol. I: *Characteristics of the population.* Part 17: Iowa. Washington: Govt. Ptg. Off., 1963. Table 103, pp. 17–333.

19. U. S. Bureau of the Census. U. S. Census Population (1960). *Detailed characteristics. United States summary.* Final Report PC(L)—1D. Washington: Govt. Ptg. Off., 1963. Table 173, pp. 1–406.
20. W. L. Warner, M. E. Meeker, and H. Eells. *Social class in America: The evaluation of status.* New York: Harper Torchbooks, 1960.
21. B. I. Wellman. Our changing concept of intelligence. *J. con. Psychol.,* 1938, 5, 97–107.
22. White House Conference on Child Health and Protection. *Addresses and Abstracts of Committee Reports, 1930.* New York: Appleton-Century, 1931.

# 29

# RECEPTIVE FIELDS OF CELLS IN STRIATE CORTEX OF VERY YOUNG, VISUALLY INEXPERIENCED KITTENS

David H. Hubel
Torsten N. Wiesel

In a series of studies on the cat over the past 5 years we have recorded from single cells in the striate cortex and mapped receptive fields using patterned retinal stimulation. The results suggest that connections between geniculate and striate cortex, and between cortical cells, must be highly specific [5]. Indeed, cells in the striate cortex respond in such a characteristic way that departures from the normal adult physiology should be easily recognizable.

In the present study we have made similar experiments in kittens ranging in age from 1 to 3 weeks. Our purpose was to learn the age at which cortical cells have normal, adult-type receptive fields, and to find out whether such fields exist even in animals that have had no patterned visual stimulation.

Source: *Journal of Neurophysiology,* 1963, 26, 994–1002. Reproduced by permission of The American Physiological Society.
Note: This work was supported in part by Research Grants GM-K3-15,304 (C2), B-2260 (C2), and B-2253-C2S1 from the Public Health Service, and in part by Research Grant AF-AFOSR-410-62 from the U.S. Air Force. The authors thank Jane Chen and Janet Tobie for their technical assistance.

## METHODS

Four kittens were included in this series. Three of these were from the same litter. The youngest was 8 days old at the time of the experiment, and had not yet opened its eyes. The second had both its eyes covered by translucent contact occluders at 9 days, at which time the eyes were just beginning to open; the experiment was done 1 week later, at 16 days of age. The third kitten had the right eye covered by a translucent occluder at 9 days, and the other eye was allowed to open normally; the experiment was done on the nineteenth day. The fourth kitten, from a different litter, was brought up normally and used in an experiment on the twentieth day, after 11 days of normal visual exposure. Thus two kittens had, at the time of the experiment, no patterned-light experience; the third had such experience in one eye only, and the fourth had normal visual stimulation in both eyes. Before the experiments the two kittens that had been exposed to patterned light were beginning to show following movements of the eyes and visually guided behavior.

Procedures for stimulating and recording have for the most part been described in previous papers [4, 5]. A few modifications were necessary for newborn and very young kittens. Since doses of barbiturate large enough to give surgical anesthesia were usually lethal, the kittens were first given a small dose of thiopental (15 to 20 mg/kg), and just before surgery the appropriate regions of skin were infiltrated with local anesthetic (Xylocaine, 2%). A few minutes after injection of the local anesthetic the animal usually fell asleep and showed no sign of discomfort during the surgery or the experiment. From observations on these and other newborn kittens we have the impression that the Xylocaine has central effects as well as local ones. Since eye movements were not troublesome, no paralyzing agent was used, and artificial respiration was not necessary. The skull, too soft to be held by ear plugs, was supported by cementing it to a modified Davies chamber [2] which was then clamped securely. The electrode was introduced through a hole in the skull and dura a few millimeters wide. Tungsten microelectrodes were used for recording, and several electrolytic lesions in each track served to identify recording sites in histological sections. All brains were examined histologically.

Patterned stimuli were shone on a diffusely lit screen which the kittens faced from a distance of 1.5 m. Background light was about 1 candle/$m^2$, and stimuli were generally 0.5 to 1.5 log units brighter. Identification of area centralis and optic discs by our usual projection method [4] was difficult because the cornea and media have a cloudy appearance and because the tapetum in cats does not develop fully until 3 to 4 weeks after birth [3]. Receptive-field position could therefore not be determined accurately, though it was our rough impression that fields were within about 10° of the center of gaze.

## RESULTS

### Cortical Activity and Responses in Kittens Without Visual Experience

*Resting Activity and Responsiveness.* Seventeen single cells were recorded from the two visually naive kittens, nine from the 8-day-old and eight from the 16-day-old. Perhaps the most marked difference between these experiments and our usual recordings from cortex in adult cats was in the maintained activity and responsiveness of the cells. With steady diffuse background illumination cells tended to be silent or to fire at a very low rate. Perhaps partly because of this paucity of maintained activity the number of cells studied in a penetration was unusually small, a few in each passage from surface to white matter as against twenty to thirty in an ordinary adult penetration. Cells were not only sluggish in their spontaneous activity but also responded grudgingly to the most effective patterned stimuli. This relative difficulty in eliciting responses reminded one of similar difficulties in driving cells in very deeply anesthetized adult cats [5, p. 122]. Just as in deeply anesthetized adults, some cells did not respond at all to patterned stimuli unless the stimuli were moving.

Finally, cortical cells, especially in the 8-day-old kitten, showed a marked tendency to fatigue. To be sure of obtaining brisk responses one sometimes had to wait for as long as a minute between stimuli. While a tendency to such fatigability is occasionally found in cells of mature cats, it is far from the rule, and when the depressed responsiveness occurs, it does not last nearly so long. The fatigue would seem to be cortical, since similar effects were not seen in geniculate cells, and since in a binocularly influenced unit the intervals between effective stimuli could not be shortened by stimulating first one eye and then the other.

*Receptive-Field Characteristics.* Except for this sluggishness, cortical cells of visually inexperienced kittens strongly resembled cells of mature cats in their responses to patterned stimuli. The cells responded poorly, and often not at all, to changes in diffuse retinal illumination. They responded best to straight-line stimuli (that is, slits, dark bars, or edges), but only when these were appropriately oriented within the receptive fields, which averaged about 2° to 5° in diameter. The optimum orientation was found by moving the stimulus back and forth across the receptive field, adjusting the orientation between stimuli. In Figure 29-1 a single-unit recording obtained from the 8-day-old kitten, a long narrow rectangle of light was moved back and forth across the receptive field as shown. Brief responses were consistently obtained when the slit was oriented in a 1 o'clock–7 o'clock direction whereas there was no response when it was oriented at 90° to this. A similar kind of preference in stimulus orientation was common to all of the units isolated. Several of the cells, especially those in the 8-day-old kitten, gave responses over a range

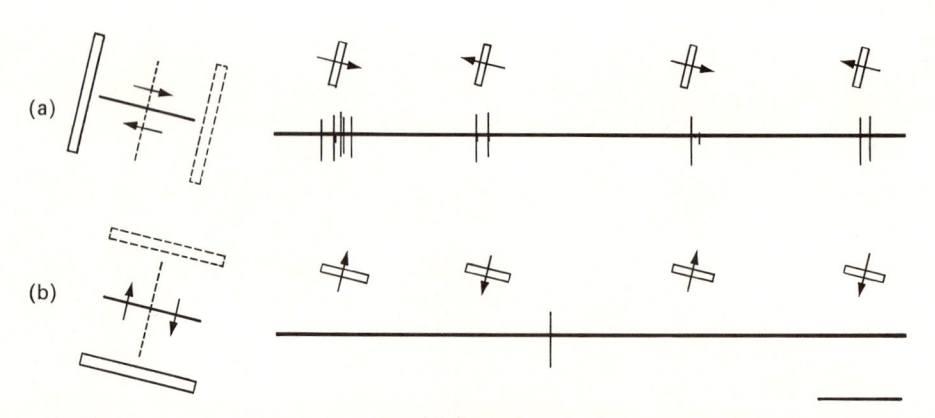

FIGURE 29-1 Single-cell responses from cortex of an 8-day-old kitten with no previous visual experience. A rectangle of light 1° × 5° is moved back and forth across the receptive field in the contralateral eye. Unit binocularly activated, ocular-dominance group 3. Receptive-field sizes about 5° × 5°; fields situated in the central part of the contralateral visual field. (a) Stimulus oriented 12:30–6:30 (parallel to receptive-field axis). (b) Stimulus oriented 9:30–3:30 (at right angles to the optimal orientation). Rate of movement, 5°/sec. Time, 1 sec.

of stimulus orientations that was unusually wide by adult standards, yet even in these cells stimulating at an orientation of 90° to the optimum evoked no response at all. Moreover, the responses to moving an optimally oriented stimulus across the receptive field were not necessarily the same for the two diametrically opposite directions of movement (see Figure 29-4). As in the adult cat, this kind of directional preference varied from cell to cell; some cells responded equally well to the two opposing directions of movement, while some responded well to one direction and not at all to the other.

The combination of sluggish responses and poor optics made it difficult to map receptive fields in a detailed way. Of those that could be mapped, however, some were clearly "simple" in type and others were "complex" [5].

*Binocular Interaction.* The great majority of cells recorded from the two immature kittens (sixteen out of seventeen) could be influenced from each eye separately. Just as in adult cats [5], the receptive fields of these cells were situated in corresponding regions in the two eyes, and the two fields were, as far as one could tell, identical in arrangement, in degree of complexity and in orientation. Furthermore, the two eyes often differed in their relative ability to influence a given cell. We have again subdivided cells into seven groups according to the relative influence of the two eyes (see Figure 29-2, legend). The distribution of cells among the groups is given in Table 29-1 and in the histogram of Figure 29-2 (shaded portion). Comparison of this histogram with the corresponding one in the adult [9, Figure 1] suggests that there is little or no difference in ocular-dominance distribution with age or visual experience.

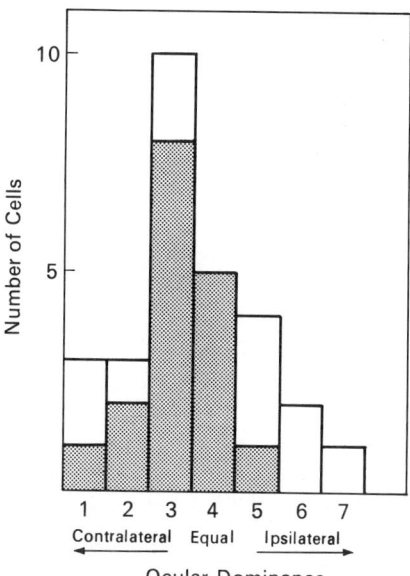

FIGURE 29-2 Distribution of twenty-eight cells among the seven ocular-dominance groups, defined as follows: cells of group 1 were driven only by the contralateral eye; for cells of group 2 there was marked dominance of the contralateral eye; for group 3, slight dominance. For cells in group 4 there was no obvious difference between the two eyes. In group 5 the ipsilateral eye dominated slightly, in group 6 markedly; and in group 7 the cells were driven only by the ipsilateral eye. The shaded portion refers to seventeen cells recorded from two kittens with no prior visual experience (aged 8 and 16 days). The unshaded portion refers to cells recorded from the 20-day-old normal kitten.

TABLE 29-1 Distribution of Cells Among the Ocular-Dominance Groups

| Kitten | Number of Cells in Each Group ||||||| 
|---|---|---|---|---|---|---|---|
| | 1 | 2 | 3 | 4 | 5 | 6 | 7 |
| 8-day-old | 1 | 2 | 3 | 3 | | | |
| 16-day-old | | | 5 | 2 | 1 | | |
| 19-day-old * | 1 | 1 | 2 | 2 | 3 | 2 | |
| 20-day-old | 2 | 1 | 2 | | 3 | 2 | 1 |
| Totals | 4 | 4 | 12 | 7 | 7 | 4 | 1 |

* Not included in histogram of Figure 29-2.

*Functional Architecture.* In penetrations perpendicular to the surface of the cortex and parallel to the radial fiber bundles there were long sequences of cells all having the same receptive-field orientation. In oblique penetrations more frequent shifts in orientation were seen. An oblique cortical penetration in the 16-day-old kitten is reconstructed in Figure 29-3. Here there were three shifts in receptive-field orientation within a relatively short distance, and between each shift cells and unresolved background activity had the same field orientation. All of this is in good agreement with previous studies of the functional architecture of the visual cortex in adult cats [5], suggesting that the organization of cortex into columns of cells having common receptive-field orientations is already present in immature kittens that have never received patterned visual stimulation.

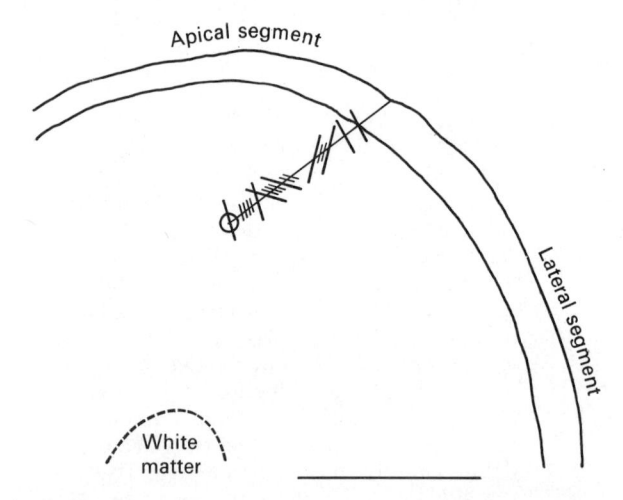

FIGURE 29-3 Reconstruction of an oblique microelectrode penetration through the postlateral gyrus of a 16-day-old kitten without previous visual experience. Longer lines intersecting the electrode track represent single well-isolated cortical cells; directions of these lines represent receptive-field orientations, a line perpendicular to the track standing for a vertical orientation. Shorter lines show regions in which unresolved background activity was observed. At the end of a penetration an electrolytic lesion was made; this is indicated by the circle. Scale, 0.5 mm.

## Kittens with Visual Experience

In their maintained activity, cortical cells of older, visually experienced kittens were much closer to normal. Most cells were active in the absence of patterned stimulation, so that isolation of single cells was much easier. Responses to restricted stimuli were brisker, and showed little of the fatigue that was so apparent in the 8-day-old kitten. As a rule the optimum stimulus was more precisely defined, especially the receptive-field orientation; in this respect these two kittens were closer to the adult than they were to the 8- and 16-day-old visually naive kittens. Both simple and complex types of fields were mapped, and reconstructions of electrode penetrations again tended to confirm the columnar organization of the cortex. In the responses to stimulation of the two eyes there were no obvious differences between the younger visually naive kittens and the older experienced ones: the eleven cells recorded from the 20-day-old normal kitten varied greatly in ocular dominance, and are included in the histogram of Figure 29-2 where they are represented by the unshaded portion.

The third, 19-day-old kitten was a useful control, since the right eye was covered from the time of normal eye opening by a translucent occluder, and the left was allowed to remain uncovered. In the cortical recordings there was, on the whole, no obvious difference between the two eyes in their ability to influence cortical cells; the previously occluded eye was dominant about as often as the normal eye (see Table 29-1). In Figure 29-4 (p.310), a two-unit recording obtained from this kitten, a slit stimulus crossed the receptive field in three different orientations. The units responded well only to the second of these; to the first and third and to orientations still further from the optimum there was little or no response. The unit from which the smaller spikes were recorded gave hardly any responses to stimulation of the right eye (which had been covered), but responded well to the left. On the contrary, the cell giving the larger spikes strongly preferred the eye that had been occluded.

There was no tendency for cells dominated by the occluded eye to have less maintained activity or to respond less briskly and precisely than the other cells. We are therefore inclined to think that the sluggishness of maintained activity and responses in the first two kittens was related to age rather than to visual experience. This is simply a tentative impression, since the difference in the two groups of kittens may be more related to differences in the animals' susceptibility to anesthesia than to a difference in properties of cortical cells, especially since we know that suppression of maintained activity and of responses is a characteristic effect of anesthesia in adult cats.

What can be concluded from this kitten is that even as late as 19 days of age a cell need not have had previous patterned stimulation from an eye in order to respond normally to it. This will be of some interest when the effects of longer periods of monocular deprivation are considered, as discussed in the accompanying paper [9].

## DISCUSSION

The main result of this study has been to show that much of the richness of visual physiology in the cortex of the adult cat—the receptive-

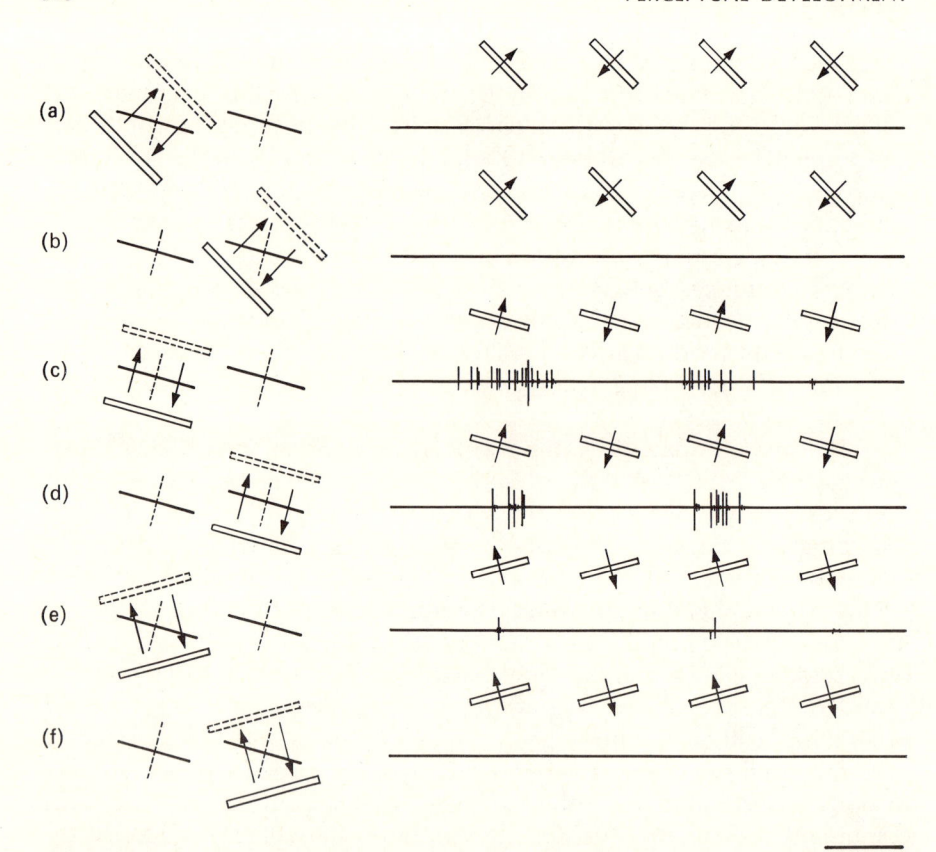

FIGURE 29-4 Two-unit recording from a 19-day-old kitten whose right eye had been covered from the time of normal eye opening by a translucent occluder. Each eye stimulated separately by a slit 0.5° × 0.4°, moved across the receptive field at a rate of about 1°/sec. Size of fields 2° × 4°. Time, 1 sec.

field organization, binocular interaction, and functional architecture—is present in very young kittens without visual experience. Our conclusion is that the neural connections subserving these functions must also be present, in large part, at or near the time of birth. This extends the work of the previous paper [8] in which we showed that visual experience was not necessary for the development of optic-nerve or geniculate receptive fields.

These findings were somewhat unexpected in view of behavioral observations in very young kittens. At birth a bright light evokes a lid reflex [10], as well as a sluggish pupillary response [1], suggesting that the visual system is to some extent functional. Nevertheless, kittens appear quite unable to use their eyes at the time of normal eye opening, which usually occurs between the sixth and the tenth day. Avoidance of objects is seen at the very earliest around 14 days, while pursuit, following movements, and visual placing appear only at 20 to 25 days [10, 7]. Visual acuity, measured by observing optokinetic nystagmus, increases rapidly from the second week and approaches adult levels by about the fourth week [7]. To parallel this behavioral development in the first weeks we have in cortical cells only the increase in briskness of responses and extent of maintained activity—which may be related to differences in reaction or our experimental procedures rather than to real differences in the physiology—and the heightened precision of responses, especially to variations in stimulus orientation. This leads one to wonder whether the inability of young kittens to use their vision is related not so much to incomplete development of the visual pathway as to a lack of visual-motor ability.

From the behavioral observations alone one might easily imagine that the improvement in visual skill during the first weeks after birth is closely paralleled by development in neural connections in the visual pathway. Such a concept has probably been reinforced by studies on the delay in development of visual ability produced by raising animals in darkness or in diffuse light (for reviews see [6]); it has been natural to assume that in the normal animal, neural connections subserving vision are developed only if pattern stimuli fall on the retina. The present results make it clear that highly complex neural connections are possible without benefit of visual experience. In interpreting the results of visual deprivation, both the behavioral and the physiological, one must therefore consider the possibility that lack of stimulation may lead not simply to a failure in forming connections, but rather to the disruption of connections that were there from the start.

## SUMMARY

Responses of single cells to visual stimuli were studied in the striate cortex of very young kittens. Two animals, aged 8 and 16 days, had had no previous exposure to patterned stimuli. Responses of cortical cells in these animals were strikingly similar to those of adult cats. Fields were simple or complex, with a clear receptive-field orientation. Cells with similar orientations appeared to be grouped in columnar regions. The majority of cells were driven by the two eyes, with patterns of binocular interaction that were similar to those in the adult. Compared with cells in the mature cat, those in young kittens responded somewhat more sluggishly to visual stimuli, and receptive-field orientations tended to be not quite so well defined.

In two other kittens, one monocularly deprived by translucent occluder from birth for 19 days, the other a normal 20-day-old, responses to patterned stimulation of either eye were entirely normal by adult standards.

It is concluded that many of the connections responsible for the highly organized behavior of cells in the striate cortex must be present at birth or within a few days of it. The development of these connections occurs even in the absence of patterned visual experience.

# REFERENCES

1. G. Abelsdorff. Bemerkungen über das Auge der neugeborenen Katze, im besonderen die retinale Sehzellenschicht. *Arch. Augenheilk.*, 1905, *53,* 257–262.
2. P. W. Davies. Chamber for microelectrode studies in the cerebral cortex. *Science,* 1956, *124,* 179–180.
3. R. Hilbert. Über die nach der Geburt eintretenden entwickelungsgeschichtlichen Veränderungen der brechenden Medien und des Augenhintergrundes der Katze. *Graefes Arch. Ophthal.,* 1884, *30,* 245–250.
4. D. H. Hubel and T. N. Wiesel. Receptive fields of optic nerve fibres in the spider monkey. *J. Physiol.,* 1960, *154,* 572–580.
5. D. H. Hubel and T. N. Wiesel. Receptive fields, binocular interaction and functional architecture in the cat's visual cortex. *J. Physiol.,* 1962, *160,* 106–154.
6. A. H. Riesen. Stimulation as a requirement for growth and function in behavioral development. In D. W. Fiske and S. R. Maddi (eds.). *Functions of varied experience.* Homewood, Ill.: Dorsey Press, 1961. Pp. 57–105.
7. J. Warkentin and K. U. Smith. The development of visual acuity in the cat. *J. genet. Psychol.,* 1937, *50,* 371–399.
8. T. N. Wiesel and D. H. Hubel. Effects of visual deprivation on morphology and physiology of cells in the cat's lateral geniculate body. *J. Neurophysiol.,* 1963, *26,* 978–993.
9. T. N. Wiesel and D. H. Hubel. Single-cell responses in striate cortex of kittens deprived of vision in one eye. *J. Neurophysiol.,* 1963, *26,* 1003–1017.
10. W. F. Windle. Normal behavioral reactions of kittens correlated with the postnatal development of nerve-fiber density in the spinal gray matter. *J. comp. Neurol.,* 1930, *50,* 479–503.

# 30

# CONSEQUENCES OF MONOCULAR DEPRIVATION ON VISUAL BEHAVIOR IN KITTENS

P. B. Dews
T. N. Wiesel

## SUMMARY

1. Kittens were raised for a period with one of their eyes closed by suture of the lids. The age at suture and the duration of deprivation were varied systematically. When the cat was a year or more old, the normal and deprived eyes were compared using behavioral procedures which made graded demands on visual function.

2. In kittens deprived from birth, the duration of eye closure determined the severity of the defect in vision with the deprived eye. A cat with an eye closed for the first 4 to 6 weeks showed as a permanent effect only a lowering of the visual acuity. When closure was extended through the first 7 weeks the visual acuity was further lowered but the animal still showed good visual guidance of paw placement. Further extension of deprivation through the first 16 weeks led to a still more severe defect; such animals showed no indication of visual guidance of paw placement or of pattern discrimination. They were influenced visually by stimuli that differed in luminosity.

3. The upper age limit of the susceptibility to deprivation was determined by varying the age at eye closure. Waiting until 1 month of age before closing the eye conferred no appreciable protection. Waiting until 2 months of age, however, reduced the damage. Deprivation starting at 4 months of age or later produced no effect we could detect. Thus, susceptibility is greatest during the second month after birth and then falls until by 4 months of age the kitten, like the adult cat, suffers no permanent consequences of monocular light and form deprivation.

4. After exclusive use of the deprived eye for a period, brought about by closure of the normal eye, visual control with the deprived eye was better than in similarly deprived cats whose normal eye was never

Source: *Journal of Physiology,* 1970, *206,* 437–455.
Note: This research was supported by Grant NB 0554-01 from the U. S. Public Health Service. We are indebted to Mrs. Marilyn Vanderhoof Bownds for help with the experiments and to Miss Eleanor Bates for help with the manuscript.

closed. Improvement in the deprived eye was also seen in an animal whose normal eye was closed after both eyes had been open for more than 1 year.

5. Relating the behavioral results to the neurophysiological findings in the visual cortex in the same or similarly deprived cats shows that the grading of visual defects with age and length of deprivation was generally paralleled by a change in proportion of cortical cells driven by stimulation of the deprived eye. The effect of reversal of eye closure in improving behavioral control was not, however, accompanied by an increase in the ability of the deprived eye to drive cortical cells.

## INTRODUCTION

Clinical observations in children with congenital cataracts have shown that lack of normal visual experience of form during early life causes severe defects in vision [9]. Similar effects have been demonstrated in behavioral studies of animals raised in darkness or under diffuse light conditions (see review [6]). Studies of the physiological and morphological effects of raising kittens with one eye closed by eyelid suture during the first few months after birth revealed changes in both the lateral geniculate and the visual cortex [10, 11]. Simple behavioral observations indicated that these animals also suffered gross and persistent defects of vision with the deprived eye.

In the present study, behavioral tests have been adapted to assess objectively and more precisely the defects produced in kittens by monocular deprivation. The dependency of the visual defects on the timing and duration of deprivation has been determined and so have the effects of closing the normal eye when the deprived eye was opened. Some of the kittens in the series and others with a similar history of deprivation were studied in acute neurophysiological experiments [4], permitting direct correlation between cortical physiology and the control of behavior by visual stimuli (visual stimulus control).

## METHODS

### Apparatus

The experiments were carried out in a plywood runway 180 cm long and 60 cm wide (Figure 30-1a). Two translucent plastic panels in the front wall were transilluminated as visual stimuli. The panels were hinged at the top. Behind each panel was a hole to which a food cup could be raised. The cats pushed back the panels with their noses, bringing their mouths over the holes for the food cups.

At the other end (the back) of the runway there was a hemispherical knob in the floor and a hole for a food cup similar to those behind the

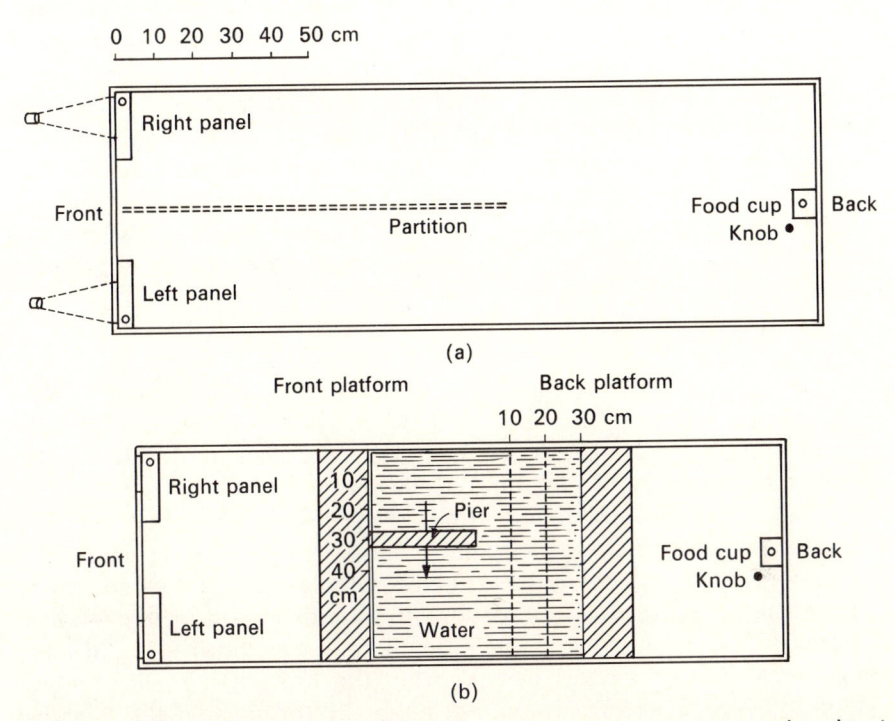

FIGURE 30-1 (a) Diagram of runway. The plastic panels were mounted in chassis on the front wall and transilluminated by the projectors. The open circles indicate the position of the holes in the floor to which the food cups could be raised. The filled circle near the back of the runway shows the knob, which was positioned so that the cat could readily put its right foot on the knob and its mouth over the hole for the food cup. The dashed lines in the runway show the position of the partition in the acuity test.

(b) Arrangement for water barrier test. The dish of water, the front and back platforms, and the pier have been added to the runway shown in (a). Between series of trials, the distance from the back platform to the end of the pier could be changed by sliding the front of the dish of water under the front platform, keeping the back platform at the back of the dish. Between trials a handle attached to the pier was used to move the pier sideways to a new position. The handle ran horizontally under the front platform to the outside of the runway.

panels. Cats shuttled from back to front of the runway pressing first the knob and then one of the panels and then the knob and so on until a series of trials was completed. Pressing an illuminated panel extinguished the panel lights and lit the knob; pressing the lighted knob darkened the knob and lit the panels. Food was presented for 3 sec when the positive panel was pushed but not when the negative panel was pushed. Food was delivered when the illuminated knob was pushed following a positive panel push but not following a negative panel push. In other words, food was delivered at both ends of the runway following presses of the positive panel but at neither end following presses of the negative panel.

Images were projected on the panels by a pair of Kodak Carousel Projectors. The image was restricted to an 11.5-cm high and 10-cm wide part of the panel as shown in Figure 30-2. Preliminary observations were made with 1, 2 and 3 log-unit neutral density filters taped in front of the projection lens. With the 2 log-unit filters the black lines of the stimuli showed against a white background of about $+2$ log cd m$^{-2}$, a reasonable and effective level of illumination, which was then used in all the reported experiments. A photocell beside the panel was activited by the positive stimulus, programing food delivery when the panel was pressed.

## The Gap Test

The positive stimuli were four continuous horizontal black lines across the lighted stimulus area (Figure 30-2). The lines were 0.5 cm wide and were separated by spaces of 1.5 cm. The negative stimuli were similar except there was a gap in the lines. Gaps about either 30 mm or 1.5 mm wide were used. An unilluminated panel was another negative stimulus. Since the cat pushed the panel with its nose, it was not possible, in the ordinary gap test, to specify the effective visual angle subtended by the gaps. Some observations were made with a modification of the gap test, referred to as an acuity test. An opaque center partition of adjustable length was inserted extending back from the front wall of the runway (Figure 30-1a). An error was scored if the cat approached the negative stimulus panel closer than the end of the partition. The visual angle subtended at the end of the partition by the gap in a line was calculated.

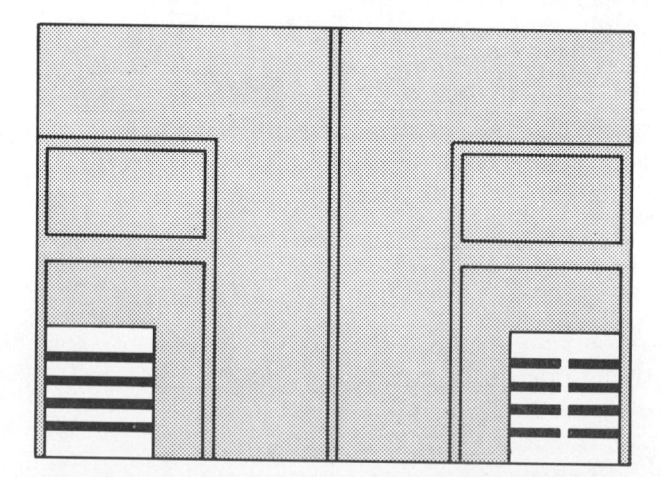

FIGURE 30-2 Cat's eye view of front wall of runway. The outline of the two panels and the areas where the stimuli appeared on the panels are shown and the position of the center partition is indicated. The stimuli are those for the gap test, with the positive stimulus on the left.

In a luminescent panel test the plastic panels were lit by electroluminescent panels (General Electric, Type FN) whose luminance depended on the voltage applied. The positive panel had a luminance of +0.7 log cd m$^{-2}$, the negative panel of −1.5 log cd m$^{-2}$.

**The Water Barrier Test**

A square metal dish was put across the middle of the runway and filled with water to a depth of about 3 cm (Figure 30-1b). The sides of the dish were vertical and fitted flush with the sides of the runway. Platforms 15 cm above the floor of the runway were arranged in front of the dish and behind it. From the front platform a pier of wood 5 cm wide projected perpendicularly backwards for 44 cm, some of that distance being over the water. As in the gap test, the cat shuttled between the back and the front of the runway, passing each time now over the water by means of the pier and platforms. The position of the pier was changed laterally to a new position each time the cat returned to the back of the runway. The distance from the back platform to the end of the pier could also be varied from 10 to 30 cm. When the distance was 10 cm, cats could stand on the rear platform and reach the pier with outstretched paw. When the distance was 30 cm, the pier could be reached only after the center of gravity of the cat had passed forward over the water under the guidance of only visual cues. In experiments with the water barrier only the positive panel was transilluminated in each trial. The room was dimly lit by reflected light, providing ambient illumination in the mesopic range. The times required for the cat to move from knob to stimulus panel were measured.

**Program**

In each projector were ten slides, five positive and five negative, arranged so that there were no more than two consecutive slides of the same kind (positive or negative). A positive slide in the right-hand projector was always accompanied by a negative slide in the left-hand projector and vice versa. The two projectors' slide holders moved together in phase from 1 to 10 and then back to 1 and so on. Slides were changed only when a panel had been pushed but not after every panel push. Whether a change would occur or not was determined by a three-position switch, ABC (programmed by an Automatic Electric Series OCS Relay), which changed after each push of the positive panel and which cycled indefinitely, ABCABC.... A push of the positive panel led to a slide change when the relay was in the A or C position but no change when it was in the B position. A push of the negative panel led to a slide change when the relay was in the C position but no change when it was in the A or B positions. Since pushing the negative panel did not change the OCS relay position, a negative stimulus on the panel on a particular side could not, two times out of three, be changed to a positive stimulus by repeatedly pushing that side following each knob press.

The positive stimulus was equally often on the right or on the left. Which side would be positive in a given trial, however, was not independent of what had happened in the previous trial because of the constraints of the sequence of slides and of the OCS program. When the positive panel was pushed, there was a 14/27 probability that the positive panel would be on the opposite side on the next trial. When the negative panel was pushed, there was a probability of 7/27 that the positive panel would be on the opposite side on the next trial. With consecutive pressings of the negative panel the probability was either 0 that the positive panel would change sides (on the two out of three occasions that the OCS was in position A or B), thus discouraging consistently going to the same side, or 7/9 that the positive panel would change sides (on the one out of three occasions that the OCS was in position C), thus discouraging alternation.

### Criteria of Stimulus Control

If the cat was equally likely to go to the right or to the left, but independently of the stimuli, the probability was 0.5 that the response on a given trial would be on the positive stimulus. From the binomial distribution, the expected number of correct responses by chance in a series of thirty trials would be 15 with a standard deviation of 2.7. Fewer than ten errors would be expected by chance, therefore, in less than 1 series in 20 ($p < 0.05$). For the gap test, the scores in three consecutive series of thirty trials have been pooled; a score of thirty errors or fewer in ninety trials has a probability of occurring by chance of less than 0.001, and has been taken as evidence of stimulus control.

### Subjects

There were fifteen cats in the main experimental series, divided into three groups depending on their history of visual deprivation. Cats in group I had their right eyes closed by lid suture [10] 8 to 15 days after birth, before they had had any significant visual experience, and then opened at various ages to determine how long initial deprivation must be continued to produce a defect (Table 30-1). Cats in group II had their right eyes closed at various ages to determine to what age susceptibility to the effects of deprivation persisted (Table 30-2). Finally, cats in group III had their right eyes closed for varying periods starting 8 to 15 days after birth, as for group I, but then the left eyes were closed when the right eyes were opened, to determine whether exclusive use of the previously deprived eye would enhance its functional capabilities (Table 30-3). One additional cat was studied, for immediate transfer of stimulus control.

TABLE 30-1 Deprivation History and Behavioral Performances of Cats in Group I

| | | Deprivation Right Eye (days) | | | Performance | | | |
|---|---|---|---|---|---|---|---|---|
| | | | | | Gap Test (errors) | | Water Barrier Test (sec) | |
| Cat No. | Litter | Closed | Opened | mm | L | R | L | R |
| 2 | A | 8 | 145 | 30 | 7 | 38 | — | — |
| 3 | B | 15 | 111 | 30 | 18 | 31 | — | — |
| 10 | C | 15 | 111 | 30 | 0 | 35 | 8.4 | ∞ |
| | | | | 1.5 | 7 | | | |
| 19 | D | 8 | 51 | 30 | 2 | 11 | 5.4 | 488 |
| | | | | 1.5 | 4 | 37 | | |
| 12 | E | 10 | 37 | 30 | 0 | 2 | 6.8 | 6.5 |
| | | | | 1.5 | 3 | 22 | | |
| 13 | E | 10 | 37 | 30 | 2 | 4 | 4.0 | 4.7 |
| | | | | 1.5 | 7 | 23 | | |
| 14 | F | 10 | 32 | 30 | 4 | 7 | 4.4 | 4.0 |
| | | | | 1.5 | 4 | 29 | | |

Note: Tables 30-1 to 30-3 give the ages in days since birth when eyes were closed and then opened. L and R refer to performances with the normal left eye and with the deprived right eye only, the other eye being occluded by an opaque contact lens. The number of errors that occurred in three consecutive series of thirty trials are given for steady-state performance in the gap test. For the water barrier test the medians of times in seconds for the animal to go from knob to stimulus panel over 30 cm of water in ten consecutive trials are given. The infinity sign means the cat did not cross the water.

After lid separation all cats had clear corneas, normal appearing fundi, and good direct and consensual pupillary light reflexes.

**Procedure**

The cats were partially deprived of food, trained to eat promptly from the food cups, and then trained to press the panels and the knob. Individual eyes were tested by occluding the other eye with an opaque contact lens. At first only the positive panel was lighted. Meanwhile the cats became accustomed to working with a contact lens in one eye.

The cats were then trained under the gap test. At first, the positive stimulus was moved slightly up and down, a maneuver which seemed to help the establishment of stimulus control. Subsequent performances under the water barrier test, the acuity test, and the luminescent panel test required essentially no additional training. Results were accepted as definitive only when the cat had been trained several months and was at least a year old. Following initial training, body weights could be returned to the normal range, without detriment to performance in the various tests.

## RESULTS

With their normal left eyes, all the eleven cats of groups I and II went predominantly to the positive stimulus with the continuous lines rather than the negative stimulus with 30-mm gaps in the lines (Figure 30-2). They made an average of 4.1 errors in ninety trials. Nine of these cats were studied with the 1.5-mm gap stimuli and, again, all were controlled by the stimuli, averaging 8.9 errors in ninety trials with no cat making as many as 20 errors. The same nine cats studied in the water barrier test completed series of trials with no trial time in excess of 30 sec, and median times less than 10 sec (Table 30-1). These results with normal eyes provide a standard for comparison with the results with deprived eyes. One great advantage of monocular closure is that conclusions can be based on differences between the normal and deprived eyes of the same individual.

### Group I Cats, with Early Monocular Closures of Graded Duration

Lids, sutured shortly after birth, were opened in two cats at about 4 months of age (cats 3 and 10) and in one cat at about 5 months (cat 2). The resulting deficiency in vision is shown by the complete lack of control with the deprived right eye by even the 30-mm gap (Table 30-1). Testing was continued for as long as 2 years without noticeable improvement.

The deficiency was dramatically demonstrated in the water barrier test with cat 10. (Cats 2 and 3 were dead before this test and the 1.5-mm gap test were introduced.) With the normal left eye open, cat 10, like all the cats studied in the test, moved from back to front of the runway, over the water, without hesitation, completing a trial in only a few seconds (Table 30-1) and then moved with equal facility from front to back of the runway, again over the water, to start a new trial. With an opaque contact lens in the normal left eye and the pier at a distance of 10 cm, cat 10 approached the water barrier slowly, over a period of more than 30 sec, then groped for the pier by extending a paw with abducted claws, in dramatic contrast to the elegant precision with which the paw was placed on the pier when the normal left eye was unoccluded. When the extended paw touched the pier, the cat passed over the water rapidly; and two subsequent trials with the pier in the same position were completed in progressively shorter times (though they were still more than 30 sec). On the next trial the pier was moved; the cat stepped forward, put its foot where the pier had been and landed with both front paws in the water.

The cat retreated and did not cross the water barrier again that session. In subsequent sessions, with the pier at 30 cm, the cat regularly gave satisfactory performances with the normal left eye uncovered but never completed the test with only the deprived right eye uncovered.

In training, cats 2, 3 and 10, with their normal left eyes occluded, went readily to the lighted rather than the darkened panel, proving some persistent visual function through the right eye. In the luminescent panel test, cat 10 made 14/90 errors with both eyes open and 12/90 errors with only the deprived right eye open; that is, cat 10 performed as well with only its deprived eye unoccluded as with its normal eye open, so there was no evidence that deprivation impaired control by the luminescent panels.

When the right eye had been closed for shorter periods, cats were controlled not only by the light and dark panels but also by other stimuli in the tests. Cat 19, deprived until 7 weeks of age, came under significant control in the 30-mm gap test with its deprived right eye (14/90). Control was better, however, through the undeprived eye (7/90 errors) (Table 30-1). The difference between the two eyes was much greater in the 1.5-mm gap test in which cat 19 was not controlled with its deprived right eye. The results in three consecutive series of thirty trials are shown in Figure 30-3, illustrating the consistency of performance. In the water barrier test, the animal performed satisfactorily with only the deprived right eye open. Thus deprivation for 7 weeks produced a severe permanent defect, but a significantly less severe defect than 4 months of deprivation.

After a still shorter period of eye closure, 4½ to 5½ weeks (cats 12, 13 and 14), stimulus control with the deprived eye was no longer limited to the water barrier test and the 30-mm gaps but now extended to the 1.5-mm gaps. The control by the 1.5-mm gaps, however, although significant with the deprived eye, was better with the normal eye (Figure 30-4). The difference between the eyes was accentuated in the acuity test on cats 12 and 13. With their normal left eyes open both cats made fewer than ten errors with partition lengths up to about 50 cm, where a 1.5-mm gap subtends a visual angle of about 10 min of arc. With their deprived right eyes both cats made more than ten errors with a partition length of only 15 cm (visual angle 33 min of arc) (Figure 30-5).

In summary, deprivation until only 4½ weeks of age produced a defect which persisted more or less unchanged over the succeeding months. The defect was progressively greater with increasing duration of deprivation until after more than 3 months there was no evidence of visual function except by light and dark panels.

## Group II Cats with Later Monocular Closure

To obtain information on the beginning and end of the period of susceptibility to visual damage by eye closure, the eyes of the cats in

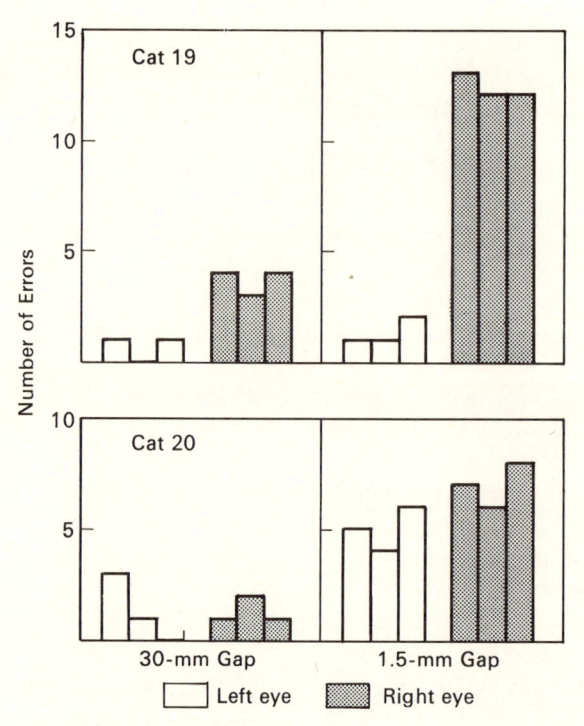

FIGURE 30-3 Performance in gap test. Performance in three consecutive series of thirty trials is shown for the 30-mm gap and the 1.5-mm gap. Note the consistency in performance in consecutive series of trials. Cat 19 made many more errors with only its deprived right eye unoccluded than with its normal left eye unoccluded. Littermate cat 20, with similar initial deprivation but subsequent normal left eye closure, performed almost as well with only its deprived right eye as with its normal left eye.

group II were closed when the kittens were already 1, 2, or 4 months of age.

Closure from 4½ weeks of age until 4 months (cat 15) produced as severe a defect as closure from the early days of life until 4 or 5 months of age. Cat 15 failed to come under control of the 30-mm gaps and did not perform the water barrier test (Table 30-2). When closure was reduced to the period from 4 weeks to 6½ weeks of age (cat 21) the animal performed well on the water barrier test and came under the control of both the 30-mm and 1.5-mm gaps (Table 30-2). With the 1.5-mm gaps, however, 24/90 errors were made, which is outside the range of errors of cats with their normal eye (three to eighteen) and is very similar to performance of cats 12 and 13 whose eyes were closed until 5½ weeks of

TABLE 30-2 Deprivation History and Behavioral Performances of Cats in Group II

| Cat No. | Litter | Deprivation Right Eye (days) Closed | Deprivation Right Eye (days) Opened | mm | Gap Test (errors) L | Gap Test (errors) R | Water Barrier Test (sec) L | Water Barrier Test (sec) R |
|---|---|---|---|---|---|---|---|---|
| 15 | F | 32 | 122 | 30 | 5 | 44 | 2.2 | ∞† |
|   |   |   |   | 1.5 | 12 |   |   |   |
| 21 | G | 30 | 47 | 30 | 3 | 13 | 2.6 | 3.0 |
|   |   |   |   | 1.5 | 11 | 24 |   |   |
| 16 | F | 63 | 147 | 30 | 4 | 4 | 4.2 | 4.5 |
|   |   |   |   | 1.5 | 16 | 28 |   |   |
| 18 | F | 114 | 199 | 30 | 0 | 0 | 3.3 | 3.0 |
|   |   |   |   | 1.5 | 16 | 11 |   |   |

† When the normal left eye of cat 15 was later closed, the cat completed the water barrier test (see Discussion).

age. Thus the period of susceptibility continues beyond the first month of life, and the severity of the defect is related to the duration of closure.

When closure was delayed until the period from 2 months of age until 5 months (cat 16), the subsequent defect was much less than that observed in animals deprived for a similar period starting earlier in life (cats 2, 3, 10, and 15); cat 16 not only completed the water barrier test but also came under the control of the 30-mm gaps and, partially, the 1.5-mm gaps. Thus, although it persists beyond 2 months of age, susceptibility is already declining by that age. Closure from 4 until 7 months of age (cat 18) produced no detectable defect, showing that susceptibility to damage from closure is lost before a kitten is 4 months old.

In an additional cat, cat 17, the right eye was closed at 6 months of age (on the 172nd day of life) and the cat was trained in the runway while the right eye was closed. After 3 months of closure (on the 262nd day) the right eye was opened under halothane anesthesia. About 3 hr later, when the animal had recovered from the anesthesia, the left eye was occluded and performance in the gap test assessed. From the outset, performance was satisfactory, one error in the first thirty trials with the 1.5-mm gap. Not only was there no detectable impairment of function of an eye closed 3 months when closure was delayed until 6 months of age, but no training specifically with the deprived eye was necessary for it to exert control in situations learned while it was closed.

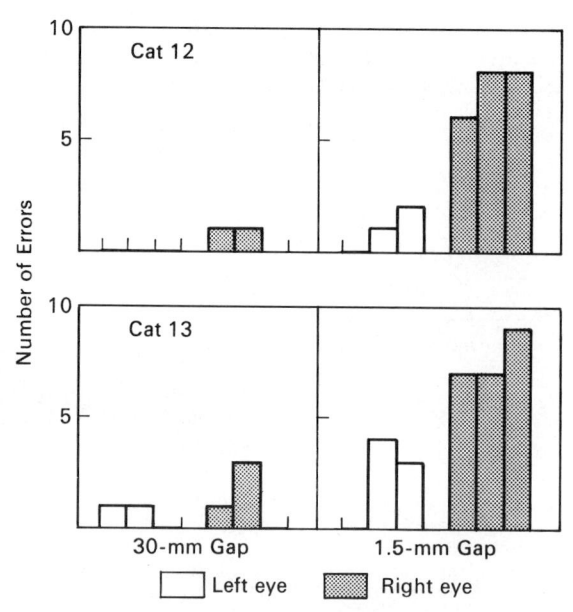

FIGURE 30-4 Performance in gap tests. Arrangement as in Figure 30-3. Note again the consistency in performance in consecutive series of trials and also the virtual identity of performance with the corresponding eyes of the littermates similarly deprived. The control exerted by the 1.5 mm gaps with the deprived eyes was statistically highly significant ($p < 0.001$); yet the difference between the control exerted by the 30-mm gap and the 1.5-mm gap, and the difference between the control with the two eyes stand out clearly.

## Group III Cats, with Right Eye Closed Early, Then Left Eye Closed When Right Eye Opened

The left eyes of the cats in groups I and II were never closed by lid suture. If a normal eye continues to suppress a deprived eye even after opening of the lids, the suppression would be removed by closing the normal eye. Closure of the normal eye might also induce some recovery in the deprived right eye that otherwise might not have occurred. To investigate these possibilities, the four cats of group III had their left eye closed when the right eye was opened (Table 30-3).

The first two cats (cats 8 and 9) were littermates of cat 10 and all three were subjected initially to similar closures of the right eye until about 4 months of age. As a result of the subsequent closure of the normal left eyes, cats 8 and 9 came to perform satisfactorily in the water barrier test over the next few months, while cat 10, which did not have reversal of eye closure, continued to fail dismally with its deprived right eye. There may be a hint of impairment in cats 8 and 9 in the water

TABLE 30-3  Deprivation History and Behavioral Performances of Cats in Group III

| Cat No. | Litter | Deprivation Right Eye (days) Closed | Opened | Deprivation Left Eye (days) Closed | Opened | Gap Test (errors) mm | L | R | Water Barrier Test (sec) L | R |
|---|---|---|---|---|---|---|---|---|---|---|
| 9 | C | 15 | 111 | 111 | 244 | 30 / 1.5 | 6 / 17 | 42 | 4.6 | 10.6 |
| 8 | C | 15 | 111 | 111 | 679† | 30 / 1.5 | 2 / 3 | 38 | 1.2 | 4.8 |
| 1 | H | 9 | 94 | 94 | 465 | 30 / 1.5 | 8 / 24 | 8 / 18 | 12.6 | 15.0 |
| 20 | D | 8 | 52 | 52 | 252 | 30 / 1.5 | 4 / 15 | 4 / 20 | 1.1 | 1.3 |

† The left eye of cat 8 was opened for testing between the 244th and 343rd days of age. There was no obvious difference in visual function between cats 8 and 9, so the second period of closure in cat 8 had little effect.

barrier test in that the times were longer with the deprived right eye than when the normal left eye was available; nevertheless, the performance of these cats was decisively better than that of littermate cat 10. Neither cat 8 nor cat 9, however, came under the control of even the 30-mm gap, showing a persistent severe visual defect.

Reversal of closure improved the visual function of kittens even when duration of deprivation was shorter and the initial defect was correspondingly less severe. While cat 19, deprived for 7 weeks, failed to come under the control of the 1.5-mm gap, littermate cat 20 with similar initial deprivation but subsequent reversal made only 20/90 errors, demonstrating highly significant control, though errors were still above the normal range (Table 30-3). Figure 30-3 illustrates the improvement produced by eye reversal by comparing cats 19 and 20 in the 30-mm and 1.5-mm gap tests. It should be remembered that the left eye of cat 20 was closed for only 3 months and that the tests were done when both eyes had been open for some months.

Cat 1, with the right eye closed for the first 3 months, then the left eye closed, represents a special case for two reasons. First, performance level in the water barrier test, and, to a lesser extent in the gap test, was below that of other cats in the series. These derelictions were almost certainly due to a mild though unmistakable ataxia in the hind limbs that also caused the cat to fall off the pier occasionally during the water barrier test. None of the other animals was so clumsy. Secondly, testing of cat 1

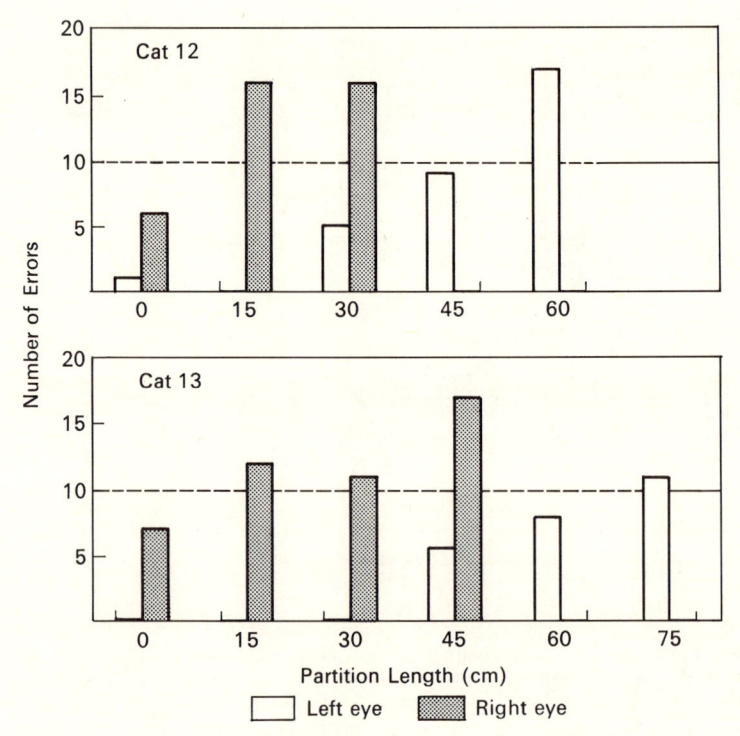

**FIGURE 30-5** Performance in acuity test. Errors in series of thirty trials with center partitions of different lengths are shown for cats 12 and 13. Significant control (less than ten errors) was exerted with the normal eye with partition lengths up to 50 cm, but the control with the deprived eye was lost at a distance of only 15 cm, confirming the difference between the eyes suggested by the results in Figure 30-4. Note again the virtual identity of performance with the corresponding eyes of littermates similarly treated.

continued over a very long period, almost 5 years. By the end of 4½ years' testing cat 1 was under the control of not only the 30-mm gaps but also the 1.5-mm gaps, representing definitely better performance than cats 8 and 9 with similar deprivation history, but shorter subsequent testing.

There was no evidence of impairment of function with the left eyes in the cats of group III in spite of prolonged closure and even though, in the case of cat 20, the eye was closed as early as 7 weeks. Cat 20 confirms that the effects of deprivation are greatly reduced by the time the kitten is 2 months old. The comparison of cat 16 (deprived from 2 to 5 months of age) and cat 20 suggests that susceptibility is still further reduced when vision with the other eye has already been damaged by deprivation. This suggestion brings to mind the neurophysiological finding that monocular closure produces more damage to vision with the deprived eye than does binocular closure [12]. A normally functioning eye seems to contribute to the damage to the other closed eye.

## DISCUSSION

The striking morphological and neurophysiological changes in the visual system of kittens deprived monocularly in early life led us to this study of the effects of deprivation on some behavioral activities depending on vision. Our results, summarized graphically in Figure 30-6, led to the following conclusions on the relations between neurophysiological and behavioral consequences of deprivation (Table 30-4). First, perma-

TABLE 30-4 Comparison of Behavioral and Neurophysiological Information on Visually Deprived Cats

| Deprivation History† | Cat Number in Behavioral Series | Visual Defect‡ in Deprived Eye | Percentage of Cells§ Driven by Deprived Eye |
|---|---|---|---|
| 4 months | 10 | + + + + | 21 (9) from Fig. 9A (same cat) |
| 7 weeks | 19 | + + | 20 (10) from Fig. 8B |
| 5½ weeks | 12 | + | 26 (25) from Fig. 7A (same cat) |
| 5½ weeks | 13 | + | 39 (38) from Fig. 7B (same cat) |
| 3 months starting at 2 months of age | 16 | + | 32 (32) from Fig. 5B |
| 3 months starting at 4 months of age | 18 | 0 | 90 (90) from Fig. 6A (same cat) |
| 4 months starting at 6 months of age | 17 | 0 | 80 (80) from Fig. 6B |
| 3 months then closure of normal eye | 1 | + | 11 (7) from Fig. 9B (same cat) |

† Starting within 2 weeks of birth unless noted otherwise.
‡ From Figure 30-6. Each test in which a cat failed to come under control was scored one + for summarizing the degree of defect.
§ From Hubel and Wiesel [4]; numbers derived from figures of that paper, as indicated. Cells refers to neurones in the visual cortex. The figures in parentheses give the percentage of cells showing normal selectivity among stimuli with different orientations and movements.

nent defects were produced only when an eye was closed during a strictly limited period of susceptibility. Normal kittens do not open their eyes until 1 to 2 weeks after birth, so visual experience is not necessary during that period. Neurophysiological studies indicate that the period of susceptibility begins around the early part of the fourth week. This suggestion accords with our finding that the behavioral defect appeared identical following closure to about 4 months of age beginning either at 1 month of age (cat 15) or shortly after birth (cats 2, 3 and 10). The period of susceptibility ends before a kitten is 4 months old; after that age closure produces neither behavioral nor neurophysiological consequences. Secondly, even within the period, susceptibility was not constant. A 2½

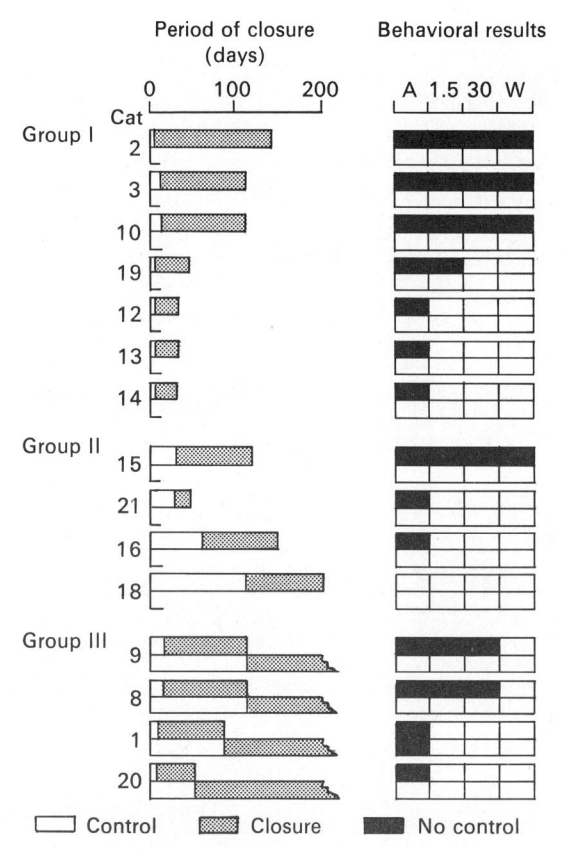

FIGURE 30-6 Graphical summary of results. The deprivation history is shown on the left and the behavioral results on the right. A, acuity test; 1.5, 1.5-mm gap test; 30, 30-mm gap test; W, water barrier test. "Closure" indicates the period the eye was closed. "Control" means significant control of the behavior of the cat by the stimuli of the test. "No control" means, for the water barrier test, failure to complete the test; for the gap tests, more than thirty errors in ninety consecutive trials; for the acuity test, more than ten errors in thirty trials. For each cat, the upper row shows the results for the right eye and the lower row for the left eye.

The purpose of the figure is to provide a general view of the results; for details see Figures 30-1, 30-2, and 30-3. Cats 2 and 3 were studied experimentally only in the 30-mm gap test.

weeks' closure during the second month (cat 21) had an effect equivalent to a 3 months' closure beginning at the end of the second month (cat 16). Again the neurophysiological results are in good agreement, showing that cells in the visual cortex are more resistant to effects of monocular deprivation after the second month. Thirdly, the severity of the permanent defect was graded, depending on the number of days of deprivation during the second and third months after birth, from mere loss of acuity (cats 12, 13 and 14) to complete loss of all visual stimulus control except to stimuli that differed in luminosity (cats 2, 3, 10 and 15). Concordantly it was shown neurophysiologically that during the period of susceptibility, even a few days' deprivation caused marked changes, and that increased duration of deprivation increased the defect [4]. Further, more cortical cells could be driven normally in cats deprived 5½ weeks than in cats deprived 3 to 4 months (compare cats 12 and 13 with cat 10, Table 30-4). Fourth and lastly, closure of the normal eye when the initially closed right eye was opened led to an improvement in the visual control of behavior with the deprived eye. This improvement was not, however, accompanied by any substantial change in the ability of the deprived eye to influence cells in the visual cortex in an acute physiological experiment (compare cats 1 and 10, Table 30-4; see also [13]).

Stimulus control, the constraint of behavior by discriminative stimuli, varies in degree, as is illustrated by the finding that the normal eye always gave better visual control than did the deprived eye (Figure 30-6). Neurophysiological results have been that more cortical neurones can be driven with a normal eye than with a deprived eye. Taken together, these results suggest that the number of cortical cells influenced by an eye determines its power to control vision-dependent behavior. The limiting condition is reached after 3 or 4 months' deprivation when behavior is influenced visually only by light and dark panels and when only a small proportion of cortical neurones are driven normally with the deprived eye (about 10%). The slowly increasing behavioral control with the deprived eye that results from closing the normal eye is most simply ascribed to the persisting cortical neurones driven by the deprived eye being able to acquire control when not chronically masked by the signal from the normal eye: but the possibility that the recovery is mediated through a less damaged noncortical component of the visual system cannot be excluded. In any event we found that once the deprived eye had acquired control it was not lost when the normal eye was reopened. Indeed, the behavioral control with the deprived eye could continue to improve after the normal eye was reopened, as in cat 1. When the deprivation effect was initially less, closing the normal eye could improve the control of the deprived eye even to the verge of the normal eye range (compare cats 19 and 20).

If the improvement in behavioral control exerted by the deprived eye when the normal eye is closed is based mainly on those neurones that persisted in their responsiveness to the deprived eye through the period of closure, it might be expected that closure of the normal eye at any time in life would result in improved visual control with the deprived eye. Preliminary observations have been made in cat 15, which showed control only by the contrast between the lighted and unlighted panels with its deprived eye up to more than a year of age. When the normal eye was then closed, within a few weeks the cat was crossing the water barrier for the first time in its life with only its deprived eye open. It appears, then, that the processes involved in recovery following reversal of eye closure are entirely different in nature from the processes maintaining functional integrity under normal circumstances through the sensitive period of the first months of life; behavioral recovery resulting from reversal can probably take place at any time in the life of the cat and is not accompanied by parallel changes in responsivity of cortical neurones.

With their normal eyes, cats were controlled by a stimulus attribute, the 1.5-mm gap in the lines, subtending a visual angle of about 10 min of arc. The object of the tests was to identify differences between normal and deprived eyes, and not to explore systematically to find the optimum stimulus configuration, level of illumination, and viewing distance for maximum visual acuity. Nevertheless, the figure of 10 min of arc agrees reasonably with the 5.5 min of arc reported by Smith [8] for a comparable "2-point" type of stimulus. Single line stimuli could exert control even when they subtended visual angles of less than 2 min of arc [8], a finding which agrees with assessment based on optokinetic responses [1]. Smith [8] remarks that "visual acuity" as measured by single lines is approximately five times more precise than when determined by the separation of two lines.

Several authors have considered the possibility of defects in visual control of movement, distinct from loss of acuity, following visual deprivation (5, 7; see review [3]). The water barrier test required visual control of paw placement but made only modest demands on visual acuity. The test was a semiautomated development of Hein and Held's prong test [2]. The differences in control with normal and deprived eyes were consistently less in the water barrier test than in the gap test. Failures in the water barrier test occurred only when the loss of acuity was gross enough to account for the incapacity. In addition, even cats which failed the gap and water barrier tests had no difficulty in guiding themselves toward the brighter of two lighted panels. Thus our results give no evidence of a persisting defect in visual-motor control following deprivation. Transient defects in visual guidance as described by Hein and Held [2] are clearly different in nature from the permanent defects in acuity found in our cats.

The partial recovery from the effects of deprivation should not be allowed to obscure the essentially permanent nature of changes in the visual system when deprivation occurs during the period of susceptibility. The effects of 2 weeks' deprivation were easily detectable behaviorally many months later and would probably continue for the life of the cat. Even after as short a period of deprivation as 3 days, the visual system shows anatomical and physiological changes [4] that may have permanent sequels. The findings suggest that, clinically, every effort should be made to avoid the interference with normal visual experience in early life which would result from covering an eye for treatment of infection or other pathology.

Finally, the studies on eye reversal suggest that some recovery in visual function after treatment of older children may not signify improvement in the primary visual pathways up to and including the striate cortex, but only the better exploitation of visual information already influencing cortical neurones.

## REFERENCES

1. L. Ganz and M. Fitch. The effect of visual deprivation on perceptual behavior. *Exp. Neurol.*, 1968, *22*, 638–660.
2. A. Hein and R. Held. Dissociation of the visual placing response into elicited and guided components. *Science*, 1967, *158*, 390–392.
3. R. Held. Dissociation of visual functions by deprivation and rearrangement. *Psychol. Forsch.*, 1967, *31*, 338–348.
4. D. H. Hubel and T. N. Wiesel (1970). The period of susceptibility to the physiological effects of unilateral eye closure in kittens. *J. Physiol.*, 1970, *206*, 419–436.
5. B. Meyers and R. A. McCleary. Interocular transfer of a pattern discrimination in pattern deprived cats. *J. comp. physiol. Psychol.*, 1964, *57*, 16–21.
6. A. H. Riesen. Sensory deprivation. In E. Stellar and J. M. Sprague (eds.). *Progress in physiological psychology.* New York: Academic Press, 1966. Vol. I, pp. 117–147.
7. A. H. Riesen, M. I. Kurke, and J. C. Mellinger. Interocular transfer of habits learned monocularly in visually naive and visually experienced cats. *J. comp. physiol. Phychol.*, 1953, *46*, 166–172.
8. K. U. Smith. Visual discrimination in the cat: IV. The visual acuity of the cat in relation to stimulus distance. *J. genet. Psychol.*, 1936, *49*, 297–313.
9. M. von Senden. *Space and sight: The perception of space and shape in the congenitally blind before and after operation.* Glencoe, Ill.: Free Press, 1960.
10. T. N. Wiesel and D. H. Hubel. Effects of visual deprivation on morphology and physiology of cells in the cat's lateral geniculate body. *J. Neurophysiol.*, 1963, *26*, 978–993.
11. T. N. Wiesel and D. H. Hubel. Single-cell responses in striate cortex of kittens deprived of vision in one eye. *J. Neurophysiol.*, 1963, *26*, 1003–1017.
12. T. N. Wiesel and D. H. Hubel. Comparison of the effects of unilateral and bilateral eye closure on cortical unit responses in kittens. *J. Neurophysiol.*, 1965, *28*, 1029–1040.
13. T. N. Wiesel and D. H. Hubel. Extent of recovery from the effects of visual deprivation in kittens. *J. Neurophysiol.*, 1965, *28*, 1060–1072.

## 31

# VISUAL EXPERIENCE MODIFIES DISTRIBUTION OF HORIZONTALLY AND VERTICALLY ORIENTED RECEPTIVE FIELDS IN CATS

H. V. B. Hirsch
D. N. Spinelli

Cats were raised from birth with one eye viewing horizontal lines and one eye viewing vertical lines. Elongated receptive fields of cells in the visual cortex were horizontally or vertically oriented—no oblique fields were found. Units with horizontal fields were activated only by the eye exposed to horizontal lines; units with vertical fields only by the eye exposed to vertical lines.

Many investigators have studied the response characteristics of single cells in the visual system in an effort to understand the neural mechanisms of perception [1, 2, 4, 6, 17]. In the visual cortex of the cat and the monkey, there are units with elongated receptive fields which respond vigorously to elongated stimuli of the same orientation as the receptive field [2, 6, 9, 17]. It is frequently assumed that such units are important in the perception of form [6, 10], but no direct test of this hypothesis has been made.[1] Ideally, one might remove all cortical units with receptive fields of a given orientation and observe the subject's visual capabilities. This would require ablation of cells on a physiological rather than an anatomical basis.

We have developed a technique for rearing kittens which results in all

---

Source: *Science*, 1970, *168*, 869–871. Copyright 1970 by the American Association for the Advancement of Science.
Note: We thank C. R. Hamilton for help and advice as the senior author's thesis adviser. Senior author supported by NIMH predoctoral fellowship 2–F1–MH–29–103. Support provided by PHS Grants NB–06501 and MH–12970. B. Bridgman and R. Phelps assisted with the electrophysiological recording.

[1] The following are examples of indirect tests of this hypothesis: [3, 14, 19, 20].

of the elongated receptive fields being oriented either vertically or horizontally, in contrast to the random arrangement present in normal cats.[2] Moreover, the units with horizontal fields respond only to stimulation of one eye, and the units with vertical fields respond only to stimulation of the other eye. Therefore, it should be possible to test the behavioral function of either class of cells by simply occluding one eye or the other.

We controlled the visual experience of kittens from birth until 10 to 12 weeks of age. Each animal's total visual experience consisted of viewing a white field containing three black vertical lines with one eye and, simultaneously viewing a field containing three horizontal lines with the other eye. The lines were 1° wide and their center points were 6° apart. These conditions were used in order to produce discordant sensory input to the binocularly activated cortical cells.

The stimuli were mounted in a mask which provided a 50° to 60° field of view for each eye. Beginning at 3 weeks of age the animals wore these devices for approximately 8 hr a day. Masks were put on and removed inside a darkroom in which the animals were housed from birth whenever they were not wearing the masks. Each set of lines in the mask was positioned at the focal plane of a lens so that small changes in the position of the mask would not affect the sharpness of focus. The kittens soon became accustomed to the masks and were active and playful during the exposure periods. To insure that the animals could not pull or rub the masks off they wore a large neck ruff similar to that used by Hein and Held [5]. The animals were checked repeatedly while they were wearing the masks. We estimate that slippage of the mask did not exceed 10° and in most cases was less than 5°; eye movements were not measured during exposure periods. It is clear from the positive results obtained that any rotations of the eyes or the mask did not interfere with the aim of the experiment.

Single unit recordings were made from the visual cortex of these animals between 10 and 12 weeks of age. We used the preparation, recording, and mapping technique developed by Spinelli [16]. In brief, thiopental sodium was injected intravenously to obtain general anesthesia and a small opening was made in the skin, bone, and dura above the visual cortex in one hemisphere. Subsequently the animal was paralyzed with Flaxedil, artificially ventilated, and held in a stereotaxic instrument. All pressure points and incisions were infiltrated with a long-acting local anesthetic (Zyljectin). The cat was positioned at 57 cm from a white tangent screen; at this distance 1 cm on the screen is equal to 1° of arc at the eye. Contact lenses were used to correct for accommodation and to

---

[2] [6]. More recent data [13] would suggest that near the visual axis vertically and horizontally oriented receptive fields may be more common than obliquely oriented receptive fields. Our observations on normal adult cats [15] would indicate that whereas there is such a preference, its magnitude may be relatively small.

protect the cornea of the eye. The projection of the optic disk onto the screen was determined with a reversible ophthalmoscope, and the position of the area centralis was inferred [18]. The estimated projections of the area centralis were centered at or near the top of the mapped region in four animals and about 5° above in the remaining animal. The units were recorded from primary visual cortex between stereotaxic coordinates anterior-posterior −1.0 to +1.0 mm and medial-lateral 0.5 to 1.5 mm. In adult cats this corresponds to the region that receives projections from the area centralis [12].

The response of single units to a black spot (1° to 4° in diameter) moving across the white background was recorded with tungsten microelectrodes. We used spots rather than line stimuli in mapping because this method should reveal the shape of the receptive field with the least bias [17]. Elongated receptive fields of single units in the visual cortex of the cat have been mapped with stationary [6] and moving [17] spots. The responsiveness to line stimuli can be predicted from maps made with spots, at least for units which have discrete excitatory and inhibitory regions within the receptive field [17]; simple cells [6] and perhaps for other types of units (for example, complex cells, diffuse cells [17]).

The spot was moved by a computer (Digital Equipment Corp., PDP-8) across a 25° × 25° field. The unit's activity was recorded at each of 2,500 points within this field and presented on an oscilloscope screen as an integral contour display. In this manner the shape of the receptive field could be visualized. All units encountered during the recording were analyzed and whenever possible each was mapped at least twelve times. The mapping was first done with both eyes open and then for each eye separately. Two vertical and two horizontal maps were made for each of these conditions. During a vertical map, for example, the spot was moved with constant speed of 10 deg/sec from bottom to top and top to bottom; fifty such scans covered the field. Data were collected separately for upward and downward motion of the spot to provide the two vertical maps. Horizontal maps were also obtained in this fashion.

Currently, a total of fifty units from five animals have been mapped in detail. Receptive fields of all units were in the lower half of the visual field. All maps were examined, but categorization of the units was based largely on the receptive field map obtained with the spot moving in the direction which elicited the strongest response from the unit [17]. Units encountered during the recording were classified as either diffuse or elongated. Diffuse receptive fields have no clearly defined boundaries, and the units responded to stimulation over a wide portion of the visual field. Twenty-seven units were of this type [Figure 31-1].

Receptive fields from twenty-three units were categorized as elongated. Their shapes ranged from somewhat elliptic to clearly edge- or bar-shaped in correspondence with elongated receptive fields described by others. Whereas normal kittens have a full complement of receptive field orientations at birth [7], all of the elongated fields found in our animals

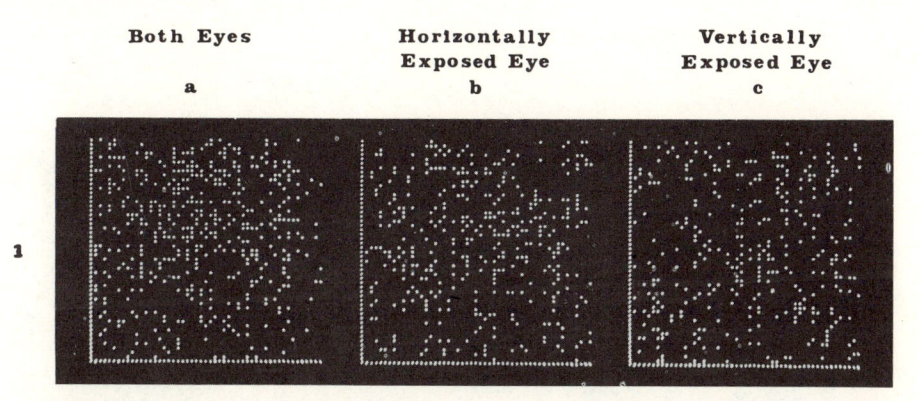

FIGURE 31-1 Cortical unit with diffuse receptive field. (Column a) Unit mapped with both eyes open. (b) Eye exposed to horizontal lines was left open. (c) Eye exposed to vertical lines was left open. The spot moved vertically during the mapping.

were oriented either vertically or horizontally [Figure 31-2]. Since diagonally oriented receptive fields have been mapped in normal animals with our recording procedure (Figure 7 in [17]), their absence here is not an artifact.

Three characteristics of these elongated receptive fields are striking when compared to elongated receptive fields found in normal cats. First, twenty-one of the twenty-three units with elongated receptive fields were predominantly or exclusively activated by only one eye, whereas normally only 10% to 20% of the units in the visual cortex of the cat respond to just one eye [6, 17]. The discordant stimulation of the two eyes might have produced this loss in binocularity [8]. The remaining two units were lost before we could determine whether they were also monocular. Second, a particular eye could activate cortical units with receptive fields of only one orientation, either vertical or horizontal, although in the normal cat receptive fields of all orientations can be activated by both eyes. Furthermore, in twenty of these twenty-one monocular units, the receptive field orientation corresponded to the orientation of the lines to which the eye that activated the unit had been exposed during rearing. Figure 31-2, rows 3 and 4, for example, shows elongated receptive fields recorded from two units found in the same cat—one unit was activated only by the eye exposed to horizontal lines, and the other only by the eye exposed to vertical lines. Third, some of the elongated receptive fields were considerably larger than those present in normal cats [6, 17].

The change in the distribution of orientations of cortical unit receptive fields that we found when kittens were raised with both eyes viewing different patterns demonstrates that functional neural connections can be selectively and predictably modified by environmental stimulation. Whether the discordant stimulation is a necessary condition is not known. A final aspect of our technique is that we succeeded in reviving our

336   PERCEPTUAL DEVELOPMENT

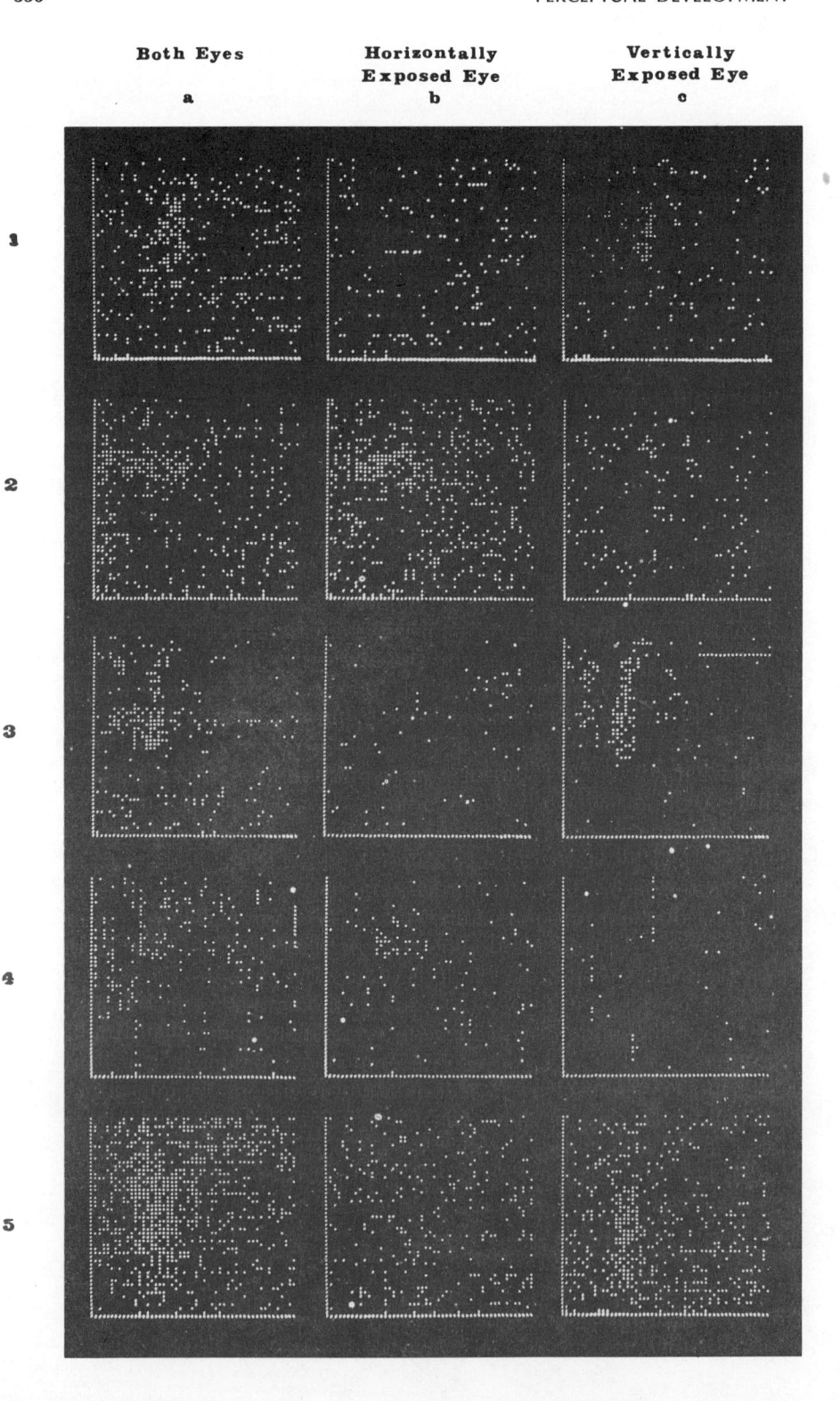

|   | Both Eyes<br>a | Horizontally<br>Exposed Eye<br>b | Vertically<br>Exposed Eye<br>c |
|---|---|---|---|
| 1 | | | |
| 2 | | | |
| 3 | | | |
| 4 | | | |
| 5 | | | |

animals after the electrophysiological recording. Therefore, we can test the performance of these same cats in the discrimination of patterns and determine the behavioral effects of the physiological manipulation.

## REFERENCES

1. H. B. Barlow, R. M. Hill, and W. R. Levick. Retinal ganglion cells responding selectively to direction and speed of image motion in the rabbit. *J. Physiol., London,* 1964, *173,* 377–407.
2. G. Baumgartner, J. L. Brown, and A. Schulz. Responses of single units of the cat visual system to rectangular stimulus patterns. *Neurophysiology,* 1965, *28,* 1–18.
3. L. Ganz and M. Fitch. The effect of visual deprivation on perceptual behavior. *Exp. Neurol.,* 1968, *22,* 638–660.
4. H. K. Hartline and F. Ratliff. Spatial summation of inhibitory influences in the eye of Limulus and the mutual interaction of receptor units. *J. gen. physiol.,* 1958, *41,* 1049–1066.
5. A. Hein and R. Held. Dissociation of the visual placing response into elicited and guided components. *Science,* 1967, *158,* 390–392.
6. D. H. Hubel and T. N. Wiesel. Receptive fields, binocular interaction, and functional architecture in the cat's visual cortex. *J. Physiol., London,* 1962, *160,* 106–154.
7. D. H. Hubel and T. N. Wiesel. Receptive fields of cells in striate cortex of very young, visually inexperienced kittens. *J. Neurophysiol.,* 1963, *26,* 994–1002.
8. D. H. Hubel and T. N. Wiesel. Binocular interaction in striate cortex of kittens reared with artificial squint. *J. Neurophysiol.,* 1965, *28,* 1041–1059.
9. D. H. Hubel and T. N. Wiesel. Receptive fields and functional architecture of monkey striate cortex. *J. Physiol., London,* 1968, *195,* 215–243.

←

FIGURE 31-2 Cortical units with elongated receptive fields. Rows 1 to 5 illustrate integral contour displays of receptive fields of five units. (Column a) The units are mapped with both eyes open. (b) Units mapped with only the eye exposed to horizontal lines open. (c) Units mapped with only the eye exposed to vertical lines open.

Rows 3 and 4 illustrate receptive fields from two units found in the same cat. Note that all receptive fields are elongated, that the units are activated by only one eye, and that the orientation of the receptive fields is identical to the orientation of the lines to which that eye was exposed during development. The unit illustrated in row 4 has one of the most poorly defined receptive fields found when mapped with both eyes open. It should, however, be noted that the receptive field is well defined when mapped with the horizontally exposed eye open (4b), whereas it is completely absent when mapped with the vertically exposed eye open (4c). During mapping the spot moved horizontally in rows 1, 3, and 5 and vertically in rows 2 and 4.

10. D. M. MacKay. Ways of looking at perception. In W. Walthen-Dunn (ed.). *Models for the perception of speech and visual form.* Cambridge, Mass.: MIT Press, 1967. Pp. 25–43.
11. W. R. A. Muntz. Mechanisms of visual form recognition in animals. In W. Walthen-Dunn (ed.). *Models for the perception of speech and visual form.* Cambridge, Mass.: MIT Press, 1967. Pp. 126–135.
12. R. Otsuka and R. Hassler. Über Aufbau und Gliederung der corticalen Sehsphäre bei der Katze. *Arch. Psychiat.,* 1962, *203,* 212–234.
13. J. D. Pettigrew, T. Nikara, and P. O. Bishop. Responses to moving slits in cat striate cortex. *Exp. Brain Res.,* 1968, *6,* 373–390.
14. R. W. Sekuler, E. L. Rubin, and W. H. Cushman. Selectivities of human visual mechanisms for direction of movement and contour orientation. *J. opt. Soc. Amer.,* 1968, *58,* 1146–1150.
15. D. N. Spinelli. Unpublished data.
16. D. N. Spinelli. Receptive field organization of ganglion cells in the cat's retina. *Exp. Neurol.,* 1967, *19,* 291–315.
17. D. N. Spinelli and T. W. Barrett. Visual receptive field organization of single units in the cat's visual cortex. *Exp. Neurol.,* 1969, *24,* 76–98.
18. G. J. Vakkur, P. O. Bishop, and W. Kozak. Visual optics in the cat, including posterior nodal distance and retinal landmarks. *Vision Res.,* 1963, *3,* 289–314.
19. T. N. Wiesel and D. H. Hubel. Single cell responses in striate cortex of kittens deprived of vision in one eye. *J. Neurophysiol.,* 1963, *26,* 1003–1017.
20. T. N. Wiesel and D. H. Hubel. Comparison of the effects of unilateral and bilateral eye closure on cortical unit responses in kittens. *J. Neurophysiol.,* 1965, *28,* 1029–1040.

# 32

# ADVANTAGE OF EARLY OVER LATE PERCEPTUAL EXPERIENCE IN IMPROVING FORM DISCRIMINATION

### Ronald H. Forgus

This study was undertaken to discover whether visual experience with specific forms will have different effects depending on the age at which it occurs. Interest in transfer of training has been re-

Source: *Canadian Journal of Psychology,* 1956, *10,* 147–155.
Note: This investigation was supported, in part, by a grant from the committee for the advancement of research at the University of Pennsylvania. The author wishes to thank his colleagues, Drs. Francis W. Irwin and Morris S. Viteles, for suggestions which materially improved the study.

vived by a renewal of research on the effects of early experience; this was largely stimulated by Hebb's [5] emphasis on the positive effects of abundant early experience. Previous studies by the present writer [3] have further suggested that the amount of transfer depends, not only on the amount of early experience but also on other factors such as the relationships between the experience and the transfer task.

Hebb has also argued that a complete theory of learning must account for the generalized effects of transfer from infant experiences, as shown in two experiments reported by him. One study found that rats with "richer" early experience had superior intelligence; the other found that late-blinded rats were superior to early-blinded rats in problem-solving ability. From the combined results of these and other studies he infers that the transfer effects of infant experience are more permanent, generalized, and important than those of adult experience [5, p. 229]. This conclusion is apparently supported by the inferiority in pattern perception of chimpanzees [7] and rats [4] reared in darkness, and of congenitally blind humans given vision at adulthood [5, pp. 31–35].

Certain questions need answering, however, before this interpretation can be fully accepted. In the first place, Hymovitch [6] did not find differences in problem solving between late- and early-blinded rats. Secondly, and more important, we cannot confidently conclude that infant experience is more important than adult experience even if we accept the evidence reported by Hebb, for in these studies the adult animals did not have experiences comparable to those of the infant group. That is, the rats blinded in infancy had no adult visual experience comparable with the infant visual experience of the late-blinded group, since the former were blind for the rest of their lives. In order to conclude that infant experience is more effective than adult experience, we must compare the performance of a group which had specific experiences during infancy with that of a group which had like experiences during adulthood. The present study was designed to permit such a comparison, and thus put Hebb's proposition to a more adequate test. Specifically, the following hypothesis was tested: *A group of rats having perceptual experience with specific two-dimensional forms during infancy will be superior in form discrimination to another group of rats having comparable experience during later life.*

## GENERAL DESIGN

To test the hypothesis four groups were used in a two-factor design. Group EF was given the specific training during early life; Group LF was given the training during later life. Groups EC and LC were the controls for Groups EF and LF, respectively, and did not receive the specific training. The experimental groups were tested at different ages, so that the delay between the end of the form experience and testing would be the same for each; hence two control groups were used.

## Rearing

Four groups of hooded rats were reared under different conditions from birth until they were tested. There were eleven rats in each group. All animals were reared in metal-walled cages 15 in. long, 9 in. wide, and 9 in. high. The top was made of ½-in. hardware cloth, and the floor of ¼-in. hardware cloth. All animals were thus unable to look at forms outside their cages, since the only openings were at the top and bottom where there were no forms. The rats, born in the psychological laboratory of the University of Pennsylvania, were all offspring of pregnant females received from the Rockland county farm in New York.

Group EF constituted the early form group. These animals, the offspring of one mother, were born in one of the cages described above. However, the cage was modified so that the animals were exposed to specific two-dimensional visual forms from the moment their eyes opened. This was done by making two grooves and inserting a transparent plastic sheet near the two short ends of the cage. The specific forms were placed between the plastic and the metal wall so that the animals could see the forms without touching them. Each plastic sheet, 8½ in. wide, 9½ in. high, and ⅛ in. thick, was located 3/16 in. from the end of the wall. The forms, approximately 3 in. high, were painted white on black cardboard 4½ in. wide, 4½ in. high, and 1/16 in. thick. Four different forms were exposed. A triangle and a cross were located side by side at one end of the cage. The other end contained a circle and a square side by side. (Form discrimination between circle and square was not tested, since the experiment took too long.) The cards were periodically moved and rotated so that the animals saw each figure at each of the two ends and also in different spatial orientations.

Although the forms were in the cages from birth onwards, the visual experience of the rats did not begin until their eyes opened when they were 16 days old. They received this visual experience for 25 days until they were 41 days old.

When the animals were weaned at 21 days old, each was transferred to a single cage, identical with the one in which it was born, and reared individually for the rest of its life.

It should be pointed out that the litter comprising the early form group was not split into components of the other three groups, since we wanted the early form group to have the visual form experience from the time when their eyes first opened, when they were too young to be weaned. However, the split-litter technique was used in forming the other three groups, so we have a fairly adequate control of genetic backgrounds.

The other three groups were split from the offspring of three pregnant females. Each litter was born in a cage identical to that housing Group EF, except that the specific two-dimensional forms were absent.

The three litters were weaned at 21 days and split into the three groups. Each rat was then reared individually until the end of the experiment.

Group LF, the late form group, were reared without the visual forms in their cages until they were 41 days old. From this date, however, the forms were inserted in their cages and remained there for 25 days, until the animals were 66 days old. These animals thus received experience with specific two-dimensional forms similar to that received by Group EF, except that it came later during their life span.

Group EC, the early control group, were reared like Group EF but never exposed to the forms.

Group LC, the late control group, were reared like Group LF but never exposed to the forms.

There were seven males and four females in Group EF, while each of the other three groups contained six males and five females.

The four groups were treated alike in all other respects. Each cage had good illumination, provided by standard fluorescent lamps located above the racks containing the cages, and by daylight coming through the windows of the laboratory. The lights were turned off at night. The animals were never deprived of water during the rearing period. One water bottle, filled daily, was located on the side of each cage. The diet consisted of Purina Dog Chow pellets and lettuce, placed in the cage. One side of the cage contained a metal door for transferring food and rats. All animals were momentarily handled once a week when the cages were cleaned.

## Procedure

The testing procedure for Group EF and Group EC began when the rats were 41 days old, whereas the testing procedure for Group LF and Group LC began when they were 66 days old.

The animals were first placed on a 23-hr food deprivation schedule for 3 days. At the end of each day they were fed Purina Dog Chow and lettuce for one hour. At the end of this 3-day period the form-discrimination training began.

A four-unit visual-discrimination apparatus, similar to one described earlier [2, p. 333] was used, except that the alleys were closed and that the rat was mildly shocked if it chose the incorrect alley.

A floor plan of one unit of the maze is presented in Figure 32-1.

The maze was built of ½-in. pine wood painted a flat black and was elevated 3 ft from the ground. The alleys were closed off from the surroundings by walls 5 in. high. The top of the maze consisted of removable sections made of ½-in. wire mesh. The swinging doors were 6 in. long and 4 in. high and contained the black discrimination cards. These were 5½ in. long, 4 in. high, with white forms 3 in. high, painted on them. A starting box 6 in. wide, 4 in. high, and 8 in. long fitted into the first discrimination unit, which was like the one shown in Figure 32-1. This was followed by three more discrimination units, making four in all. The last unit led directly to the goal box, which had the same dimensions as the starting box. Each discrimination unit was wired so that the incorrect alley could be electrically charged by throwing a knife switch.

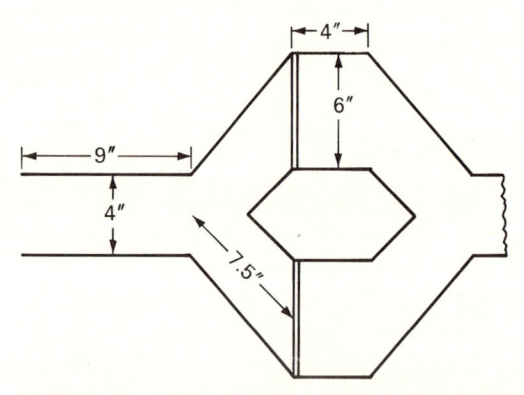

FIGURE 32-1 Floor plan of one unit of the discrimination apparatus. The solid double lines indicate the positions of the swinging doors which contained the discrimination cards.

The animals received 4 days of preliminary training on this maze. They were always trained after having been deprived of food for 23 hr. During the first 3 days the animals were trained merely to push through the light-metal swinging doors. There were no forms on the doors and no shock was given. The animal was placed in the starting box and could choose any alley, since both swinging doors were unlocked. If the animal hesitated at the doorway, the experimenter helped it by partially pushing the door open. Each animal received one daily trial of pushing through the doors of all four units before it was rewarded with Purina Dog Chow in the goal box. At the end of each daily trial it was fed for 1 hr. On the fourth day the discrimination cards were inserted on the swinging doors. In each discrimination unit one door contained an upright triangle; the other door contained an upright cross. The door containing the triangle, which was positive, was unlocked, whereas the one containing the cross, which was negative, was locked. However, the animal was not shocked for an incorrect choice but was permitted to correct itself and go to the next unit. After the last choice it was rewarded and fed for an hour.

After this preliminary training the following two discrimination tests were carried out using the same apparatus. In both tests each animal was given one trial per day after 23-hr food deprivation, was rewarded with a Purina Dog Chow pellet in the goal box, and then fed for 1 hr.

## Form Discrimination

The animal was required to discriminate between the upright triangle, which was positive, and the upright cross, which was negative. The forms were identical with the ones which had been located in the living cages of the experimental group. The rat was placed in the starting box and ran to the bifurcation from which it was to make its choice. If it chose the triangle, it could push through the one-way swinging door quite easily. If it chose the cross it was shocked, and also found the door locked. There were four possible errors in one trial. The correction method was used and backtracking was not scored an error. The left-right positions of the positive and negative forms were randomized according to a predetermined sequence. The criterion of learning was two consecutive errorless trials, that is, eight consecutive correct choices. Time scores were also recorded from trial 5 onwards.

## Form Generalization

After each animal had reached the form discrimination criterion the forms were rotated clockwise through 90°. The number of errors each rat made in ten trials was recorded.

## RESULTS

Because the results of the two tests exhibited similar trends they are presented together. Table 32-1 shows the mean number of errors for each group on each test; Table 32-2 shows the $p$ values obtained when the major differences between groups were tested for significance by $t$ ratios.

These tables show that (a) the animals with specific visual experi-

TABLE 32-1 Means and Standard Deviations for the Four Groups on Form-Discrimination and Generalization Tests Form

| Group | Form Discrimination Trials | SD | Form Generalization Errors | SD |
|---|---|---|---|---|
| EF | 33.8 | 4.2 | 4.7 | 2.0 |
| LF | 39.4 | 5.9 | 11.1 | 1.7 |
| EC | 48.2 | 3.5 | 19.7 | 3.2 |
| LC | 46.5 | 5.9 | 19.6 | 3.4 |

TABLE 32-2  Significance (t test) of Differences Between Groups in Form Discrimination and Form Generalization

| Groups Compared | Form Discrimination | Form Generalization |
|---|---|---|
| EF vs. EC | < 0.001 | < 0.001 |
| LF vs. LC | < 0.01 | < 0.001 |
| EF vs. LF | < 0.05 | < 0.001 |
| EC vs. LC | > 0.1 | > 0.1 |

ence (experimental groups) were superior in form discrimination and generalization to the animals without this experience (controls); and (b) the animals with earlier visual experience (group EF) were superior to those having the experience later (group LF). The interaction between age and experience suggested by the latter finding was tested for significance by a double-classification analysis of variance. The F ratio obtained for interaction was 5.21, which is significant ($p < 0.05$).

It will be noted that the experimental groups exhibited good form generalization whereas the control groups did not. This is in agreement with the author's previous finding [2] that form generalization as well as form discrimination can be improved by early perceptual experience. These results are interesting, since Fields' [1] adult rats showed form generalization only after special and prolonged training.

It is also clear from the scores of groups EC and LC that age of testing did not significantly affect the performance of the rats on the two tests used in this study.

The age at which the animals were tested did, however, make a difference in their speed of running, as can be seen from the graph in Figure 32-2.

Running times for the first four trials were very long and are not shown; the graph shows running times for the remaining discrimination trials during which every rat was still being tested. It can be seen that there was no difference in the running times of the two older groups (LF and LC), and that the older rats were much faster runners than the younger during the early part of the testing procedure. However, the early experimental group improved rapidly and were running as fast as the older rats by trial 18, whereas the early control group was still much slower even at trial 27.

## DISCUSSION

We may conclude that rats who have perceptual experience with specific two-dimensional forms are superior in discrimination and form

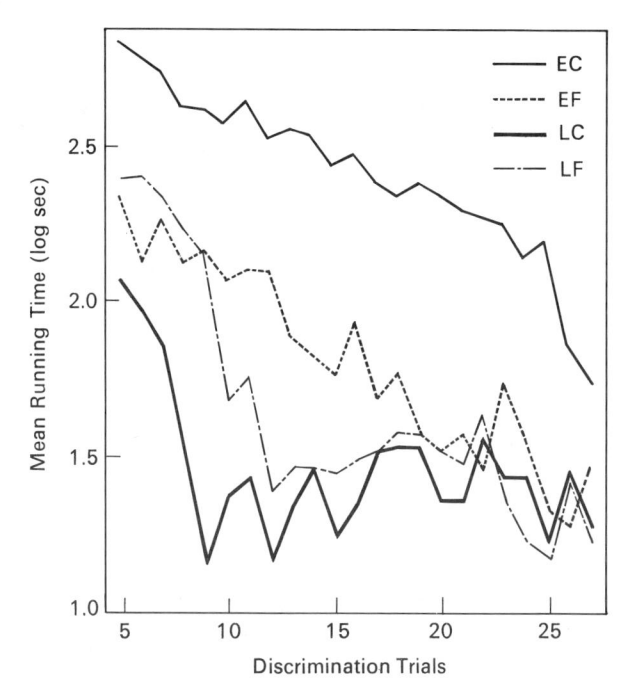

FIGURE 32-2  Mean running time per trial for each of the four groups between trial 5 and trial 27.

generalization (of those forms) to rats who do not have such experience. Moreover, the specific hypothesis we set out to test has also been confirmed: rats who have this experience during infancy are superior in form discrimination and generalization to rats who have this experience in later life. This is in agreement with Hebb's position.

Confirmation of the hypothesis might conceivably be questioned because of the fact that the early form group was tested at 41 days of age, whereas the late form group was tested at 66 days. It has already been shown, however, that age at testing made no difference in discrimination or generalization; the two control groups performed similarly, except as regards running speed. Whether the early form group would still have been superior if these animals had also been tested at 66 days of age is a question of retention which the present experiment was not designed to answer. A study might well be done along such lines to test the permanence of the effects, but for comparing the effects of early and late experience on form discrimination learning the present design seemed the most adequate.

Why learning is more effective when it occurs earlier in life is problematic; Hebb [5] has offered a neurological explanation. He suggests that infant learning produces changes in the central nervous system, particularly in the cerebral cortex, which permanently influence the course of later learning, whereas learning occurring later, when cortical organization is relatively complete, has less marked effects.

The present experiment, which varied the time of experience without destroying receptors or the central nervous system, shows that Hebb's psychological theory can be adequately tested on the psychological level, without specific reference to the underlying neurological conditions.

Whatever these may be, it appears that the development of form perception, which is one of the important bases of cognitive development, is a continuous process, at least in the early years of life. That is, the nature of early experience with form determines the effectiveness of later experience in such a manner that later training may be less effective if certain important experiences are meager or lacking during infancy. Whether early ages are crucial in the sense that the specific learning will only occur during that age period, or whether they are crucial because the early learning is a base for what comes later, is an open question to be answered experimentally; such research is being planned.

The above relationship may have some bearing on the concept of psychological readiness as used in education, that is, the notion that training of any kind will be most effective if it is initiated when the organism is maturationally ready for it, rather than earlier or later. The present results suggest that the hooded rat might be ready for visual form experience soon after its eyes open, and that delay makes such experience less effective as a basis for form discrimination and generalization. Just when the organism is ready for other types of experience can best be answered by empirical studies on a variety of species. Many more experiments will be needed to determine the precise nature of the age-experience interaction for other cognitive, and also emotional, experiences.

Finally, we have the fact that the younger animals ran much more slowly than the older animals during the early stages of the discrimination test. Observation suggested that the reason for this longer running time was that the younger animals hesitated longer and more frequently at the discrimination doors, as if they were more afraid of pushing through them, and they appeared, in general, more timid than the older rats. The early form-experienced group, however, quickly adjusted to the situation and ultimately ran as fast as the older groups, whereas the early control group did not. If the assumption of greater fear in the younger rats is accepted, one might suggest that the presence of familiar forms on the discrimination doors led to more rapid emotional adaptation in the form-experienced group than in the young control group, with consequent more rapid increase in running speed.

Lest it be argued that the entire results could be explained in "emotional" terms, let us hasten to point out that there appeared to be little relationship between error scores and time scores; for example, there was a significant difference between the two older groups in errors but not in running times.

## SUMMARY

This study tested the hypothesis that rats which had perceptual experience with specific two-dimensional forms during infancy would be superior in form discrimination to rats having comparable experience during later life.

One group of animals was exposed to triangles, crosses, circles, and squares from the age of 16 days to the age of 41 days. Another group received the same training between the age of 41 days and 66 days. Two control groups, receiving no visual training, were used. All animals were then tested for visual form discrimination and form generalization of a triangle and cross.

The results indicated that both form-experienced groups were superior to the control groups, and that the early experienced group was superior to the late experienced group. The findings are discussed with respect to Hebb's theory and to the general problem of cognitive and emotional development.

## REFERENCES

1. P. E. Fields. Studies in concept formation: I. The development of the concept of triangularity by the white rat. *Comp. psychol. Monogr.*, 1932, 9, 1–70.
2. R. H. Forgus. The effect of early perceptual learning on the behavioral organization of adult rats. *J. comp. physiol. Psychol.*, 1954, 47, 331–336.
3. R. H. Forgus. Influence of early experience on maze-learning with and without visual cues. *Canad. J. Psychol.*, 1955, 9, 231–238.
4. D. O. Hebb. The innate organization of visual activity: I. Perception of figures by rats reared in total darkness. *J. genet. Psychol.*, 1937, 51, 101–126.
5. D. O. Hebb. *The organization of behavior.* New York: Wiley, 1949.
6. B. Hymovitch. The effects of experimental variation on problem solving in the rat. *J. comp. physiol. Psychol.*, 1952, 45, 313–326.
7. A. H. Riesen. The development of visual perception in man and chimpanzee. *Science*, 1947, 106, 107–108.

# 33

# MOVEMENT-PRODUCED STIMULATION IN THE DEVELOPMENT OF VISUALLY GUIDED BEHAVIOR

Richard Held
Alan Hein

*Full and exact adaptation to sensory rearrangement in adult human Ss requires movement-produced sensory feedback. Riesen's work suggested that this factor also operates in the development of higher mammals but he proposed that sensory-sensory associations are the prerequisite. To test these alternatives, visual stimulation of the active member (A) of each of 10 pairs of neonatal kittens was allowed to vary with its locomotor movements while equivalent stimulation of the second member (P) resulted from passive motion. Subsequent tests of visually guided paw placement, discrimination on a visual cliff, and the blink response were normal for A but failing in P. When other alternative explanations are excluded, this result extends the conclusions of studies of adult rearrangement to neonatal development.*

Hebb's writing [1] has stirred interest in the effects of exposure to the environment on the development of spatial perception and coordination. The main experimental attack on the problem has used the technique of rearing animals in restricted environments (deprivation) from the time of birth or shortly thereafter. An alternative approach consists in experimentally analyzing the conditions for modifying certain sensorimotor coordinations in adults on the assumption that they are similarly plastic during the entire exposure history of the organism [3, 4, 5]. If this supposition is true, the analysis carried out on adults must also define the kind of contact with the environment required for

Source: *Journal of Comparative and Physiological Psychology*, 1963, 56, 872–876. Copyright 1963 by the American Psychological Association. Reprinted by permission.
Note: This research was supported by a grant from the National Science Foundation.

development. Use of the rearrangement technique for studying plasticity in adult human subjects has yielded results which suggest its complementarity to the procedures of neonatal deprivation [6]. This experiment demonstrates the convergence of the two approaches.

In the human adult, change in stimulation dependent upon the natural movements of the subject has been shown essential to the achievement of full and exact compensation for sensory rearrangements [2, 4, 6, 11]. A suggestive parallel between these findings and those of deprivation studies comes from two experiments on kittens reared under different conditions of deprivation. In one experiment subjects were allowed visual experience in an illuminated and patterned environment only while they were restrained in holders which prevented them from freely moving about [16]. When subsequently tested they showed deficiencies in visually guided behavior compared with their normally reared littermates. Related deficits followed rearing in a second experiment in which subjects were allowed to move about freely in light but with diffusing hoods over their eyes [15]. The exposure factor lacking under both conditions was the variation in visual stimulation produced by the full range of the subject's movement in normal circumstances; a result consistent with our findings.

Riesen has suggested that his deprived subjects showed deficits because they lacked sufficient opportunity for developing sensory-sensory associations in the manner proposed by Hebb [15]—even the patterned surroundings viewed by the holder-restrained subjects may not have provided sufficient variation in visual stimulation for forming the necessary associations. This interpretation agrees with ours in asserting that the variation in visual stimulation accompanying movement is essential for the development of certain coordinations but it omits our qualification that this variation can be effective only when it is concurrent with and systematically dependent upon self-produced movements [3, 5]. The alternative to our interpretation asserts that changes in stimulation irrespective of their relation to self-produced movements are sufficient. To decide between these two alternatives, we reared different sets of kittens from birth under the two implied conditions of exposure and subsequently compared their development. Under one condition stimulation varied as a result of the subjects own locomotion whereas under the other it was equivalently varied by transporting subjects through an equivalent range of motion while they were restrained from locomoting.

## METHOD

### Subjects

Ten pairs of kittens were used, each pair from a different litter.

## Exposure Apparatus and Procedure

The exposure apparatus diagramed in Figure 33-1 was designed to equate the visual stimulation received by each member of a pair of subjects. Stimulation varied with the locomotor movements of the active subject (A in Figure 33-1) but varied with equivalent motion of the passive subject (P). To attain this equivalence, the gross motions of A were mechanically transferred to P. These movements were restricted to rotations around three axes. The radial symmetry of the visible environment made variations in visual stimulation, contingent upon these movements, equal over time for the two subjects.

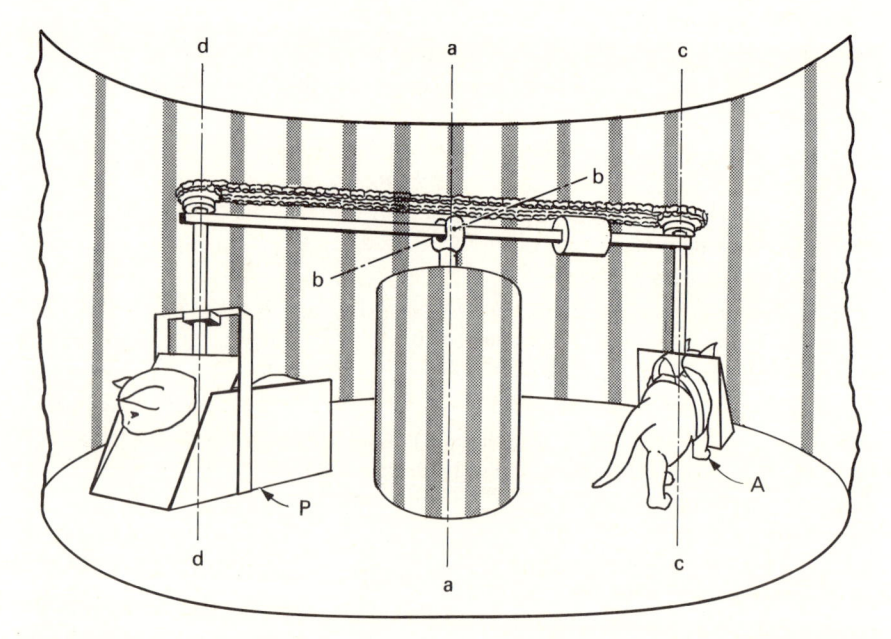

FIGURE 33-1 Apparatus for equating motion and consequent visual feedback for an actively moving (A) and a passively moved (P) subject.

The P was placed in the gondola and held there by a neck yoke and body clamp. The lever from which the gondola was suspended was then balanced by appropriate placement of a counterweight. When attached to the opposite end of the lever by a second neck yoke and body-clamp assembly, A was free to move itself in both directions around the three axes of rotation a-a, b-b, and c-c while pulling P through the equivalent movements around a-a, b-b, and d-d by means of the mechanical linkages to the gondola. The distance between c-c and d-d was 36 in. The range of motions normally performed by subjects was somewhat reduced by the experimental apparatus. Use of ball bearings and aluminum in the construction of the apparatus reduced friction and inertia insofar as possible. The importance of these restraints is mitigated, we believe, by previous findings in rearrangement studies which indicate that similar restraints, and constant changes in the inertia overcome by muscular movement, do not affect the adaptation process [7, 8]. Head motion was not restricted for either A or P. This restriction seemed unnecessary since Riesen and Aarons [16] have shown that kittens reared from birth with variation in visual stimulation consequent upon free head motions, but otherwise restricted, failed to learn a simple spatial discrimination. Because of its constraints, P could not locomote. However, its limbs were free to move and to slide along the smooth floor of the gondola. According to our observations these movements frequently occurred.

The apparatus was surrounded by a galvanized iron cylinder that was 24 in. high with a diameter of 48 in. The lever support mechanism was enclosed within a second cylinder that was 11 in. high with a diameter of 12 in. The smaller cylinder served to obscure each subject's view of its mate. Patterning was provided by vertically oriented 1-in-wide stripes of black and white masking tape separated by 1 in. of bare metal. Additional texture was provided by the rough side of a piece of masonite which served as the floor. The floor was uniform throughout, thus providing equivalent visual stimulation for the two subjects. Sight of the paws and other body parts was excluded by appropriate extensions of the neck stocks.

**Testing Apparatus and Procedure**

We used tests of visually guided behavior that minimized the subject's gross movements in the visible environment in order not to confound the conditions of testing with those of exposure, a confusion which past investigators have generally disregarded. For this purpose responses to stimuli were used that require no conditioning with repetition of movements but which are nonetheless contingent upon a capacity to make visual-spatial discriminations. Following the leads of earlier work, we have used three such tests:

1. Visually guided paw placement [15]. The subject's body was held in the experimenter's hands so that its head and forelegs were free. It was slowly carried forward and downward towards the edge of a table or some other horizontal surface. A normally reared subject shows visually mediated anticipation of contact by extending its paws as it approaches the edge.

2. Avoidance of a visual cliff [18]. The visual cliff consists essentially of a narrow platform supported by vertical sides that drop a few inches to a large plate of glass. The subject placed on the platform can descend to the glass on either one of two sides. Its view on the deep side is through the glass to a patterned surface 30 in. below. On the other side it views a similarly patterned surface attached to the underside of the glass. In our apparatus, both surfaces were illuminated from below and

hence the clean glass surface was practically invisible. For the vertical sides of the platform, we substituted planes inclined 35° from the vertical.

3. Blink to an approaching object [12]. The subject was held in a standing position in a neck yoke and body clamp with a large sheet of Plexiglas positioned directly in front of its face. The experimenter moved his hand quickly toward the subject, stopping just short of contact with the Plexiglas.

Several additional tests were performed to check the status of peripheral receptor and response mechanisms. These included observations of pupillary reflex to light, the tactual placing response, and visual pursuit of a moving object. The subject, held in a standing position in a neck yoke and body clamp, was light-adapted in the normally illuminated laboratory prior to observation of the pupillary reflex. Change in pupillary size was then noted when a light beam from a penlight was moved across the eye from outer to inner canthus. To determine the presence of the tactual paw-placing response the subject was supported as in the visual paw-placing test. It was then carried to the edge of a table where the dorsa of its front paws were brought into contact with the vertical edge of the table. Observations of experimental subjects were compared with those of normals which, in response to this stimulus, place the paws on the horizontal surface of the table. Visual pursuit was elicited by the experimenter's hand moving slowly across the subject's visual field.

## General Procedure

The ten pairs of subjects were divided into two groups, X and Y, whose members were reared with minor differences. Each of the eight pairs of group X was reared in darkness from birth until member A attained the minimal size and coordinational capacity to move itself and its mate in the apparatus. This age varied between 8 and 12 weeks. They then began exposure in the apparatus for 3 hr daily. The two pairs of group Y received 3 hr daily exposure, beginning at 2 and ending at 10 weeks of age, to the patterned interior of the laboratory while restrained in holders that allowed some head movement but prevented locomotion. They then began exposure in the apparatus for 3 hr daily. When not exposed, all subjects were kept in lightless cages together with their mothers and littermates. We had found in pilot studies that subjects reared in this fashion did not show the freezing, agitation, or fear responses reported to follow social isolation by Melzack [10] and Riesen [13].

Six repetitions of the paw-placement test were performed after each daily exposure period for all subjects. On the first day that one subject of each pair in group X displayed visual paw placement, both were tested on the visual cliff. They were retested on the following day. For each test and retest the subject was required to descend from the central platform six times. Immediately following trials on the visual cliff on the second day, member P of each pair was put in a continuously illuminated room for 48 hr. Retesting of visual placing and renewed trials on the visual cliff followed this unrestricted exposure. The testing procedure differed slightly for pairs of group Y. On the first day that A displayed visual paw placing, it was tested on the visual cliff and retested on the following day. However, its mate (P) was not placed on the cliff at this time; instead, the passive exposure procedure was continued for 3 hr daily for a total of 126 hr. The paw-placing and visual cliff tests were then administered to P.

## RESULTS

The principal results of this experiment are summarized in Table 33-1. The amount of time required for the development of a visually guided paw placement in the members of each pair of littermates is indicated in the column under the heading "Exposure in Apparatus." After those periods of exposure required by A, every P mate failed to display the response. Observations suggest a tendency for the placing response to develop in the livelier of the active subjects with fewer hours of exposure than required by the quieter ones. The blink response to an approaching hand developed concurrently with the placing response. Pupillary reflex to light, tactual placing response, and visual pursuit were each noted on first elicitation, just prior to the initial exposure in the apparatus.

TABLE 33-1 Ratio of Descents to Shallow and Deep Sides of Visual Cliff

| Pair Number | Age (Weeks)† | Exposure in Apparatus (hr) A | P | Ratio of Descents Shallow/Deep A | P |
|---|---|---|---|---|---|
| 1X | 8 | 33 | 33 | 12/0 | 6/6 |
| 2X | 8 | 33 | 33 | 12/0 | 4/8 |
| 3X | 8 | 30 | 30 | 12/0 | 7/5 |
| 4X | 9 | 63 | 63 | 12/0 | 6/6 |
| 5X | 10 | 33 | 33 | 12/0 | 7/5 |
| 6X | 10 | 21 | 21 | 12/0 | 7/5 |
| 7X | 12 | 9 | 9 | 12/0 | 5/7 |
| 8X | 12 | 15 | 15 | 12/0 | 8/4 |
| 1Y | 10 | 30 | 126 | 12/0 | 6/6 |
| 2Y | 10 | 33 | 126 | 12/0 | 8/4 |

† At the beginning of exposure in the experimental apparatus.

On the day that the visually guided placing response was shown by A, he was tested on the modified visual cliff. All A's behaved like normally reared subjects which had been observed previously in a pilot experiment. As shown by the totals of Table 33-1, each A descended to the shallow side of the cliff on every trial of the first day and repeated this performance on the trials of the following day. The P members of group X were tested on the cliff on the same days as their actively exposed littermates. They showed no evidence of discriminating the shallow from the deep side. Observations of the P members of group Y on the cliff, after their prolonged passive exposure, gave similar results, and they also failed to perform visual paw placement. Following the 48 hr period of freedom in an illuminated room, the P members of group X were re-tested. They then displayed normal visually guided paw placement and performed all descents to the shallow side of the visual cliff.

## DISCUSSION

The results are consistent with our thesis that self-produced movement with its concurrent visual feedback is necessary for the development of visually guided behavior. Equivalent, and even greatly increased, variation in visual stimulation produced by other means is not sufficient. However, before concluding that our thesis is valid we must consider other alternative explanations of the deficits in the behavioral development of neonates following deprivation. These alternatives assert that loss of function does not reflect deficiencies in a process of the central nervous system that depends upon exposure for its development. Instead, the capacity to perform is allegedly present but prevented from operating by either peripheral blockage or other suppressive effects of the special rearing conditions. Such negative effects fall into two categories: (a) anatomical or physiological deterioration, and (b) behavioral inhibition.

Included under anatomical or physiological deterioration said to result from deprivation, are the findings of atrophy in peripheral parts of the visual nervous system, a literature reviewed by Riesen [14]; the assumption that maturation of the retina is prevented [18]; and the suggestion that general debility results from lack of use of various organs [9]. In the present experiment, the relevance of peripheral atrophy is contraindicated by the presence of pupillary and pursuit reflexes and the rapid recovery of function of the passive subjects once given their freedom. Debility specific to the motor systems of these subjects can be ruled out on the grounds that their tactual placing responses and other motor activities were indistinguishable from those of normals. In addition, differential losses in the periphery or differential debility could hardly be expected to result from those differences between active and passive exposures which occurred in the experimental apparatus.

Inhibition of performance attributable to the effects of shock, fright, or overactivation upon exposure to the novel and increased stimulation that follows release from the deprived state has been suggested by Sutherland [17] and Melzack [10]. Sutherland has also suggested that habits developed during deprivation may compete with and inhibit the normal response. However, both our active and passive subjects were raised under very similar conditions insofar as restriction was concerned and under the rather mild conditions of deprivation of this experiment we did not observe any signs of shock, excitement, or fright. Moreover, the passive subjects were not observed performing responses that might have competed with the expected response.

These findings provide convincing evidence for a developmental process, in at least one higher mammal, which requires for its operation stimulus variation concurrent with and systematically dependent upon self-produced movement. This conclusion neither denies nor affirms that other processes, such as maturation, occur concomitantly. The results demonstrate the complementarity of studies of adult rearrangement and neonatal deprivation.

REFERENCES

1. D. O. Hebb. *The organization of behavior.* New York: Wiley, 1949.
2. A. Hein and R. Held. Minimal conditions essential for complete relearning of hand-eye coordination with prismatic distortion of vision. Paper read at Eastern Psychological Association, Philadelphia, 1958.
3. A. Hein and R. Held. A neural model for labile sensorimotor coordinations. In E. E. Bernard and M. R. Kare (eds.). *Biological prototypes and synthetic systems.* New York: Plenum Press, 1962. Vol. 1, pp. 71–74.
4. R. Held. Shifts in binaural localization after prolonged exposures to atypical combinations of stimuli. *Amer. J. Psychol.,* 1955, *68,* 526–548.
5. R. Held. Exposure-history as a factor in maintaining stability of perception and coordination. *J. nerv. ment. Dis.,* 1961, *132,* 26–32.
6. R. Held and J. Bossom. Neonatal deprivation and adult rearrangement: Complementary techniques for analyzing plastic sensory-motor coordinations. *J. comp. physiol. Psychol.,* 1961, *54,* 33–37.
7. R. Held and A. Hein. Adaptation of disarranged hand-eye coordination contingent upon reafferent stimulation. *Percept. mot. Skills,* 1958, *8,* 87–90.
8. R. Held and M. Schlank. Adaptation to optically increased distance of the hand from the eye by reafferent stimulation. *Amer. J. Psychol.,* 1959, *72,* 603–605.
9. E. H. Hess. Ethology: An approach toward the complete analysis of behavior. In R. Brown, E. Galanter, E. H. Hess, and G. Mandler (eds.). *New directions in psychology.* New York: Holt, Rinehart & Winston, 1962. Pp. 159–266.
10. R. Melzack. Effects of early perceptual restriction on simple visual discrimination. *Science,* 1962, *137,* 978–979.
11. H. Mikaelian and R. Held. Two types of adaptation to an optically rotated visual field. *Amer. J. Psychol.,* 1964, *77,* 257–263.
12. A. H. Riesen. Plasticity of behavior: Psychological aspects. In H. F. Harlow and C. N. Woolsey (eds.). *Biological and biochemical bases of behavior.* Madison: University of Wisconsin Press, 1958. Pp. 425–450.

13. A. H. Riesen. Excessive arousal effects of stimulation after early sensory deprivation. In P. Solomon, P. E. Kubzansky, P. H. Leiderman, J. H. Mendelson, R. H. Trumbull, and D. Wexler (eds.). *Sensory deprivation*. Cambridge: Harvard University Press, 1961. Pp. 34–40.
14. A. H. Riesen. Stimulation as a requirement for growth and function in behavioral development. In D. W. Fiske and S. R. Maddi (eds.). *Functions of varied experience*. Homewood, Ill.: Dorsey Press, 1961. Pp. 57–80.
15. A. H. Riesen. Studying perceptual development using the technique of sensory deprivation. *J. nerv. ment. Dis.*, 1961, *132*, 21–25.
16. A. H. Riesen and L. Aarons. Visual movement and intensity discrimination in cats after early deprivation of pattern vision. *J. comp. physiol. Psychol.*, 1959, *52*, 142–149.
17. N. S. Sutherland. Stimulus analyzing mechanisms. In *Mechanization of thought processes*. National Physical Laboratory Symposium No. 10. London: HMSO, 1959. Vol. 2, pp. 575–609.
18. R. D. Walk and E. J. Gibson. A comparative and analytical study of visual depth perception. *Psychol. Monogr.*, 1961, *75*(15, whole no. 519).

# 34

# INDEPENDENCE OF THE CAT'S SCOTOPIC AND PHOTOPIC SYSTEMS IN ACQUIRING CONTROL OF VISUALLY GUIDED BEHAVIOR

Alan Hein
Rhea M. Diamond

*Neonatal kittens were exposed at scotopic levels of illumination while freely locomoting in an enclosure. Subsequently, visually guided behaviors were displayed at scotopic levels of illumination but were absent at photopic*

Source: *Journal of Comparative and Physiological Psychology*, 1971, *76*, 31–38. Copyright 1971 by the American Psychological Association. Reprinted by permission.
Note: This research was supported by Grant GB-17045 from the National Science Foundation and Grant 1 RO1 N509279-01 from the National Institutes of Health. The authors are grateful to Lewis Harvey for assistance in measuring the luminance levels used in this study.

*levels. This result is attributed to the fact that visual feedback from movement was restricted to the rod system. It is suggested that the capacity to mediate visually guided behaviors can be acquired independently by scotopic and photopic systems.*

Experiments with neonatal kittens have identified the exposure conditions which support development of a number of visually controlled behaviors. Among the behaviors studied are those guided by visual information which localizes objects in three-dimensional space. Exposure in light is not by itself sufficient for acquisition of these visually guided behaviors [14]; self-produced movement systematically associated with changes in patterned visual stimulation appears essential [11]. All coordinations need not develop simultaneously; it has previously been suggested that the visually guided behaviors displayed during testing are specified by the particular feedback opportunities provided during exposure [5]. The technique of selective exposure provides a means to test this assertion and has permitted the identification of components of visually guided behavior which may be independently acquired.

When gross locomotory movements are systematically associated with the motion of images across the retina, visually guided locomotion develops [11]. View of the limbs does not appear to be necessary for acquisition of this capacity. Visually guided reaching to a small target such as a swinging ball, or to the solid portion of an interrupted surface, develops only if a kitten views its moving limbs [8]. The essential feature of this exposure is the systematic association of self-produced movements with the motion of images of the limbs across the retina [7].

The use of exposure conditions which provide restricted opportunities for motor-visual feedback has also permitted analysis of visually guided reaching into independent components. In both monkeys [10] and cats [6] the acquisition of visually guided reaching may be restricted to one limb and guided reaching mediated by one eye may develop without acquisition of control by the other eye [9].

The present study uses the technique of selective exposure to explore the possibility that coordinations acquired by the young animal may be specific to level of illumination during exposure and may not be exhibited when that level changes. The particular question asked is whether the capacity to mediate certain coordinations may be acquired by the scotopic visual system independently of acquisition by the photopic system. This possibility was raised by a result of a visual rearrangement study [4]. In one of their experiments human adults viewed their moving hands through prisms in bright light. When hand-eye coordination was tested in dim light the subjects showed substantially less adaptation to the prisms than when tested in bright light. It seemed possible that kittens reared in dim light would display visually guided behaviors when tested at scotopic levels of illumination but not when tested at photopic levels. The present paper reports three experiments using this paradigm. In the first, a small bright portion of the generally dim environment provided photopic-level stimulation but light reflected from the paws was sufficient to stimulate only the rods. In the second, all light reflected from the environment, as well as from the limbs, was below photopic levels. In the third, all light provided during movement was within the scotopic range but the kittens were given daily exposure in bright light while immobilized.

## EXPERIMENT 1

Stationary environmental targets were present at both scotopic and photopic levels of luminance. Thus, locomotory movements were accompanied by systematic changes in the pattern of stimulation of both rods and cones. However, luminance of the limbs was below the photopic threshold, so that retinal images of the moving limbs stimulated only the rods.

### Method

*Subjects.* Eleven kittens from seven litters were used as subjects. They were kept with their mothers and littermates in total darkness until they were 6 to 8 weeks old. At that time the vibrissae were cut and the animals, in groups of two or three, were placed in a dimly illuminated enclosure where they remained until removed for testing. (Each animal was handled for 5 min daily in the dark to facilitate later testing.)

*Apparatus.* The exposure apparatus is shown in Figure 34-1a. It is a light-tight enclosure 90 × 60 × 50 cm. A circular aperature 5 cm in diameter at one end permits light to enter. The source is a 50-w incandescent bulb transmitted through a blue-pass filter (Kodak Wratten 47B) with intensity controlled by a Variac. Illumination was adjusted so that light reflected from the forelimbs would stimulate rods but not cones. Maximum luminance of a paw was calibrated with a Macbeth illuminometer at $1.13 \times 10^{-4}$ ft-l. If it is assumed that cones in a kitten are not stimulated until luminance reaches $1.0 \times 10^{-2}$ ft-l, light reflected from the paws was always well below the photopic range [1]. Luminance at the source was estimated at $1.5 \times 10^{-1}$ ft-l; thus the luminance of the 5-cm aperature itself was well above the cone threshold. All measurements were made without the blue-pass filter in place and then corrected by the factor 0.004 to estimate effective luminance. This factor was derived from a comparison of the luminance of a test patch with and without filter.

Visually guided reaching was tested with the aid of the interrupted

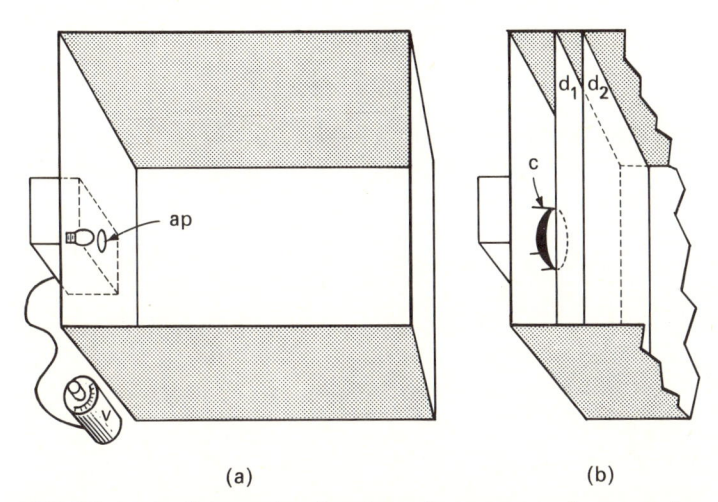

FIGURE 34-1 Schematic drawing of apparatus for exposing kittens in dim light. (a) Luminance at aperture (ap) is within the photopic range. (b) Addition of reflecting cone (c) and 0.3-cm-thick vinyl screens ($d_1$ and $d_2$) diffuses incoming light so that luminance of all surfaces is within the scotopic range.

surface used by Hein and Held [8]. The apparatus consists of a board with cutouts spaced to form parallel prongs. The kitten is carried downward with one forelimb free and its head is directed alternately to a prong or to a space. Six trials are given with each forelimb. The dimensions of the board assure that approximately half of unguided limb extensions will contact a prong. Normally reared kittens contact a prong on 95% of all trials [8].

The apparatus used for observing visually guided locomotion consists of an obstacle course. Wooden blocks inserted into a perforated base in an irregular arrangement provide narrow channels of passage. The kitten is placed at various points in the course and observed as it walks about.

*Procedure.* Kittens were kept in the dimly illuminated enclosure for 7 to 17 days before being tested. In this, as in all subsequent experiments, the vibrissae were cut again before testing. Both visually guided reaching and visually guided locomotion were examined under dim illumination; then the illumination level was raised and the tests repeated, with visually guided reaching assessed first.

Before conducting tests in dim light the experimenters remained in the dark for 30 min. Illumination for testing at scotopic levels was provided by 50-w bulbs housed in two Kodak adjustable safelights fitted with blue-pass filters (Kodak Wratten 47B) with intensity regulated by a Variac. The lamps were placed about 0.5 m from the interrupted surface and positioned to minimize variation in luminance of the prongs. Immediately after testing with the interrupted surface the animal was observed in the obstacle course. For this test the safelights were directed upward so that light was reflected downward from the ceiling onto the obstacles. In all dim-light testing the luminance of visual targets was approximately $1.0 \times 10^{-4}$ ft-l as measured with a Macbeth illuminometer.

Before testing under photopic illumination each kitten was permitted to adapt to light for 10 min while being held by an experimenter so that it could not locomote or see its limbs. During the period of light adaptation, normal room illumination was gradually increased by the successive addition of light from three 3200° K incandescent bulbs housed in lamps equipped with reflectors. For testing in bright light these three lamps were placed approximately 0.5 m above the surfaces to be illuminated, directed downward, and positioned to minimize variation in luminance. This high level of illumination was intended to bleach the rods so that only cones could be used.

## Results

All animals readily negotiated the obstacle course in dim light, moving rapidly without bumping into the objects. As indicated in Table 34-1, in dim light the kittens reached accurately to the solid portion of the interrupted surface. Of 132 limb extensions, 127 hit a prong.

When tested in bright light the kittens appeared neither frightened nor dazed and showed the normal forelimb extension response when carried downward toward a broad surface. However, when the interrupted surface was employed, the extended forelimb fell into the space between prongs about as often as it struck a prong. Of 132 limb extensions, only 64 were hits, indicating that performance was at chance level. The animals that had shown accurate guided reaching in dim light appeared unable to guide their limbs to the same targets in bright light. In contrast to this deficiency in visually guided reaching, there was no apparent impairment of visually guided locomotion. The kittens moved rapidly and avoided the objects; their performance on the obstacle course in bright light was indistinguishable from their performance in dim light.

The capacities acquired by the neonatal animal were specified by the exposure conditions during rearing. Locomotion was accompanied by systematic changes in the pattern of stimulation of cones as well as rods and visually guided locomotion was exhibited at both photopic and scotopic levels of illumination. In contrast, light reflected from the limbs stimulated only the rods. Visually guided reaching was displayed at scotopic levels of illumination and was absent at photopic levels.

## EXPERIMENT 2

The presence of a bright area in the enclosure used in experiment 1 was believed essential to development of visually guided locomotion

TABLE 34-1  Visually Guided Reaching at Scotopic and Photopic Levels of Illumination

|  |  | Scotopic |  | Photopic |  |
|---|---|---|---|---|---|
| Experiment | Subject | Prongs: Hits/Misses | Bridge: Hits/Misses | Prongs: Hits/Misses | Bridge: Hits/Misses |
| 1 | 1 | 12/0 |  | 5/7 |  |
|  | 2 | 12/0 |  | 5/7 |  |
|  | 3 | 11/1 |  | 7/5 |  |
|  | 4 | 11/1 |  | 3/9 |  |
|  | 5 | 12/0 |  | 8/4 |  |
|  | 6 | 11/1 | (not used) | 6/6 | (not used) |
|  | 7 | 12/0 |  | 9/3 |  |
|  | 8 | 11/1 |  | 3/9 |  |
|  | 9 | 11/1 |  | 5/7 |  |
|  | 10 | 12/0 |  | 6/6 |  |
|  | 11 | 12/0 |  | 7/5 |  |
| 2 | 1 | 11/1 | 6/0 | 5/7 | 3/3 |
|  | 2 | 12/0 | 6/0 | 6/6 | 3/3 |
|  | 3 | 12/0 | 6/0 | 6/6 | 2/4 |
|  | 4 | 12/0 | 6/0 | 5/7 | 2/4 |
|  | 5 | 12/0 | 6/0 | 7/5 | 1/5 |
| 3 | 1 | 12/0 | 6/0 | 3/9 | 3/3 |
|  | 2 | 11/1 | 6/0 | 7/5 | 3/3 |
|  | 3 | 11/1 | 6/0 | 5/7 | 3/3 |
|  | 4† | 12/0 | 6/0 | 4/8 | 1/5 |
|  | 5† | 11/1 | 6/0 | 5/7 | 3/3 |
| Normal light-reared | 1 | 12/0 | 6/0 | 12/0 | 6/0 |
|  | 2 | 12/0 | 6/0 | 12/0 | 6/0 |
|  | 3 | 11/1 | 6/0 | 12/0 | 6/0 |
|  | 4 | 12/0 | 6/0 | 11/1 | 6/0 |
|  | 5 | 12/0 | 6/0 | 12/0 | 6/0 |
|  | 6 | 12/0 | 6/0 | 11/1 | 6/0 |

† Exposed in enclosure without blue-pass filter over light source and tested in unfiltered light.

mediated by the photopic system. In experiment 2 the bright area was eliminated so that stimulation from the environment during locomotion, as well as light reflected from the paws, fell below the cone threshold. Under these conditions the photopic system should fail to acquire the capacity to mediate visually guided locomotion. Visually guided locomotion, as well as visually guided reaching, would be displayed only when the scotopic system was being used.

## Method

*Subjects.* Five kittens from two litters were kept in total darkness until placed in the dimly lit enclosure at 7 weeks of age. Except for a change in apparatus all rearing procedures were identical to those of experiment 1.

*Apparatus.* The enclosure described in experiment 1 was modified to eliminate photopic-level luminance at the light source. As shown in Figure 34-1b (p. 359) an opaque reflecting cone in front of the aperture and two white vinyl screens served to diffuse incoming light. The luminance of the source was adjusted with the Variac so that no part of panel $d_2$ was above the cone threshold.

As in experiment 1, visually guided reaching was tested with the interrupted surface and visually guided locomotion was observed in the obstacle course. In addition, an alternate test of visually guided reaching was employed. As stipulated by Hein and Held [8], when the interrupted surface is used to test visually guided reaching, two principal criteria must be met before a hit or miss may be scored. The animal's head must be pointed forward and forelimb extension must be discrete. In dim light, it is difficult to be certain these criteria have been met. The apparatus illustrated in Figure 34-2 was used to provide additional data on the accuracy of guided reaching. The device is referred to as a bridge box. Dews and Wiesel [3] have used a similar apparatus as an alternative to the inter-

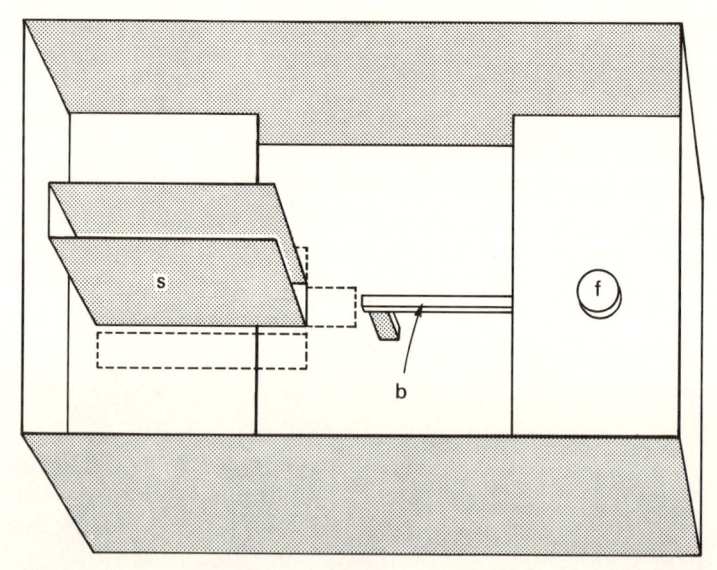

FIGURE 34-2 Schematic drawing of bridge box for assessing visually guided reaching. Kitten leaves start box(s) and steps across gap to bridge (b) leading to food (f). For test trials the start box is moved with respect to the bridge as indicated by dashed lines.

rupted surface. The kitten is required to step from the start box across a gap onto a bridge 2.5 cm wide. The start box can be moved to change its position with respect to the bridge. For dim-light testing, light from the safelight lamps was directed upward and reflected from the ceiling into the bridge box. Luminance of the bridge was equivalent to that of the visual targets in the other test procedures. For testing in bright light three lamps housing 3200° K bulbs were placed approximately 0.5 m above the bridge to the left, right, and directly ahead of the start box. These lamps directed light downward onto the bridge and other interior surfaces of the box.

*Procedure.* After 10 days of exposure at scotopic levels of illumination the kittens were tested for visually guided behavior. As in experiment 1, all tests were conducted in dim light and then, following light adaptation, repeated in bright light. The animals were tested first with the interrupted surface, next in the bridge box, and, finally, observed in the obstacle course. The procedure used with the interrupted surface and obstacle course was identical to that of experiment 1.

Use of the bridge box for testing visually guided reaching required a brief period of preliminary training with the bridge directly ahead of the start box. The kittens were deprived of food for 24 hr and then trained in dim light to walk across the bridge to a dish of fish. Then a small gap was introduced between the start-box platform and the bridge and the animals were required to extend a limb across the gap to reach the bridge. If swiping or leaping occurred, the kitten was returned to the start box without being permitted to reach the food. The gap was gradually increased to the maximum distance the animal would step without jumping. Training ended and testing began after six consecutive reaches across the maximum gap. This criterion was met following 2 to 3 days with one 15-min training session a day. Six test trials in dim light were given with the bridge kept at the maximum distance and positioned successively right-left-center-right-left-center with respect to the start box. Reaching was considered accurate if the animal made a single direct placement of the paw on the bridge.

Before testing in bright light, a brief period of retraining was given with the bridge directly ahead of the start box. All animals met the criterion for testing within 3 to 5 min and six test trials followed immediately.

## Results

In dim light the kittens of experiment 2 reached accurately to the solid portion of the interrupted surface (Table 34-1). Of sixty limb extensions, fifty-nine were hits. In bright light, performance was at chance level; of sixty limb extensions only twenty-nine were hits. Testing of visually guided reaching in the bridge box confirmed the results obtained with the interrupted surface. The animals crossed the bridge accurately on all thirty trials in dim light but on only eleven of thirty trials in bright light. Errors consisted of reaches to one or the other side of the bridge. On several trials in bright light the kittens fell from the start-box platform to the surface below the bridge.

Like the kittens of experiment 1, these animals readily negotiated the obstacle course in dim light. However, in contrast to the results of experiment 1, in bright light the kittens of experiment 2 were deficient in visually guided locomotion. They repeatedly walked into the obstacles and frequently startled in response to this contact.

The capacities acquired by the young animal matched the opportunities for motor-visual feedback provided during exposure. Only the rods were stimulated by light reflected from the environment and from the moving limbs. Visually guided locomotion and visually guided reaching were exhibited at scotopic levels of illumination and both capacities were absent at photopic levels.

## EXPERIMENT 3

The fact that feedback from movement was available only to the scotopic system during exposure was believed to account for the subsequent restriction of visually guided behavior to scotopic levels of testing. Regardless of feedback, however, 10 days of exposure restricted to scotopic levels of illumination might produce this result, perhaps by inducing degeneration in the cone system.

Experiment 3 was designed to provide a direct test of the critical role of feedback. Kittens were exposed in dim light as in experiment 2 but were also provided daily exposure in bright light while immobilized. This procedure was intended to minimize the possibility of degeneration of the cones and associated neural structures. It was expected that the results would not differ from those of experiment 2—visually guided behaviors would be displayed only at scotopic levels of illumination. This result would support the hypothesis that the scotopic and photopic systems each require appropriate feedback in order to develop the capacity to mediate these behaviors.

### Method

*Subjects.* Five kittens from three litters were kept in total darkness until placed in the dimly lit enclosure at 7 to 8 weeks of age. With the exception of a daily period of exposure in bright light all rearing procedures were identical with those of experiment 2.

*Apparatus.* The dimly lit enclosure used in experiment 2 was again employed; all light provided to the animals fell below the cone threshold re 34-1b). Two kittens were exposed with the blue-pass filter removed and intensity of the source reduced to compensate for absence of the filter. When these two animals were tested no filter was used. Unfiltered light was used to minimize the difference in distribution of wavelengths between dim and bright light.

For daily exposure in bright light, room illumination was supplemented by light from three 300-w bulbs. These were located 0.5 m to the right, left, and directly in front of the animal's head. The kitten was placed in a holder which prevented movements of head, torso, and limbs, according to the procedure described by Hein, Gower, and Diamond [7].

*Procedure.* The animals remained in the dimly lit enclosure except for 3-hr daily exposure in bright light while immobilized. Visually guided behavior was examined following 12 to 16 days of exposure. The order of tests and details of training and testing procedures were identical to those of experiment 2.

## Results

In dim light the kittens of experiment 3 displayed visually guided behaviors on all three tests. Negotiation of the obstacle course was rapid and accurate. Of sixty limb extensions to the interrupted surface, fifty-seven were hits. Accurate crosses were observed on all thirty test trials in the bridge box (Table 34-1).

Repetition of these tests at photopic levels of illumination yielded results similar to those of experiment 2. Only twenty-four of sixty limb extensions to the interrupted surface were hits. Accurate crosses of the bridge were observed on only thirteen of thirty trials. Negotiation of the obstacle course in bright light was also deficient; the animals repeatedly bumped into objects and frequently showed startle responses. The two animals raised and tested in dim light without blue filters behaved like the others and their data have not been segregated. Despite 3-hr daily exposures in bright light while immobilized, the kittens of this experiment displayed the same deficiencies when tested at photopic levels of illumination as the animals of experiment 2.

## DISCUSSION

Deficiencies in visual-motor coordination at photopic levels of illumination followed exposure in which motor-visual feedback was restricted to rod vision. When feedback from locomotory movements was restricted to rod vision, the capacity to mediate visually guided locomotion was gained only by the scotopic system. When light reflected from the moving limbs stimulated only the rods, accurate guided reaching was subsequently displayed only when using the scotopic system. The results were confirmed when exposure conditions minimized the likelihood of damage to the cones or associated neural structures.

Additional evidence that peripheral atrophy cannot account for the results was provided when the deficiencies observed at photopic levels of illumination were shown to be transient. Five animals used in experiment 1 were retested in bright light after they had spent 10 days freely locomoting in a normally illuminated room. No deficiencies were observed after this exposure period. In experiment 2, following initial testing all the kittens were permitted 3 hr of free locomotion in a brightly illuminated room and then retested in bright light. If at that time a kitten failed to exhibit visually guided behaviors, exposure was continued and the animal was retested after each additional hour (with a maximum of 6 hr of bright-light exposure a day). All animals of experiment 2 exhibited coordinated behaviors mediated by cone vision following 3 to 10 hr in bright light. After initial testing under both levels of illumination, the animals of experiment 3 were permitted 3 hr of free locomotion in bright light and then returned to the dimly illuminated enclosure for 16 hr. Following this period in dim light, the kittens were light-adapted while prevented from moving, and then retested in bright light. If visually guided behaviors were not displayed at this time, the kittens were permitted additional exposure while locomoting in bright light. Each additional hour of bright light was followed by 23 hr in the dimly illuminated enclosure, light adaptation as above, and retesting in bright light. This sequence was repeated until testing was completed. All animals displayed visually guided behaviors at photopic levels of illumination following 4 to 9 hr in bright light. These data suggest that the transient deficiencies exhibited by the experimental animals may be attributed to absence of opportunity for feedback from movement to the photopic system.

An alternate possibility is that the behavior of the experimental animals when first observed in bright light is due either to insufficient light adaptation or to some special disturbing feature of that testing procedure. The kittens of experiment 1 negotiated the obstacle course as well in bright light as in dim light, evidence against a generalized impairment of performance in bright light. Although all of the experimental kittens failed to show accurate guided reaching in bright light, limb extension responses were readily elicited. This suggests that the coordination failures cannot be attributed to emotionality induced by testing in bright light. Moreover, the kittens of experiment 3 displayed visually coordinated movements in bright light under these same test conditions, after they had been permitted a few hours of motor-visual feedback at photopic levels of illumination. This implies that the initial deficiency was not due to exigencies of the bright-light testing situation. To confirm this suggestion, the behavior of six normally reared kittens was examined under both dim and bright light using the test procedures employed in experiment 3. After 16 hr of dark adaptation the animals were tested in dim light, then light adapted for 10 min while immobilized, and then tested in bright light. No performance decrement was associated with testing in bright light; under both levels of illumination performance on all tests of coordination was excellent. Individual data on guided reaching are given in Table 34-1.

The contribution of the spectral difference between dim illumination (blue) and bright illumination may also be examined. Normally reared animals performed equally well under both conditions, making it appear unlikely that any effect specific to wavelength strongly influenced these behaviors. In addition, two animals of experiment 3 were kept without a blue-pass filter in the enclosure and subsequently tested in dim light without blue filters. Their data were similar to those obtained from animals exposed with a filter, implying that prior exposure with short wavelengths was not critical to the performance decrement in bright light. A similar point could be made with regard to the display of visually guided locomotion under bright light in experiment 1, since all light provided during exposure was transmitted through the blue-pass filter.

This series of studies has demonstrated that the capacity to mediate visually guided behaviors may be acquired by the scotopic system independently of acquisition by the photopic system. Under normal rearing conditions, coincidental development involving both parts of the visual system obscures this independence. The separability of control by rod and cone vision provides another instance in which the capacities acquired are precisely specified by exposure conditions during rearing. The results add a new dimension of support to the hypothesis that motor-visual feedback opportunities during exposure determine the course of development of visually guided behaviors. Experiments now in progress will determine whether the cone system may gain control of visually guided behaviors without acquisition by the rod system.

Behavioral evidence for the separability of scotopic and photopic systems implies that inputs from these systems are differentiated in the central nervous system. The convergence of receptor elements upon ganglion cells does not preclude physiologic differentiation. Changes in firing rate of single cells in the lateral geniculate nucleus of macaques have been shown to follow change in wavelength impinging upon the eye [2]. Although there is no comparable evidence for the cat, it is possible that neurons of the lateral geniculate nucleus may respond differentially to scotopic and photopic stimulation.

A possible anatomic basis for differentiation of scotopic and photopic systems is suggested by the work of Klüver [12] and Malmo [13] with macaques. These investigators have reported that the effect of striate cortex ablation upon intensity discrimination at scotopic levels is substantially less than at photopic levels. Accordingly, Malmo suggests a subcortical locus for the discrimination of intensity at low luminance levels. Alternately, the critical region could be cortical but extrastriate. In the cat, there might be a striate focus for visually guided behavior in bright light and a subcortical or extrastriate focus for these behaviors in dim light. The behavioral evidence presented here does not demand complete separation of scotopic and photopic systems but does reveal that they acquire control of certain visual-motor coordinations independently.

REFERENCES

1. N. W. Daw and A. L. Pearlman. Cat colour vision: One cone process or several? *J. Physiol., London,* 1969, *201,* 745–764.
2. R. L. DeValois and G. H. Jacobs. Primate color vision. *Science,* 1968, *162,* 533–540.
3. P. B. Dews and T. N. Wiesel. Consequences of monocular deprivation on visual behaviour in kittens. *J. Physiol., London,* 1970, *206,* 437–455.
4. A. M. Graybiel and R. Held. Prismatic adaptation under scotopic and photopic conditions. *J. Psychol.,* 1970, *85,* 16–22.
5. A. Hein. Recovering spatial motor coordination after visual cortex lesions. *Percept. Dis.,* 1970, *48,* 163–175.
6. A. Hein. Visual-motor development of the kitten. *Optom. Weekly,* 1970, *61,* 890–892.
7. A. Hein, E. C. Gower, and R. M. Diamond. Exposure requirements for developing the triggered component of the visual placing response. *J. comp. physiol. Psychol.,* 1970, *73,* 188–192.
8. A. Hein and R. Held. Dissociation of the visual placing response into elicited and guided components. *Science,* 1967, *158,* 390–392.
9. A. Hein, R. Held, and E. C. Gower. Development and segmentation of visually controlled movement by selective exposure during rearing. *J. comp. physiol. Psychol.,* 1970, *73,* 181–187.
10. R. Held and J. Bauer. Visually guided reaching in infant monkeys after restricted rearing. *Science,* 1967, *155,* 718–720.
11. R. Held and A. Hein. Movement-produced stimulation in the development of visually guided behavior. *J. comp. physiol. Psychol.,* 1963, *56,* 872–876.
12. H. Klüver. Visual functions after removal of the occipital lobes. *J. Psychol.,* 1941, *11,* 23–45.
13. R. B. Malmo. Effects of striate cortex ablation on intensity discrimination and spectral intensity distribution in the rhesus monkey. *Neuropsychologia,* 1966, *4,* 9–26.
14. A. H. Riesen. Stimulation as a requirement for growth and function in behavioral development. In D. W. Fiske and S. R. Maddi (eds.). *Functions of varied experience.* Homewood, Ill.: Dorsey Press, 1961. Pp. 57–80.

# 35
# ABSENCE OF SIZE CONSTANCY IN VISUALLY DEPRIVED RATS

## Donald P. Heller

*Effects of visual deprivation on the manifestation of size constancy was investigated in a series of experiments. Normally reared rats possessed size constancy, but visual deprivation from the time of parturition precluded its appearance. Rats reared under visual deprivation learned a size discrimination in terms of retinal image size, and, although possessing adequate depth perception, did not coordinate the 2 processes in order to achieve size constancy. This coordination was accomplished with approximately 10 days of visual experience.*

Size constancy has been demonstrated in the monkey [5], cat [2], duck [6] and carp [3, 4]. In these experiments, when a visual size discrimination had been established, the larger object was moved away from the subject, making the visual angle it subtended equal to or less than the visual angle of the smaller stimulus. Continued, consistent response by the subject to the previously rewarded stimulus indicated size constancy.

The present study is concerned with the role of prior visual experience on the manifestation of size constancy. The problem suggested an experimental design in which animals were deprived of visual experience from birth and subsequently tested for size constancy. However, testing for size constancy in animals involves training in a visual size discrimination. It is conceivable that in the process of learning a size discrimination the subject might also obtain the experience which leads to the presence of size constancy. For example, the subject approaches the stimuli giving it experience with objects at varying distances.

Since the empiricists postulate that visual experience with objects

Source: *Journal of Comparative and Physiological Psychology*, 1968, 65, 336–339. Copyright 1968 by the American Psychological Association. Reprinted by permission.
Note: I would like to thank Irvin Rock for his many suggestions during the actual process of these experiments and for his invaluable help in preparation of this manuscript.

at various distances is needed for the development of size constancy, some training procedure must be found which precludes this experience. If an organism could be trained in a visual size discrimination while seeing the stimuli at only one specified distance, and at all other times be kept in total darkness, then the ontogenesis of size constancy could be investigated.

## EXPERIMENT 1

Experiment 1 was designed (a) to demonstrate that young, visually experienced rats can learn a size discrimination under restricted conditions, and (b) to show that once having learned the discrimination they would exhibit size constancy.

### Method

*Subjects.* The subjects were five normally reared Sprague-Dawley rats, 34 days old at the inception of the experiment.

*Apparatus.* A ½-in. board was placed down the center of a 7 ft × 8½ in. × 1 ft box, dividing it into two 4-in.-wide parallel alleys. A start box, 4 in. wide and 8 in. long, with a Plexiglas guillotine door, formed a common entrance to the left and right alleys. A telegraph key was recessed in the start-box floor immediately in front of the alleys. Depression of this key turned on two movable 7½-w bulbs, one in each alley, which illuminated the two stimuli from the rear and produced the appearance of two luminous circles, one 1 in. and the other 2 in. in diameter. The alleys in front of the stimuli were also illuminated to some extent. The stimuli, constructed from heavy black cardboard and backed by ¼-in. milk plastic, were placed 18 in. behind the guillotine door. Combination goal boxes and running alleys were constructed by placing clear plastic partitions across each alley, 8 in. behind the guillotine door. Reinforcement wells were constructed by cutting 1-in. circles in the Masonite floor immediately in front of each partition. To prevent undue scattering of light, the apparatus was painted flat black and the top of the alleys was covered with a double thickness of heavy black felt.

*Procedure.* The subjects were placed on 23-hr food deprivation 2 days before training. Under standard training procedures, subjects were given ten noncorrection discrimination trials per day until they reached a criterion of eight correct responses on 3 consecutive days. A correct response was defined as selecting the positive goal box immediately after the stimulus lights were turned off. The 2-in. circle was positive for 3 subjects and the 1-in. circle was positive for 2 subjects. The rewarded stimulus was placed in the left or right alley according to a Gellermann series. To prevent the subject from learning a brightness discrimination rather than a size discrimination, the stimulus lights were randomly positioned in each alley. This made the rewarded stimulus appear darker than the nonrewarded stimulus on half of the trials and brighter than the nonrewarded stimulus on the other half of the trials.

Most important, to avoid visual experience with objects at varying distances during training, subjects could observe the stimuli only when they depressed the telegraph key by standing in one particular position. At other times during training, the room was in total darkness. Thus, subjects were exposed to the training stimuli only at one specific distance.

Then subjects were tested for size constancy on ten trials identical to the training trials except (a) the reward was placed in both alleys, and (b) the larger stimulus was moved to a position 36 in. from the subject, equating the visual angles of the two stimuli.

## Results

Every subject learned the size discrimination. The subjects trained with the larger circle positive took a mean of 100 trials to reach criterion, while subjects trained with the smaller stimulus positive required a mean of 105 trials. A Mann-Whitney $U$ test indicated that this difference was not significant ($p = 0.645$). Size constancy was demonstrated when every subject continued to respond as in training; that is, no subject went below the criterion of eight out of ten correct responses.

## EXPERIMENT 2

Experiment 2 was concerned with the effects of visual deprivation on size constancy and depth perception.

## Method

*Subjects.* Of fifteen visually deprived rats available at the start of training, six were lost due to difficulties in handling subjects in the dark.

*Procedure.* Pregnant Sprague-Dawley rats were placed in individual breeding cages in a dark room. Weanling subjects were removed from the breeding cages to individual cages in the same room 34 days after parturition. Then subjects were trained in a size discrimination and tested for size constancy using the procedures and apparatus described in experiment 1. The small circle was positive for five subjects and the large was positive for four subjects. It is important to note that transfer, feeding, and testing were accomplished in complete darkness.

After the size constancy test, subjects were placed on a visual cliff for 5 min to test for depth perception. Then they were placed in individual cages in an illuminated animal room for 7 days during which they remained on 23-hr food deprivation. On days 8 to 10, each subject was tested for retention of the size discrimination, and returned to the illuminated room. On day 11 subjects were again tested for size constancy.

**Results**

All subjects learned the size discrimination. The mean number of trials to learn the discrimination (143.55) was significantly greater than the mean reported in experiment 1 ($p < 0.05$, Mann-Whitney $U$). As in experiment 1, the mean number of trials to learn the discrimination did not differ for the large circle (143.6) and the small circle (143.5).

When tested for size constancy, no subject reached the criterion of eight out of ten correct responses. The mean number of correct responses was 5.1. The dark-reared subjects were significantly inferior to the light-reared subjects of experiment 1 in demonstrating size constancy ($p < 0.01$, Fisher exact probability test).

On the visual cliff, a significant preference was shown for the shallow side; eight out of nine subjects descended to that side first (binomial $p < 0.05$). Also, the mean time spent on the shallow side was 188 sec, while the mean time spent on the deep side was 35 sec ($p < 0.002$, sign test).

All subjects retained the size discrimination after being placed in the illuminated animal room. Their performance on the last day of retention testing was not significantly different from that on the last day of size discrimination training. After subjects were exposed to illumination, however, there was a change in the results of the size constancy test. Every subject now reached the criterion.

## EXPERIMENT 3

The initial failure of dark-reared rats to show size constancy can be interpreted in two ways: (a) Subjects lack size constancy and, therefore, have no basis for discriminating between the retinally identical stimuli, or (b) Subjects possess size constancy, but dark-rearing prevents its demonstration by reducing their ability to transfer from the learning task to the constancy test.

If the retinal and physical size of the stimuli were placed in opposition during constancy testing, then one could distinguish between the two interpretations. Opposition is achieved by placing the 1-in. circle 9 in. from the subject and the 2-in. circle 36 in. from the subject. Now the 1-in. circle is retinally twice as large as the 2-in. circle. Three predictions are now possible: (a) If subjects have size constancy, they should continue to respond to the objectively positive stimulus regardless of position. (b) If subjects suffer from a transfer difficulty, they should respond randomly. (c) If subjects do not possess constancy, and do not suffer from transfer difficulty, they should respond to the retinal size rather than the physical size of the stimuli.

This design has two advantages: (a) the retinal size relationship existing during training was maintained, permitting the greatest possibility of continued responding on this basis. (b) A substantial change was introduced by altering the position of both stimuli, maximizing the opportunity of demonstrating transfer difficulties.

## Method

*Subjects.* Of seven albino rats reared under the visual deprivation conditions of experiment 2, three were trained with the 2-in. circle positive and four with the 1-in. circle positive.

*Apparatus and Procedure.* The apparatus and procedure were the same as in experiment 2, except for positioning of stimuli during testing. In testing for size constancy, the 1-in. circle was 9 in. in front of the guillotine door and the 2-in. circle 36 in.

## Results

The mean number of 121 trials to learn the size discrimination was not significantly different from the mean number of trials to learn in experiment 1 (Mann-Whitney $U$ converted to $Z = 1.55, p = 0.06$).

The results of the constancy test were as follows: Six out of seven subjects continued to respond at criterion to the "retinally" positive stimulus rather than the objectively positive stimulus. These results when assessed by a Fisher's combined probabilities test, show a significant preference for the retinally positive stimulus ($p < 0.01$).

## DISCUSSION

Experiment 1 demonstrated size constancy in normally reared rats 50 days old. Thus not only human infants [1] but also weanling rats exhibit size constancy. This demonstration indicates that the experimental apparatus and procedures were effective in revealing size constancy and that the animals were maturationally ready to reveal size constancy. Since, at testing, dark-reared subjects were the same age as normally reared subjects, the absence of size constancy cannot be attributed to maturational variables. Instead, the failure of dark-reared rats indicates that visual experience is necessary for the development of size constancy. In fact, as established in experiment 3, without visual experience with objects at varying distances, rats will respond in terms of retinal size rather than physical size. Furthermore, the visual cliff data of experiment 2, in line with the findings of Walk and Gibson [7], suggest that the difficulty is not due to a lack of depth perception. Thus the three experiments together indicate that size constancy is not innate in the albino rat, but rather that size constancy develops with 10 days of visual exposure to a normal laboratory environment. Thus the acquisition of size constancy is extremely rapid.

## REFERENCES

1. T. G. R. Bower. Discrimination of depth in premotor infants. *Psychon. Sci.,* 1964, *1,* 368.
2. R. Gunter. Visual size constancy in the cat. *Brit. J. Psychol.,* 1951, *42,* 288–293.
3. K. Herter. Weitere Dressurversuche an Fischen. *Z. Wiss. Biol. Apt.,* 1930, *11,* 730–748.
4. K. Herter. *Die Fischdressüre und ihre Sinnes physiologischen Grundlagen.* Berlin: Akademie-Verlag, 1953.
5. N. A. Locke. Comparative study of size constancy. *J. genet. Psychol.,* 1937, *51,* 255–265.
6. N. Pastore. Form perception and size constancy in the duckling. *J. Psychol.,* 1958, *45,* 259–261.
7. R. D. Walk and E. J. Gibson. A comparative and analytical study of visual depth perception. *Psychol. Monogr.,* 1961, *75*(15, whole no. 519).

PART III

# Higher Perceptual Processes

# THE BRAIN—DOES IT HAVE A MIND OF ITS OWN?

This final part presents a number of articles about what are often called higher perceptual processes. One of the most widely researched topics falling under this rubric is memory and closely related phenomena. In the article by Shiffrin and Atkinson a theoretical, three-stage memory model is described. The principal components of the proposed system are (a) a sensory register that functions for initial processing of incoming sensory information, (b) a short-term store that retains information for a limited period of time, after which decay occurs unless the item is used or rehearsed by the individual, and (c) a long-term store that draws information from the short-term store and is capable of retaining it permanently. This article emphasizes the mechanisms thought to be involved in the storage and retrieval of information in the long-term store. It is an example of "black-box" theorizing. The various components of the system are assigned unspecified locations within the brain, and within these regions or boxes the mechanisms of action are not detailed. Neither exact locations nor exact mechanisms are essential for the formal aspects of the theory.

A different manner of studying memory can be seen in the selection by Luria, in which he describes an individual whose recall abilities were extraordinary. The excerpt included here discusses the capabilities of the individual and the methods he used to remember events and items. It is an interesting exercise to attempt to place the feats of this person into the model described in the previous article. It is also useful to consider how typical the mnemonist's memory system is in terms of techniques of recall.

It is apparent that most people are limited in their capacity to process perceptual information. (A discussion of the limitations of the perceptual system can be found in an article by Miller [4]. Therefore, some sort of selective process occurs that determines which stimuli are processed. The next several articles are concerned with this problem of selection of stimuli. One way in which particular information can be dealt with is by attentional mechanisms. The word attention has been used in a variety of contexts in psychology; Treisman bases her discussion of attention on a model proposed by the British psychologist D. E. Broadbent [1]. According to Broadbent, information reaches a person by various communication channels. Which channel is used is determined by some attribute of the incoming stimulus. Among these attributes may be the modality of the stimulus, or within a specific modality, some specific characteristics. For example, in the auditory system the information coming into the right ear may involve a different channel than the information coming into the left ear, or men's and women's voices may utilize different channels. Broadbent argues that an individual can display selective attention by filtering out input arriving via certain channels and allowing other input access to the short-term store area. In Treisman's article, details of the various components of Broadbent's model are described and relevant experiments are discussed that have somewhat modified this model.

A special case of selective attention—perceptual defense—is discussed in the next three papers. McGinnies presents a study demonstrating that anxiety-eliciting stimuli result in a form of perceptual screening manifested by a raised threshold for that particular class of stimuli. This study, like some in Part I, is also an example of perceptual research and subliminal stimulation. Considerable controversy exists about the nature of perceptual defense, in particular, about whether the phenomenon results from a response bias (for example, a tendency not to want to say taboo words) or from a perceptual block. Zajonc supports the former, while evidence for the latter is presented by Worthington.

The final paper on memory concerns an aspect of the topic that has been rather difficult to study in an experimental situation. Eidetic imagery, a very vivid visual recollection of a stimulus, differs from conventional memory in that fine detail is maintained and the image tends to be scanned by the subject. Eidetic imagery seems to be restricted primarily to children, and the study selected here, by Haber and Haber, is a rigorous attempt to determine the frequency of occurrence of this phenomenon. Interested students are urged to read a recent paper by Hebb [3] in which various types of imagery are considered from a physiological point of view.

In the paper referred to above, Hebb postulated that eye movement is important as an organizing factor in imagery. Eye movement has also been found to be of importance in the perception of movement. In the next selection Gregory suggests that two cues provide information for the perception of motion: movement of the eyes to follow a moving object, and the firing of various cells in the retina as a moving object stimulates them sequentially. In response to the puzzle of why the world doesn't appear to spin around when we move our heads, Gregory argues quite persuasively that in such a case both cues are being elicited but they are working in opposition to one another and therefore cancel one another out. Students are encouraged to try the experiments that Gregory suggests to demonstrate his points. The importance of specific units in the retina in the perception of motion is demonstrated in the Masland selection. He found that if subjects stare at a moving object for a length of time and then observe that object twenty hours later when it is stationary, an illusion of motion in the opposite direction occurs and that this illusion depends upon the same portion of the retina being stimulated in both cases. For a further discussion of cues that are important in the perception of movement, an article by Gibson [2] is recommended.

As do the papers considering the perception of motion, the next three articles also emphasize physiological mechanisms. Sperry reports on the effects on human beings of having most of the anatomical connections between the two cerebral hemispheres surgically destroyed. These patients were all suffering from severe epilepsy and the operations were performed to alleviate the convulsions. The data presented by Sperry further the understanding of some of the neurological substrates of perception, particularly the integrative properties both within and between various sense modalities required for normal perceptual behavior. A second major point in Sperry's article is that the two hemispheres in man do not perform in identical ways. This functional asymmetry is particularly evident in verbal tasks, where the dominant hemisphere, the hemisphere contralateral to the preferred hand (that is, in a right-handed person, normally the left hemisphere), seems to be essential for communication. The results demonstrated that patients with "split brains" have, instead of the typical single stream of consciousness, separate perceptions and memories, each associated with one hemisphere and not accessible to the opposite hemisphere.

The study by Kimura and Folb is an experimental investigation of hemispheric asymmetry and the perception of speech sounds discussed by Sperry. Verbal stimuli presented to both ears are perceived more efficiently by the ear opposite the dominant hemisphere. Kimura and Folb's experiment was designed to determine whether the neural mechanisms which result in superior processing of speech by the dominant hemisphere, and superior processing of nonverbal material such as melodies by the nondominant hemisphere, are based upon the meaningfulness of speech. They found that speech sounds played backwards on a tape recorder were still identified more accurately by the right ear (left hemisphere dominant). As evidence has suggested that the fibers connecting the ear to the hemisphere on the opposite side are the most important tracts for speech perception, their conclusion was that the right ear–left hemisphere superiority in verbal identification was *not* based on the meaningfulness of the sound.

G. von Békésy examines a different aspect of auditory perception—backward masking—in the selection included here. This masking occurs when one stimulus follows another within approximately 60 msec; the first stimulus is then not perceived. Von Békésy relates backward masking to the architectural difficulty of designing concert halls. His paper is a good example of applying what appears to be purely a laboratory finding to the real world.

The final group of papers are concerned with the complex issue of individual differences. The topics are chosen to present examples of the variables that can result in differences in perception among individuals exposed to the same stimuli. In the paper by Delk and Fillenbaum the apparent color of objects was shown to be significantly affected by the subjects' "knowing" what color the object should be. Lambert, Solomon, and Watson demonstrate that the perception of the size of an object is influenced by the value attributed to it. Another variable among individuals that affects perception may be the obesity of the person. This surprising finding is detailed in the paper by Schachter, in which data derived from both inside and outside of the laboratory suggest that cues that elicit eating behavior are different for obese individuals and for normal persons. The evidence indicates that eating in overweight subjects is influenced to a greater extent than in normal subjects by nonphysiological cues such as taste, appearance, and time of day. The eating habits of normal subjects are dictated to a greater degree by physiological variables such as stomach motility and food deprivation. Schachter discusses these differences in terms of the varied effects of external and internal cues on the two types of individuals.

Another variable affecting the differential perception of stimuli among individuals is cultural upbringing. An example is shown by Bagby, who presented two different visual stimuli for 10 sec at the same time using a stereoscope. The subjects were either American or Mexican, and the visual stereograms were paired so that each pair of pictures had scenes depicting both cultures. Binocular rivalry resulted, with the visual scene from the subject's own culture predominating. The results were interpreted as indicating that past experience can modify present perception.

The final article, by Gardner, is a critique of studies purporting to have demonstrated dermoperception (vision through the skin) in certain rare cases. The author, an amateur magician, argues, in a very readable paper, that this unusual form of perception is probably nothing more than a "peek down the nose" by the blindfolded subjects being tested.

## REFERENCES

1. D. E. Broadbent. *Perception and communication.* New York: Pergamon, 1958.
2. J. J. Gibson. What gives rise to the perception of motion? *Psychol. Rev.,* 1968, *75,* 335–346.
3. D. O. Hebb. Concerning imagery. *Psychol. Rev.,* 1968, *75,* 466–477.
4. G. A. Miller. The magical number seven, plus or minus two: Some limits on our capacity for processing information. *Psychol. Rev.,* 1956, *63,* 81–97.

## 36
# STORAGE AND RETRIEVAL PROCESSES IN LONG-TERM MEMORY

R. M. Shiffrin
R. C. Atkinson

*A theory of human memory is described in which a distinction is made between three memory stores: the sensory register, the short-term store, and the long-term store. Primary emphasis is given to the processes by which information is stored in and retrieved from the long-term store, a store which is considered to be a permanent repository for information. Forgetting and related phenomena are attributed to a failure of the retrieval process, in which the search through some memory area becomes less efficient as new information is placed in it. Storage and retrieval in the long-term store are conceived of as parallel processes, one mirroring the other, and each is divided into three stages for conceptual clarity. The memory trace is viewed as an ensemble of information stored in some memory location, the location of storage determined largely by the components of the ensemble itself. The ability of the system to cope with diverse phenomena is demonstrated by a consideration of a number of selected experimental paradigms.*

... We begin by describing the overall conception of the memory system.... It should be emphasized that our hypotheses about the various memory stores do not require any assumptions regarding the physiological locus of these stores; the system is equally consistent with the view that the stores are separate physiological struc-

Source: *Psychological Review*, 1969, 76, 179–193. Copyright 1969 by the American Psychological Association. Reprinted by permission.
Note: Preparation of this article was supported by a grant from the National Aeronautics and Space Administration and is an outgrowth of ideas first developed in two earlier reports [4, 40]. This paper, in combination with previous papers by Atkinson and Shiffrin [2, 3], represents an attempt to formulate a general schema within which to analyze memory and learning.

tures as with the view that the short-term store is simply a temporary activation of information permanently stored in the long-term store. The control processes listed in Figure 36-1 are a sample of those which the subject can call into play at his discretion, depending upon such factors as the task and the instructions. Control processes govern informational flow, rehearsal, memory search, output of responses, and so forth.

The sensory register is a very short-lived memory store which temporarily holds incoming sensory information while it is being initially processed and transferred to the short-term store. In the visual modality, for example, information will decay from the sensory register in a period of several hundred milliseconds [41]. Information in the short-term store, if not attended to by the subject, will decay and be lost in a period of about 30 sec or less, but control processes such as rehearsal can maintain information in STS for as long as the subject desires (the buffer process in Figure 36-1 is one highly organized rehearsal scheme). While information resides in STS, portions of it are transferred to LTS. The long-term store is

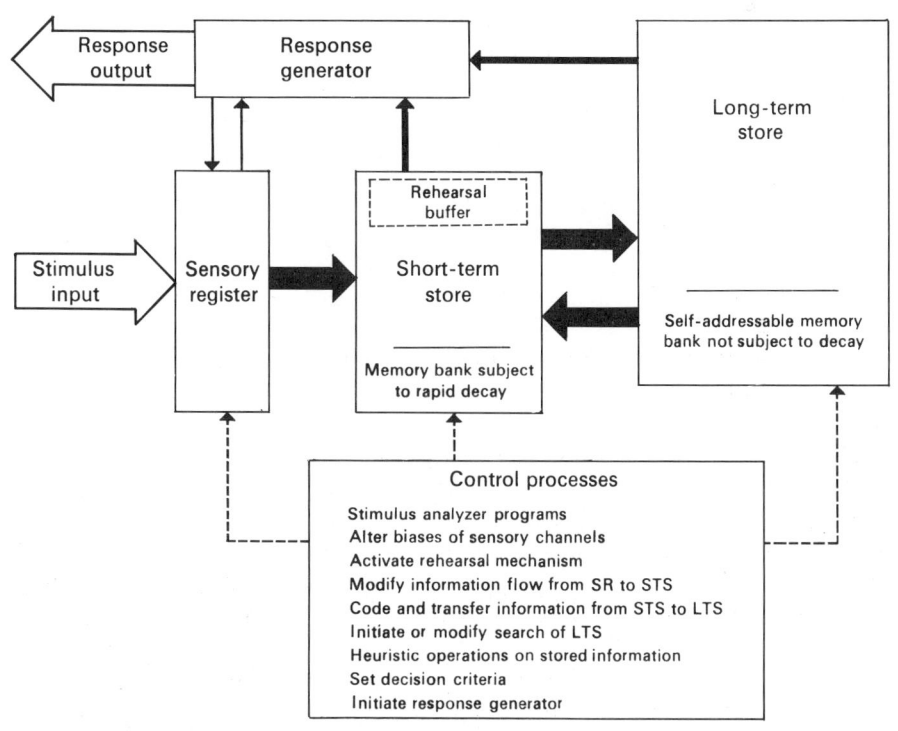

FIGURE 36-1   A flow chart of the memory system. Solid lines indicate paths of information transfer. Dashed lines indicate connections which permit comparison of information arrays residing in different parts of the system; they also indicate paths along which control signals may be sent which activate information transfer, rehearsal mechanisms, and so on.

assumed to be a *permanent* repository of information; we realize that factors such as traumatic brain damage, lesions, and deterioration with extreme age must lead to memory loss, but such effects should be negligible in the types of experiments considered in this paper. Thus it is hypothesized that information, once stored in LTS, is never thereafter destroyed or eliminated. Nevertheless, the ability to retrieve information from LTS varies considerably with time and interfering material.

The short-term store serves a number of useful functions. On the one hand it decouples the memory system from the external environment and relieves the system from the responsibility of moment-to-moment attention to environmental changes. On the other hand, STS provides a working memory in which manipulations of information may take place on a temporary basis. Because STS is a memory store in which information can be maintained if desired, it is often used as the primary memory device in certain types of tasks; in these tasks the information presented for retention is maintained in STS until the moment of test and then emitted. Tasks in which STS is utilized for this purpose, and the mechanisms and control processes that may come into play, have been examined extensively in Atkinson and Shiffrin [3]. In this report we are primarily interested in STS as a temporary store in which information is manipulated for the purposes of storage and retrieval from LTS, rather than as a store in which information is maintained until test. In the remainder of this paper, discussion is limited to that component of memory performance which involves LTS retrieval, and the components arising from STS and the sensory register will not be considered.

## LONG-TERM STORE

In describing the structure of LTS, an analogy with computer memories is helpful. The usual computer memory is location-addressable: If the system is given a certain location, it will return with the contents of that location. When given the contents of a word ("word" refers to a single computer memory location), such a system must be programed to examine each location in turn in order to find the possible locations of these contents in the memory. It seems untenable that an exhaustive serial search is made of all of LTS whenever retrieval is desired. An alternative type of memory may be termed content-addressable: If the system is given the contents of a word, it will return with the locations in memory containing those contents. One way in which such a memory may be constructed utilizes a parallel search through all memory locations; the system then returns with the locations of all matches. If this view is adopted, however, an additional process is needed to select the desired location from among the many returned by the parallel search. Thus, if we feed the system the word *red,* it would not be useful for the system to return with all references or locations of *red:* there are simply too many and the original retrieval problem would not be significantly reduced in scale. There is, however, an alternative method for forming a content-addressable memory; in this method, the contents to be located themselves contain the information necessary to specify the storage location(s). This can occur if the information is originally stored in locations specified by some master plan dependent upon the contents of the information. Such a system will be termed self-addressing. A self-addressing memory may be compared with a library shelving system which is based upon the contents of the books. For example, a book on caulking methods used for twelfth century Egyptian rivercraft will be placed in a specific library location (in the Egyptian room, and so on). If a user desires this book, it may be located by following the same shelving plan used to store it in the first place. We propose that LTS is to a large degree just such a self-addressable memory. An ensemble of information presented to the memory system will define a number of memory areas in which that information is likely to be stored; the memory search will therefore have certain natural starting points. The system is assumed to be only partially self-addressing in that the degree to which the storage locations are specified will vary from one ensemble to the next and one moment to the next, in much the way as proposed in stimulus sampling theory [17]. Thus it may be necessary to embark upon a memory search within the specified locations, a search which may proceed serially from one location to the next. This conception of LTS leads to a number of predictions. For example, a recognition test of memory will not proceed via exhaustive scanning of all stored codes, nor will a recognition test eliminate in all cases the necessity for an LTS search. If information is presented and the subject must indicate whether this information has been presented previously, then the likely storage location(s) is queried. To the degree that the information has highly salient characteristics which precisely identify the storage location, the extent of the LTS search will be reduced. Thus, for items with highly salient characteristics, the subject should be able to identify quickly and accurately whether the item was presented previously, and the identification might not require a memory search which interrogates more than a single storage location. The less well-specified the storage location, the greater the memory search needed to make an accurate recognition response. . . .

The term location is used in relation to the organizational schema; an LTS location is defined by the place in the organizational structure occupied by an information ensemble. The location will be defined in terms of the modality of the information (for instance, visual versus auditory), the level of analysis (for instance, spelling versus syntactic structure), and all other dimensions of organization that may be relevant. Two locations will be said to be close if the information in them tends to be retrieved together. In particular, we shall refer to a *code*, or an *image*, as an ensemble of information that is closely related and very likely to be retrieved together. . . .

## STORAGE AND RETRIEVAL

Since LTS is self-addressing, storage and retrieval have many features in common, one process mirroring the other. Storage is assumed to consist of three primary mechanisms: *transfer, placement,* and *image production.* The transfer mechanism includes those control processes by which the subject decides what to store, when to store, and how to store information in LTS. The placement mechanism determines the locations in which the ensemble of information under consideration will be stored. To a large degree, the components of the ensemble itself will determine the location of storage. That is, in the action of encoding the desired information for storage, the subject may supplement the information currently in STS with pertinent information retrieved from LTS; the resultant ensemble in STS determines the storage location. The image-production mechanism determines what proportion of the current ensemble of information in STS will be placed in the designated LTS location(s). The proportion stored should be a function of the duration of the period that the ensemble is maintained in STS. Retrieval, like storage, is assumed to consist of three primary mechanisms: *search, recovery,* and *response generation.* The search process is a recursive loop in which locations or images are successively selected for examination. As each image is examined, the recovery process determines how much information will be recovered from the image and placed in STS. The response generation process then examines the recovered information and decides whether to continue the search or terminate and emit a response. If the search does not terminate, the selection of the next location or image for examination may depend upon information already uncovered during the search.

Although storage and retrieval are treated separately in this paper, we do not wish to imply that these processes are separated in time, one following the other. Rather, long-term storage is continually occurring for the information residing in short-term store. In addition, retrieval is continually occurring during storage attempts by the subject; for example, he may try to store a paired associate by searching LTS for prominent associations to the stimulus, associations which could then be used as mediators....

### Storage Processes

*Transfer.* ... The decision concerning when to store information is especially important in situations where a large amount of information is being input rapidly to STS. Such a situation taxes the capacity of the system and forces the subject to select a subset of the presented information for special attention and coding. There are a number of factors that determine the information so selected. Important or easily stored information is likely to be given preference....

The decisions concerning how to store information will also affect performance: Storage via visual images may be more effective than auditory storage [39]; overt and covert rehearsal methods may result in very different effects [10]; and mediating versus nonmediating instructions may give rise to considerable performance differences [38]. . . .

*Placement.* The location in which an image will be stored is determined by the contents of that image; the subject therefore controls the storage location by manipulating the information complex in STS. . . .

The primary mechanism determining storage location is in all cases an organizational framework. . . .

In most cases, the subject's placement strategy involves choosing one of many pre-existing organizational dimensions for storage. In these cases, an organizational clue contained in the experimental design may prove useful. In categorized free recall, for example, the subject will be induced to store (and retrieve) in the given categories [8; 12; 13]. Thus the location in which the word *division* will be stored will be quite different if preceded by *multiplication, addition,* and *subtraction* than if preceded by *platoon, regiment,* and *battalion.* . . .

**Retrieval Processes**

The retrieval mechanism forms the crux of the present theory, since it enables a permanent long-term store to exhibit the characteristics of a failing memory. The basic mechanism by which memory loss occurs involves a partially random search through an increasingly large set of images in some local set of memory locations. This local area may be defined by one or more dimensions in the organizational structure of LTS; as the number of images in the local area increases, the search for the desired information will become increasingly ineffective. For example, consider two areas, one consisting of three images, the other consisting of ten images, and both containing the desired code. A random search through the smaller set will result in successful retrieval in a shorter period of time than a search through the larger set.

The retrieval process begins with the presentation of an information complex which places constraints on the response desired and also provides a number of clues, or delimiting information, concerning that desired output (that is, a stimulus). On the basis of this presented information, or as the result of an external search strategy, the subject is led to look in some local memory area and select (possibly randomly) an image for examination. The process by which information is recovered from this image is called recovery. The recovered information will be placed in the short-term store, which may also contain other information such as the search strategy being employed, salient information recovered previously in the search, the LTS locations that have been examined already, and some of the links to other images that have been examined already, and some of the links to other images that have been noted in the search but not yet examined. The short-term store thus acts as a "window" upon LTS, allowing the subject to deal sequentially with a manageable amount of information. The current contents of STS are now examined and various decisions made concerning whether the desired response has been found, whether to emit it, whether to terminate the search unsuccessfully, or whether to continue the search. These decisions and the generation of the response are called the response-generation process. If a decision is made to continue the search, then a new location is selected either randomly, on the basis of information just recovered, or in accord with an overriding external search strategy. The process which continues cycling in this manner until termination is called the search process.

*Search.* Each cycle in the search recursion begins with a mechanism which locates the next image for examination. This mechanism may be separated into *directed* and *random* components. The directed component includes strategies controlled by the subject and depends upon the input information and the self-addressing nature of the system. As a result of the directed component, a number of locations in some area of memory are marked for examination. The locations and images so marked will be referred to as the *examination subset,* and the directed component of the search may be characterized by the probability that the sought-after code is in the examination subset. . . .

In its most general form the search process can be viewed as a series of stages in which searches are made successively in different examination subsets. . . . On the other hand, there are models which emphasize the probabilistic search through an examination subset of items in some memory area [2]. It is upon this latter type of model that attention will be focused in this paper.

*Recovery.* Once an image has been located, it is appropriate to ask what information contained in the image will be entered into the short-term store. This process is called recovery. The amount of information recovered from an image is assumed to be probabilistic, depending upon the current noise level in the system and the amount of information in the image. In particular, the amount of information recovered should be an increasing function of the amount of information in the image.

*Response Generation.* Having recovered information from LTS, the subject is faced with decisions as to whether to terminate the search and respond or to continue to search. These decisions must first of all depend upon the consistency of the recovered information with that indicated by the test information. Inconsistent information can be ruled out at once. If information consistent with the test stimulus is found, and a recognition response is desired, then the response will be given when temporal or contextual information is recovered indicating that the image was stored recently. . . .

A decision can be made to terminate the search unsuccessfully if response time has run out, or if response time is expected to run out and the subject wishes to make a guess before it does, or if he decides that further search would not be useful. Termination schemes of the latter type are quite varied. One simple rule would terminate the search when all images in the examination subset have been interrogated unsuccessfully. Other schemes would end the search when some fixed time limit expired, or some fixed number of items examined. These schemes are described in more detail in Atkinson and Shiffrin [2]. . . .

## APPLICATIONS OF THE SYSTEM

### Forgetting

Decrements in performance occur in the system as a result of the input of additional information to LTS. . . .

## REFERENCES

1. R. C. Atkinson, J. W. Brelsford, Jr., and R. M. Shiffrin. Multiprocess models for memory with applications to a continuous presentation task. *J. math. Psychol.,* 1967, *4,* 277–300.
2. R. C. Atkinson and R. M. Shiffrin. *Mathematical models for memory and learning.* Institute for Mathematical Studies in the Social Sciences, Stanford University, Tech. Rep. No. 79. 1965. (Republished: D. P. Kimble (ed.). *Proceedings of the third conference on learning, remembering, and forgetting.* New York: New York Academy of Science, 1967.)
3. R. C. Atkinson and R. M. Shiffrin. Human memory: A proposed system and its control processes. In K. W. Spence and J. T. Spence (eds.). *The psychology of learning and motivation: Advances in research and theory.* New York: Academic Press, 1968. Vol. 2, pp. 89–195.
4. R. C. Atkinson and R. M. Shiffrin. *Some speculations on storage and retrieval processes in long-term memory.* Institute for Mathematical Studies in the Social Sciences, Stanford University, Tech. Rep. No. 127. 1968.
5. H. A. Bernbach. Decision processes in memory. *Psychol. Rev.,* 1967, *74,* 462–480.
6. J. R. Binford and C. Gettys. Nonstationarity in paired-associate learning as indicated by a second guess procedure. *J. math. Psychol.,* 1965, *2,* 190–195.
7. A. Bjork. *Learning and short-term retention of paired associates in relation to specific sequences of interpresentation intervals.* Institute for Mathematical Studies in the Social Sciences, Stanford University, Tech. Rep. No. 106. 1966.
8. W. A. Bousfield and B. H. Cohen. Clustering in recall as a function of the number of word categories in stimulus-word lists. *J. gen. Psychol.,* 1956, *54,* 95–106.

9. G. H. Bower. A multicomponent theory of the memory trace. In K. W. Spence and J. T. Spence (eds.). *The psychology of learning and motivation.* New York: Academic Press, 1967. Vol. 1, pp. 229–325.
10. J. W. Brelsford, Jr. and R. C. Atkinson. Short-term memory as a function of rehearsal procedures. *J. verb. Learning verb. Behavior,* 1968, *7,* 730–736.
11. J. W. Brelsford, Jr., R. M. Shiffrin, and R. C. Atkinson. Multiple reinforcement effects in short-term memory. *Brit. J. math. stat. Psychol.,* 1968, *21,* 1–19.
12. C. N. Cofer. On some factors in the organizational characteristics of free recall. *Amer. Psychol.,* 1965, *20,* 261–272.
13. B. H. Cohen. Recall of categorized word lists. *J. exp. Psychol.,* 1963, *66,* 227–234.
14. K. M. Dallet and L. D'Andrea. Mediation instructions versus unlearning instructions in the A-B, A-C paradigm. *J. exp. Psychol.,* 1965, *69,* 460–466.
15. F. J. DaPolito. Proactive effects with independent retrieval of competing responses. Unpublished doctoral dissertation, Indiana University, 1966.
16. J. Deese. *The structure of associations in language and thought.* Baltimore: Johns Hopkins University Press, 1966.
17. W. K. Estes. The statistical approach to learning theory. In S. Koch (ed.). *Psychology: A study of a science.* New York: McGraw-Hill, 1959. Vol. 2, pp. 380–491.
18. E. A. Feigenbaum. Information processing and memory. In *Proceedings of the fifth Berkeley symposium on mathematical statistics and probability, 1966.* Vol. 4. Berkeley: University of California Press, 1966.
19. J. G. Greeno. *Some attempts to locate associative information.* Department of Psychology, Indiana University, Tech. Rep. 1967.
20. W. F. Harley, Jr. The effect of monetary incentive in paired-associate learning using an absolute method. *Psychon. Sci.,* 1965, *3,* 141–142.
21. S. Hellyer. Supplementary report: Frequency of stimulus presentation and short-term decrement in recall. *J. exp. Psychol.,* 1962, *64,* 650.
22. D. L. Hintzman. Explorations with a discrimination net model for paired-associate learning. *J. math. Psychol.,* 1968, *5,* 123–162.
23. G. Keppel. Retroactive and proactive inhibition. In T. R. Dixon and D. L. Horton (eds.). *Verbal behavior and general behavior theory.* Englewood Cliffs, N. J.: Prentice-Hall, 1968. Pp. 172–213.
24. W. Kintsch. Memory and decision aspects of recognition learning. *Psychol. Rev.,* 1967, *74,* 496–504.
25. J. B. McGovern. Extinction of associations in four transfer paradigms. *Psychol. Monogr.,* 1964, *78* (16, whole no. 593).
26. G. Mandler. Association and organization: Facts, fancies, and theories. In T. R. Dixon and D. L. Horton (eds.). *Verbal behavior and general behavior theory.* Englewood Cliffs, N. J.: Prentice-Hall, 1968. Pp. 109–119.
27. E. Martin. Stimulus recognition in aural paired-associate learning. *J. verb. Learning verb. Behavior,* 1967, *6,* 272–276.
28. A. W. Melton. Implications of short-term memory for a general theory of memory. *J. verb. Learning verb. Behavior,* 1963, *2,* 1–21.
29. A. W. Melton and J. M. Irwin. The influence of degree of interpolated learn-

ing on retroactive inhibition and the overt transfer of specific responses. *Amer. J. Psychol.,* 1940, *53,* 173–203.
30. R. Millward. An all-or-none model for noncorrection routines with elimination of incorrect responses. *J. math. Psychol.,* 1964, *1,* 392–404.
31. B. B. Murdock, Jr. The serial position effect of free recall. *J. exp. Psychol.,* 1962, *64,* 482–488.
32. D. A. Norman. Toward a theory of memory and attention. *Psychol. Rev.,* 1968, *75,* 522–536.
33. C. E. Osgood. Psycholinguistics. In S. Koch (ed.). *Psychology: A study of a science.* New York: McGraw-Hill, 1963. Vol. 6, pp. 244–316.
34. J. L. Phillips, R. M. Shiffrin, and R. C. Atkinson. Effects of list length on short-term memory. *J. verb. Learning verb. Behavior,* 1967, *6,* 303–311.
35. H. R. Pollio. *The structural basis of word association behavior.* The Hague: Mouton, 1966.
36. L. Postman. The present status of interference theory. In C. N. Cofer (ed.). *Verbal learning and verbal behavior.* New York: McGraw-Hill, 1961. Pp. 152–196.
37. D. E. Rumelhart. *The effects of interpresentation intervals in a continuous paired-associate task.* Institute for Mathematical Studies in the Social Sciences, Stanford University, Tech. Rep. No. 116. 1967.
38. W. N. Runquist and F. H. Farley. The use of mediators in the learning of verbal paired associates. *J. verb. Learning verb. Behavior,* 1964, *3,* 280–285.
39. J. Schnorr and R. C. Atkinson. Repetition versus imagery instructions in the short- and long-term retention of paired associates. *Psychon. Sci.,* 1969, *15,* 183–184.
40. R. M. Shiffrin. *Search and retrieval processes in long-term memory.* Institute for Mathematical Studies in the Social Sciences, Stanford University, Tech. Rep. No. 137. 1968.
41. G. Sperling. The information available in brief visual presentations. *Psychol. Monogr.,* 1960, *74* (11, whole no. 498).
42. W. J. Thompson. Recall of paired-associate items as a function of interpolated pairs of different types. *Psychon. Sci.,* 1967, *9,* 629–630.
43. E. Tulving. Subjective organization in free recall of "unrelated" words. *Psychol. Rev.,* 1962, *69,* 344–354.
44. E. Tulving. The effects of presentation and recall of material in free-recall learning. *J. verb. Learning verb. Behavior,* 1967, *6,* 175–184.
45. B. J. Underwood. Interference and forgetting. *Psychol. Rev.,* 1957, *64,* 49–60.
46. B. J. Underwood. Stimulus selection in verbal learning. In C. N. Cofer and B. S. Musgrave (eds.). *Verbal behavior and learning: Problems and processes.* New York: McGraw-Hill, 1963. Pp. 33–70.
47. W. A. Wickelgren and D. A. Norman. Strength models and serial position in short-term recognition memory. *J. math. Psychol.,* 1966, *3,* 316–347.

# 37

# THE MIND OF A MNEMONIST: HIS MEMORY

### A. R. Luria

This study of S.'s memory was begun in the mid-1920s, when he was still working as a newspaper reporter. It continued for many years, during which S. changed jobs several times, finally becoming a professional mnemonist who gave performances of memory feats....

### THE INITIAL FACTS

Throughout the course of our research S.'s recall was always of a spontaneous nature. The only mechanisms he employed were one of the following: Either he continued to see series of words or numbers which had been presented to him, or he converted these elements into visual images.

The simplest structure was one S. used to recall tables of numbers written on a blackboard. S. would study the material on the board, close his eyes, open them again for a moment, turn aside, and, at a signal, reproduce one series from the board. Then he would fill in the empty squares of the next table, rapidly calling off the numbers. It was a simple matter for him to fill in the numbers for the empty squares of the table either when asked to do this for certain squares I chose at random, or when asked to fill in a series of numbers successively in reverse order. He could easily tell me which numbers formed one or another of the vertical columns in the table and could "read off" to me numbers that formed the diagonals; finally, he was able to compose a multidigit number out of the one-digit numbers in the entire table.

In order to imprint an impression of a table consisting of twenty numbers, S. needed only 35 to 40 sec, during which he would examine the chart closely several times. A table of fifty numbers required somewhat more time, but he could easily fix an impression of it in his mind in 2½ to 3 min, staring at the chart a few times, then closing his eyes as he tested himself on the material in his mind.

Source: Excerpted from Chapter 3 of *The Mind of a Mnemonist: A Little Book About a Vast Memory* by A. R. Luria. (c) 1968 by Basic Books, Inc., Publishers, New York, and Jonathan Cape, Ltd., London.

The following is a typical example of one of dozens of experiments that were carried out with him (experiment of May 10, 1939):

TABLE 1

| | | | |
|---|---|---|---|
| 6 | 6 | 8 | 0 |
| 5 | 4 | 3 | 2 |
| 1 | 6 | 8 | 4 |
| 7 | 9 | 3 | 5 |
| 4 | 2 | 3 | 7 |
| 3 | 8 | 9 | 1 |
| 1 | 0 | 0 | 2 |
| 3 | 4 | 5 | 1 |
| 2 | 7 | 6 | 8 |
| 1 | 9 | 2 | 6 |
| 2 | 9 | 6 | 7 |
| 5 | 5 | 2 | 0 |
| x | 0 | 1 | x |

He spent 3 min examining the table I had drawn on a piece of paper (Table 1), stopping intermittently to go over what he had seen in his mind. It took him 40 sec to reproduce this table (that is, to call off all the numbers in succession). He did this at a rhythmic pace, scarcely pausing between numbers. His reproduction of the numbers in the third vertical column took somewhat longer—1 min, 20 sec—whereas he reproduced those in the second vertical column in 25 sec, and took 30 sec to reproduce this column in reverse order. He read off the numbers which formed the diagonals (the groups of four numbers running zigzag through the chart) in 35 sec, and within 50 sec ran through the numbers that formed the horizontal rows. Altogether he required 1 min, 30 sec to convert all fifty numbers into a single fifty-digit number and read this off.

As I have already mentioned, an experiment designed to verify S.'s "reading" of this series, which was not carried out until after several months had elapsed, indicated that he could reproduce the table he had "impressed" in his mind just as fully as in the first reproduction and at about the same rates. The only difference in the two performances was that for the later one he needed more time to "revive" the entire situation in which the experiment had originally been carried out: to "see" the room in which he had been sitting; to "hear" my voice; to "reproduce" an image of himself looking at the board. But the actual process of "reading" the table required scarcely any more time than it had earlier....

## SYNESTHESIA

... S. had remarked on a number of occasions that if the examiner said something during the experiment—if, for example, he said *yes* to confirm that S. had reproduced the material correctly or *no* to indicate he had made a mistake—a blur would appear on the table and would spread and block off the numbers, so that S. in his mind would be forced to "shift" the table over, away from the blurred section that was covering it. The same thing happened if he heard noise in the auditorium; this was immediately converted into "puffs of steam" or "splashes" which made it more difficult for him to read the table.

This led us to believe that the process by which he retained material did not consist merely of his having preserved spontaneous traces of visual impressions; there were certain additional elements at work. I suggested that S. possessed a marked degree of synesthesia. If we can trust S.'s recollections of his early childhood ... these synesthetic reactions could be traced back to a very early age. As he described it:

> When I was about 2 or 3 years old I was taught the words of a Hebrew prayer. I didn't understand them, and what happened was that the words settled in my mind as puffs of steam or splashes. . . . Even now I *see* these puffs or splashes when I hear certain sounds.

Synesthetic reactions of this type occurred whenever S. was asked to listen to tones. The same reactions, though somewhat more complicated, occurred with his perception of voices and with speech sounds.

The following is the record of experiments that were carried out with S. in the Laboratory on the Physiology of Hearing at the Neurological Institute, Academy of Medical Sciences.

> Presented with a tone pitched at 30 cps and having an amplitude of 100 db, S. stated that at first he saw a strip 12 to 15 cm in width the color of old, tarnished silver. Gradually this strip narrowed and seemed to recede; then it was converted into an object that glistened like steel. Then the tone gradually took on a color one associates with twilight, the sound continuing to dazzle because of the silvery gleam it shed.
>
> Presented with a tone pitched at 50 cps and an amplitude of 100 db, S. saw a brown strip against a dark background that had red, tongue-like edges. The sense of taste he experienced was like that of sweet and sour borscht, a sensation that gripped his entire tongue.
>
> Presented with a tone pitched at 100 cps and having an amplitude of 86 db, he saw a wide strip that appeared to have a reddish-orange hue in the center; from the center outwards the brightness faded with light gradations so that the edges of the strip appeared pink.
>
> Presented with a tone pitched at 250 cps and having an amplitude of 64 db, S. saw a velvet cord with fibers jutting out on all sides. The cord was tinged with a delicate, pleasant pink-orange hue.
>
> Presented with a tone pitched at 500 cps and having an amplitude of 100 db, he saw a streak of lightning splitting the heavens in two. When the intensity of the sound was lowered to 74 db, he saw a dense orange color which made him feel as though a needle had been thrust into his spine. Gradually this sensation diminished.
>
> Presented with a tone pitched at 2,000 cps and having an amplitude of 113 db, S. said: "It looks something like fireworks tinged with a pink-red

hue. The strip of color feels rough and unpleasant, and it has an ugly taste—rather like that of a briny pickle.... You could hurt your hand on this."

Presented with a tone pitched at 3,000 cps and having an amplitude of 128 db, he saw a whisk broom that was of a fiery color, while the rod attached to the whisks seemed to be scattering off into fiery points.

The experiments were repeated during several days and invariably the same stimuli produced identical experiences.

What this meant was that S. was one of a remarkable group of people, among them the composer Scriabin, who have retained in an especially vivid form a complex synesthetic type of sensitivity....

S. also experienced synesthetic reactions when he listened to someone's voice. "What a crumbly, yellow voice you have," he once told L. S. Vygotsky[1] while conversing with him. At a later date he elaborated on the subject of voices as follows:

> You know there are people who seem to have many voices, whose voices seem to be an entire composition, a bouquet. The late S. M. Eisenstein[2] had just such a voice: Listening to him, it was as though a flame with fibers protruding from it was advancing right toward me. I got so interested in his voice, I couldn't follow what he was saying....

From an objective standpoint these synesthetic components were important to his recall, for they created, as it were, a background for each recollection, furnishing him with additional, "extra" information that would guarantee accurate recall. If, as we shall see later, S. was prompted to reproduce a word inaccurately, the additional synesthetic sensations he experienced would fail to coincide with the word he produced, leaving him with the sense that something was wrong with his response and forcing him to correct the error.

> ... I recognize a word not only by the images it evokes but by a whole complex of feelings that image arouses. It's hard to express ... it's not a matter of vision or hearing but some overall sense I get. Usually I experience a word's taste and weight, and I don't have to make an effort to remember it—the word seems to recall itself. But it's difficult to describe. What I sense is something oily slipping through my hand ... or I'm aware of a slight tickling in my left hand caused by a mass of tiny, lightweight points. When that happens I simply remember, without having to make the attempt.... [Record of May 22, 1939.]

Hence, the synesthetic experiences that clearly made themselves felt when he recalled a voice, individual sounds, or complexes of sound were not of major importance but served merely as information that was secondary in his recall of words. Let us consider S.'s responses to words now in greater detail.

---

[1] The well-known Russian psychologist.
[2] The famous producer.

## WORDS AND IMAGES

As we know, there are two aspects to the nature of words. On the one hand, words are composed of conventional groupings of sounds having various degrees of complexity—the feature of language phonetics deals with. On the other hand, words also designate certain objects, qualities, or activities; that is, they have specific meanings—that aspect of words with which semantics and other related branches of linguistics, such as lexicology and morphology, are concerned. A person in a healthy, alert state of awareness will generally not notice the phonetic elements in words, so that given two words such as *skripka* and *skrepka* (Russian: "violin" and "paper clip"), which differ by virtue of one minor alteration of vowel sounds, he may be completely unaware of their resemblance phonetically and observe only that they stand for two completely different things.[3]

For S., too, it was the meaning of words that was predominantly important. Each word had the effect of summoning up in his mind a graphic image, and what distinguished him from the general run of people was that his images were incomparably more vivid and stable than theirs. Further, his images were invariably linked with synesthetic components (sensations of colored "splotches," "splashes," and "lines") which reflected the sound structure of a word and the voice of the speaker.

It was only natural, then, that the visual quality of his recall was fundamental to his capacity for remembering words. For when he heard or read a word it was at once converted into a visual image corresponding with the object the word signified for him. Once he formed an image, which was always of a particularly vivid nature, it stabilized itself in his memory, and though it might vanish for a time when his attention was taken up with something else, it would manifest itself once again whenever he returned to the situation in which the word had first come up. As he described it:

> When I hear the word *green*, a green flowerpot appears; with the word *red* I see a man in a red shirt coming toward me; as for *blue*, this means an image of someone waving a small blue flag from a window.... Even numbers remind me of images. Take the number 1. This is a proud, well-built man; 2 is a high-spirited woman; 3 a gloomy person (why, I don't know); 6 a man with a swollen foot; 7 a man with a mustache; 8 a very stout woman—a sack within a sack. As for the number 87, what I see is a fat woman and a man twirling his mustache. [Record of September 1936.]

One can easily see that the images produced by numbers and words represent a fusion of graphic ideas and synesthetic reactions. If S. heard

---

[3] It is only in certain pathological states that the phonetic elements of words predominate and meaning becomes unimportant. See [1].

a word he was familiar with, the image would be sufficient to screen off any synesthetic reactions; but if he had to deal with an unfamiliar word, which did not evoke an image, he would remember it "in terms of lines." In other words, the sounds of the word were transformed into colored splotches, lines, or splashes. Thus, even with an unfamiliar word, he still registered some visual impression which he associated with it but which was related to the phonetic qualities of the word rather than to its meaning.

When S. read through a long series of words, each word would elicit a graphic image. And since the series was fairly long, he had to find some way of distributing these images of his in a mental row or sequence. Most often (and this habit persisted throughout his life), he would "distribute" them along some roadway or street he visualized in his mind. Sometimes this was a street in his home town, which would also include the yard attached to the house he had lived in as a child and which he recalled vividly. On the other hand, he might also select a street in Moscow. Frequently he would take a mental walk along that street—Gorky Street in Moscow—beginning at Mayakovsky Square, and slowly make his way down, "distributing" his images at houses, gates, and store windows. At times, without realizing how it had happened, he would suddenly find himself back in his home town (Torzhok), where he would wind up his trip in the house he had lived in as a child. The setting he chose for his "mental walks" approximates that of dreams, the difference being that the setting in his walks would immediately vanish once his attention was distracted but would reappear just as suddenly when he was obliged to recall a series he had "recorded" this way.

This technique of converting a series of words into a series of graphic images explains why S. could so readily reproduce a series from start to finish or in reverse order; how he could rapidly name the word that preceded or followed one I'd select from the series. To do this, he would simply begin his walk, either from the beginning or from the end of the street, find the image of the object I had named, and "take a look at" whatever happened to be situated on either side of it. S.'s visual patterns of memory differed from the more commonplace type of figurative memory by virtue of the fact that his images were exceptionally vivid and stable; he was also able to "turn away" from them, as it were, and "return" to them whenever it was necessary.[4]

It was this technique of recalling material graphically that explained why S. always insisted a series be read clearly and distinctly, that the words not be read off too quickly. For he needed some time, however slight, to convert the words into images. If the words were read too quickly, without sufficient pause between them, his images would tend

---

[4] S.'s technique of a "graphic distribution" and "reading" of images closely resembled that of another mnemonist, Ishihara, who was studied and written about in Japan. See [2].

to coalesce into a kind of chaos or "noise" through which he had difficulty discerning anything.

In effect, the astonishing clarity and tenacity of his images, the fact that he could retain them for years and call them up when occasion demanded it, made it possible for him to recall an unlimited number of words and to retain these indefinitely. Nonetheless, his method of recording also had certain drawbacks.

Once we were convinced that the capacity of S.'s memory was virtually unlimited, that he did not have to memorize the data presented but merely had to register an impression, which he could read on a much later date... (10 or even 16 years after the original presentation), we naturally lost interest in trying to "measure" his memory capacity. Instead, we concentrated on precisely the reverse issue: Was it possible for him to forget? We tried to establish the instances in which S. had omitted a word from a series.

Indeed, not only were such instances to be found, but they were fairly frequent. Yet how was one to explain forgetting in a man whose memory seemed inexhaustible? How explain that sometimes there were instances in which S. omitted some elements in his recall but scarcely ever reproduced material inaccurately (by substituting a synonym or a word closely associated in meaning with the one he'd been given)?

The experiments immediately turned up answers to both questions. S. did not "forget" words he'd been given; what happened was that he omitted these as he "read off" a series. And in each case there was a simple explanation for the omissions. If S. had placed a particular image in a spot where it would be difficult for him to discern—if he, for example, had placed it in an area that was poorly lit or in a spot where he would have trouble distinguishing the object from the background against which it had been set—he would omit this image when he "read off" the series he had distributed along his mental route. He would simply walk on without noticing the particular item, as he explained.

These omissions (and they were quite frequent in the early period of our observation, when S.'s technique of recall had not developed to its fullest) clearly were not defects of memory but were, in fact, defects of perception. They could not be explained in terms of established ideas on the neurodynamics of memory traces (retroactive and proactive inhibition, extinction of traces, and so on) but rather by certain factors that influence perception (clarity, contrast, the ability to isolate a figure from its background, the degree of lighting available). His errors could not be explained, then, in terms of the psychology of memory but had to do with the psychological factors that govern perception.

Excerpts from the numerous reports taken on our sessions with S. will serve to illustrate this point. When, for example, S. reproduced a long series of words, he omitted the word *pencil;* on another occasion he skipped *egg;* in a third series it was the word *banner,* and in a fourth, *blimp*. Finally, S. omitted from another series the word *shuttle,* which he was not familiar with. The following is his explanation of how this happened:

> I put the image of the *pencil* near a fence ... the one down the street, you know. But what happened was that the image fused with that of the fence and I walked right on past without noticing it. The same thing happened with the word *egg*. I had put it up against a white wall and it blended in with the background. How could I possibly spot a white egg up against a white wall? Now take the word *blimp*. That's something gray, so it blended in with the gray of the pavement.... *Banner*, of course, means the Red Banner. But, you know, the building which houses the Moscow City Soviet of Workers' Deputies is also red, and since I'd put the banner close to one of the walls of the building I just walked on without seeing it.... Then there's the word *putamen*. I don't know what this means, but it's such a dark word that I couldn't see it ... and, besides, the street lamp was quite a distance away.... [Record of December 1932.]

> Sometimes I put a word in a dark place and have trouble seeing it as I go by. Take the word *box*, for example. I'd put it in a niche in the gate. Since it was dark there I couldn't see it.... Sometimes if there is noise, or another person's voice suddenly intrudes, I see blurs which block off my images. Then syllables are liable to slip into a word which weren't there originally and I'd be tempted to say they really had been part of the word. It's these blurs which interfere with my recall.... [Record of December 1932.]

Hence, S.'s defects of memory were really defects of perception or concentration. An analysis of them allowed us to get a better grasp of the characteristic devices this amazing man used to recall words, without altering our former impressions with respect to the power of his memory.

## REFERENCES

1. A. S. Luria and O. S. Vinogradova. An objective investigation of the dynamics of semantic systems. *Brit. J. Psychol.,* 1959, *50* (no. 2), 89–105.
2. Tukasa Susukita. Untersuchung eines ausserordentlichen Gedächtnisses. *Japan Tohoku Psychol. Fol.* Vol. 1 (no. 2–3) and Vol. 2 (no. 1). Sendai: Tohoku Imperialis Universitas, 1933.

# 38
# SELECTIVE ATTENTION IN MAN

Anne M. Treisman

Fifty years ago psychologists thought of attention as "the focalization of consciousness" or "the increased clearness of a particular idea." But these and other definitions in terms of mental faculties or subjective experience proved sterile for empirical research and ended in a series of inconclusive controversies. Recently interest in this problem has revived, prompted both by the urgent practical need, with the increasing use of machines in industry, to define man's characteristics as an information-handling system, and by two conceptual advances: the rejection of introspective reports as a source of explanation, and the development of scientific models dealing not with the conservation and transmission of energy but with control and communication. There has been a parallel development of interest in the neurophysiological bases of attention and selectivity of response, and the prospect is that the neural structures underlying the functional processes inferred from psychological studies will ultimately be identified; but this paper is confined to behavioral research.

## METHODS, PROBLEMS, AND APPROACH

Various experimental methods have been used to investigate behavior in tasks requiring selective attention. Our examples are mainly of human subjects responding to passages of speech. A subject is presented with two or more messages which can differ in physical characteristics such as intensity, frequency, or spatial localization, in features of the language such as similarity, meaningfulness, importance to the subject, or contextual probability, and finally in the degree to which the messages overlap or are separated in time. He may be asked to respond to one message or to several, or to monitor all messages and respond only to some. The response required may be immediate or delayed; it may coincide with further messages or alternate with them; and it may vary in complexity, for example it may be repeating back the message or replying to questions—the two most common tasks—or translating, writing, summarizing or recalling the message.

Examples of problems which arise are the nature of the limits in

Source: *British Medical Bulletin*, 1964, 20, 12–16. Reprinted by permission.

man's ability to respond to competing messages; the form of selective system used by the brain and the stage at which irrelevant data are discarded; finally, the way in which incoming data are analyzed from sound to word and meaning, stored in short-term or long-term memory, and used to determine the appropriate response. A useful approach is to start with a general descriptive model, making it more precise as evidence accumulates. The alternatives at this level are usually qualitative and the evidence relates to the type of function rather than to the actual mechanisms which carry it out, and to the order in which the processes occur rather than to their spatial lay-out. Broadbent [7] made an important contribution with his "filter" and "information flow" theory (see Figure 38-1), which provides the basis and starting point for this paper. Some alternative accounts of attention are given by Hebb [16], Sutherland [29], Berlyne [1], and Deutsch and Deutsch [13].

## LIMITS TO PERFORMANCE WITH COMPETING INPUTS

Many experiments [2, 11, 21, 23, 34] have shown that if a man must deal with competing messages, there is a limit at which his performance will break down. For example, Broadbent asked his subjects to answer questions about a changing visual display and found that their efficiency was lower if two questions (in different voices) were given simultaneously. Cherry showed that subjects who repeated back a passage of prose heard through one ear were unable to report any of the verbal content of another passage presented at the same time to the other ear. They were aware of the general physical characteristics—that it was speech in a man's voice—but they failed to notice when the English changed to German or to speech played in the reverse direction.

What sets the limits to performance in tasks like these? Peripheral masking is unlikely to be the whole answer, since subjects are quite able to handle either of the two messages if no response is required to the other. Moreover, very similar results are obtained when one message is visual and one auditory [21]. Competition between motor responses may be avoided by requiring successive responses to simultaneous messages, for instance asking subjects to repeat one, then recall the other, as in Cherry's experiment. Thus part at least of the interference must occur at some central stage, either in identification of the words or in memory storage....

## BROADBENT'S "FILTER" AND "INFORMATION FLOW" MODEL

To summarize these findings, Figure 38-1 shows the relevant parts of Broadbent's model. A number of messages may reach the receptors together and pass along different input channels to a selective system

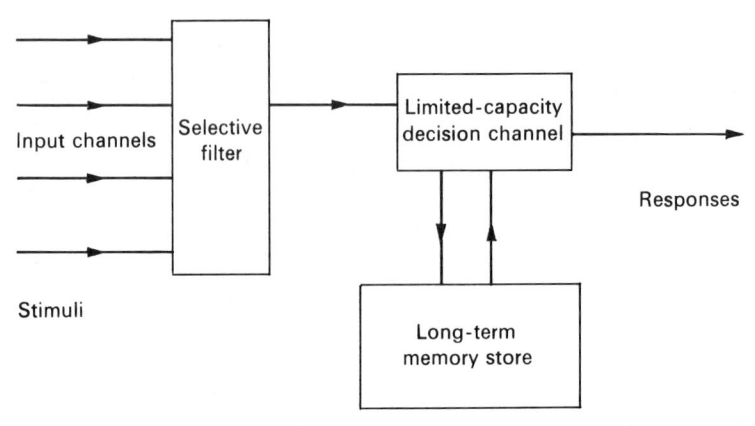

FIGURE 38-1 Broadbent's "Filter" and "Information Flow" Model for Selective Attention [7]. The diagram illustrates a model in which man is represented as an information-handling system. The successive parts of the model are discussed in the text.

which he calls the *filter*. This blocks some and passes others to a single-decision channel of limited capacity, which has access to information in a long-term memory store and which determines the appropriate response. The next problem is to specify the parts of the model and their interrelations in more detail.

**Input Channels**

The word *channel* normally implies a discrete physical system with defined properties, and might be used to describe different sense organs, like eye and ear. However, many experiments have shown that messages can be selected or rejected on the basis of characteristics other than the receptors at which they arrive. Subjects can respond efficiently to one of two auditory messages if these differ in spatial position, whether real [3] or apparent [3, 32], in frequency range [28], in intensity [14]—in short, in any general physical feature. The efficiency of selective response declines as the difficulty of discrimination between selected and irrelevant messages is increased along any of these dimensions [7]. Thus, in terms of the model, the input channels are functionally defined as carrying classes of sounds distinguished by one or more physical features which allow the filter to select between them.

Broadbent originally suggested that classes of words distinguished by their meaning might also be thought of as coming in different channels; for example, the filter might select names of food or reject taboo words. Cherry [11] has shown that subjects can use the contextual probabilities of words to pick out one of two messages in the absence of any other cue. But this type of selection is much less efficient than that based on general physical features, for Cherry's subjects needed many trials to separate the two messages completely. If bilingual subjects are presented once only with two messages in different languages, they are hardly more efficient in repeating back one of the two than when both are in the same language, and do much worse than when the two are in different voices, despite the extreme difference at the linguistic level [32]. Since no message can be discarded on the basis of features still to be discriminated, rejection of classes of words could occur only during or after word identification. This allows much less economy in analysis than selection by a physical feature in the sounds of the messages, which may be discriminated at an earlier stage.

This leaves the problem of how the brain separates out the single, complex sound-wave reaching both ears into two or more channels, of which it can select one for further analysis. There have been some attempts to specify in more detail how these discriminations are carried out. For example, Cherry and Sayers [12] have put forward a model for auditory localization in which the signals reaching the two ears are cross-correlated to determine which constitute the same message; the delay interval giving maximum correlation for each message then indicates the apparent position of each source of sound. Another example is the suggestion by Broadbent and Ladefoged [10] that the cue distinguishing different voices is the larynx tone or pulse modulation rate of the frequency spectrum. When this is the same, different frequencies in the same or opposite ears are heard as one sound; when it differs, two sounds are heard. This pulse rate may be coded by the nervous system as a rate of firing, so that the channels are not necessarily identifiable with separate neural pathways.

## Stages of Input Analysis and Level of Filter

It is plausible to suppose that different features of the input messages are discriminated successively, and that the filter selects on the basis of past analyses which inputs will be passed on for further processing and which discarded. Both the order in which the different features are analyzed and the stage at which the selection is made could be fixed or variable. There is some evidence that in human selective listening the channel discriminations based on general physical features are always made, and that the filter can operate only at a later stage; Cherry's subjects could report all these features of the message to which they were not attending [11]. I have shown that the interference with response to a selected message was determined not by the number of irrelevant messages or verbal sequences but by the number of channels in which they were presented, although the minimum physical difference between selected and irrelevant channels was kept constant [32]. This suggests that all the physical features distinguishing the irrelevant channels were being discriminated, whether they were needed for the task or not.

On the other hand, there is little evidence that differences in the purely verbal content of irrelevant messages are noticed or produce differences in interference, provided that they arrive in separate channels from the selected message. For example, Moray's subjects showed no trace of recognition of a repeated series of words presented in an irrelevant channel, and failed to recall digits that they had specifically been told to listen for [19]. To ensure that this was not a limit in memory only, I asked subjects to make an immediate manual response to any digit on either channel while repeating back one message only [32]. The information in the manual response was the same for both channels, but subjects responded only to digits in the selected message. I also failed to produce any change in efficiency of selective response by varying the information content, the meaningfulness or the similarity of irrelevant messages, provided that no consistent differences were produced in nonlinguistic features of the sounds [32]. (This last factor was not controlled in experiments by Webster and Thompson [33] or by Peters [22], who claimed to find effects on performance of the content of competing messages.)

However, there are a few interesting exceptions to the rule that the verbal content is never reported. Moray [19] showed that subjects sometimes noticed their own names if these occurred in the irrelevant message, and suggested that there might be a specific system, before the filter, for analyzing patterns and for identifying highly important signals. I found that subjects occasionally repeated a word from the irrelevant message if it was made highly probable in the context of the message to which they had been attending [31]. This is more difficult to attribute to a specific pattern analyzer, since the range of words which could be made highly probable is very large. Cherry [11] showed that if identical messages were presented to the two ears a few seconds out of step, subjects became aware that the two were the same. To determine at what level the identity was recognized, I presented the same messages in different voices and also two messages with the same meaning in different languages, using bilingual subjects in the latter case [32]. In both conditions subjects still noticed the identity. Deutsch and Deutsch [13] argue that these examples of recognition of the verbal content of rejected messages imply that selection is made only after full analysis of all inputs. As further support for this idea they quote studies of habituation by Sharpless and Jasper [25] and by Sokolov [26].

## HABITUATION

If the same stimulus is presented repeatedly, the response originally made tends to decrease or disappear; this change is known as habituation. Like selective attention to competing messages, it implies some form of selectivity or filtering, and Broadbent originally attributed both to the same filter system. He postulated that this had an intrinsic bias for passing novel stimuli (novel implying both stimuli which had not been present before and those which had not recently been selected by the filter). As the stimuli to which the subject is being habituated are repeated, they become less novel, and the filter will shift to new channels.

Sokolov [26] reports some interesting studies of habituation in the arousal response or "orienting reflex." He examined the decrease or disappearance of alpha blocking in the electroencephalogram and the galvanic skin response in human subjects on repeated presentations of the same stimulus. He then altered the stimulus in various ways and found that the arousal response reappeared not only when the intensity or duration of the habituated stimulus increased but also when they decreased. This makes it unlikely that the habituation is due to perceptual blocking or attenuation of the stimulus, and he concluded that the recurrence of the arousal response was produced not by the stimulus as such, but by a mismatch between the new stimulus and a neural record representing the features of the habituated stimulus. He found, moreover, that this mismatch could imply complex levels of analysis, such for instance as a change in meaning with words. Deutsch points out that selection in these experiments must follow more complex analysis of the signals than discrimination of the simple features which distinguish functional input channels. Broadbent's original account is probably not inconsistent with Deutsch's, since his concepts both of novelty and of filtering were very general and flexible. However, it does not follow that selection must always be made at this late stage, and a different system may control habituation from that which controls selective attention with competing and highly informative inputs.

## WORD IDENTIFICATION AND SELECTIVE RESPONSE

I have suggested an alternative explanation of the few occasions when the verbal content is identified [31, 32]. It may be that the channel filter attenuates irrelevant messages rather than blocks them completely. If so, words which were highly important or relevant to the subject could be picked out when the threshold for identifying them was permanently or temporarily lowered within the word-identification system itself, in spite of their reduced signal-to-noise ratio. A possible system for identifying words is a hierarchy of tests carried out in sequence and giving a unique outcome for each word or other linguistic unit. The decision at each test point could be thought of as a signal detection problem (cf. [30]): A certain adjustable cut-off or criterion point is adopted on the dimension being discriminated, above which signals are accepted and below which they are rejected as noise. The criteria determining the results of the tests would be made more liberal for certain outcomes if favored by contextual probabilities, by recent use or by importance. Messages attenuated by the filter would pass the tests only if the criteria had been lowered in their favor and, if not, would pass no further through the hierarchy. This would be more economical than Deutsch's full analysis, since most irrelevant words would fail tests early in the hierarchy. Broadbent and Gregory [9] recently showed that the auditory threshold of one ear is raised if subjects are asked to attend to simultaneous digits in the other ear, and that this change is in the internal signal-to-noise ratio, not in the decision criterion. The complementary test is to show that thresholds are lowered for particular important or probable words and that this change is in the decision criterion, not the signal-to-noise ratio. There is certainly considerable evidence that, with a single message masked by noise, the threshold is lowered both for contextually probable words [18] and for one's own name [17]; moreover when two competing messages are presented in the same channel, selection is determined by the transition probabilities between words [11, 32]. But it has not yet been determined whether this is owing, as predicted, to a change in decision criterion.

It seems likely that the channel filter will be used only when two or more competing inputs would together overload the central decision channel. If so, it would not be brought into play in the usual restricted and monotonous environment of an habituation experiment. Habituation could then be attributed not to attenuation of certain input channels but to a change in the criteria for particular test outcomes at any level in the identification hierarchy, depending on the common features of the habituation stimuli used. This change could thus be as specific as the effects found by Sokolov, leaving the criteria for all other features unaffected.

## SHIFTING OF ATTENTION

The final problems raised relate to the setting and shifting of the filter from one channel to another and to the retrieval of temporarily rejected messages. Does the filter take time to shift to a new channel, and can one message be held temporarily in store while another is handled? In an ingenious series of experiments Broadbent [3, 5, 6, 8] reached an affirmative answer to both questions. He presented subjects with three pairs of simultaneous digits to be recalled, one of each pair in a different input channel (either the two ears; or ear and eye; or a frequency-filtered and a normal voice). He found that at rates faster than one digit per ear per second, subjects always recalled the digits from one channel first, followed by the other, rather than alternating between the channels to approximate the correct temporal order. The alternating order was possible only when the presentation rate was reduced to half a digit per ear per second where different sense organs were used, and two thirds of a digit per ear per second with voices differing in frequency spectrum. Two conclusions can be drawn: (1) There is a limit to the rate at which the filter can shift from one input channel to another, which is probably faster the less distinct the channels. (2) There is a short-term store prior to the filter in which the digits from the second channel are held while those from the first are identified.

Moray [20] questioned the first conclusion: he showed that if the digits were staggered in time, his subjects could alternate between their ears at rates much higher than those in Broadbent's experiments. But his own results also show that the subjects did worse when the digits alternated between the ears than when all were given to one ear. This again implies a limit in switching rate, although the shifts appear to be faster for staggered than for simultaneous digit pairs. Perhaps the filter shifts are facilitated by the presence of an external stimulus rather than a stored trace (as with the simultaneous digits). Gray and Wedderburn [15] also raise a difficulty for Broadbent's account by their finding that when the words of a common phrase such as "Who goes there?" are used instead of digits, subjects are as likely to group their responses by meaning as by input channel. In this case, subjects appear to select at a later stage, perhaps to take advantage of the transition probabilities between the words and thus to compensate for any extra interference in identifying them.

## SHORT-TERM STORAGE

Two main questions arise about the nature of the short-term store: (1) whether it is limited primarily by decay of items with time, or by interference between items held in it; (2) whether it is used only to cope with temporary overloading caused by momentary peaks of information or as a normal stage through which all inputs must pass. Broadbent varied both the time for which the digits in the second channel had to be stored before recall (by increasing the number given in the first channel) and the number of items to be held in store (by increasing the number in the second channel). Both these changes impaired recall, suggesting that the store is limited both by a short decay time (of the order of 1 or 2 sec) and by a small capacity. He also compared recall when subjects were told in advance which series of digits they were to repeat first and when they were told only after presentation of the digits. If all digits were automatically held in store, there should be no difference between these conditions, while if digits in one channel were sent straight through, advance knowledge of the order of recall would allow subjects to choose which to send first and should thus give better results. Broadbent [6] found that his subjects could perform in either way, but tended to change from an initial strategy of storing all digits to one of sending some through immediately, perhaps because it proves less efficient to hold all digits in the limited peripheral store.

Other recent findings may throw more light on this relatively peripheral "buffer" storage. Rabbitt [24] has shown that two aspects of a single visual stimulus (its shape and its color) may be treated in the same way as the digits sent to right and left ears in Broadbent's experiment on the order of recall. Thus the model for storage and selection can apply to any feature of the input which is as yet uncategorized as well as to inputs coming from one particular channel or source. Sperling [27] reports an ingenious method of estimating the information available in a temporary store immediately after presentation of a visual display, and of measuring its decay with time. He used a sampling technique to see whether the normal limit of five or six items in the span of apprehension is set by the initial intake capacity or by a central selection. At different intervals after a short exposure he gave a signal to instruct subjects which one of several rows of items they should recall; then used the partial recall to estimate the total number of items available. He found that this was initially two or three times the number in the normal span, but declined rapidly in less than a second to the normal limit. His finding seems closely related to the change from multichannel to single-channel functioning in Broadbent's model, although the decay time for vision may be more rapid than for hearing. Finally I compared the storage time for selected and rejected auditory messages: I repeated Cherry's experiment, presenting identical speech messages to the two ears, separated by a variable time interval, and noted the interval at which subjects recognized the identity, both with the selected message leading in time and with the rejected one leading [32]. In the first case the selected message had to be stored for comparison with the rejected one, and the interval for recognition was 5 sec; in the second case the rejected message was stored, and the interval fell to 1 or 2 sec. This result is consistent with Broadbent's estimate of the decay time for as yet uncategorized signals, and shows that identification of the sounds as words may treble their memory survival time.

## CONCLUSION

The traditional model of attention has become both more general and more precise: It has been related to the mechanisms of perception as such and has been defined in the language of channels, information, filtering processes and storage. This clarification may open the way to a more exact linking of behavioral concepts with underlying physiological mechanisms which are now being investigated. Developments of great interest are to be expected from the convergence of these two approaches.

## REFERENCES

1. D. E. Berlyne. *Conflict, arousal, and curiosity.* New York: McGraw-Hill, 1960.
2. D. E. Broadbent. *J. exp. Psychol.,* 1952, *43,* 267ff.
3. D. E. Broadbent. *J. exp. Psychol.,* 1954, *47,* 191ff.
4. D. E. Broadbent. *Brit. J. Psychol.,* 1956, *47,* 51ff.
5. D. E. Broadbent. *Quart. J. exp. Psychol.,* 1956, *8,* 145ff.

6. D. E. Broadbent. *Quart J. exp. Psychol.*, 1957, *9*, 1ff.
7. D. E. Broadbent. *Perception and communication.* Oxford: Pergamon, 1958.
8. D. E. Broadbent and M. Gregory. *Quart. J. exp. Psychol.*, 1961, *13*, 103ff.
9. D. E. Broadbent and M. Gregory. *Proc. roy. Soc.* (ser. B), 1963, *158*, 222ff.
10. D. E. Broadbent and P. Ladefoged. *J. acoust. Soc. Amer.*, 1957, *29*, 708ff.
11. E. C. Cherry. *J. acoust. Soc. Amer.*, 1953, *25*, 975ff.
12. E. C. Cherry and B. M. Sayers. *J. acoust. Soc. Amer.*, 1956, *28*, 889ff.
13. J. A. Deutsch and D. Deutsch. *Psychol. Rev.*, 1963, *70*, 80ff.
14. J. P. Egan, E. C. Carterette, and E. J. Thwing. *J. acoust. Soc. Amer.*, 1954, *26*, 774ff.
15. J. A. Gray and A. A. Wedderburn. *Quart. J. exp. Psychol.*, 1960, *12*, 180ff.
16. D. O. Hebb. *The organization of behavior: A neuropsychological theory.* London: Chapman & Hall, 1949.
17. C. I. Howarth and K. Ellis. *Quart. J. exp. Psychol.*, 1961, *13*, 236ff.
18. G. A. Miller, C. A. Heise, and W. Lichten. *J. exp. Psychol.*, 1951, *41*, 329ff.
19. N. Moray. *Quart. J. exp. Psychol.*, 1959, *11*, 56ff.
20. N. Moray. *Quart. J. exp. Psychol.*, 1960, *12*, 214ff.
21. G. H. Mowbray. *J. exp. Psychol.*, 1953, *46*, 365ff.
22. R. W. Peters. *Competing messages: The effect of interfering messages upon the reception of primary messages.* USN School Aviat. Med., Naval Air Station, Pensacola, Fla., Joint Proj. Rep. No. 27. 1954.
23. E. C. Poulton. *J. exp. Psychol.*, 1953, *46*, 91ff.
24. P. M. Rabbitt. *Nature, London,* 1962, *195*, 102ff.
25. S. Sharpless and H. Jasper. *Brain,* 1956, *79*, 655ff.
26. E. N. Sokolov. In M. A. B. Brazier (ed.). *The central nervous systems and behavior.* Transactions of the Third Conference, Princeton, February 1960. New York: Josiah Macy, Jr., Foundation, 1960.
27. G. Sperling. *Psychol. Monogr.*, 1960, *74* (no. 11).
28. W. Spieth and J. C. Webster. *J. acoust. Soc. Amer.*, 1955, *27*, 866ff.
29. N. S. Sutherland. Stimulus analyzing mechanisms. In *Mechanization of thought processes.* National Physical Laboratory Symposium No. 10. London: HMSO, 1959. Vol. 2, pp. 575–609.
30. W. P. Tanner, Jr., and J. A. Swets. *Psychol. Rev.*, 1954, *61*, 401ff.
31. A. M. Treisman. *Quart. J. exp. Psychol.*, 1960, *12*, 242ff.
32. A. M. Treisman. Attention and speech. Unpublished doctoral dissertation, Oxford University, 1961.
33. J. C. Webster and P. O. Thompson. *J. audio Engng. Soc.*, 1953, *1*, 171ff.
34. J. C. Webster and P. O. Thompson. *J. acoust. Soc. Amer.*, 1954, *26*, 396ff.

# 39
# EMOTIONALITY AND PERCEPTUAL DEFENSE

## Elliott McGinnies

During the past decade, a number of experimental investigations have progressively revealed the so-called dynamic, or motivational, aspects of perceptual behavior. No longer do we view perception as organized solely in terms of the structural characteristics of stimulus objects or the frequency with which the individual has been exposed to these objects. Perceptions are structured not only with respect to the limiting stimulus conditions but also with regard to the possibilities of reward [11, 12], need fulfillment [1, 7], attitudinal orientation [10], potential anxiety [4], symbolic value [3], and release from tension [2], to mention just a few. In order to describe such facts as the perceptual selection and accentuation of valued objects and the elimination or distortion of inimical stimulus objects, it has been found convenient to invoke mechanisms of sensitization, defense, and value resonance [10], vigilance [2], and primitivation [4]. Finally, playing host to these varied and intricate functions is the "ego," in whose service, presumably, the various perceptual adjustments operate.

It seems well established, then, that the perceptual filtering of visual stimuli serves, in many instances, to protect the observer as long as possible from an awareness of objects which have unpleasant emotional significance for him. Does this process, however, entirely insulate him from the emotion-provoking qualities of the stimulus situation? It is to this problem that the present discussion is addressed.

If we view emotion essentially as a motivating condition of the individual [6], the critical nature of the relationship between emotion and perception becomes apparent. Emotion does appear to represent a highly organized and directed state of the organism. Consequently emotion-inducing stimuli may be expected to initiate those perceptual responses which will be consistent with the general picture of emotional adaptation. Several exploratory investigations have indicated that the individual both perceives and reacts in a manner consistent with his emotional response to stimulation. That tension (defined as reactivity to threat, deprivation, or thwarting) will induce perceptual accentuation of objects previously associated with the anxiety-producing situation has been dem-

Source: *Psychological Review*, 1949, 56, 244–251. Copyright 1949 by the American Psychological Association. Reprinted by permission.

onstrated by Bruner and Postman [2]. More recently the same authors have shown that frustration, induced by sarcasm and criticism, will raise the perceptual thresholds of observers to tachistoscopically presented words. When, on the other hand, individuals are faced with stimulus objects which are not actually threatening, but which represent for them areas of little interest or some antipathy, they also generally display raised thresholds of recognition [10]. This process of perceptual screening apparently is acquired by the individual as a technique for organizing perceptions around value expectancies so as to produce maximum reinforcement of those expectancies.

One question intrudes repeatedly into interpretations of these experimental findings, namely, How is a raised or lowered threshold of recognition for inimical stimulus objects accomplished before the observer discriminates them and is thereby made aware of their threatening character? While the answer to this question will follow eventually only from fuller knowledge of the neurophysiological processes underlying perceptual response, detection of any one aspect of physiological reaction accompanying perceptual behavior should throw some light upon the processes by which perceptual defense is effected. One might conjecture, for example, that stimuli of an appropriate sort will arouse autonomic reactions characteristic of anxiety or pleasure *prior* to conscious awareness of the nature of the stimulus. If this is the case, we might expect to find a change in galvanic skin response in reaction to visually presented stimuli with emotion-provoking connotations before the subject is able to report the exact nature of the stimulus. In short, autonomic reactivity may have a lower threshold to threat than do those neural systems which mediate consciousness. Study of such reactions, therefore, should hold significant possibilities for adding to our understanding of the process by which discriminatory evaluation of visually sensed objects is accomplished before accurate perception occurs.

## THE EXPERIMENT

Because of the ease and precision with which it can be measured, the galvanic skin response was selected in the present study as an index of emotionality[1] in response to affectively charged verbal symbols. A list of eleven neutral and seven critical, or emotionally toned, words was first devised. The words are listed in Table 39-1 in their order of presentation to the subjects. Exposure of the words was accomplished by means of a Gerbrand's mirror tachistoscope, which allowed controlled variation of the exposure interval from 0.01 sec upward. This was done silently,

[1] The term emotionality is employed here in the sense of autonomic response without regard to presence or absence of phenomenological content.

TABLE 39-1   Stimulus Words in the Experiment in Order of Their Presentation to Each Observer

| apple | kotex |
|---|---|
| dance | broom |
| *raped* | stove |
| child | *penis* |
| *belly* | music |
| glass | trade |
| river | *filth* |
| *whore* | clear |
| sleep | *bitch* |

Note: Critical, or emotional, words are in italics.

since exposure duration in this apparatus is controlled by the activation of fluorescent tubes rather than by a shutter arrangement.

Subjects in the experiment were eight male and eight female undergraduates drawn from an elementary psychology class at the University of Alabama. All were naive as to the purpose of the experiment. The procedure consisted, first, in seating the subject before the viewing mirror of the tachistoscope and strapping electrodes onto both his palms. These were connected in series with a potentiometric circuit described by Lacey and Siegel [5] for measuring galvanic skin response. A 32-cm scale microammeter accurate to 0.5% made it possible to read current changes of 1 $\mu$a with precision. The subject's threshold was first determined for four trial words in order to accustom him to the apparatus and to allow his level of resistance to stabilize. In all cases, thresholds were determined by exposing the stimulus word once at 0.01 sec, once at 0.02 sec, and so on, until it was correctly reported by the subject.

Prior to experimentation, the subjects were told that they would be shown words which they might not be able to recognize at first. They were instructed to report whatever they saw or thought they saw on each exposure, regardless of what it was. One additional injunction was that they fix their hypothesis upon exposure of the stimulus, but withhold stating it verbally until they received a signal from the experimenter. In this manner we were able to expose the stimulus word, note the maximum deflection of the microammeter pointer during the 6-sec period following exposure, and then record the subject's response. Two experimenters cooperated in the procedure, one operating the tachistoscope, the other recording galvanic skin response and readjusting the current through the subject to 40 $\mu$a after recognition of each word.[2]

---

[2] Miss Billie Sue Talantis, a graduate student in psychology at the University of Alabama, assisted in the experimental procedure. The author is also grateful to Rosemary T. McGinnies for her generous assistance in organizing the data.

## EXPERIMENTAL FINDINGS

### Emotionality

Since we were interested primarily in the galvanic skin response of our subjects during the period *preceding correct recognition* of the stimulus words, we have based our analysis upon just those microammeter readings which were recorded on exposure trials up to, but not including, the trial on which recognition finally occurred. Assuming that the GSR may properly be considered an index of emotionality, we have succeeded in measuring emotional, or autonomic, reactivity to verbal symbols during the period preceding accurate recognition of the stimulus. That emotionality, so defined, is significantly greater during prerecognition exposures of the critical than of the neutral words is confirmed by statistical analysis of the findings. Testing the null hypothesis that no differences other than those attributable to random fluctuations in the data would exist between mean galvanic skin responses of the observers to the neutral and critical words, we obtained a $t$ value of 5.10 for 15 degrees of freedom. This permits rejection of the null hypothesis at the 0.01 level of confidence, and indicates a highly significant relationship between GSR and word meaning during the prerecognition period. The results are presented graphically in Figure 39-1, while the experimental findings are summarized in Table 39-2.

### Thresholds

Of equal interest are the data relating to thresholds of the observers for the neutral and critical words. The relationship here is depicted in Figure 39-2. Without exception, the mean thresholds of the observers were greater for the critical than for the neutral stimulus words. The significance of the individual differences in thresholds between critical and neutral words was tested statistically, the results yielding in this case a $t$

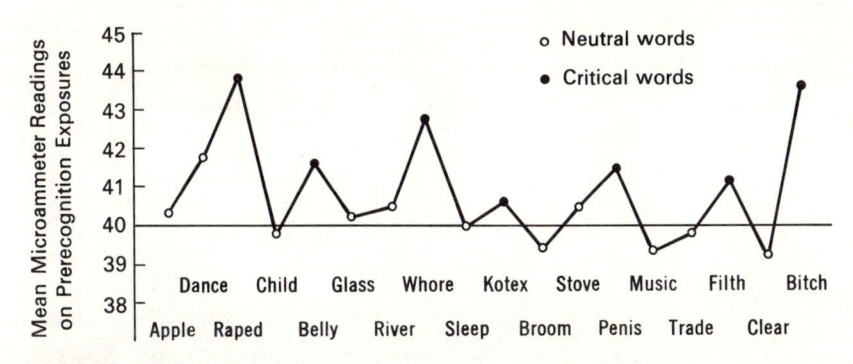

FIGURE 39-1 Group averages of galvanic skin response to neutral and critical words during prerecognition exposures.

TABLE 39-2 Summary of the Raw Data and Statistical Tests for All Observers with Respect to Both Galvanic Skin Response and Thresholds of Recognition for Neutral and Critical Stimulus Words

| Observer | Mean Microammeter Readings During Prerecognition Exposures | | Mean Thresholds of Recognition | |
|---|---|---|---|---|
| | Neutral Words | Critical Words | Neutral Words | Critical Words |
| 1 | 37.80 | 40.46 | 0.055 | 0.184 |
| 2 | 40.96 | 41.53 | 0.044 | 0.094 |
| 3 | 39.31 | 42.06 | 0.054 | 0.080 |
| 4 | 38.34 | 40.80 | 0.103 | 0.126 |
| 5 | 41.48 | 43.76 | 0.040 | 0.064 |
| 6 | 41.41 | 47.08 | 0.070 | 0.130 |
| 7 | 40.75 | 39.94 | 0.057 | 0.104 |
| 8 | 39.98 | 42.85 | 0.063 | 0.076 |
| 9 | 39.44 | 42.68 | 0.059 | 0.130 |
| 10 | 40.02 | 42.71 | 0.049 | 0.223 |
| 11 | 39.88 | 41.55 | 0.046 | 0.077 |
| 12 | 41.27 | 44.02 | 0.057 | 0.091 |
| 13 | 40.56 | 41.37 | 0.033 | 0.037 |
| 14 | 40.19 | 41.42 | 0.034 | 0.054 |
| 15 | 40.85 | 40.63 | 0.046 | 0.056 |
| 16 | 40.83 | 41.84 | 0.036 | 0.046 |

Mean diff. = 1.98.
$t = 5.10$.
$p < 0.01$.

Mean diff. = 0.045.
$t = 3.96$.
$p < 0.01$.

value of 3.96 for 15 degrees of freedom. In short, the observers displayed significantly higher thresholds of recognition for the emotionally toned words than they did for the neutral words. The threshold measures are also summarized in Table 39-2.

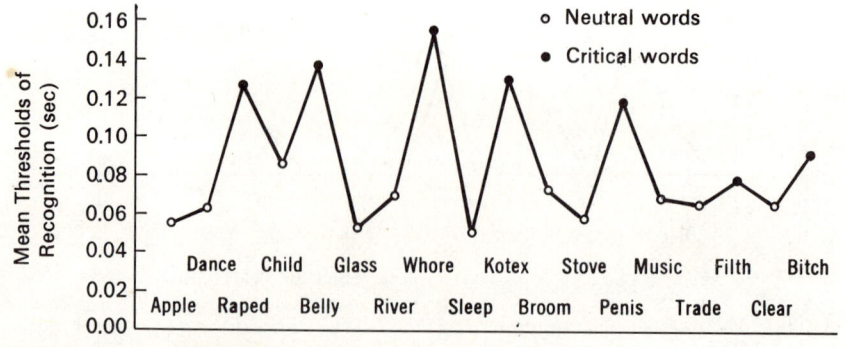

FIGURE 39-2 Mean thresholds of recognition of the observers to the neutral and emotionally charged words.

A breakdown of the data with respect to sex of the observers was also done. The male subjects, on the average, had significantly lower thresholds for both the neutral and critical words. Since the factor of individual differences in visual acuity was not controlled, these results cannot be accepted as more than suggestive of a sex difference in threshold of visual recognition. The mean difference between thresholds for neutral and critical words, however, did not differ significantly in magnitude for the male and female observers. Neither group, in other words, displayed greater evidence of perceptual defense than the other. In addition it was found that no significant sex differences existed with respect to absolute magnitude of galvanic skin response to the critical and neutral words or to differential GSR to the two types of words. Emotionality during the prerecognition period was of equal degree in both the men and the women.

## Content Analysis

Since the observers were instructed to report whatever they saw, they characteristically volunteered a number of prerecognition "hypotheses" before recognition occurred. These were recorded and later analyzed in terms of four general response categories. In order to simplify and objectify as much as possible the coding of these perceptual "guesses," the content categories were limited to the following:

1. *Structurally similar.* Hypotheses coded under this heading resembled in structure the stimulus word. For example, the observer may have guessed *trace* for *trade,* or *whose* for *whore.*
2. *Structurally unlike.* Coded here were hypotheses that were unlike, or dissimilar, in structure to the stimulus word, as, for example, *roared* for *belly,* or *ideal* for *glass.*
3. *Nonsense.* This category included responses that simply had no dictionary meanings. Such would be the case in guessing *egtry* for *kotex,* or *widge* for *stove.*
4. *Part.* These were fractional, or incomplete, hypotheses consisting of any disconnected group of letters.

Figure 39-3 shows the percentage of responses in each of the content categories made to neutral and critical stimulus words for the group of observers as a whole. A chi-square test of independence between type of hypothesis and meaning of the stimulus words indicates a relationship significant below the 0.01 level of confidence. The tabulation of observed and theoretical frequencies with the obtained value of chi-square is reproduced in Table 39-3. Inspection of Figure 39-3 in the light of the statistical evidence reveals that the observers made proportionately more similar and part responses to the neutral words and proportionately more unlike and nonsense hypotheses to the critical words. An additional breakdown of the nonsense category into responses which were similar

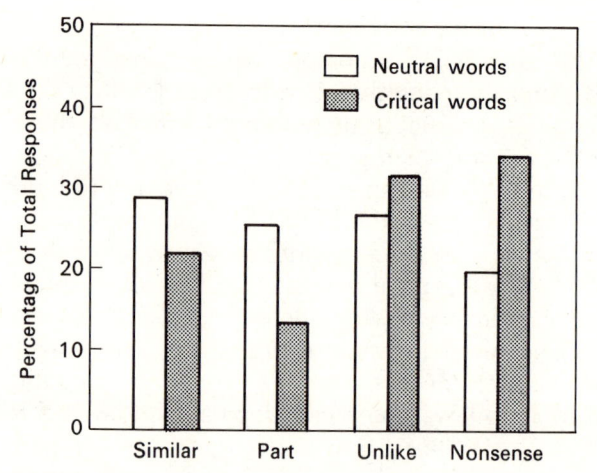

FIGURE 39-3 Percentage frequencies with which hypotheses to neutral and critical stimulus words appeared in the response categories.

to and those which were unlike the stimulus word failed to reveal any difference in frequency of occurrence to neutral and critical words. For this reason it was concluded that more detailed analysis of the content of responses would be unwarranted and would merely introduce an additional degree of arbitrariness to the scoring of the prerecognition guesses.

The subjects were queried following the experimental session as to whether they had reported their perceptions of the words promptly and

TABLE 39-3 Chi-Square Test of Independence Between Stimulus Words and Response Categories

|  | Neutral | Critical |  |
|---|---|---|---|
| Similar | 89 (76.36) | 93 (105.64) | 182 |
| Part | 79 (57.06) | 57 (78.94) | 136 |
| Unlike | 83 (91.89) | 136 (127.11) | 219 |
| Nonsense | 62 (87.69) | 147 (121.31) | 209 |
|  | 313 | 433 | 746 |

$\chi^2 = 31.260$.
$p < 0.01$.
Note: Theoeretical frequencies are in parentheses.

accurately. In all cases, they assured the experimenters that with the occasional exception of the first charged word, they did not withhold or modify their verbal response because of reluctance to say the word. In measuring the GSR, then, we apparently were recording genuine prerecognition reactions to the stimulus words.

## IMPLICATIONS FOR PERCEPTUAL THEORY

Armed with the findings thus far reported, we can readdress ourselves to the problem of "discrimination without awareness," to employ a term used by J. G. Miller [8]. It seems clear that emotional reactivity, as measured by the galvanic skin response, is an accompaniment of perceptual defense. The existence of such a state of affairs has previously been suggested by H. A. Murray, who states that "... certain features of the object which the subject does not consciously perceive are nevertheless physically affecting his body, and though he may be unable to report upon these internal happenings, they are nevertheless affecting his conscious appraisal of the object" [9, p. 312]. Although Murray was speaking without laboratory evidence, his phrasing of the matter in terms of emotional conditioning is essentially correct.

Early in life, most individuals learn that words like *whore* and *bitch* are socially taboo. Since the use of such words by the child will generally result in chastisement by the parent, a conditioned emotional reaction to these verbal symbols is soon established. This pattern of conditioned emotional response may be considered one of fear or anxiety aroused by symbols having sexual, excretory, or otherwise unpleasant or "immoral" connotations. Despite the fact that these words may be employed frequently at a later age, especially when communicating with members of one's own sex, the early emotional reaction persists, as revealed by the GSR, even when overt signs of anxiety or embarrassment are not observable.

Despite evidence of unconscious emotional arousal, perceptual defense against these anxiety-arousing symbols is still accomplished, as witnessed by the heightened limens of our observers when they were confronted with the charged words. This poses a problem for neurophysiological explanation which cannot be answered here. However, we might consider two possibilities: Is the galvanic skin response preceding recognition of critical words a result of feedback from the cortical association centers? Or is autonomic response initiated as the visual impulses reach the optic thalamus? In this case, one might conjecture that rerouting of afferent activity then takes place in the several visual centers so that cortical integration is effectively modified in the direction of phenomenological distortion. Evidence for this latter hypothesis is found in the greater frequency of nonsense and unlike hypotheses in response to the charged words. Formulation of these prerecognition perceptions represents tactics apparently designed to delay accurate recognition of the stimulus word. The relatively higher frequency of part responses to the neutral words, on the other hand, may indicate effort toward recognition. That is, hypotheses based upon the neutral words are not as frequently distorted into nonsense or structurally dissimilar percepts, but are based upon whatever fractional discriminations the observer can make. Such an explanation, of course, is ad hoc and is presented as such.

It has been suggested to the author by Dr. Jerome Bruner that an alternative explanation of the findings might be summarized as follows: The critical words appear less frequently in print, and the increase in thresholds for these words is a function of their unfamiliarity. Greater effort is required to recognize them, and this, in turn, causes a heightened GSR to the critical words. Such an explanation, however, seems untenable on several grounds. First, the critical words are quite common in conversational usage despite their infrequent appearance in print. Second, there is no reason why unfamiliarity with these words should generate a preponderance of nonsense and structurally unlike hypotheses. Third, if GSR is merely an accompaniment of the increased effort expended in recognizing words which show higher thresholds, one should expect a correlation between mean GSR's and mean thresholds for both the neutral and critical words. Pearson $r$'s were calculated in each case. Correlations of $-0.002$ and $+0.077$ were obtained between mean GSRs and mean thresholds for the neutral and critical words respectively. Clearly, no significant relationship exists within the two groups of words between GSR and threshold. The results, therefore, may be viewed as reflecting genuine emotional response rather than mere autonomic reactivity accompanying effort at recognition.

Perceptual defense apparently is based upon conditioned avoidance of unpleasant or dangerous stimulus objects. That the individual actually discriminates the stimulus before he fully perceives it is evident in his increased emotionality before recognition. Inimical stimuli, then, may serve as cues which are appropriately evaluated by the central nervous system even though integration of the afferent impulses is such as to delay recognition, either through distortion or an increase in threshold or both. Almost without exception, the galvanic skin response of the observers was greatest following the final exposure of the critical words; that is the one during which recognition occurred. Clearly, the process of perceptual defense is designed to delay the greater anxiety that accompanies actual recognition of the stimulus. As suggested previously, some integrational processes may occur at the thalamic level which are effective in delaying or modifying cortical integration of visual patterns, while at the same time causing autonomic reaction to emotionally meaningful stimuli. The conditioned response, anxiety, is not entirely circumvented, even though perceptual avoidance is in some measure achieved.

## SUMMARY

Recognition thresholds and galvanic skin responses during the prerecognition period were measured for sixteen observers presented tachistoscopically with eleven neutral and seven emotionally toned words, randomly ordered. The observers reacted with GSRs of significantly greater magnitude during the prerecognition presentation of the critical words than they did before recognizing the neutral words. In addition, the observers displayed significantly higher thresholds of recognition for the critical than for the neutral words. Hypotheses made before recognition of the charged words were of such a nature as to indicate resistance to recognizing these words. The findings are interpreted as representing conditioned avoidance of verbal symbols having unpleasant meanings to the observer. The stimulus word serves as a cue to deeply imbedded anxiety which is revealed in autonomic reactivity as measured by the GSR. Avoidance of further anxiety is contemporaneously aroused in the form of perceptual defense against recognition of the stimulus object.

## REFERENCES

1. J. S. Bruner and C. Goodman. Value and need as organizing factors in perception. *J. abnorm. soc. Psychol.*, 1947, *42*, 33–44.
2. J. S. Bruner and L. Postman. Tension and tension release as organizing factors in perception. *J. Pers.*, 1947, *15*, 300–308.
3. J. S. Bruner and L. Postman. Symbolic value as an organizing factor in perception. *J. soc. Psychol.*, 1948, *27*, 203–208.
4. J. S. Bruner and L. Postman. Perception under stress. *Psychol. Rev.*, 1948, *6*, 314–323.
5. O. L. Lacey and P. S. Siegel. An improved potentiometric circuit for measuring galvanic skin response. *Amer. J. Psychol.*, 1948, *61*, 272–274.
6. R. W. Leeper. A motivational theory of emotion to replace "emotion as disorganized response." *Psychol. Rev.*, 1948, *55*, 5–21.
7. R. Levine, I. Chein, and G. Murphy. The relation of a need to the amount of perceptual distortion: a preliminary report. *J. Psychol.*, 1942, *13*, 283–293.
8. J. G. Miller. Discrimination without awareness. *Amer. J. Psychol.*, 1939, *52*, 562–578.
9. H. A. Murray. The effect of fear upon estimates of the maliciousness of other personalities. *J. soc. Psychol.*, 1933, *4*, 310–329.
10. L. Postman, J. S. Bruner, and E. McGinnies. Personal values as selective factors in perception. *J. abnorm. soc. Psychol.*, 1948, *43*, 142–154.
11. H. Proshansky and G. Murphy. The effects of reward and punishment on perception. *J. Psychol.*, 1942, *13*, 295–305.
12. R. Schafer and G. Murphy. The role of autism in a visual figure-ground relationship. *J. exp. Psychol.*, 1943, *32*, 335–343.

# 40
# RESPONSE SUPPRESSION IN PERCEPTUAL DEFENSE

## Robert B. Zajonc

Recent theorizing maintains that the phenomenon of perceptual defense can be accounted for in terms of response processes. Elevated thresholds to taboo words are now generally regarded as reflecting a response bias deriving from either previous experience [4], set [8], or conflict [2], rather than a defensive perceptual blocking. Although the core of the issue deals with the relative contributions of the stimulus and response to the perceptual defense effect, studies attempting to evaluate such relative contributions have been rather few [5, 7]. It is the purpose of this experiment to determine the extent to which both recognition threshold and the galvanic skin response (GSR) are influenced by the stimulus and to what extent by the response, using a procedure first suggested by Garner, Hake, and Eriksen [3]. First, threshold and GSR data for a set of taboo and neutral words were obtained by means of standard methods. Secondly, a paired-associate list was constructed using the previously exposed words as stimulus terms and a new set of taboo and neutral words as response terms. Some taboo stimuli were paired with taboo, others with neutral response terms. Neutral stimuli too, were sometimes paired with neutral and sometimes with taboo response terms. All subjects learned the paired-associate list to a criterion. The third step consisted of a repeated threshold and GSR assessment of the original stimuli. Now, however, one group was required to indicate recognition as before, that is, by reading out loud the word presented tachistoscopically, and another by saying the appropriate response term which they have learned in the previous paired-associate task. Thus, the second group was given an opportunity to indicate recognition by means of responses whose emotional significance was either positively or negatively correlated with the emotional significance of the stimulus.

Source: *Journal of Experimental Psychology*, 1962, 64, 206–214. Copyright 1962 by the American Psychological Association. Reprinted by permission.
Note: This work was supported by Grants AS 49(638)-367 and G-4951 from the Air Force Office of Scientific Research and the National Science Foundation. I wish to thank James Taylor for his assistance in this study, and Dorwin Cartwright and Arthur Platz for reading the manuscript.

## METHOD

### Subjects

Forty male subjects, all enrolled at the University of Michigan, participated in the experiment. They were randomly assigned to two experimental groups consisting of twenty subjects each. The subjects were paid $1.25 per hour for participation in the experiment.

### Apparatus

Gerbrand's transparent mirror tachistoscope with an instant start fluorescent lamp circuit was employed to present stimuli. Skin resistance changes were observed by means of a Lafayette psychogalvanometer Model 603-A.

### Materials

Stimulus words were printed in black 2-in. block letters and presented in the center of the exposure field on gray 10 × 12 in. cards (54.5% reflectance). Stimulus-response pairs in the paired-associated task were shown in the same manner. Twelve taboo and twelve neutral words were selected from McGinnies' [6] original list of eighteen words to which equivalent neutral and taboo stimuli were added. Half of the taboo and half of the neutral words were used as stimuli in the threshold assessment and as stimulus terms in the paired-associate training task. The remainder of the list was used as response terms in the paired-associate task. Three taboo stimuli were paired with three taboo responses, three taboo stimuli were paired with three neutral responses, three neutral stimuli were paired with three taboo responses, and three neutral stimuli with three neutral responses. These sets of words will be referred to as the TT, TN, NT, and NN sets. The twenty-four words were *apple, broom, candy, chair, child, floor, music, rains, river, shelf, stove, trade, balls, belly, bleed, fairy, filth, hymen, kotex, penis, pubic, raped, vomit, whore.*

### Procedure

As briefly outlined above, the procedure consisted of two recognition threshold and GSR assessment sessions separated by an intervening paired-associate learning task. The subjects were divided into two groups of twenty each, one of which was required during the second threshold assessment session to indicate recognition in terms of the stimuli presented (group S), the other in terms of the response terms paired with the stimuli (group R).

Thresholds were obtained by the ascending method of limits in

0.01-sec steps beginning with 0.05 sec below the subject's threshold to a neutral training word. The intertrial intervals were approximately 30 sec. Some of the words were shown more than once in order to eliminate prerecognition guesses during the second threshold assessment, when full knowledge of the list was already available to subjects. For those words data from the first presentation alone were included in the analysis. The criterion of threshold was the first correct recognition of the word in group S and the first emission of the correct response term in group R.

The subject was seated with his head against the eyepieces and with his hand to which electrodes were affixed lying relaxed on the table. A rest period of 1 min was given after the first threshold assessment session and after the paired-associate training.

The tachistoscope was operated by an adult male and the psychogalvanometer by an adult female. The GSR readings were taken in terms of reduction in resistance from the basal resistance level, which was adjusted for each stimulus exposure. Only those reactions which occurred within 5 sec following stimulus exposure, and only those for which the resistance returned to the immediate neighborhood of the pre-exposure level were recorded. GSR readings were taken on every presentation of the stimulus word. Since some subjects recognized the word on the fourth exposure, only two prerecognition trials and the recognition trial were considered. Thus, for each subject three GSR scores were computed for each set of stimuli, and for the purposes of analysis all were converted to standard scores with a mean of 50 and SD of 10 for all forty subjects.

The paired-associate task was conducted using a 2-sec interval for the presentation of the stimulus and a 2-sec interval for the presentation of the pair, with 20 sec between trials. All terms were presented tachistoscopically. The order of the stimuli was randomly altered from trial to trial. Three consecutive correct anticipations of the entire list were used as the criterion.

## RESULTS

### Recognition Threshold and GSR Before Paired-Associate Training

Mean recognition thresholds obtained before paired-associate training are shown in Table 40-1. The analysis of variance for these results showed that the only significant effect is due to the difference between taboo and neutral words ($F = 17.08$, $p < 0.001$). Although the mean recognition thresholds for group R are somewhat higher than those for group S, this difference is not significant. Also, no significant differences were obtained between taboo words to be later used with taboo responses (TT) and taboo words to be later used with neutral responses (TN). Nor was there any difference between neutral words to be later used with taboo responses (NT) and neutral words to be later used with neutral responses (NN).

TABLE 40-1  Mean Recognition Thresholds (sec) Before Paired-Associate Training

| Group | Later PA Conditions |  |  |  | Words |  |
|---|---|---|---|---|---|---|
|  | TT | TN | NT | NN | All Taboo | All Neutral |
| S | 0.219 | 0.228 | 0.193 | 0.198 | 0.223 | 0.196 |
| R | 0.234 | 0.233 | 0.206 | 0.213 | 0.234 | 0.210 |
| Both | 0.227 | 0.231 | 0.200 | 0.206 | 0.229 | 0.203 |

The GSRs are shown in Figure 40-1. Again no difference between the experimental groups was found. It is evident from the results that on all trials taboo words exceed neutral words in GSR ($F = 30.99$, $p < 0.001$). It is also clear that there is a considerable rise in the GSR on the recognition trial ($F = 32.94$, $p < 0.001$). No significant differences between TT and TN words as well as between NN and NT words were found for either of the two groups.

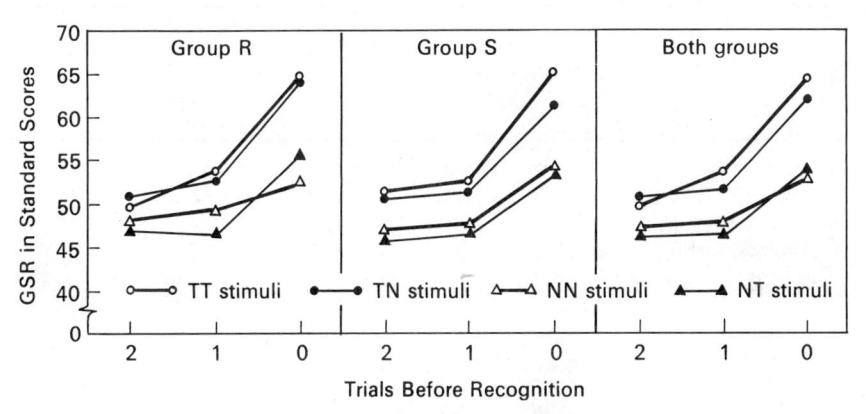

FIGURE 40-1  GSR before paired-associate training.

## Paired-Associate Learning

Average number of trials to learn the four sets of associations are presented in Table 40-2. The means represent the number of trials which subjects required to learn a given association to a criterion of three correct anticipations, averaged for the three items in each set. Shown in Table 40-2 is also the average number of errors for each set of pairs. The results indicate that the four sets of associations were not learned at the same rate (see Table 40-3). In particular, the TN pairs seem to be the most difficult, and the TT easiest. The analysis of variance presented in Table 40-3 shows a significant effect due to differences between word sets, which is primarily due to the type of response. In general, pairs with a

TABLE 40-2  Mean Trials and Errors to Criterion in Paired-Associate Learning

| Group | Pairs TT | Pairs TN | Pairs NT | Pairs NN | Words Taboo Stimuli | Words Neutral Stimuli | Words Taboo Responses | Words Neutral Responses |
|---|---|---|---|---|---|---|---|---|
| **Group S** | | | | | | | | |
| Trials | 4.56 | 5.62 | 4.37 | 5.13 | 5.09 | 4.75 | 4.47 | 5.38 |
| Errors | 4.55 | 7.10 | 3.70 | 6.10 | 5.83 | 4.90 | 4.13 | 6.60 |
| **Group R** | | | | | | | | |
| Trials | 4.21 | 4.95 | 4.48 | 4.28 | 4.58 | 4.38 | 4.35 | 4.62 |
| Errors | 2.90 | 5.00 | 3.80 | 3.55 | 3.95 | 3.68 | 3.35 | 4.28 |
| **Both** | | | | | | | | |
| Trials | 4.39 | 5.29 | 4.43 | 4.71 | 4.84 | 4.57 | 4.41 | 5.00 |
| Errors | 3.73 | 6.05 | 3.75 | 4.83 | 4.89 | 4.29 | 3.74 | 5.44 |

TABLE 40-3  Analysis of Variance for Data in Table 40-2

| Source | df | Trials to Criterion MS | Trials to Criterion F | Errors MS | Errors F |
|---|---|---|---|---|---|
| Treatments (A) | 1 | 8.06 | 0.83 | 96.09 | 1.09 |
| Words | 3 | 6.69 | 6.03*** | 48.54 | 6.23*** |
| S component ($B_1$) | 1 | 3.11 | 3.27 | 14.40 | 2.68 |
| R component ($B_2$) | 1 | 13.40 | 8.93** | 115.60 | 11.73** |
| $B_1 \times B_2$ | 1 | 3.57 | 4.12 | 15.62 | 1.92 |
| Treatments × Words | 3 | 1.78 | 1.60 | 13.45 | 1.73 |
| A × $B_1$ | 1 | 0.24 | 0.25 | 4.23 | 0.79 |
| A × $B_2$ | 1 | 3.93 | 2.62 | 24.03 | 2.44 |
| A × $B_1$ × $B_2$ | 1 | 1.18 | 1.37 | 12.10 | 1.49 |
| Error (b) | 38 | 9.76 | | 88.91 | |
| Error (w) | 114 | 1.11 | | 7.79 | |
| Subjects × $B_1$ | 38 | 0.95 | | 5.38 | |
| Subjects × $B_2$ | 38 | 1.50 | | 9.85 | |
| Subjects × $B_1$ × $B_2$ | 38 | 0.86 | | 8.13 | |

** $p = 0.01$.
*** $p = 0.001$.

taboo response require fewer trials and lead to fewer errors than pairs with neutral responses. Of particular importance to the present experiment is the difference between the TN and NT pairs. If speed of learning and number of errors reflect the degree to which a given response has become attached to the stimulus word, the TN stimuli should, during the subsequent threshold and GSR assessment of group R, be more handicapped than NT stimuli. The differences between these pairs in both trials to criterion and average number of errors are significant at the 0.001 level.

## Recognition Threshold and GSR After Paired-Associate Training

*Group R.* Table 40-4 shows recognition thresholds for the four sets of words for the condition in which subjects indicated recognition by means of the response term acquired during the paired-associate training. It is apparent that compared with those obtained before the paired-associate training, the thresholds to all the words are considerably reduced. It is also clear that no longer does the recognition threshold totally depend on the stimulus. There is a considerable effect due to the response which the subject utilizes in indicating recognition. It should be pointed out that the subject's ability to give evidence of recognition, not by means of a word which is presented but by means of a response previously learned, depends on the degree to which these responses were fixated. It will be recalled that the learning of the four types of associations was not uniform. In particular there was a considerable difference between the TN and the NT pairs, in favor of the latter. Moreover, the examination of the results on paired-associate learning disclosed a significant effect due to individual differences. The $F$ ratios evaluating the individual difference effect were 8.79 for trials to criterion, and 11.41 for errors, which for the degrees of freedom given are significant well beyond the 0.001 level. We would expect a more reliable test of the relative contributions of the stimulus shown and of the response given from subjects who learned these responses well. Group R was therefore divided at the median number of trials to criterion, and the recognition thresholds for the rapid and slow learners are shown in Table 40-4, and the analysis of variance in Table 40-5. It is clear from Table 40-4 that slow learners manifest considerably higher recognition thresholds for *all* the words. The differ-

TABLE 40-4 Mean Recognition Thresholds (sec) in Group R After Paired-Associate Learning

| Group | PA Pairs TT | TN | NT | NN | Taboo Stimuli | Neutral Stimuli | Taboo Responses | Neutral Responses |
|---|---|---|---|---|---|---|---|---|
| Rapid learners | 0.151 | 0.138 | 0.145 | 0.138 | 0.145 | 0.142 | 0.148 | 0.138 |
| Slow learners | 0.178 | 0.180 | 0.174 | 0.172 | 0.179 | 0.173 | 0.176 | 0.176 |
| All subjects | 0.165 | 0.159 | 0.160 | 0.155 | 0.162 | 0.158 | 0.163 | 0.157 |
| Adjusted means for all subjects | 0.168 | 0.153 | 0.160 | 0.157 | 0.161 | 0.159 | 0.164 | 0.155 |

TABLE 40-5  Analysis of Variance for Data in Table 40-4

| Source | df | MS | F |
|---|---|---|---|
| Groups (rapid vs. slow) (A) | 1 | 24,945 | 6.72* |
| Words | 3 | 338 | 2.54 |
| S component ($B_1$) | 1 | 466 | 2.13 |
| R component ($B_2$) | 1 | 546 | 5.00* |
| $B_1 \times B_2$ | 1 | 1 | <1.00 |
| Groups × words | 3 | 131 | <1.00 |
| $A \times B_1$ | 1 | 35 | <1.00 |
| $A \times B_2$ | 1 | 536 | 4.91* |
| $A \times B_1 \times B_2$ | 1 | 122 | 1.67 |
| Error (b) | 18 | 3,711 | |
| Error (w) | 54 | 133 | |
| Subjects × $B_1$ | 18 | 218 | |
| Subjects × $B_2$ | 18 | 109 | |
| Subjects × $B_1 \times B_2$ | 18 | 73 | |

* $p = 0.05$.

ence between groups is significant at better than the 0.05 level. It appears that the slow learner's recognition threshold depends primarily on the type of stimulus presented, while that of rapid learners on the response which they were required to make. However, the groups × stimulus × response interaction was not significant. The overall results, however, indicate that the effects due to the stimulus component were not significant while those due to the response were significant. Further support for the conclusion that recognition threshold depends primarily on the type of response required is obtained when the data are adjusted for differences in learning the four types of associations. The mean recognition thresholds, adjusted by means of the regression equation relating the former to the number of trials, are shown at the bottom of Table 40-4. Analysis of covariance performed on these results disclosed a significant effect due to the response component ($F = 8.78$, $df = 1/17$) and no effects due to stimulus.

The GSR data shown in Figure 40-2 follow a similar pattern. Again, as compared with the results obtained before paired-associate training, the GSRs are weaker. The analysis of variance (Table 40-6) shows a significant effect due to the differences between words which seems to be a function of the stimulus and of the response component as well. The results of both groups combined indicate that on the second prerecognition trial the GSRs do not follow any particular pattern. However, the curves for the rapid learners show a pattern of particular interest. On the second prerecognition trial the GSRs seem to depend primarily on the stimulus component; their order is TN, TT, NN, and NT. As the subjects approach recognition the stimulus effect is gradually replaced by the

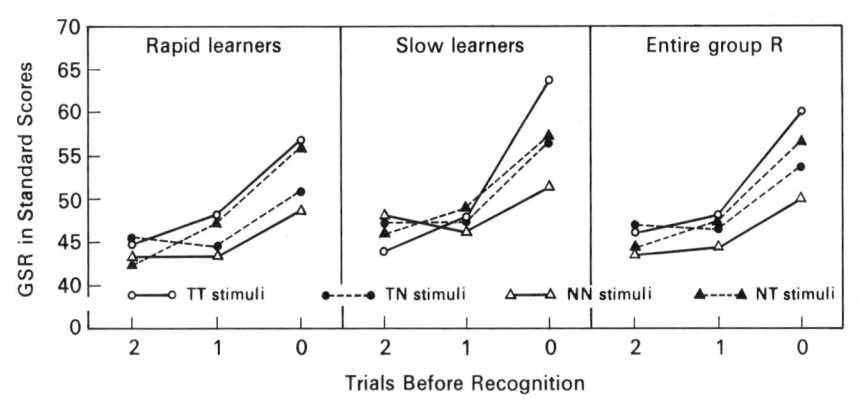

## FIGURE 40-2  GSR after paired-associate training (group R).

TABLE 40-6  Analyses of Variance for Data in Figures 40-2 and 40-3

| Source | df | Group R MS | Group R F | Group S MS | Group S F |
|---|---|---|---|---|---|
| Groups (rapid vs. slow) (A) | 1 | 522.4 | 1.19 | 161.7 | <1.00 |
| Words | 3 | 171.1 | 6.35** | 78.6 | 3.48* |
| S component ($B_1$) | 1 | 149.6 | 7.03* | 227.0 | 7.73* |
| R component ($B_2$) | 1 | 356.5 | 10.57** | 2.5 | <1.00 |
| $B_1 \times B_2$ | 1 | 7.3 | <1.00 | 6.3 | <1.00 |
| Trials (C) | 2 | 2,235.6 | 28.97*** | 942.5 | 12.57*** |
| Groups × words | 3 | 9.6 | <1.00 | 26.1 | 1.16 |
| $A \times B_1$ | 1 | 0.3 | <1.00 | 16.9 | <1.00 |
| $A \times B_2$ | 1 | 27.8 | <1.00 | 51.4 | 1.92 |
| $A \times B_1 \times B_2$ | 1 | 0.8 | <1.00 | 10.1 | <1.00 |
| Words × trials | 6 | 136.7 | 5.44*** | 38.6 | 3.08** |
| $B_1 \times C$ | 2 | 87.8 | 4.27* | 79.0 | 4.71* |
| $B_2 \times C$ | 2 | 319.6 | 12.47*** | 6.6 | <1.00 |
| $B_1 \times B_2 \times C$ | 2 | 2.8 | <1.00 | 30.4 | 4.94* |
| Groups × trials | 2 | 25.3 | <1.00 | 39.4 | <1.00 |
| Groups × words × trials | 6 | 32.6 | 1.30 | 22.2 | 1.77 |
| $A \times B_1 \times C$ | 2 | 77.5 | 3.77* | 36.7 | 2.19 |
| $A \times B_2 \times C$ | 2 | 5.7 | <1.00 | 4.8 | <1.00 |
| $A \times B_1 \times B_2 \times C$ | 2 | 14.7 | <1.00 | 25.1 | 4.09* |
| Error (b) | 18 | 439.1 | | 441.1 | |
| Error (w)$_1$: subjects × words | 54 | 27.0 | | 22.6 | |
| Subjects × $B_1$ | 18 | 21.3 | | 29.4 | |
| Subjects × $B_2$ | 18 | 33.7 | | 26.8 | |
| Subjects × $B_1 \times B_2$ | 18 | 25.9 | | 11.6 | |
| Error (w)$_2$: subjects × words × trials | 36 | 77.2 | | 75.0 | |
| Error (w)$_3$: subjects × words × trials | 108 | 25.1 | | 12.6 | |
| Subjects × $B_1 \times C$ | 36 | 20.6 | | 16.8 | |
| Subjects × $B_2 \times C$ | 36 | 25.6 | | 14.7 | |
| Subjects × $B_1 \times B_2 \times C$ | 36 | 29.2 | | 6.2 | |

* $p < 0.05$.  ** $p < 0.01$.  *** $p < 0.001$.

response effect and the GSRs are ordered according to the response. One may interpret this result to mean that stimulation present two trials before recognition is probably too weak to call out strong anticipatory partial responses. As soon as the stimulation gains in strength and becomes capable of evoking some parts of the learned response, the autonomic reactions lose their dependence upon the stimulus and begin to be dominated by the response component.

The mean GSR reaction for rapid learners was 47.55 and for slow learners 50.53, but as is evident from Table 40-6 this difference was not significant.

*Group S.* The principal purpose of the paired-associate learning task was to enable subjects to give evidence of recognition of the stimulus words without having to say them. However, it is possible to argue that the training simultaneously produced temporary changes in the emotional quality of the stimulus words. Thus, taboo stimuli which were paired with neutral responses could, by virtue of the repeatedly reinforced association, have become emotionally neutralized. Similarly, conditioning a taboo response to a neutral stimulus word might have affected the emotional quality of the latter. These eventualities are of course quite remote because of the small number of conditioning trials involved. If conditioning of the type suggested has in fact taken place then the recognition thresholds and the GSR data should show the same patterns in groups S and R. The average recognition thresholds for group S are shown in Table 40-7, and the analysis of variance for these results has shown effects only due to the stimulus component. It is of interest to note that as was the case in group R slow learners in group S also showed somewhat higher recognition thresholds than rapid learners. However, this difference failed to reach an acceptable level of significance.

TABLE 40-7 Mean Recognition Thresholds (sec) in Groups After Paired-Associate Training

| Group | PA Pairs |   |   |   | Words |   |   |   |
|---|---|---|---|---|---|---|---|---|
|  | TT | TN | NT | NN | Taboo Stimuli | Neutral Stimuli | Taboo Responses | Neutral Responses |
| Rapid learners | 0.153 | 0.151 | 0.143 | 0.141 | 0.152 | 0.142 | 0.148 | 0.146 |
| Slow learners | 0.167 | 0.175 | 0.154 | 0.162 | 0.171 | 0.158 | 0.160 | 0.168 |
| All subjects | 0.160 | 0.163 | 0.149 | 0.152 | 0.161 | 0.150 | 0.154 | 0.157 |

Neither do the GSR results shown in Figure 40-3 suggest any conditioning effect. Besides the increase in reactions over trials, the only significant effect is that due to the stimulus component. The analysis of

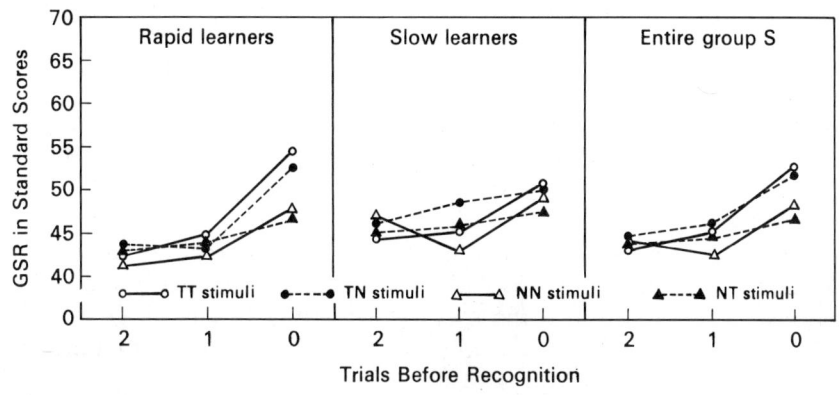

FIGURE 40-3  GSR after paired-associate training (group S).

variance in Table 40-8 shows an F ratio significant at the 0.05 level for the stimulus component. On the trials immediately preceding recognition there is a slight but not significant response effect for rapid learners. Also, as observed before, the GSRs of rapid learners are somewhat less than those of slow learners (45.69 and 47.16, respectively), but this difference is decidedly not reliable.

## DISCUSSION

The evidence presented failed to disclose perceptual effects of any significance. The recognition threshold was found to be a function not of

TABLE 40-8  Analysis of Variance for Data in Table 40-7

| Source | df | MS | F |
| --- | --- | --- | --- |
| Groups (rapid vs. slow learners) (A) | 1 | 10,160 | 3.12 |
| Words | 3 | 896 | 3.03 |
| S component ($B_1$) | 1 | 2,532 | 5.34* |
| R component ($B_2$) | 1 | 157 | <1.00 |
| $B_1 \times B_2$ | 1 | 0 | <1.00 |
| Groups × words | 3 | 150 | <1.00 |
| $A \times B_1$ | 1 | 131 | <1.00 |
| $A \times B_2$ | 1 | 419 | 1.68 |
| $A \times B_1 \times B_2$ | 1 | 1 | <1.00 |
| Error (b) | 18 | 3,088 | |
| Error (w) | 54 | 296 | |
| Subjects × $B_1$ | 18 | 474 | |
| Subjects × $B_2$ | 18 | 250 | |
| Subjects × $B_1 \times B_2$ | 18 | 164 | |

* $p = 0.05$.

what the subject saw but what he had to say. Moreover, GSR data follow an identical pattern. The GSRs were found to be produced not by the stimulus alone, but depended primarily on the response required of the subject. The results are best accounted for by Brown's [2] competing response theory. Irrespective of the stimulus, if the responses were in conflict with an inhibitory tendency, that is, if the subject had to make a vulgar response, both recognition threshold and GSR were elevated. Stimuli arousing no response conflict failed to produce differential thresholds and GSRs irrespective of their emotionality. Further support for the response competition hypothesis is seen in the GSR data. In general, the differences in the GSRs were found to increase over trials, reaching their peak upon recognition. To the extent that the GSRs reflect response conflict, one would expect that with increasing exposure time both the positive and the negative tendencies increase, thus generating a stronger conflict.

There is evidence in the data that recognition threshold and GSR are also subject to variation as a result of not only a conflict between a positive and negative tendency but also as a result of a conflict between competing excitatory tendencies. First we note that both are markedly reduced after familiarization with the stimuli. Before paired-associate learning the response alternatives available to subjects are many, and all of these are in competition. The training reduces them to twelve, thus reducing the extent of response competition involved. Secondly, consistent differences in the overall recognition threshold and GSR reactions between the rapid and slow learner were found. If one views the speed of the paired-associate learning and the mean number of errors as an index of the amount of response competition present, these results become quite meaningful.

It is not claimed here that the perceptual defense phenomenon has been disproven. But if the phenomenon is empirically demonstrable its proof must be established by experimental methods other than those commonly used. Perhaps Blum's [1] forced-choice technique of threshold assessment holds best promise since it eliminates possible effects due to the response process.

## SUMMARY

The role of stimuli and responses in perceptual defense was examined by first obtaining recognition thresholds and GSRs to taboo and neutral words. Subsequently, subjects learned a paired-associate list with the original words serving as stimulus terms and a new set of words as response terms. Half of the neutral stimuli were paired with neutral and half with taboo responses. The same was true of taboo stimuli. Following training, recognition thresholds and GSRs were again measured with one group required to indicate recognition by means of response terms and another by means of stimulus terms. Both recognition threshold and GSR were found to depend primarily on the response required of the subjects in indicating recognition.

## REFERENCES

1. G. S. Blum. An experimental reunion of psychoanalytic theory with perceptual vigilance and defense. *J. abnorm. soc. Psychol.*, 1954, *13*, 94–99.
2. J. S. Brown. *The motivation of behavior.* New York: McGraw-Hill, 1961.
3. W. R. Garner, H. W. Hake, and C. W. Eriksen. Operationism and the concept of perception. *Psychol. Rev.*, 1956, *63*, 149–159.
4. I. Goldiamond and W. F. Hawkins. Vexierversuch: The log relationship between word frequency and recognition obtained in the absence of stimulus words. *J. exp. Psychol.*, 1958, *56*, 457–463.
5. A. Mathews and M. Wertheimer. A "pure" measure of perceptual defense uncontaminated by response suppression. *J. abnorm. soc. Psychol.*, 1958, *57*, 373–376.
6. E. McGinnies. Emotionality and perceptual defense. *Psychol. Rev.*, 1949, *56*, 244–251.
7. U. Neisser. An experimental distinction between perceptual process and verbal response. *J. exp. Psychol.*, 1954, *47*, 399–402.
8. L. Postman, W. C. Bronson, and G. L. Gropper. Is there a mechanism of perceptual defense? *J. abnorm. soc. Psychol.*, 1953, *48*, 215–224.

# 41
# PAIRED COMPARISON SCALING OF BRIGHTNESS JUDGMENTS: A METHOD FOR THE MEASUREMENT OF PERCEPTUAL DEFENSE

A. G. Worthington

Thirty-two subjects made paired comparison judgments of the relative brightness of stimuli presented 0.1 log ft-1 below recognition threshold. All stimuli were objectively equal in brightness. Half the subjects made judgments under conditions of simultaneous presentation and half under conditions of successive presentation. The stimuli had previously been scaled for "emotionality" by a sample of subjects drawn from the same population as the subjects who made perceptual judgments. A scale of apparent brightness was derived from the data obtained under the successive condition but the data from the simultaneous condition were not scalable. The scale for the successive condition was significantly correlated with the emotionality scale. These results support an arousal interpretation of perceptual defense and indicate that where appropriate techniques are employed it is possible to measure the perceptual component of perceptual defense. The method described would seem potentially powerful for further investigations in this and related areas.

Recent reviews of perceptual defense by Bevan [1] and Minard [6] indicate that there is increasing acceptance by experimental psychologists that under certain conditions a true *perceptual* component of the effect may be isolated.

This position is in marked contrast to the conclusions reached earlier by Goldiamond [4], Eriksen [3], and Zajonc [11]. The techniques used by Mathews and Wertheimer [5] and Minard [6] have been generally

Source: British Journal of Psychology, 1969, 60, 363–368.
Note: This research was financed by a research grant from Queen's University, Kingston, Ontario.

accepted as considerable improvements over conventional methods in this area. Among the improvements are techniques for estimating the effects of conscious suppression, differential frequency of usage, and so on, and for applying appropriate corrections such that any remaining effect can be considered a "pure" index of perceptual defense.

Concern with the development of methods to eliminate response bias has led also to the development of rather different procedures which seem to preclude the possibility of response factors leading to an equivocal interpretation of perceptual defense effects. For example, Dixon [2] demonstrated that the threshold for material presented to one eye was modified in terms of the emotionality or otherwise of stimuli contemporaneously presented below recognition threshold to the *other*. In addition, Worthington [9] used rate of dark adaptation as the dependent variable so that at no stage could the subject have been aware that verbal material was being presented.

The technique to be described below was developed following an earlier study by Worthington [10]. This study used two distinct but related approaches. One of these utilized the classical perceptual defense experiments where thresholds (ascending limits) were obtained for words judged to be of differing degrees of emotionality. The results showed the classical perceptual defense effect. The second approach was based on the assumption that if a more intense signal is required to recognize an emotional word, then emotional stimuli would be seen as subjectively *less bright* than neutral stimuli. This assumption led to the deduction that it should therefore be possible to scale the stimuli in terms of their subjective brightnesses. An experiment was conducted using a paired-comparison procedure where subjects were required to make brightness judgments of pairs of words presented simultaneously below recognition threshold. Each word transmitted the same amount of light. No differences in subjective brightness were found.

The conflicting results from the two parts of this study seem to support a response-bias interpretation of perceptual defense. Response bias would be maximized in the classical situation and minimized in the scaling situation. Such an interpretation is premature, however, since an essential condition was omitted.

In the experiment to be reported below the missing condition was included. Two perceptual situations were used. In the first, the subjects were required to make paired-comparison brightness judgments of pairs of stimuli objectively equal in brightness and presented *simultaneously*. In the second situation an identical procedure was used except that the stimuli were presented *successively*. The rationale for the procedure was as follows:

1. If perceptual defense reflects a change in perceptual sensitivity, then in the simultaneous condition any such change would apply to both

words of any pair and hence within any pair the subject would be forced to guess. Under the successive condition, however, any change in sensitivity would be stimulus specific and should be reflected in systematic differences in subjective brightness.

2. Although any effects of response factors should be minimized by the response required, any bias due to such factors that might be present should occur under both conditions, and if these factors are important in this situation discriminations between stimuli should be observed under both conditions.

3. If response factors are not involved in a task of this type and if these factors completely account for the perceptual defense effect, then no systematic discriminations should be obtained under either experimental condition.

## METHOD

### Subjects

All subjects in this study (160) were male and were drawn from the summer-school populations of Queen's University during 1963 and 1964.

### Stage 1

Twenty words, each of six letters, considered to cover a range from high to low subjective emotionality, were selected. Each stimulus was paired with every other stimulus (190 pairs) and a random sequence of these 190 pairs generated. Three additional orders based on this original sequence were prepared such that order and position were counterbalanced. Sixty-four subjects (sixteen for each order) were each shown a list (one pair at a time) and requested to indicate which member of a pair they considered more emotional. Responses were scaled using the Torgerson Class II procedure [8] and a scale value (z score) obtained for each word. Since this preliminary scaling was merely to examine the range of the scale values obtained and to select stimuli most likely to produce a subjective emotionality scale, no attempt to apply a goodness-of-fit test to the data was made at this stage.

### Stage 2

Nine words (*orgasm, virgin, cancer, coffin, urchin, tartar, fathom, icebox,* and *branch*) were selected from the original twenty used in stage 1. Each stimulus was paired with every other (thirty-six pairs) and the procedure described for stage 1 was repeated. Once again, sixty-four subjects were used. The resultant scale values for each of the stimuli are given in the first column of Table 41-1.

TABLE 41-1  Scale Values (z Scores): Conscious Judgment Task and Experiments I and II

| Stimulus† | Conscious Judgment | Experiment I | Experiment II |
|---|---|---|---|
| Orgasm | 2.14 | −0.16 | 0.00 |
| Virgin | 1.82 | 0.15 | 0.54 |
| Cancer | 1.70 | 0.07 | 0.97 |
| Coffin | 1.64 | 0.23 | 0.41 |
| Urchin | 0.95 | 0.05 | −0.17 |
| Tartar | 0.56 | −0.19 | −0.13 |
| Fathom | 0.37 | −0.09 | −0.59 |
| Icebox | 0.26 | −0.12 | −0.38 |
| Branch | 0.00 (Arbitrary origin) | −0.32 | −0.64 |
| Range | 2.14 SD | 0.55 SD | 1.61 SD |
| Goodness of fit, $\chi^2$ | 33.1 | 65.37 | 39.59 |
| df | 28 | 28 | 28 |
| $= 0.05, \chi^2$ | 41.34 | 41.34 | 41.34 |
| Decisions | Accept | Reject | Accept |

† The stimuli are ordered in terms of the conscious judgment scale. *Orgasm* was judged most emotional and *branch* least emotional. The more the positive score on the brightness judgment scales, the *less* bright the stimulus was judged.

The Mosteller goodness-of-fit test [7] was applied ($\chi^2 = 33.1$; $df = 28$; $p > 0.05$). It was therefore concluded that the nine words selected formed a scale of subjective emotionality and could be used in stage 3 of the experiment.

### Stage 3

Sixteen subjects were employed in each of the two experiments of stage 3.

## EXPERIMENT I

### Simultaneous Condition

Recognition thresholds were obtained for each subject, utilizing the method of ascending limits. Twenty slides, transmitting the same amount of light as the slides to be used in the experiment proper, were used. It should be noted that the only light produced was by the stimuli. The background was in darkness. Each slide contained two six-letter words. Words used in threshold measurement were *killer, lesson, magpie, nicety,* and *detour* and the twenty slides contained each possible pair of these five words counterbalanced for position. The two words on each slide transmitted equal amounts of light. Both here and in the two experiments subsequently described the words were constructed entirely of lower-case letters. Each of the twenty slides was presented twice. Recognition threshold was defined as the lowest illumination level at which the subject recognized *either* of the stimulus words on any trial. The level of illumination for each slide started at a point where the subject could just detect light on the screen and was increased in steps of 0.02 log ft = 1 until the subject recognized a word. The testing was conducted in a darkened room. The subject was given a 5-min adaptation period before threshold judgments were obtained. During the intertrial interval the screen was in darkness.

During the brightness judgment scaling task the stimuli consisted of slides each of which contained two words transmitting the same amount of light. The light transmitted was checked by standard photometric measurement techniques.

Seventy-two slides were prepared. Each of the nine words found to scale for subjective emotionality in stage 2 was paired with every other (thirty-six basic pairs), and an additional set consisting of these pairs with position reversed was also prepared. In determining the original basic pairs position was determined by reference to a table of random numbers.

A random order was obtained for the basic thirty-six slides. This order formed the basis for an additional three orders whereby order and position were counterbalanced.

Each subject was required to make judgments of 144 pairs of words. The 144 pairs consisted of the four sets of thirty-six described above. The order of the sets was randomly determined for each subject. Subjects were instructed to fixate a small cross marked on a screen positioned 4 ft in front of the subject. This fixation cross could be seen when a slide was present. Slides were presented by backward projection on to the screen so that one word appeared on either side of the fixation point. Exposure time was 2 sec with a 12-sec interval between pairs. Half the subjects were instructed to report which of the two patches of light, the left or the right, seemed the brighter. The other half were required to report which stimulus was the dimmer. A hardboard partition was placed between the experimenter and the subject. The experimenter simply recorded the "left" or "right" judgment on a score sheet which contained details of order number, trial number, and instruction type.

Stimuli were projected at a level 0.1 log ft = 1 below the lowest illumination level at which the subject recognized one or the other word during the threshold testing session. Subjects were not told that the stimuli were words, merely that they consisted of patches of light. They were also told that although the differences in intensity of the two patches were extremely small, there were real differences and that if the subject could not detect a difference he was to guess. At the end of the session the subjects were questioned to determine if at any stage they noticed that words had been presented. None of the subjects indicated that they had been aware of words.

## EXPERIMENT II

### Successive Condition

In this experiment the slides consisted of single words only. In the threshold-testing session the same five words were used as in the comparable session of experiment I. Recognition threshold was obtained using a similar procedure to that employed in experiment I. Each slide used transmitted approximately the same amount of light as the slides used in experiment I, and each of the five words used to obtain recognition thresholds transmitted the same amount of light. Each slide was presented eight times (forty trials in all). Recognition threshold was defined as the lowest level of illumination at which the subject recognized a word during the testing session.

Stimuli used during the brightness judgment scaling task were the same as in experiment I. In this case, however, only nine slides were prepared. Each slide transmitted the same amount of light as those used in the threshold-testing period. The light transmitted by each slide was again checked by standard photometric techniques.

Each subject was required to make 144 brightness judgments. The same random order used in experiment I was employed. Identical counterbalancing procedures were employed. In this case, however, counterbalancing for position was to control for temporal rather than spatial effects. Each trial consisted of the presentation of one stimulus for a period of 2 sec, a 10-sec interval, and then the presentation of the second stimulus of a pair. The intertrial interval was 12 sec. The 10-sec interval between members of a pair was chosen somewhat arbitrarily but after discussion with various individuals. It seemed likely that any "arousal" change would be complete by 5 or 6 sec. The 10-sec interval seemed likely to produce a safe margin for the purpose of this study. The subjects' task was to report which of the slides appeared brighter. As in experiment I, half the subjects were given instructions requiring them to choose the brighter and half the dimmer. Equality judgments were not permitted.

The level of illumination used for the presentation of slides during the experimental session was 0.1 log ft = 1 below the recognition threshold obtained to the test slides. Again, subjects were not told that words were being presented and at the end of the experiment were questioned as to whether they had noticed words during the session. No subject reported seeing a word. The physical separation of experimenter and subject in experiment I was maintained.

*Apparatus.* The basic apparatus used for the presentation of stimuli consisted of a standard 2 × 2 in. slide projector and a circular neutral density wedge connected to a control knob operated by the experimenter. A protractor calibrated in log ft = 1 enabled the experimenter to set the filter at any desired position and thus vary the amount of light transmitted by the projector to the screen. Timing was controlled by an endless tape which enabled contacts to be made and broken to trigger the projector shutter at the appropriate intervals. A 12 × 12 in. ground glass screen was positioned 2 ft from the projector shutter and the stimuli were presented at its center. A fixation cross ensured that the subject was fixating on the appropriate area.

## RESULTS

The data from both experiments were analyzed utilizing the Thurstone paired-comparisons procedure. The appropriate model is that described by Torgerson as a class III procedure where multiple observations (in this case, four) are obtained from each subject for each pair [8].

After obtaining the appropriate scale score (z value) for each stimulus in both experiments the goodness of fit of the resultant scale was tested using the Mosteller technique. For experiment I the resultant chi-square was significant ($\chi^2(28) = 65.37$; $p < 0.001$), while for experiment II chi-square was not significant ($\chi^2 = 39.59$; $p > 0.05$). The decision based on these results is therefore that the data from experiment II are scalable, whereas those of experiment I are not. The z values for each experiment are detailed in columns 2 and 3 of Table 41-1.

Examination of the respective rank orders of the nine stimuli on the conscious judgment task and on the two brightness judgment tasks indicates a large and significant correlation between the emotionality scale rank and the rank for experiment II ($p = 0.85$; $p < 0.01$). The correlation between the emotionality scale and experiment I rank orders is not significant ($p = 0.35$, n.s.).

## DISCUSSION AND CONCLUSIONS

The results obtained in this study favor the hypothesis that the perceptual defense effect has a significant perceptual component and cannot be accounted for entirely by differences in response probability between the critical and noncritical stimuli. In view of the task used it is difficult to see how differences in response probability due to such factors as conscious suppression, word frequency, and word familiarity could be involved. If, however, they did play a role in brightness judgments, it would be expected that the effects would occur under both simultaneous and successive conditions. The absence of a scale for simultaneous exposures suggests no systematic differences between the judged brightnesses of the various stimuli. Reference to Table 41-1 shows the restricted range of differences between stimuli under this condition and the apparent randomness of the brightness differences. In contrast, it can be noted that there was an expanded range for the successive condition. Further, the scale scores for the four stimuli most emotional under the conscious judgment task indicate that these are all judged less bright than the five more neutral stimuli.

Although the correlation between the emotionality scale and the experiment II scale is large and significant, it is not perfect. The largest perceptual defense effect is shown to the word *cancer*. No unequivocal explanation of why this word showed the greatest effect is possible. The position of the word *orgasm* on the brightness scale is also discrepant from its position on the emotionality scale. The precise reason for this is again uncertain.

The finding that a brightness scale is obtainable under the conditions of experiment II and the fact that this scale correlates so highly with the emotionality scale provide evidence that the presentation of emotional material modifies the overall sensitivity of the perceptual system. The scaling method used in this study would seem potentially useful in parametric studies. Using the procedure it would be possible to check the reliability of the effect in the same individual over time. The technique may be used just as readily to derive I (Individual) scales as it can be used to estimate a population scale. Having obtained such I scales the experimenter can then subject the subjects to specific treatments and measure effects in terms of the amount of change in the I scales.

## REFERENCES

1. W. Bevan. Subliminal stimulation: A pervasive problem for psychology. *Psychol. Bull.*, 1964, *61*, 81–99.
2. N. F. Dixon. Apparent changes in the visual thresholds: central or peripheral? *Brit. J. Psychol.*, 1960, *51*, 297–309.
3. C. W. Eriksen. Discrimination and learning without awareness: A methodological survey and evaluation. *Psychol. Rev.*, 1960, *67*, 279–300.
4. I. Goldiamond. Indicators of perception: I. Subliminal perception, subception, unconscious perception: An analysis in terms of psychophysical indicator methodology. *Psychol. Bull.*, 1958, *55*, 373–411.
5. A. Mathews and M. A. Wertheimer. A "pure" measure of perceptual defense uncontaminated by response suppression. *J. abnorm. soc. Psychol.*, 1958, *57*, 373–376.
6. J. G. Minard. Response bias interpretation of "perceptual defense": A selective review and evaluation of recent research. *Psychol. Rev.*, 1965, *72*, 74–88.
7. F. Mosteller. Remarks on the method of paired comparisons: III. A test of significance for paired comparisons when equal standard deviations and equal correlations are assumed. *Psychometrika*, 1951, *16*, 207–218.

8. W. S. Torgerson. *Theory and methods of scaling.* New York: Wiley, 1958.
9. A. G. Worthington. Differential rates of dark adaptation to "taboo" and "neutral" stimuli. *Canad. J. Psychol.,* 1964, *18,* 257–265.
10. A. G. Worthington. An attempt to scale subliminal visual stimuli. *Psychon. Sci.,* 1964, *1,* 291–294.
11. R. B. Zajonc. Response suppression in perceptual defense. *J. exp. Psychol.,* 1962, *64,* 206–214.


# 42
# EIDETIC IMAGERY: I. FREQUENCY

Ralph Norman Haber
Ruth B. Haber

*Eidetic imagery, defined as a visual image persisting after stimulation, relatively accurate in detail, colored positively, and capable of being scanned, was measured in nearly all children in an elementary school in New Haven, Conn. Care was taken to specify and follow precise methods for the measurement, and strict criteria were used for the discrimination of eidetic images from afterimages and from memory. Discontinuous distributions of scores were found on all of the measures used to define eidetic category on each measure. Their images lasted as long as 4 min., during which nearly all of the details of the stimulus could be reproduced. However, their memory of the stimulus was not much better after their imagery had faded than that of subjects who did not have eidetic imagery. These results were discussed in terms of models of translation of stimulation into memory, and further research was outlined.*

Source: Reprinted with permission of author and publisher. R. N. Haber and R. B. Haber, *Eidetic Imagery: I. Frequency. Perceptual and Motor Skills,* 1964, *19,* 131–138.

Note: This research was supported in part by Grant MH-03244 from the National Institute of Mental Health to Yale University, under the direction of the first author. We would like to thank Miss May White, the Superintendent of Schools for Elementary Education of the City of New Haven, Miss Margaret R. Fitzsimons, Principal, and each of the teachers of the Roger Sherman Elementary School of New Haven, for their permission to test the children, and for their kind support throughout the project.

Some children (and a very few adults) are able to maintain a complete visual image of a stimulus from which they can describe the stimulus in detail. This eidetic imagery is notably different from most adult perception, in which the visual image of a stimulus fades almost immediately and any description of the stimulus must be based on a normally incomplete memory. These two characteristics of eidetic imagery—long-term visual imagery and accurate reports without memory—should have given it great theoretical interest. However, current theories of perception have not considered visual imagery to be very important. Sperling [8], in perhaps the most comprehensive model of the translation of stimulation into memory, does not mention visual imagery, with the exception of afterimages. For him, the offset of the stimulus energy is the end of the stimulus, and all further processing of that stimulation uses different aspects of encoded memory. While he shows [7] that a dark pre-exposure field increases the duration of what he calls short-term memory (presumably because of the long afterimages produced), in other places both he [8] and Averbach [1] talk of short-term memory as already having undergone some encoding.

Eidetic imagery is important in this connection because it is sufficiently long and accurate to allow extensive and complete reports of the stimulus to be made without benefit of the intervening processes described in Sperling's model. Indeed, if eidetic imagery is as prevalent as the literature indicates, then perhaps initially in the life of the child, all translations from stimulation to reports may be through eidetic images, and not until later are the elaborate encoding and rehearsal processes necessary. Of course, any report in words of a visual stimulus requires encoding into words, but if the image of the stimulus is long, this encoding does not have to be accomplished from an imperfect memory.

With these issues in mind, this research was designed first to ascertain whether eidetic imagery occurs, and then to examine the nature of the imagery, specifically how it is used by the perceiver in reporting what he sees. This report presents data relevant primarily to the first question.

Eidetic images have been distinguished from memory by their preservation of fine detail (which is usually lost in memory), by the subject's report that a visual image still persists after the stimulus has been removed, and by behavior which indicates that he is indeed attending to such an image. Eidetic images have been distinguished from afterimages by their persistence (afterimages fade rather rapidly), by their reliability of evocation from even low-contrast stimuli (afterimages are usually difficult to arouse from such stimuli), by their positive representation of color (afterimages, especially long ones, are usually negative), by their independence of visual fixation (afterimages usually require fixation to form, while eidetic images do not), and by the lack of effects of eye movements during report (afteriamges move with the eye, while eidetic images can be scanned visually).

Perhaps 200 empirical, semiempirical, and clinical studies, mostly

German, have been made of this phenomenon, although by 1925 as many were being done in this country as abroad. Kluever has been the major reviewer of this work, with extensive reviews in 1928, 1931, and 1932, while Jaensch has been the primary systematizer, as a representative of the Marburg School, with a major book in 1925 and another in 1930. By 1937, however, interest and research, as judged by publications, had nearly ended, with only twelve papers listed in *Psychological Abstracts* during the past 25 years. The reasons for so sharp a change probably included the lack of a sound theoretical base, the behavioristic climate against this introspective subject, and the strangeness and unusualness of the behavior, at least as viewed by adult psychologists. No serious doubts were raised about the validity of eidetic imagery as a phenomenon, even though the methodology of assessment has been both poorly described and poorly executed. Eidetic imagery just ceased to excite scientists. The majority of the dozen references since 1937 are clinical reports of individual eidetic persons, usually patients.

A review of all of the research findings of eidetic imagery would be out of place here, in view of able earlier reviews of Kluever, and because of the many serious methodological deficiencies of the early work. Percentages of children said to possess some form of eidetic imagery ranged from 30 to 90, depending upon the age and population sampled, with a rough average of all studies around 50%. Nearly every investigator has reported that eidetic imagery was common, and that eidetic subjects could easily be found among any population of children. Different investigators have reported different peak ages; some have indicated a negative correlation with age, while others have pointed to puberty or shortly before as the age of greatest prevalence. All investigators have reported zero or near-zero frequencies among adults, although, as far as is known, no longitudinal studies have been reported.

## METHOD

### Subjects

All subjects were students in the Roger Sherman Elementary School of New Haven, Conn., during the academic year 1961–1962. The school had 245 children registered, of whom 179 were tested. Those missed were either consistently absent ($N = 14$) or because of time pressures were not included in the random samples drawn from the lower grades. Of the 179 subjects tested, 28 were not scorable, due to malfunctions of the tape recorder, leaving 151 in the sample.

### Testing Situation

The subject was brought into a small room which contained a table with an easel on it. The easel (30 in. wide by 24 in. high, in a neutral grey finish) was tilted away from the subject slightly, and had a narrow ledge along the bottom on which the pictures were rested. The subject was seated 20 in. away from the easel, his eyes level with the middle of it. Room illumination was normal, with strong sunlight blocked by curtains when necessary. A tape recorder transcribed both the subject's and the experimenter's voices.

**Procedure**

The sequence of events was the same for each subject. He first was shown a 4-in. red square, mounted on a board 10 in. by 12 in., of the same material as the easel. The experimenter placed the stimulus on the easel, left it there for 10 sec., and then removed it rapidly. The subject reported what he still saw on the easel. Three other colored squares (blue, black, and yellow), always in this order, were presented in a similar fashion. After the fourth square was shown, four pictures were presented for 30 sec each, in the same manner.

The following instructions were given to the subject at the beginning.

> We are going to play a game with colors and with pictures. Here on this easel I am going to show you some colors and some pictures, and then we are going to talk about them. When I put a colored square here (pointing), I want you to stare at the center of it as hard as you can, and try not to move your eyes at all as long as I leave the square there. When I take the square away, I want you to continue to stare as hard as you can where the square was. If you stare hard enough, you will still be able to see something there. It is very much like when you stare hard at a light bulb, and then look away—you can still see something out there in front of your eyes. (If any child acted as if he was unfamiliar with this demonstration, he was instructed to try it then with one of the overhead lights in the room.) The important thing is to stare hard at the colored square when I put it on the easel!—do not take your eyes away or move them around. When I remove the square, do not look at me, or follow the color as I take it away, but keep staring at the place where it was on the easel. As soon as I take the color away, I want you to tell me what you still see there, if you see anything. You do not have to wait until I ask you—you can begin telling me right away. OK, here is the first colored square.

The experimenter was watching carefully during the exposure to be sure the subject did not move his eyes. If the subject reported that he saw nothing at all after the square was removed, he was encouraged by being assured that it was all right to see things after the color was removed. If he still said he saw nothing, he was reminded to stare hard, and not to move his eyes at all, and he was questioned again as to whether he knew what these instructions meant. Then the experimenter presented the next square, increasing the duration by 10 sec over the previous exposure.

If the subject said he saw something, he was allowed to report spontaneously. When he stopped, he was questioned on whichever of the following items he had not reported: Was the image still visible? What was its color and shape? Did color and shape change, and if so, how? In what direction did the image move? How did it disappear? Did it move when the eyes moved (he was instructed to try to move his eyes to the top of the easel)? After these points had been covered, and the image had faded completely, the experimenter gave the initial instructions again, and showed another square. The same procedure was followed for the four squares.

After the last square was shown and the subject had finished his response, the instructions for the pictures were given.

> Now, I am going to show you some pictures. For these, however, I do not want you to stare in one place, but to move your eyes around so that you can be sure you can see all of the details. When I take the picture away, I want you to continue to look hard at the easel where the picture was, and tell me what you can still see after I take it away. After I take it away, you also can move your eyes all over where it was on the easel. And be sure while the picture is on the easel that you move your eyes around it to see all of the parts.

All four pictures were presented for 30 sec each. The experimenter watched closely to be sure the pictures were scanned and not fixated. The first picture was of a family scene, black pictures pasted on a grey board to form a silhouette. The second, constructed in the same way, was of an Indian hunting, with a deer, other animals, and some birds. The third, in full color, showed an Indian fishing in a canoe, with many fish in the water. The fourth, also in color, from *Alice in Wonderland,* depicted Alice standing at the base of a large tree staring up at the Cheshire cat. A number of similar pictures had been used in pretesting and in extra testing with some of the same subjects.

After the first picture was removed, the subject was told to continue to look at the easel, and to tell whatever he could still see. He was reminded that he could move his eyes. If he reported seeing something, the experimenter asked if he was actually seeing it then or remembering it from when the picture was still on the easel. The experimenter asked frequently if he was still seeing it, since subjects often would not report the fading of the image but would continue reporting it from memory. If the subject stopped his report, he was asked if he could see anything else. If he said no, but said he was still seeing an image, he was asked if he could describe anything else about that image. The experimenter probed for further description and attributes of all objects still visible in the image. The subject also was asked to move his eyes if he had not done so spontaneously. The experimenter noted the relation between direction of gaze and details of report. Whenever the subject said the entire image had faded, he was asked to describe the picture from memory, with as many details as possible. The same kind of probing questions were asked.

If, after the picture was removed, the subject said that he saw nothing, he was asked to describe the picture from memory with as many details as possible. The probing questions described above were asked.

This process was repeated for all four pictures. The average time for testing varied from 10 min with a young subject having no visual imagery to more than 30 min for an older subject with extensive imagery.

At the beginning of the next academic year, thirty-four subjects were retested using the same procedures and the same pictures and colors. They were selected so as to include most of the subjects who had earlier produced long-term and accurate images, some subjects with partial images, and a few subjects who never had reported an image to any of the pictures.

## Scoring

The tape recordings were encoded onto specially prepared data sheets, which indicated the content of all responses (images and memory). The reliability of this condensation of the data was nearly perfect, since the coding sheets had categories for every object and most of their attributes for each stimulus; the coder rarely had to make any scoring decision. All further scoring was done from these data sheets except the durations of responses, which were taken directly from the tape recordings.

For the results to be reported here, eight scores were assigned to each subject by the first author. His scoring reliability was checked by a second judge, who also scored each subject on the same eight indices. In each case, the reliability exceeded $r = +0.81$ for the continuous ratings, and 99% agreement for the dichotomous ratings. Two scores indicated whether or not the images for the squares and the pictures were colored positively. Two scores indicated the durations of the images for the pictures and for the squares. Two scores, on a five-point scale, indicated the accuracy of the coloring of the images for the pictures and for the memory of the pictures. Finally, two scores, on a nine-point scale, indicated the accuracy of the details of the images for the pictures and the memories for the pictures. The four scores assigned to rating scales were summary ratings made of the completeness of the images and memories.

## RESULTS

Eighty-four of the 151 subjects (55%) reported images of at least one of the pictures. As might be expected, a positive relationship between accuracy and duration was found, although the only subjects who had both very high accuracy and duration scores were those who saw images of all four pictures. The twelve most extreme subjects in that group were discontinuous from the remaining seventy-two on several measures.

They were the only ones who saw four images, all forty-eight of which lasted over 40 sec, all of which had an accuracy of six or greater (the majority were eight or nine), 90% of which were positively colored (as compared to 34% for the remaining subjects), and 100% of which could be scanned with the eyes (as compared to 2%). Since these latter two scores had been proposed as criteria to distinguish eidetic images from afterimages, and because of their far superior accuracy and duration, these twelve subjects seemed to be reporting eidetic images of the pictures, while the remaining seventy-two subjects seemed to be reporting afterimages or weak visual images of some other kind. Given this discontinuity on nearly every measure relevant to a definition of eidetic imagery, these twelve subjects appeared to possess an imagery which was qualitatively different from that of all of the other subjects in the sample.

The most striking aspect of the eidetic child's report was the vividness and completeness of an image that was "out there" in front of him. There was no qualification in his speech, such as "I think I see," nor did he ever use the past tense as he might have if he were combining imagery and memory. He was able to report very fine detail, such as the number of feathers worn by each of the ten Indians in one pretest picture, the different colors in a multicolored Indian blanket, the expressions on the faces, and the various poses of the persons, and all from the same image. Even if these reports were based on memory, which they did not seem to be, it would be quite unusual. One of the clearest examples of eidetic imagery occurred when the experimenter showed the next picture, mistakenly thinking that the subject had indicated that the image to the previous one had faded. After the second picture had been removed, the subject described her eidetic image, which was clearly a fusion of the images of the two stimuli. She said that she knew this was happening, but was still seeing it.

In addition to the differences in accuracy and duration between the twelve eidetic subjects and the seventy-two other subjects who produced some kind of imagery (noneidetic image), the eidetic subjects also had more positive (black) images to the two silhouette pictures (92% versus 28%, $t = 6.53$, $p < 0.001$), and greater accuracy of color in their images of the two remaining pictures than the noneidetic-image subjects ($t = 4.30$, $p < 0.001$). For the responses to the colored squares, and for the memory of the pictures, the eidetic subjects were compared with the seventy-two noneidetic-image subjects who produced some images to the pictures, and with the other sixty-seven subjects who never reported an image of any of the pictures (no-image subjects). The differences between the eidetic subjects and the other two groups were not quite so striking, but they were still highly significant (all $t$ tests exceeded 3.00, $p < 0.01$). In no instance did the noneidetic-image and the no-image subjects differ significantly. The eidetic subjects saw more afterimages to the colored squares (3.8 as compared with 3.2 and 3.0), more of which were positively colored (43% as compared to 19% and 14%), and which lasted more than twice as long as those of either of the noneidetic groups (35 sec as compared with 14 and 13 sec). The differences in memory among the three groups were much smaller than expected, although for both the accuracy of detail and of color, the eidetic subjects were significantly superior to both of the other groups (all $t > 2.10$, $p < 0.05$).

The eidetic subjects did not differ from the school population in their sex or race. Their ages varied from 8 to 12 years. Since no children older than these were tested, no indication was available of the upper age limit. No eidetic children were found below the second grade. However, since there were so few eidetic children at all, conclusions regarding their distribution throughout the population must be very cautious. Further, clear evidence of difficulty was found in the younger children (ages 4 through 6 or 7) in understanding what was expected of them and in their communication of what they were seeing and remembering. On the basis of these observations and results in this age range, previous positive results of eidetic imagery in children this young or younger should be viewed with extreme caution.

Nine of the twelve eidetic subjects were retested 8 months later, along with twenty-five other subjects. None of the noneidetic subjects, based on the original classification, produced any images in the retest to any of the pictures that were as long or as accurate as the poorest image of the eidetic subjects. Of the original nine who were retested, all but one showed the same type of imagery. While the relationships between original and retest scores for these nine subjects were generally low, they were all off the distributions on both testings. One subject failed to produce any eidetic images on the retest, even though she had an average of nearly 3 min of imagery originally, with very fine accuracy. The experimenter reported that she seemed extremely anxious on the retest, and was very concerned as to the reason she was being tested again. With this one exception, the retesting further supported the classification of subjects into eidetic and noneidetic.

## IMPLICATIONS

Contrary to a voluminous literature, the prevalence of eidetic imagery in an elementary school in New Haven was quite low—about 8%. However, the twelve subjects who were classified as eidetic were not merely the end of a continuous distribution, but rather were children who showed qualitatively different behavior on this simple perceptual task. Therefore, eidetic imagery does exist as a verifiable, identifiable characteristic in children. This first study has not attempted to explore further how these children were different from the 92% of children without this ability. That is to be followed up.

The most likely explanation of the discrepancy from previously reported frequencies is in terms of the methodological differences in the techniques used to assess the presence of eidetic imagery. This study used very strict criteria and very careful observation of the behavior of subjects' eyes, as well as their verbalizations. Many experiments in the literature classified subjects as eidetic if they produced *any* images of pictures. Following this criterion, 55% of the children would be eidetic in this study. However, it seems apparent that most of these images were afterimages—they persisted for very short periods of time, they were usually negative in color, they could not be scanned with the eye, and they included very little detail of the stimulus. Therefore, it is assumed that these results represent a closer approximation to the prevalence of eidetic imagery in the general population of children than does the previous literature.

It has not been possible to differentiate afterimages from other kinds of weak imagery in this study, if in fact they can be differentiated at all. To be able to have done so would have required that the imagery last long enough so that the effects of eye movements and the accuracy of representation could have been assessed. While neither of these would have been conclusive, it might have been possible to offer a better distinction than we can now.

Evidence has been presented, however, that 55% of the children had some kind of imagery to the pictures, with 8% having eidetic imagery. These 8% could use their imagery to report details of the stimulus, very much as if they had a nearly perfect memory lasting for the duration of the imagery. It was somewhat surprising that their actual memory for the stimulus, after the imagery had faded, was not also strikingly better than that of the noneidetic subjects. Apparently, the eidetic subjects were not using the time during which the image was present to encode the stimulus for later recall, nor were they taking advantage of their practice in reporting the stimulus from their imagery.

The presence of imagery of this fidelity and duration certainly requires inclusion in any kind of theory or model of the translation of stimulation into memory. Originally, it had been hoped we could carry out extensive experiments with large groups of eidetic subjects, so as to provide data for the construction of such a model. However, because of the small percentage found, this has not been feasible. Therefore, work is proceeding with detailed examination of these twelve subjects. This effort will provide a short-term longitudinal study, in which a number of different aspects of the relationship between perception, imagery, encoding, and memory can be analyzed.

REFERENCES

1. E. Averbach and A. S. Coriell. Short-term memory in vision. *Bell Syst. tech. J.*, 1961, *40*, 1–20.
2. E. R. Jaensch. *Die Eidetik*. Leipzig: Quell & Meyer, 1925.

3. E. R. Jaensch. *Eidetic imagery and typological methods of investigation.* New York: Harcourt, Brace, 1930.
4. H. Kluever. Studies on the eidetic type and eidetic imagery. *Psychol. Bull.,* 1928, *25,* 69–104.
5. H. Kluever. The eidetic child. In C. Murchison (ed.). *A handbook of child psychology.* Worcester, Mass.: Clark University Press, 1931. Pp. 643–668.
6. H. Kluever. Eidetic phenomena. *Psychol. Bull.,* 1932, *29,* 181–203.
7. G. Sperling. The information available in brief visual presentations. *Psychol. Monogr.,* 1960, *74* (11, whole no. 498).
8. G. Sperling. A model for visual memory tasks. *Hum. Factors,* 1963, *5,* 19–31.

# 43
# SEEING MOVEMENT

## R. L. Gregory

... Those eyes, like our own, which move in the head can give information of movement in two distinct ways. When the eye remains stationary, the image of a moving object will run across the receptors and give rise to velocity signals from the retinas: but when the eyes follow a moving object, the images remain more or less stationary upon the retinas, and so *they* cannot signal movement, *but we still see the movement of the object.* If the object is viewed against a fixed background, there may be velocity signals from the background, which now sweep across the retinas as the eyes follow the moving object, *but we still see movement even when there is no background.* This can be demonstrated with a simple experiment. Ask someone to wave a lighted cigarette around slowly in a dark room; and follow it with the eyes. The movement of the cigarette is seen although there is no image moving across the retinas. Evidently, the rotation of the eyes in the head can give perception of movement, and fairly accurate estimates of velocity, in the absence of movement signals from the retinas.

There are, then, two movement systems, and we name them (a) the *image-retina system,* and (b) the *eye-head system* (Figure 43-1). (These names follow those used in gunnery, where similar considerations apply when guns are aimed from the moving platform of a ship. The gun turret

Source: *Eye and Brain* by R. L. Gregory, (c) R. L. Gregory, 1966. Used with permission of McGraw-Hill Book Company and Weidenfeld and Nicolson Publishing Co. Ltd.

may be stationary or following, but movement can be detected in either case.)

We may now take a look at the image-retina system, and then see how the two systems work in collaboration.

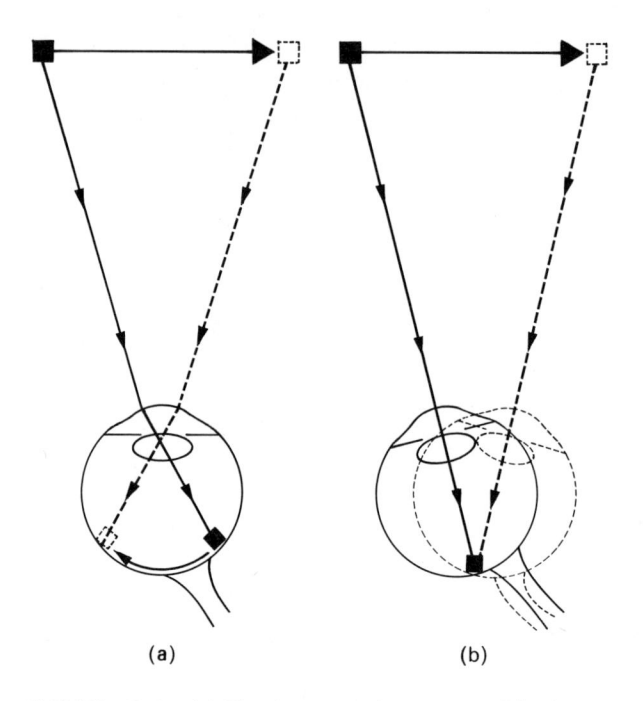

FIGURE 43-1 (a) The image-retina system. The image of a moving object runs along the retina when the eyes are held still, giving information of movement through sequential firing of the receptors in its path. (b) The eye-head movement system. When the eye follows a moving object the image remains stationary upon the retina, but we still see the movement. The two systems can sometimes disagree, giving curious illusions.

## THE IMAGE-RETINA MOVEMENT SYSTEM

It is found, by recording the electrical activity from the retinas of animals, that there are various kinds of receptors, almost all signaling only changes of illumination and very few giving a continuous signal to a steady light. Some signal when a light is switched on, others when it is switched off, while others again signal when it is switched on or off. Those various kinds are named, appropriately enough, "on," "off," and "on-off" receptors. It seems that these receptors sensitive only to change of illumination are responsible for signaling movement, and that *all eyes are primarily detectors of movement.* The receptors signaling only changes will respond to the leading and trailing edges of images, but will not signal the presence of stationary images unless the eyes are in movement.

By placing fine wires (electrodes) in the retinas of excised frogs' eyes, it has been found that analysis of the receptor activity takes place in the retina before the brain is reached. A paper [2] charmingly titled "What the Frog's Eye Tells the Frog's Brain" by Lettvin, Maturana, McCulloch, and Pitts, of the Research Laboratory of Electronics at MIT, describes a retinal "bug detector," and three classes of fibers sending different kinds of information to the brain. The "bug detector" elicits a reflex movement of the tongue when a small shadow, corresponding to a fly, falls on the retina, and so the retina is serving in this respect as a brain. In addition to this system, which responds essentially to curved lines, they find:

1. Fibers responding only to sharply defined boundaries between objects.
2. Fibers responding only to changes in the distribution of light.
3. Fibers responding only to a general dimming of illumination, such as might be caused by the shadow of a bird of prey.

The frog's eye signals only changing light patterns and moving curved edges; everything else is ignored and never reaches the brain. The frog's visual world is thus limited to movement of certain kinds of objects.

The physiologists Hubel and Wiesel [1] have conducted important experiments recording from the visual region of the cat's brain, and they find that there are some single cells which respond only to movement across the retina, and to movement in only a certain direction. They show actual records of the activity of selected single cells from the cat's brain during stimulation of the eye by movements of various kinds, and it is seen that some cells are sensitive only to movement in certain directions.

The physiological discovery that movement is coded into neural activity in the retina, or immediately behind the retina in the visual projection areas of the brain, is important in many respects; but in particular it shows that *velocity can be perceived without involving an estimate of time.* It is, however, often assumed that the neural systems giving perception of velocity must resort to an internal biological clock. Velocity is defined in physics as the time taken for an object to travel a given distance ($v = d/t$). It is then assumed that a time estimate is always required to estimate velocity. But the speedometer of a car has no clock associated with it. A clock is needed for calibrating such an instrument in the first place, but once calibrated it will give velocity measures without the use of a clock, and the same is evidently true of the eye. The image running across the retina sequentially fires the receptors, and the faster the image travels, up to a limit, the greater the velocity signal this gives. Analogies with other velocity detectors (speedometers and so on) show that velocity could be perceived without reference to a clock, but they do not tell us precisely how the neural system works. Some day it should be possible to draw a complete circuit diagram of the retina and make a working electronic model of it, but this we cannot do with any confidence as yet for the human eye. A model has been suggested for the compound eye of beetles. This has been made and is now sometimes used in aircraft to detect drift due to wind blowing the machine off course. This movement detector was developed by biological evolution some hundred million years ago, discovered by applying electronic ideas, and then built with electronic components and used for flight by man.

## THE EYE-HEAD MOVEMENT SYSTEM

The neural system giving perception of movement by shift of images across the retinas must be very different from the way movement is signaled by relation of the eyes in the head. The eye movements are controlled by six extrinsic muscles for each eye; somehow the fact that the eye is being moved is signaled to the brain and used to indicate the movement of external objects. That this really does happen is demonstrated with the cigarette experiment we have just described, for in that situation there is no systematic movement across the retina and yet the movement of the cigarette is seen when it is followed by the eyes (Figure 43-1b).

The most obvious kind of signal would be feedback from the muscles so that when they stretch, signals would be fed back to the brain indicating movement of the eyes, and so of objects followed by the eyes. This would be the engineer's solution, but is it Nature's? We find the answer when we look at what may seem a different question.

## WHY DOES THE WORLD REMAIN STABLE WHEN WE MOVE OUR EYES?

The retinal images run across the receptors whenever we move our eyes, and yet we do not experience movement—the world does not spin round whenever we move our eyes. Why should this be?

We have seen that there are neural systems for signaling movement, the image-retina and the eye-head systems and it seems that during normal eye movements, these cancel each other out to give stability to the visual world. The idea of cancellation to give stability was discussed by the physiologist who did most to unravel the spinal reflexes, Sir Charles Sherrington, and by Helmholtz, but they had very different ideas as to how it comes about, and especially how what we have called the eye-head velocity system functions. Sherrington's theory is known as the *inflow theory* and Helmholtz's as the *outflow theory* (Figure 43-2). Sherrington thought that signals from the eye muscles are fed back into the brain when the eye moves to cancel the movement signals from the retina. This idea is familiar to engineers as feedback, but neural signals from the eye muscles would take rather a long time to arrive, and we would expect a sickening jolt just after we move our eyes, before the inflow signals reach the brain to cancel the retinal movement signals. Helmholtz had a very different idea. He thought that the retinal movement signals are canceled *not* by signals from the muscles, but by central signals from the brain commanding the eyes to move.

The issue can be decided by very simple experiments, which the reader can try himself. Try pushing an eye gently with the finger, while the other is closed by holding a hand over it. When the eye is rotated passively in this way, the world will be seen to swing round in the opposite direction to the movement of the eye. Evidently stability does not hold for *passive* eye movements, though it does for the normal *voluntary* movements. Since the world swings round *against* the direction of

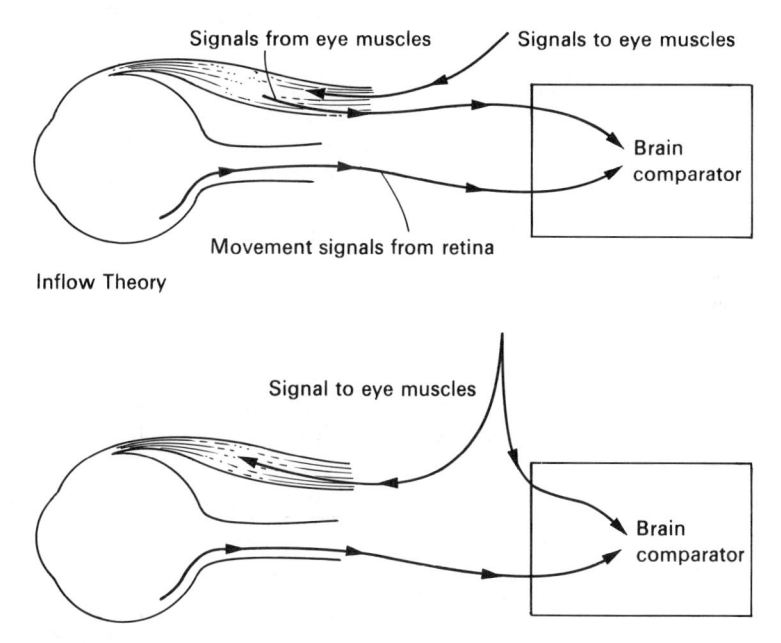

FIGURE 43-2 Why does the world remain stable when we move our eyes? The *inflow theory* suggests that the movement signals from the retina (image-retina system) are canceled by (afferent) signals from the eye muscles. The *outflow theory* suggests that the retinal movement signals are canceled by the (efferent) command signals to move the eyes, through an internal monitoring loop. The evidence favors the outflow theory.

the passive eye movements, it is evident that the image-retina system still works; it is the eye-head system which is not operating. We may well ask: Why should the eye-head system work only for voluntary and not for passive eye movements? Sherrington thought that it works by sending down signals from stretch receptors in the eye muscles. Such stretch receptors are well known and serve to give feedback signals from the muscles which move the limbs. But it looks as though the eye-head system does not work this way, for the stretch receptors should surely provide some signals during passive movements of the eyes.

We may stop all retinal movement signals and see what happens during passive movements of the eye. This is easily done by staring at a bright light (or a photographic flash) to get an afterimage. This produces a local area of fatigue like a photograph stuck on the retina, and it will move precisely with the eye, and so cannot give any image-retina movement signals however the eye moves. If we observe the afterimage in darkness (to avoid a background), it is found that if the eyes are pushed with the finger to move passively *the afterimage does not move*. This is very strong evidence against the inflow theory, for stretch receptor activity should cause the afterimage to shift with the eye, if it is normally responsible for canceling the retinal movement signals.

If the eye is now moved voluntarily, you will find that *the afterimage moves with the eye*. Wherever the eye is moved, the afterimage will follow. Helmholtz explained this by supposing that it is not activity *from* the eye muscles which is involved, but *commands to move the eyes*. The outflow theory, as we have seen, holds that the command signals are monitored by an internal loop in the brain and canceled against the retinal movement signals. When these are absent, as in the case of afterimages viewed in darkness, the world swings round with the eyes because the command signals go uncanceled by the retina. Passive movements of the eye give no movement of afterimages for neither system gives a movement signal.

In clinical cases where something has gone wrong with the eye muscles or their nerve supply, the world swings round for these patients when they try to move their eyes. Their world moves in the direction their eyes should have moved. This also occurs if the muscles are prevented from functioning by curare, the South American arrow poison. The German scientist Ernst Mach bunged up his eyes with putty so that they could not move, and he got the same result.

The eye-head system, then, does not work by actual movement of the eyes, but by commands to move them. It works even when the eyes do not obey the command. It is surprising that command signals can give rise to perception of movement: We usually think of movement perception as coming from the eyes, not from a source deep in the brain controlling them.

Why should such a peculiar system have evolved? It is even more surprising, when we find that there are in fact stretch receptors in the eye muscles. An inflow or feedback system would appear to be too slow: by the time a feedback signal got back to the brain for canceling against the retinal movement signal, it would be too late.

The canceling signal could start at the same moment as the command, and so could oppose the retinal signal with no delay. Actually, the signal from the retina takes a little time to arrive (the retinal action time), and so the command signal could arrive for canceling too soon; but it is delayed to suit the retina, as we may see by studying carefully the movement of the afterimage with voluntary eye movements. Whenever the eye is moved, the afterimage takes a little time to catch up, and this is evidently the delay put into the monitored command signal so that it does not arrive before the signal from the retina. Can one imagine a more beautiful system? . . .

## REFERENCES

1. D. H. Hubel, and T. N. Wiesel. Receptive fields, binocular interaction, and functional architecture in the cat's visual cortex. *J. Physiol.*, 1962, *160*, 106–154.
2. J. Y. Lettvin, H. R. Maturana, W. S. McCulloch, and W. H. Pitts. What the frog's eye tells the frog's brain. *Proc. Inst. Radio. Engr.* 1959, *47*, 1940–1951.

# 44
# VISUAL MOTION PERCEPTION: EXPERIMENTAL MODIFICATION

## R. H. Masland

*If a human observer fixates a moving spiral pattern for 15 minutes, a negative aftereffect of motion is perceived when he inspects a stationary spiral 20 hours later. The illusory motion is seen only when the stationary test stimulus falls upon the portion of the retina which had been stimulated by real motion. Thus previous stimulation can cause a relatively long-term modification of vision.*

In the classic aftereffect of visual motion the observer views a repetitively moving pattern for a short time, the motion of the pattern is then stopped, and an illusion of the pattern moving in the opposite direction is experienced. (For reviews see [9, 3].) Under the usual conditions the aftereffect dissipates within a few seconds, and perhaps for this reason the effect was considered by nineteenth-century physiologists as a "motion afterimage," similar to the familiar negative color afterimages. However, I have found that it is possible to generate a motion aftereffect, which is seen hours or days after exposure to real movement, when the observer inspects the stimulus which he originally viewed in real motion. This demonstration suggests the existence of a long-term storage capability in vision.

Observers were forty-five male university students who had no previous knowledge of the motion aftereffect. They were seated 2.4 m from a black and white spiral pattern (3.5 turn) on a disk 20.3 cm (5.1° visual angle) in diameter. A black knob (0.6 cm in diameter) provided a fixation point at the center of the spiral. The spiral was aligned vertically, with its center 55 cm from the floor, and was surrounded by a white screen 100 cm$^2$. It was illuminated at 13.9 lu/m$^2$ by a tungsten photoflood lamp located above and behind the observer. Motion was generated by rotating the disk clockwise at 80 rpm.

Source: *Science*, 1969, *165*, 819–821. Copyright 1969 by the American Association for the Advancement of Science.
Note: Supported by National Research Council of Canada grant to Dr. D. Donderi, whose guidance is acknowledged.

The observer was told only that the experiment was concerned with visual perception and that he would simply be asked to report what he saw. He heard the following instructions: "In a minute I am going to turn on a motor which will make the spiral turn. You see that there is a black knob in the center of the spiral. I would like you to look at the knob, and keep looking there until I tell you to stop. It is extremely important that you keep looking right at the center and not look away at all." Each observer then fixated the center of the spiral for 15 min. At the end of this period, alternate observers were assigned to one of two experimental groups.

In group 1 ($N = 15$), the spiral was stopped and the observer was permitted to observe the aftereffect at will for 10 min before leaving the room. For group 2 ($N = 15$), the lights were turned out and the observer sat in the dark for 10 min, after which the lights were turned on again and he left the room. He was then asked if he noticed anything unusual about his vision, which none did. A third group of fifteen observers underwent a control procedure identical to that of group 2, except that the spiral was not rotated—the observer simply fixated the center of a stationary spiral for 15 min, then sat in the dark for 10 min.

All observers returned for a second session between 20 and 26 hr later. They had been told on the first day that there was "another part of this experiment." The stimulus was covered before the observer entered the room. He was seated as in the first session and given the following instructions: "In a minute I will take the card away and you will see the spiral that you looked at yesterday. I want you to look back at the center of the spiral, where you looked before, and tell me what you see."

All observers in both experimental groups reported apparent movement of the spiral on the second day. The typical observer in group 1 would exclaim "It's still moving," and observers in group 2, who had not been allowed to see the aftereffect on the first day, reported that the spiral definitely seemed to be moving. In all cases the motion described was in the opposite direction to the previous real motion of the spiral. None of the control observers, who had inspected a stationary spiral in the first session, reported the motion aftereffect on the second day. The basic finding described above has been replicated with an additional 121 observers in other experiments [5].

The strength (speed) of the motion aftereffect can be measured by means of a compensation method in which the observer controls, with a rheostat, an objective motion of the spiral in the direction opposite of the aftereffect. The null point, where aftereffect and real motion cancel, is taken as the speed of the aftereffect.[1] Seventy-two additional observers were given a 15-min exposure to real movement under conditions similar

---

[1] This procedure could not be used in the first experiment because the instructions to the observer might be construed as suggesting the result. For details of the tracking method see [4] and [8].

to those for group 2. The speed of the resulting apparent movement was measured after a period between exposure and testing of 0.6, 7.5, 15, or 60 min, or 24 hr (Figure 44-1). Each observer served in a single delay condition.

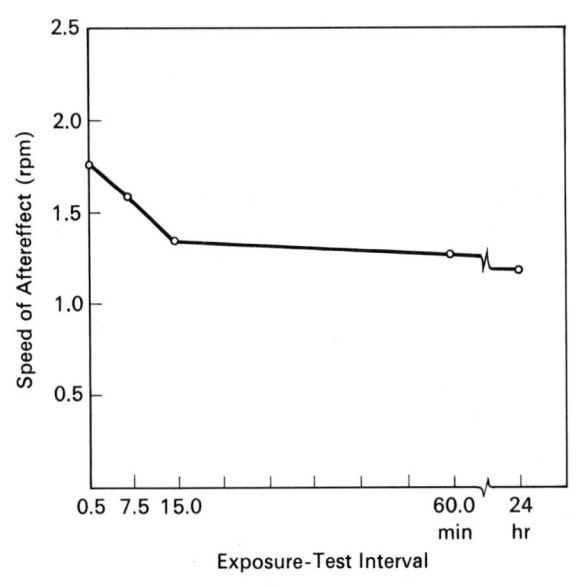

FIGURE 44-1 Speed of aftereffect as a function of exposure-test delay.

Subjectively the apparent movement is striking and unambiguous. One sees a clear aftereffect like the one following short exposure to real motion in the classic demonstration. Although the instructions merely request description of the stimulus, it is conceivable that some observers may have expected to see motion on the second day. This seems unlikely because the effect was not reported by control observers, and was reported by observers in experimental group 2, who never experienced the aftereffect before the second test session and should have had no way to suggest to themselves the direction of the apparent motion. More importantly, they were clearly taken by surprise to find the spiral moving.

Another explanation would involve eye movements. A tendency for the eye to counteract the original rotation might become an actual (torsional) eye movement during later inspection of the stationary stimulus. But the effect described above has also been obtained under conditions of optical stabilization (Hepler and Masland, 1969) and in any event one would expect the whole visual field to tilt when the eye movement occurred, rather than its effect being limited to producing an apparent rotation of the test spiral. Thus it seems likely that this result reflects a long-term modification of the responsiveness of the nervous system.

This suggestion is supported by the fact that the presence of the effect is limited to the part of visual system which was stimulated by real movement (Figure 44-2). Fourteen observers fixated a point 6.1° lateral

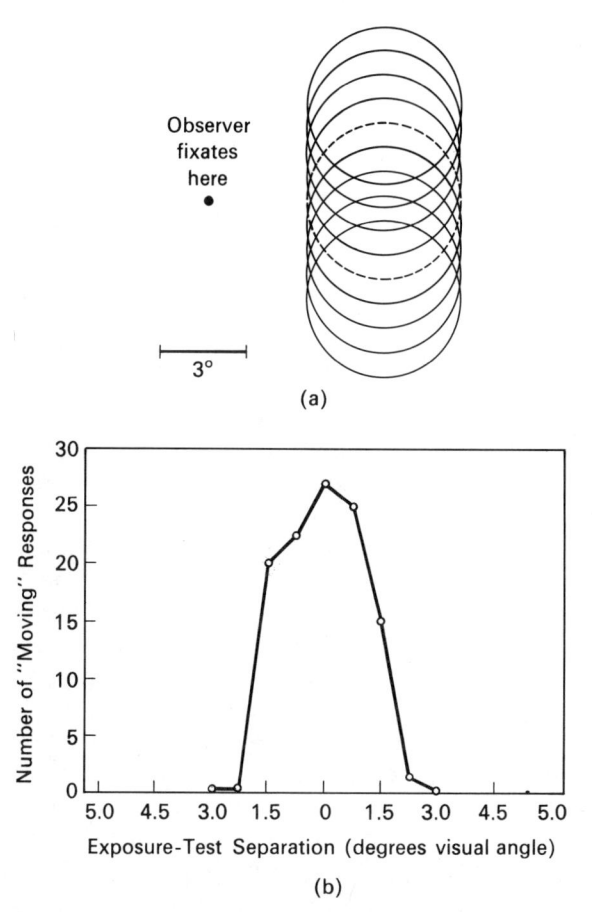

FIGURE 44-2 (a) Test for topographic specificity of the aftereffect. During both real movement and test for aftereffect the observer fixated at the indicated point. During stimulation with real movement the spiral was located in the position indicated by the dashed circle. The stationary test spiral was later presented at one of the positions indicated by the solid circles, or at the position where the moving spiral had been. Since the fixation point was constant, this procedure varies the overlap between the retinal area stimulated by real motion and that stimulated by the stationary pattern. (b) Number of reports of movement as a function of the center-to-center separation between the location of the moving spiral and the location of the stationary test spiral.

to the moving spiral during a 15-min exposure. After a 30-min delay[2] each reported on the presence or absence of apparent motion when the spiral was presented in one of nine positions (in random order) relative to the position of the originally moving stimulus. Each position was tested twice for each observer, with the stationary stimulus exposed for 2 sec on each trial. The results show that unless the stationary test stimulus falls within about 1.5° of the location where the objectively moving stimulus had been shown there is no aftereffect.[3] In free observation the specificity of the perceptual change is quite compelling. Looking directly at the stimulus one sees nothing unusual, but when the eyes return to the fixation point the spiral suddenly begins to move; the motion can be started and stopped merely by shifting one's line of regard by a few degrees.

Thus an observer exposed to the rotating spiral for 15 min under these experimental conditions leaves the laboratory with a localized change in his vision. His perception is apparently unchanged, but if he looks at a pattern identical to the one he watched rotate, and if the pattern falls on the same part of his retina—and its topographic central projection—his perception is altered and he sees an illusory motion.

These findings show that at least in a simple case vision can be modified by previous visual stimulation. It may be that the phenomenon is best considered as a form of habituation, specific both to stimulus and to place.[4]

The physiological basis of such a visual storage mechanism is obscure, although Morrell [6] and Chow and others [1] have shown evidence of plasticity in firing patterns of single units of cat visual cortex and dorsal lateral geniculate body. The topographic specificity of the modification of perception seems to suggest that at least some of the events responsible for the long-term effects of localized stimulation occur in the same population of cells which was stimulated by real motion. An electrophysiological study of motion-sensitive cortical neurons during prolonged stimulation and testing might yield information on this problem.

REFERENCES

1. K. L. Chow, D. F. Lindsley and M. Gollender. Modification of response patterns of lateral geniculate neurons after paired stimulation of contralateral and ipsilateral eyes. *J. Neurophysiol.*, 1968, *31*, 729–739.

---

[2] Figure 44-1 shows that there is little change in the strength of the aftereffect during the additional time between 30 min and 24 hr. This experiment has also been made using 24-hr delay and central fixation, with the same results [4].

[3] An independent similar experiment on the immediate aftereffect of short exposure to motion has yielded results similar to those reported here [7].

[4] Inasmuch as the phenomenon represents form-contingent motion adaptation it may be related to the specific color-adaptation effects shown by Hepler [2] and McCollough [5].

2. N. Hepler. Colour: A motion-contingent aftereffect. *Science,* 1968, *162,* 376–377.
3. H. C. Holland. *The spiral aftereffect.* New York: Pergamon, 1965.
4. R. H. Masland. Unpublished thesis, McGill University, 1968.
5. C. McCollough. Colour adaptation of edge-detectors in the human visual system. *Science,* 1965, *149,* 1115–1116.
6. F. Morrell. Electrical signs of sensory coding. In G. C. Quarton, T. Melnechuk, F. O. Schmitt (eds.). *The neurosciences.* New York: Rockefeller University Press, 1967. Pp. 452–468.
7. R. Sekuler and A. Pantle. A model for after-effects of seen movement. *Vision Res.,* 1967, *7,* 427–439.
8. M. M. Taylor. Tracking the neutralization of seen rotary movement. *Percept. mot. Skills,* 1963, *16,* 513–519.
9. A. Wohlgemuth. On memory and the direction of associations. *Brit. J. Psychol.,* 1911 (suppl. 1), *5,* 447–465.

# 45

# HEMISPHERE DECONNECTION AND UNITY IN CONSCIOUS AWARENESS

## R. W. Sperry

The following article is a result of studies my colleagues and I have been conducting with some neurosurgical patients of Philip J. Vogel of Los Angeles. These patients were all advanced epileptics in whom an extensive midline section of the cerebral commissures had been carried out in an effort to contain severe epileptic convulsions not controlled by medication. In all these people the surgical sections included division of the corpus callosum in its entirety, plus division also of the smaller anterior and hippocampal commissures, plus in some instances the massa intermedia. So far as I know, this is the most radical disconnection of the cerebral hemispheres attempted thus far in

Source: *American Psychologist,* 1968, *23,* 723–733. Copyright 1968 by the American Psychological Association. Reprinted by permission.
Note: Original work referred to in this article by the writer and his coworkers was supported by Grant MH–03372 from the National Institute of Mental Health, United States Public Health Service, and by the Hixon Fund of the California Institute of Technology.

human surgery. The full array of sections was carried out in a single operation.

No major collapse of mentality or personality was anticipated as a result of this extreme surgery: Earlier clinical observations on surgical section of the corpus callosum in man, as well as the results from dozens of monkeys on which I had carried out this exact same surgery, suggested that the functional deficits might very likely be less damaging than some of the more common forms of cerebral surgery, such as frontal lobotomy, or even some of the unilateral lobotomies performed more routinely for epilepsy.

The first patient on whom this surgery was tried had been having seizures for more than 10 years with generalized convulsions that continued to worsen despite treatment that had included a sojourn in Bethesda at the National Institutes of Health. At the time of the surgery, he had been averaging two major attacks per week, each of which left him debilitated for another day or so. Episodes of *status epilepticus* (recurring seizures that fail to stop and represent a medical emergency with a fairly high mortality risk) had also begun to occur at 2- to 3-month intervals. Since leaving the hospital following his surgery over 5½ years ago, this man has not had, according to last reports, a single generalized convulsion. It has further been possible to reduce the level of medication and to obtain an overall improvement in his behavior and well being [3].

The second patient, a housewife and mother in her 30s, also has been seizure-free since recovering from her surgery, which was more than 4 years ago [2]. Bogen related that even the EEG has regained a normal pattern in this patient. The excellent outcome in the initial, apparently hopeless, last-resort cases led to further application of the surgery to some nine more individuals to date, the majority of whom are too recent for therapeutic evaluation. Although the alleviation of the epilepsy has not held up 100% throughout the series (two patients are still having seizures, although their convulsions are much reduced in severity and frequency and tend to be confined to one side), the results on the whole continue to be predominantly beneficial, and the overall outlook at this time remains promising for selected severe cases.

The therapeutic success, however, and all other medical aspects are matters for our medical colleagues, Philip J. Vogel and Joseph E. Bogen. Our own work has been confined entirely to an examination of the functional outcome, that is, the behavioral, neurological, and psychological effects of this surgical disruption of all direct cross-talk between the hemispheres. Initially we were concerned as to whether we would be able to find in these patients any of the numerous symptoms of hemisphere deconnection that had been demonstrated in the so-called splitbrain animal studies of the 1950s [12, 15, 16]. The outcome in man remained an open question in view of the historic Akelaitis [1] studies that had set the prevailing doctrine of the 1940s and 1950s. This doctrine maintained that no important functional symptoms are found in man following even complete surgical section of the corpus callosum and anterior commissure, provided that other brain damage is excluded.

These earlier observations on the absence of behavioral symptoms in man have been confirmed in a general way to the extent that it remains fair to say today that the most remarkable effect of sectioning the neocortical commissures is the apparent lack of effect so far as ordinary behavior is concerned. This has been true in our animal studies throughout, and it seems now to be true for man also, with certain qualifications that we will come to later. At the same time, however—and this is in contradiction to the earlier doctrine set by the Akelaitis studies—we know today that with appropriate tests one can indeed demonstrate a large number of behavioral symptoms that correlate directly with the loss of the neocortical commissures in man as well as in animals [4, 15, 16, 19]. Taken collectively, these symptoms may be referred to as the syndrome of the neocortical commissures or the syndrome of the forebrain commissures or, less specifically, as the syndrome of hemisphere deconnection.

One of the more general and also more interesting and striking features of this syndrome may be summarized as an apparent doubling in most of the realms of conscious awareness. Instead of the normally unified single stream of consciousness, these patients behave in many ways as if they have two independent streams of conscious awareness, one in each hemisphere, each of which is cut off from and out of contact with the mental experiences of the other. In other words, each hemisphere seems to have its own separate and private sensations; its own perceptions; its own concepts; and its own impulses to act, with related volitional, cognitive, and learning experiences. Following the surgery, each hemisphere also has thereafter its own separate chain of memories that are rendered inaccessible to the recall processes of the other.

This presence of two minds in one body, as it were, is manifested in a large number and variety of test responses which, for the present purposes, I will try to review very briefly and in a somewhat streamlined and simplified form. First, however, let me take time to emphasize that the work reported here has been very much a team project. The surgery was performed by Vogel at the White Memorial Medical Center in Los Angeles. He has been assisted in the surgery and in the medical treatment throughout by Joseph Bogen. Bogen has also been collaborating in our behavioral testing program, along with a number of graduate students and postdoctoral fellows, among whom M. S. Gazzaniga, in particular, worked closely with us during the first several years and managed much of the testing during that period. The patients and their families have been most cooperative, and the whole project gets its primary funding from the National Institute of Mental Health.

Most of the main symptoms seen after hemisphere deconnection can be described for convenience with reference to a single testing setup, shown in Figure 45-1. Principally, it allows for the lateralized testing of

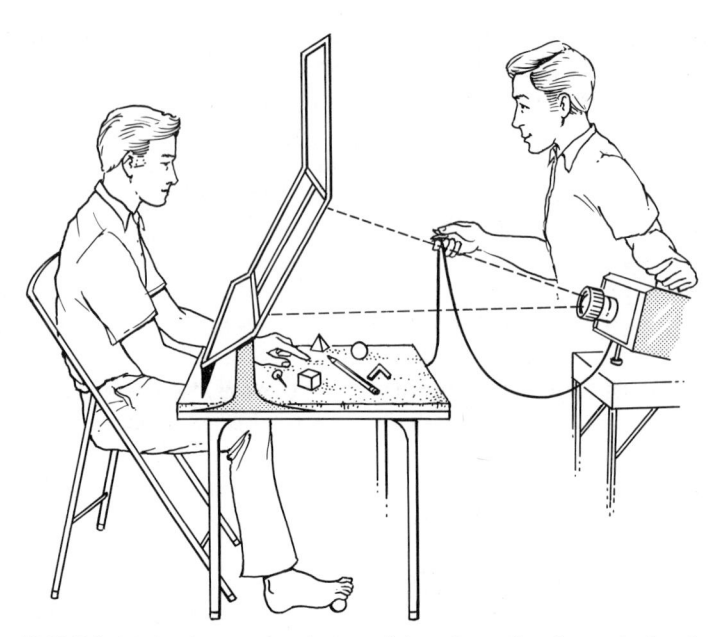

FIGURE 45-1 Apparatus for studying lateralization of visual, tactual, lingual, and associated functions in the surgically separated hemispheres.

the right and left halves of the visual field, separately or together, and the right and left hands and legs with vision excluded. The tests can be arranged in different combinations and in association with visual, auditory, and other input, with provisions for eliminating unwanted stimuli. In testing vision, the subject with one eye covered centers his gaze on a designated fixation point on the upright translucent screen. The visual stimuli on 35-mm transparencies are arranged in a standard projector equipped with a shutter and are then back-projected at 0.10 sec or less—too fast for eye movements to get the material into the wrong half of the visual field. Figure 45-2 is merely a reminder that everything seen to the left of the vertical meridian through either eye is projected to the right hemisphere and vice versa. The midline division along the vertical meridian is found to be quite precise without significant gap or overlap [17].

When the visual perception of these patients is tested under these conditions the results indicate that these people have not one inner visual world any longer, but rather two separate visual inner worlds, one serving the right half of the field of vision and the other the left half—each, of course, in its respective hemisphere. This doubling in the visual sphere shows up in many ways: For example, after a projected picture of an object has been identified and responded to in one half field, we find that it is recognized again only if it reappears in the same half of the field of vision. If the given visual stimulus reappears in the opposite half of the visual field, the subject responds as if he had no recollection of the previous exposure. In other words, things seen through the right half of the visual field (through the left hemisphere) are registered in mental experience and rememberd quite separately from things seen in the other half of the field. Each half of the field of vision in the commissurotomized patient has its own train of visual images and memories.

This separate existence of two visual inner worlds is further illustrated in reference to speech and writing, the cortical mechanisms for which are centered in the dominant hemisphere. Visual material projected to the right half of the field—left-hemisphere system of the typical right-handed patient—can be described in speech and writing in an essentially normal manner. However, when the same visual material is projected into the left half of the field, and hence to the right hemisphere, the subject consistently insists that he did not see anything or that there was only a flash of light on the left side. The subject acts as if he were

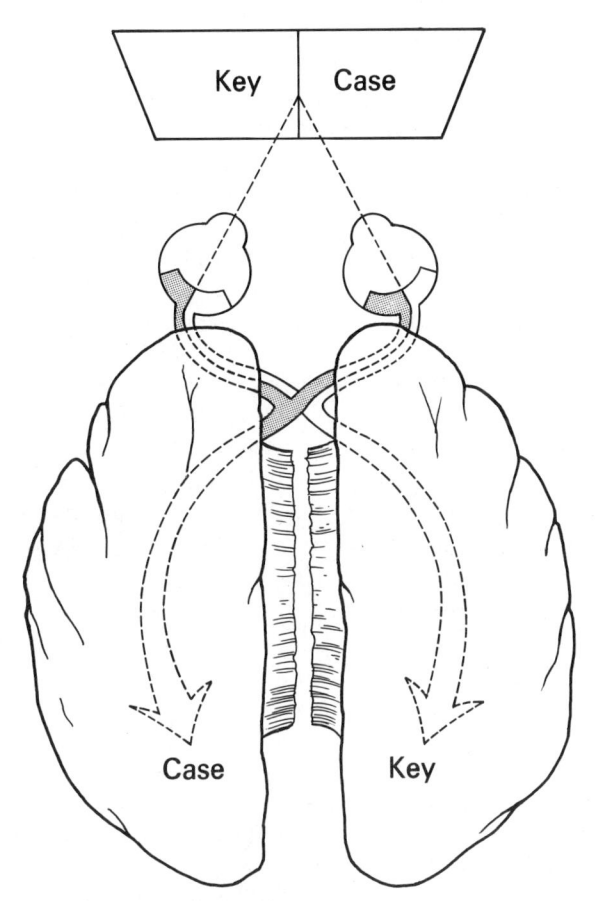

FIGURE 45-2 Things seen to the left of a central fixation point with either eye are projected to the right hemisphere and vice versa.

blind or agnostic for the left half of the visual field. If, however, instead of asking the subject to tell you what he saw, you instruct him to use his left hand to point to a matching picture or object presented among a collection of other pictures or objects, the subject has no trouble as a rule in pointing out consistently the very item that he has just insisted he did not see.

We do not think the subjects are trying to be difficult or to dupe the examiner in such tests. Everything indicates that the hemisphere that is talking to the examiner did in fact not see the left-field stimulus and truly had no experience with, nor recollection of, the given stimulus. The other, the right or nonlingual hemisphere, however, did see the projected stimulus in this situation and is able to remember and recognize the object and can demonstrate this by pointing out selectively the corresponding or matching item. This other hemisphere, like a deaf mute or like some aphasics, cannot talk about the perceived object and, worse still, cannot write about it either.

If two different figures are flashed simultaneously to the right and left visual fields, as for example a dollar sign on the left and a question mark on the right and the subject is asked to draw what he saw using the left hand out of sight, he regularly reproduces the figure seen on the left half of the field, that is, the dollar sign. If we now ask him what he has just drawn, he tells us without hesitation that the figure he drew was the question mark, or whatever appeared in the right half of the field. In other words, the one hemisphere does not know what the other hemisphere has been doing. The left and the right halves of the visual field seem to be perceived quite separately in each hemisphere with little or no cross-influence.

When words are flashed partly in the left field and partly in the right, the letters on each side of the midline are perceived and responded to separately. In the key case example shown in Figure 45-2 the subject might first reach for and select with the left hand a key from among a collection of objects indicating perception through the mirror hemisphere. With the right hand he might then spell out the word *case* or he might speak the word if verbal response is in order. When asked what kind of case he was thinking of here, the answer coming from the left hemisphere might be something like *in case of fire* or *the case of the missing corpse* or *a case of beer,* and so on, depending upon the particular mental set of the left hemisphere at the moment. Any reference to key case under these conditions would be purely fortuitous, assuming that visual, auditory, and other cues have been properly controlled.

A similar separation in mental awareness is evident in tests that deal with stereognostic or other somesthetic discriminations made by the right and left hands, which are projected separately to the left and right hemispheres, respectively. Objects put in the right hand for identification by touch are readily described or named in speech or writing, whereas, if the same objects are placed in the left hand, the subject can only make wild guesses and may often seem unaware that anything at all is present. As with vision in the left field, however, good perception, comprehension, and memory can be demonstrated for these objects in the left hand when the tests are so designed that the subject can express himself through nonverbal responses. For example, if one of these objects which the subject tells you he cannot feel or does not recognize is taken from the left hand and placed in a grab bag or scrambled among a dozen other test items, the subject is then able to search out and retrieve the initial object even after a delay of several minutes is deliberately interposed. Unlike the normal subject, however, these people are obliged to retrieve such an object with the same hand with which it was initially identified. They fail at cross-retrieval. That is, they cannot recognize with one hand something identified only moments before with the other hand. Again, the second hemisphere does not know what the first hemisphere has been doing.

When the subjects are first asked to use the left hand for these stereognostic tests they commonly complain that they cannot "work with that hand," that the hand "is numb," that they "just can't feel anything or can't do anything with it," or that they "don't get the message from that hand." If the subjects perform a series of successful trials and correctly retrieve a group of objects which they previously stated they could not feel, and if this contradiction is then pointed out to them, we get comments like "Well, I was just guessing," or "Well, I must have done it unconsciously."

With other simple tests a further lack of cross-integration can be demonstrated in the sensory and motor control of the hands. In a symmetric handpose test the subject holds both hands out of sight symmetrically positioned and not in contact. One hand is then passively placed by the examiner into a given posture, such as a closed fist, or one, two, or more fingers extended or crossed or folded into various positions. The subject is then instructed verbally or by demonstration to form the same pose with the other hand, also excluded from vision. The normal subject does this quite accurately, but the commissurotomy patient generally fails on all but the very simplest hand postures, like the closed fist or the fully extended hand.

In a test for crossed topognosis in the hands, the subject holds both hands out of sight, forward and palm up with the fingers held apart and extended. The examiner then touches lightly a point on one of the fingers or at the base of the fingers. The subject responds by touching the same target point with the tip of the thumb of the same hand. Cross-integration is tested by requiring the patient to use the opposite thumb to find the corresponding mirror point on the opposite hand. The commissurotomy patients typically perform well within either hand, but fail when they attempt to cross-locate the corresponding point on the opposite hand. A crude cross-performance with abnormally long latency may be achieved in some cases after practice, depending on the degree of ipsilateral motor control and the development of certain strategies. The latter breaks down easily under stress and is readily distinguished from the natural performance of the normal subject with intact callosum.

In a related test the target point is presented visually as a black spot on an outline drawing of the hand. The picture is flashed to the right or left half of the visual field, and the subject then attempts as above to touch the target spot with the tip of the thumb. The response again is performed on the same side with normal facility but is impaired in the commissurotomy patient when the left visual field is paired with a right-hand response and vice versa. Thus the duality of both manual stereognosis and visuognosis is further illustrated; each hemisphere perceives as a separate unit unaware of the perceptual experience of the partner.

If two objects are placed simultaneously, one in each hand, and then are removed and hidden for retrieval in a scrambled pile of test items, each hand will hunt through the pile and search out selectively its own object. In the process each hand may explore, identify, and reject the item for which the other hand is searching. It is like two separate individuals working over the collection of test items with no cooperation between them. We find the interpretation of this and of many similar performances to be less confusing if we do not try to think of the behavior of the commissurotomy patient as that of a single individual, but try to think instead in terms of the mental facilities and performance capacities of the left and the right hemispheres separately. Most of the time it appears that the major, that is, the left, hemisphere is in control. But in some tasks, particularly when these are forced in testing procedures, the minor hemisphere seems able to take over temporarily.

It is worth remembering that when you split the brain in half anatomically you do not divide in half, in quite the same sense, its functional properties. In some respects cerebral functions may be doubled as much as they are halved because of the extensive bilateral redundancy in brain organization, wherein most functions, particularly in subhuman species, are separately and rather fully organized on both sides. Consider for example the visual inner world of either of the disconnected hemispheres in these patients. Probably neither of the separated visual systems senses or perceives itself to be cut in half or even incomplete. One may compare it to the visual sphere of the hemianopic patient who, following accidental destruction of an entire visual cortex of one hemisphere, may not even notice the loss of the whole half sphere of vision until this has been pointed out to him in specific optometric tests. These commissurotomy patients continue to watch television and to read the paper and books with no complaints about peculiarities in the perceptual appearance of the visual field.

At the same time, I want to caution against any impression that these patients are better off mentally without their cerebral commissures. It is true that if you carefully select two simple tasks, each of which is easily handled by a single hemisphere, and then have the two performed simultaneously, there is a good chance of getting better than normal scores. The normal interference effects that come from trying to attend to two separate right and left tasks at the same time are largely eliminated in the commissurotomized patient. However, in most activities that are at all complex the normally unified cooperating hemispheres still appear to do better than the two disconnected hemispheres. Although it is true that the intelligence, as measured on IQ tests, is not much affected and that the personality comes through with little change, one gets the impression in working with these people that their intellect is nevertheless handicapped in ways that are probably not revealed in the ordinary tests. All the patients have marked short-term memory deficits, which are especially pronounced during the first year, and it is open to question whether this memory impairment ever clears completely. They also have orientation problems, fatigue more quickly in reading and in other tasks requiring mental concentration, and presumably have various other impairments that reduce the upper limits of performance in functions that have yet to be investigated. The patient that has shown the best recovery, a boy of 14, was able to return to public school and was doing passing work with B to D grades, except for an F in math, which he had to repeat. He was, however, a D student before the surgery, in part, it would seem, for lack of motivation. In general, our tests to date have been concerned mostly with basic cross-integrational deficits in these patients and the kind of mental capacities preserved in the subordinate hemisphere. Studied comparisons of the upper limits of performance before and after surgery are still needed.

Much of the foregoing is summarized schematically in Figure 45-3. The left hemisphere in the right-handed patients is equipped with the expressive mechanisms for speech and writing and with the main centers for the comprehension and organization of language. This major hemisphere can communicate its experiences verbally and in an essentially normal manner. It can communicate, that is, about the visual experiences of the right half of the optic field and about the somesthetic and volitional experiences of the right hand and leg and right half of the body generally. In addition, and not indicated in the figure, the major hemisphere also communicates, of course, about all of the more general, less lateralized cerebral activity that is bilaterally represented and common to both hemispheres. On the other side we have the mute aphasic and agraphic right hemisphere, which cannot express itself verbally, but which through the use of nonverbal responses can show that it is not agnostic; that mental processes are indeed present centered around the left visual field, left hand, left leg, and left half of the body; along with the auditory, vestibular, axial somatic, and all other cerebral activities that are less lateralized and for which the mental experiences of the right and left hemispheres may be characterized as being similar but separate.

It may be noted that nearly all of the symptoms of cross-integrational impairment that I have been describing are easily hidden or com-

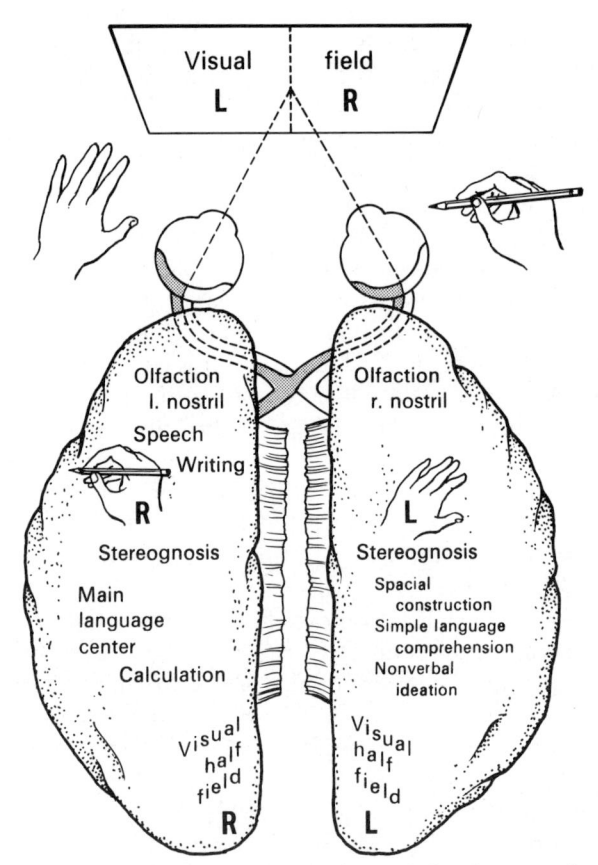

FIGURE 45-3 Schematic outline of the functional lateralization evident in behavioral tests of patients with forebrain commissurotomy.

pensated under the conditions of ordinary behavior. For example, the visual material has to be flashed at 0.10 sec or less to one half of the field in order to prevent compensation by eye movements. The defects in manual stereognosis are not apparent unless vision is excluded; nor is doubling in olfactory perception evident without sequential occlusion of right and left nostril and elimination of visual cues. In many tests the major hemisphere must be prevented from talking to the minor hemisphere and thus giving away the answer through auditory channels. And, similarly, the minor hemisphere must be prevented from giving nonverbal signals of various sorts to the major hemisphere. There is a great diversity of indirect strategies and response signals, implicit as well as overt, by which the informed hemisphere can be used to cue in the uninformed hemisphere [11].

Normal behavior under ordinary conditions is favored also by many other unifying factors. Some of these are very obvious, like the fact that these two separate mental spheres have only one body, so they always get dragged to the same places, meet the same people, and see and do the same things all the time and thus are bound to have a great overlap of common, almost identical, experience. Just the unity of the optic image—and even after chiasm section in animal experiments, the conjugate movements of the eyes—means that both hemispheres automatically center on, focus on, and hence probably attend to, the same items in the visual field all the time. Through sensory feedback a unifying body schema is imposed in each hemisphere with common components that similarly condition in parallel many processes of perception and motor action onto a common base. To get different activities going and different memory chains built up in the separated hemispheres of the bisected mammalian brain, as we do in the animal work, requires a considerable amount of experimental planning and effort.

In motor control we have another important unifying factor, in that either hemisphere can direct the movement of both sides of the body, including to some extent the movements of the ipsilateral hand [10]. Insofar as a response involves mainly the axial parts and proximal limb segments, these patients have little problem in directing overall response from sensory information restricted to either single hemisphere. Control of the distal limb segments and especially of the finer finger movements of the hand ipsilateral to the governing hemisphere, however, are borderline functions and subject to considerable variation. Impairments are most conspicuous when the subject is given a verbal command to respond with the fingers of the left hand. The absence of the callosum, which normally would connect the language processing centers in the left hemisphere to the main left-hand motor controls in the opposite hemisphere, is clearly a handicap, especially in the early months after surgery. Cursive writing with the left hand presents a similar problem. It may be accomplished in time by some patients using shoulder and elbow rather than finger movement. At best, however, writing with the left hand is not as good after as before the surgery. The problem is not in motor coordination per se, because the subject can often copy with the left hand a word already written by the examiner when the same word cannot be written to verbal command.

In a test used for more direct determination of the upper limits of this ipsilateral motor control, a simple outline sketch of a finger posture (see Figure 45-4) is flashed to a single hemisphere, and the subject then tries to mimic the posture with the same or the opposite hand. The sample posture can usually be copied on the same side (through the main, contralateral control system) without difficulty, but the performance does not go so easily and often breaks down completely when the subject is obliged to use the opposite hand. The closed fist and the open hand with all fingers extended seem to be the two simplest responses, in that these can most often be copied with the ipsilateral hand by the more adept patients.

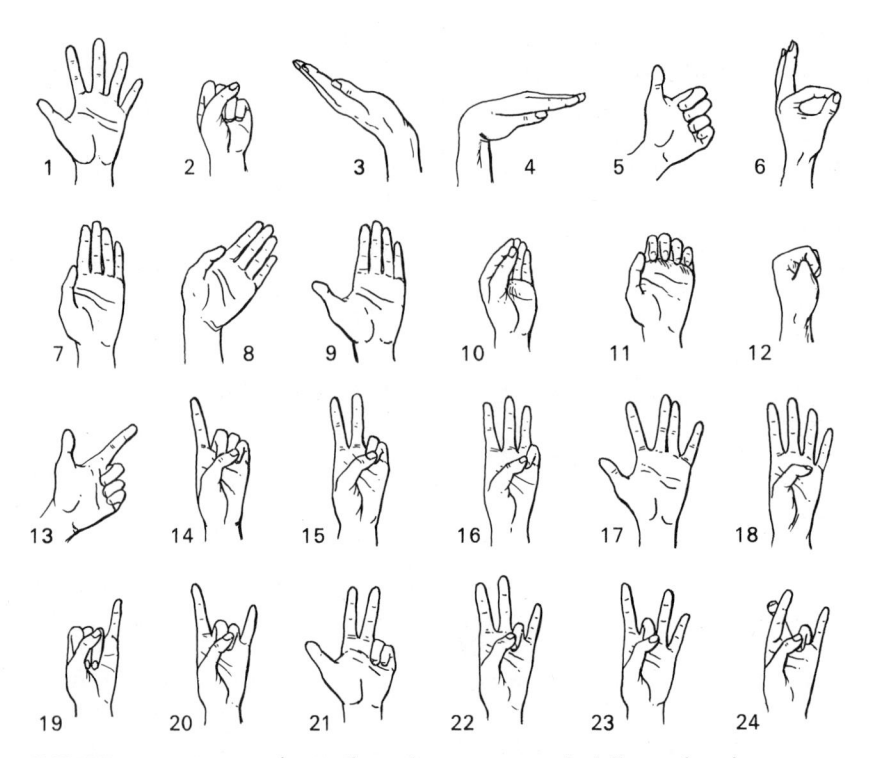

FIGURE 45-4 In tests for ipsilateral motor control, different hand postures in outline drawing are projected one at a time to left or right visual field (see Figure 45-1). Subject attempts to copy the sample hand pose with the homolateral and the contralateral hand.

The results are in accord with the thesis [5] that the ipsilateral control systems are delicate and marginal and easily disrupted by associated cerebral damage and other complicating factors. Preservation of the ipsilateral control system in varying degree in some patients and not in others would appear to account for many of the discrepancies that exist in the literature on the symptoms of hemisphere deconnection, and also for a number of changes between the present picture and that described until 2 years ago. Those acquainted with the literature will notice that the present findings on dyspraxia come much closer to the earlier Akelaitis observations than they do to those of Liepmann or of others expounded more recently (see [8]).

To try to find out what goes on in that speechless agraphic minor hemisphere has always been one of the main challenges in our testing program. Does the minor hemisphere really possess a true stream of conscious awareness or is it just an agnostic automaton that is carried along in a reflex or trancelike state? What is the nature, the quality, and the level of the mental life of this isolated subordinate unknown half of the human brain—which, like the animal mind, cannot communicate its experiences? Closely tied in here are many problems that relate to lateral dominance and specialization in the human brain, to the functional roles mediated by the neocortical commissures, and to related aspects of cerebral organization.

With such in mind, I will try to review briefly some of the evidence obtained to date that pertains to the level and nature of the inner mental life of the disconnected minor hemisphere. First, it is clear that the minor hemisphere can perform intermodal or cross-modal transfer of perceptual and mnemonic information at a characteristically human level. For example, after a picture of some object, such as a cigarette, has been flashed to the minor hemisphere through the left visual field, the subject can retrieve the item pictured from a collection of objects using blind touch with the left hand, which is mediated through the right hemisphere. Unlike the normal person, however, the commissurotomy patient is obliged to use the corresponding hand (i.e., the left hand, in this case) for retrieval and fails when he is required to search out the same object with the right hand (see Figure 45-5). Using the right hand the subject recognizes and can call off the names of each object that he comes to if he is allowed to do so, but the right hand or its hemisphere does not know what it is looking for, and the hemisphere that can recognize the correct answer gets no feedback from the right hand. Hence, the two never get together, and the performance fails. Speech and other auditory cues must be controlled.

It also works the other way around: that is, if the subject is holding

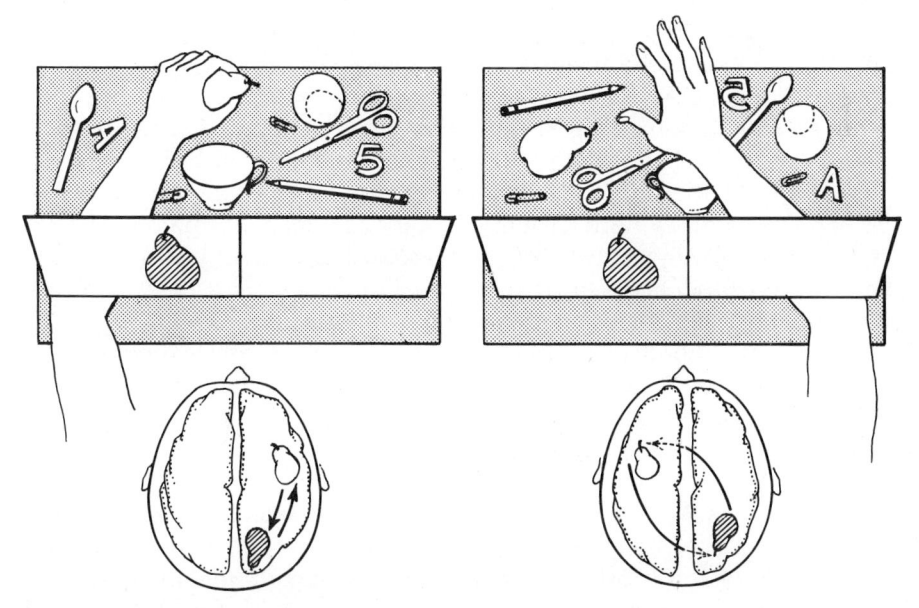

FIGURE 45-5 Visuotactile associations succeed between each half of the visual field and the corresponding hand. They fail with crossed combinations in which visual and tactual stimuli are projected into opposite hemispheres.

an object in the left hand, he can then point out a picture of this object or the printed name of the object when these appear in a series presented visually. But again, these latter must be seen through the corresponding half of the visual field; an object identified by the left hand is not recognized when seen in the right half of the visual field. Intermodal associations of this sort have been found to work between vision, hearing and touch, and, more recently, olfaction in various combinations within either hemisphere but not across from one hemisphere to the other. This perceptual or mnemonic transfer from one sense modality to another has special theoretical interest in that it is something that is extremely difficult or impossible for the monkey brain. The right hemisphere, in other words, may be animal-like in not being able to talk or write, but in performances like the foregoing and in a number of other respects it shows mental capacities that are definitely human.

Other responses from the minor hemisphere in this same testing situation suggest the presence of ideas and a capacity for mental association and at least some simple logic and reasoning. In the same visuotactual test described above, the minor hemisphere, instead of selecting objects that match exactly the pictured item, seems able also to select related items or items that "go with" the particular visual stimulus, if the subject is so instructed. For example, if we flash a picture of a wall clock to the minor side and the nearest item that can be found tactually by the left hand is a toy wrist watch, the subjects significantly select the watch. It is as if the minor hemisphere has an idea of a timepiece here and is not just matching sensory outlines. Or, if the picture of a dollar sign is flashed to the minor side, the subject searches through the list of items with the left hand and finally selects a coin such as a quarter or a 50-cent piece. If a picture of a hammer is presented, the subject may come up with a nail or a spike after checking out and rejecting all other items.

The capacity to think abstractly with symbols is further indicated in the ability of the minor hemisphere to perform arithmetical problems. When confronted with two numerals each less than 10, the minor hemisphere was able in four of six subjects so tested to respond with the correct sum or product up to 20 or so. The numbers were flashed to the left half of the visual field or presented as plastic block numerals to the left hand for identification. The answer was expressed by pointing to the correct number in columns of seen figures, or by left-hand signals in which the fingers were extended out of the subject's sight, or by writing the numerals with the left hand out of sight. After a correct left-hand response had been made by pointing or by writing the numeral, the major hemisphere could then report the same answer verbally, but the verbal report could not be made prior to the left-hand response. If an error was made with the left hand, the verbal report contained the same error. Two different pairs of numerals may be flashed to right and left fields simultaneously and the correct sum or products signaled separately by right and left hands. When verbal confirmation of correct left-hand signals is required under these conditions, the speaking hemisphere can only guess fortuitously, showing again that the answer must have been obtained from the minor and not from the major hemisphere. This has been demonstrated recently in a study still in progress by Biersner and the present writer. The findings correct an earlier impression [7] in which we underestimated the capacity for calculation on the minor side. Normal subjects and also a subject with agenesis of the callosum [13] were able to add or to multiply numerals shown one in the left and one in the right field under these conditions. The commissurotomy subjects, however, were able to perform such calculations only when both numerals appeared in the same half of the visual field.

According to a doctrine of long standing in the clinical writings on aphasia, it is believed that the minor hemisphere, when it has been disconnected by commissural or other lesions from the language centers on the opposite side, becomes then "word blind," "word deaf," and "tactually alexic." In contradiction to this, we find that the disconnected minor hemisphere in these commissurotomy patients is able to comprehend both written and spoken words to some extent, although this comprehension cannot be expressed verbally [7, 14, 18]. If the name of some object is flashed to the left visual field, like the word *eraser*, for example, the subject is able then to search out an eraser from among a collection of objects using only touch with the left hand. If the subject is then asked what the item is after it has been selected correctly, his replies show that he does not know what he is holding in his left hand—as is the general rule for left-hand stereognosis. This means of course that the *talking* hemisphere does not know the correct answer, and we concluded accordingly that the minor hemisphere must, in this situation, have read and understood the test world.

These patients also demonstrate comprehension of language in the minor hemisphere by being able to find by blind touch with the left hand an object that has been named aloud by the examiner. For example, if asked to find a piece of silverware, the subject may explore the array of test items and pick up a fork. If the subject is then asked what it is that he has chosen, he is just as likely in this case to reply *spoon* or *knife* as fork. Both hemispheres have heard and understood the word *silverware,* but only the minor hemisphere knows what the left hand has actually found and picked up. In similar tests for comprehension of the spoken word, we find that the minor hemisphere seems able to understand even moderately advanced definitions like *shaving instrument* for razor or *dirt remover* for soap and *inserted in slot machines* for quarter.

Work in progress shows that the minor hemisphere can also sort objects into groups by touch on the basis of shape, size, and texture. In some tests the minor hemisphere is found to be superior to the major, for example, in tasks that involve drawing spatial relationships and performing block design tests. Perceptive mental performance in the minor hemisphere is also indicated in other situations in which the two hemispheres function concurrently in parallel at different tasks. It has been found, for example, that the divided hemispheres are capable of perceiving different things occupying the same position in space at the same time, and of learning mutually conflicting discrimination habits, something of which the normal brain is not capable. This was shown in the monkey work done some years ago by Trevarthen [20] using a system of polarized light filters. It also required section of the optic chiasm, which of course is not included in the human surgery. The human patients, unlike normal subjects, are able to carry out a double voluntary reaction-time task as fast as they carry out a single task [6]. Each hemisphere in this situation has to perform a separate and different visual discrimination in order to push with the corresponding hand the correct one of a right and left pair of panels. Whereas interference and extra delay are seen in normal subjects with the introduction of the second task, these patients with the two hemispheres working in parallel simultaneously perform the double task as rapidly as the single task.

The minor hemisphere is also observed to demonstrate appropriate emotional reactions as, for example, when a pinup shot of a nude is interjected by surprise among a series of neutral geometric figures being flashed to the right and left fields at random. When the surprise nude appears on the left side the subject characteristically says that he or she saw nothing or just a flash of light. However, the appearance of a sneaky grin and perhaps blushing and giggling on the next couple of trials or so belies the verbal contention of the speaking hemisphere. If asked what all the grinning is about, the subject's replies indicate that the conversant hemisphere has no idea at this stage what it was that had turned him on. Apparently, only the emotional effect gets across, as if the cognitive component of the process cannot be articulated through the brainstem.

Emotion is also evident on the minor side in a current study by Gordon and Sperry [9] involving olfaction. When odors are presented through the right nostril to the minor hemisphere the subject is unable to name the odor but can frequently tell whether it is pleasant or unpleasant. The subject may even grunt, make aversive reactions or exclamations like *phew!* to a strong unpleasant smell, but not be able to state verbally whether it is garlic, cheese, or some decayed matter. Again it appears that the affective component gets across to the speaking hemisphere, but not the more specific information. The presence of the specific information within the minor hemisphere is demonstrated by the subject's correct selection through left-hand stereognosis of corresponding objects associated with the given odor. The minor hemisphere also commonly triggers emotional reactions of displeasure in the course of ordinary testing. This is evidenced in the frowning, wincing, and negative head shaking in test situations where the minor hemisphere, knowing the correct answer but unable to speak, hears the major hemisphere making obvious verbal mistakes. The minor hemisphere seems to express genuine annoyance at the erroneous vocal responses of its better half.

Observations like the foregoing lead us to favor the view that in the minor hemisphere we deal with a second conscious entity that is characteristically human and runs along in parallel with the more dominant stream of consciousness in the major hemisphere [14]. The quality of mental awareness present in the minor hemisphere may be comparable perhaps to that which survives in some types of aphasic patients following losses in the motor and main language centers. There is no indication that the dominant mental system of the left hemisphere is concerned about or even aware of the presence of the minor system under most ordinary conditions except quite indirectly as, for example, through occasional responses triggered from the minor side. As one patient remarked immediately after seeing herself make a left-hand response of this kind, "Now I know it wasn't me did that!"

Let me emphasize again in closing that the foregoing represents a somewhat abbreviated and streamlined account of the syndrome of hemisphere deconnection as we understand it at the present time. The more we see of these patients and the more of these patients we see, the more we become impressed with their individual differences, and with the consequent qualifications that must be taken into account. Although the general picture has continued to hold up in the main as described, it is important to note that, with respect to many of the deconnection symptoms mentioned, striking modifications and even outright exceptions can be found among the small group of patients examined to date. Where the accumulating evidence will settle out with respect to the extreme limits of such individual variations and with respect to a possible average "type" syndrome remains to be seen.

## REFERENCES

1. A. J. Akelaitis. A study of gnosis, praxis, and language following section of the corpus callosum and anterior commissure. *J. Neurosurgery,* 1944, *1,* 94–102.
2. J. E. Bogen, E. D. Fisher, and P. J. Vogel. Cerebral commissurotomy: A second case report. *J. AMA,* 1965, *194,* 1328–1329.
3. J. E. Bogen and P. J. Vogel. Cerebral commissurotomy: A case report. *Bull. L. A. neurol. Soc.,* 1962, *27,* 169.
4. M. S. Gazzaniga. The split brain in man. *Sci. Amer.,* 1967, *217,* 24–29.
5. M. S. Gazzaniga, J. E. Bogen, and R. W. Sperry. Dyspraxia following division of the cerebral commissures. *Arch. Neurol.,* 1967, *16,* 606–612.
6. M. S. Gazzaniga and R. W. Sperry. Simultaneous double discrimination following brain bisection. *Psychon. Sci.,* 1966, *4,* 262–263.
7. M. S. Gazzaniga and R. W. Sperry. Language after section of the cerebral commissures. *Brain,* 1967, *90,* 131–148.
8. N. Geschwind. Disconnexion syndromes in animals and man. *Brain,* 1965, *88,* 237–294, 584–644.

9. H. W. Gordon and R. W. Sperry. Olfaction following surgical disconnection of the hemispheres in man. *Proc. psychon. Soc.,* 1968, *7,* 111–120.
10. C. R. Hamilton. Effects of brain bisection on eye-hand coordination in monkeys wearing prisms. *J. comp. physiol. Psychol.,* 1967, *64,* 434–443.
11. J. Levy-Agresti. Ipsilateral projection systems and minor hemisphere function in man after neocommissurotomy. *Anat. Rec.,* 1968, *160,* 384.
12. R. E. Myers. Corpus callosum and visual gnosis. In J. F. Delafresnaye (ed.). *Brain mechanisms and learning.* Oxford: Blackwell, 1961. Pp. 481–505.
13. R. Saul and R. W. Sperry. Absence of commissurotomy symptoms with agenesis of the corpus callosum. *Neurology,* 1968, *18,* 307.
14. R. W. Sperry. Brain bisection and mechanisms of consciousness. In J. C. Eccles (ed.). *Brain and conscious experience.* New York: Springer-Verlag, 1966. Pp. 298–313.
15. R. W. Sperry. Mental unity following surgical disconnection of the hemispheres. *The Harvey lectures.* Ser. 62. New York: Academic Press, 1967. Pp. 293–323.
16. R. W. Sperry. Split-brain approach to learning problems. In G. C. Quarton, T. Melnechuk, and F. O. Schmitt (eds.). *The neurosciences.* New York: Rockefeller University Press, 1967. Pp. 714–722.
17. R. W. Sperry. Apposition of visual half-fields after section of neocortical commissures. *Anat. Rec.,* 1968, *160,* 498–499.
18. R. W. Sperry and M. S. Gazzaniga. Language following surgical disconnection of the hemispheres. In C. H. Millikan (ed.). *Brain mechanisms underlying speech and language.* New York: Grune and Stratton, 1967. Pp. 108–121.
19. R. W. Sperry, M. S. Gazzaniga, and J. E. Bogen. Function of neocortical commissures: Syndrome of hemisphere deconnection. In P. J. Vinken and G. W. Bruyn (eds.). *Handbook of neurology.* Vol. 4. Amsterdam: North Holland, 1969. Pp. 273–290.
20. C. B. Trevarthen. Double visual learning in split-brain monkeys. *Science,* 1962, *136,* 258–259.

# 46
# NEURAL PROCESSING OF BACKWARDS-SPEECH SOUNDS

D. Kimura
S. Folb

*When sounds such as those produced by reverse playback of recorded speech are presented to left and right ears of normal subjects, the sounds arriving at the right ear are more accurately identified than those arriving at the left. These findings are comparable to the right-ear superiority demonstrated with normal speech sounds, and contrast with the left-ear superiority for musical and other non-speech sounds. It is suggested that the neural mechanisms underlying the perception of speech and nonspeech sounds are not differentiated along the dimension of conceptual content.*

The perception of verbal material is known to be mediated primarily by the left half of the brain in man. Previous studies have indicated that the dominance of the left hemisphere for perception of speech can be detected in normal persons by the more accurate report of verbal stimuli presented to the right (contralateral) ear compared with the left [2]. In contrast, melodic patterns are more accurately identified when they are presented to the left ear [3]; this fact reflects the known predominance of the right hemisphere in the processing of nonverbal sounds [7].

These auditory asymmetries appear to occur only with dichotic presentation: that is, with different sounds presented to the two ears simultaneously—not with monaural stimulation. They are not due to differences in acuity of the two ears, but rather to the advantageous neural connections of each ear with the opposite cerebral hemisphere. The probable neuroanatomical mechanism for asymmetry with dichotic presentation has been described [4].

The right-ear superiority has been demonstrated for digits, words,

Source: *Science*, 1968, *161*, 395–396. Copyright 1968 by the American Association for the Advancement of Science.
Note: Supported by a grant from the National Research Council of Canada.

and nonsense syllables [4]; left-ear superiority, for both familiar and unfamiliar melodic patterns [4] as well as for environmental nonspeech sounds [1]. All these results are consistent with the demonstrated division of labor between the left and right hemispheres in the processing of speech and nonspeech stimuli, respectively.[1]

The technique of dichotic presentation is thus demonstrably sensitive to the differential neural processing of verbal and nonverbal stimuli in the two hemispheres of the brain. Varying the stimulus characteristics of dichotically presented sounds should then enable us to form some conclusions regarding the factors involved in this differential processing.

Backwards-speech sounds were presented dichotically with the aim of discovering whether such highly unfamiliar, meaningless sounds would be processed in the same way as other speech sounds; that is, whether there would be more accurate perception of those sounds arriving at the right ear. The backwards speech was obtained by recording trisyllabic nonsense words on a half-track, dual-channel tape recorder, and then inverting the tape and playing it back in the normal direction. The result is something quite unusual and unfamiliar, somewhat resembling a Slavic language.

The subjects were fourteen female and ten male undergraduates in psychology; all were right-handed and had no known hearing defects.

On each trial the subject was first presented with two different backwards-speech sounds simultaneously: one to the left ear and one to the right. After a 4-sec interval, four more backwards-speech sounds were played one at a time, two of them being identical with those played dichotically. The subject's task was to identify which two of the four he had heard presented dichotically. Each of the four positions of the sequence was used equally often for each ear. There were twelve trials, yielding a maximum possible score of 12 for each ear. For half the subjects the earphones were reversed from normal so that any asymmetry in the tape or apparatus was counterbalanced over ears.

This multiple-choice recognition procedure is identical with that used for melodic patterns, for which it yields a left-ear superiority [3] and for trisyllabic nonsense speech for which it yields a right-ear superiority [4]. The backwards-speech sounds were never referred to as speech, but as nonsense sounds.

The mean score for the left ear was 4.6 or 38% correct (SD, 2.1); for the right ear, 7.6 or 63% correct (SD, 2.8). The difference between ears is significant beyond the 0.001 level ($t$, 4.05; correlated means). Eighteen subjects showed right-ear superiority, four showed left-ear superiority, and two showed no difference between ears. Table 46-1 compares these

---

[1] For a review of relevant studies of impairment after lesions of the left and right hemispheres, see [6].

TABLE 46-1 Comparison of Left and Right Ears for Trisyllabic Nonsense Speech Under Two Conditions—Forwards and Backwards

| Left | Right | p |
|---|---|---|
|  | Forwards |  |
| 5.6 (47%) | 8.1 (68%) | < 0.01 |
|  | Backwards |  |
| 4.6 (38%) | 7.6 (63%) | < 0.001 |

data with data from the earlier study [4] employing normal nonsense speech.

The right-ear superiority for backwards-speech sounds indicates that they are processed by neuropsychological systems overlapping those for normal speech sounds, rather than by systems for nonspeech sounds; it provides strong support for the suggestion that the critical distinguishing characteristics of speech sounds are not related to meaningfulness, familiarity, or conceptual content [4]. In a consideration of the acoustic characteristics to which the speech-processing system may selectively respond, Liberman et al. [5] have proposed that the auditory signals are perceived via the same motor-command signals as those responsible for producing speech. This suggestion implies that only sounds that can be articulated should be processed by the speech system. Our intention in making backwards-speech stimuli was to have inarticulable sounds, but in this we were only partly successful. Although these stimuli are extremely difficult to reproduce, the subjective impression when one tries to hold them in storage for the few seconds until they are identified is that one is treating them as though they were sounds that one could produce. Several spontaneous reports of this kind came from the subjects also. Thus we may not have ruled out the participation of some kind of articulatory mechanism during the "holding" period.

# REFERENCES

1. F. K. W. Curry. A comparison of left-handed and right-handed subjects on verbal and non-verbal dichotic listening tasks. Cortex, 1967, 3, 343–352.
2. D. Kimura. Cerebral dominance and perception of verbal stimuli. Canad. J. Psychol., 1961, 15, 166–171.
3. D. Kimura. Left-right differences in the perception of melodies. Quart. J. exp. Psychol., 1964, 14, 355–358.
4. D. Kimura. Functional asymmetry of the brain in dichotic listening. Cortex, 1967, 3, 163–178.
5. A. M. Liberman, F. S. Cooper, D. P. Shankweiler, and M. Studdert-Kennedy. Perception of the speech code. Psychol. Rev., 1967, 74, 431–461.

6. C. H. Millikan and F. L. Darley (eds.). *Brain mechanisms underlying speech and language.* New York: Grune and Stratton, 1967.
7. B. Milner. Laterality effects in audition. In V. Mountcastle (ed.). *Interhemispheric relations and cerebral dominance.* Baltimore: Johns Hopkins University Press, 1962. Pp. 177–195.

# 47
# AUDITORY BACKWARD INHIBITION IN CONCERT HALLS

## Georg von Bekesy

Immersed as we are in the cacophony of an overcrowded world, perhaps a good musical performance in a grand concert hall is one of the last auditory stimuli that is still desirable. Unfortunately, however, sound transmission in a concert hall is greatly complicated by the reflections from the walls of the structure.

The problems of the concert hall are of three major types.

1. The performance of the musician and his instrument. Many experiments have been made to determine the reasons for the differences in sound transmission of individual stringed instruments of a given type. There seems to be, for every instrument, a typical direction in which the sound radiates. Even today it is not clear whether, for instance, the sound from a violin should radiate directly toward the audience as a whole or more toward the ceiling so that it can be reflected from there to the audience in the back of the concert hall. Furthermore, is the optimum direction of radiation the same for all the frequencies emitted by the violin? It is obvious that for the violin which radiates a large part of its sound, for all frequencies, toward the ceiling, any absorption by the ceiling should be avoided. The same thing holds true for the side walls. This is just one example of the close interaction between the musical instrument and the architecture of the concert hall. Most of the musical instruments developed during the eighteenth century were built to fulfill the requirements of a small concert hall. Today we have larger audiences, and we would

Source: *Science,* 1971, *171,* 529–536. Copyright 1971 by the American Association for the Advancement of Science.
Note: Supported by NFS Grant GB-5768 and PHS Grant NS-06890 from the Institute of Neurological Diseases and Blindness.

therefore like to improve upon the construction of earlier musical instruments so that the sound of today's instruments can fill large concert halls.

2. The physical transmission of a sound from the performer to the listener in a concert hall. The ancient Romans were interested in this problem; the first treatise on the subject was probably that of [39]. In Vitruvius' time, the transmission of sound was considered similar to the transmission of a light beam, and reflections from a wall were considered very important. This approach to acoustical problems was very successful, especially for high frequencies. It was already known at that time that a musical performer should have a reflecting wall behind him. Whereas in outdoor theaters the role of a reflecting wall can be easily controlled, in a closed room like a concert hall much more is involved. It was mainly the work of Sabine [30] which demonstrated the concept of room reverberation—that is, that the sound reflected from one wall in a closed room is again and again reflected from the other walls, so that a diffused sound field is created. This sound field represents acoustic energy accumulated in every cubic foot of the room. The time interval within which this accumulated sound energy can be dissipated is of great importance in determining the acoustic quality of a structure. The only way to dissipate the accumulated energy is to have, in addition to the absorbent surfaces of the audience, absorbent walls.

Later work in the field of architectural acoustics by Knudsen [20, 21] and by many other researchers in the United States and Europe indicated that the two concepts—that of reflected sound and that of reverberant sound—should be combined. The ratio between the loudness of direct sound and the loudness of reverberant sound is an important factor in determining the quality of concert halls. A description of concert halls throughout the world which are considered to be of excellent quality is given by Beranek [7].

3. The most complex factor in concert hall acoustics is the reaction of the listener to the complicated mixture of direct and reverberant sound. He definitely does not act as a microphone, but he is able to partially reject (inhibit) sound waves or completely cancel them out, depending on their direction of impact, their intensity, and the interval between the times of emission and of arrival.

## FIVE DIFFERENT TYPES OF INHIBITION

There are at least five different types of inhibition in the auditory system which modify the loudness, the location, the volume density, and the apparent extension of a sound source. All five differ for a continuous tone and for a transient one. Besides being inhibitory, the nervous system integrates some of the sounds into a single sensation. When the architecture of a room enhances this sensation of integration, we say that the room has good acoustics. Most of the pertinent experiments indicate that inhibition can be just as important as the sensations produced by the stimuli themselves. Let us consider the five types.

First, if we consider only two sound stimuli—for example, the direct sound and the sound reflected from one wall—we find that inhibition is present even if there is no delay between the arrival of the two sounds. The localization of the sound source then depends on the relative loudness of the direct and the reflected sound.

The second type of inhibition is very well known. It is produced by small differences (of the order of 1 msec or less) in the time a sound reaches the two ears, and it is responsible for directional hearing. If both ears are stimulated by a sound simultaneously, we localize the sound source in the median plane of the head. But if there is a time difference, we localize the sound source to the side which receives the sound first. With a time difference of 1 msec we have the impression that we hear the sound only with one ear. This type of inhibition was well described by von Hornbostel and Wertheimer [17] and later fully discussed by von Hornbostel [14, 15, 16]. We may call this type of inhibition *forward inhibition* because the first stimulus inhibits all the stimuli that are later presented to the other ear. It is a continuous type of inhibition: An increase in the difference in the times of arrival of a sound at the two ears produces a continuous movement of the localization of the apparent sound source. The maximum time interval for this activity is only about 2 msec. If the delay is greater than 2 msec, we have two separate sound sensations, one in each ear. This second type of inhibition makes it possible for us to separate in space the sounds from the different instruments of an orchestra.

The third type of inhibition might be called *backward inhibition*. It is also often associated with the phenomena of masking or metacontrast. Backward inhibition is active in the time-difference range between 30 and 120 msec. It is a peculiar type of inhibition: a second stimulus presented about 60 msec after presentation of the first stimulus is able to inhibit or apparently erase the first stimulus. It is a type of erasure related to short-term memory. The phenomenon is not new; Exner [10] was probably the first to describe it, in 1868. The description was elaborated by Bant [3] and by Monjé [25]. A summary of backward inhibition, including more modern research, has been given by Raab [28].

Inclined as we are to believe that events in the brain occur in an orderly sequence, we have always been somewhat amazed by a phenomenon in which one stimulus can be completely erased by a second stimulus arriving much later (about 60 msec later). But if we assume that every stimulus starts a process in the brain which lasts perhaps 200 msec, we can make backward inhibition acceptable if we further suppose that this process can be inhibited at any moment during the 200-msec interval by the onset phenomenon of the second stimulus. With a delay greater than 200 msec no inhibition occurs and both stimuli are recognized, separately.

Backward inhibition is illustrated in Figure 47-1. There the interval

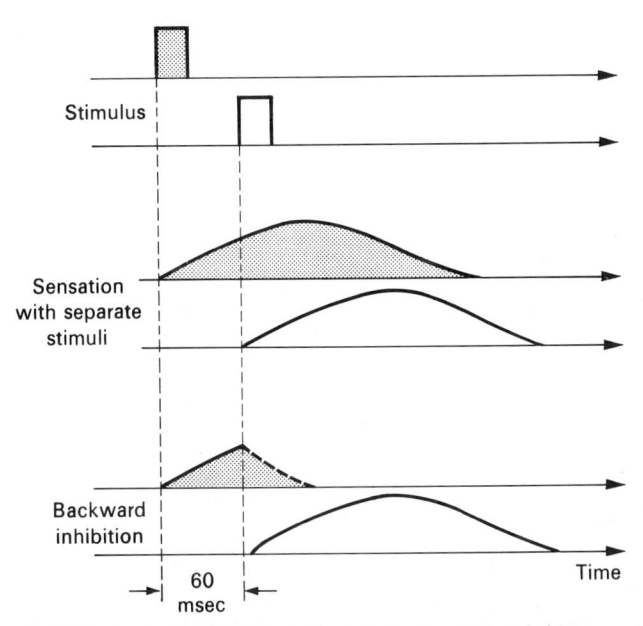

FIGURE 47-1 The principle of backward inhibition. A short stimulus (shaded area in top diagram) produces a neural activity (shaded area in middle diagram) of much longer duration than the stimulus. This neural activity can be stopped by the action of a second stimulus presented much later than the first. The neural activity produced by the first stimulus is thereby reduced in magnitude and duration (shaded area in bottom diagram).

between the times of arrival of the two stimuli is 60 msec; the shaded areas represent brain processes. The bottom graph of the figure illustrates how the onset of the second stimulus shortened the process initiated by the first stimulus and reduced the magnitude of the sensation.

It is well known, from demonstrations of lateral inhibition in Mach bands, that a stimulus can be reduced by a second stimulus in its neighborhood in space [5, 29]. Pertinent experiments show that every stimulus at one point of a sense organ with a large surface area produces an area of sensation which is surrounded by an area of inhibition; thus, a second stimulus applied in this area is inhibited. In the case of Mach bands, no time difference between presentation of the two stimuli is involved. In backward inhibition we have only to assume that the onset phenomenon of the second stimulus can inhibit and block out the neighboring processes already occurring in the nervous tissue. In this way backward inhibition becomes a consequence of the well-observed lateral inhibition, such as is seen in Mach bands. Backward inhibition is only one of the phenomena which indicate the importance of the onset phenomena in sensory perception.

A fourth type of inhibition becomes obvious when we listen to a tone with a constant amplitude. Despite the fact that there is no change in the stimulus, we have the impression that the loudness is periodically interrupted or decreased for short moments. It was Lehmann [23] who pointed out that the pattern of brain processes suggests series of time quanta. The length of the time quantum is between 800 and 1,200 msec. Whenever a phenomenon starts, the brain integrates it to that length of time. After that there is a short pause, and then the integration starts afresh. We know this phenomenon well from listening to telegraph signals. Its application to room acoustics was illustrated in experiments [4] in which it was demonstrated that the apparent length of a decaying reverberant sound can be shortened by this type of blackout. It is a type of inhibition that exerts its influence mainly on stimuli which last about 800 msec.

Another type of inhibition is central inhibition. It can produce a longer-lasting blackout or decrease in the magnitude of a sensation. It is often called shift of attention.

All these different kinds of inhibition play a role in one situation or another. Since they are central processes they seem to be analogous for the various sense organs [6]. This sometimes makes investigation very easy and, to a certain degree, better established, since observations obtained for one sense organ corroborate results obtained for a different sense organ. In the next section I discuss the role of backward inhibition in vision, and I then go on to discuss its application in the field of room acoustics.

## BACKWARD INHIBITION IN VISION

In recent decades there has been increased interest in backward inhibition in vision [1, 2, 8, 11, 22, 37]. There are many ways of showing that backward inhibition is a powerful phenomenon and that it can lead to complete cancellation of the stimulus presented first. A method of showing the magnitude of the inhibition is given in Figure 47-2, for binocular vision. Two black frames with diagonal shading are placed before the observer's eyes, one before each eye. The two frames are of exactly the same size, but, as Figure 47-2a shows, the direction of the shading is different. When looking at these two frames in a binocular stereoscope the observer experiences a rivalry between the two fields; he may see the stripes going from left to right, or he may see the reverse pattern.

In our experiment a large black disk with a slit about 3 mm wide is rotated before the observer's eyes as he views the square frames. According to the direction of rotation of the disk, the left eye or the right eye receives the picture first. The speed of rotation of the disk determines the time difference between the two presentations. With a time difference of about 60 msec between the presentations, the two black frames fuse per-

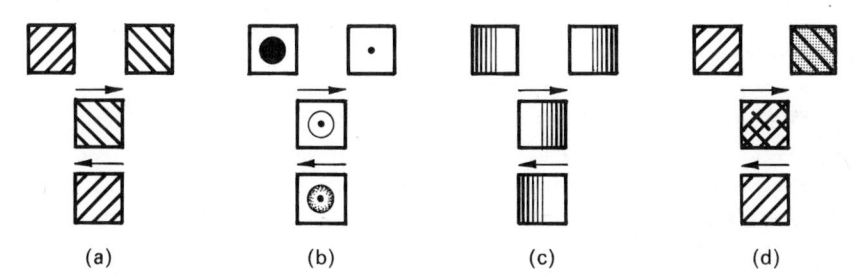

FIGURE 47-2 The principle of backward inhibition in vision. (a) If the two top frames are presented to the two eyes simultaneously, they are fused and produce one or the other of the sensations shown in the middle and bottom frame. It is possible to switch the observer's sensation from one diagonal pattern to the other by introducing an interval of about 60 msec between presentation of the two frames. This is accomplished by placing a disk with a 3-mm slit between the observer's eyes and the frames, rotating the disk, and changing the direction of rotation. (b) Similar phenomena can be obtained with a large dot and a small dot (see text), and also (c) when no edges are involved but only a slowly increasing brightness pattern (see text). As (a), (b), and (c) indicate, in vision the second stimulus can completely inhibit the first. (d) This is the case even if the strength of the second stimulus is reduced by a density filter of 2.0. It is not the case with a density filter of 2.3.

fectly, and the observer sees, inside the fused frames, the stripes going in the direction of those in the square presented last. The eye which saw the stripes first seems to be completely eliminated. By reversing the direction of rotation (Figure 47-2a) the experimenter can reverse the direction of the stripes. If the fusion of the frame is well adjusted in the stereoscopic viewer, the effect is quite surprising and easy to repeat. In our experiment the square was 2 cm on a side and was viewed from a distance of 30 cm. Observers who are trained to fuse images of the two eyes do not need a stereoscopic viewer for this experiment; isolating the field of view of each eye by placing a black paper between the two eyes is sufficient. The rotating disk was 10 cm before the eyes. The stripes were drawn in black on translucent plastic and homogeneously illuminated from the back.

The backward inhibition represented in Figure 47-2b is well known and demonstrates especially well the way in which contours influence each other. If, first, in place of the stripes in the frame a large black dot is presented to one eye and later a small black dot surrounded by a white surface is presented to that eye, the white surface around the small black dot can produce a white ring surrounded by a gray ring as a remaining image of the large black dot. This indicates that the white surface around the small black dot that was presented later is able to dominate, to a certain degree, the brightness pattern. The inhibition around the edge of a small dot has often been described as an edge effect. But, as is shown in Figure 47-2c, if in the two frames the luminance fades out in opposite directions from the center, we still do not see, when there is a delay between presentations to the two eyes, a homogeneous gray surface inside the frame, as a result of stereoscopic fusion. Maximum brightness is seen on the same side as the maximum luminance in the image presented second.

We can go even farther, placing a milky plastic, or half of a Ping-Pong ball, before each eye and flashing a different color before each eye. In this case we have a homogeneous illumination of the whole retina, and no edges are seen. Even in this case with binocular vision there was no fusion of red and green to a gray; rather, the color last presented appeared just as bright as if it alone had been presented.

If we use the pattern shown in Figure 47-2a, but cover the right-hand frame with a gray density filter of 2.0, which reduces the luminance ten times, we can still see the stripes when the slit is rotated from left to right. This indicates that even when the luminance of the second stimulus is reduced by a factor of 10, the second stimulus can still inhibit the effect of the stimulus presented 60 msec earlier. However, with a density filter of 2.3, for most observers the backward inhibition is partial, as is shown in Figure 47-2d for left-to-right movement of the slit. Most stripes are seen as intermingled, and only for a movement from right to left is the pattern of the darker frame completely inhibited. This was to have been expected. The strength of the density filter with which intermingling occurs depends on many variables—on the luminance of the white stripes inside the frame, on the luminance of the surrounding area, on the time difference between the two exposures, and also on some individual differences. In the case of our experiments the luminance of the white stripes and of the surrounding area was 5.4 mL, and the eye was light-adapted to this luminance.

The question arose, Does backward inhibition on one section of the retina involve the whole retina or only the particular portions of it? To test this we duplicated the two frames of Figure 47-2a so that there were, in all, four frames. We placed the two with stripes tilted in the same direction in front of the upper half of the retina and the two with oppositely tilted stripes in front of the lower half of the retina. By using two rotating disks with slits and rotating them in opposite directions, we obtain in the upper and lower half of the eye an opposite inhibition. It is always the stimulus that is presented second that dominates.

Many experiments were performed to determine what time difference would result in an optimum backward inhibition. Under the conditions described, it was found that 60 msec $\pm$ 30% was the value that most observers considered to be optimum. In general, if the delay is longer than 120 msec, two separate sensations are produced, which can be distinguished. For shorter delays there is a combination of the two patterns.

Due to the simplicity of the equipment, the experiments mentioned were performed stereoscopically, with both eyes, but when a tachistoscope was used and both stimuli were presented to one eye only, the same phenomena were obtained.

## BACKWARD INHIBITION IN HEARING

Backward inhibition in hearing is well known and easy to demonstrate for bursts of tone or noise if they are presented to both ears by earphones. In such experiments, instead of using disks with slits, we used rotating disks to each of which two contacts had been fixed to present tone bursts to the two ears, with a delay between the bursts. Reversal of the direction of rotation of the disk easily demonstrates backward inhibition similar to that found for vision. (For literature on this subject see [9, 13, 24, 26, 27, 31, 32, 33].) In the 1960s, Samoilova [31, 32, 33] was the main investigator of backward inhibition; recently Elliott [9] has made more expansive studies in this field. Backward inhibition in hearing can be achieved monaurally or binaurally, and the results are about the same in the two cases. The magnitude of the inhibition depends to a very large extent on the length of the delay, the loudness of the stimuli, the difference in the loudnesses of the two stimuli, and the frequency range involved. Generally speaking, it is found that a time difference of 60 msec is effective in hearing as well as in vision.

Inhibitory phenomena observed by means of earphones differ in many ways from the inhibitions occurring in room acoustics. In room acoustics we have a three-dimensional sound field and we always have forward inhibition of the 1-msec type, producing localization of the sound source, combined with backward inhibition of the 60-msec type. Only in very rare cases do we have pure backward inhibition rather than a combination of forward and backward inhibitions.

Therefore, to simulate room acoustics we have to use loudspeakers. As is shown in Figure 47-3, we used one loudspeaker (no. 1) to simulate the original sound source in the concert hall and a circle of loudspeakers (nos. 2) to simulate the reflections from the walls. All the loudspeakers in the circle had exactly the same phase, and the delay relative to loudspeaker no. 1 was the same for all of them. In further research, obviously, the small delays between the arrival times of sounds from the various loudspeakers in the circle and any small changes that may occur in their sound output must be investigated. In our experiments the circle had a radius of 60 cm and was formed by twelve loudspeakers of sequential serial numbers. The loudspeakers were mounted with wires on a ring, so there were only small reflections from the mounting. Bursts of tone and noise of 35-msec duration were used, and the time difference between the arrival of sound from loudspeaker no. 1 and from the loudspeakers in the ring was 60 msec.

The observer, who stood 2.5 m outside and in front of the circle, was first asked to describe the local sound density of loudspeaker no. 1 and to make a drawing of the way the sound faded at the sides. To make such a drawing of the local sound density, a certain amount of training is needed. One can readily realize that a click has a very small area of ex-

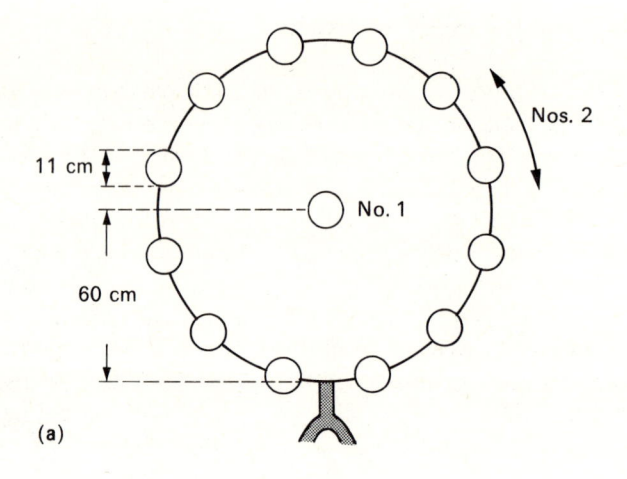

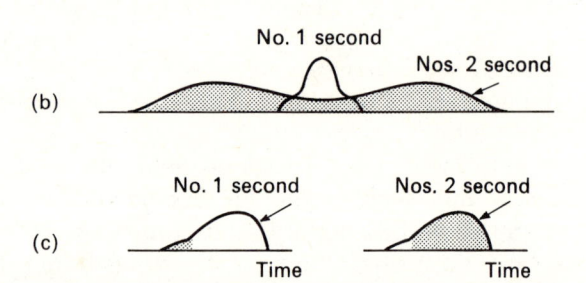

FIGURE 47-3 (a) A central loudspeaker (no. 1) and a ring of loudspeakers (nos. 2) are used in combination, with an interval of 60 msec between arrival of the sound of speakers 2 and 1, or vice versa. (b) If the central speaker is presented second, this inhibits to a very large degree the sound of the speakers in the ring, and the extension of the sound image around the central speaker is reduced. If the speakers in the ring are presented second, they almost completely inhibit the sound of the central speaker and we have an apparent extension of a sound image, represented by the shaded area in (b). (c) Diagram showing that the stimulus presented second accounts for a longer time interval in the perception than the stimulus presented first does.

tension and a very high local loudness density. Thus, in a drawing in which the loudness density is represented by heights on the ordinate, we have a curve that is narrow and high. A 1,000-H tone burst, on the other hand, will have a much greater extension than a click, and, for the same overall loudness, a much lower loudness density. Low-frequency sounds in general have a much greater extension and lower density than noise bursts. In studies of vision, observers can be trained well for this type of experiment. We can illuminate a grayish surface with a flashlight and ask the observer to describe, with a sketch, the way the brightness fades at the edges of the illuminated spot. Later we compare the observer's brightness drawings with the actual luminance measurements for different areas of the screen. By changing the absolute value of the luminance and the extension of the illuminated spot, it is easy to train an observer to make reproducible observations.

Figure 47-3b shows schematically how the local loudness density is distributed if the sound from speaker no. 1 is presented 60 msec after the equally loud sound from speakers in the ring. For this situation the extension of the sound source seems to be quite small and the sound seems to come mainly from speaker no. 1 (unshaded area). But if we present the sound from the speakers in the ring second, the sound image has a large extension (Figure 47-3b, shaded area). In this case the effect of lateral inhibition is so strong that (Figure 47-3c, right) the sound from speaker no. 1 is hardly recognized, except in the beginning, when there is a hint that it is present; later the sound from speakers in the ring account for the whole sensation. On the other hand if the sound from speaker no. 1 is presented second, the sound from the speakers in the ring seems to disappear (Figure 47-3c, left).

Since, in room acoustics, the echoes from the walls arrive later than the direct sound, it is to be expected that backward inhibition plays an important role and that it can reduce the loudness of the original sound source, as Figure 47-3c, right, indicates.

The curves of Figures 47-3b and c represent mean values for three observers for a loudness level of 90 db and a pure tone of 1,500-H frequency for the speakers in the ring and of 1,000-H frequency for speaker no. 1. The measurements were made in a room that was lined with absorptive material, to keep reflections from wall and ceiling to a minimum. The loudness-density distribution represented by the ordinate in Figure 47-3b is projected to the plane of the speakers in the ring—the plane in which speaker no. 1 is also located. When asked to sketch the time pattern of Figure 47-3c, the observer was given a certain length (representing duration of the sound) and asked to draw within this length the time dominated by sound from speaker no. 1 and that dominated by sound from the speakers in the ring.

The relative apparent lengths of the sound presented first and the sound presented second (Figure 47-3c) are influenced by many factors. If one of the tones is clipped so as to produce squares waves, adjusted to the earlier loudness, and presented second, a further increase in dominance is obtained. A frequency-dependent absorption by the wall can play an important role in determining the quality of a concert hall.

Varying the time difference between 30 and 120 msec indicated that 60 msec is an effective time interval for backward inhibition. In general, with an interval of 60 msec, the tone presented second shortens the time of the whole sound pattern more than it does when the interval is shorter or longer than 60 msec. A decrease in the apparent length of the inhibited tone burst is always accompanied by a decrease in its loudness.

The loudspeakers were placed as shown in Figure 47-3 to represent the bowl of a concert hall, with a sound source and nearby reflecting walls, represented by the ring of speakers. But in many of our experiments speaker no. 1 was placed outside the ring of speakers. If speaker no. 1 was moved laterally in the horizontal plane, the position of the loudness density curve for speaker no. 1 moved correspondingly.

In the experiment of Figure 47-4 the speakers were placed so as to simulate the diffused reflections from (a) the back wall and (c) the ceiling of a room. The dimensions of the ring of speakers was the same as in the

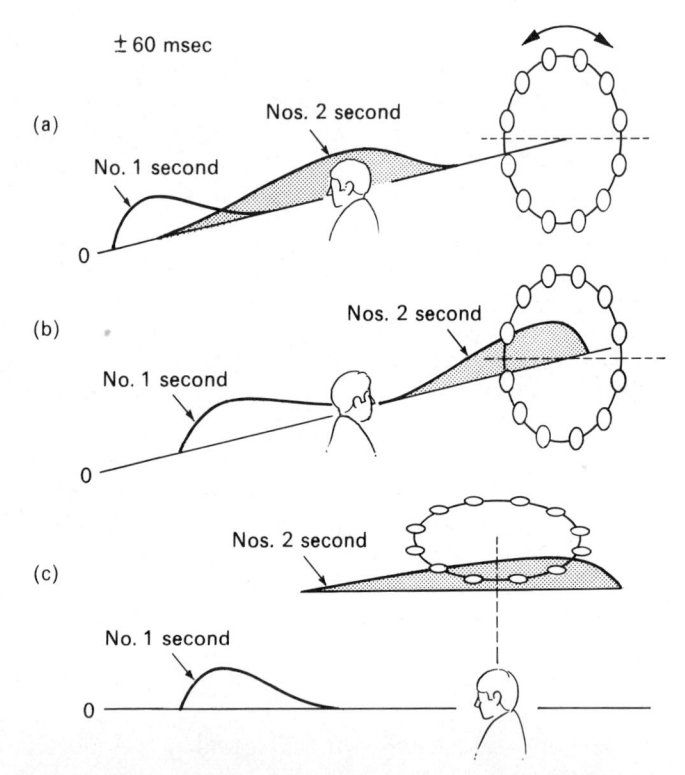

FIGURE 47-4 (a) Loudspeaker no. 1 is in front of the observer and the ring of speakers (nos. 2) is behind him. If speaker no. 1 is presented second, it eliminates the loudness sensation produced by the speakers in the ring. But if the speakers in the ring are presented second, then the loudness area (shaded area) shifts to the vicinity of the observer. (b) The observer faces the ring of speakers; otherwise the experimental conditions are the same as in (a). (c) The ring of speakers is above the head of the observer; otherwise the experimental conditions are the same as in (a).

earlier experiments, but the observer was between the two sound sources, 2.5 m from speaker no. 1 and 2.5 m from the ring of speakers. The local loudness density for different distances is illustrated in Figure 47-4a. When the sound from speaker no. 1 is presented second, the whole sound image is in the neighborhood of that speaker; the effect of the speakers in the ring is practically negligible. But if the sound from the speakers in the ring is presented second (a situation which corresponds to the reflection of sound from the back wall in a concert hall), the sound image is pulled away from the original sound source and comes closer to the observer. This effect seems to be optimal when the delay between the sound from the single speaker and that from the ring speakers is about 60 msec. If we imitate the reflections from the ceiling of the concert hall, again (Figure 47-4c) the sound image is drawn away from the initial sound source (the single speaker) to the ring speakers, whose sounds represent sounds reflected from the ceiling. In all these cases, for the observer the loudness of the sound from the single speaker was the same as the loudness of the sound from the ring speakers when the two sounds were presented separately. Again, the frequencies of the tone for the single speaker and the ring speakers were 1,000 and 1,500 H, respectively. This type of shift in the localization of sound makes the sound image produced by a single singer or violinist in a concert hall much larger than the sound image we observe in a chamber without echoes, or outdoors where there are no reflections from walls.

The time pattern of loudness is, in the cases of Figure 47-4, the same as that shown in Figure 47-3c. When sound from the ring speakers behind the observer reaches him 60 msec later than the sound from the single speaker, the second stimulus reduces the loudness of the first, and shortens its duration as shown in Figure 47-3c. But it must be pointed out that in the three-dimensional situation, where forward inhibition is combined with backward inhibition, in the case of sound the first presentation is not completely suppressed, as it is in vision.

Very similar results were obtained when the frequency of both tones was 1,000 H, but in one case the waves were sinusoidal, and in the other case square waves, so that the tones could be discriminated.

## BACKWARD INHIBITION IN CONCERT HALLS

In a concert hall there are basically three different types of sounds which are transmitted from the performer to the listener: the direct sound, the reflected sound, and the reverberant sound, which is the integration of all the back-and-forth reflections between the walls and ceiling and the audience. The physical part of this sound transmission has recently been very successfully investigated, and the result has been improvement in transmission from the performer to the listener. The progress was mainly achieved by taking onset and offset phenomena into consideration, as Jordan [18, 19] pointed out. For discussion of this latest development in architectural acoustics, see [12, 34, 35, 38].

But now that the physical problem seems to be solved, room acoustics is becoming more and more a psychological problem and, to a certain degree, a problem of inhibition. All five known types of inhibition play a role in judgments of the quality of a concert hall. Apparently backward inhibition is a major factor.

Knowing that a difference of 60 msec between the arrival times of direct sound and the first reflected sound can reduce the direct sound that emanates from the performer, we have determined the difference between these two arrival times for a listener in two different concert halls. Figure 47-5a (p. 494) is a longitudinal section of Symphony Hall in Boston. If S is the sound source and B is an observer, the solid line SB represents the direct sound for that observer. Sixty msec corresponds to a sound-propagation distance of 20 m; the solid ellipse with focal points S and B gives the locus of possible reflecting surfaces from which the first reflection would arrive at B 60 msec later than the direct sound. As may be seen, the actual ceiling (shaded area) might produce many such reflections.

Some observers are of the opinion that acoustics in the upper balcony of Symphony Hall are much better than those on the ground floor. In Figure 47-5a the direct sound to an observer seated in the upper balcony is represented by the dashed line SC, and the locus of surfaces from which the first reflection would arrive at C 60 msec later than the direct sound is given by the dashed ellipse. As may be seen, a listener in the balcony does not receive reflections of 60-msec delay time from the ceiling. The reflections that reach him are those that are delayed a much shorter time. This difference can account for the relatively smaller amount of backward inhibition for an observer in the balcony.

Figure 47-5b shows schematically a bird's-eye view of the ground floor of Symphony Hall. If the listener is at A, and if the sound sources on the stage are at S, he will receive many reflections of 60-msec delay time from the opposite wall. This can explain the observation that a listener sitting at one side of the concert hall sometimes finds it difficult to hear an orchestral instrument which is on the same side of the hall. An amateur cellist far back in the audience on the ground floor, supposing that the sound should be transmitted easily along the side wall, may complain when he does not hear the cello on his side of the hall. At the same time, a listener may hear an instrument in the orchestra very well if he and the performer are near opposite side walls of the concert hall. The dashed ellipse in Figure 47-5b indicates that a listener at B in Boston's Symphony Hall would receive very few reflections of 60-msec delay time.

Similar drawings were made for the Colón Opera House in Buenos Aires. Figure 47-5c is very different from the corresponding diagram for Symphony Hall in Boston. Again, the acoustics seem to be less good for listeners in seats on the main floor than for listeners in the upper balcony —for example, at C, where there seems to be little backward inhibition in the 60-msec delay range for sounds made by a singer on the stage. Since in this auditorium the orchestra is in the pit, the direct sound from the orchestra is small and the singer's voice is dominant—a characteristic for which this opera house is well known. Figure 47-5d—a schematic bird's-eye view of the ground floor—shows the expected difference in the amounts of backward inhibition at locations A and B.

In judging the importance of direct sound relative to reflected sound, we have to take into consideration the fact that, because of its longer path, the reflected sound is, in general, weaker, even under the best reflecting conditions. This difference in the strength of the sound is relatively small for listeners in the back seats, since an increase of 20 m in the pathway is a small percentage of the increase in path length. This is not the case for listeners in seats close to the sound source. In those seats, as Figure 47-5a indicates for a seat at A, the pathway of the reflected sound is 2½ times the length of the pathway of the direct sound. In this case the strength of the sound will be decreased by a factor of about 6. This will naturally decrease the role of backward inhibition.

In the preceding description only backward inhibition for the listener has been considered, but it should not be forgotten that in a good concert hall, one of the second main requirements is that the performer receive from the concert hall an acoustic feedback which enables him to judge the quality of his performance. It is very difficult for a performer to play in a concert hall that has too large a damping effect because, as they say, the hall does not respond. In most concert halls the delay between the production of sound by the performer and its reflection back to him from the walls and the back of the hall is so long that backward inhibition does not play a role. It is different in small rooms.

## OUTLOOK

Since the introduction of a large variety of sound-absorbing materials and the increase in our knowledge of sound pathways and reverberation in concert halls, the physical part of the transmission of sound from the performer to the listener seems to be under control. If the size of concert halls has to be increased further, loudspeakers can be added, and, as the Hall of Congress in Moscow demonstrates, the quality of the sound can be extremely good.

The interesting thing is that seemingly we do not want to have perfect sound transmission. There would be no difficulty today in developing a violin with an electric loudspeaker instead of a wooden sounding board. But for some reason we definitely prefer a Stradivarius to an electric violin. The same thing seems to hold true for concert halls. We expect our concert hall to have a certain personality, just as we expect this of a conductor or a well-known orchestra or a violin. There are many music lovers who have traveled around the world and who remember

**494**      HIGHER PERCEPTUAL PROCESSES

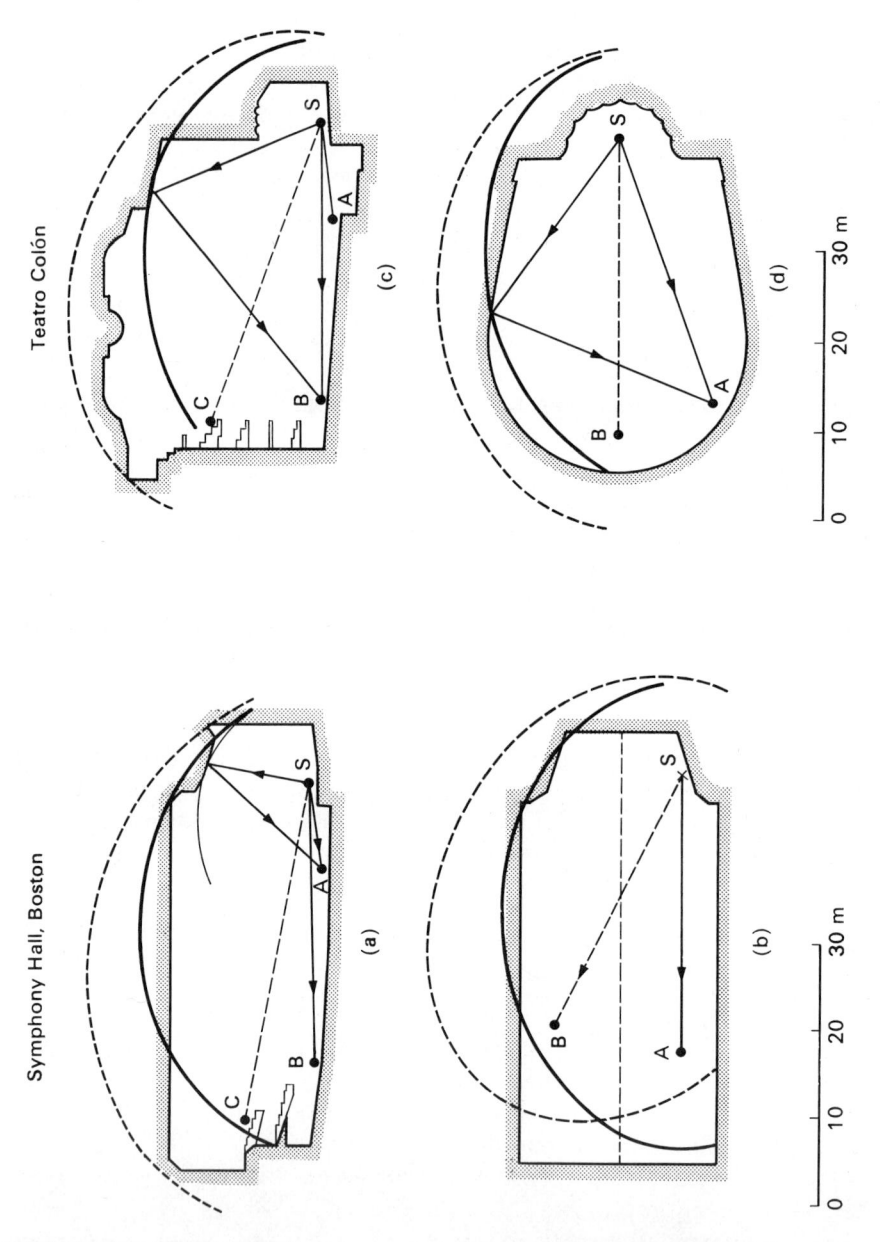

FIGURE 47-5 Longitudinal sections of Symphony Hall, Boston, and of the Colón Opera House, Buenos Aires. (a) B is a listener on the ground floor of Symphony Hall, and S is the sound source. The solid ellipse shows the locus of all the points for which the reflected sound would arrive at B about 60 msec later than the directly transmitted sound (SB). These points seem to coincide with the surface of the ceiling, so backward inhibition is expected in this situation. C is a listener seated in the top balcony. The dashed ellipse (corresponding to the solid ellipse for B) indicates that, for listener C, backward inhibition is of less importance than it is for listener B. (b) Schematic bird's-eye view of Symphony Hall, showing that

well how a performance sounded in a particular concert hall. An opera singer in the Colón is something absolutely different from the same singer in the Vienna Opera House. Nobody seems to want standardization in this field, even when we take into account the fact that by introducing artificial reverberation, we could adjust the reverberation to the needs of the musical piece and even change it during the performance. For an engineer, a hall with such a capability would seem to be an improvement over an auditorium of fixed acoustics. The attitude of concert-goers might change if, through electronics, we could make an ordinary violin sound like a Stradivarius.

Under these circumstances, room acoustics becomes a psychological problem in the area of hearing. We are only in the early stages of this development, and at this time it is even difficult to determine whether a direct sound is more important than the first reflected sound, or what ratio we would like to have for the loudness of these two sounds.

With development of the computer, there are new experimental possibilities, as Schroeder [36] has pointed out, for creating artificial echoes and reverberations. Another improvement can easily be made by describing the concert halls of known good quality in a more precise way, with a more or less standardized vocabulary, which does not now exist in the field of music. To become more definitive, the vocabulary of the musician has to approach that for the physical properties of sound.

The measuring techniques in acoustics are still not appropriate for measuring changes like onset and offset phenomena, just as in vision it is only recently that equipment has been deveolped to measure the contours of a picture. Unfortunately, the nervous system reacts mainly to changes. The study of room acoustics will contribute to the development of physical instruments that will come closer to measuring the phenomena that are important to the nervous system, rather than the phenomena that are easily measured by a physicist. Unfortunately we have no equipment for directly measuring inhibition, especially in situations where inhibition consists of a combination of forward and backward inhibition. The two types seem to oppose each other to a certain degree. We can investigate that opposition by judging the acoustics of a concert hall, not under normal conditions, but with one ear stopped. With monaural hearing the grading of a hall is, in general, different from the grading done

---

the degree of backward inhibition for listeners A and B, both seated on the ground floor, can be quite different, because for A the interval between the arrival of direct sound and of sound reflected from the side walls is 60 msec, and this is not the case for B [7].

The Colón Opera House is well known for its good acoustics, especially for singers. Here again (c) backward inhibition is of less importance for a listener seated in the balcony than for one seated on the ground floor. (d) Backward inhibition is of more importance for a listener near the side wall of the theater than for one in a central position.

under normal conditions, because, with monaural hearing, forward inhibition is decreased. The interaction between forward and backward inhibition is one of the psychological problems of the future in the field of room acoustics.

REFERENCES

1. M. Alpern. Metacontrast. *J. opt. Soc. Amer.*, 1953, *43*, 648–657.
2. E. Averbach and A. S. Coriell. Short-term memory in vision. *Bell Syst. tech. J.*, 1961, *40*, 309–328.
3. N. Bant. *Pflügers Arch. Gesamte Physiol. Menschen Tiere*, 1871, *4*, 325ff.
4. G. von Békésy. *Experiments in hearing.* New York: McGraw-Hill, 1960.
5. G. von Békésy. *Sensory inhibition.* Princeton, N. J.: Princeton University Press, 1967.
6. G. von Békésy. Similarities of inhibition in the different sense organs. *Amer. Psychol.*, 1969, *24*, 707–719.
7. L. L. Beranek. *Music, acoustics, and architecture.* New York: Wiley, 1962.
8. B. H. Crawford. Visual adaptation in relation to brief conditioning stimuli. *Proc. roy. Soc.* (ser. B), 1947, *134*, 283–302.
9. L. L. Elliott. Backward masking: monotic and dichotic conditions. *J. acoust. Soc. Amer.*, 1962, *34*, 1108–1115.
10. S. Exner. Über die zu einer Gesichtswahrnehmung nöthige Zeit. *Sitzungsber. Wien. Akad. Wiss.*, 1868, *58*, 601–632.
11. G. A. Fry. Depression of the activity aroused by a flash of light by applying a second flash immediately afterwards to adjacent areas of the retina. *Amer. J. Physiol.*, 1934, *108*, 701–707.
12. W. Furrer. *Raum- und Bauakustik für Architekten.* Basel: Birkhauser, 1956.
13. I. J. Hirsh. Auditory perception of temporal order. *J. acoust. Soc. Amer.*, 1959, *31*, 759–767.
14. E. M. von Hornbostel. Beobachtungen über ein- und zweiohriges Hören. *Psychol. Forsch.*, 1923, *4*, 64–114.
15. E. M. von Hornbostel. Das raümliche Hören. In *Handbuch der normalen und pathologischen Physiologie.* Vol. 11. Berlin: Springer-Verlag, 1926. Pp. 602–618.
16. E. M. von Hornbostel. Neue Beiträge zur physiologischen Hörtheorie. *Jahresber. phys. exp. Pharmakol.*, 1928, *9*, 753.
17. E. M. von Hornbostel and M. Wertheimer. Über die Wahrnehmung der Schallrichtung. *Sitzungsber. Akad. Wiss. Berlin*, 1920, *15*, 388–396.
18. V. L. Jordan. Einige Bemerkungen über Anhall und Anfangsnachhall in Musikräumen. *Appl. Acoust.*, 1968, *1*, 29–36.
19. V. L. Jordan. Room acoustics and architectural acoustics development in recent years. *Appl. Acoust..* 1969, *2*, 59–81.
20. V. O. Knudsen. *Architectural acoustics.* New York: Wiley, 1932.
21. V. O. Knudsen and C. M. Harris. *Acoustical designing in architecture.* New York: Wiley, 1962.

22. P. A. Kolers. Intensity and contour effects in visual marking. *Vision Res.*, 1962, *2*, 277–294.
23. A. Lehmann. *Die köperlichen Äusserungen psychischer Zustände.* Leipzig: O. R. Reisland, 1905.
24. R. L. Miller. Masking effect of periodically pulsed tones as a function of time and frequency. *J. acoust. Soc. Amer.*, 1947, *19*, 798–807.
25. M. Monjé. Die Empfindungszeitmessung mit der Methode des Löschreizes. *Z. Biol.*, 1928, *87*, 23–40.
26. M. Pickett. Backward masking. *J. acoust. Soc. Amer.*, 1959, *31*, 1613–1615.
27. D. H. Raab. Forward and backward masking between acoustic clicks. *J. acoust. Soc. Amer.*, 1961, *33*, 137–139.
28. D. H. Raab. Backward masking. *Psychol. Bull.*, 1963, *60*, 118–129.
29. F. Ratliff. *Mach bands: Quantitative studies on neural networks in the retina.* San Francisco: Holden-Day, 1965.
30. W. C. Sabine. *Amer. Archit.*, 1913, *104*, 257ff.
31. I. K. Samoilova. Effekt maskirouki sil'nym zuukouym razdrazhitelem predshestvuiushchego slabogo. *Biofizika*, 1956, *1*, 79–87.
32. I. K. Samoilova. Masking of short tone signals as a function of the time interval between masked and masking sounds. *Biophysics*, 1959, *4*, 44–52.
33. I. K. Samoilova. Masking of brief tonal signals which precede the masking sounds. *Probl. fiziol. Akust.*, 1959, *4*, 38–44.
34. M. R. Schroeder. Complementarity of sound buildup and decay. *J. acoust. Soc. Amer.*, 1966, *40*, 549–551.
35. M. R. Schroeder. Architectural acoustics. *Science*, 1966, *151*, 1355–1359.
36. M. R. Schroeder. Digital simulation of sound transmission in reverberant spaces. *J. acoust. Soc. Amer.*, 1970, *47*, 424–431.
37. R. Stigler. Chronophotische Studien über den Umgebungskontrast. *Pflügers Arch. Gesamte Physiol. Menschen Tiere*, 1910, *134*, 365–435.
38. R. Thiele. Richtungsverteilung und Zeitfolge der Schallrückwürfe in Räumen. *Acustica*, 1953, *3*, 291–302.
39. M. Vitruvius. *De architectura.*

48

# DIFFERENCES IN PERCEIVED COLOR AS A FUNCTION OF CHARACTERISTIC COLOR

John L. Delk
Samuel Fillenbaum

The evidence on the problem of memory color is far from clear. Duncker [3] and Bruner, Postman, and Rodrigues [2] have shown that under impoverished or marginal conditions of observation, the apparent color of an object may shift in the direction of its characteristic color. Bolles, Hulicka, and Hanly [1] have suggested, however, that such effects may be obtained only under conditions in which no exact color match can be made and where, therefore, a true "psychophysical equation is impossible." Since the critical figure and the adjustable color mixer were not contiguous but viewed successively in these studies, the effects obtained could have been on remembered color rather than on perceived color.

Harper [5] placed the critical figures, one at a time, directly in front of the color mixer, which served as ground. Using cutouts of red-associated and neutral objects, he found significantly more red needed to match the former than the latter. Fisher, Hull, and Holtz [4] repeated and extended Harper's study, but were only able in part to replicate his results. Whatever differences were found between red-associated and neutral objects tended to be rather small.

## METHOD

The procedure of the present experiment was patterned after those of the latter two, but there were several changes with regard to experimental arrangements and instructions. In the earlier experiments, the stimulus figures were very small, but those of the present experiment were considerably larger (by a factor of 5 to 10). Harper was unable to illuminate his figures evenly, and because of the technique used to mount them, the figures used by Fisher may not have been identical in color. In the present experiment, by contrast, there was even illumination for the figures, which were all of exactly the same color. Furthermore, the in-

Source: From *American Journal of Psychology*, 1965, 78, 290–293.

structions given to the subjects of the present experiment were varied systematically to assess the possible biasing effects of the instructions used in the earlier experiments. Three different instructions were employed: (a) instructions similar to those used previously with red-associated figures called reddish and the other figures called yellowish-orange; (b) instructions verbally identifying or naming each figure, as in (a), but with nothing whatsoever said about color; and (c) instructions without any verbal identification or naming of any of the figures. Finally, while Harper and Fisher used only two classes of figures, red-associated figures and abstract neutral figures, a third class—characteristically nonred figures—was used here.

**Apparatus and Materials**

Ten figures were cut from the same sheet of orange-red cardboard—see Munsell chip R/5/12 for approximate color[1]—in the shapes of a heart, an apple, a pair of lips, an oval, a circle, an ellipse, a horse's head (front view), a bell, a mushroom, and a square. These figures, identical in color, were of approximately the same area, ranging from about 28 to 32 $cm^2$. The first three of these figures (heart, apple, and lips) usually are associated with the color red. The second three (oval, circle, and ellipse) usually are associated with no particular color. The third three (horse, bell, and mushroom) usually are associated with colors other than red. The tenth figure (square) was used only as a practice or demonstrational figure and was not included in the experiment proper.

A differential color mixer which permits the mixing of two colors to produce continuously varying intermediate shades was used. The mixture could be varied from 360° red (Munsell chip R/3/8) and 0° yellow-orange (Munsell chip YR/6/10) to 0° red and 360° yellow-orange. Each of the figures could be mounted directly in front of the center of the color mixer, which thus served as ground for each figure.

The color mixer was placed upon a table in the corner of the experimental room. About 6.5 in. in front of the color mixer was a black screen, 2 × 4 ft, in which there was a 5.5-in. aperture. On the inside of the screen, over the aperture, a sheet of waxed paper was pasted to reduce visual acuity and to obtain a better blend of figure and ground. Both the figure and ground were illuminated by a 9-in. circular fluorescent lamp so attached to the inside of the screen that it formed a circle around the aperture. This lighting arrangement provided even, soft illumination of both figure and ground, and cast no shadows of the figure on the ground. The overhead lights in the room were turned off and the window shade

---

[1] In the Munsell notation, the letter indicates hue, the first number indicates value (saturation), and the second number indicates chroma (intensity or strength) [6]. Two observers independently matched the orange-red cardboard to the same Munsell chip.

drawn, leaving the room quite dimly illuminated. From his seated position, the subject could see only the black screen, the aperture, and, through the aperture, the figure upon a field of orange-red.

## Subjects

The subjects of this experiment were sixty undergraduate men at the University of North Carolina, recruited from a course in introductory psychology.

## Procedure

The subjects were randomly assigned to the three instructional conditions, with twenty serving in each condition. All were told that they would see a number of figures, one at a time, against a background that could be changed from a light red to a dark red, or vice versa. They were to instruct the experimenter to make the background darker or lighter until it was the same color as the figure, that is, until the figure could no longer be distinguished from the background. For subjects in group I (the color-label group), as each figure appeared it was called a yellowish-orange horse, a yellowish-orange oval, and so forth, except for the three red-associated forms which were described as a reddish heart, a reddish apple, and a reddish pair of lips. The subjects in group II (the label-only group) were told the name of each figure as it was presented, but there was no reference to color. The subjects of group III (the self-labeling group) were not instructed either as to the name or the color of any figure, but were asked to tell the experimenter the name of each figure.

Two matches (one ascending trial and one descending trial) were obtained for each figure. For every subject in each condition, the square was presented first as a practice figure. The remaining nine figures then were presented in a randomized order. The random orders of presentation used with group I were used also for the other two groups.

## RESULTS

Table 48-1 presents the mean settings for each figure and each group. Analysis of variance reveals only one significant effect, that of figures, with $F = 56.18$, $df = 8/456$, $p < 0.01$. Although differences in instructions had no appreciable effect on the judgments, there were considerable differences between the figures, with red-associated figures requiring more red in the ground for the match than neutral or nonred-associated figures; there was no interaction between instructions and figures.

Table 48-2 contrasts the various means.[2] It reveals that each of the

---

[2] The analysis was based on procedures outlined in [7, pp. 80–85].

TABLE 48-1  Mean Setting (in Degrees of Red) for Each Figure Under Each Instructional Condition

| Group | Red-associated |||| Neutral |||| Nonred ||||
|---|---|---|---|---|---|---|---|---|---|---|---|---|
| | Heart | Apple | Lips | Combined | Oval | Circle | Ellipse | Combined | Horse | Bell | Mushroom | Combined |
| Color-label | 265 | 284 | 272 | 273 | 241 | 244 | 243 | 243 | 243 | 241 | 228 | 237 |
| Label-only | 263 | 271 | 255 | 263 | 240 | 232 | 238 | 237 | 237 | 226 | 225 | 230 |
| Self-labeling | 269 | 280 | 254 | 268 | 245 | 236 | 248 | 243 | 248 | 231 | 230 | 237 |
| Means | | | | 268 | | | | 241 | | | | 235 |

TABLE 48-2  Tests of Mean-Differences by the Newman-Keuls Procedure

| Figure:<br>Ordered<br>Means: | | Mushroom<br>1<br>227.8 | Bell<br>2<br>232.1 | Circle<br>3<br>237.0 | Oval<br>4<br>242.0 | Ellipse<br>5<br>242.6 | Horse<br>6<br>242.7 | Lips<br>7<br>259.9 | Heart<br>8<br>265.4 | Apple<br>9<br>278.7 |
|---|---|---|---|---|---|---|---|---|---|---|
| Differences<br>between<br>pairs | Mushroom<br>Bell<br>Circle<br>Oval<br>Ellipse<br>Horse<br>Lips<br>Heart | | 4.3 | 9.2*<br>4.9 | 14.2**<br>9.9*<br>5.0 | 14.8**<br>10.5*<br>5.6<br>0.6 | 14.9**<br>10.6*<br>5.7<br>0.7<br>0.1 | 32.1**<br>27.8**<br>22.9**<br>17.9**<br>17.3**<br>17.2** | 37.6**<br>33.3**<br>28.4**<br>23.4**<br>22.8**<br>22.7**<br>5.5 | 50.9**<br>46.6**<br>41.7**<br>36.7**<br>36.1**<br>36.0**<br>18.8**<br>13.3** |
| q critical at 0.05 level:<br>q critical at 0.01 level: | | | 6.27<br>8.29 | 7.53<br>9.41 | 8.27<br>10.08 | 8.78<br>10.55 | 9.18<br>10.91 | 9.50<br>11.22 | 9.77<br>11.47 | 10.04<br>11.67 |

\* Significant at the 0.05 level.
\*\* Significant at the 0.01 level.

three red-associated figures was seen as significantly more red than any of the other six figures, and that the apple was seen as significantly more red than the heart or lips. The mean differences between the red-associated figures and the other figures are not only highly significant statistically but also of substantial magnitude perceptually. This becomes evident if one compares the Munsell chips which approximately match (to the eyes of two independent judges) the mean settings for the three classes of figure. For red-associated figures, the Munsell chip is R/4/12; for the neutral figures, R/5/12; and for the nonred figures, R/5/13. The difference between chip R/4/12 and the other two chips is considerable. The other two chips are also perceptually distinct, although the difference between them is smaller.

Why were the identically colored figures responded to as though they were actually different in color? All figures were cut from the same colored paper; were of approximately the same area (the correlation between setting and area was only −0.05); had relatively smooth contours; and were viewed under the same conditions of illumination, against the same ground. One is led to the conclusion that past association of color and form does in some way influence perceived color, since that is the one respect in which the figures did clearly differ. To interpret the results in terms of memory color does not, of course, explain them, since little can be said at this time as to the mechanism by which an interaction of sensory and associative factors might occur.

## SUMMARY

This experiment had two purposes: (1) to investigate the possible effect of characteristic color upon perceived color; and (2) to assess the possible biasing effects of instructions on color-matching judgments. Although differences in instruction had no effect upon the judgments, there was a highly significant effect attributable to characteristic color. Each of the three red-associated figures was seen as redder than each of the other six figures (three neutral figures and three nonred figures). There was no interaction of characteristic color with instructions.

REFERENCES

1. R. C. Bolles, I. M. Hulicka, and B. Hanly. Color judgments as a function of stimulus conditions and memory color. *Canad. J. Psychol.,* 1959, *13,* 175–185.
2. J. S. Bruner, L. Postman, and J. Rodrigues. Expectation and the perception of color. *Amer. J. Psychol.,* 1951, *64,* 216–227.
3. K. Duncker. The influence of past experience upon perceptual properties. *Amer. J. Psychol.,* 1939, *52,* 255–265.
4. S. C. Fisher, C. Hull, and P. Holtz. Past experience and perception: Memory color. *Amer. J. Psychol.,* 1956, *69,* 546–560.
5. R. S. Harper. The perceptual modification of colored figures. *Amer. J. Psychol.,* 1953, *66,* 86–89.
6. A. H. Munsell. *The atlas of the Munsell color system.* Baltimore: Munsell Color Comp., Inc., 1929.
7. B. J. Winer. *Statistical principles in experimental design.* New York: McGraw-Hill, 1962.

# 49
# REINFORCEMENT AND EXTINCTION AS FACTORS IN SIZE ESTIMATION

William W. Lambert
Richard L. Solomon
Peter D. Watson

In recent experiments on the psychology of perceiving, there has been a noticeable tendency to emphasize determinants which might be classed as motivational in character. The work of Sanford [6, 7] involving the relationship between drive states and autistic perceiving, and the extension of this work by Murphy and his collaborators [3, 5, 8], and by McClelland and Atkinson [4], illustrate this trend. More closely related to the present problem is the work of Bruner, Postman, and their collaborators [1, 2] dealing with the selection and accentuation of perceived objects relative to the value systems of an individual. Two of their experiments in particular illustrate the operation of the conceptualized value dimension. Bruner and Postman [2] found that circles of the same diameter, embossed with (1) a high-valued social symbol, and (2) a low-valued social symbol, were judged to be larger than circles embossed with (3) a neutral symbol. This might indicate that perceptual accentuation is a U-shaped function of a value dimension varying from −1 to +1, with a minimum of accentuation at neutrality. Bruner and Goodman [1] have shown that poor children tend to overestimate the size of coins more than rich children do. These experimenters stated: "The reasonable assumption was made that poor children have a greater subjective need for money than rich ones." [1, p. 39] They further asserted that "the greater the value of the coin, the greater is the deviation of *apparent* size from *actual* size." [1, p. 38]

The multitude of influences correlated with being rich or poor makes it difficult to analyze the specific determinants of size overestimation. It was thought that some light could be shed on this problem by experimentally controlling the life history of children with respect to an initially neutral object. Specifically, we wished to associate a relatively

Source: *Journal of Experimental Psychology*, 1949, 39, 637–641. Copyright by the American Psychological Association. Reprinted by permission.
Note: This research was facilitated by the Laboratory of Social Relations, Harvard University. The authors wish to thank Miss Winifred Lydon, director of the Harvard Veteran's Nursery School, and Major Gertrude Atkinson of the Salvation Army Nursery School, Boston, for their indispensable help and cooperation in carrying out this study.

neutral poker chip[1] with candy reward and later extinguish this association by removal of reward and to measure the effects of such procedures on the estimated size of the poker chip. Our hypothesis was that 'value,' as defined by changes in apparent size, is a function of both reinforcement and extinction procedures.

## SUBJECTS AND PROCEDURE

In the first study, 32 children from the Harvard Nursery School (ages three to five) were divided into 22 experimental subjects and 10 control subjects. In the second study, 22 children of comparable age from a Salvation Army Nursery School provided 15 experimental subjects and 7 control subjects.

The experimental subjects were individually introduced to a token-reward situation where they turned a crank 18 turns in order to receive a white poker chip which, when put into a slot, led to the automatic delivery of a piece of candy. The control subjects were introduced into the same situation, but candy came directly after work, *without* the mediation of a poker chip. In the first study, both groups worked (and were rewarded) once a day for 10 days; in the second study, the subjects worked (and were rewarded) five times a day for 10 days.

Size estimates of the white poker chip token were made by the subjects (1) prior to the experiment; (2) after 10 days of reward; (3) after extinction had occurred (eleventh day); and (4) after reward had been reinstated (twelfth day).

Measurements were taken with the equipment designed and used by Bruner and Goodman [1]. This equipment was composed of a rectangular wooden box (9 × 9 × 18 in.) with a 5-in. square ground-glass screen in the center of the front panel, and a control knob at the lower right-hand corner. At the center of the ground-glass screen the subject was presented with a circular patch of light (16.2 app. ft-c) the diameter of which was under the control of the knob. The light source was a 60-w incandescent light shining through an iris diaphragm which could be varied (in terms of the visible light patch) from ⅓ to 2 in. As Bruner and Goodman reported: "The circle was not truly round, containing the familiar nine-elliptoid sides found in the Bausch and Lomb iris diaphragm. It was so close, however, that subjects had no difficulty making the subjective equations required of them." [1, p. 37]

The subjects stood in front of the apparatus with the light patch at or slightly below eye level, and about 12 to 18 in. away. The token, pasted on a 5-in. square gray cardboard, was held by the experimenters so that

---

[1] Only one of our children knew what a poker chip was. It was called a circle in our experiment.

it was parallel to the circular patch. About 7 in. separated the centers of the two objects to be compared.

The judgment problem was presented to the children of both groups as a game. Each child made his estimates alone. Two judgments starting from the open and two starting from the closed position of the iris were obtained from each child at each measurement session; these judgments were made in an order which was counterbalanced for direction of turning of the control knob. The children were not informed of their success in approximating the actual size of the poker chip.

On the eleventh day—after 10 days of rewarded trials—extinction was instituted. The children of both groups worked, but no candy was forthcoming. They worked until they met the arbitrary criterion of extinction: 3 min during which they did not turn the handle of the work machine. The size estimates were made immediately after the subject had met the extinction criterion.

On the twelfth day the subjects were reintroduced to the reward sequence, and the work brought candy to the control group and token plus candy to the experimental group. Size estimates were made immediately after this twelfth session.

## RESULTS

The results for both nursery schools were combined and they are shown graphically in Figure 49-1. The four size estimation sessions are

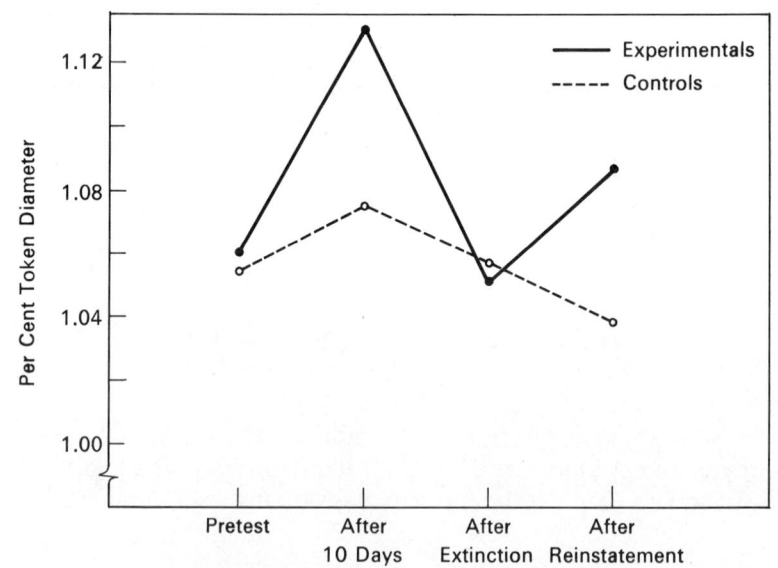

FIGURE 49-1 Effects of the experimental conditions upon children's estimates of the diameter of a token when these estimates are taken as per cents of the true diameter.

distributed on the x axis; the mean estimate of the token size in terms of per cent of actual size is shown on the y axis. The actual size is indicated by the horizontal line parallel to the x axis. The means for the experimental group are connected by the solid lines, and the means for the control group are connected by the dotted lines. The connecting lines are meant to increase legibility; they do not imply a continuous function of any sort.

It would appear that the control group showed no significant changes with experience. The experimental group, however, showed a rise in the apparent size of the token after 10 days of using the token to obtain reward. The estimates dropped to the level of the beginning estimates following the extinction procedure in which the token no longer led to candy reward. The estimates went back in the direction of overestimation when reward was reinstated on the twelfth day.

The mean size estimates in arbitrary units of the comparison-stimulus diameter are given in Table 49-1, together with the corresponding per cent of the actual token diameter, for each of the four points in our experiment. The results for our two studies are combined, since there were no appreciable differences between the ten-reinforcement and the fifty-reinforcement experiments.

Analyses of variance[2] were performed on the data which are summarized in Table 49-1. The following differences are of interest: (1) In the experimental group, the estimated size of the token after 10 days of reinforcement was significantly greater than at the pretest. This difference is reliable at the 0.01 level of confidence. (2) In the experimental group, the size estimates after extinction were significantly smaller than they were after the 10 days of reinforcement. This difference is reliable at the 0.01 level of confidence. (3) In the experimental group the rise in estimated size following reinstatement of reward is significant at the 0.01 level of confidence. (4) In the control group, none of the four mean estimates is significantly different from any other. (5) The mean estimates for the experimental and control groups after 10 days of reinforcement are significantly different from one another with a reliability between the 0.01 and 0.05 levels of confidence. (6) The mean estimates for the experimental and control groups after reinstatement of reward are not significantly different from one another even though a marked trend seems evident.

## DISCUSSION

Several alternative theoretical interpretations for our results could be made. Since experiments are in progress to study further the factors involved, these possibilities will merely be listed at this time. These views

---

[2] These analyses are uncorrected for the correlation between successive sets of estimates. They are thus conservative.

TABLE 49-1  The Alteration of Size Estimation with Experience in the Experimental Situation

|  | Experimental Group |  |  |
|---|---|---|---|
|  | Mean Estimated Size† | $\sigma_m$ | Per Cent Actual Size |
| Pretest | 66.8 | 1.2 | 1.06 |
| After 10 days | 70.9 | 1.1 | 1.13 |
| After extinction | 66.3 | 1.3 | 1.05 |
| After reinstatement | 68.5 | 1.8 | 1.09 |

|  | Control Group |  |  |
|---|---|---|---|
|  | Mean Estimated Size† | $\sigma_m$ | Per Cent Actual Size |
| Pretest | 66.4 | 1.5 | 1.05 |
| After 10 days | 67.7 | 1.2 | 1.07 |
| After extinction | 66.6 | 1.2 | 1.06 |
| After reinstatement | 65.4 | 1.4 | 1.04 |

† Actual size of poker chip is 63.0 in arbitrary units of diameter. The error of measurement of diameter by experimenter is ±0.2 units.

are not mutually exclusive, but overlap, as do so many formulations in this field.

1. The estimation changes in the experimental group may be compatible with a generalized pattern of behavior which we could call the "cookie effect." That is, the effect may be peculiar to our culture where, for example, a bigger cookie is *better* than a little one. Bigness and value, or bigness and goodness, may be acquired equivalencies for our children, particularly at the ages of the subjects used here. Experiments have been planned which may provide evidence on whether this phenomenon is culture-bound or not.

2. These results may provide a measure reflecting some of the secondary reinforcing characteristics taken on by the token during the reinforced trials. These characteristics become lost when reinforcement is not maintained, as during extinction, but are restored when reward is reinstated. This formulation, if further bulwarked with evidence, could serve to integrate perceptual distortion phenomena with learning theory and possibly provide a valuable indirect measure of secondary reinforcement.

3. It is possible that the size enhancement phenomenon can provide us with inferences about perceptual processes as envisioned by Bruner and his collaborators [1, 2]. They hypothesize: "The greater the social value

of an object, the more will it be susceptible to organization by behavioral determinants." [1, p. 36] In its learning aspects, however, overestimation of size may reflect either expectancy or hypothesis formation (and decay) or it may, as stated above, reflect learned needs which operate in the workings of this conceptualized perceptual process. The actual mechanism which produces overestimation following reinforcement is, however, entirely obscure at the present stage of our research.

In view of the fact that relatively neutral poker chips were used in the experiment, our data cannot be legitimately compared with the coin-size data of Bruner and Goodman [1]. In addition, our two nursery school groups do not fulfill the criteria of distinct economic class differences. In no sense can we call one group rich children, and the other group poor children.

It is interesting to note the possibility that effects such as those discussed here depend on a difficult or ambiguous judgment situation. Probably, the more ambiguous the stimulus situation, the more strongly can reinforcement and motivational factors operate in determining size judgments.

4. It is interesting to note that following extinction procedures, the estimates of the experimental group do not increase above the original level, when the chip was neutral. This could mean that the U-shaped function postulated to relate accentuation and value does not apply here. Or it could mean that extinction removes positive value without producing negative value. Perhaps extinction by punishment is necessary for producing negativity and an increase in size estimates at the negative end of the U-shaped function.

## SUMMARY

We have described the results of an experiment which was designed to investigate the effects of reinforcement and extinction on size estimation. It was found that the establishment of a token reward sequence results in relative overestimation of the token size. Extinction of the sequence removes this overestimation tendency to a great extent. The results are thought to have relevance for both learning and perception theory.

## REFERENCES

1. J. S. Bruner and C. C. Goodman. Value and need as organizing factors in perception. *J. abnorm. soc. Psychol.*, 1947, *42*, 33–44.
2. J. S. Bruner and L. Postman. Symbolic value as an organizing factor in perception. *J. soc. Psychol.*, 1948, *27*, 203–208.
3. R. Levine, I. Chein, and G. Murphy. The relation of the intensity of a need

to the amount of perceptual distortion: A preliminary report. *J. Psychol.,* 1942, *13,* 283–293.
4. D. C. McClelland and J. W. Atkinson. The projective expression of needs: I. The effect of different intensities of hunger drive on perception. *J. Psychol.,* 1948, *25,* 205–222.
5. H. Proshansky and G. Murphy. The effects of reward and punishment on perception. *J. Psychol.,* 1942, *13,* 295–305.
6. R. N. Sanford. The effect of abstinence from food upon imaginal processes: A preliminary experiment. *J. Psychol.,* 1936, *2,* 129–136.
7. R. N. Sanford. The effect of abstinence from food upon imaginal processes: A further experiment. *J. Psychol.,* 1937, *3,* 145–159.
8. R. Shafer and G. Murphy. The role of autism in a visual figure-ground relationship. *J. exp. Psychol.,* 1943, *32,* 335–343.

# 50
# OBESITY AND EATING

## Stanley Schachter

Current conceptions of hunger control mechanisms indicate that food deprivation leads to various peripheral physiological changes such as modification of blood constituents, increase in gastric motility, changes in body temperature, and the like. By means of some still debated mechanism, these changes are detected by a hypothalamic feeding center. Presumably some or all facets of this activated machinery lead the organism to search out and consume food. There appears to be no doubt that peripheral physiological changes and activation of the hypothalamic feeding center are inevitable consequences of food deprivation. On the basis of current knowledge, however, one may ask, when this biological machinery is activated, do we necessarily describe ourselves as hungry, and eat? For most of us raised on the notion that hunger is the most primitive of motives, wired into the animal and unmistakable in its cues, the question may seem farfetched, but there is increasing reason to suspect that there are major individual differences in

Source: *Science,* 1968, *161,* 751–756. Copyright 1968 by the American Association for the Advancement of Science.
Note: Much of the research described in this article was supported by Grants G23758 and GS73Z from the National Science Foundation.

the extent to which these physiological changes are associated with the desire to eat.

On the clinical level, the analyst Hilde Bruch [3] has observed that her obese patients literally do not know when they are physiologically hungry. To account for this observation she suggests that during childhood, these patients were not taught to discriminate between hunger and such states as fear, anger, and anxiety. If this is so, these people may be labeling almost any state of arousal "hunger," or alternatively, labeling no internal state "hunger."

If Bruch's speculations are correct, it should be anticipated that the set of physiological symptoms which are considered characteristic of food deprivation are not labeled "hunger" by the obese. In other words the obese literally may not know when they are physiologically hungry. For at least one of the presumed physiological correlates of food deprivation, this does appear to be the case. In an absorbing study, Stunkard [13, 15] has related gastric motility to self-reports of hunger in thirty-seven obese subjects and thirty-seven subjects of normal size. A subject, who had eaten no breakfast, came to the laboratory at 9 a.m.; he swallowed a gastric balloon, and for 4 hr Stunkard continuously recorded gastric motility. Every 15 min the subject was asked if he was hungry. He answered *yes* or *no,* and that is all there was to the study. We have, then, a record of the extent to which a subject's self-report of hunger corresponds to his gastric motility. The results show (a) that obese and normal subjects do not differ significantly in degree of gastric motility, and (b) that when the stomach is not contracting, the reports of obese and normal subjects are quite similar, both groups reporting hunger roughly 38% of the time. When the stomach is contracting, however, the reports of the two groups differ markedly. For normal subjects, self-report of hunger coincides with gastric motility 71% of the time. For the obese, the percentage is only 47.6. Stunkard's work seems to indicate that obese and normal subjects do not refer to the same bodily state when they use the term hunger.

## EFFECTS OF FOOD DEPRIVATION AND FEAR

If this inference is correct, we should anticipate that if we were to directly manipulate gastric motility and the other symptoms that we associate with hunger, we would, for normal subjects, be directly manipulating feelings of hunger and eating behavior. For the obese there would be no correspondence between manipulated internal state and eating behavior. To test these expectations, Goldman, Gordon, and I [11] performed an experiment in which bodily state was manipulated by two means: (a) by the obvious technique of manipulating food deprivation, so that some subjects had empty stomachs and others had full stomachs before eating; (b) by manipulating fear, so that some subjects were badly frightened and others were quite calm immediately before eating. Carlson

[5] has indicated that fear inhibits gastric motility; Cannon [4] also has demonstrated that fear inhibits motility, and has shown that it leads to the liberation, from the liver, of sugar into the blood. Hypoglycemia and gastric contractions are generally considered the chief peripheral physiological correlates of food deprivation.

Our experiment was conducted under the guise of a study of taste. A subject came to the laboratory in midafternoon or evening. He had been called the previous evening and asked not to eat the meal (lunch or dinner) preceding his appointment at the laboratory. The experiment was introduced as a study of "the interdependence of the basic human senses —of the way in which the stimulation of one sense affects another." Specifically, the subject was told that this study would be concerned with "the effects of tactile stimulation on the way things taste."

It was explained that all subjects had been asked not to eat a meal before coming to the laboratory because "in any scientific experiment it is necessary that the subjects be as similar as possible in all relevant ways. As you probably know from your own experience," the experimenter continued, "an important factor in determining how things taste is what you have recently eaten." The introduction over, the experimenter then proceeded as follows.

For the "full stomach" condition he said to the subject, "In order to guarantee that your recent taste experiences are similar to those of other subjects who have taken part in this experiment, we should now like you to eat exactly the same thing they did. Just help yourself to the roast beef sandwiches on the table. Eat as much as you want—till you're full."

For the "empty stomach" condition, the subjects, of course, were not fed.

Next, the subject was seated in front of five bowls of crackers and told, "We want you to taste five different kinds of crackers and tell us how they taste to you." The experimenter then gave the subject a long set of rating scales and said, "We want you to judge each cracker on the dimensions (salty, cheesy, garlicky, and so on) listed on this sheet. Taste as many or as few of the crackers of each type as you want in making your judgments; the important thing is that your ratings be as accurate as possible."

Before permitting the subject to eat, the experimenter continued with the next stage of the experiment—the manipulation of fear.

"As I mentioned," he said, "our primary interest in this experiment is the effect of tactile stimulation on taste. Electric stimulation is the means we use to excite your skin receptors. We use this method in order to carefully control the amount of stimulation you receive."

For the "low fear" condition the subject was told, "For the effects in which we are interested, we need to use only the lowest level of stimulation. At most you will feel a slight tingle. Probably you will feel nothing at all. We are only interested in the effect of very weak stimulation."

For the "high fear" condition the experimenter pointed to a large black console loaded with electrical junk and said, "That machine is the one we will be using. I am afraid that these shocks will be painful. For them to have any effect on your taste sensations, the voltage must be rather high. There will, of course, be no permanent damage. Do you have a heart condition?" A large electrode connected to the console was then attached to each of the subject's ankles, and the experimenter concluded, "The best way for us to test the effect of tactile stimulation is to have you rate the crackers now, before the electric shock, and then rate them again, after the shock, to see what changes in your ratings the shock has made."

The subject then proceeded to taste and rate crackers for 15 min under the impression that this was a taste test; meanwhile we were simply counting the number of crackers he ate.[1] We then had measures of the amounts eaten by subjects who initially had either empty or full stomachs and who were initially either frightened or calm. There were of course, two types of subjects: obese subjects (from 14% to 75% overweight) and normal subjects (from 8% underweight to 9% overweight).

To review expectations: If we were correct in thinking that the obese do not label as hunger the bodily states associated with food deprivation, then our several experimental manipulations should have had no effects on the amount eaten by obese subjects; on the other hand, the eating behavior of normal subjects should have directly paralleled the effects of the manipulations on bodily state.

It will be a surprise to no one to learn, from Figure 50-1, that the normal subjects ate considerably fewer crackers when their stomachs were full than when their stomachs were empty. The results for obese subjects stand in fascinating contrast. They ate as much—in fact, slightly more—when their stomachs were full as when they were empty (interaction $p < 0.05$). Obviously the actual state of the stomach has nothing to do with the eating behavior of the obese.

In Figure 50-2, pertaining to the effect of fear, we note an analogous picture. Fear markedly decreased the number of crackers the normal subjects ate but had no effect on the number eaten by the obese (interaction $p < 0.01$). Again, there was a small, though nonsignificant, reversal: The fearful obese ate slightly more than the calm obese.

It seems clear that the set of bodily symptoms the subject labels "hunger" differs for obese and normal subjects. Whether one measures gastric motility, as Stunkard did, or manipulates it, as I assume my co-workers and I have done, one finds, for normal subjects, a high degree of correspondence between the state of the gut and eating behavior and,

---

[1] It is a common belief among researchers in the field of obesity that the sensitivity of their fat subjects makes it impossible to study their eating behavior experimentally—hence this roundabout way of measuring eating; the subjects in this study are taking a "taste test," not "eating."

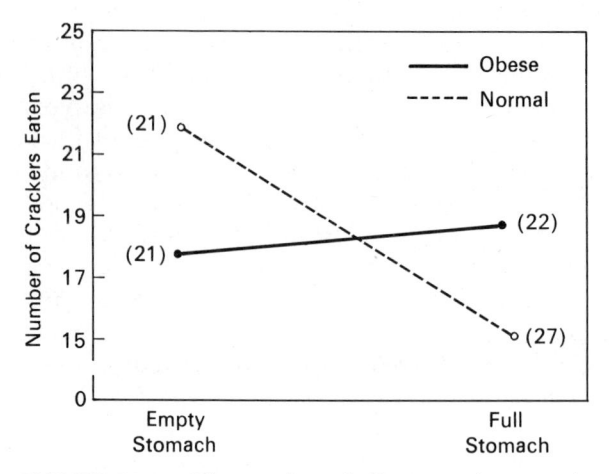

FIGURE 50-1 Effects of preliminary eating on the amounts eaten during the experiment by normal and obese subjects. Numbers in parentheses are numbers of subjects.

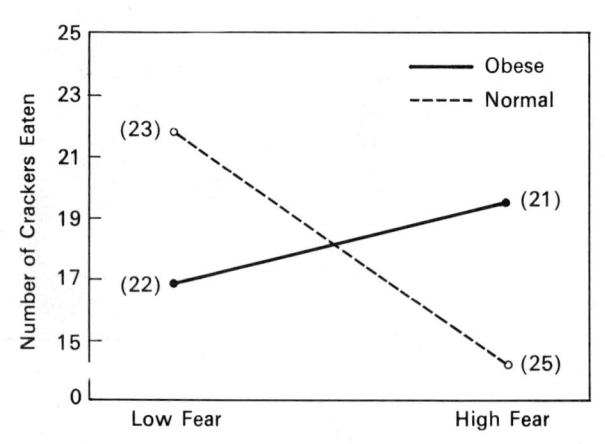

FIGURE 50-2 Effects of fear on the amounts eaten by normal and obese subjects. Numbers in parentheses are numbers of subjects.

for obese subjects, virtually no correspondence. While all of our manipulations have had a major effect on the amounts eaten by normal subjects, nothing that we have done has had a substantial effect on the amounts eaten by obese subjects.

## EFFECTS OF THE CIRCUMSTANCES OF EATING

With these facts in mind, let us turn to the work of Hashim and Van Itallie [8] of the Nutrition Clinic, St. Luke's Hospital, New York City. Their findings may be summarized as follows: Virtually everything these workers do seems to have a major effect on the eating behavior of the obese and almost no effect on the eating behavior of the normal subject.

These researchers have prepared a bland liquid diet similar to commercial preparations such as vanilla-flavored Nutrament or Metrecal. The subjects are restricted to this monotonous diet for periods ranging from a week to several months. They can eat as much or as little of it as they want. Some of the subjects get a pitcher full and pour themselves a meal any time they wish. Other subjects are fed by a machine which delivers a mouthful every time the subject presses a button. With either feeding technique, the eating situation has the following characteristics: (a) The food itself is unappealing. (b) Eating is entirely self-determined; whether or not the subject eats, how much he eats, and when he eats are matters decided by him and no one else. Absolutely no pressure is brought to bear to limit his consumption. (c) The eating situation is devoid of any social or domestic trappings. It is basic eating; it will keep the subject alive, but it's not much fun.

To date, six grossly obese and five normal individuals have been

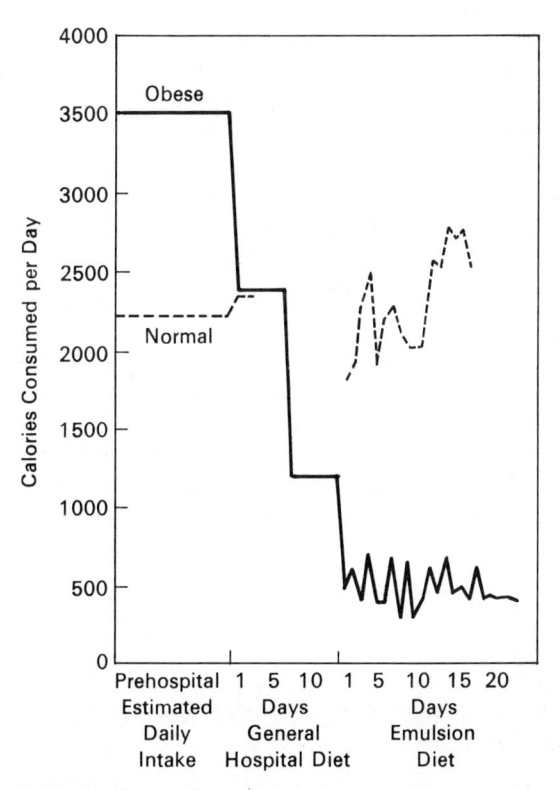

FIGURE 50-3 The effects of an emulsion diet on the amounts eaten by an obese and a normal subject.

subjects in these studies. In Figure 50-3 the eating curves for a typical pair of subjects over a 21-day period are plotted. Both subjects were healthy people who lived in the hospital during the entire study. The obese subject was a 52-year-old woman, 5 ft 3 in. (1.6 m) tall, who weighed 307 lb (138 kg) on admission. The normal subject was a 30-year-old male, 5 ft 7 in. tall, who weighed 132 lb.

The subject's estimated daily caloric intake before entering the hospital (as determined from a detailed interview) is plotted at the left in Figure 50-3. Each subject, while in the hospital but before entering upon the experimental regime, was fed a general hospital diet. The obese subject was placed on a 2,400-calorie diet for 7 days and a 1,200-calorie diet for the next 8 days. As may be seen in Figure 50-3, she ate everything on her tray throughout this 15-day period. The normal subject was placed on a 2,400-calorie diet for 2 days, and he too ate everything.

With the beginning of the experiment proper, the difference in the eating behavior of the two subjects was dramatic and startling. The food consumption of the obese subject dropped precipitately the moment she entered upon the experimental regime, and it remained at an incredibly low level for the duration of the experiment. This effect is so dramatic that the weight of one obese subject who took part in the experiment for 8 months dropped from 410 to 190 pounds. On the other hand, the food consumption of the normal subject of Figure 50-3 dropped slightly on the first 2 days, then returned to a fairly steady 2,300 g or so of food a day. The curves for these two subjects are typical. Each of the six obese subjects has manifested this marked and persistent decrease in food consumption during the experiment; each of the normal subjects has steadily consumed about his normal amount of food.

Before suggesting possible interpretations, I should note certain marked differences between these two groups of subjects. Most important, the obese subjects had come to the clinic for help in solving their weight problem and were, of course, motivated to lose weight. The normal subjects were simply volunteers. Doubtless this difference could account for the observed difference in eating behavior during the experiment, and until obese volunteers, unconcerned with their weight, are used as subjects in similar studies, we cannot be sure of the interpretation of this phenomenon. However, I think we should not, solely on grounds of methodological fastidiousness, dismiss these findings. It was concern with weight that brought these obese subjects to the clinic. Each of them, before entering the hospital and while in the hospital before being put on the experimental diet, was motivated to lose weight. Yet, despite this motivation, none of these subjects had been capable of restricting his diet at home, and each of them, when fed the general hospital diet, had eaten everything on his tray. Only when the food was dull and the act of eating was self-initiated and devoid of any ritual trappings did the obese subject, motivated or not, severely limit his consumption.

## INTERNAL AND EXTERNAL CONTROL

On the one hand, then, our experiments indicate virtually no relationship between internal physiological state and the eating behavior of the obese subject; on the other hand, these case studies seem to indicate a close tie between the eating behavior of the obese and what might be called the circumstances of eating. When the food is dull and the eating situation is uninteresting, the obese subject eats virtually nothing. For the normal subject, the situation is just the reverse: His eating behavior seems directly linked to his physiological state but is relatively unaffected by the external circumstances or the ritual associated with eating.

Given this set of facts it seems clear that eating is triggered by different sets of stimuli in obese and normal subjects. Indeed, there is growing reason to suspect that the eating behavior of the obese is relatively unrelated to any internal state but is, in large part, under external control, being initiated and terminated by stimuli external to the organism. Let me give a few examples. A person whose eating behavior is under external control will stroll by a pastry shop, find the food in the window irresistible, and, even if he has recently eaten, go in and buy something. He will pass by a hamburger stand, smell the broiling meat, and, even though he has just eaten, buy a hamburger. Obviously such external factors—smell, sight, taste, other people's actions—to some extent affect anyone's eating. However, in normal individuals such external factors interact with internal state. They may affect what, where, and how much the normal individual eats, but they do so chiefly when he is in a state of physiological hunger. For the obese, I suggest, internal state is irrelevant and eating is determined largely by external factors.

This hypothesis obviously fits the data presented here, as well it should, since it is an ad hoc construction designed specifically to fit these data. Let us see, then, what independent support there is for the hypothesis, and where the hypothesis leads.

## EFFECTS OF MANIPULATING TIME

Among the multitude of external food-relevant cues, one of the most intriguing is the passage of time. Everyone "knows" that 4 to 6 hr after eating his last meal he should eat his next one. Everyone "knows" that, within narrow limits, there are set times for eating regular meals. We should, then, expect that if we manipulate time we should be able to manipulate the eating behavior of the obese subjects. In order to do this, Gross and I [12] simply gimmicked two clocks so that one ran at half normal speed and the other, at twice normal speed. A subject arrives at 5:00 p.m., ostensibly to take part in an experiment on the relationship of base levels of autonomic reactivity to personality factors. He is ushered into a windowless room containing nothing but electronic equipment and a clock. Electrodes are put on his wrists, his watch is removed "so that it will not get gummed up with electrode jelly," and he is connected to a polygraph. All this takes 5 min, and at 5:05 he is left alone, with nothing to do for a true 30 min, while ostensibly we are getting a record of galvanic skin response and cardiac rate in a subject at rest. There are two experimental conditions. In one, the experimenter returns after a true 30 min and the clock reads 5:20. In the other, the clock reads 6:05, which is normal dinner time for most subjects. In both cases the experimenter is carrying a box of crackers and nibbling a cracker as he comes into the room; he puts the box down, invites the subject to help himself, removes the electrodes from the subject's wrists, and proceeds with personality testing for exactly 5 min. This done, he gives the subject a personality inventory which he is to complete and leaves him alone with the box of crackers for another true 10 min. There are two groups of subjects—normal and obese—and the only datum we collect is the weight of the box of crackers before and after the subject has had a chance at it.

If these ideas on internal and external controls of eating behavior are correct, normal subjects, whose eating behavior is presumably linked to internal state, should be relatively unaffected by the manipulation and should eat roughly the same number of crackers regardless of whether the clock reads 5:20 or 6:05. The obese, on the other hand, whose eating behavior is presumably under external control, should eat very few crackers when the clock reads 5:20 and a great many crackers when it reads 6:05.

The data of Figure 50-4 do indeed indicate that the obese subjects eat almost twice as many crackers when they think the time is 6:05 as they do when they believe it to be 5:20. For normal subjects, the trend

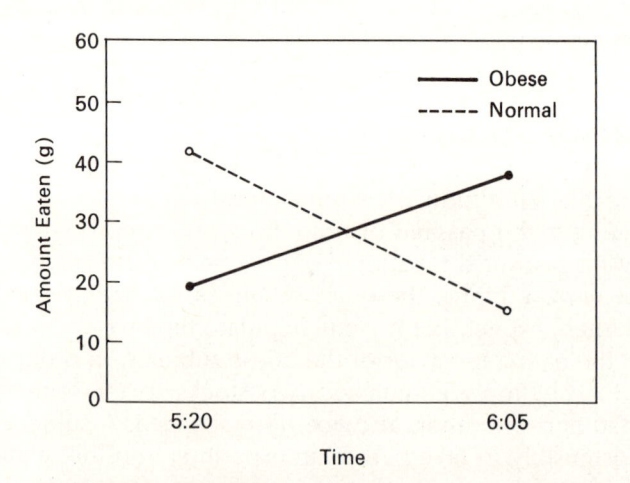

FIGURE 50-4 The effects of manipulation of time on the amounts eaten by obese and normal subjects.

is just the reverse (interaction $p = 0.002$)—an unanticipated finding but one which seems embarrassingly simple to explain, as witness the several normal subjects who thought the time was 6:05 and politely refused the crackers, saying, "No thanks, I don't want to spoil my dinner." Obviously cognitive factors affected the eating behavior of both the normal and the obese subjects, but there was a vast difference. While the manipulation of the clock served to trigger or stimulate eating among the obese, it had the opposite effect on normal subjects, most of whom at this hour were, we presume, physiologically hungry, aware that they would eat dinner very shortly, and unwilling to spoil their dinner by filling up on crackers.

## EFFECTS OF TASTE

In another study, Nisbett [10] examined the effects of taste on eating behavior. Nisbett reasoned that taste, like the sight or smell of food, is essentially an external stimulus to eating. Nisbett, in his experiment, also extended the range of weight deviation by including a group of underweight subjects as well as obese and normal subjects. His purpose in so doing was to examine the hypothesis that the relative potency of external versus internal controls is a dimension directly related to the degree of overweight. If the hypothesis was correct, he reasoned, the taste of food would have the greatest impact on the amounts eaten by obese subjects and the least impact on the amounts eaten by underweight subjects. To test this, Nisbett had his subjects eat as much as they wanted of one of two kinds of vanilla ice cream; one was a delicious and expensive product, the other an acrid concoction of cheap vanilla and quinine which he called vanilla bitters. The effects of taste are presented in Figure 50-5, in which the subjects ratings of how good or bad the ice cream is are plotted against the amount eaten. As may be seen in Figure 50-5, when the ice cream was rated "fairly good" or better, the obese subjects ate considerably more than the normal subjects did; these, in turn, ate more than the underweight subjects did. When the ice cream was rated "not very good" or worse, the ordering tended to reverse: The underweight subjects ate more than either the normal or the obese subjects. This experiment, then, indicates that the external, or at least nonvisceral, cue of taste does have differential effects on the eating behavior of underweight, normal, and obese subjects.

The indications, from Nisbett's experiment, that the degree of dependence on external cues relative to internal cues varies with deviation from normal weight are intriguing, for, if further work supports this hypothesis, we may have the beginnings of a plausible explanation of why the thin are thin and the fat are fat. We know from Carlson's work [5] that gastric contractions cease after a small amount of food has been introduced into the stomach. To the extent that such contractions are directly related to the hunger experience—to the extent that a person's

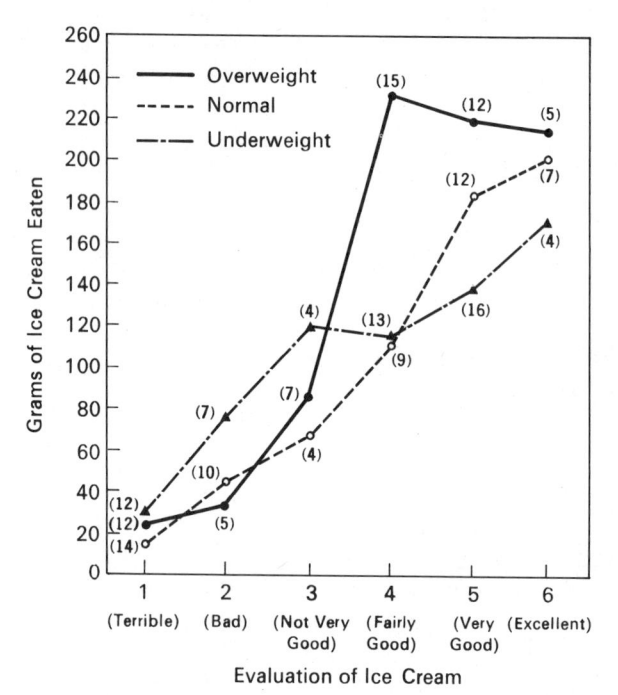

FIGURE 50-5 The effects of food quality on the amounts eaten by obese, normal, and underweight subjects. Numbers in parentheses are numbers of subjects.

eating is under internal control—he should "eat like a bird," eating only enough to stop the contractions. Eating beyond this point should be a function of external cues—the taste, sight, and smell of food. Individuals whose eating is externally controlled, then, should find it hard to stop eating. This hypothesis may account for the notorious "binge" eating of the obese [14] or the monumental meals described in loving detail by students [1] of the great, fat gastronomic magnificoes.

This rough attempt to explain why the obese are obese in itself raises intriguing questions. For example, does the external control of eating behavior inevitably lead to obesity? It is evident, I believe, that not only is such a linkage logically not inevitable but that the condition of external control of eating may in rare but specifiable circumstances lead to emaciation. A person whose eating is externally controlled should eat and grow fat when food-related cues are abundant and when he is fully aware of them. However, when such cues are lacking or when for some reason, such as withdrawal or depression, the individual is unaware of the cues, the person under external control would, one would expect, not eat, and if the condition persisted, would grow "concentration-camp" thin. From study of the clinical literature one does get the impression that there is an odd but distinct relationship between obesity and extreme emaciation. For example, eleven of twenty-one subjects of case studies discussed by Bliss and Branch in *Anorexia Nervosa* [2] were, at some time in their lives, obese. In the case of eight of these eleven subjects, anorexia was preceded and accompanied by either marked withdrawal or intense depression. In contrast, intense attacks of anxiety or nervousness (states which our experiment [11] suggests would inhibit eating in normal individuals) seem to be associated with the development of anorexia among most of the ten subjects who were originally of normal size.

At this point, these speculations are simply idea-spinning—fun, but ephemeral. Let us return to the results of the studies described so far. These can be quickly summarized as follows.

1. Physiological correlates of food deprivation, such as gastric motility, are directly related to eating behavior and to the reported experience of hunger in normal subjects but unrelated in obese subjects [11, 15].
2. External or nonvisceral cues, such as smell, taste, the sight of other people eating, and the passage of time, affect eating behavior to a greater extent in obese subjects than in normal subjects [8, 10, 12].

## OBESITY AND FASTING

Given these basic facts, their implications have ramifications in almost any area pertaining to food and eating, and some of our studies have been concerned with the implications of these experimental results for eating behavior in a variety of nonlaboratory settings. Thus, Goldman, Jaffa, and I [7] have studied fasting on Yom Kippur, the Jewish Day of Atonement, on which the orthodox Jew is supposed to go without food for 24 hr. Reasoning that, on this occasion, food-relevant external cues are particularly scarce, one would expect obese Jews to be more likely to fast than normal Jews. In a study of 296 religious Jewish college students (defined as Jewish college students who had been to a synagogue at least once during the preceding year on occasions other than a wedding or a bar mitzvah), this proves to be the case, for 83.3% of obese Jews fasted, as compared with 68.8% of normal Jews ($p < 0.05$).

Further, this external-internal control schema leads to the prediction that fat, fasting Jews who spend a great deal of time in the synagogue on Yom Kippur will suffer less from fasting than fat, fasting Jews who spend little time in the synagogue. There should be no such relationship for normal fasting Jews. Obviously, there will be far fewer food-related cues in the synagogue than on the street or at home. Therefore, for obese Jews, the likelihood that the impulse to eat will be triggered is greater outside of the synagogue than within it. For normal Jews, this distinction is of less importance. In or out of the synagogue, stomach pangs are stomach pangs. Again, the data support the expectation. When the number of hours in the synagogue is correlated with self-ratings of the unpleasantness of fasting, for obese subjects the correlation is $-0.50$, whereas for normal subjects the correlation is only $-0.18$. In a test of the difference between correlations, $p = 0.03$. Obviously, for the obese, the more time the individual spends in the synagogue, the less of an ordeal fasting is. For normals, the number of hours in the synagogue has little to do with the difficulty of the fast.

## OBESITY AND CHOICE OF EATING PLACE

In another study [7] we examined the relationship of obesity to choice of eating places. From Nisbett's findings on taste, it seemed a plausible guess that the obese would be more drawn to good restaurants and more repelled by bad ones than normal subjects would be. At Columbia, students have the option of eating in the university dining halls or in any of the many restaurants that surround the campus. At Columbia, as probably at every similar institution in the United States, students have a low opinion of the institution's food. If a freshman elects to eat in a dormitory dining hall, he may, if he chooses, join a prepayment food plan at the beginning of the school year. Any time after November 1 he may, by paying a penalty of $15, cancel his food contract. If we accept prevailing campus opinion of the institution's food as being at all realistically based, we should anticipate that those for whom taste or food quality is most important will be the most likely to let their food contracts expire. Obese freshmen, then, should be more likely to drop out of the food plan than normal freshmen. Again, the data support the expectation: 86.5% of fat freshmen cancel their contracts as compared with 67.1% of normal freshmen ($p < 0.05$). Obesity does to some extent serve as a basis for predicting who will choose to eat institutional food.

## OBESITY AND ADJUSTMENT TO NEW EATING SCHEDULES

In the final study in this series [7] we examined the relationship of obesity to the difficulty of adjusting to new eating schedules imposed by time-zone changes. This study involved an analysis of data collected by the medical department of Air France in a study of physiological effects of time-zone changes on 236 flight personnel assigned to the Paris–New York and Paris–Montreal flights. Most of these flights leave Paris around noon, French time; fly for approximately 8 hr; and land in North America sometime between 2:00 and 3:00 P.M. Eastern time. Flight-crew members eat lunch shortly after takeoff and, being occupied with landing preparations, are not served another meal during the flight. They land some 7 hr after their last meal, at a time that is later than the local lunch hour and earlier than the local dinner time.

Though this study was not directly concerned with eating behavior, the interviewers systematically noted all individuals who volunteered the information that they "suffered from the discordance between their physiological state and meal time in America" [9]. One would anticipate that the fatter individuals, being sensitive to external cues (local meal hours) rather than internal ones, would adapt most readily to local eating schedules and be least likely to complain of the discrepancy between American meal times and physiological state.

Given the physical requirements involved in the selection of aircrews, there are, of course, relatively few really obese people in this sample. However, the results of Nisbett's experiment [10] indicate that the degree of reliance on external relative to internal cues may well be a dimension which varies with the degree of deviation from normal weight. It seems reasonable, then, to anticipate that even within a restricted sample, there will be differences in response between the heavier and the lighter members of the sample. This is the case. In comparing the 101 flight personnel who are overweight (0.1 to 29% overweight) with the 135 who are not overweight (0 to 25% underweight), we find that 11.9% of the overweight complain as compared with 25.3% of the nonoverweight ($p < 0.01$). It does appear that the fatter were less troubled by the effects of time changes on eating than the thinner flyers.[2]

These persistent findings that the obese are relatively insensitive to variations in the physiological correlates of food deprivation but highly sensitive to environmental, food-related cues is, perhaps, one key to understanding the notorious long-run ineffectiveness of virtually all attempts to treat obesity [16]. The use of anorexigenic drugs such as amphetamine or of bulk-producing, nonnutritive substances such as methyl cellulose is based on the premise that such agents dampen the intensity of the physiological symptoms of food deprivation. Probably they do, but these symptoms appear to have little to do with whether or not a fat person eats. Restricted, low-calorie diets should be effective just so long as the obese dieter is able to blind himself to food-relevant cues or so long as he exists in a world barren of such cues. In the Hashim and Van Itallie study [8], the subjects did, in fact, live in such a world. Restricted to a Metrecal-like diet and to a small hospital ward, all the obese subjects lost impressive amounts of weight. However, on their return to normal living, to a man they returned to their original weights.

---

[2] Obviously, I do not mean to imply that the *only* explanation of the results of these three nonlaboratory studies lies in this formulation of the external-internal control of eating behavior. These studies were deliberately designed to test implications of this general schema in field settings. As with any field research, alternative explanations of the findings are legion, and, within the context of any specific study, impossible to rule out. Alternative formulations of this entire series of studies are considered in the original papers [7, 10, 11, 12].

## REFERENCES

1. L. Beebe. *The big spenders.* New York: Doubleday, 1966.
2. E. L. Bliss and C. H. Branch. *Anorexia nervosa.* New York: Hoeber, 1960.
3. H. Bruch. Transformation of oral impulses in eating disorders: A conceptual approach. *Psychiat. Quart.,* 1961, *35,* 458–481.
4. W. B. Cannon. *Bodily changes in pain, hunger, fear, and rage.* New York: Appleton, 1915.
5. A. J. Carlson. *Control of hunger in health and disease.* Chicago: University of Chicago Press, 1916.
6. A. R. Feinstein. The treatment of obesity: An analysis of methods, results, and factors which influence success. *J. chron. Diseases,* 1960, *11,* 349–393.
7. R. Goldman, M. Jaffa, and S. Schacter. Yom Kippur, Air France, dormitory food, and the eating behavior of obese and normal persons. *J. Pers. soc. Psychol.,* 1968, *10,* 117–123.
8. S. A. Hashim and T. B. Van Itallie. Studies in normal and obese subjects with a monitored food dispensing device. *Ann. N.Y. Acad. Sci.,* 1965, *131,* 654–661.
9. J. Lavernhe and E. Lafontaine (Air France), personal communication.
10. R. E. Nisbett. Taste, deprivation, and weight determinants of eating behavior. *J. Pers. soc. Psychol.,* 1968, *10,* 107–116.
11. S. Schacter, R. Goldman, and A. Gordon. Effects of fear, food deprivation, and obesity on eating. *J. Pers. soc. Psychol.,* 1968, *10,* 91–97.
12. S. Schacter and L. Gross. Manipulated time and eating behavior. *J. Pers. soc. Psychol.,* 1968, 98–106.
13. A. Stunkard. Obesity and the denial of hunger. *Psychosomat. Med.,* 1959, *21,* 281–289.
14. A. Stunkard. Hunger and satiety. *Amer. J. Psychiat.,* 1961, *118,* 212–217.
15. A. Stunkard and C. Koch. The interpretation of gastric motility: I. Apparent bias in the reports of hunger by obese persons. *Arch. genet. Psychiat.,* 1964, *11,* 74–82.
16. A. Stunkard and M. McLaren-Hume. The results of treatment for obesity. *Arch. intern. Med.,* 1959, *103,* 79–85.

# 51
# A CROSS-CULTURAL STUDY OF PERCEPTUAL PREDOMINANCE IN BINOCULAR RIVALRY

## James W. Bagby

Only recently has research on binocular rivalry and fusion begun to explore the influence that objects which possess particular significance or meaning for an observer have upon him. Most former work had used abstract figures, circles, squares, colored patches, discrepant lines and the like. Consequently the principles of binocular fusion were elaborated on the basis of studies employing such abstract forms. A recent series of investigations by Engel [3], which employed photographs of people and objects, has demonstrated that there are important empirical and theoretical consequences when meaningful content is introduced in fusion and rivalry experimentation. This work strongly suggests that meaning for the perceiver is influential in the binocular resolutions achieved.

Binocular presentation of materials of disparate content and of varying subjective significance thus appears to be a technique of considerable value for psychology [1, 2, 4]. The binocular conflict method offers an approach for ascertaining the role of a variety of factors in the perceptual processes. The nature of the specific resolution of two affectively charged pictures which Engel [3] presented to his subjects, for example, appeared to derive from an unconscious and spontaneous choice on the part of the subject. Although a large number of resolutions were possible, the perceptual choices were shown to reflect the subject's actual feelings and dispositions. There is need, however, for much further work to clarify the phenomena encountered in such situations of binocular conflict.

The present investigation is concerned with discovering whether the cultural characteristics of conflicting visual presentations are differentially perceived by members of different societies. Presented with a situation of simultaneous binocular rivalry, do subjects perceive more readily and consistently visual presentations of content drawn from their own culture than presentations of similar content from another society? The present study investigated this question with respect to Mexicans and Americans.

Source: *Journal of Abnormal and Social Psychology*, 1957, 54, 331–334. Copyright 1957 by the American Psychological Association. Reprinted by permission.
Note: This research was made possible through a Rockefeller Foundation Grant to Princeton University for perceptual research.

## METHOD

### Subjects

There were two experimental groups, one composed of twelve Mexican subjects, and the other composed of twelve American subjects. Half of each experimental group were males and the other half females. They ranged in age from 16 to 42 years. All had 20-20 vision. Each subject in the Mexican group was matched with an American counterpart as to sex, age, education, occupation, and socioeconomic status. Table 51-1 presents some characteristics of the matched subjects.

An examination of Table 51-1 reveals that the Mexicans were largely middle-class residents of interior provincial centers and that they possessed superior educational backgrounds. The Americans were residents from Northeast, Middle Atlantic, and Midwestern states with similar educational and socioeconomic backgrounds. With the exception of one matched pair, no subject had traveled outside his own country. Thus, for both Mexicans and Americans, the knowledge of the opposite culture was limited to books, the mass communication media, secondhand experience, and other similar sources.

### Stimulus Material

Ten pairs of photographic slides were presented. In each pair, one photograph was of a typical Mexican scene including one or more persons, and the other was a photograph of a similar American scene. The picture had been reduced or enlarged to occupy a standard 2 in. × 2 in. area. An attempt was made to attain similarity in the form, contour of major mass, texture, definition, and light and shadow of the paired scenes.

The following were the ten stereogram slide pairs:

1. An American businessman and a Mexican peasant.
2. A blonde American girl and a dark Mexican girl.
3. An old farm woman and an Indian peasant woman.
4. An old farm man and an old Mexican peon.
5. An American miner and a Latin American miner.
6. An American wedding scene of a bride and groom and a traditional Mexican wedding scene.
7. An American farm couple and an Indian couple.
8. A blonde American mother with children and a dark Indian mother with children.
9. A baseball scene and a bullfight scene.
10. A young American boy and a Mexican boy.

TABLE 51-1  Some Characteristics of Mexican and American Subjects

| Subjects[†] | Age | Education[‡] | Occupation | SES[§] | Geographic Residence |
|---|---|---|---|---|---|
| Male | | | | | |
| A | 32 | 17 | Statistician | Middle | Chihuahua |
| A' | 30 | 16 | Accountant | Middle | New York |
| B | 19 | 13 | Student | Middle | Durango |
| B' | 18 | 13 | Student | Middle | Connecticut |
| C | 20 | 15 | English Student | Upper | Coahuila |
| C' | 20 | 15 | English Student | Upper | Wisconsin |
| D | 19 | 13 | Mathematics Student | Middle | Jalisco |
| D' | 18 | 13 | Mathematics Student | Middle | Pennsylvania |
| E | 20 | 14 | Education Student | Middle | Morelia |
| E' | 20 | 14 | Education Student | Middle | New York |
| F | 23 | 12 | Fine Artist | Upper | Mexico City |
| F' | 22 | 13 | Commercial Artist | Upper | Massachusetts |
| Female | | | | | |
| G | 27 | 17 | College Teacher | Upper | Torreon |
| G' | 27 | 16 | High School Teacher | Middle | Kentucky |
| H | 42 | 16 | Language Teacher | Middle | Coahuila |
| H' | 40 | 17 | Language Teacher | Middle | New England |
| I | 33 | 16 | Elementary Teacher | Middle | Chihuahua |
| I' | 32 | 16 | Elementary Teacher | Middle | Illinois |
| J | 16 | 11 | Student | Upper | Guadalajara |
| J' | 17 | 12 | Student | Upper | New Jersey |
| K | 27 | 12 | Artist | Middle | Jalisco |
| K' | 30 | 16 | Art Teacher | Middle | Iowa |
| L | 29 | 16 | Teacher | Middle | Guanajuato |
| L' | 31 | 16 | Teacher | Middle | Colorado |

[†] Subjects matched: A, Mexican—A', American; B, Mexican—B', American, and so on.
[‡] Numeral refers to years of formal education. Thus, 11 is equivalent to junior year in high school, 17 is equivalent to one year beyond college graduation, and so on.
[§] SES refers to socioeconomic status in three groupings: upper, middle, and lower classes.

## Apparatus

The stereogram slide pairs were presented to the subject by means of a prism lens stereoscope enclosed in a light-tight box, like that more fully described by Bagby and Engel [2, 4]. Each side was independently presented with but one photograph of a pair. The slide holder was adjustable to permit the proper setting for a normal binocular fusion of the two stimuli. The intensity of illumination upon either slide could be independently varied, but for the present set of data it was equated.

## Procedure

The subject was informed that he was to view a series of slides in the apparatus and was to tell the experimenter what he saw. He was cautioned to look with both eyes and to keep his forehead pressed against the metal eyepiece. When the preliminary questions regarding procedure were answered to his satisfaction he was placed in viewing position.

The initial presentation was stereoscopic slide 33 of the Titchener series [7]. The subject was asked to adjust the setting so the white circle (in one visual field) was centered as nearly as possible in the black circle (presented to the other field). When this had been achieved a slide from the series of Engel's "male faces" [3] was presented and the subject was asked what he saw. All described a single male face. The subject was then asked if the face appeared in clear focus. Ordinarily there was some minor adjustment to be made in the setting of the apparatus to obtain proper fusion.

At this point the subject was told that the apparatus was adjusted for his own vision and that the experiment per se was to begin. The sequence of Mexican-American stereogram slides was then presented, each being exposed for a 60-sec viewing period. To control for eye dominance, the left-eye-right-eye positions of the Mexican and American scenes were randomized within the series. In terms of the subjects running descriptive report of what he saw, the experimenter recorded the relative predominance of the right or left stimulus object. The basic data, however, derive from the initial view or first 15-sec exposure of the slides.

## RESULTS AND DISCUSSION

A variety of reports was obtained from subjects:

1. In the simplest (and relatively infrequent) case the subject reported seeing but one slide of a pair, and solely described its features. This slide could readily be classified as "predominant" or "preferred" by the subject.
2. In other cases one slide of the pair would be described very thor-

oughly, after which the subject would begin to say he saw "something else," gradually describing the features of the other slide while reporting that each picture "comes and goes." In the case of such rivalry, the preference or predominance of one slide was determined by (a) the picture first reported, and (b) the subject's statements as to which picture seemed to be present most of the time.

3. There were also reports of a single picture which was an "admixture" of the two pictures presented. "Admixture" reports were rare for the initial view; usually they came during total exposure after a transition from marked predominance. It was not difficult to determine the preferred slide since the subject's report of content was definitive.

4. There were also reports of the two pictures being seen at once with one superimposed on the other. This condition was reported for first view on only three occasions.

Table 51-2 gives the overall results. The Wilcoxon [8] test was used for determining the significance of differences between the selections made by the Mexican and American subjects. Significance was at the 0.01 level of confidence.

Since the initial time interval was rather short, it may be suggested that culturally familiar subject matter was preferentially reported in cases 3 and 4 without the selection being strictly perceptual. This possibility was checked by excluding these cases from the analysis; the overall results remain unchanged, with significance at the 0.02 level.

An additional check on the preferential reports for cases 3 and 4 was conducted on all subjects using the same stimulus materials. This consisted of re-exposing the materials and varying the intensity of light on the two pictures [2, pp. 10–11]. The degree to which illumination of the less preferred picture had to be increased to offset the advantage of the other provided a quantitative measure of perceptual predominance. The direction only, and not the relative strength of the indexes, was used in further support of the predominance report derived from the first-view-in-time. In no instance were the original criteria for determining preference, more especially cases 3 and 4, contraindicated.

TABLE 51-2 Differential Selection of American Content in Ten Stereograms

| Nationality | 8–10 | 5–7 | 2–4 | 0–1 | Total |
| --- | --- | --- | --- | --- | --- |
| Mexican subjects | 0 | 0 | 5 | 7 | 12 |
| American subjects | 9 | 3 | 0 | 0 | 12 |
| Total | 9 | 3 | 5 | 7 | 24 |

*No. of Subjects Selecting American Content in Given Number of Stereograms*

TABLE 51-3 Overall Perceptual Predominance in the Ten Stereogram Pairs

|  | No. Where Mexicans Dominate | No. Where Americans Dominate | Total (6 × 10) |
|---|---|---|---|
| Mexican males (6) | 44 | 16 | 60 |
| Mexican females (6) | 45 | 15 | 60 |
| American males (6) | 7 | 53 | 60 |
| American females (6) | 12 | 48 | 60 |

Table 51-3 gives the results from the intensity variation.

Since the probability of equal perceptual predominance was rejected at the 0.01 level for both subjects and content, the conclusion seems justified that subjects report scenes of their own culture as predominant in binocular rivalry over scenes from another culture. The national cultural differences appear critical in affecting perceptual predominance in the majority of the stereogram slide pairs. There were only three pairs in which cultural preference was not marked (pairs 1, 5, and 10). One can only speculate concerning the less marked cultural influence in the latter pairs, which could involve the physical characteristics of the photographs (for instance, greater clarity or better definition of the prints), or possibly greater appeal of the particular individuals depicted regardless of cultural setting. However, the major finding is clear.

Various theoretical interpretations are possible for describing the findings of the present investigation. The position here favored, however, is that advanced by Ames, Cantril, and the transactional school, who regard perception as being fundamentally determined by previous, rather than present, experience [5, 6]. In transactional perceptual theory the role of meaning is accorded a central position in the perceptual processes. Differences in ways of perceiving come about as a consequence of differences in past experiences and purposes. These in turn emerge from influences in the home, in the school, and in the various groups with which an individual identifies. Thus, under conditions of perceptual conflict as found in the binocular rivalry situation, those impingements possessing the more immediate first-person meaning would be expected to predominate in visual awareness. The findings of the present experiment seem accountable in these terms. While greater familiarity with the objects and scenes from the subject's own culture provided a more dominant set for perceiving those materials in preference to the relatively less familiar, other variables such as mood, need, and self-reference values undoubtedly entered into the actual selections. The best explanation of the present data, therefore, would seem to be in terms of past experience. The accumulated past experience of the individual within the characteristic settings and with typical individuals of his own culture should make pictorial scenes from his own culture possess greater personal significance at the visual level than that possessed by the less familiar situations and individuals of another society.

## SUMMARY

Twelve Mexican and twelve matched American subjects were simultaneously presented with a series of ten stereogram slide pairs of similar scenes, one from Mexico and one from the United States. Under these conditions of experimentally induced binocular rivalry, it was found that scenes from the subject's own culture tended to be perceptually predominant. The findings were accounted for in terms of the demonstrable role of personal significance in perceptual processes.

## REFERENCES

1. J. W. Bagby. The relative roles of information and action in the genesis of a perception. Unpublished doctoral dissertation, Columbia University, 1955.
2. J. W. Bagby. A perceptual study of cross-cultural attitudes in Mexico and the United States. Advance report, Psychology Dept., Princeton University. March 1956.
3. E. Engel. Binocular conflict and resolution. Unpublished doctoral dissertation, Princeton University, 1955.
4. E. Engel. The role of content in binocular resolution. Amer. J. Psychol., 1956, 69, 87–91.
5. W. Ittelson and H. Cantril. *Perception: a transactional approach.* New York: Doubleday, 1954.
6. F. P. Kilpatrick. Human behavior from the transactional point of view. Hanover, N.H.: Institute for Associated Research, 1952.
7. *Stereoscopic slides.* Titchener Series. Chicago: C. H. Stoelting Co., 1942.
8. F. Wilcoxon. *Some rapid approximate statistical procedures.* New York: American Cyanamid, 1949.

# 52
# DERMO-OPTICAL PERCEPTION: A PEEK DOWN THE NOSE

## Martin Gardner

Science reporting in United States newspapers and mass-circulation magazines is more accurate and freer of sensationalism than ever before, with pseudoscience confined largely to books. A reverse situation holds in the Soviet Union. Except for the books that defended Lysenko's theories, Soviet books are singularly free of pseudoscience, and now that Lysenko is out of power, Western genetics is rapidly entering the new Russian biology textbooks. Meanwhile, Russian newspapers and popular magazines are sensationalizing science much as our Sunday supplements did in the 1920s. The Soviet citizen has recently been presented with accounts of fish brought back to life after having been frozen 5,000 years, of deep-sea monsters that leave giant tracks across the ocean floor, of absurd perpetual-motion devices, of extraterrestrial scientists who have used a laser beam to blast an enormous crater in Siberia, and scores of similar stories.

By and large, the press in the United States has not taken this genre of Soviet science writing seriously. But in 1963 and 1964 it gave serious attention to a sudden revival, in Russia's popular press, of ancient claims that certain persons are gifted with the ability to "see" with their fingers.

The revival began with a report, in the summer of 1962, in the Sverdlovsk newspaper *Uralsky Rabochy*. Isaac Goldberg, of First City Hospital in Lower Tagil, had discovered that an epileptic patient, a 22-year-old girl named Rosa Kuleshova, could read print simply by moving a fingertip over the lines. Rosa went to Moscow for more testing, and sensational articles about her abilities appeared in *Izvestia* and other newspapers and popular magazines. The first report in the United States was in *Time*, January 25, 1963.

When I first saw *Time*'s photograph of Goldberg watching Rosa, who was blindfolded, glide her middle finger over a newspaper page, I broke into a loud guffaw. To explain that laugh, I must back up a bit. For 30 years, my principal hobby has been magic. I contribute to conjuring journals, write treatises on card manipulation, invent tricks, and, in brief, am conversant with all branches of this curious art of deception, including a branch called mentalism.

Source: *Science*, 1966, *151*, 654–657. Copyright 1966 by the American Association for the Advancement of Science.

For half a century professional mentalists—performers, such as Joseph Dunninger, who claim unusual mental powers—have been entertaining audiences with "eyeless vision" acts. Usually the mentalist first has a committee from the audience seal his eyes shut with adhesive tape. Over each eye is taped something opaque, such as a powder puff or a silver dollar. Then a large black cloth is pulled around the eyes to form a tight blindfold. Kuda Bux, a Mohammedan who comes from Kashmir, is perhaps the best known of today's entertainers who feature such an act. He has both eyes covered with large globs of dough, then many yards of cloth are wound like a turban to cover his entire face from the top of his forehead to the tip of his chin. Yet Kuda Bux is able to read books, solve mathematical problems on a blackboard, and describe objects held in front of him.

## THE NOSE PEEK

Now I do not wish to endanger my standing in the magic fraternity by revealing too much, but let me say that Kuda Bux and other mentalists who feature eyeless vision do obtain, by trickery, a way of seeing. Many ingenious methods have been devised, but the oldest and simplest, surprisingly little understood except by magicians, is known in the trade as the nose peek. If the reader will pause at this point and ask someone to blindfold him, he may be surprised to discover that it is impossible, without injury to his eyes, to prepare a blindfold that does not permit a tiny aperture, on each side of the nose, through which light can enter each eye. By turning the eyes downward one can see, with either eye, a small area beneath the nose and extending forward at an angle of 30° to 40° from the vertical. A sleep-mask blindfold is no better; it does not fit snugly enough around the nose. Besides, slight pressure on the top of the mask, under the pretense of rubbing the forehead, levers out the lower edge to permit even wider peeks. The great French magician Robert-Houdin (from whom Houdini took his name), in his memoirs [17] tells of watching another conjuror perform a certain card trick while blindfolded. The blindfold, Robert-Houdin writes, "was a useless precaution... for whatever care may be taken to deprive a person of sight in this way, the projection of the nose always leaves a vacuum sufficient to see clearly." Pushing wads of cotton or cloth into the two apertures accomplishes nothing. One can always, while pretending to adjust the blindfold, secretly insert his thumb and form a tiny space under the wadding. The wadding can actually be an asset in maintaining a wider aperture than there would be without it. I will not go into more subtle methods currently used by mentalists for overcoming such apparent obstacles as adhesive tape criss-crossed over the eyelids, balls of dough, and so on.

If the mentalist is obtaining information by a nose peek (there are other methods), he must carefully guard against what has been called the sniff posture. When the head of a blindfolded person is in a normal position, the view down the nose covers anything placed on the near edge of a table at which the person is seated. But to extend the peek farther forward it is necessary to raise the nose slightly, as though one is sniffing. Practiced performers avoid the sniff posture by tilting the head slightly under cover of some gesture, such as nodding in reply to a question, scratching the neck, and other common gestures.

One of the great secrets of successful blindfold work is to obtain a peek in advance, covered by a gesture, quickly memorize whatever information is in view, then later—perhaps many minutes later—to exploit this information under the pretense that it is just then being obtained. Who could expect observers to remember exactly what happened five minutes earlier? Indeed, only a trained mentalist, serving as an observer, would know exactly what to look for.

Concealing the "sniff" demands much cleverness and experience. In 1964, on a television show in the United States, a girl who claimed powers of eyeless vision was asked to describe, while blindfolded, the appearance of a stranger standing before her. She began with his shoes, then went on to his trousers, shirt, and necktie. As her description moved upward, so did her nose. The photograph in *Time* showed Rosa wearing a conventional blindfold. She is seated, one hand on a newspaper, and sniffing. The entire newspaper page is comfortably within the range of a simple nose peek.

## OTHER DOP CLAIMANTS

After the publicity about Rosa, Russian women of all sorts turned up, performing even more sensational feats of eyeless vision. The most publicized of these was Ninel Sergyeyevna Kulagina. The Leningrad newspaper *Smena,* January 16, 1964, reported on her remarkable platform demonstration at the Psychoneurological Department of the Lenin-Kirovsk District. The committee who examined Ninel's blindfold included S. G. Fajnberg (Ninel's discoverer), A. T. Alexandrov, rector of the University of Leningrad, and Leonid Vasiliev, whose laboratory at the University is the center of parapsychology research in Russia. No magicians were present, of course. While "securely blindfolded," Ninel read from a magazine and performed other sensational feats. Vasiliev was reported as having described her demonstration as "a great scientific event."

There were dozens of other DOP claimants. The magazine *USSR* (now *Soviet Life*), published here in English, devoted four pages to some of them in its February 1964 issue [22]. Experiments on Rosa, this article said, made it unmistakably clear that her fingers were reacting to ordinary light and not to infrared heat rays. Filters were used which could block either light or heat. Rosa was unable to "see" when the light (but not heat) was blocked off. She "saw" clearly when the heat rays (but not light) were blocked off. "The fingers have a retina," biophysicist Mikhail Smirnov is quoted as saying. "The fingers 'see' light."

Accounts of the women also appeared in scientific publications. Goldberg contributed a report on his work with Rosa to *Voprossy Psikhologii* in 1963 (English translation, [6]). Biophysicist N. D. Nyuberg wrote an article about Rosa for *Priroda,* May 1963 (English translation [11]). Nyuberg reports that Rosa's fingers, just like the human eye, are sensitive to three color modes, and that, after special training at the neurological institute, she "succeeded in training her toes to distinguish between black and white." Other discussions of Rosa's exploits appeared in Soviet journals of philosophy and psychology.

Not only did Rosa read print with her fingers, she also described pictures in magazines, on cigarette packages, and on postage stamps. A *Life* correspondent reported that she read his business card by touching it with her elbow. She read print placed under glass and cellophane. In one test, when she was "securely blindfolded," scientists placed a green book in front of her, then flooded it with red light. Exclaimed Rosa: "The book has changed color!" The professors were dumbfounded. Rosa's appearance on a TV program called "Relay" flushed out new rivals. *Nedelya,* the supplement of *Izvestia,* found a 9-year-old Kharkov girl, Lena Bliznova, who staggered a group of scientists by reading print ("securely blindfolded") with fingers held a few inches *off* the page. Moreover, Lena read print just as easily with her toes and shoulders. She separated the black from the white chess pieces without a single error. She described a picture covered by a thick stack of books (see my remarks above about exploiting previously memorized information).

In the United States, *Life* (June 12, 1964) published a long uncritical article by Albert Rosenfeld [19], the writer whose card Rosa had read with her elbow. The Russian work is summarized and hailed as a major scientific breakthrough. Colored symbols are printed on one page so the reader can give himself a DOP test. Gregory Razran, who heads the psychology department at Queens College, New York, is quoted as saying that perhaps "some entirely new kind of force or radiation" has been detected. Razran expected to see "an explosive outburst of research in this field. . . . To see without the eyes—imagine what that can mean to a blind man!"

Let us hope that Razran, in his research, will seek the aid of knowledgeable mentalists. In a photograph of one of his DOP tests, shown in the *Life* article, the subject wears a conventional sleep-mask, with the usual apertures. She is reaching through a cloth hole in the center of an opaque partition to feel one of two differently colored plates. But there is nothing to prevent her from reaching out with her other hand, opening the cloth a bit around her wrist, then taking a nose peek through the opening.

The most amusing thing about such experimental designs is that there is a simple, but never used, way to make sure all visual clues are eliminated. A blindfold, in any form, is totally useless, but one can build a light-weight aluminum box that fits over the subject's head and rests on padded shoulders. It can have holes at the top and back for breathing, but the solid metal must cover the face and sides, and go completely under the chin to fit snugly around the front of the neck. Such a box eliminates at one stroke the need for a blindfold, the cumbersome screen with arm holes, various bib devices that go under the chin, and other clumsy pieces of apparatus designed by psychologists unfamiliar with the methods of mentalism. No test made without such a box over the head is worth taking seriously. It is the only way known to me by which all visual clues can be ruled out. There remain, of course, other methods of cheating, but they are more complicated and not likely to be known outside the circles of professional mentalism.

In its 1964 story *Life* did not remind its readers of the three pages it had devoted, in 1937, to Pat Marquis, "the boy with the X-ray eyes" [12]. Pat was then 13 and living in Glendale, California. A local physician, Cecil Reynolds, discovered that Pat could "see" after his eyes had been taped shut and covered with a blindfold. Pat was carefully tested by reporters and professors, said *Life,* who could find no trickery. There are photographs of Pat, "securely blindfolded," playing Ping-Pong, pool, and performing similar feats. Naturally he could read. Reynolds is quoted as saying that he believed that the boy "saw" with light receptors in his forehead. Pat's powers were widely publicized at the time by other magazines and by the wire services. He finally agreed to being tested by J. B. Rhine, of Duke University, who caught him nose peeking [16].

The truth is that claims of eyeless vision turn up with about the same regularity as tales of sea serpents. In 1898 A. N. Khovrin, a Russian psychiatrist, published a paper on "A rare form of hyperaesthesia of the higher sense organs" [9], in which he described the DOP feats of a Russian woman named Sophia. There are many earlier reports of blind persons who could tell colors with their fingers, but "blindness" is a relative term, and there is no way now to be sure how blind those claimants really were. It is significant that there are no recent cases of persons known to be totally blind who claim the power to read ordinary print, or even to detect colors, with their fingers, although it would seem that the blind would be the first to discover and develop such talents if they were possible.

## JULES ROMAINS' WORK

Shortly after World War I the French novelist Jules Romains, interested in what he called paroptic vision, made an extensive series of tests with French women who could read while blindfolded. His book, *Vision Extra-Rétinienne* [18] should be read carefully by every psychologist tempted to take the Russian claims seriously, for it describes test after test exactly like those that have been given to today's Russians. There are the same lack of controls, the same ignorance of the methods of mentalism, the same speculations about the opening of new scientific frontiers, the same unguarded predictions about how the blind may someday learn to "see," the same scorn for those who remain skeptical. Romains found that DOP was strongest in the fingers, but also present in the skin at any part of the body. Like today's Russian defenders of DOP, Romains is convinced that the human skin contains organs sensitive to ordinary light. His subjects performed poorly in dim light and could not see at all in total darkness. Romains thought that the mucous lining of the nose is especially sensitive to colors, because in dim light, when colors were hard to see, his subjects had a marked tendency to "sniff spontaneously."

The blindfolding techniques Romains used are similar to those used by the more recent investigators. Adhesive tape is crossed over the closed eyes, then folded rectangles of black silk, then the blindfold. At times cotton wool is pushed into the space alongside the nose, at times a projecting bib is placed under the chin. (Never a box over the head.) Anatole France witnessed and commented favorably on some of Romains' work. One can sympathize with the novelist when he complained to a U.S. reporter [2] that both Russian and American psychologists had ignored his findings and had simply "repeated one twentieth of the discoveries I made and reported."

It was Romains' book that probably aroused magicians in the United States to devise acts of eyeless vision. Harlan Tarbell, of Chicago, worked out a remarkable act of this type which he performed frequently [21]. Stanley Jaks, a professional mentalist from Switzerland, later developed his method of copying a stranger's signature, upside down and backward, after powder puffs had been taped over his eyes and a blindfold added [3, 4, 7]. Kuda Bux uses still other techniques. (A description of an early eyeless vision act by Kuda Bux is given in [15].) At the moment, amateurs everywhere are capitalizing on the new wave of interest in DOP. In my files is a report on Ronald Coyne, an Oklahoma boy who lost his right eye in an accident at the age of 7. When his left eye is "securely blindfolded," his empty right eye socket reads print without hesitation. Young Coyne has been appearing at revival meetings to demonstrate his miraculous power. "For thirteen years he has had continuous vision where there is no eye," reads an advertisement in a Miami newspaper for an Assembly of God meeting. "Truly you must say 'Mine eyes have seen the glory of God.'"

## TESTS IN THE UNITED STATES

The most publicized DOP claimant in the United States is Patricia Stanley. Richard P. Youtz, of the psychology department at Barnard College, was discussing the Soviet DOP work at a faculty lunch one day.

Someone who had taught high school in Owensboro, Kentucky, recalled that Patricia, then a student, had astounded everyone by her ability to identify objects and colors while blindfolded. Youtz traced Patricia to Flint, Michigan, and in 1963 he made several visits to Flint, tested her for about sixty hours, and obtained sensational results. These results were widely reported by the press and by such magazines of the occult as *Fate* [20]. The soberest account, by science writer Robert K. Plumb, appeared in the *New York Times,* January 8, 1964 ([13]; see also [14] and [1]). Mrs. Stanley did not read print, but she seemed able to identify the colors of test cards and pieces of cloth by rubbing them with her fingers. Youtz's work, together with the Russian, provided the springboard for Leonard Wallace Robinson's article "We have more than five senses" in the *New York Times Magazine,* March 15, 1964.

Youtz's first round of tests, in my opinion, were so poorly designed to eliminate visual clues that they cannot be taken seriously. Mrs. Stanley wore a conventional sleep-mask. No attempt was made to plug the inevitable apertures. Her hands were placed through black velvet sleeves, with elastic around the wrists, into a lightproof box constructed of plywood and painted black. The box could be opened at the other side to permit test material to be inserted. There was nothing to prevent Mrs. Stanley from picking up a test card or piece of colored cloth, pushing a corner under the elastic of one sleeve, and viewing the exposed corner with a simple nose peek. Youtz did have a double-sleeve arrangement that might have made this difficult, but his account [23] of his first round of tests, on which Mrs. Stanley performed best, indicate that it was attached only on the rare occasions when a photomultiplier tube was used. Such precautions as the double sleeve, or continuous and careful observation from behind, seemed unnecessary because Mrs. Stanley was securely blindfolded. Moreover, there was nothing to prevent Mrs. Stanley from observing, by nose peeks, the test material as it was being placed into the light-tight box.

Here is a description of Mrs. Stanley's performance by the *New York Times* reporter who observed her: "Mrs. Stanley concentrates hard during the experiments.... Sometimes she takes three minutes to make up her mind.... She rests her forehead under the blindfold against the black box as though she were studying intently. Her jaw muscles work as she concentrates" [8]. While concentrating, she keeps up a steady flow of conversation with the observers, asking for hints on how she is doing.

Youtz returned to Flint in late January 1964 for a second round of tests, armed with more knowledge of how blindfolds can be evaded (we exchanged several letters about it [5, 24]) and plans for tighter controls. I had been unsuccessful in persuading him to adopt a box over the head, but even without this precaution, results of the second round were not above chance expectation. These negative results were reported by the *New York Times* [8] but not by any other newspaper or news magazine that had publicized the positive results of the first round of tests. Youtz was disappointed, but he attributed the failure to cold weather [25].

A third series of tests was made on April 20, 1964, for an observing committee of four scientists. Results were again negative. In the warm weather of June, Youtz tested Mrs. Stanley a fourth time, over a three-day period. Again, performance was at chance level. Youtz attributes this last failure to Mrs. Stanley's fatigue [25]. He remains convinced that she does have the ability to detect colors with her fingers and suspects that she does this by sensing delicate differences in temperature [26]. Although Russian investigators had eliminated this as an explanation of Rosa's powers, Youtz believes that his work with Mrs. Stanley, and later with less skillful Barnard students, will eventually confirm this hypothesis. He strongly objects to calling the phenomenon vision. None of his subjects has displayed the slightest ability to read with the fingers.

## NINEL IS CAUGHT CHEATING

In Russia, better-controlled testing of Rosa has strongly indicated nose peeking. Several articles have suggested this, notably those by L. Teplov, author of a well-known book on cybernetics, in the March 1–7, 1964, issue of *Nedelya,* and in the May 25, 1964, issue of the Moscow *Literaturnaya Gazeta.* Ninel Kulagina, Rosa's chief rival, was carefully tested at the Bekhterev Psychoneurological Scientific Research Institute in Leningrad. B. Lebedev, the institute's head, and his associates summarize their findings as follows [10]:

> In essence, Kulagina was given the same tasks as before, but under conditions of stricter control and in accordance with a plan prepared beforehand. And this was the plan: to alternate experiments in which the woman could possibly peek and eavesdrop with experiments where peeking would be impossible. The woman of course did not know this. As was to be expected, phenomenal ability was shown in the first instance only. In the second instance [under controls] Kulagina could distinguish neither the color nor the form. . . .
> Thus the careful checking fully exposed the sensational "miracle." There were no miracles whatever. There was ordinary hoax.

In a letter to *Science* [27] Joseph Zubin, a biometrics researcher at the New York State Department of Mental Hygiene, reported the negative results of his testing of an adolescent who "read fluently" after blindfolds had been secured around the edges with adhesive tape. Previous testing by several scientists had shown no evidence of visual clues. It became apparent, however, that the subject tensed muscles in the blindfold area until "a very tiny, inconspicuous chink appeared at the edge. Placing an opaque disk in front of the chink prevented reading, but not immediately. The subject had excellent memory and usually continued for a sentence or two after blocking of the reading material." Applying zinc ointment to the edges of the adhesive proved only temporarily effective, because muscle tensing produced new chinks (made easier to detect by the white ointment). A professional magician, Zubin reports, participated in the investigations.

The majority of psychologists, both here and in the Soviet Union, have remained unimpressed by the latest revival of interest in DOP. In view of the failures of subjects to demonstrate DOP when careful precautions were taken to rule out peeks through minute apertures, and in view of the lack of adequate precautions in tests that yielded positive results, this prevailing scepticism appears to be strongly justified.

## REFERENCES

1. Can fingers "see"? (editorial) *New York Times,* February 6, 1964.
2. J. Davy. *Observer,* February 2, 1964.
3. M. Gardner. *Sphinx,* February 1949, *12,* 334–337.
4. M. Gardner. *Linking Ring,* October 1954, *34,* 23–25.
5. M. Gardner. Letter. *New York Times Magazine,* April 5, 1964.
6. I. Goldberg. *Soviet Psychol. Psychiat.,* 1963, *2,* 19ff.
7. G. Groth. He writes with your hand. *Fate,* October 1952, *5,* 39–43.
8. Housewife is unable to repeat color "readings" with fingers. *New York Times,* February, 2, 1964.
9. A. N. Khovrin. In *Contributions to neuropsychic medicine.* Moscow, 1898.
10. B. Lebedev. Article in *Leningradskaya Pravda,* March 15, 1964. Trans. Albert Parry, Dept. Russian Studies, Colgate University.
11. N. D. Nyuberg. *Federation Proc.,* 1964, *22,* T 701.
12. Pat Marquis of California can see without his eyes. *Life,* April 19, 1937, pp. 57–59.
13. R. K. Plumb. Woman who tells color by touch mystifies psychologist. *New York Times,* January 8, 1964.
14. R. K. Plumb. Sixth sense is hinted in ability to "see" with fingers. *New York Times,* January 26, 1964.
15. H. Price. *Confessions of a ghost-hunter.* New York: Putnam, 1936.
16. J. B. Rhine. *Parapsychol. Bull.,* 1963, *66,* 2–4.
17. J. E. Robert-Houdin. *Confidences d'un prestidigitateur.* Blois, 1958. Eng. trans. *Memoirs of Robert-Houdin: Ambassador, author, and conjuror.* London, 1859. Reprinted *Memoirs of Robert-Houdin: King of the conjurors.* New York: Dover, 1964.
18. J. Romains. *Vision extra-rétinienne.* Paris, 1919. Eng. trans. C. K. Ogden, *Eyeless vision.* New York: Putnam, 1924.
19. A. Rosenfeld. Seeing color with the fingers. *Life,* June 12, 1964, pp. 102–113.
20. P. Saltzman. *Fate,* May 1964, *17,* 38–48.
21. H. Tarbell. X-ray eyes and blindfold effects. *The Tarbell course in magic.* New York: Tannen, 1954. Vol. 6, pp. 251–261.

22. *USSR,* February 1964, *89,* 32ff.
23. R. P. Youtz. Aphotic digital color sensing: A case under study. Photocopied for the Bryn Mawr meeting of the Psychonomic Society, August 29, 1963.
24. R. P. Youtz. Letter. *New York Times Magazine,* April 26, 1964.
25. R. P. Youtz. The case for skin sensitivity to color, with a testable explanatory hypothesis. Photocopied for the Psychonomic Society, Niagara Falls, Ontario, October 9, 1964.
26. R. P. Youtz. Letter. *Sci. Amer.,* 1965, *212,* 8–10.
27. J. Zubin. Dermooptical perception: A cautionary report. Letter to editor. *Science,* 1965, *147,* 985.

# Index

Acoustics
 and backward inhibition in hearing, 487–491
 and feedback, 493
 measuring, 495–496
Act, action, 7, 16, 34
 at a distance, 38–39
 of figures, 254
 and hemispheric deconnection, 461–475
 motor, 267–282
 neural cell, and learning, 36
 retinal, time, 453
 and schema, 223
 and visual image, 250–252
Adaptation-level theory, 3, 52–59, 121, 135
 definition, 53–55
 of animals, 6
 emotional, 346
 and Ganzfeld, 260
 sensory, 11–12
 and social psychology, 69
Afterimages
 and eidetic images, 439
 motion, 454–458
Age
 and attention, 221–235
 and depth perception, 240–244
 and discrimination, 296
 and eidetic memory, 377
 and experience, 137–138, 300–301, 332–347
 and form, 314, 338–347
 and learning, 134–135
 and monocular deprivation, 313–331
 and part-whole recognition, 134–135, 165–174
 and physiology, 231, 303–312
 and psychological change, 221–235, 346
 and representation of events, 223
 and response, 198–222
 and self-produced movement, 349, 355
 and sensory deprivation, 284–289
 and size constancy, 369–374
 and social deprivation, 290–299
 and specificity theory, 182–183
 and visual reception, 333
 and visually guided behavior, 357
Anchor effect, 52, 56–58, 121–125
Anxiety
 potential, and perception, 408
 and stimuli, 377
Arousal
 and habituation, 403

and hunger, 511
 and imagery, 439
 and memory, 188
 and perceptual defense, 430
 and sensory isolation, 281–282
 and subliminal stimulation, 123–125
 unconscious emotional, 415
Association theory, associationism, 135, 177, 190–193, 195
 and color, 499–503
 and identifying response, 190
 and identity, 144–145, 193
 and language, 188–189, 191–192
 and meaning, 14, 197
 and minor hemisphere, 472
 and nervous system, 189–190
 and paired associate learning, 421–427
 and perceptual learning, 135, 187–198
 physiological, 190–194
 psychological, 190–192
 sensory-sensory, 348–355
Attention, 135, 398–406
 definition, 398
 and age, 221–235
 and image, 247, 250
 mechanisms of, 376–377
 selective, 377
 shift of, 484
Attitudes, 176–177, 408
Auditory modality. See Hearing
Awareness, conscious, 4, 97–102
 discrimination without, 415–417
 and hemispheric deconnection, 459–475

Behavior, behavior theory, 2, 5, 121, 135, 190
 and attention, 398–406
 criterion, 190
 and eating, 379, 519–523
 and eidetic imagery, 439, 445
 and Gestalt theory, 35
 and hemispheric deconnection, 460–475
 ideal, optional, 80, 83
 and inhibition, 354–355
 mechanisms of, 221–235
 molar, 10
 and monocular deprivation, 318–331
 and performance, 222
 and sensory deprivation, 288
 species-specific, 222
 and stimulus, 6–8, 348–355
 and subliminal stimulation, 97–106

and visual deprivation, 285, 313–331
 visually guided, 348–368
"Black box" theorizing, 376
Brain
 hemispheric deconnection, 459–475
 major (dominant) hemisphere, 463–475
 minor hemisphere, 470–475
 and perception, 378
 and sensory isolation, 280–282
 and time, 484
 and verbal material, 477–479
 and vision, 303–312, 462–475
Cell assemblies, theory of, 254–255, 288–289
Change
 and brain, 41–52
 emotional, 273–282
 and experience, 225
 and learning, 3
 orientation to, 225
 physiological, 36–40, 314–331, 495–496
 psychological, 221–235
 and response system, 27
 and schema, 223–224
 and stimulus, 11
Channels, communication, 376–377, 400–404
 definition, 400
Clues, cues
 definition, 13–14
 and eating, 379, 519–523
 and memory, 385–387
 and motion, 377
 and perceptual defense, 416–417
 and stimulus, 13–14, 178–179
 utilization of, 194
 visual, 243–244, 287
Coding, encoding
 definition, 383
 cells and learning, 137
 and eidetic image, 439, 446
 and memory, 383
 and neural activity, 449
 and stimuli, 14
Cognition. See also Cognitive dissonance, theory of
 and competence, 222
 and hemispheric deconnection, 461–475
 and learning, 287–289
 mechanisms, 221–225
 and stimulus, 15–16
Cognitive dissonance, theory of
 definition, 62
 and social psychology, 62, 69

# INDEX

Color perception, 498–503
  and Ganzfeld, 259–265
  and imagery, 247, 439
  and individuality, 379
  and sensory isolation, 268–282
  and synesthesia, 392–397
  and visual inhibition, 486
Completion, closure
  and monocular deprivation, 313–331
  and perception, 255
  and visual image, 250–251
  and visual perception, 253
Conditioning. See also Learning
  definition, 222
  and nervous system, 106–107
  and perceptual defense, 415, 426–427
  and species-specific behavior, 222
Conflict
  binocular, 379, 525–531
  and threshold, 418
Consciousness
  and associationism, 189–190
  measurement formula for, 6
Context, 177
  and memory response generation, 386
  and probability, 398–404
  Titchener's theory, 188–190
Contour
  and attention, 224–225
  and backward visual inhibition, 484–486
  and information, 72–73
  measuring, 495
Control
  hunger, 510, 517
  and memory, 384–387
  motor, 469–475
  sensory, and hemispheric deconnection, 464–475
Coordination
  motor-visual, 357–368
  and sensory deprivation, 284–289
  spatial, 348–355
Criterion
  and perceptual learning, 190–192
  and signal detection theory, 81–95
  and stimulus, 194–195, 224
  and testing statistical hypothesis theory, 83
Cultural characteristics
  of binocular conflict, 525–531
  and individuality, 379
Cutaneous modality. See Skin

Darkness. See Light deprivation
Data, sensory, 188
  and attention, 399
  and inference, 14
  and observation, 84
  and signal detection theory, 85
Density
  and Ganzfeld, 257–265

and hearing inhibition, 481–491
and visual inhibition, 488–489
Deprivation
  foot, 510–523
  light, 266–282, 348
  monocular, 313–331
  neonatal, 348–355
  sensory, 137–138, 284–290, 348
  social, 290–299
  visual, 285–289, 313–331, 370–374
Depth perception, 135–138, 237–246, 351–355
  and sensory isolation, 267–282
  and size, 371–374
  and visual perception, 252–255
Development
  emotional, 290–299
  perceptual, 178
  and reflexes, 287
  sexual, 291–299
  social, 300–301
Differentiation
  and associationism, 194–195
  and Gestalt theory, 178
  and operationism, 25–26
  and specificity theory, 178
Direction
  and sensory deprivation, 288
  and sound, 481–484
  and vision, 455–458, 484–486
Discrepancy principle, 225–231
  definition, 225
Discrimination
  and associationism, 190, 195
  auditory, 136, 267–282
  without awareness, 101–102, 415–417
  and depth perception, 237–246
  and form, 338–347
  and monocular deprivation, 313–331
  and operationism, 21–23
  and perceptual defense, 432–437
  and perceptual learning, 179, 185–186
  and selective response, 400–404
  and size, 138, 369–374
  and social deprivation, 296
  somesthetic, 464–475
  and specificity theory, 188
  and threshold of recognition, 409
  and visual deprivation, 287–289
Distance
  and Ganzfeld, 257–265
  and sensory deprivation, 288
  and size constancy, 369–370
Dreams, and sensory isolation, 273–282
Duration. See Time

Eating, 379, 517–523
Emotion
  definition, 408–409
  and arousal, 415
  and eating, 511–514
  and experience, 346

and minor hemisphere, 474
and operationism, 26
and perception, 408–409
and perceptual defense, 408–417, 426, 430–437
and sensory isolation, 273–282
and social deprivation, 290–299
and stimuli, 377
and visually guided behavior, 366
and transactional theory, 530
Empiricism, 176–177, 225
  and associationism, 193–194
  and attention, 398
  and Gestalt theory, 29–31
  and size, 369–370
Energy
  and signal detection theory, 92
  as stimulus, 5, 13, 15
Enrichment theory of perceptual learning, 177–198
  and memory, 135, 188
  and physiological associationism, 193
Environment
  and age, 222
  and brain changes, 41–52
  and Gestalt theory, 29
  and sensory deprivation, 284–289, 348
  and short-term memory, 382
  and sounds, 478
  and space, 348–355
  and specificity theory, 195–197
  and stimulus, 9–18
  and transactional theory, 530
  and visually guided behavior, 357–368
Examination subset
  definition, 386
Experience, 5, 18, 121, 175–186, 225
  and age, 137–138, 300–301, 332–347
  and associationism, 191
  and brain changes, 41–52
  and change, 225
  and enrichment theory, 188
  and Gestalt theory, 3, 29–35, 143–144
  and hemispheric deconnection, 461–475
  and identity, 134, 144–145
  and learning, 3
  and organization, 142–144
  and primitive unity, 140–142
  and schema, 222–225
  and sensory isolation, 136
  and species-specific behavior, 222
  and stimulus, 7
  and threshold, 418
  and transactional theory, 530–531
  visual, 306–312, 369–374
Experiments
  and adaptation-level theory, 56–57
  and associationism, 190

# INDEX

Experiments (cont.)
  and binocular rivalry, 526–531
  and brain changes, 41–52
  and cognitive dissonance theory, 63–67
  and color perception, 498–503
  and depth perception, 237–246
  and eidetic image, 440–445
  and experience, 134–138
  and Ganzfeld, 257–265
  and genesis of perception, 134
  and Gestalt theory, 32–34
  and habituation, 249
  and hearing, 487–491
  and interpretation of results, 2
  and monocular deprivation, 313–331
  and operationism, 23–26
  and part-whole perception, 165–174
  and perceptual defense, 409, 436
  and perceptual learning, 179–184, 198–221
  psychophysical, 26, 190
  receptive visual field, 303–312
  and recognition, 154–164
  and redundancy, 70–74
  and sensory deprivation, 285–289
  and sensory isolation, 266–282
  and signal detection theory, 85
  and size, 369–374, 504–509
  social deprivation, 290–299
  and speech sounds, 478–479
  and stimulus, 6, 8, 19
  and subliminal stimuli, 55–56
  visual, 246–256, 333–338, 348–355, 358–364, 454–458
Extinction, 504–509

Fechner's law, 6, 121
  reformulated, 53–54
Figures. See also Form
  and binocular rivalry, 525
  complexity of, 249–255
  figure-ground segregation, 262–265
  and Ganzfeld, 258–265
  and Gestalt theory, 254
  "good," 250–254
  perception of, 140–152
  and sensory isolation, 267–282
  simple, 247–256
  and visual perception, 252–253
Filter and information flow model, 399–405
Form
  and age, 314
  discrimination, 338–347
  generalization, 343–349
  and light, 314
  and minor hemisphere, 473

Ganzfeld, 136, 257–265
Generalization, of form, 145, 149, 343–349
Gestalt theory, 11, 29–35
  definition, 2–3

  and behaviorism, 35
  and differentiation, 178
  and experience, 3, 29–35, 143–144
  and figure perception, 142–144
  and grouping, 32–34
  and information, 30–32, 74–75
  and learning, 3, 32, 134–136
  and meaning, 30
  and nervous system, 34–35
  and part-whole recognition, 165–174
  and sensory input, 176–177
  and stimulus, 10, 12, 15
  and time, 34
  and visual perception, 252–255
Grouping, laws of, 75
  and figure recognition, 141
  and Gestalt theory, 32–34
  and visual perception, 254–255

Habituation
  and attention, 402–403
  physiology of, 403
  and retinal image, 249
  and visual aftereffect, 458
Hemispheres. See Brain
Hearing, auditory modality. See also Speech and attention, 224–225, 398–407
  and discrimination, 136
  field, 462–475
  and hemispheric deconnection, 462–475
  "holding," 255
  and inhibition, 480–496
  and integration, 481–484
  and minor hemisphere, 472
  and model for localization, 401
  and response, 400–401
  and sensory isolation, 267–282
  and signals, 401
  and stimuli, 227, 249, 377
  and subliminal stimuli, 109
Holt, E. B. and stimuli, 15
Homogeneity
  and Ganzfeld, 257–265
  grouping, law of, 75

Identification
  and associationism, 190
  and responses, 179–184, 403–404
  and signals, 402
  word, 403–404
Identity, 144–148
  definition, 144
  and associationism, 144–145, 193
  and experience, 144–145
  and figure recognition, 146–148
Illumination. See Light
Image
  definitions, 383, 438
  and arousal, 439
  and associationism, 176–177, 188, 190
  and color, 439
  and eidetic image, 438–446

  and eidetic memory, 377
  and enrichment theory, 188
  and memory, 176, 188, 383–387, 438
  and mnemonist, 390–397
  and movement, 377, 447–450
  and organization, 377
  retinal, 246–256
  and time, 439, 443–445
  and sensory isolation, 273–282
Individuality
  and hemispheric deconnection, 475
  and perception, 378–379
Information, information theory, 70–77
  and attention, 398
  and brain, 175–177
  and channels, 376–377
  and content, 402
  and contours, 72–73
  and depth perception, 237
  and memory, 376, 381–387
  and minor hemisphere, 471–475
  processing perceptual, 376–377
  redundant, 3–4
  sensory, 376, 383–385
  and short-term storage, 405–406
  and stimuli, 5, 13–14, 18, 178–179
  and time, 70
  and vision, 70–77, 356–368
Information flow theory, 399–402
Inherited factor, 222
Inhibition
  behavioral, 354–355
  sensory, 480–496
Inflow theory of eye-head velocity, 450–451
Innate factor
  and Gestalt theory, 143–144
  and learning, 3
  and primitive unity, 140–142
  and reflexes, 285, 287
Input. See also Stimulus
  competing, 399–401
  and filter and information flow model, 399–401
  and hemispheric deconnection, 462–475
  and memory search, 386
  and stimulus, 2, 14
Integration
  and hearing, 481–484
  and senses, 378
Intellectual capacity
  and experience, 300–301
  and sensory isolation, 281–282
  and social deprivation, 296
Intensity
  and sound inhibition, 481–484
  and speech, 398
  and visual deprivation, 287
Interaction
  binocular, 306–312
  between forward, backward inhibition, 491, 496
  social, 291–299
Introspection theory, 189–194, 398

INDEX 545

Isolation
  sensory, 136–137, 266–284, 348
  social, 352

Judgment
  in adaptation-level theory, 56–57
  psychophysical, 52–54
  and signal detection theory, 80–81
  and stimulus, 8
  and subliminal stimulation, 105, 121–125

Knowledge. See Information

Language. See Words
Learning. See also Learning, perceptual
  definitions, 191–192, 339
  and age, 134–135
  and associationism, 135, 191–192
  and change, 3
  and conditioning, 106–107, 221–235
  and experience, 3
  and figure perception, 142–144, 148–152
  and Gestalt theory, 3, 32, 134–136
  and hemispheric deconnection, 461–475
  and nervous system, 3, 36–40, 106–107, 137
  neurological basis of, 345–346
  and perception, 3, 143
  and perceptual defense, 421–427
  and response, 134
  and sensory deprivation, 287–289
  and size estimation, 509
  and stimulus, 3, 143
  and subliminal stimulation, 102, 106
  verbal, 179
  and visual deprivation, 287
Learning, perceptual. See also Learning
  definitions, 175, 190–192, 194
  and association theory, 187–198
  classical theory of, 179
  and enrichment theory, 177–198
  Hebb's neurophysiological theory of, 140–153, 193
  and perceptual distortion theory, 508
  specificity theory of, 175–198
Light
  and backward visual inhibition, 485–486
  and cortical cells, 305–306
  deprivation, 266–282, 348
  and Ganzfeld, 257–265
  and perceptual defense, 430–437
  reflex to, 352–355

  and retinal image, 246–256
  and retinal receptors, 449–450
  and sensory isolation, 279–282
  and sound, 481
  and stimulus, 5, 13
  and visually guided behavior, 356–368
  and vision, 314
Limen. See Threshold
Localization
  model for auditory, 401
  spatial, 398
  visual, 356–368
Location
  and auditory inhibition, 481–484
  and memory storage, 383–387

Mach, Ernst, and eye movement, 452
Mach bands, and backward inhibition of sound, 483
Machine theory (Gestalt), 29
Meaning
  and associationism, 14, 197
  and attention, 398, 405
  and binocular rivalry, 525–531
  and figure perception, 143
  and Gestalt theory, 30
  and identifying response, 179
  and selective response, 402
  and sensory isolation, 282
  and speech sounds, 479
  and stimulus, 6–19
  and symbols, 195–197
  and transactional theory, 530
  and visual image, 250–251
  and visual perception, 253
  and words, 394, 399
Measurement
  of perceptual defense, 430–437
  techniques, 495–496
Mechanisms
  and associationism, 188–189, 192–195
  and attention, 376–377
  and behavior, 221–225
  and cognitive structure, 221–235
  mediating, 7, 192–235
  of mnemonist, 390–391
  and model, 399
  neural, of perception, 109, 332–333
  of perceptual defense, 408
  physiological, 378
  of response, 194–195, 198–221
  of retrieval, 399
  and sensory deprivation, 137–138
Memory, 376–387
  and anchors, 56–58
  and color, 498–503
  eidetic, 377
  and eidetic imagery, 438–446
  and enrichment theory, 135, 188
  and hemispheric deconnection, 461–475

  long-term, 382–385, 399–402
  of mnemonists, 390–397
  and minor hemisphere, 471
  and neural cells, 56–58
  and perceptual learning, 135, 176, 177, 186
  and response generation, 386
  and selective response, 402
  and sensory isolation, 281–282
  short-term, 382, 399, 439, 467–475
  theory of, 446
  and time, 376, 382–387, 399–402, 405–406
Mill, James, 193
Mill, John Stuart, 193
Model mechanisms, 399
  of attention and perception, 398–406
  of auditory localization, 401
  of compound eye of beetle, 450
  at memory search process, 386
  and order, 399
  and spatial layout, 399
Motion, movement
  and afterimage, 454
  deprivation of, 138
  and eye, 377, 447–456
  and image-retina system, 447–450
  and perception, 136
  and perceptual learning, 223–224
  physiological cue, 377–378
  and retina, 246–256, 449
  and response, 192
  self-produced, 348–357
  and stimulus, 348–355
  and time, 449–453
  and visual deprivation, 286–289
  and visual perception, 377, 454–455
  and visual pursuit, 352–355
  and visually guided behavior, 348–368
Motivation, 504
  and sensory isolation, 274–282
  and transactional theory, 530
Motor activity
  and control, 469–475
  and identifying response, 179
  and learning, 191
  visual, 148–152, 286–289
  visual-motor coordination, 357–358
  visual-motor reflexes, 286–289
Müller, Johannes, 5, 9, 17
Music
  and left-ear superiority, 478
  and mnemonist, 392–393
  and sound, 480–481

Nativism, 176
Need
  and perception, 408
  and size, 509
  and transactional theory, 530
Nervous action, law of, 190, 192
Neurophysiology. See Physiology.

## INDEX

Noise
 and memory recovery, 386
 and relevant response, 222
 and sensory isolation, 279–282
 and signal detection theory, 83–95
 and stimulus, 4

Obesity, 510–523
Objects
 and Gestalt theory, 29–35
 moving, 352–355
 properties of, 194
 and size, 369–370
 and space, 356–368
 and stimulus, 8–10
 visual, 247–255
Occupation, and early experience, 301
Olfactory modality
 and minor hemisphere, 474
 and sensory adaptation, 11–12
Onset, offset phenomena, 224, 483, 491–495
Operationism
 and associationism, 190, 192
 converging operations, 2, 23–29
 definition of conditioning, 222
 discrimination in, 22
 parallel operations, 24
 and perception, 21–29
 and response, 25–26
 and stimulus, 22–23
Optic modality. *See* Visual modality
Order
 and Gestalt theory, 29
 and model, 399
 and perceptual defense, 433–436
 and retinal image, 249–255
 serial, 255
 and signal detection theory, 85
 and time, 78
Organization
 and behavior, 221–235
 figure-ground, 140–144
 and Gestalt theory, 10, 29–35, 176–177
 and imagery, 377
 and language, 467
 and memory, 383–387
 and perception, 177
 and speech, 79
 and vision, 285, 303–312
Orientation
 to change, 225
 and hemispheric deconnection, 467–475
 to a visual event, 223–224
Outflow theory of eye-head velocity, 450–451

Pattern
 and blindness, 339
 and brain processes, 484
 and environment, 16
 and Gestalt theory, 34–35
 melodic, 478

 and retinal stimulation, 303–312
 and selective response, 402
 and sound, 490–491
 and stimulus, 10–11, 16
 and vision, 2, 198–221
 and visual aftereffect, 458
 and visual deprivation, 286–287
 and visual inhibition, 486
 and visual perception, 252–253
 and visual stimulation, 357
 and visually guided behavior, 348–349
Perception
 acquired or innate, 134
 and associationism, 192–193
 and attention, 398–406
 and binocular conflict, 525
 and binocular rivalry, 525–531
 and brain, 378
 classical theory of, 179
 dermoperception, 379
 dermo-optical, 532–540
 and eidetic image, 439, 446
 and emotion, 408–409
 and experimental results, 2
 and figures, 142–144
 genesis of, 135
 and Gestalt theory, 2–3, 176–177
 and grouping, 75
 and hemispheric deconnection, 461–475
 and individuality, 378–379
 and information theory, 70
 and learning, 3, 143
 and meaning, 253
 and minor hemisphere, 471–475
 and movement, 377
 and mnemonist, 396–397
 and operationism, 21–29
 part-whole, 134–135, 140, 149, 165–174
 and perceptual defense, 430–437
 psychology of, 504
 and sensation, 188
 and size, 508–509
 and speech, 79
 and stimulus, 6–10, 15, 177, 408
 and subliminal stimuli, 109–111
 theories on, 177
 Titchener's context theory, 188
Perception, visual, 246–265
 and brain, 377
 and experiment, 333–338
 and hemispheric deconnection, 462–475
 and reflex responses, 285
 and sensory deprivation, 285–289
 and visual motion, 454–455
Perceptual defense, 377, 408–437. *See also* Selective attention
Perceptual distortion theory, and learning theory, 508
Personality
 and hemispheric deconnection, 460
 and subliminal perception, 109–111

Philosophy
 and perception, 2
 and psychology, 111
 and stimulus, 5
Physics
 ecological, 16, 18
 of sound transmission, 481, 491–496
 and stimulus, 5–18
Physiology
 and age, 231
 and associationism, 188–190
 and attention, 398–406
 and brain, 459–475
 and change, 495–496
 and conditioning, 106–107
 and eating, 379, 512, 517, 523
 and food deprivation, 510–511
 and Gestalt theory, 34–35
 and habituation, 403
 and hemispheric deconnection, 460–475
 and interaction, 10
 and learning, 3, 36–40, 106–107, 137, 345–346
 and light, 305–306
 mechanism of, 378
 and memory, 380–381
 and monocular deprivation, 314–331
 and movement, 377–378, 447–453
 and neonatal deprivation, 354–355
 neurobiotaxis, 37–38
 and observation, 84
 and perception, 2, 332–338
 and perceptual defense, 415
 and perceptual response, 409
 and primitive unity, 134, 140
 and receptor system, 137, 188, 303–312
 and reflex response, 285
 and retina, 246–256, 303–312, 377–378, 449–450
 and schema, 223
 sensory, 6, 137–138
 and sensory isolation, 276–282
 and signal detection theory, 85–86
 and sound, 477–479
 and speech, 477–479
 and stimulus, 5, 9, 36–40
 and subliminal stimulation, 109
 and time, 223–224
 and visual aftereffect, 458
 and visual behavior, 356–368
 and visual experience, 306
 and visual systems, 137, 308–312, 367–368
Place. placement, position
 and memory storage, 384–387
 of perceptual defense, 433–436
 and sensory deprivation, 285–286
 tactile, 285
 and visual aftereffect, 458
Pooling theory, 54, 124–125
Primitivation, 408

# INDEX

Probability
  conditional, 87–95
  and descriptive classification, 222
  and examination subset, 386
  of joint occurrence, 81–95
  and memory recovery, 386
  and perceptual defense, 436–437
  and selective response, 398–404
  and signal detection theory, 81–95
Projection, and stimulus, 14
Psychology
  and age, 221–235
  animal, 6
  as applied discipline, 97–115
  and associationism, 188–189
  and concert halls, 495–496
  and hemispheric deconnection, 460–475
  and perception, 2, 504
  and philosophy, 111
  and positivism, 196–197
  and response, 15
  social, 61–69
  and stimulus, 6, 15–16, 103–104
Psychophysics, 6, 121–126
  of classes (frame of reference), 52–53
  classical, 52, 80–81
  and perceptual learning, 184–185
  and specificity theory, 187–197
  and stimulus, 8, 15, 103
  and threshold, 121–125

Rationalism, 176
Receptors, 137, 188
  field, 303–312, 332–338
  peripheral, 352
  and responses, 194–195
  retinal, 449–450
  and stimulus, 2–13
Recognition, 145, 154–173
  mean threshold, 420–429
  test of memory, 383
  threshold, 409, 423
Redundancy
  complexity and, 224–225
  information, 3–4
  language, 79
  visual stimulation, 70–77
Reflexes
  innate or developed, 287
  to light, 352–355
  and stimuli, 6–7
  and visual deprivation, 286–289
Reinforcement, 504–509
  secondary, 508
Response
  and age, 222–235
  and associationism, 190
  autonomic, 192
  bipolar, 53
  differentiation, 25–26, 190
  generation, 384–387
  and Gestalt theory, 34–35

and hemispheric deconnection, 461–475
identifying, 179
and learning, 134, 194–195
mechanisms of, 194–195, 198–221
molecular, 11
and operationalism, 21–27
physiology of, 409, 456–458
and pooling, 54
preferential, 26, 218–221
and psychology, 15
and receptors, 194–195
and relations, 11
selective, 398–406
and signal detection theory, 85–86, 91–95
skin, 398–429
and specificity theory, 178
and stimulus, 2, 7, 198–222
and subliminal stimulation, 101–102, 121–125
and vision, 134–138, 154–164, 198–221
and visual aftereffect, 456–458
and visual deprivation, 285–286
Rorschach test, and structure of stimuli, 12

Schema
  definition, 222–223
  and change, 223–224
  and experience, 222–235
  and hypothesis (cognitive structure), 231
  and neuronal model, 223
  and Piaget's sensory-motor scheme, 223
  and spatial relations, 222
  and time, 222
Scriabin, 393
Senses, sense organs
  and channel, 400
  and deprivation, 284–290, 348
  and hemispheric deconnection, 462–475
  and information, 376, 383
  and inhibition, 484
  and integrative properties, 378
  and isolation, 266–282, 348
  and memory, 376, 381–385
  and minor hemisphere, 472
  and perception, 483
  and rearrangement, 348
  and vision, 249–250
Sensation
  and context theory, 188
  and hemispheric deconnection, 461–475
Sensory system. See Physiology
Sequence. See also Time
  and environment, 16, 195–197
  and response, 26
  and stimulus, 11–12, 377
  and visual perception, 255
Sherrington, Sir Charles, 5, 18–19, 450
Signal, 14, 222, 401–404

signal detection theory, 4, 80–95
signal plus noise (SN), 83–95
Signs and symbols, 14, 196–197
  and Gestalt theory, 30
  and meaning, 195–197
  and minor hemisphere, 472–473
  and patterns, 273
  and specificity theory, 195–197
  and stimulus, 14
  and value, 408
Size, 369–374, 379, 504–509
  and Ganzfeld, 264
  and minor hemisphere, 473
  and sound, 480–481
Skin (cutaneous modality)
  and sensory adaptation, 11–12
  and subliminal stimulation, 109
  and stimuli, 9
Social
  deprivation, 290–299
  development, 291–301
  interaction, 291–299
  isolation, 352
  psychology, 61–69
Sound, 5, 399, 402, 477–484, 490–496
Space
  and environment, 348–355
  and Ganzfeld, 257–265
  and Gestalt theory, 34
  and localization, 356–368, 398
  and minor hemisphere, 473–474
  and model, 399
  and schema, 222
  and sound inhibition, 483
Specificity theory, 177–190. See also Learning, perceptual hypothesis, 194–197
  and psychophysical correspondence, 187–190, 194–197
  and stimulus, 17–19, 188
Speech, language. See also Words
  and associationism, 188–192
  and dominant hemisphere, 467
  and hemispheric deconnection, 463–475
  and learning, 179, 191
  and organization, 79
  and perception, 77–79
  redundancy in, 79
  and stimulus, 16–17
Statistical decision, theory of, 80–83. See also Signal detection, theory of
Stimulus theory, 6–20
  definitions, 2, 7–9, 17, 34–35
  and age, 222–235
  and anxiety, 377
  and associationism, 190
  auditory, 227, 249, 377, 398–407
  and behavior, 348–355
  and channels, 376–377
  and clue cue, 13–14, 178–179
  deprivation, 135
  and depth perception, 237
  and eating, 517
  electrical, 121–125

## INDEX

Stimulus theory (cont.)
  and energy, 177
  and enrichment, 135
  and Ganzfeld, 264–265
  and habituation, 402
  and homogeneity, 136–137
  and information, 13–14, 18–19, 178–179
  interpolated, 121–125
  and judgment, 8, 54–55
  and learning, 6, 16–19, 177–186, 188, 194–195
  and memory, 385, 446
  movement-produced, 348–355
  and perception, 6–10, 15–19, 22–23, 177, 408
  and perceptual defense, 416–437
  and physiology, 3, 6, 9, 36–40, 103
  potential, 2, 8, 16–19
  preferential, 198–221, 305–306
  and psychology, 6, 15–16, 103–104
  and psychophysics, 8, 15, 52–55, 103
  and recognition threshold, 423
  and redundancy, 70–77
  and response, 6, 16, 34–35, 54, 179–186, 191
  selection of, 376–377
  and sensory inhibition, 281–282
  and sequence, 377
  subliminal, 377, 430–437
  verbal, 378, 398–432, 477–479
  visual, 247, 303–312, 332–338, 348–357, 408–432, 458, 484–486
Stimulus sampling theory, 383
Stimuli, subliminal
  and adaptation-level theory, 55–56
  application of, 97–120
  and behavior, 97–106
  ethics of, 111–115
  and hearing, 109
  and learning, 102–106
  and response, 101–102, 121–125
  and threshold, 97–105
  and unconsciousness, 106–107
  and vision, 109

Threshold, limen, 4–6, 8, 17
  definitions, 93, 104
  and conflict, 418
  and experience, 418
  limen, 104, 121
  mean recognition, 409, 420–429
  and operationism, 23–25
  and perceptual defense, 411–413

and psychophysics, 121–125
and selective response, 404
and set, 418
and signal detection theory, 80, 92–95
and stimulus preference, 198–217
and subliminal stimulation, 97–125
Time
  and attention, 398, 405–506
  and brain processes, 484
  and eating, 517–523
  and Ganzfeld, 260
  and Gestalt theory, 34
  and hearing, 487–491
  and hemispheric deconnection, 474
  and imagery, 439, 443–445
  and information, 70
  and memory, 376, 382–387, 399–402, 405–406
  and movement, 449–453
  and nervous system, 223–224
  and order, 78
  and response, 222
  and reverberation, 481
  and schema, 222
  and sensory deprivation, 287
  and sensory isolation, 268–282
  and signal detection theory, 83
  and sound inhibition, 481–484
  and vision, 250, 313–331, 453, 484–486
Transactional theory, 530–531

Unit, unity
  and figure, 252–253
  and Gestalt theory, 29
  and hemispheric deconnection, 459–469
  and nervous system, 134, 140
  and visual image, 250–253

Value
  and extinction, 509
  self-reference, 530
  and size, 504–509
  social, 508–509
  and symbolism, 408
Verbal communication. See Words
Vernon, M. D., 7
Vision
  and aftereffect, 454–458
  and anticipation of contact, 351–355
  and backward inhibition, 484–489
  and behavior, 285–289, 311–331, 348–374

and brain, 303–312
and cues, 243–244
and deprivation, 137–138, 285–289, 370–374
and experience, 261, 303–312
and field, 257–265, 303–312, 462–475
and figure perception, 148–152
and fixation, 246–256, 439
and form, 314
and Ganzfeld, 136, 257–265
and Gestalt theory, 29–35
and hemispheric deconnection, 462–475
and image, 247–256, 390–397
and information, 70–77, 356–368
and isolation, 136
and long-term storage, 454–458
and measuring, 495
and minor hemisphere, 472
and mnemonist, 390–397
and monocular deprivation, 313–331
and neonatal deprivation, 354
and object, 247–255
and pattern, 2, 218–221
and perception, 253, 285–289, 377, 454–455
and physiology, 137, 447–453
and response, 134–138, 154–164, 198–221
and sensory isolation, 267–282
and stimulus, 11–12, 17
and subliminal stimulation, 109

Words, verbal communication
  definition, 394
  and brain, 477–479
  and computer, 382
  and emotion, 415, 426
  and dominant hemisphere, 467, 477–478
  and frequency, 436–437
  and identification, 403–404
  and meaning, 394
  and mnemonist, 391–397
  and perceptual defense, 426, 436–437
  and selective response, 400–404
  and sounds, 394, 399
Writing
  and dominant hemisphere, 467
  and hemispheric deconnection, 463–475

Zero
  and adaptation-level theory, 54
  confidence, 100–101
  Fechner's law, 6, 53–54, 121